Preventing & Reducing Juvenile Delinquency

To our daughter, Megan Q. Howell, the youngest "Comp Strat" thinker and future criminologist, whose compassion for the field inspires me

Preventing & Reducing Juvenile Delinquency

A Comprehensive Framework

James C. Howell

SAGE Publications
International Educational and Professional Publisher
Thousand Oaks ▪ London ▪ New Delhi

For information:

 Sage Publications, Inc.
2455 Teller Road
Thousand Oaks, California 91320
E-mail: order@sagepub.com

Sage Publications Ltd.
6 Bonhill Street
London EC2A 4PU
United Kingdom

Sage Publications India Pvt. Ltd.
B-42 Panchsheel Enclave
Post Box 4109
New Delhi 110 017 India

Printed in the United States of America

Library of Congress Cataloging-in-Publication Data

Howell, James C.
Preventing and reducing juvenile delinquency: A comprehensive framework /
by James C. Howell.
    p. cm.
Includes bibliographical references and index.
ISBN 0-7619-2508-2
ISBN 0-7619-2509-0 (pbk.)
    1. Juvenile delinquency—United States—Prevention. 2. Youth and
violence—United States—Prevention. 3. Violent crimes—United States—Prevention.
4. Juvenile delinquents—Rehabilitation—United States. I. Title.
HV9104 .H76 2003
364. 36—dc21

                                                        2003000428

This book is printed on acid-free paper.

03   04   05   06   10   9   8   7   6   5   4   3   2   1

Acquisitions Editor:	Jerry Westby
Editorial Assistant:	Vonessa Vondera
Production Editor:	Denise Santoyo
Copy Editor:	Judy Selhorst
Typesetter:	C&M Digitals (P) Ltd.
Indexer:	Pamela Van Huss
Cover Designer:	Michelle Lee

CONTENTS

PREFACE

My juvenile justice career began shortly after I completed my doctoral work at the University of Colorado, under the tutelage of Dr. Delbert Elliott. I was ready to begin a university-based teaching and research career. That never happened. A fellow graduate student who had planned a similar career convinced me that we should spend a year in Washington, D.C., exploring the federal side of things, to be better prepared for teaching and research. That anticipated year in the nation's capital turned out to be 23 years. Shortly after I had taken a research position at the National Institute of Justice (NIJ) in the U.S. Department of Justice (DOJ), the DOJ created the first major federal juvenile justice office, the Office of Juvenile Justice and Delinquency Prevention (OJJDP), established in 1975. My research division in NIJ became part of the new OJJDP. I had the unusual experience of helping to establish the OJJDP and of working toward implementing the progressive legislation that authorized it, the Juvenile Justice and Delinquency Prevention Act of 1974 (P.L. 93-415).

When the OJJDP was established, its functions were very broad; they included research, data collection, development of demonstration programs, training, information dissemination, program evaluation, juvenile justice system improvement, and (somewhat futilely, I must say) coordination of all federal efforts focused on juvenile delinquency. As subsequently amended, the JJDP Act contained four "core" protections: removal of juvenile "status" (noncriminal) offenders from secure confinement, separation of juveniles from adults in confinement, jail and lockup removal, and reduction in the disproportionate confinement of minorities (Howell, 1997, pp. 24-46). In addition, the JJDP Act steadfastly supported the critical role of the juvenile justice system as an alternative to criminal justice system handling of juveniles.

I immensely enjoyed the next 21 years at OJJDP, where I held several positions; for most of my time there, I was director of research and program development. Fortunately, the office was given the opportunity to allocate a significant portion of program resources for the integration of basic research, program evaluation, and program development. Some 15 years after OJJDP was established, a colleague and I realized that we needed to disseminate the available knowledge on juvenile justice in a more widespread manner, rather than as we had been doing, on a project-by-project basis. This recognition was occasioned by several important developments in the field. Reported juvenile violence had increased sharply, beginning in the mid-1980s, and a "moral panic" over juvenile delinquency came into full bloom. The "get tough on juveniles" movement was growing, along with a penchant among policy makers for "quick fixes" or piecemeal solutions that often were stimulated by knee-jerk reactions to perceived problems. Rehabilitation programs were falling by the wayside, while boot camps, detention centers, and juvenile reformatories were increasingly populating the nation's landscape.

A colleague and I at the OJJDP recognized that we had an obligation to take stock of what was known about delinquency and about ways to prevent and reduce it, and to attempt to package this information in a user-friendly format. We thought such a product might assist practitioners and policy makers in the juvenile justice field in taking a more balanced approach to dealing with growing juvenile violence. Over my years at DOJ and OJJDP, I had formed a rewarding collegial relationship with my partner in this endeavor, John J. Wilson, a lawyer with an MBA degree and 8 years of social service agency experience. He was OJJDP's special counsel on legal matters at the time, but soon he would be made the office's deputy administrator, and later its acting administrator.

We both saw the need for a holistic, systemwide approach to juvenile delinquency as an alternative to reactive, after-the-fact solutions that were not proving to be effective. A proactive approach was required, with a balanced emphasis on prevention, early intervention, and a system of graduated sanctions, in what we called a *comprehensive strategy.* Our in-house review of research, programs, and management tools for dealing with serious, violent, and chronic juvenile offenders began in 1990. John's legal training and social work experience blended well with my research background. For 3 years, we worked collaboratively to develop a framework for implementing best practices. We enjoyed many work sessions, both alone and with staff, going back and forth between research and evaluation results and the program implications that flowed from them.

We developed and circulated many iterations of our comprehensive strategy approach to researchers and practitioners, and presented it for feedback at juvenile justice conferences and professional meetings such as those held by the American Society of Criminology. We would then return to the office and make modifications. It was a labor of love. We named our product the Comprehensive Strategy for Serious, Violent, and Chronic Juvenile Offenders (Wilson & Howell, 1993), to convey the message that these offenders should be the main target group for juvenile justice system services and sanctions.

U.S. Department of Justice policy at the time called for harsh sanctions for first-time juvenile offenders, a position stated in a policy paper issued by U.S. Attorney General William Barr. The policy paper contended that the best way to prevent juvenile offenders from becoming adult career criminals is

> by imposing tough, smart sanctions that are carefully tailored for the first-time juvenile offender. . . . Such punishment actually benefits the juvenile more than lenient sanctions, or no sanctions at all. Excessive leniency can result in additional transgressions, culminating in a life of crime. . . . A juvenile justice system that is too lenient can become, in effect, a conveyor belt for career criminals. (McBride, Scott, Schlesinger, Dillingham, & Buckman, 1992, p. 26)

The paper recommended that states "establish a range of tough juvenile sanctions that emphasize discipline and responsibility to deter nonviolent first-time offenders from further crimes. . . . These sanctions should include the option of institutional settings. . . . One possibility is boot camps" (McBride et al., 1992, p. 27). In addition, the paper recommended that those persons making up the small group of chronic violent juvenile offenders should be treated as adults—contending that they "are as hardened as any adult offender" (p. 28).

The Comprehensive Strategy shifted the U.S. Department of Justice's orientation to include prevention and its intervention policy to give priority to juvenile offenders who have histories of serious or violent offenses. This position was based on self-report studies showing that only a fraction of all juvenile offenders are serious chronic offenders (Elliott, Huizinga, & Morse, 1986) or violent chronic offenders (Thornberry, Huizinga, & Loeber, 1995). The attorney general's policy paper ignored the issue of prevention; in contrast, the Comprehensive Strategy placed top priority on prevention, especially through the strengthening of social institutions, beginning with families.

The Comprehensive Strategy framework has been used to guide three subsequent national reviews of juvenile delinquency research and programs, providing valuable information for this book. The first national review, conducted in 1993-1994, focused on prevention and graduated sanctions programs. A group of researchers at the University of Washington reviewed prevention programs, and another group of researchers at the National Council on Crime and Delinquency reviewed graduated sanctions and rehabilitation programs. These reviews were published in the OJJDP's *Guide for Implementing the Comprehensive Strategy for Serious, Violent, and Chronic Juvenile Offenders* (Howell, 1995) and in the *A Sourcebook: Serious, Violent, and Chronic Juvenile Offenders* (Howell, Krisberg, Hawkins, & Wilson, 1995).

The second national review was conducted under the auspices of the OJJDP Study Group on Serious and Violent Juvenile Offenders, under the leadership of Drs. Rolf Loeber and David Farrington. The group of 22 leading juvenile justice and criminology scholars conducted a 2-year assessment of research and programs on and for serious and violent offenders in the period 1995-1997. The resulting volume, *Serious and Violent Juvenile Offenders: Risk Factors and Successful Interventions* (Loeber & Farrington, 1998c), refined and expanded the national assessment of promising and effective programs that was earlier published in the *Guide* and *Sourcebook*. The study group focused specifically on research and programs pertaining to serious and violent juvenile offenders (for an excellent summary of the volume, see Gibbons, 1999). Several other products of the study group's work have also been published (see Chapter 12).

The third national review was conducted under the auspices of the OJJDP Study Group on Very Young Offenders (1998-1999). This review, again carried out under the leadership of Drs. Loeber and Farrington, was an outgrowth of the recognition by members of the initial Study Group on Serious and Violent Juvenile Offenders that although many of these offenders begin their careers of antisocial behavior before they are teenagers, little was known about child delinquency. The Study Group on Very Young Offenders consisted of 16 scholars who work in the fields of juvenile delinquency and child problem behaviors, and an equal number of other scholars contributed to the group's book. The work of this study group was published in the volume *Child Delinquents: Development, Intervention, and Service Needs* (Loeber & Farrington, 2001a; for the executive summary of the volume, see Loeber & Farrington, 2001b). Both of the study groups commissioned secondary analyses of existing data sets to fill knowledge gaps.

In this book, I draw heavily on these state-of-the-art reviews of research and programs and use the broad Comprehensive Strategy framework to guide the selection of material. I also draw extensively from the results of three major longitudinal studies of juvenile delinquency: the Pittsburgh Youth Study (directed by Dr. Rolf Loeber), the Denver Youth Survey (directed by Dr. David Huizinga), and the Rochester Youth Development Study (directed by Dr. Terence P. Thornberry). These are the first major prospective studies (measuring causal variables in advance of outcomes) of the causes and correlates of juvenile delinquency in the United States (I describe each of the studies in some detail in Chapter 4). All of the studies used large, representative samples of urban youngsters. Among the many powerful features of these studies are the facts that they were implemented simultaneously and they use common measures across sites for comparison of similarities and differences in findings. These three studies have made numerous landmark contributions to our understanding of delinquency and delinquent careers, only a few of which I am able to cover in this book.

A personal disclaimer is in order: To pretend that I am a dispassionate observer of the juvenile justice system would be misleading. The juvenile court system in the United States was founded on the recognition that children are not little adults, and, in all justice and fairness, should not be treated as such. Because of their diminished capacity, deviant children and adolescents should be given "room to reform," to keep their life chances intact (Scott, 2000). Thus the juvenile justice system was created as an alternative to the harsh, punishment-oriented criminal justice system, whose prisons serve as "schools for crime" and whose failure to rehabilitate criminal offenders disqualifies it as a model that should be used for juvenile offenders. The juvenile court is a unique American invention that has since been replicated around the world. As Zimring (2002) notes: "No developed nation tries its youngest offenders in its regular criminal courts. . . . No legal institution in Anglo-American legal history has achieved such universal acceptance among the diverse legal systems of the industrialized democracies" (p. 142). How a society treats its young is an important measure of its claim to civilization. Juvenile courts are a cornerstone of our society.

However, to say that this system is without significant flaws would also be misleading. It is not, and most of them are exposed in this book. Two of my major aims in this book are to familiarize readers with the strengths and weaknesses of the juvenile justice system and to suggest a comprehensive framework for improving it.

ACKNOWLEDGMENTS

A large number of people contribute to the work that goes into producing this type of book. I would be remiss if I did not personally express a debt of gratitude to several of them. The contributions a couple of these individuals made to my career's work extend far back. Charles Norman, my first graduate sociology professor, taught me to think critically about social issues and the value of applied research. I thank him for this. I am also indebted to Delbert Elliott, who fueled my interest in juvenile delinquency and instilled in me the importance of longitudinal studies and research-based theory.

I am grateful to John J. Wilson, former head of the Office of Juvenile Justice and Delinquency Prevention, for several things. His steadfast support of the principles and legal requirements of the Juvenile Justice and Delinquency Prevention Act of 1974 is admirable. He remains the strongest advocate of juvenile justice that I have had the pleasure of knowing. His example inspired me during my tenure at OJJDP and made my collegial work with him all the more rewarding. As I explain in the preface to this book, we collaborated in developing the Comprehensive Strategy for Serious, Violent, and Chronic Juvenile Offenders.

Marion Kelly, former juvenile justice specialist with the Virginia Department of Criminal Justice Services, helped enrich this book. We worked together to develop material to update the original *Guide for Implementing the Comprehensive Strategy*. Some of the material on which we collaborated appears in this volume. This book has benefited from her keen insights into practical applications of the Comprehensive Strategy framework.

The juvenile justice field owes a debt of gratitude to Rolf Loeber and David Farrington ("Sir David," I prefer to call him) for "putting the meat on the bones" of the Comprehensive Strategy. They directed both of the national study groups (the Study Group on Serious and Violent Juvenile Offenders and the Study Group on Very Young Offenders) that took stock of research (while also adding new findings) and information on effective programs. The extremely rich body of knowledge the two groups synthesized under their tutelage is unparalleled; I have been able to weave only small bits of it throughout this book. The extremely high scholarship standards exhibited by Drs. Loeber and Farrington constantly challenge me.

Rolf Loeber (Pittsburgh), Terry Thornberry (Rochester), and David Huizinga (Denver) are the directors of the three major U.S. longitudinal studies of the causes and correlates of delinquency. They provided me with their published products and prepublication copies in many instances. In addition, they inspired me enormously through their ingenious research. These studies are truly landmark ones.

Mark Lipsey helped me understand meta-analysis and the practical application of his pioneering work in the real world. I am very grateful to him for the opportunity to work with him in the North Carolina experiment, using his meta-analysis results as a template for evaluating existing programs and guiding efforts to improve them. The way he combines his meta-analytic genius with a very practical orientation to the field never ceases to amaze me.

John P. Moore, director of the National Youth Gang Center, kindly extended from time to time my commitments to the NYGC to complete this book. More important, he helped me improve my ability to communicate research findings to practitioners. Arlen Egley, Jr., at the NYGC, contributed the national youth gang trend data and related text in Chapter 5. In addition, he often upstages me in discovering newly published gang studies, helping to keep me up-to-date on current research.

David Farrington not only supplied me with important products of his landmark Cambridge Study of Delinquent Development, he thoughtfully sent to me, from across the Atlantic Ocean, one of his editor's copies of outstanding scholarly works he had stewarded. These are works that any criminologist would be delighted to add to his or her library, such as *Building a Safer Society: Strategic Approaches to Crime Prevention* (Tonry & Farrington, 1995a) and *A Century of Juvenile Justice* (Rosenheim, Zimring, Tanenhaus, & Dohrn, 2002). I am grateful to him for his largesse in assisting my research.

Dr. George Pratt, a pioneer in the development of community-based adolescent mental health treatment, helped me understand a variety of mental health issues and how these should be addressed in home and community settings. Several other colleagues helped me with particular chapters. John Wilson provided sage advice on the chapter on transfer of juveniles to the criminal justice system. Kimberly-Kempf Leonard reviewed several of the chapters and appropriately cautioned me in proposing a unique pathway to serious and violent offenders for girls in Chapter 4. Barbara Burns helped me enormously in constructing the history of comprehensive services, both in our collaborative work on the Study Group on Very Young Offenders and in her review of Chapter 11. David Hawkins provided reports on the implementation and evaluation of Communities That Care. Gary Waint provided information on Missouri's Comprehensive Strategy implementation and reviewed my account of it. Cynthia Burke and Susan Pennell saw to it that I got an early copy of their evaluation of the San Diego Comprehensive Strategy project and checked my summary of it. Scott Henggeler helped me access published reports on his renowned Multisystemic Therapy program.

Jerry Regier, a former OJJDP administrator, provided information on Oklahoma's implementation of the strategy. My dear friend the late Gwen Kurz and Michael Schumacher, pioneers of the first Comprehensive Strategy implementation, gave me unpublished material on the Orange County, California, model. After Gwen's untimely death, Shirley Hunt provided unpublished evaluation results. Yvonne Day, program director, and Dave Sheppard provided information on the Baton Rouge Comprehensive Strategy implementation, called Operation Eiger. Rick Wiebush and Dennis Wagner contributed material on the structured decision-making model (Chapter 12). Donna Hamparian provided unpublished reports on the Cuyahoga County, Ohio, Probation Graduated Sanctions System. Dave Curry gave me unpublished reports on the St. Louis SafeFutures project. Alice Wilkins at the Katharine Boyd Library, Sandhills Community College, in Southern Pines, North Carolina, and Janet Martin, librarian, Health Sciences Library, First Health of the Carolinas, in Pinehurst, North Carolina, assisted my research greatly by obtaining books and articles from other sources.

I owe a special debt of gratitude to Secretary George Sweat, Ed Taylor, Donn Hargrove, Susan Whitten, and Kathy Dudley, North Carolina Department of Juvenile Justice and Delinquency Prevention. They kindly gave me the wonderful opportunity to work with them in implementing the new North Carolina juvenile justice legislation that implements the Comprehensive Strategy throughout the state. Because of their unwavering commitment to effective juvenile justice and delinquency prevention programs and to a comprehensive system, the experience of working with them gave vitality to this book.

I am indebted to my wife and life-course partner, Karen, for her tolerance of the disruptions to our lives that a project like this naturally causes, and for many lively discussions that helped me communicate numerous topics more clearly. I am especially grateful for assistance I received from our daughter, Megan, a recent graduate of the University of North Carolina–Charlotte, and a criminal justice major. She helped me build the reference database, critiqued several chapters, and helped me improve the presentation of material. She was especially helpful in reorganizing and sharpening the unique pathway for females. More important, the satisfaction I got from discussing the Comprehensive Strategy with her inspired me to introduce it to university classrooms.

Sage editor Jerry Westby's vigilant oversight of the production of the book and management of the outside review process was invaluable to its quality. He coached me in using various new techniques for effectively presenting complicated research material for classroom use. Heidi Van Middlesworth, associate editor at Sage, helped me with development of the manuscript, expertly sifting through and synthesizing the numerous outside reviews Sage obtained. Vonessa Vondera, editorial assistant at Sage, and Denise Santoyo, production editor, skillfully managed the production process. Judy Selhorst masterfully edited the volume and provided invaluable assistance to me in referencing works. Any errors in the volume are mine. I also thank the outside reviewers for wading through rough drafts of material and providing thoughtful advice on how I could organize and present it more effectively.

—James C. Howell
Pinehurst, North Carolina

PART I

The Historical Context of Current Juvenile Justice System Policies and Practices

This first section provides some historical context for an understanding of current juvenile justice system policies and practices. The chapters in Part I present an overview of juvenile delinquency—particularly serious and violent delinquency—from three perspectives. Chapter 1 examines serious and violent juvenile delinquency trends from 1980 to the present and addresses the distinguishing features of serious and violent juvenile delinquency to help put these forms into proper perspective. This chapter presents an analysis of delinquency trends as indicated by three main data sources: official records, victimization reports, and self-reports of delinquency involvement. Chapter 2 considers several key myths about juvenile violence and the ability of the juvenile justice system to handle modern-day juvenile delinquents. The "super-predator" myth—that a new breed of juvenile offenders emerged in the late 1980s and the 1990s—is a predominant one examined in the chapter. Chapter 3 examines the current moral panic over juvenile delinquency and the consequences of this so-called crisis for both juvenile offenders and juvenile justice system operations. The chapter shows that this moral panic has created a crisis in juvenile justice system policies and practices.

1

■

SERIOUS AND VIOLENT JUVENILE DELINQUENCY TRENDS AND UNIQUE FEATURES OF JUVENILE VIOLENCE

An unprecedented juvenile violence "epidemic" is said to have occurred in the late 1980s and early 1990s (Blumstein, 1995a, 1995b; Cook & Laub, 1998; Fox, 1996b). In this chapter I examine the so-called epidemic, focusing on serious and violent juvenile delinquency trends in two time periods: from 1980 to the present and from the late 1980s through the early 1990s. The longer time frame serves to put in proper perspective the increases in violent juvenile delinquency reported for the period of the late 1980s and early 1990s. In the first section of the chapter, I examine in detail the rates of serious and violent delinquency in both of the time periods; I then provide information on the distinguishing features of serious and violent delinquency.

Serious and Violent Juvenile Delinquency Trends

Three different kinds of measures are used to gauge changes in the levels of serious and violent delinquency: police arrests, victimization surveys, and delinquency self-report surveys. Observers can draw different conclusions regarding juvenile violence trends during the late 1980s and early 1990s, depending on the data sources they use to measure changes. The patterns of delinquency suggested by victimization reports, arrest data, and self-report measurements are distinctly different from one another for this period.

Arrest Data

The number of violent juvenile delinquency arrests increased in the late 1980s and early 1990s.

Arrest data reported in the Federal Bureau of Investigation's annual compilation of data reported by localities across the country (*Uniform Crime Reports*) are the most widely recognized juvenile delinquency trend data. State and federal legislators, the broadcast and print news media, and state and local policy makers most commonly refer to these FBI data in tracking juvenile delinquency trends and in making policy changes. It is important to note, however, that arrest data indicate society's *response* to juvenile delinquency, not the actual level of delinquency. Police choose to make arrests depending on local policies, and arrest rates vary from community to community for the same kinds of offenses (Shannon, 1968, 1988).

Arrest data show that, after years of stability, the violent juvenile delinquency arrest rate began to increase in the late 1980s (see Figure 1.1). This focused national attention on the juvenile violence problem. In 1989, the violent juvenile arrest rate increased to its highest level since the 1960s (Snyder & Sickmund, 1999, p. 120). This rate continued to climb each year thereafter, until it reached a peak in 1994. In the period 1988 through 1994, the violent juvenile arrest rate increased 62% (Snyder & Sickmund, 1999, p. 120). From 1984 through 1994, the *number* of juvenile homicide offenders tripled (Snyder & Sickmund, 1995, p. 56; Snyder, Sickmund, & Poe-Yamagata, 1996, p. 22). This development grabbed headline attention, and it was repeatedly cited as evidence that juvenile delinquency was out of control in the United States. However, the juvenile murder arrest *rate* barely doubled, from just under 6 to 14 per 100,000 juveniles ages 10-17 (Snyder & Sickmund, 1999, p. 122). The murder rate for young adults (ages 18-24) was much higher: 25 in

Box 1.1
Uniform Crime Reports

The Federal Bureau of Investigation's *Uniform Crime Reports* (*UCR*), publications produced by a program begun in the 1930s, are based on voluntary reports that thousands of law enforcement agencies across the United States make each year on the following information:

- Number of reported index crimes (see explanation below)
- Number of arrests and the most serious charge involved in each arrest
- Age, sex, and race of arrestees
- Proportion of reported index crimes cleared by arrest and the proportion of these cleared by the arrest of persons under age 18
- Dispositions of juvenile arrests
- Detailed victim, assailant, and circumstance information in homicide cases

UCR data are not fully representative of the juvenile population. Agencies contributing data on reported crime in 1997 represented 95% of the U.S. population, but those contributing data on arrests represented only 68% of the population. Nevertheless, *UCR* data can provide estimates of the annual number of arrests of juveniles and certain information on them. The *UCR* program monitors the number of crimes that come to the attention of law enforcement agencies. Thus it is important to keep in mind that *UCR* crime data reflect only crimes that are actually reported to law enforcement, and therefore cannot be used to measure the number or proportion of crimes actually committed by juveniles or adults. Crimes are more likely to be reported if they involve serious injuries or large economic losses. The willingness of victims to report crimes and the inclination of the police to make records of incidents reported by victims are other factors that affect the actual number of reported crimes.

Crime Indexes of the Uniform Crime Reports

The *UCR* Crime Index is divided into two components: the Violent Crime Index and the Property Crime Index. The Violent Crime Index includes murder and nonnegligent manslaughter, forcible rape, robbery, and aggravated assault. Definitions of these crimes are as follows:

- Murder and nonnegligent manslaughter is the willful (nonnegligent) killing of one human being by another.
- Forcible rape is the carnal knowledge of a female forcibly and against her will.
- Robbery is the taking or attempting to take of anything of value from the care, custody, or control of a person or persons by force or threat of force or violence and/or by putting the victim in fear.
- Aggravated assault is an unlawful attack by one person upon another for the purpose of inflicting severe or aggravated bodily injury. This type of assault is usually accompanied by the use of a weapon, and attempts to harm another are included in this category.

The Property Crime Index includes burglary, larceny-theft, motor vehicle theft, and arson. Definitions of these crimes are as follows:

- Burglary is the unlawful entry of a structure to commit a felony or theft.
- Larceny-theft is the unlawful taking, carrying, leading, or riding away of property from the possession or constructive possession of another. It includes shoplifting, theft from motor vehicles, and other thefts in which no use of force, violence, or fraud occurs.

- Motor vehicle theft is the theft or attempted theft of a motor vehicle of any type.
- Arson is any willful or malicious burning or attempt to burn a dwelling house, public building, motor vehicle, or personal property of another.

The overall Crime Index includes all eight crimes included in the Violent Crime Index and Property Crime Index.

Although the Violent Crime Index excludes some violent crimes, such as kidnapping and extortion, it contains most of the crimes generally considered to be violent. In contrast, a substantial proportion of the crimes in the Property Crime Index are generally considered less serious crimes, such as shoplifting, theft from motor vehicles, and bicycle theft, all of which are included in the larceny-theft category. Otherwise, the Property Crime Index contains what are generally considered to be "serious" crimes.

Other Important Features of the *UCR* Program

There are several drawbacks to using national arrest data published in the *Uniform Crime Reports* as a measure of delinquency (McCord, Widom, & Crowell, 2001, pp. 26-27). For example, not everyone who is arrested actually committed the offense for which he or she was arrested. In addition, the accuracy and completeness of the data are affected by the voluntary nature of *UCR* reporting (Maltz, 1999), and all states and localities do not report data every year. A person can be arrested more than once in a year. The *UCR* data reflect the numbers of arrests each year, but not the numbers of persons arrested. Each arrest is counted separately in the UCR data, and one arrest can represent many crimes. For instance, if a person is arrested for allegedly committing 40 burglaries, the arrest would show up in the *UCR* data as one arrest, with no indication of the number of burglaries. Also, one crime may result in multiple arrests. For example, three youths may be arrested for one burglary. A single crime with multiple arrests is more likely to occur with juveniles than with adults, because juveniles are more likely than adults to commit crimes in groups. In addition, *UCR* arrest data reflect only the most serious offense for which a person was arrested.

UCR data capture the proportion of crimes that were "cleared" (solved) by a juvenile arrest. Assessments of the juvenile contribution to the U.S. crime problem are often based on this proportion. Arrest and clearance statistics give a very different picture of the juvenile contribution to crime. A crime is considered cleared if someone is formally *charged* with the crime. To use the *UCR* data properly, one must understand this difference (for an excellent illustration, see Snyder & Sickmund, 1999, pp. 113-114).

In the late 1980s, the *UCR* program began to move from aggregate statistics to detailed incident-based reporting. The redesigned data-reporting protocol was labeled the National Incident-Based Reporting System (NIBRS). NIBRS is designed to allow law enforcement agencies to report to the FBI information on many attributes of an incident, including the following (Snyder & Sickmund, 1999, p. 114):

- The demographic characteristics of the victim
- All the offenses involved
- The date, time, and place(s) of the incident
- The level of victim injury
- The weapon involved
- The type and dollar value of property lost
- The victim's perception of the demographic characteristics of the offender(s)

NIBRS data have myriad uses (see Maxfield & Maltz, 1999). As of August 2001, the FBI had certified a total of 21 states for NIBRS reporting, representing 16% of the U.S. population and 13% of crimes (for information on NIBRS status, see the Web site of the Bureau of Justice Statistics at www.ojp.usjoj.gov/bjs/nibrsstatus.htm). This reporting system is expected to replace the *UCR* program in the future.

SOURCE: Snyder and Sickmund (1999, pp. 112-114).

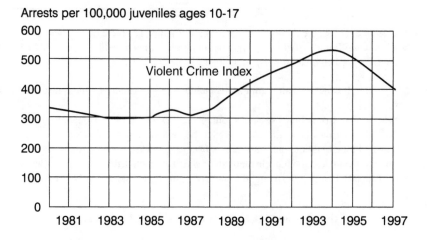

Figure 1.1   Juvenile Violent Crime Index Arrest Rates: 1981-1997

SOURCE: *Juvenile Offenders and Victims: 1999 National Report* (p. 120), by H. N. Snyder and M. Sickmund, 1999, Washington, DC: Office of Juvenile Justice and Delinquency Prevention. ©1999 by National Center for Juvenile Justice. Reprinted with permission.

1994, having increased from 15 in 1984 (Fox, 1996b, p. 4).

It is interesting to note that juvenile arrest rates for Property Crime Index offenses (larceny-theft, burglary, motor vehicle theft, and arson) changed little from the late 1980s to the early 1990s (Snyder & Sickmund, 1999, p. 126). These offenses showed a different pattern over the period 1988-1993 (pp. 128-129). Arrest rates for burglary declined consistently over the 6-year period, larceny-theft arrest rates remained rather constant, and both the motor vehicle theft and arson rates increased sharply. Both motor vehicle theft and arson are low-rate offenses among juveniles, however; thus increases in these rates did not appreciably affect the overall trend for Property Crime Index offenses. Because juvenile violence arrest rates increased and juvenile serious property arrests did not increase noticeably, the delinquency increase was characterized as a juvenile violence epidemic—not an epidemic of overall juvenile delinquency. The possible occurrence of an "epidemic" of juvenile violence without a similar increase in nonviolent delinquency suggests that juvenile offenses deemed violent were specifically targeted for arrest and prosecution (Zimring, 1998a).

Violent juvenile arrests have been in a sharp downturn since 1994 (Snyder & Sickmund, 1999). In 1999, the United States experienced its fifth consecutive year of an unprecedented drop in the rate of juvenile arrests for violent offenses. The juvenile arrest rate (the number of arrests per 100,000 juveniles ages 10 through 17) for murder in the United States fell 68% from 1993 to 1999, reaching its lowest level since 1966 (Snyder, 2000). The overall juvenile arrest rate for Violent Crime Index offenses dropped 36% from 1994 to 1999, its lowest level since 1988. In addition to decreases in juvenile murders, there were substantial drops in the juvenile arrest rate for every other violent crime in this period:

- Forcible rape was down 31% from 1991 to 1999, the lowest level since 1980.
- Robbery was down 53% from 1994 to 1999, the lowest level since 1980.
- Aggravated assault was down 24% from 1994 to 1999, the lowest level since 1989.

The juvenile arrest rate for Property Crime Index offenses, which had remained fairly level for most of the 1990s, fell 23% from 1997 to 1999. Each individual property crime also showed declines:

- Burglary was down 60% from 1980 to 1999.
- Larceny-theft was down 23% from 1997 to 1999.
- Motor vehicle theft was down 52% from 1990 to 1999.
- Arson was down 25% from 1994 to 1999.

Box 1.2

National Crime Victimization Survey

Since 1972, the National Crime Victimization Survey (NCVS) has collected data on nonfatal crimes against persons age 12 or older, reported and not reported to the police, from a nationally representative sample of U.S. households. In 2000, 86,800 households and 159,420 people age 12 or older were interviewed. The NCVS provides information about the following:

- Victims (age, gender, race, ethnicity, marital status, income, and educational level)
- Offenders (gender, race, approximate age, and victim-offender relationship)
- Criminal offenses (time and place of occurrence, use of weapons, nature of injury, and economic consequences)

With all its strengths, the NCVS has two significant limitations in describing the extent of juvenile victimizations. First, the NCVS does not collect information from, or about, victims below age 12 (because designers of the survey believed that younger respondents are not able to provide the requested information). Thus juvenile victimizations reported by the NCVS cover only those involving juveniles ages 12-17.

Second, despite the national attention that juvenile violence has received over the past 20 years, the U.S. Bureau of Justice Statistics (BJS) normally does not provide separate data on juvenile (ages 10-17) victimization in its NCVS reports. The ages commonly used for measurement of "juvenile" delinquency are 10 to 17, but BJS's adolescent reporting categories are ages 12-15 and 16-19 (Rennison, 2001). The latter category includes two age groups that every state considers adults (ages 18 and 19). To generate data that cover the full range of the juvenile years (10-17), researchers must access the BJS data and separate juveniles from these two adult age groups. Therefore, separate data are not currently available for 2000. In 1999-2000, violent victimization decreased among 12- to 15-year-olds by 19%, and by 17% among 16- to 19-year-olds (Rennison, 2001, p. 4).

In addition, the juvenile arrest rate for weapons law violations fell by 39% from 1993 to 1999—its lowest level since 1988. Even juvenile arrest rates that increased during most of the 1990s have declined in recent years. The rate for drug abuse violations dropped by 13% from 1997 to 1999, and the rate for curfew and loitering violations dropped 17% over the same period. However, when we examine the more long-term trend (1994-2000), we see that juvenile arrests for a number of high-volume offenses—drug abuse violations, liquor law violations, nonserious assaults, and curfew violations—increased sharply, indicating that more and more juveniles are being arrested and brought into the juvenile justice system for minor offenses.

The decrease in juvenile violence persisted into 2000, marking 6 consecutive years. The added drop from 1999 to 2000 brought the overall violent juvenile crime arrest rate down to the 1980 level—before the sharp increase (Butts & Travis, 2002, p. 5). Moreover, the juvenile arrest rate for murder dropped to a level below the 1980 rate. From 1994—the peak year of violent juvenile arrests—to

2000, juvenile arrests for Violent Crime Index offenses dropped 34%, and Property Crime Index arrests dropped 31% (Butts & Travis, 2002).

The violent crime arrest rate for juveniles dropped twice as much as the adult rate from 1994 to 2002 (Butts & Travis, 2002, pp. 4-5). The juvenile arrest rate for murder plummeted 71% during this period, whereas the drop in rate for young adults, ages 18-24, was about half that. This sharp decrease in the juvenile arrest rate for murder dropped it even below the 1980 rate.

Victimization Trends

Victimization data collected in the National Crime Victimization Survey (NCVS) conducted by the Bureau of Justice Statistics show that violent juvenile victimizations increased during the late 1980s and early 1990s. In an analysis of NCVS data covering the period 1987-1992, Moone (1994) found that the juvenile violent victimization rate increased 23%. However, two-thirds of the violent juvenile victimizations (rape, robbery, aggravated

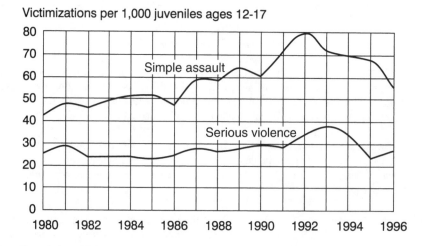

Figure 1.2   Violent Juvenile Victimization Rate: 1980-1996

SOURCE: *Juvenile Offenders and Victims: 1999 National Report* (p. 26), by H. N. Snyder and M. Sickmund, 1999, Washington, DC: Office of Juvenile Justice and Delinquency Prevention. ©1999 by National Center for Juvenile Justice. Reprinted with permission.

assault, and simple assault) during this period were simple assaults that did not involve weapons and resulted in nothing more than minor injuries. Juvenile serious violent victimizations (rape, robbery, aggravated assault) did not increase significantly in this period. In fact, the proportion of violent juvenile victimizations that resulted in serious injury declined from 11% to 7% from 1987 to 1992, and the percentage of serious violent incidents resulting in injury and hospital stays and that involved the use of weapons remained essentially the same (Snyder & Sickmund, 1995). Figure 1.2 shows that the increase in assaults was accounted for mainly by simple assaults that did not result in serious injury.

The 23% increase in reported violent victimizations from 1987 to 1992 shown in Moone's (1994) analysis is only about one-third as large as the increase (62%) in juvenile arrests for violent crimes between 1988 and 1994 (Snyder & Sickmund, 1999, p. 120). These sources would not show such a large discrepancy if both of them were valid measures of delinquent activity. Remember that arrests are official police *responses* to delinquency; arrest rates are not an actual measure of delinquency. Because of the limitations of national arrest data (see Box 1.1), victims' reports are more valid than arrest rates as a measure of delinquency (see Box 1.2).

Violent juvenile victimizations began dropping before the mid-1990s. From 1993 through 1997, the number of serious violent victimizations with at least one juvenile offender dropped 33%; the drop in such victimizations in which all offenders were adults was lower, 25% (Snyder & Sickmund, 1999, pp. 62-63). Thus serious violent victimizations involving juvenile offenders dropped at a much faster rate than those involving adults.

Self-Reported Delinquency Trends

In self-reports obtained through surveys of juvenile populations, respondents give information on their own delinquent acts. These data are generally recognized as the most valid measure of delinquent *behavior* (Dunford & Elliott, 1984; Huizinga, Esbensen, & Weiher, 1996).

Data from two national self-report studies show that there was no sharp increase in juvenile violence in the 1980s and early 1990s (see Box 1.3). In an examination of trends in the Monitoring the Future (MTF) survey over the 1982-1994 period, Johnston, Bachman, and O'Malley (1995) found that high school seniors did not report more significant involvement in any of the 15 behaviors (except theft over $50) over the course of the 13 years of the survey; in fact, they reported modest decreases in involvement in most of the behaviors measured by the survey (Maguire & Pastore, 1995, pp. 258-259). The MTF violence Index offenses also remained relatively stable for the longer period 1980-1998 (U.S. Department of Health and Human Services, 2001, p. 27).

Box 1.3

National Self-Reported Delinquency Surveys

The most direct method of measuring the incidence and volume of juvenile delinquency is through self-report surveys in which adolescents are asked to admit what offenses they have committed. Unfortunately, there currently is no standardized national self-report survey of juveniles that can be considered to be fully representative of both the juvenile population and the full range of delinquency offenses.

The National Youth Survey (NYS) is the most cited and analyzed self-report survey. It was a prospective longitudinal study of a national probability sample of 1,725 youths ages 11-17 in 1976. The researchers designed the survey to measure delinquent behavior and drug use, and they selected youths from a national probability sample of U.S. households. The panel was interviewed annually from 1976 to 1980 and every 3 years thereafter. At the time of the last interview, in 1993, the members of the panel were ages 27-33. Official arrest record data are available for all respondents.

The Monitoring the Future (MTF) study continues to measure illicit drug use and delinquency among a national sample of high school seniors (eighth and tenth graders were added in 1991). Beginning in 1982, students have been asked to report their involvement during the preceding 12 months in 15 behavioral areas. The survey includes six questions covering violent acts (called the MTF Violence Index): arguing or fighting with parents, hitting an instructor or supervisor, getting into a serious fight at school or work, group fighting, hurting someone so seriously they needed medical attention, and using a weapon to take something. (More information about the MTF study is available online at www.monitoringthefuture.org.)

The National Longitudinal Survey of Youth (NLSY) began surveying a nationally representative sample of 9,000 youth between the ages of 12 and 16 in 1997. The main purpose of the NLSY is to study school-labor market issues. The survey also asks youth to self-report having engaged in a variety of deviant and delinquent behaviors. The NLSY is conducted every 2 years.

The Youth Risk Behavior Surveillance (YRBS) system was designed to determine the prevalence and age of initiation of health risk behaviors; to assess whether health risk behaviors increase, decrease, or remain the same over time; and to provide comparable national, state, and local data. Developed by the Centers for Disease Control (CDC) in collaboration with federal, state, and private-sector partners, this voluntary system includes a national survey and surveys conducted by state and local education and health agencies. School-based surveys were last conducted in 1999 among students in grades 9 through 12 in 42 states, 16 large cities, and 4 territories. The average sample size was 2,200. In addition to assisting states, CDC conducts a national survey every 2 years to produce data representative of students in grades 9 through 12 in public and private schools in the 50 states and the District of Columbia. The 1999 survey included more than 15,000 respondents.

Self-report surveys that measure delinquency have limitations (McCord et al., 2001, pp. 30-31). First, the surveys of student samples (the MTF and YRBS) miss three important groups of students: (a) those who are absent from school when the surveys are taken, (b) those who have dropped out of school, and (c) homeless juveniles who are not attending school. Second, the behaviors covered in self-report surveys often are not directly comparable with arrest and court crime categories. And finally, the validity of self-report data may not be consistent among persons of different races and genders.

Other self-report studies that include younger adolescents suggest a slightly different pattern. Elliott (1994b) notes that, based on the National Youth Survey (NYS) and other self-report studies, it appears there was a relatively small increase (8-10%) in the proportion of adolescents involved in some type of serious violent offending in the late 1980s and early 1990s, but the frequency of offending remained about the same. In other words, Elliott suggests that the prevalence of adolescent violence increased during this period, but the violent incidence rate did not. Thus in the early 1990s, compared with the late 1980s, a slightly larger proportion of juveniles were committing serious violent acts, but they were not committing those acts at a higher rate.

Box 1.4
Defining Juvenile Offenders

Unless otherwise noted, juvenile offenders are defined throughout this book as follows (these definitions are generally equivalent to the FBI's *UCR* definitions, shown in Box 1.1).

- *Serious juvenile offenders* are those who commit the following felony offenses: larceny or theft, burglary or breaking and entering, extortion, arson, and drug trafficking or other controlled dangerous substance violations.
- *Violent juvenile offenders* are those who commit the following felony offenses: homicide, rape or other felony sex offenses, mayhem, kidnapping, robbery, or aggravated assault. (The researchers cited in this book often refer to these as *serious violent* offenses.)
- *Chronic juvenile offenders* are those who commit four or more offenses of any type, including nonfelony offenses such as truancy and running away.
- *Serious, violent, chronic juvenile offenders* are those who commit four or more serious or violent offenses.

In sum, juvenile arrests for violent crimes increased much more sharply than either violent victimizations or self-reported serious violent offenses in the period from the mid-1980s through the mid-1990s. These comparisons suggest that arrest data tend to exaggerate changes in violent juvenile offenses during this period. As Snyder and Sickmund (1995) note, arrest data reflect law enforcement agencies' policy responses to juvenile delinquency, whereas victimization and self-report measures reflect actual behaviors.

The Tyranny of Small Numbers Principle

The phrase *tyranny of small numbers* refers to the fact that when a small increase occurs in a small number, a large percentage increase results. For example, if a person has one automobile and buys another one, this represents a 100% increase in the number of automobiles the person owns. Because only one-third of 1% of juveniles are arrested for violent offenses (Snyder, 2000), the base rate for juvenile violence is very low. Thus any change in either direction, when reported as a ratio or percentage, takes the form of a relatively large number. Snyder and his colleagues (1996) illustrate the tyranny of small numbers principle as it applies to rates of juvenile violence:

Of the 100 violent crimes committed in 1985 in a small town, assume that juveniles were responsible for 10, and adults for 90. If the number of juvenile crimes increased 70% in 1994, juveniles would be committing 17 (or 7 more)

violent crimes. A 50% increase in adult violent crimes would mean that adults were committing 135 (or 45 more) violent crimes. If each crime resulted in an arrest, the percentage increase in juvenile arrests would be more than the adult increase (70% versus 50%). However, 87% of the increase in violent crime (45 of the 52 additional violent crimes) would have been committed by adults. Juvenile arrests represent a relatively small fraction of the total; consequently, larger percentage increases in juvenile arrests does not necessarily translate into a large contribution to overall crime growth. (p. 20)

Snyder and his colleagues show how the tyranny of small numbers principle applies in a comparison of juvenile and adult contributions to murders during the 1985-1994 period. They demonstrate that if juveniles had committed no more murders in 1994 than in 1985, murders in the United States would have increased 15% instead of 23%. Therefore, juveniles were responsible for about one-third of the increase in murders during the period 1985-1994. The tyranny of small numbers led the media and others to exaggerate the contribution of juveniles both to the total volume of violent crime in the United States and to the increase over the previous decade.

The tyranny of small numbers principle also applies to misinterpretation of the juvenile contribution to total increases in reported violent crimes. Using FBI-reported crime and clearance statistics, Snyder et al. (1996, p. 20) estimated that juveniles committed 137,000 more violent offenses in 1994 than in 1985, and adults committed an additional 398,000. Therefore, juveniles were responsible for about one-fourth (26%) of the growth in violent crime between 1985 and 1994, and adults were responsible for nearly three-fourths (74%) of the increase in violent crime clearances during this period.

Other Ways of Producing
Misleading Juvenile Delinquency Statistics

A common way in which some observers distort crime trend data is by focusing on a very short time period and ignoring long-term trends. As the discussion above shows, many dramatized the increase in juvenile homicide offenders between 1984 and 1994 as a tripling of the number. The effect of focusing only on the short period of the mid-1980s through the mid-1990s is an exaggeration of the magnitude of the increase. When viewed in a longer-term perspective, the increase in the juvenile homicide rate is not nearly as dramatic.

Zimring (1998a, pp. 31-47) made such a comparison for 13- to 17-year-olds from 1980 through 1995. He found that two of the four Violent Crime Index offenses were essentially trendless over that 16-year period. Robbery and rape rates fluctuated, without any discernible long-range trend. Arrests for robbery dropped by 21%, and rape arrests remained at a relatively low level. Aggravated assault increased 56% above the 1980 level, and a 34% gain was recorded for homicide. Thus the major change in violent juvenile arrests over this period was for aggravated assaults.

However, most of the increase in aggravated assault arrests from 1980 through 1995 occurred at the nonserious end of the seriousness scale (Zimring, 1998a, p. 41). As Zimring (1998a) notes, the counting and classification of assaults are essentially matters of police discretion: "For the period since 1980, there is significant circumstantial evidence from many sources that changing police thresholds for when assault should be recorded and when the report should be for aggravated assault are the reason for most of the growth in arrest rates" (p. 39). Police standards for recording juvenile assaults shifted toward "upgrading" simple assaults to aggravated assaults in the 16-year period (p. 41). Zimring's conclusion is supported by Moone's (1994) analysis of juvenile victimization rates. Most of the increase in juvenile assault victimization rates during 1987-1992 was accounted for by an increase in minor assaults.

Another misleading way of depicting juvenile violence trends is to use the very lowest points in

juvenile violence as the base year. As Zimring (1998a) observes, "Picking a low period in a cyclically fluctuating time series will generate the greatest difference between baseline rates and the current rates of violence, but it also risks confusing the up-and-down movements in a cyclical patterns with trends that represent changes in the average volume of violence to be expected over time" (p. 34). Several analysts have done this, picking 1984 or 1985 as their base year because it was a low point of juvenile violence rates (Blumstein, 1995a, 1995b; Fox, 1996b).

Distinguishing Features of Juvenile Violence

Juvenile violence has several distinguishing features. First, very few juveniles are arrested for violent offenses. In 1999, the juvenile arrest rate for violent crime was 339 arrests per 100,000 juveniles (Snyder, 2000). Juvenile Violent Crime Index arrests in 1999 represented only 16% of all violent crime arrests in the United States, and only 9% of all arrests for murder. Even at the height of the so-called juvenile crime wave (1993), only about 6% of all juvenile arrests were for violent crimes, and about two-tenths of 1% were for homicide (McCord, Widom, & Crowell, 2001, p. 33). The overwhelming majority of juvenile arrests are for minor property offenses. In addition, the relatively small proportion of all violent offenses that violent juvenile arrests represent are, by and large, nonserious acts that result in little injury.

Very few juvenile violent offenders officially record subsequent violent offenses. In an Arizona study of the court careers of 151,000 juvenile offenders, Snyder (1998) found that only 17% were brought to court for second violent offenses. However, a sizable proportion of juveniles are involved in at least one violent act. In the 1997 National Longitudinal Survey of Youth (NLSY), 18% of 12- to 16-year-olds self-reported that they had ever committed an assault (Snyder & Sickmund, 1999, pp. 58-59), and some 30% of twelfth graders report having committed at least one of the violent offenses in the MTF survey (U.S. Department of Health and Human Services, 2001, p. 27).

Second, juvenile violence is largely limited to the latter part of the adolescent period. Violence spreads in the latter part of adolescence, especially in three social contexts where adolescents interact: in peer groups, at school, and in youth gangs (Howell & Hawkins, 1998). In the National Youth Survey, serious violence prevalence rates for aggravated assault, robbery, and rape peaked at age 17 for black males and white males and at age 15 for white females and age 16 for black females (Elliott, 1994a, p. 6). However, this does not mean that the incidence (or offense rate) of serious violent crimes is higher among adolescent delinquents than among adult criminals. There is a difference between prevalence (the proportion of persons offending) and incidence (the number of offenses per person) of offending. Some observers often use the two measures interchangeably (and erroneously) in addressing issues of age and crime. The important distinction is that "the peak in the crime rate in the teenage years reflects a peak in prevalence [but] incidence does not vary consistently with age" (Farrington, 1986a, p. 219). This observation is related to the next two points.

Third, juvenile violence produces low death rates and less serious injuries than adult crime (Zimring, 1998a). In 1998, murdered adults were more likely to have been killed with firearms (68%) than were murdered juveniles (48%) (Snyder, 1999, p. 3). Among violently victimized persons, adult victims are twice as likely as juvenile victims to be injured seriously (Snyder & Sickmund, 1995, p. 21). More than four-fifths of the persons with violence-related injuries treated in hospital emergency departments are adults (Rand & Strom, 1997). Finally, rates of youth gang violence are higher when adults are involved (Howell, Egley, & Gleason, 2000; Parsons & Meeker, 1999; Wiebe, Meeker, & Vila, 1999). In a nutshell, adult crime has far more serious consequences than juvenile crime.

Fourth, adults are far more likely than juveniles to use guns in attacks and to use more lethal ones. Media portrayals of juvenile "superpredators" (see Chapter 2) have created the impression that juveniles are most likely to be armed—heavily armed—and to use guns in attacks. The increase in juvenile and young adult homicides from the mid-1980s through the mid-1990s prompted the U.S. Department of the Treasury to launch the Youth Crime Gun Interdiction Initiative (YCGII), which gathered valuable information on the ages of illegal gun carriers. Under the YCGII, the Bureau of Alcohol, Tobacco and Firearms in the Department of the Treasury supported 27 cities in developing systems that would allow them to trace all recovered crime guns. Surprisingly, nearly 9 out of 10 (89%) of the illegal guns recovered by police in the 27 cities in 1997-1998 were in the hands of adults (ages 18 and older); only 11% were recovered from juveniles (Bureau of Alcohol, Tobacco and Firearms, 1999). Nearly three times more recovered guns (32%) were in the hands of young adults, ages 18-24, than were in the hands of juveniles.

Moreover, in a recent St. Louis study concerning guns recovered from juveniles, Ruddell and Mays (in press) found that most of the firearms carried by juveniles had a low capacity for lethality. Most of the seized firearms in the hands of juveniles were pellet guns, .22 caliber firearms, and "Saturday night specials." Very few were large-caliber assault weapons, sawed-off rifles, or shotguns, all weapons more widely used by adult offenders.

Fifth, adolescent violence is characterized by group involvement (Reiss, 1988; Warr, 2002; Zimring, 1981). In an analysis of National Longitudinal Survey of Youth data (Gold & Reimer, 1975), Warr (1996) found that most adolescent offenders committed their offenses with two to three others, and that four others typically were involved in group fights. National victimization data show that more than one-half of serious violent juvenile offenses involve groups of offenders, compared with one-third of adult offenses (Snyder & Sickmund, 1995, p. 47).

Still, group arrests of juveniles serve to inflate juvenile arrest statistics (Snyder, 1999, p. 2; Snyder & Sickmund, 1999, pp. 113-114). In a Philadelphia study that made an adjustment for co-offending, McCord and Conway (2000) found that the number of offenses committed by juveniles was reduced by about 40% when co-offending was taken into account. Thus the clearance statistic is a better indicator than arrest of the proportion of crime committed by juveniles (see Box 1.1). The clearance statistic would typically show that a smaller number of juveniles in a presumed group-related crime were actually charged with the crime.

Sixth, there is no common pattern for juvenile violent arrests when viewed in the long term because rates of such arrests change substantially in the short run (Zimring, 1998a, p. 33). Zimring (1998a) analyzed more than 16 year-to-year changes (from 1980 to 1996) and found that juvenile homicide arrest rates increased or decreased by more than 20% four times, and by more than 15% a total of seven times. Aggravated assault arrest rates fluctuated similarly, with 1-year increases of 34%, 19%, and 17% in the 16 year-to-year changes. As noted earlier in this chapter, the four most serious violent offenses (homicide, robbery, rape, and aggravated assault) showed four different statistical stories among juveniles from 1980 to 1996.

Seventh, it is important to recognize that juvenile and young adult arrest rates were driven up during the 1980s and 1990s by four U.S. "wars": the "war on crime" (Bittner, 1970; Caplan, 1976; Milakovich & Weis, 1975; Tonry, 1994a), the "war on drugs" (Austin, Marino, Carroll, McCall, & Richards, 2000; Gardiner & McKinney, 1991; Tonry, 1994b), the "war on gangs" (Fleisher, 1995, p. 7), and the "war on juveniles" (Howell, 1997; Zimring, 1998a). As Bittner (1970) has observed, the rhetorical war language signifies the transition from a routine concern to a state of emergency and "is supposed to indicate that the community is seriously imperiled by forces bent on its destruction and calls for the mounting of efforts that have claims on all available resources to defeat the peril" (p. 48).

All four of these "wars" targeted young inner-city black males. Violent arrests increased the most for members of this group from the mid-1980s to the early 1990s (Blumstein, 1995a, 1995b, 1996; Fox, 1996b). From 1983 to 1992, arrest rates for both white and black juveniles increased sharply (Snyder & Sickmund, 1995, p. 104). In absolute terms, however, the rate for black juveniles grew much more than that for white juveniles; as Snyder and Sickmund (1995) note, "A typical 100,000 white juveniles experienced 110 more arrests in 1992 than in 1983, while a comparable group of black juveniles experienced 470 more arrests for a violent crime" (p. 104).

Finally, it can be misleading to consider only juvenile violence trends and ignore violence trends in other age groups. In an analysis of the FBI *Supplemental Homicide Reports,* Cook and Laub (1998) found that the homicide commission and victimization rates for 13- to 17-year-old and 18- to 24-year-old males during the late 1980s and early 1990s increased similarly. Yet the increase in juvenile violence was given far more media attention than the similar growth in young adult crime. In fact, the Violent Crime Index arrest rate increased among all age groups in the 1980s and 1990s (Snyder & Sickmund, 1999, p. 130), and the increase was larger (66%) among 30- to 49-year-olds than in any other age group, including teenagers (Males, 1997). The largest absolute increase in the homicide rate was among black males ages 18 to 24 (Cook & Laub, 1998).

Summary

The decade from the mid-1980s through the mid-1990s saw sharp increases in violent crime rates among all age groups; the increase for overall serious violent crime was largest among 30- to 49-year-olds, and the increase for homicide was largest among 18- to 24-year-olds. When one examines the data from a short-term perspective, the increase in juvenile violence is exaggerated, in part, because of the tyranny of small numbers principle. Long-term arrest data for the period from 1980 through 1996

show that only two of the four major violent juvenile crimes increased during this period: aggravated assault and murder. Aggravated assault arrests increased the most; however, most of this increase was at the nonserious end of the assault scale.

For several reasons, arrest data are not as reliable as either victimization data or self-report survey data as a measure of actual crimes for juvenile offenders. First, juveniles are more likely than adults to be arrested in groups, and they may be more easily apprehended because of their group offending and lack of criminal stealth (Reiss, 1988). Second, juveniles are more likely than adults to be arrested for certain crimes that are reported to police. Finally, it appears that many minor juvenile offenses were upgraded to more serious charges during the 1988-1992 period (Zimring, 1998a) because of the lower degree of tolerance of juvenile delinquency that ensued following the publicized increases in serious and violent delinquency. The lower tolerance is attributable, in particular, to the "wars" on crime, drugs, juveniles, and gangs.

If we employ more reliable measures of delinquency, we see a much different picture of violent juvenile crime trends. Self-report data suggest that in the early 1990s, compared with the late 1980s, a slightly larger proportion (only 8-10%) of juveniles were committing serious violent acts, but not at a higher rate. Victimization data show that violent juvenile victimizations resulting in serious injury actually declined from the late 1980s to early 1990s. (Of course, homicide cannot be measured in victim surveys.)

Thus the main feature of juvenile violence trends during the 1980-1996 period is the increase in gun use in homicides. Recall that non-gun homicides did not evidence a similar increase. Much of the increase in adolescent and young adult homicides appears to be attributable to an increase in gang-related homicides (Howell, 1999). The contribution of gang-related violence and homicides to the total volume of juvenile and young adult violence is perhaps the most overlooked factor in analysis of crime trends. The size and number of youth gangs, overall gang violence, and gang-related homicides all grew enormously from the mid-1980s to the mid-1990s (see Chapter 5). Unfortunately, *Uniform Crime Reports* data do not provide an accurate accounting of gang-related homicides (Maxson, Curry, & Howell, 2002). The few city studies that have been conducted have found that up to 6 out of 10 of all homicides committed by juveniles and young adults are gang related (see Chapter 5). The numbers of youth gang homicides rose sharply in the late 1980s (Howell,

1999), then tapered off in the early 1990s (Maxson et al., 2002), consistent with the national juvenile and young adult homicide trends. Although the absence of reliable national gang homicide data in the late 1980s and early 1990s precludes our making a firm determination, it appears certain that changes in gang homicide trends were a major factor influencing overall trends in homicides committed by juveniles and young adults.

Nothing I have said in this chapter should be taken as an attempt to minimize the severity of juvenile violence. Rather, my aim is to put such violence into proper perspective—historically and in relation to adult crime. Juveniles are part and parcel of the very high rates of violence in the United States. Ours is an extremely violent country, and juvenile violence rates are particularly high—higher than in other industrialized countries (U.S. Department of Health and Human Services, 2001, p. 28).

Both the total numbers and rates of violent crime juvenile arrests have dropped for 6 consecutive years since 1994, bringing these rates to their lowest levels in 20 years. In addition, violent victimization rates of juveniles ages 12-17 were at about at the same low level in 1996 as in 1980 (Snyder & Sickmund, 1999, p. 26). Homicides by juveniles have plummeted since 1993 (Butts & Travis, 2002).

Violence rates dropped among all age groups from 1994 to 2000, similar to the populationwide increase in the 1980s and early 1990s. No one knows why violence rates rise and fall at the same time in all sectors of society. Suggested explanations include the following (Blumstein & Wallman, 2000; Steffensmeier & Harer, 1999):

- Improved economic conditions
- Changes in crime opportunities
- Tougher laws and enforcement that have deterred and incapacitated offenders
- Longer sentences for violent crime involving guns
- Growing intolerance for violent behavior
- Expanded problem-oriented and community policing

- Police crackdowns on gun carrying and illegal gun purchases
- Expanded crime and violence prevention programs
- Gang suppression strategies
- Reductions in drug abuse and stabilization of illegal drug markets

Unfortunately, it is impossible to measure either the independent or the collective effects of such factors. Put simply, criminology cannot explain the peaks and valleys in crime rates.

Discussion Questions

1. What are the three different data sources that observers use to gauge changes in the levels of serious and violent delinquency? What are the strengths and weaknesses of each of these sources?

2. What is the tyranny of small numbers principle? Why is it important to understand this principle when one is attempting to assess juvenile delinquency trends?

3. Aside from the inappropriate use of data sources, what are some other ways of producing misleading juvenile crime trend statistics?

4. What are the distinguishing features of juvenile violence? Why are these important?

5. What is the main change in juvenile violence that occurred in the period of the late 1980s through the early 1990s?

6. How have domestic "wars" contributed to changing crime rates?

2

■

MYTHS ABOUT JUVENILE DELINQUENCY
AND THE JUVENILE JUSTICE SYSTEM

In this chapter, I address several key myths about juvenile violence that have had serious impacts on public responses and juvenile justice policies over the past 10-15 years. These myths are centered on the increase in violent juvenile arrests that began to occur in the mid-1980s and the projected increase in the number of juveniles in the U.S. population from the 1990s to 2010. Predominant among these myths is the myth of the emergence of a new breed of juvenile offenders often called *superpredators*. In conjunction with this pejorative label, other myths about juvenile violence have also contributed to distortions of reality about juvenile delinquency and appropriate juvenile justice system responses to it.

The Superpredator Myth

John DiIulio (1995b) coined the term *superpredator* to refer to a "new breed" of offenders, "kids that have absolutely no respect for human life and no sense of the future. . . . these are stone-cold predators!" (p. 23). Elsewhere, DiIulio and coauthors have described these young people as "fatherless, Godless, and jobless" and as "radically impulsive, brutally remorseless youngsters, including ever more teenage boys, who murder, assault, rob, burglarize, deal deadly drugs, join gun-toting gangs, and create serious communal disorders" (Bennett, DiIulio, & Walters, 1996, p. 27).

The superpredator myth gained further popularity when it was linked to forecasts of increased levels of juvenile violence made by James Q. Wilson and John DiIulio. Wilson (1995) asserted that "by the end of this decade [i.e., by 2000] there will be a million more people between the ages of 14 and 17 than there are now. . . . Six percent of them

will become high rate, repeat offenders—thirty thousand more young muggers, killers and thieves than we have now. Get ready" (p. 507). DiIulio (1995a, p. 15) made the same prediction.

A year later, DiIulio (1996a) pushed the horizon back 10 years and raised the ante, projecting that "by the year 2010, there will be approximately 270,000 more juvenile super-predators on the streets than there were in 1990" (p. 1). To come up with this number, he made the mistake of applying the 6% figure generated by the Philadelphia Birth Cohort Study (Wolfgang, Figlio, & Sellin, 1972; see Chapter 4 for discussion of this study) to the entire youth population, not just those in the delinquency-prone group, ages 10-17. By including infants and children ages 0-10 in his projection, DiIulio came up with a number eight times larger than the estimate he and Wilson had made earlier (see Box 2.2).

DiIulio based his projection of 270,000 on two factors. First, he assumed that the 6% figure that the Philadelphia Birth Cohort Study found in relation to Philadelphia boys who were chronic offenders in the 1960s would remain constant. Second, he factored this figure in with projections of the growth of the juvenile population made by the U.S. Bureau of the Census (see Figure 2.1). According to these projections, the ages 0-17 population group in the United States was expected to grow by 14% (4.5 million) between 1996 and 2010.

The illogical nature of DiIulio's projection is readily apparent. He assumed that 6% of babies and children as well as juveniles would be chronic offenders (Zimring, 1996). If we were to apply the 6% figure to the 1996 population under age 18, according to DiIulio's analysis, there already were 1.9 million "superpredator" juvenile offenders in

---

Box 2.1

Myths About Juvenile Delinquency

Bernard (1992) describes myths as "beliefs about the past that are strongly held and convenient to believe but are based on little actual information. Myths are not necessarily false—people generally just don't know or care whether they are true or false. They hold the belief because it is convenient to do so" (p. 11). Following are some common myths about juvenile delinquency (Bernard, 1992, p. 12):

- *The myth of progress: Delinquency in the past was much more serious than it is today.* Few people believe this myth; rather, they fear that if they let their guard down, delinquency will get worse.
- *The myth that nothing changes: Delinquency in the past was about the same as it is today.* More people believe this myth than believe the first one. It is supported by the view that delinquency is part and parcel of human nature—"boys will be boys."
- *The myth of the good old days: Delinquency in the past was much less serious than it is today.* More people likely believe this myth than believe the first and second ones combined. This myth is true some of the time and false at other times. The view that delinquency was better controlled at one time implies that relatively simple solutions (quick fixes) should solve the problems associated with juvenile delinquency today.

Box 2.2

The Logic of DiIulio's (1995b) Superpredator Prediction

- From 1996 through 2010, the number of boys under age 18 would increase by a total of 4.5 million (from 32 million to 36.5 million).
- The Philadelphia Birth Cohort Study found that 6% of the boys in the study sample were chronic offenders.
- Therefore, by 2010, the United States would have 270,000 (.06 × 4.5 million) more superpredators, perpetrators of the "coming wave of teen violence."

---

the United States. This number is nearly twice the number of children and adolescents referred to juvenile courts each year (for discussion of other errors in logic made by both Wilson and DiIulio, see Zimring, 1998a, pp. 61-65). In addition, DiIulio and Wilson apparently were not aware that the majority of the 6% "chronic" offenders in the Philadelphia Birth Cohort Study were never arrested for a Violent Crime Index offense (Weitekamp, Kerner, Schindler, & Schubert, 1995). This oversight served to exaggerate further the potential dangerousness of future offenders.

Speaking at a meeting of the American Association for the Advancement of Science, Fox warned of a "bloodbath" of teen violence (quoted in Associated Press, 1996). He also warned elsewhere

of a juvenile "crime wave storm" (Fox, 1996a). In a report to the U.S. Attorney General, Fox (1996b) said, "Our nation faces a future juvenile violence problem that may make today's epidemic pale in comparison" (p. 3). He called attention in particular to the projected growth in the black teenage (ages 14-17) population, which would increase 26% by 2005. He also noted: "There is, however, still time to stem the tide, and to avert the coming wave of teen violence. But time is of the essence" (p. i). DiIulio (1996b) warned that juvenile superpredators would be "flooding the nation's streets," coming "at us in waves over the next 20 years. . . . Time is running out" (p. 25). He also used inflammatory language similar to Fox's, warning, "We must therefore be prepared to contain the ['crime bomb'] explosion's

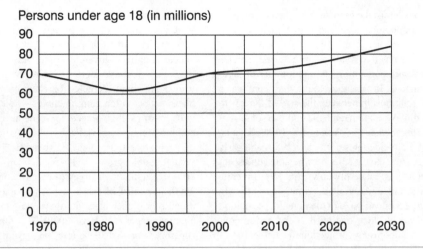

Figure 2.1   U.S. Juvenile Population Trend

SOURCE: *Juvenile Offenders and Victims: 1999 National Report* (p. 2), by H. N. Snyder and M. Sickmund, 1999, Washington, DC: Office of Juvenile Justice and Delinquency Prevention. ©1999 by National Center for Juvenile Justice. Reprinted with permission.

force and limit its damage" (DiIulio, 1995a, p. 15). However, he expressed hopelessness, saying, "This crime bomb probably cannot be defused," and asserting that the superpredators would be here within 5 years (i.e., by the year 2000) (p. 15).

Analyses conducted by others, such as Blumstein (1995a, 1995b, 1996) and Fox (1996b), lent support to DiIulio's and Wilson's formulations. Blumstein's analysis showed that the homicide rates among juveniles, the numbers of gun homicides, and the arrest rates of nonwhite juveniles for drug offenses all doubled in the late 1980s and early 1990s, and he tied these three findings together. He, too, feared that the youth violence epidemic would continue with the growth of the young population and warned that "children who are now younger (about ages 5 to 15) represent the future problem" (Blumstein, 1996, p. 2; see also Blumstein & Rosenfeld, 1999, pp. 161-162). Fox (1996b) also put the spotlight on juveniles and tied drugs, guns, and gangs together more explicitly in a causal connection.

Snyder and Sickmund (1995, p. 111) made projections using a "constant rate" assumption in which violent crimes by juveniles between the years 1992 and 2010 would increase by 22%, commensurate with the expected increase in the juvenile population ages 10 to 17. They also made an "increasing rate" forecast in which the rates of juvenile violence would continue to increase as they had in recent years prior to 1992. Under this increasing-rate assumption, the number of juvenile arrests for violent crime could be

predicted to double by the year 2010, with an increase of 145% for murder. To their credit, Snyder and Sickmund (2000) later retracted their projection, for the reason that is explained shortly.

Aggregate (group) data can be misleading when used to explain causal relationships at the individual level, because an apparent correlation may turn out to be simply chance. For example, although gang homicides increased in cities hit hard by the crack cocaine epidemic, and gangs are known to be active in drug trafficking, studies in seven such cities showed only a weak correlation between gang homicides and gang involvement in drug trafficking (Howell, 1999; see also Rosenfeld, Bray, & Egley, 1999). That is, the apparent gangs-drugs-homicide connection lacks empirical support. Studies have shown that youth gang violence has many sources unrelated to drugs (Howell & Decker, 1999), mainly turf battles for prominence over the constricted boundaries of small neighborhood areas (Block & Block, 1993) and retaliatory responses to violence—real or perceived—against rival gangs (Decker, 1996). Some youth gangs do engage in drug market wars, but most of these drug wars involve adult drug cartels or syndicates and other adult criminal organizations (Eddy, Sabogal, & Walden, 1988; Gugliotta & Leen, 1989). It is interesting to note that in Canada juvenile homicide rates increased sharply in the mid- to late 1980s without the presence of any crack cocaine epidemic (Hagan & Foster, 2000).

It also is a mistake to assume a direct correlation between population size and crime rates (Levitt, 1999). As Cook and Laub (1998) have shown, there is no strong positive relationship between the size of the juvenile population and the number of juvenile homicides. In fact, they found that there was a *negative* relationship between the size of the 13- to 17-year-old population and the number of homicides during the late 1980s and early 1990s. That is, "the high homicide rates of the late 1980s and early 1990s occurred during a period when the adolescent population was relatively low" (p. 59). Juvenile homicides and other violent crimes currently are *decreasing,* while the size of the juvenile population is *increasing.* In fact, one-third of the period covered in the doomsday projections (1995-2010) of waves of juvenile violence already has passed, and juvenile violence has been decreasing since 1994, not increasing (Snyder & Sickmund, 1999). In fact, the magnitude of the decline in violent crime arrests in the period 1994-1997 was greater than the projected growth in the juvenile population over the next 20 years (Snyder & Sickmund, 1999, p. 6). Now, after six consecutive year-to-year decreases in overall juvenile violence arrests, and with arrest rates at a 20-year low, it is obvious that Wilson, DiIulio, and Fox were seriously wrong in their forecasts (see Butts & Travis, 2002). Many other researchers have debunked their superpredator concept and doomsday projections (e.g., Howell, 1998c; Males, 1996; Snyder, 1998; Snyder & Sickmund, 2000, p. 130; Zimring, 1998a).

Forecasting juvenile delinquency rates—and adult crime rates, for that matter—is risky business. As McCord, Widom, and Crowell (2001) note, criminologists' capacity to forecast crime rates is very limited, and "errors in forecasts over even relatively short periods of two to three years, let alone for a decade or more, are very large" (p. 65). When observers attempt to make such forecasts, they should be careful to include both warnings about the inherent inaccuracy of projected estimates in this area and cautions about the limited appropriate use of such estimates. In addition, juvenile justice policy makers should guard against giving much credence to forecasts made by reputed "experts" from outside the field of juvenile justice who are unfamiliar with the implications of using arrest data to measure juvenile delinquency. Uncritical acceptance of juvenile arrest data is a common problem in the juvenile justice field (Elliott, 1995, 2000).

In spite of the problems noted above with Wilson's, DiIulio's, and Fox's doomsday forecasts, they were taken seriously for a number of years. The two images foremost in these forecasts, of "superpredators" and a growing "crime bomb," were powerful, and they played well in the broadcast media and with politicians who wanted to appear tough on juvenile crime. Several popular magazines featured stories on the predicted crime wave, and many depicted on their covers young black thugs—often gang members—holding handguns. Stories that played to readers' fears were common (e.g., Guest & Pope, 1996). Articles spoke of "baby-faced criminals" (Lyons, 1997). Fear of young people grew in the public's mind (Soler, 2001). In a national survey of parents conducted in 2000, one-third of those responding said that the threat of violence affecting their own children was a major concern (Villalva, 2000). The images of the superpredator and the crime bomb stimulated the assumptions about youth violence discussed below.

Assumptions Tied to
the Superpredator Myth

The superpredator myth generated three assumptions that have been misleading to the juvenile justice field:

1. That the relative *proportion* of serious and violent offenders among all juvenile delinquents is growing

2. That juvenile offenders are becoming younger and younger

3. That juveniles are committing more and more violent crimes

Snyder (1998) tested all three of these assumptions by examining the juvenile court careers of members of 16 annual birth cohorts in Maricopa County, Arizona (this county includes Phoenix and several smaller surrounding cities). He analyzed the juvenile court careers of all persons born from 1962 through 1977 who were referred to the court from 1980 through 1995—up to the point when they graduated from the jurisdiction of the juvenile court (i.e., once they turned 18, they no longer were legally eligible for juvenile court jurisdiction). Some 151,000 offender careers were represented in the 16 cohorts.

First, did the relative proportion of serious and violent offenders increase? Snyder found only a 4% increase (from about 13% of all careers to about 17%) in the proportion of chronic offender careers in the juvenile justice graduating classes of the 1990s compared with the classes of the 1980s. However, the serious nature of the individual chronic career remained about the same. That is to say, the later classes contained more chronic offender careers, but they were not more significantly more active, more serious, or more violent than chronic offenders in the graduating classes of the 1980s. Compared with offender careers in the 1980s, a slightly greater proportion of offender careers in the 1990s included violent offenses (10% versus 8%). This proportion increased about 5% from 1988 to 1992—hardly a change of epidemic proportions.

Second, was the onset of officially recognized juvenile violence and serious offending occurring at younger age in the 1990s than in the 1980s? Snyder found no evidence that the juveniles in his study were beginning their court careers at younger ages. Across all cohorts, the first delinquency and serious-nonviolent referrals occurred at age 15, and the first violent referrals occurred at age 16. These average entry ages did not change over the 16 years. Moreover, there was no significant increase in the proportion of juveniles who began their offending careers or violent offending before age 14.

Third, were serious and violent offenders in recent years being referred for more crimes? Snyder did not find any increase in the numbers of crimes for which serious and violent offenders were charged. The violent offense rate in the careers of youth with violent offense referrals remained constant over the 16 graduating classes, averaging 1.2 violent referrals per career. Also, the serious delinquency (serious-nonviolent referrals) rate did not change from the early 1980s to the late 1990s. The overall delinquency referral rate did increase over the 16 graduating classes, but, as Snyder (1998) observes, "much of the growth in referrals for the more recent graduating classes was a growth in referrals for nonserious offenses, an indication that the juvenile justice system may be spreading its net wider, bringing in more juveniles, not more serious juvenile offenders" (p. 443).

Other Myths About Juvenile Violence

- *Myth 1:* A juvenile violence "epidemic" occurred in the late 1980s and early 1990s.

This is a questionable assertion. Public health scientists use the word *epidemic* to refer to particular health problems that affect numbers of the population above expected levels, but they do not specify what constitutes an "epidemic level." The evidence does not necessarily support the conclusion that

there was an epidemic of *overall* juvenile violence in the late 1980s and early 1990s; only the increase in homicides might be considered to have reached such a level. At the height of the "juvenile violence epidemic" (in 1993), only about 6% of all juvenile arrests were for violent crimes (McCord et al., 2001, p. 33). If a youth violence epidemic had occurred, the rates of all forms of youth violence would have increased sharply, not just gun homicides. Although increases shown in arrest data could be taken as evidence of a juvenile violence epidemic, more reliable measures of juvenile violence trends (victimization and self-report data) do not support such a conclusion—as seen in Chapter 1. Victimization and self-report data show only a modest increase in juvenile violence during this period, with the exception of homicide. Although there was a 23% increase in juvenile violent victimization, most of these were simple assaults, and the proportion of victimizations that resulted in serious injury actually declined during this period. The proportion of juveniles who self-reported having committed violent acts is estimated to have increased about 8-10% in the late 1980s and early 1990s (Elliott, 1994b)—hardly an epidemic.

It can properly be said that a gun homicide epidemic occurred in the late 1980s and early 1990s, and juveniles were a part of this. From 1984 through 1993, the number of juveniles killed with firearms tripled, and the number of nonfirearm homicides remained relatively constant (see Figure 2.2). However, the gun homicide epidemic was by no means limited to juveniles. Although adolescents showed the biggest proportional increase in homicide commission and victimization (due to the "tyranny of small numbers"), the biggest absolute change was for young adults (Cook & Laub, 1998, p. 60).

It can also be said that a gun *suicide* epidemic occurred in the 1980s and early 1990s. The rate of youth (ages 0-19) suicides involving firearms increased 39% from 1980 through 1994, whereas the rate of suicides not involving firearms remained virtually unchanged during this period (Snyder & Sickmund, 1999, p. 24). These data are illustrated in Figure 2.3. For every two young people (ages 0-19) who are murdered, one commits suicide (Snyder & Sickmund, 1995, p. 27). The gun suicide epidemic was most evident among black adolescent males, the very group that DiIulio singled out as fearless, "stone-cold predators." From 1979 through 1994, the rate of juvenile suicides involving firearms increased by one-third among young white males; during this same period the rate almost tripled among young black males (Sickmund, Snyder, & Poe-Yamagata, 1996, p. 3). Thus it would be accurate to say that an adolescent gun suicide

Juvenile homicide victims

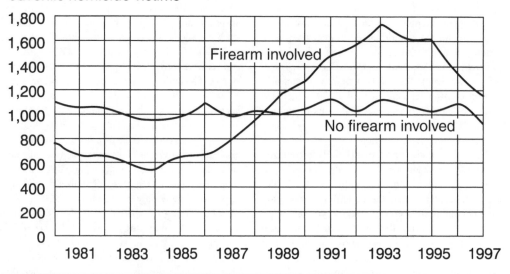

Figure 2.2   Firearm and Nonfirearm Juvenile Homicide Victims

SOURCE: *Juvenile Offenders and Victims: 1999 National Report* (p. 19), by H. N. Snyder and M. Sickmund, 1999, Washington, DC: Office of Juvenile Justice and Delinquency Prevention. ©1999 by National Center for Juvenile Justice. Reprinted with permission.

epidemic occurred at the same time as the adolescent gun homicide epidemic—particularly among young black males. Any explanation for the increase in adolescent gun homicides in the late 1980s and early 1990s must also account for the increase in adolescent gun suicides during that period. The crack cocaine epidemic is not a plausible explanation for both phenomena.

- *Myth 2:* Juveniles frequently carry guns and traffic in them.

The reality is that juveniles very rarely carry firearms or use them. The 1997 National Longitudinal Survey of Youth (NLSY) found that 10% of 12- to 16-year-olds had ever carried a handgun, only 3% had done so in the past 30 days, and fewer than 1 in 200 had carried a handgun to school during the past 30 days (cited in Snyder & Sickmund, 1999, p. 58). As noted in Chapter 1, the Bureau of Alcohol, Tobacco and Firearms (1999) has found that 89% of illegal guns that police recover on the streets are recovered from adults. The BATF has found also that only 19% of juvenile gun carriers are involved in gun trafficking.

- *Myth 3:* Juvenile violence is the top crime problem in the United States.

Actually, adult violence is our nation's top crime problem. FBI data show that juveniles accounted for only 6% of the murders and only 12% of violent crimes in the United States cleared by arrests in 1999 (Snyder, 2000, p. 2). These figures are far below juveniles' proportional representation (19%) in the age range of the total population that commits most crime (ages 10-49) (Snyder & Sickmund, 1999, p. 116). Young adult offenders ages 18-24 have the highest violent crime arrest rates (Cook & Laub, 1998).

Violence rates are very high among juveniles, but adult violence produces far more harm to victims. The majority of the most serious form of violence—homicide—involves adults killing adults. Most homicide offenders are ages 18 to 34, as are their victims (Snyder & Sickmund, 1999, p. 22). The greatest numbers of homicides involve 19- and 20-year-olds killing others of the same ages. In addition, many very young children are killed by persons in their 20s and 30s (mostly cases in which children are killed by their parents). The overwhelming majority of gun homicides and gun assaults in the United States involve adult perpetrators and victims (Cook & Ludwig, 2001).

- *Myth 4:* Juveniles were the driving force behind the increase in violence in the

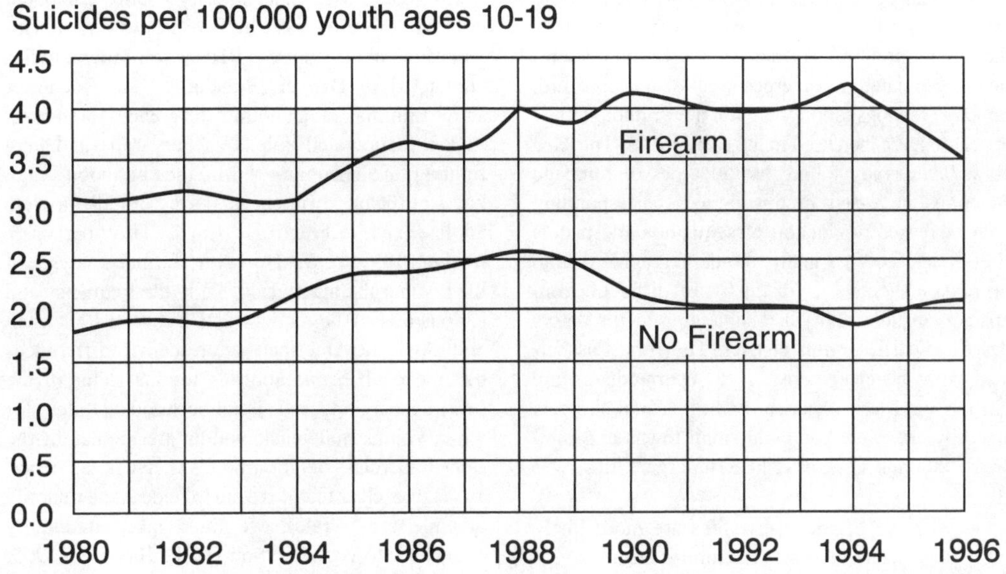

Suicides per 100,000 youth ages 10-19

Figure 2.3   Firearm and Nonfirearm Juvenile Suicides

SOURCE: *Juvenile Offenders and Victims: 1999 National Report* (p. 24), by H. N. Snyder and M. Sickmund, 1999, Washington, DC: Office of Juvenile Justice and Delinquency Prevention. ©1999 by National Center for Juvenile Justice. Reprinted with permission.

United States from the mid-1980s through the early 1990s.

In reality, studies conducted by researchers at the National Center for Juvenile Justice have shown that adults, not juveniles, accounted for two-thirds of the increase in murders in the late 1980s and early 1990s, and that adults were responsible for nearly three-fourths of the increase in violent crime arrests during this period (Snyder et al., 1996, p. 20). Murders increased 23% from 1985 through 1994 (Snyder et al., 1996, p. 20). If murders by juveniles had remained constant over this period, murders in the United States would have increased by 15%. Violent crime arrests rose 66% from 1980 through 1994 among 30- to 49-year-olds—the largest increase in any age group (Males, 1997).

- *Myth 5:* Juvenile offenders are committing more and more violent crimes at younger and younger ages.

OJJDP's Study Group on Very Young Offenders concluded that there is no empirical evidence to support this claim (see the chapters collected in Loeber & Farrington, 2001a; see also Butts & Snyder, 1997; Snyder, 1998). The proportion of all

juvenile violent arrests involving children ages 10-12 remained essentially constant in the 1980s and 1990s (Snyder & Sickmund, 1999, p. 121). Just 2% of all juvenile arrests involved youth under age 10 in 1998 (Snyder, 1999, p. 11). After reviewing self-report studies, Elliott (1994b) concluded that the proportion of adolescents involved in some type of serious violent offending increased slightly from the late 1980s through the early 1990s, but the frequency of offending remained about the same.

- *Myth 6:* School shootings represent a "second wave" of the juvenile violence (Wickham, 1998) that doomsday forecasters Fox and DiIulio prophesied.

First, it is important to recognize that student school shooters represent only a fraction of all mass killers, a group that is overwhelmingly made up of adults (Fessenden, 2000; Fox & Levin, 1994). A large proportion of rampage killings are motivated by domestic problems. A study conducted for the *New York Times* found that even when domestic cases are excluded, school shootings represent only one in five rampage killings (Fessenden, 2000). Second, few school shootings are random acts. In a study of the 105 school-associated deaths in the

United States in the period 1992-1994, Kachur et al. (1996) found that only 18% were random events—the same proportion as suicides. Most school shootings are related to interpersonal disputes. Third, rampage school shootings are not new, although they appear to have increased in the early 1990s. The *New York Times* study found that all types of rampage shootings increased in this period, corresponding with increased production of semiautomatic pistols (Fessenden, 2000). Finally, the demographic profile of school shooters is distinctively different from characterizations of mythical juvenile superpredators described earlier in this chapter. The youths associated with the characteristics of superpredators are inner-city African American males; school shooters typically are white youths in small towns and rural areas, although some have lived in larger cities.

- *Myth 7:* Minority juveniles are more likely than white juveniles to commit crimes.

In a national poll conducted by the organization Building Blocks for Youth, just over one-third (34%) of respondents agreed with the statement "Black juveniles are more likely to commit crime than white juveniles" (Soler, 2001). The reality is that studies have shown no substantive differences in age-specific prevalence rates nationwide for serious and violent offenses during the adolescent period (Elliott, 1994a; Huizinga & Elliott, 1987). In the National Youth Survey, Elliott (1994a) found that it was not until adulthood that the self-reported serious and violent offense rates for blacks greatly exceeded the rates for whites. However, national data appearing in the FBI's (1992) *Uniform Crime Reports* showed a 5-to-1 difference in arrest rates for violent offenses for black versus white youths at about the time Elliott's study was completed. Elliott concluded that the small self-reported differences were not sufficient to explain the large differences in arrest rates (p. 18). Huizinga and Elliott (1987) examined racial differences among high-frequency juvenile offenders and among offenders who inflicted greater physical injury to victims or used weapons; they conclude that "even at the very high end of the delinquent behavior continuum there is almost no evidence of a racial difference" (p. 215). Thus black youth are overrepresented in arrest, court referral, and incarceration data. This is one of the main reasons that researchers who have used police records to study chronic juvenile offenders have found race to be a defining characteristic (see Tracy, Wolfgang, & Figlio, 1990; Wolfgang et al., 1972; Wolfgang, Thornberry, & Figlio, 1987).

But could it be that minority youths, compared with white youths, have higher rates of serious violent crime in large cities? Recent self-report studies conducted in Denver, Pittsburgh, and Rochester show minimal racial/ethnic differences in serious violent (aggravated assault, robbery, rape, and gang fights) prevalence rates during the childhood years, but significant differences during middle to late adolescence (Kelley, Huizinga, Thornberry, & Loeber, 1997, p. 8). However, further analysis of the Pittsburgh data reveals that in the frequency and seriousness of delinquent acts between Caucasian and African American adolescents, differences disappear when one controls for the status of the juveniles' residential neighborhoods: Rates for white youths and black youths are similar in the same underclass neighborhoods (Peeples & Loeber, 1994). It is clear that if we are to understand minority juvenile crime rates, we must take community contexts into consideration (D. F. Hawkins, 1995; Hawkins, Laub, & Lauritsen, 1998).

- *Myth 8:* The juvenile justice system in the United States is a failure; it is collapsing because it cannot handle today's more serious offenders.

In the midst of the moral panic over delinquency, such unusually critical statements were made about the juvenile courts—including charges that they are "kiddie courts," too lenient, and quaint, and that probation is a farce (Butterfield, 1997)—that some critics proposed scrapping them altogether (see Chapter 8). The notion that the juvenile justice system has become ineffective is based on the following three assumptions (Tracy & Kempf-Leonard, 1998):

1. Sanctions in juvenile courts are neither certain enough nor severe enough to deter serious delinquents from continually committing serious crimes.

2. The rehabilitative techniques used by juvenile courts have not sufficiently reduced recidivism.

3. The preponderance of noncustodial sanctions (such as probation) and/or the very short institutional sanctions that are applied allow delinquents to pose a continued and severe risk to public safety.

None of these assumptions is supported by empirical evidence, as I will show in later chapters of this book. Juvenile court studies (which I review in

Chapter 9) show relatively low recidivism rates. Sanctions alone are not effective, but juvenile court sanctions are adequate to control delinquency, particularly when combined with treatment options. There is some evidence that neither the certainty nor the severity of punishment decreases recidivism among most juveniles (Schneider, 1990; Schneider & Ervin, 1990), and deterrence strategies such as shock incarceration and boot camps have been shown to increase recidivism instead of reducing it (see Chapter 7). Most juvenile court programs, even everyday programs, reduce recidivism, and many of them produce large reductions—even for serious and violent offenders (see Chapter 9). Probation combined with certain treatment interventions appears to be most effective. In addition, juvenile recidivism rates are higher among offenders sent to training schools than for those the courts assign to community-based alternative programs. Thus incarceration of juveniles provides less long-term protection for the public than treatment and rehabilitation programs aimed at young offenders.

- *Myth 9:* Transferring juveniles to the criminal justice system is the way to reduce juvenile delinquency.

A philosophical shift concerning the aim of incarceration of juvenile offenders (from rehabilitation to punishment) and the presumption that the juvenile justice system cannot mete out sufficiently long sentences to deter the presumed new breed of juvenile offenders have led to the notion that imprisonment will deter these offenders from their criminal tendencies. However, studies have shown that juveniles who are transferred to criminal court and placed in adult prisons are actually more likely to recidivate than juveniles retained in the juvenile justice system, and their recidivism rates, offense rates, and offense severity appear to increase after they are released from prison (see Chapter 8). Equally important, the criminal justice system does not have the capacity necessary to handle juvenile offenders, and its performance record with adult offenders does not inspire confidence in its ability to deal with juveniles as well. (I discuss the topic of transfer of juveniles to the criminal justice system in detail in Chapter 8.)

Summary

The most damaging and egregiously erroneous myth propagated in the 100-year history of the juvenile justice system in the United States is that concerning the emergence of a new breed of juvenile offenders pejoratively called superpredators. Observers have linked this mythical image with forecast increases in the size of the juvenile population. Frightening images of "waves of violent adolescents coming at us over the next decade," producing a "bloodbath," have been disseminated by the popular press. As shown in this chapter, juvenile violence rates are not directly tied to the population size of juvenile age groups.

Over the past 10-15 years, many other myths about juvenile violence and the juvenile justice system have also changed public perceptions of juvenile delinquents and the ability of the juvenile justice system to handle them. One of these myths is that a juvenile violence "epidemic" occurred in the late 1980s and early 1990s. Those who try to defend this myth mainly use arrest data to support their claim. However, if we use other, more reliable measures of actual levels of juvenile violence— self-report and victimization surveys—we can see that the claim is erroneous. Four domestic U.S. "wars" (on crime, drugs, gangs, and juveniles) drove juvenile arrests up during the late 1980s and early 1990s (see Chapter 1), creating the perception of an overall epidemic of violence among juveniles. Actually, violence increased across the board, in all age groups, with the largest increase among adults in their 30s and 40s. Yet the public perception was that juveniles were driving the increase in violence, and many came to believe that juvenile violence must be the country's top crime problem. Neither perception corresponded with reality. Adults—not juveniles—are the perpetrators of most serious violence in the United States. Moreover, victims of adult crime are twice as likely as the victims of juvenile crime to be injured seriously (Snyder & Sickmund, 1995, p. 21), and death rates related to juvenile violence are low (Zimring, 1998a).

Other myths about juvenile violence fit well with the superpredator myth and the myth of an epidemic of juvenile violence, such as the myth that juvenile offenders are committing more and more violent crimes at younger and younger ages and the myth that the juvenile justice system lacks the capacity to deal effectively with the new breed of superpredators and the coming juvenile violence epidemic. Such myths have led to a perception of juvenile delinquency as equivalent to adult crime, and some observers have come to believe that turning juvenile offenders over to the criminal justice system is a solution. This has proved to be a flawed policy, however (see Chapter 8).

Box 2.3

Myths About Juvenile Violence

- A juvenile violence "epidemic" occurred in the late 1980s and early 1990s.
- Juveniles frequently carry guns and traffic in them.
- Juvenile violence is the top crime problem in the United States.
- Juveniles were the driving force behind the increase in violence in the United States from the mid-1980s through the early 1990s.
- Juvenile offenders are committing more and more violent crimes at younger and younger ages.
- School shootings represent a "second wave" of the juvenile violence that doomsday forecasters Fox and DiIulio prophesied.
- Minority juveniles are more likely than white juveniles to commit crimes.
- The juvenile justice system in the United States is a failure; it is collapsing because it cannot handle today's more serious offenders.
- Transferring juveniles to the criminal justice system is the way to reduce juvenile delinquency.

In sum, the best available evidence suggests that the decade from the mid-1980s to the mid-1990s saw the following changes:

- A doubling of the low juvenile homicide rate
- An 8-10% increase in the proportion of juveniles who committed violent acts
- A 5% increase in the proportion of juvenile court careers that included violent offenses
- A 4% increase in the proportion of chronic offenders (offenders who did not commit violent offenses)

The current crisis in juvenile justice has nothing to do with superpredators or new waves of violent juvenile offenders, as DiIulio, Fox, and Wilson have suggested. Rather, the erroneous perceptions of these observers have contributed to a "moral panic" over juvenile delinquency that has led to a crisis of overload in the juvenile justice system; I turn to this topic in Chapter 3.

Discussion Questions

1. Explain the superpredator hypothesis. How is the logic DiIulio used to support this concept flawed?

2. Why is forecasting juvenile delinquency rates a risky business?

3. Why might the increase in overall violent juvenile arrests from the mid-1980s to the early 1990s not be considered an epidemic? What, specifically, about that increase could be called epidemic?

4. Of the nine myths about juvenile violence discussed in this chapter, which one do you find most surprising? Why?

3

■

MORAL PANIC OVER JUVENILE DELINQUENCY AND THE CONSEQUENCES

As Chapter 1's examination of trends in serious and violent juvenile delinquency has shown, there was an increase in violent delinquency—particularly juvenile homicides—in the United States from the mid-1980s through the early 1990s. As discussed in Chapter 2, several important myths about juvenile delinquency, including the super-predator myth and the myth of a coming increase in juvenile crime, have been principal factors contributing to a moral panic over juvenile delinquency. That moral panic is the topic of this chapter.

In addition to the myths discussed in Chapter 2, other developments have contributed to and helped to sustain the current moral panic over juvenile delinquency. This chapter addresses the origins and history of this moral panic, which I characterize as the seventh moral panic over delinquency in the United States. The previous six moral panics occurred in the 1920s and around 1932, 1946, 1954, 1964, and 1977 (Bernard, 1992, pp. 31-37). In each of these eras, the current cohort of delinquents was described as "worse than ever before." As Hamparian, Schuster, Dinitz, and Conrad (1978) have observed, "From antiquity every generation has entertained the opinion that many if not most of its youth are the most vicious in the history of the race" (p. 11). I begin this chapter with a discussion of the history and development of the current moral panic, and then address the consequences of this panic for today's juvenile offenders and for the juvenile justice system.

Origins of the Current Moral Panic

The current moral panic over juvenile delinquency has its origins in three main factors. The first is often referred to as the *cycle of juvenile justice,* a strangely unique feature of American juvenile justice. The second factor contributing to this seventh moral panic is the recentness of the sixth moral panic over juvenile delinquency, which occurred in the late 1970s, preceding the beginning of the current panic by only about 10 years. The third contributing factor is the philosophical shift from rehabilitation to punishment in the criminal justice system that began in the 1970s; rather than rehabilitation, the main purpose of criminal justice intervention became punishment.

The enduring cycle of juvenile justice is a major contributor to the current moral panic over juvenile delinquency. Bernard (1992, pp. 37-39) explains the cycle as follows: Americans have strongly held, and conflicting, views about juvenile delinquency policies and the philosophy of juvenile justice historically applied in the United States. Juveniles are treated more leniently than adults for the same offenses based on jurisprudence (legal policies) in the American juvenile justice system; concepts such as *diminished capacity, proportionality,* and *room to reform* are applied to juveniles (Zimring, 1998a; for explanations of these concepts, see Chapter 8). Some of the young offenders who go through the juvenile justice system later go on to commit serious crimes, and many people believe that this would not happen if the juvenile justice system were not so lenient. They contend that the leniency of the system "encourages juveniles to laugh at the system, to believe they will not be punished no matter what they do, and to feel free to commit more frequent and serious crimes" (Bernard, 1992, p. 37). These views lead to public support for more punitive policies, less lenient responses, and the imposition of harsh punishments on juveniles. Despite such "get tough" measures, juvenile crime rates invariably remain high. Thus many observers are prompted to oppose harsh punishments, pointing out that they do not appear to reduce juvenile crime. These arguments lead to the return of more lenient treatment of juvenile offenders, beginning the cycle all over again. Thus the essence of "the cycle of juvenile justice arises from the fact that juvenile crime rates remain high regardless of juvenile justice policies that are in effect at the time" (Bernard, 1992, p. 38). In sum, Bernard asserts, the current (seventh) moral panic was to be expected; such panics are regularly occurring events, beginning anew every decade or so.

Even before the superpredator myth and other myths about juvenile delinquency and violence began to take hold in the mid-1990s, juvenile justice policies, practices, and laws had already begun to change. This wave of policy changes grew, in part, out of the sixth juvenile delinquency moral panic. It was stimulated by the manufacturing of a juvenile delinquency "epidemic" in the late 1970s (Hamparian et al., 1978) and was supported by the notion that a new subgroup of "chronic" juvenile offenders had emerged. This group was identified in the Philadelphia Birth Cohort Study (Wolfgang, Figlio, & Sellin, 1972) and in other studies that suggested the existence of young "monsters" (for a review of these studies, see Hamparian et al., 1978; Tracy, Wolfgang, & Figlio, 1990; Tracy & Kempf-Leonard, 1996).

Mainly as a result of the sixth moral panic over delinquency, nearly half of the states enacted some form of tougher responses to deal with the "new" group of serious and chronic juvenile offenders between 1978 and 1981 (McCord, Widom, & Crowell, 2001, pp. 161-162). Many of the changes these states initiated were patterned after the punitive measures that had been adopted in the criminal justice system. Juveniles charged with certain offenses were excluded from juvenile court jurisdiction. Making it easier to prosecute juveniles in adult criminal courts was a key change that signaled the beginning of a punishment trend that would drastically change U.S. juvenile justice policy (see Chapter 8).

The third factor contributing to the current moral panic, the philosophical shift from rehabilitation to punishment in the criminal justice system, has filtered down to the juvenile justice system (Howell, 1997). Attacks on criminal justice policies in the 1970s and 1980s came from both liberal and conservative ends of the political spectrum (Travis & Petersilia, 2001). Liberals viewed indeterminate sentences and disparate sentences for the same offenses as unjust. They wanted to see more consistency in criminal justice policies. Conservatives

viewed the criminal justice system as too lenient; they wanted to see more punishment elements in criminal justice policies. They advocated the "just desert" principle, a retributive philosophy that holds that offenders should suffer the infliction of deserved pain (von Hirsch, 1976). According to the just desert principle, criminal behavior should elicit punishment commensurate with the severity of the offense. An OJJDP administrator (a just desert advocate) put it thus: "The only way to deal with [chronic juvenile offenders] is to let them feel the sting of the justice system" (Regnery, 1986, p. 44).

The just desert philosophy produced in the adult segment of the justice system such innovations as determinate sentences, longer sentences, mandatory minimum sentences, and "truth in sentencing" (i.e., guarantees that offenders would serve their full sentences). Advocates of this philosophy also pushed for the revival of capital punishment, more use of incarceration (in jails and prisons) for adults and, more recently, punitive "three strikes" laws. Almost all of these policies were installed in the criminal justice system in the 1970s and 1980s, and adoption of many of these policies in the juvenile justice system was soon to follow.

The convergence of the three historical factors discussed above produced the most pronounced of the moral panics over juvenile delinquency in the 100-year history of the American juvenile justice system. Had but one of the three factors been present, that would have been sufficient for a sizable moral panic, but the convergence of the three forces generated a powerful impact on juvenile justice. The recurring cycle of juvenile justice that gave rise to the seventh moral panic was compounded by the aftereffects of the sixth moral panic. Indeed, the effects of the sixth moral panic were extended by the just desert reforms that had occurred in the criminal justice system and were filtering down to the juvenile justice system. The panic was further fueled by the inflammatory superpredator myth and related forecasts of a "coming wave" of juvenile violence.

The New Moral Panic
Over Juvenile Delinquency

It is difficult to capture in words the depth of the emotion that was part of the new moral panic of the early 1990s. The superpredator myth and the mistaken belief that "waves" of predatory youth were to "come at us" over the next decade, producing a "bloodbath," engendered enormous fear (Coalition for Juvenile Justice, 1994). The demonization of juveniles and catchy phrases about the dangers they

Box 3.1
Moral Panic Over Juvenile Delinquency

Definition

The term *moral panic* (Cohen, 1980) refers to circumstances in which the perceived threat from some group or situation is greatly exaggerated compared with the actual threat (Jackson & Rudman, 1993, p. 271). Put simply, moral crusaders in a society, offended by the social actions of a certain group or groups, create moral panics to stigmatize as evil the persons or actions they find offensive (Becker, 1963, pp. 147-148).

The Stages of Moral Panic

Brendtro and Long (1994) describe the four stages of moral panic. In the first stage, *stress* evokes irrational beliefs. For example, in the case of the current moral panic over juvenile delinquency, the stress engendered by frightening myths about violent juveniles leads to the view among adults that nothing can be done to diminish youth violence; adults come to fear adolescents because of their belief that adolescents cannot be controlled, and feelings of helplessness emerge.

In the second stage, feelings of helplessness trigger distressed, *furious feelings.* As Brendtro and Long describe it, "The natural human response in such situations is to 'down-shift' our brains from rational thought to lower brain survival mechanisms of fight/flight" (p. 4). If the distressed person cannot escape the source of stress, he or she will likely experience anger or rage. In the case of the moral panic over juvenile delinquency, Brendtro and Long note, "rage is a primitive hostile feeling that drives adults to want to get even. The person in this state is a blink away from striking out at the slightest provocation" (p. 4).

In the third stage, furious feelings drive *behavior.* The common behavioral response is to "make the transgressor suffer." Such behavior occurs when juveniles' offending so violates adults' standards of decency that adults feel justified in punishing the offending adolescents. A primitive part of humans even "enjoys" meting out punishment under such conditions.

In the fourth stage, punishment provokes a *reaction by the punished individuals.* Harsh punishment increases the likelihood that counteraggression will be triggered by rage on the part of the punished. Thus adolescent offenders who feel that they have been treated unfairly given what they have done, even when guilty, are likely to take part in further aggression against society. "Violence begets violence" in this stage (p. 4).

posed were repeated over and over in the media and by politicians in the early 1990s (Zimring, 1998a). As Torbet and Szymanski (1998) explain: "Extensive media coverage of violent crimes by juveniles—especially homicides with firearms—fueled perceptions of a juvenile violence epidemic. This, in turn, led to a response by governors and legislators to 'get tough' on juvenile crime" (p. 1). From 1992 through 1996, 48 (90%) of 51 state legislatures (including the District of Columbia) made substantive changes to their criminal statutes, mainly targeting juveniles who commit violent or serious crimes (Torbet et al., 1996). By the end of the decade, all states had enacted laws that made their juvenile justice systems more punitive or made it easier to transfer juveniles to the criminal justice system (Griffin, Torbet, & Szymanski, 1998; Moon, Sundt, Cullen, & Wright, 2000; Lyons, 1997; National Conference of State Legislatures, 1999a; National Criminal Justice Association, 1997; Snyder & Sickmund, 1999, p. 89; Torbet et al., 1996; Torbet, Griffin, Hurst, & MacKenzie, 2000; Torbet & Szymanski, 1998). Brendtro and Long (1994) have specified the psychological processes—that is, the stages of moral panic—through which legislators and other adult members of the public, outraged by youth violence, became hooked into an aggressive panic mode (see Box 3.1).

During this period, legislators lined up to introduce or support legislation aimed at stopping the coming wave of youth violence. Whenever a very young offender picked up a handgun, legislators were quick to lower the age of transfer to the criminal justice system, and even to provide the possibility of capital punishment. The states of Washington and Vermont enacted legislation allowing sentences of life without the possibility of parole for juveniles as young as ages 8 and 10, respectively (Logan, 1998). Despite the sharp drop in juvenile homicides and other violent crimes for 6-7 years running, in 2000 Virginia legislators acted to allow the death penalty for 16- and 17-year-olds convicted of certain felonies (Burton, 2001), in clear violation of international laws (were the United States to adopt such progressive human rights legislation; see Chapter 8).

Aphorisms such as "If you're old enough to do the crime, you're old enough to do the time" became the mantras of the leaders of the moral panic. Variations on this theme were "Do adult crime, do adult time," "Do the crime, do the time," and "If they are going to act like adults, treat them as adults" (Hunzeker, 1995; National Conference of State Legislatures, 1999a; Torbet et al., 1996; Torbet & Szymanski, 1998). *Accountability* became a euphemism for deserved punishment (i.e., just desert). But much of this posturing was part of an effort by prosecutors and other politicians to shift public policy toward harsher, more repressive solutions to youth crime (Beckett & Sasson, 2000). Zimring (2002, p. 154) argues that the exceptional performance of juvenile courts in the 1970s and 1980s rendered them vulnerable to attacks by those who had succeeded in radically altering punishments in the criminal justice system; they saw a "punishment gap" between the two systems. In this sense, juvenile offenders became "the last significant battleground for a get-tough orientation that had permeated the rest of the peno-correctional system" (Zimring, 2002, p. 154).

The new breed of superpredator juvenile offenders, by virtue of their "adult" offenses, presumably could not be controlled by the juvenile justice system or by any other conventional methods. Just deserts advocates put forth proposals to abolish the juvenile court system and promoted the use of punitive laws, policies, and practices in the juvenile justice system, including three-strikes laws, determinate sentences, longer sentences, sentencing to boot camps, electronic monitoring, drug testing, shock incarceration, and restorative justice (Howell, 1997). Such policies and practices, which de-emphasize prevention of juvenile crime and rehabilitation of juvenile offenders, are now commonplace in the juvenile justice system. Three-strikes laws are the failed attempt of the criminal justice system to use confinement for serious, chronic adult offenders (Austin, Clark, Hardyman, & Henry, 1999). The changes in many states' juvenile codes (laws governing juvenile delinquency) had the following effects:

- They designated larger proportions of juveniles as serious and violent offenders, resulting in the incarceration of more juveniles in detention centers, juvenile corrections facilities, and adult jails and prisons.
- They extended periods of confinement in juvenile correctional facilities.
- They lowered the ages at which juvenile offenders could be transferred to the criminal justice system.
- They excluded more juvenile offenders from juvenile court jurisdiction.
- They expanded the lists of crimes for which juveniles can be transferred to the criminal justice system.

The new laws also "criminalized" juvenile courts—that is, they changed procedures in juvenile courts so that these courts now operate much like adult criminal courts. The changes include the introduction of adversarial procedures, an increased role for prosecutors, formalization of due process, elimination of confidentiality for offenders, the use of fingerprinting, the use of "blended sentencing" (see Chapter 8), the exclusion of many kinds of serious and violent offenders from juvenile courts, and an emphasis on offense-based sanctioning rather than the traditional individualized, rehabilitation focus of juvenile courts (Fagan & Zimring, 2000; Feld, 1993, 1998a, 1998b; Singer, 1996). The increased criminalization of juvenile courts calls into question the rationality of such reforms (Mears, 2000, 2001).

Texas, Florida, and Minnesota stand out as states that have increasingly criminalized their juvenile courts (Torbet et al., 1996), and evaluations in these three states raise serious questions about the success of this criminalization (on Texas, see Mears, 1998, 2001; Mears & Field, 2000; Mears & Kelly, 1999; on Florida, see Bishop, Frazier, Lanza-Kaduce, & Winner, 1996; Winner, Lanza-Kaduce, Bishop, & Frazier, 1997; and on Minnesota, see Podkopacz & Feld, 1995, 1996). It seems unlikely that legislatures can move juvenile courts completely away from their traditional focus on rehabilitation and individualized attention to young offenders because this approach has been shown to be effective—even with serious, violent, and chronic juvenile offenders (see Chapter 9). But there is no question that prosecutors and legislatures have succeeded in their assault on juvenile courts, restricting their role in the criminal justice apparatus and making them much more punitive, like criminal courts (Fagan & Zimring, 2000).

Lawmakers and policy makers in the United States have a tendency to "declare war" on social problems, leading them to apply policies and other strategies that are characterized by aggression (Zimring, 1998a). Feelings of stress, anger, and even rage on the part of policy makers are evident in the juvenile justice policies that have ensued from the seventh juvenile delinquency panic, in which punishment is a central theme. Legislators, prosecutors, and other politicians seemingly have been unable to control their urges to add more punishments as well as punishments of greater severity. For example, in 1999 some U.S. senators proposed a bill, the Violent and Repeat Juvenile Offender Accountability and Rehabilitation Act, that would have transferred some 10-year-olds accused of particular crimes to criminal court. Some 200 criminologists wrote a joint letter to the U.S. Senate in 1999 opposing this legislation. The letter urged the senators to cease using outdated juvenile crime trend data and called their attention the fact that, at that point, the juvenile homicide arrest rate had dropped again for the fourth straight year. The letter also urged the senators to reject the superpredator myth and the false prediction of "a coming bloodbath" promulgated by Fox and DiIulio. In this context, the letter advised the senators "to resist the temptation to replace sound data and rational review with soundbites and rhetoric" (Butts, 1999).

This is not to say that most legislators have lost a balanced perspective on juvenile justice issues. Many state legislators have championed some of the very progressive policies embodied in comprehensive juvenile justice strategies (National Conference of State Legislatures, 1999a), including delinquency prevention and early intervention along with combinations of early childhood education and parent training. A sizable cadre of individuals in the law enforcement community also opposes the use of mean-spirited, "lock'em up" juvenile justice policies. Fight Crime: Invest in Kids, a national anti-crime organization comprising more than 1,800 police chiefs, sheriffs, prosecutors, crime survivors, and leaders of rank-and-file police officer organizations, advocates a balanced approach to crime control. This organization takes the position that "America's anti-crime arsenal contains no weapons more powerful than the proven programs that help

kids get the right start in life—programs like school readiness child care, youth development programs for the after-school and summer hours, child abuse prevention, and intervention programs to help kids get back on track" (Fight Crime: Invest in Kids, 2002, p. 1). One of the organization's members, George Sweat, a former police chief and current Secretary of the North Carolina Department of Juvenile Justice and Delinquency Prevention, says that "America's fight against violence must begin in the high chair, not the electric chair. Anything less leaves America's police fighting with one hand behind their back" (p. 2).

Moral Panic and Hysteria in Public Schools

During the 1997-1998 school year, the American public was riveted by print and broadcast media images of school shootings in Pearl, Mississippi; West Paducah, Kentucky; Jonesboro, Arkansas; Edinboro, Pennsylvania; Richmond, Virginia; and Springfield, Oregon (Donohue, Schiraldi, & Ziedenberg, 1999). Then the 1999 shootings at Columbine High School in Littleton, Colorado, dramatized further the horrifying vulnerability of schools to gun attacks by mass killers. As Brooks, Schiraldi, and Ziedenberg (2001) have observed, responses across the nation to the killing of 12 children and a teacher at Columbine included panic and "desperate fear" for the safety of children in schools (p. 3). Congress chimed in on the issue of school shootings, and some U.S. senators erroneously stated that "Congress finds that children between the ages of 10 and 14 are committing increasing numbers of murders and other serious crimes. . . . The tragedy of Jonesboro, Arkansas, is, unfortunately an all too common occurrence in the United States" (Violent and Repeat Juvenile Offender Accountability and Rehabilitation Act, 1999, S. 254, passed in the Senate in May 1999, quoted in Brooks et al., 2001, p. 1).

The extent of the panic over school shootings is evident when one contrasts the reality of this form of violence with public perceptions of the problem. Brooks et al. (2001, p. 6) report that school-associated violent deaths dropped 40% between school years 1997-1998 and 1998-1999, juvenile homicide arrests declined 56% between 1993 and 1998, and the chance that a school-aged child would die in a school in 1998-1999 was 1 in 2 million. Yet 71% of individuals responding to a public poll in 1998 said that they thought a school shooting was "likely" to happen in their community, and the proportion of survey respondents who feared a school shooting in their community increased 49% from 1993 to 1998.

Brooks et al. (2001) found that "even after . . . well-publicized studies reported school crime to be on the decline, seven months after Columbine, more than 60% of Americans said school safety 'worried them a great deal'" (p. 3). Parents and school boards continued to call for more metal detectors, locker searches, and other security measures in schools, even though these measures, in and of themselves, likely will not solve the problem. Other interventions need to be implemented along with school security measures to promote a safe school environment and make all students feel safe (Gottfredson & Gottfredson, 2001). Some individuals have advocated the development of screening instruments to identify potential school shooters, but, as I have noted in Chapter 2, school shooters do not fit the profile of mythical superpredators—or any other high-risk profile, for that matter. No instrument has ever been developed that can be used reliably to predict such violent behavior by specific individuals (Le Blanc, 1998). (It is possible that some school shooting incidents involve "copycatting." There is some evidence that serious violent juvenile offenders involved in gun offenses are more likely to report copycat behaviors; see Surette, 2002.)

The panic over school shootings led to hysteria, which contributed significantly to the growth of "zero-tolerance" school policies, a trend that had already begun as a result of the general panic over youth violence. Zero-tolerance policies specify predetermined mandatory consequences or punishments for specific offenses. By 1997, at least three-fourths of all schools reporting to the National Center for Education Statistics (1997) said that they had zero-tolerance policies in place for various student offenses, including bringing firearms or other weapons to school; alcohol, drug, and tobacco offenses; and physical attacks or fighting. In 1997, 100,324 students were expelled from schools and more than 363,464 were given out-of-school suspensions lasting 5 days or more for violations of these policies; most of the disciplinary actions were taken as the result of physical attacks or fights. Several cases in which zero-tolerance policies played a part serve to illustrate the hysteria that extended to minor infractions (Brooks et al., 2001, pp. 16-17). In one case, five African American students who had been playfully throwing peanuts at one another on a school bus were arrested and suspended from school after one of the peanuts accidentally hit the white bus driver. In another case, a 9-year-old on the way to school found a manicure set that included a one-inch knife and brought the set onto the school grounds; when it was discovered, the student was suspended from school for a day. A high school junior was expelled from school for having a can of pepper spray on a key chain. All told, about 3 million students were suspended from schools across the United States in the 1996-1997 school year—up from 1.7 million in 1974 (Brooks et al., 2001, p. 18). (For a fuller discussion of zero-tolerance policies as they apply to juveniles, see Chapter 7.)

Consequences of the New Moral Panic for the Juvenile Justice System

In the pages that follow, I present an assessment of the consequences of the seventh panic over juvenile delinquency for the American juvenile justice system. This assessment, however, is hampered by the incompleteness of juvenile justice system data (descriptions of the existing data systems are provided in Box 3.2). Unfortunately, there are no complete national data on juvenile offenders in any component of the juvenile justice system. With these cautions noted, I examine below the national data that are available on the juvenile justice system. As will become clear, the effects of the seventh moral panic over juvenile delinquency are very apparent in these data.

Police Arrests and Court Referrals

As noted in Chapter 1, the juvenile arrest rate for Violent Crime Index offenses began falling in 1994, yet the rate of police referrals to juvenile court increased 31% from 1980 through 1997 (Butts & Adams, 2001, p. 6). During this period, the proportion of arrested juveniles referred to juvenile court by police increased from one-half to almost two-thirds. This higher proportion was reached in 1992 (Snyder & Sickmund, 1995), and referrals have remained at that level since then (Snyder & Sickmund, 1999). Thus a much higher proportion of arrested juveniles was referred to court in the 1990s than in prior years. One would expect that most of this increase would be accounted for by serious juvenile offenders, but a much higher proportion of nonserious offenders also was referred to court by police during this period (Butts & Adams, 2001; Snyder, 1999).

Arrests of girls for serious youth violence have increased; however, this does not necessarily mean that rates of violent offenses have actually increased for females (Chesney-Lind & Paramore, 2001). From 1987 through 1994, the female juvenile violent crime arrest rate more than doubled; during the same period, the rate for male juveniles increased by two-thirds (Snyder &

Box 3.2
National Data on the Juvenile Justice System

The federal Office of Juvenile Justice and Delinquency Prevention has statutory responsibility for collecting and reporting nationwide data on youths in the juvenile justice system. OJJDP maintains two reporting systems for this purpose: the National Juvenile Court Data Archive and the Census of Juveniles in Residential Placement (CJRP). To understand these data, one needs a fundamental understanding of the structure and processes of the juvenile justice system; Snyder and Sickmund (1999, pp. 85-100) provide a clear explanation, complete with a case flowchart illustrating the juvenile justice system's processing stages (p. 98).

Juvenile Court Data

Juvenile court data are gathered for the National Juvenile Court Data Archive through a voluntary reporting system. The extent to which the data in this archive are representative of juvenile courts nationwide is unknown; in 1997, data were collected from courts that had jurisdiction over 71% of the juvenile population in the United States in that year (Sickmund, 2000). This archive makes available a wide variety of data on juvenile court referrals, methods of handling, and dispositions, including placements in detention centers and commitments to residential facilities.

Juvenile Corrections Data

The federal government no longer collects nationwide data on admissions of juveniles to detention and corrections facilities (for a brief history of federal juvenile correctional data collection, see Krisberg & Howell, 1998). Therefore, the numbers and characteristics of juvenile admissions to detention and correctional facilities are unknown. The National Council on Crime and Delinquency collected such data in the early 1990s. See DeComo (1998) for an interesting analysis of racial and ethnic characteristics of youths admitted to detention and corrections facilities.

In 1997, OJJDP launched an alternative reporting system, the 1-day Census of Juveniles in Residential Placement. The CJRP collects individual data such as race, sex, and most serious offense on all juveniles held in residential facilities (short-term detention and long-term state correctional facilities) on a given day each year. In addition, facilities are asked to provide information about the legal status of each juvenile held.

The biases that may exist in the CJRP data are unknown. Any census of incarcerated offenders taken on a single day has an inherent flaw: It overstates the number of more serious offenders because they are in the system longer and thus are more likely to be there on the day the census is taken (Lynch & Sabol, 1997, p. 6; McCord, Widom, & Crowell, 2001). This factor, combined with key juvenile justice policy variables, means that it is impossible to make nationwide projections of juvenile justice system cases with a high degree of confidence (Butts & Adams, 2001; McCord et al., 2001).

Sickmund (2002) used CJRP responses to report that 108,931 juvenile offenders were in residential placement on October 27, 1999. Only 25% of all juveniles in residential correctional facilities on that day in 1999 were placed there because of a Violent Crime Index offense, and only 24% were charged with a Property Crime Index offense. Thus the majority of juvenile offenders in detention and correctional facilities at that time were not charged with serious property offenses or serious violent offenses.

Key Publications

In 1995, OJJDP began to publish a regular series of "national reports" on juvenile offenders and victims that include comprehensive information on existing data on the juvenile justice system from a wide variety of sources. Two such reports have been published to date (Snyder & Sickmund, 1995, 1999). The 1999 report, along with a "statistical briefing book" that contains valuable information on various aspects of juvenile justice system handling of children and adolescents, is available on OJJDP's Web site at http://ojjdp.ncjrs.org/facts/facts.html.

Sickmund, 1999, p. 121). Even so, the 1997 Violent Crime Index arrest rate for male juveniles was more than five times the arrest rate for female juveniles. In Chapter 4, I discuss a possibly unique pathway that girls may follow to serious, violent, and chronic delinquency.

Court Referrals and Out-of-Home Placements

Increasing numbers of juvenile offenders are being referred to juvenile court and are receiving out-of-home placements. The total number of delinquency cases handled by juvenile courts increased 48% from 1988 through 1997 (Stahl, 2000). The numbers of cases more than doubled for drug law violations (125%), simple assault (124%), and disorderly conduct (107%). Person offense cases almost doubled (97%). The Monitoring the Future study found that the overall proportions of juveniles reporting *any illicit drug use* in the prior year peaked among younger teens in 1996 and among older teens in 1997 (Johnston, O'Malley, & Bachman, 1999), thus it seems that confinements for drug use among juveniles should have peaked in 1997, but they did not (Sickmund, 2002).

Juvenile court referrals of females for delinquent offenses also have increased in the past decade. In the period 1988-1997, referrals for females increased 83%, compared with a 39% increase for males (Stahl, 2000, p. 1). A similar pattern is evident in the detention rates for juvenile females and males. From 1988 through 1997, the number of cases involving detention increased 65% among females versus 30% among males (Porter, 2000). (For additional information on female offenders in the juvenile justice system, see Poe-Yamagata & Butts, 1996.)

In 1997, more than one-fourth (28%) of the defendants in juvenile cases that were formally adjudicated were placed in residential facilities; 19% were detained, and more than half (55%) were placed on probation. From 1988 through 1997, the number of cases in which the courts ordered adjudicated delinquents to be placed in residential facilities increased 56%, and the number of formal probation cases increased 67%. Thus juvenile court judges apparently responded to the outcry for more punitive sanctioning of juvenile offenders by formally adjudicating and placing more of them in confinement. Much of the growth in the numbers of detained and confined juveniles has been in cases involving younger offenders—that is, offenders under age 15 (Sickmund, 2002, p. 2).

Correctional Facilities: Overcrowding and Other Conditions of Confinement

Overcrowding has worsened in juvenile correctional facilities in recent years. The juvenile commitment population in detention centers and training schools increased 39% from 1993 through 1997 (Butts & Adams, 2001); in the same period, the proportion of females grew 65%, and the proportion of black youth increased 52% (Porter, 2000). Although the detention rate has remained about the same, more youths are being detained, largely because of the increase in the number of juvenile court cases over the past decade. Several other system policy factors have contributed to these increases (Butts & Adams, 2001), including increases in the adjudication rate and the average length of stay.

Because of the increase in use of detention, more juveniles are placed in overcrowded facilities today than was the case in the past. In 1995, nearly two-thirds (60%) of incarcerated juveniles were in overcrowded detention centers (Wordes & Jones, 1998), and more than 70% of juveniles locked up in training schools were held in overcrowded facilities (Snyder & Sickmund, 1999, p. 206). A 1995 study published by the National Institute of Corrections concluded that the "get tough on crime" policies of the 1990s were overwhelming both juvenile correctional facilities and adult prisons in a "chain reaction."

The conditions of confinement for juveniles have worsened over the past decade or more. In a 1993 national study of the conditions of confinement in juvenile detention and correctional facilities, Parent, Leiter, Livens, Wentworth, and Stephen (1994) found that many such facilities were not meeting minimal professional standards concerning the inmates' health and living conditions. These researchers also found that overcrowding in such facilities contributes to higher rates of institutional violence and suicidal behavior.

In several states, juveniles who have been transferred to criminal court and sentenced to imprisonment are held in juvenile training schools until they reach the age of majority and are then sent to adult prisons. These training schools thus experience buildups of juveniles who face extended prison terms on their departure. Minority youths are most severely affected by these practices (Males & Macallair, 2000). Many such juveniles pose serious management problems for training school staff, perhaps because they have nothing to lose—their misconduct in the juvenile facility has no real consequences for them (Parent, Dunworth, McDonald, & Rhodes, 1997, p. 3).

Residents in overcrowded facilities have also been found to spend more time in lockdown, and this leads to lower program quality (Previte, 1997). When staff must focus primarily on safety and security, effective intervention and treatment are compromised (Roush & McMillen, 2000, p. 3).

More and more detention and corrections facilities are being constructed because of increasing demands for punitive confinement and growing overcrowding in existing facilities. As Roush and McMillen (2000) have observed, the United States is experiencing "a building surge [in juvenile corrections facilities] that has begun to rival the exponential growth of adult facilities in the 1970s and 1980s" (p. 2; for a history of the adult prison building boom, see Schlosser, 1998).

The federal Civil Rights of Institutionalized Persons Act provides protection from dangerous, unlawful conditions and practices of confinement for youths in detention and correctional facilities. Juveniles in state juvenile corrections facilities have been subjected to abuse in Louisiana (Human Rights Watch, 1995), Georgia (Human Rights Watch, 1996b), Colorado (Human Rights Watch, 1997b), and Virginia (Joint Legislative Audit and Review Commission of the Virginia General Assembly, 1997). A commission appointed by the Virginia General Assembly found instances of "shackling," use of the "four-point restraint," and use of long periods of confinement in isolation (Boyle, 1999; Joint Legislative Audit and Review Commission of the Virginia General Assembly, 1997). In 1997, as a result of investigations and negotiations to remedy certain confinement conditions, 61 consent decrees were in place requiring state and local jurisdictions to take corrective actions in 108 facilities throughout the United States (National Conference of State Legislatures, 1999a).

Criminal charges against staff for abuse of children or civil lawsuits related to conditions in juvenile boot camps are pending in at least seven states (Krajicek, 2000). The deaths of several youngsters in boot camps have raised further questions about abusive conditions in such facilities (Blackwood, 2001).

In 2001, concern over the conditions of confinement to which juveniles are subjected reached a high enough level that a bill was introduced in the U.S. Congress that would require a General Accounting Office study of the prevalence and effects of the worst conditions (S. 1174, 107th Congress, 1st Session, July 12, 2001). It would mandate investigation of the use of electroshock weapons, four-point restraints, chemical restraints, restraint chairs, and solitary confinement of juvenile offenders in the federal and state criminal and juvenile corrections systems. This bill would help ensure safe incarceration of juvenile offenders, but its future is uncertain; as of this writing, Congress has not yet acted on it.

Mental Health Problems

There is nothing new about the fact that the mental health needs of children and adolescents are going unmet in the United States. In a landmark study conducted in the early 1980s, Knitzer (1982) documented the enormous gap between the mental health treatment needs of youth and the services traditionally offered to them. The mental health system in the United States relies excessively on hospitalization for adolescent clients; nearly one-third of adolescents receiving mental health care are institutionalized, at a cost of as much as $500 per day, amounting to 50% of the total amount spent on child and adolescent services (Burns, 1991; Sondheimer, Schoenwald, & Rowland, 1994). Yet up to half of these hospitalized youths do not have any severe or acute mental illness; most are admitted to residential facilities and psychiatric hospitals for behavioral disorders or because their parents cannot control them and other crisis intervention options are not available in their communities (Weithorn, 1988). As Sondheimer et al. (1994) put it, most of them are "troublesome rather than 'troubled'" (p. 8). Worse yet, those youths who are presumably most in need of hospitalization are least likely to benefit from inpatient treatment (Pfeiffer & Strzelecki, 1990).

In sum, the mental health system has the same problem as the juvenile justice system: overreliance on deep-end solutions and placement of the wrong youngsters in long-term residential care. Many seriously emotionally disturbed youngsters are in state juvenile correctional facilities, and a large proportion of facilities are inappropriately configured to meet the needs of this population (Roush & McMillen, 2000). As Arredondo et al. (2001) have observed, these circumstances raise two legally and medically indefensible problems: First, "undiagnosed and untreated serious mental illness or incapacity may constitute a circumstance of diminished competence or culpability" (p. 3); and second, "locking up a child who is hallucinating or delusional may be a violation of the constitutional right to be free from cruel and unusual punishment" (p. 3).

A high proportion of the young people in the juvenile justice system have diagnosable mental health disorders. Several studies have found that 80% or more of the individuals making up the juvenile justice population have been diagnosed with conduct disorders (see Cocozza & Skowyra, 2000, p. 6). Many of these youth qualify for more than one diagnosis, whether they are in detention centers (Virginia Policy Design Team, 1994) or correctional facilities (McGarvey & Waite, 2000). In one study of incarcerated boys convicted of mostly violent offenses, using a sample that was representative of the California Youth Authority population, Steiner, Garcia, and Matthews (1997) found that nearly a third of the boys met all of the criteria for a diagnosis of posttraumatic stress disorder.

It has been estimated that at least 20% of youth who come in contact with the juvenile justice system have serious mental health disorders (Cocozza & Skowyra, 2000, p. 6). The prevalence of mental health problems among incarcerated youngsters may well be higher. In a study of nearly 2,000 delinquents detained in the Cook County (Illinois) Juvenile Temporary Detention Center, Teplin (2001) found that two-thirds of the subjects had one or more alcohol, drug, or mental health disorders (known as ADM disorders). Based on these findings, Teplin estimates that 670,000 youths processed in the juvenile justice system each year could meet diagnostic criteria for one or more ADM disorders that require mental health and/or substance abuse treatment. In Teplin's sample, females showed far greater mental health needs and greater risk than males.

There is some evidence that the mental health treatment needs of incarcerated youngsters may be increasing. For example, McGarvey and Waite (2000) conducted a study of 10,000 offenders committed to the Virginia juvenile corrections system over a the period 1993-1998 and found that the percentage of incarcerated adolescents who had been prescribed medication for mental health problems nearly doubled over the 6-year period, from about one-fourth to almost one-half. However, the youth committed in 1998 were no more violent than those committed in 1993. Of course, these data may well reflect society's growing reliance on medication to treat child and adolescent problem behavior rather than an increase in the incidence of mental health problems.

Reliance on residential facilities is also increasing. By the 1990s, all types of residential placements for youths were used more often (Lerman, 2002), including child welfare (foster care), mental health (private facilities, hospitals, residential treatment facilities, and community treatment centers), and substance abuse placements (rehabilitation/residential facilities). More youths were admitted to detention centers than to any other type of secure facility, but among those admitted to facilities associated with treatment or rehabilitation programs, more were admitted to mental health facilities, often for "disorders" of some sort (Lerman, 2002, pp. 104-105). For an examination of mental health problems as a risk factor for serious and violent delinquency, see Chapter 6.

Transfer to the Criminal Justice System

In 1996, Torbet et al. noted, "More juveniles are being charged and tried in criminal court, detained longer, and incarcerated more frequently in the adult correctional system than ever before" (p. 6). Since 1987, every state has made it easier to transfer adolescents under the maximum age for juvenile court jurisdiction to criminal court under some circumstances (Griffin et al., 1998; National Conference of State Legislatures, 1999a; Torbet et al., 1996; Torbet & Szymanski, 1998; U.S. General Accounting Office, 1995).

The number of delinquency cases judicially waived to criminal court reached a peak in 1994 with 11,700 cases—a 73% increase over the number of cases waived in 1988 (Puzzanchera, 2000). The majority of transferred juveniles are not violent offenders. In 1997, the proportion of formally processed person offense cases (40%) that were waived was about the same as for property offense cases (38%), and 15% involved drug law violations (Stahl, 2000). I examine the issues surrounding the policy of transferring juveniles to the criminal justice system in detail in Chapter 8.

Jailing and Imprisonment

The number of juveniles held in adult jails nearly tripled from 1993 through 1997 (Gilliard & Beck, 1996, p. 10; Strom, 2000, p. 2). At midyear in 1997, nearly twice as many juveniles (9,100) were held in local adult jails as were held in prisons (Strom, 2000, p. 2). About 7,000 of them were held as "adults," and about 2,100 were held as juveniles (Gilliard, 1999). A juvenile is considered to be an adult for the purposes of the justice system when the maximum age for juvenile court jurisdiction in the juvenile's state is below age 18, when the juvenile is excluded by law from juvenile court jurisdiction because of the specific offense with which he or she is charged, or when the juvenile has been transferred to the criminal justice system and thus is legally redefined as an adult.

Relative to the number of arrests of juvenile offenders, the likelihood of their incarceration in state prison increased from 1985 through 1997 (Strom, 2000, p. 1). Admissions of juveniles to adult prisons have increased 7% per year since 1985, faster than the growth rate for adults (5%; Strom, 2000, p. 3). The number of juvenile admissions to state prisons more than doubled from 1985 through 1997. In 1997, 5,400 juveniles were in state prisons (Strom, 2000, p. 1).

Juveniles are being sentenced to adult prisons at younger and younger ages. In 1997, 26% of persons under age 18 who were admitted to adult prisons were 16 or younger at time of admission; in 1990, 20% of offenders under age 18 were 16 or younger at the time of admission to prison (Strom, 2000, p. 6). More than half (58%) of the juveniles admitted to prisons in 1997 were black; 25% were white. Of these offenders, 9 out of 10 had not graduated from high school at the time of admission. The average amount of time served in jails and prisons by juveniles in 1997 was 37 months (33 months in prison and 4 months in jail; Strom, 2000, p. 9).

Conditions of Confinement in Adult Prisons

The deplorable state of physical health, mental health, and safety conditions in many state prisons is well known (Jones, 1997; Rosenblatt, 1996). Conditions in super-maximum-security prisons have drawn a great deal of attention (Human Rights Watch, 1997a; Riveland, 1999). The number of prisoners held in conditions of extreme isolation in "supermax" prisons has grown to more than 20,000 (Amnesty International, 2002). Sexual assaults and abuse have also emerged as major concerns. Both rape and sexual harassment of males (Human Rights Watch, 2001b; Robertson, 1999) and sexual abuse of females by other women and correctional officers (Human Rights Watch, 1996a) are all too common in state prisons. In a few states, sexual abuse of incarcerated women is routinely tolerated or even condoned. Prison gangs are also a major concern. Although no reliable national data are available on the prevalence and membership of prison gangs, the first collection of articles published on them indicates that experts agree that prison gangs got bigger and became more entrenched in the 1980s and 1990s (Fleisher, Decker, & Curry, 2001; see also Jacobs, 2001). Another serious problem affecting the conditions of confinement in state prisons is the decreasing availability of rehabilitation programs; only about one-third of inmates currently receive vocational training or other education while in prison (Travis &

Petersilia, 2001). Overcrowding is another growing problem. According to the Bureau of Justice Statistics (2002), as of December 31, 2001, state prisons were operating at between 1% and 16% above capacity, and federal prisons were operating at 31% above capacity. The growing number of juveniles held in adult prisons is contributing to the deterioration of conditions of confinement and creating housing and programming problems (National Institute of Corrections, 1995; Parent et al., 1997). A survey conducted by the National Institute of Corrections (1995) has shown that few prisons provide special programming for juvenile inmates. I discuss prison conditions and their consequences for juveniles in more detail in Chapter 8.

The federal Juvenile Justice and Delinquency Prevention Act of 1974, as amended, prohibits the housing of juvenile offenders in adult facilities. Although the act permits placement of juveniles in adult jails after their transfer to criminal court, human rights advocacy organizations urge that juveniles be kept out of adult jails and other secure facilities prior to their conviction as adults (Coalition for Juvenile Justice, 1998).

Most states (36 as of 1997) allow juveniles to be housed in prisons with adult offenders, and only 6 states never house them with adults (Parent et al., 1997, pp. 2, 5). In 12 states, convicted juveniles serve their sentences in juvenile facilities until they reach a certain age, usually 18 (Strom, 2000, p. 10). Only 8 states segregate juveniles from adults in programs for "youthful offenders." Research has found that housing juvenile offenders in adult prisons may aggravate recidivism ("Adult Treatment," 1996), exposes juveniles to undesirable criminal influences, and increases their risk of violent victimization (see Chapter 8).

Minority Overrepresentation

Overrepresentation of minority youths in both juvenile and adult justice systems is a serious problem. As noted in Chapter 2, the superpredator myth created a demonic image of black, inner-city males, linking them with drugs, guns, and gangs. This image of black youths persists and is played out daily in the punitive reforms that have been put in place over the past decade. Black juveniles are the main victims of the injustices that take place in the juvenile and criminal justice systems (Building Blocks for Youth, 2000; Poe-Yamagata & Jones, 2000).

Black youths are far more likely than white youths to be arrested for similar offenses, to be referred to juvenile court, to be confined in detention facilities while awaiting court appearances,

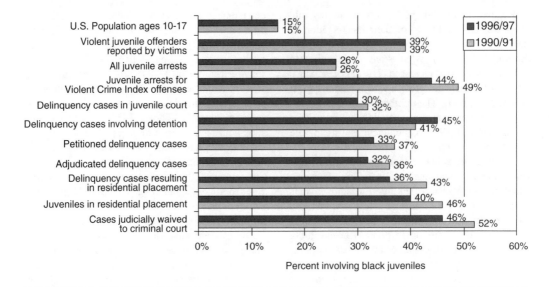

Figure 3.1   Proportion of Black Youth in the Juvenile Justice System

SOURCE: *Juvenile Offenders and Victims: 1999 National Report* (p. 192), by H. N. Snyder and M. Sickmund, 1999, Washington, DC: Office of Juvenile Justice and Delinquency Prevention. ©1999 by National Center for Juvenile Justice. Reprinted with permission.

to be adjudicated "delinquent," to be placed on probation, to be committed to out-of-home placements, and to be confined in less desirable public facilities rather than in private ones (D. F. Hawkins, 1995; Hawkins, Laub, & Lauritsen, 1998; Pope & Feyerherm, 1990, 1991; Snyder & Sickmund, 1995). Racial/ethnic disparities appear at every point in the juvenile justice system (see Box 3.3), with minorities consistently receiving harsher dispositions, even when offense severity and other factors are taken into account (Fagan, Slaughter, & Hartstone, 1987; see also Austin, 1995; Dean, Hirschel, & Brame, 1996).

Although black youths represent only 15% of the 10- to 17-year-old population in the United States, in 1996-1997, 45% of detained juveniles, 40% of juveniles in long-term correctional facilities, and nearly half (46%) of juveniles judicially waived to criminal court were black (Snyder & Sickmund, 1999, p. 192). Figure 3.1 shows these and other disparities. It is interesting to note that the figure shows some improvements in the representation of black juveniles between 1990-1991 and 1996-1997 in almost all stages of the juvenile justice system. The major exception is delinquency cases involving detention.

Currently, Hispanics make up the fastest-growing minority group in juvenile facilities (Smith, 1998,

p. 535). Custody rates for Latino and Native American youths exceed the rate for white youths by 2.5 times (Poe-Yamagata & Jones, 2000, p. 3). However, custody rates for black youths are 5 times as high as those for white youths.

Data on transfers to the criminal justice system of minority and nonminority juveniles show a more inequitable situation. Note that Figure 3.1 does not illustrate any data on criminal justice system handling of minorities, except for cases waived to criminal court by juvenile court judges. These judges now transfer only a small proportion of all juveniles transferred to the criminal justice system. When all three methods of transfer (by juvenile court judges, by prosecutors, and by legislative mandate) are taken into account, three out of four youths admitted to state prisons in 1997 were minorities. More than half of these (58%) were black, 25% were white, 15% were Latino, and the remaining 2% were young people of other ethnicities (Poe-Yamagata & Jones, 2000, p. 25).

In a study of 18 jurisdictions with large numbers of transfers, the organization Building Blocks for Youth (2000) found that African American (43%) and Latino (37%) youths were more likely than white youths (26%) to receive sentences of incarceration. This pattern held true even when offense seriousness was taken into account. For example, of those convicted of violent offenses, 58% of African Americans and 46% of Latinos received sentences of incarceration, compared with 34% of whites.

Is the overrepresentation of juvenile racial/ ethnic minorities in the juvenile and criminal justice systems a result of disproportionate involvement of these juveniles in serious and violent delinquency? Given the findings of studies that have compared the offense rates of black youths and white youths, the answer to this question is no. As noted in Chapter 2, black youths and white youths have similar self-reported serious and violent offense rates, and self-report data provide evidence that arrest records seriously overstate the actual offense rates of minorities relative to whites.

Why are the arrest rates for minority juveniles so much higher than those for whites? Aside from the obvious answer—racial/ethnic prejudice and discrimination—minority youth are easier for police to arrest. As Tonry (1994b) notes, police find inner-city minority youths easier to arrest for drug offenses than white suburban and urban working-class youths because of three factors: First, drug sales in poor minority areas are likely to take place outdoors, or in public places such as bars, where transactions are visible to police; second, drug dealers in inner-city areas have little choice but to sell to strangers and new acquaintances; and third, arrested drug dealers in inner-city minority communities are soon replaced because of the "nearly inexhaustible potential supply of young minority Americans to be arrested" (p. 487). There is no question that the "wars" on drugs, crime, gangs, and juveniles have targeted inner-city areas in general, and minority youths in particular.

Racial profiling is another factor that helps to account for the differential representation of minority youth in the juvenile and criminal justice systems. This police practice often takes the form of the use of stereotypical images of minority offenders to identify the most likely criminals. Although the superpredator myth emphasizes the dangerous nature of inner-city black youngsters, Latino youths are often stereotyped along with African Americans in the youth gang context (Klein, 1995; Zatz, 1987), and their likelihood of arrest is also higher than that of whites. Hence juveniles who are members of these racial/ethnic minorities are more likely than Caucasian juveniles to appear in arrest records and to have longer arrest histories.

The International Convention on the Elimination of All Forms of Racial Discrimination (known as CERD), to which the United States is a party, defines race discrimination as conduct that has the "purpose or effect" of restricting rights on the basis of race (Human Rights Watch, 2000b). Under CERD, governments may not engage in "malign neglect"; that is, they may not ignore the need to secure equal treatment of all racial and ethnic groups, but rather must act affirmatively to prevent or end policies that have unjustified discriminatory impacts. The United States has acted affirmatively through the federal Disproportionate Minority Confinement Initiative (see Box 3.3).

Sentences of Life Without Possibility of Parole

Being sentenced to a life term without the possibility of parole is a realistic possibility for some juvenile offenders. Life without parole, or LWOP, is the harshest penalty now imposed on those under age 16 at the time of their offenses, because states are restrained from executing such young offenders by a Supreme Court decision, as explained below (Logan, 1998). In 1997, 3% (222) of 7,400 juveniles admitted to adult prisons received life sentences (Strom, 2000, p. 7); how many of these sentences included no possibility of parole is unknown. Among the 13 juveniles convicted of murder/nonnegligent manslaughter and admitted to prison in 1997, 32% (4) were sentenced to life without parole.

Only a handful of states have statutes that expressly prohibit LWOP for individuals under age 16; the overwhelming majority of states appear to permit such sentences or make LWOP mandatory upon conviction in criminal court (Logan, 1998, pp. 690-691). In the state of Washington, for instance, offenders as young as 8 years of age can be sentenced to LWOP; in Vermont, 10-year-olds can draw such terms. Except in those states that expressly prohibit LWOP, youths transferred to the criminal justice system can be required to spend the rest of their lives in adult prisons without a chance of meaningful appellate review of their sentences (Logan, 1998, pp. 708-709). The U.N. Convention on the Rights of the Child, Article 37(a), 1995, prohibits life imprisonment without the possibility of parole for offenses committed by persons under 18 years of age. As noted earlier, the United States is one of only two countries that have not ratified this convention.

Juvenile Executions

The International Covenant on Civil and Political Rights (ICCPR) and the U.N. Convention on the Rights of the Child (CRC) both forbid the execution of persons for crimes they

---

Box 3.3

The Disproportionate Minority Confinement Initiative

The reduction of disproportionate minority confinement became official U.S. juvenile justice policy when the 1992 amendments to the Juvenile Justice and Delinquency Prevention (JJDP) Act of 1974 (P.L. 93-415) were enacted into law. The JJDP Act amendments (42 U.S.C. Sec. 5633[a][23]) required that states receiving JJDP Act formula grants provide assurances that they will develop and implement plans to reduce the overrepresentation of minorities in the juvenile justice system—that is, where the proportion of minority youth in confinement exceeds the proportion those minority groups represent in the general population. Congress incorporated a financial incentive to accelerate states' progress toward full compliance with the mandate by requiring that 25% of a state's annual formula grant allocation from OJJDP be withheld for noncompliance. States that failed to make progress, or at least show a good-faith effort, would be required to allocate the remaining 75% of their formula grant funds toward achieving compliance. To meet the mandate of the Disproportionate Minority Confinement (DMC) Initiative, states must complete the three phases required in the OJJDP Formula Grants Regulation (28 CFR 31)— problem identification, problem assessment, and program intervention—within established time frames. The DMC Initiative was based on prior research on the issue of disproportionate minority confinement (Pope & Feyerherm, 1990, 1991) and the efforts of advocacy groups (see Howell, 1997, pp. 37-38).

Leiber (2002) recently completed a comprehensive assessment of the results of the DMC Initiative that focuses on the first two key components of the DMC mandate and states' efforts to comply— problem identification and problem assessment. Leiber reports the following key findings concerning the problem identification stage:

- Minority youth overrepresentation was evident in 32 states.
- Minority youth overrepresentation existed at all of the decision points.
- The decision point where minority youth overrepresentation was greatest varied from state to state.
- Where states differentiated among minority groups, overrepresentation existed for African Americans and Hispanics.

The problem assessment stage—that is, uncovering explanations for minority overrepresentation—proved to be very difficult for states to accomplish. Because the instructions OJJDP provided lacked specificity, Leiber (2002) notes, "states often did not understand how to do an assessment study and/or were not in position to conduct the kind of research needed to identify the causes of DMC" (p. 17). Thus the sophistication of the assessment strategies used varied from state to state. Leiber reports that "OJJDP has begun to address these deficiencies, and these efforts may result in a greater number of states becoming more committed to DMC and [thus obtaining] information to better inform strategies to reduce the disproportionate representation of minority youth in our juvenile justice system" (p. 19). Owing to the problems noted, the prospects for success of the DMC Initiative in the program intervention stage are uncertain at this time.

Latino and Latina youth are catching up with black youth as victims of disproportionate minority representation (Villarruel & Walker, 2002). Building Blocks for Youth has developed an "action packet" that includes suggested steps that youth advocates can take to eliminate the disparate treatment of Latino and Latina youth in the justice system as well as sample materials. The action packet is available on the Building Blocks for Youth Web site at http://www.buildingblocksforyouth.org/latino_rpt/act_pk_main.html.

committed in their juvenile years (Amnesty International, 1998a, 1998b). Article 6(5) of the ICCPR states that the death penalty must not be imposed for crimes committed by people when they were under 18 years of age. Although the United States ratified the ICCPR in 1992, it reserved the right to impose the death penalty for crimes committed by those under age 18. Article 37(a) of the CRC states that "neither capital punishment nor life imprisonment without the possibility of release shall be imposed for offenses committed by persons below eighteen years of age." President Clinton signed the CRC in 1995 with a reservation to Article 37(a). The U.S. Senate has not yet ratified the CRC. Of the 154 members of the United Nations, the United States and Somalia are the only countries that have not yet ratified the CRC (Cothern, 2000, p. 9).

Unfortunately, the execution of juvenile offenders continues in the United States. As of the end of 2001, 83 juveniles were on death rows in 15 states; 26 of them were in Texas prisons (Human Rights Watch, 2002a, 2002b). A total of 18 persons have been put to death for offenses they allegedly committed while under the age of 18 since the U.S. Supreme Court reinstated the death penalty in 1976 (Human Rights Watch, 2002b; see also Snell, 1999; Streib, 1983, 1998). Such executions are permitted because of the 1989 U.S. Supreme Court case *Stanford v. Kentucky,* in which the Court upheld the death penalty for 16- and 17-year-olds as consistent with U.S. "standards of decency," even though this is a violation of international law. At the present time, 16- and 17-year-olds can be executed in 22 U.S. states. Executions of juveniles are continuing at a steady pace even though several states are considering legislative proposals to abolish capital punishment for juveniles (Human Rights Watch, 2002a). Indiana has already done so. The only other countries known to execute juvenile offenders are Iran, Nigeria, Pakistan, Saudi Arabia, and Congo (Human Rights Watch, www.hrw.org); however, only Congo and Iran are known to have executed juvenile offenders in the past 3 years (Human Rights Watch, 2002a). Both of these countries now explicitly repudiate the practice, making the United States the only country that continues to claim the legal authority to execute juvenile offenders. As Claude W. Pettit of the College of Law at Ohio Northeastern University has observed, "Sooner or later the United States will have to [stop defying] the whole world's notion of what is proper behavior" (quoted in "Executioners Kick Off," 2000, p. 8). More juvenile offenders were executed in the United States in the 1990s than in all other countries combined. This U.S. policy is not likely to change in the foreseeable future. The Bush administration fervently defended the practice at a May 2002 meeting of the United Nations ("Sewer of the Summit," 2002). Recently, Virginia won the competition to determine which state gets to execute juvenile John Lee Malvo, companion of adult sniper John Allen Muhammad, in the "grisly game of death-penalty shopping" (Mauro, 2002, p. 15A). Virginia is second only to Texas in executions of juveniles and adults, and it has a new law that makes it easier to impose the death penalty (Locy, 2001).

Summary

Phenomenal changes occurred in the administration of juvenile justice in the United States from the late 1970s through the late 1990s. Two waves of punitive changes spread across the nation during this 20-year span. The first wave was ushered in by a combination of changes in criminal justice system philosophy—a shift from rehabilitation to just desert punishments—that filtered down to the juvenile justice system, by the "cycle of juvenile justice" (Bernard, 1992), and by the sixth moral panic over juvenile delinquency. The seventh moral panic over delinquency, along with the propagation of frightening myths about juvenile violence, incited legislators across the country to enact more punitive measures against youthful offenders than U.S. history has seen since the colonial era, when barbaric punishments were commonplace. In general, as Torbet et al. (2000) note, "the traditional rehabilitative goals of juvenile sanctioning have been de-emphasized in favor of straightforward, adult-style punishments and long-term incapacitation with fewer allowances for the individual and special needs of juveniles" (p. 1). This is something of an overstatement. Hemmens, Fritsch, and Caeti analyzed state juvenile codes in 1997 and found that about half of them still adhered to the traditional model of juvenile justice. As the remainder of this book will show, the rehabilitative mission of the juvenile justice system is far from dead (Howell, 1997; Lederman, 1999; Moon et al., 2000; Zimring, 2002). Juvenile courts are a cornerstone of our society, and new democracies all over the world frequently choose to implement juvenile justice systems rather than rely exclusively on criminal courts (Shepherd, 1999). Indeed, the United States is the only developed nation in the world that tries its youngest offenders in the regular criminal courts (Zimring, 2002).

Unfortunately, the overreactions to the myths about juvenile violence have produced a crisis of overload in many state juvenile justice systems, particularly in juvenile correctional facilities. As Smith (1998) has observed, because of the lingering myths, "it is difficult to imagine how the number of children in custody will not continue to increase over the next several years" (p. 539). J. A. Butts (1999), a leading researcher for a Washington, D.C., policy research organization, has described working in the juvenile justice field in the current era as much like being inside a walled village with a monster (the "get tough" movement) just outside the gates. To satisfy the hunger of the monster, fearful villagers throw juveniles over the wall—first the most violent youths in the village, and then all the 16- and

17-year-olds, then kids with prior adjudications, and so on. But the monster's hunger is never satisfied.

Consistent with the application of the just desert principle in the criminal justice system, *accountability* has become a synonym for retribution against juveniles. Legislatures have applied the accountability principle to a wide variety of violent offenses characterized as "adult" crimes. The new state juvenile codes have designated more juveniles as serious offenders, extended periods of confinement in juvenile correctional facilities, lowered the ages at which juvenile offenders can (or must) be transferred to the criminal justice system, excluded more juvenile offenders from juvenile court jurisdiction, and expanded the lists of crimes for which juveniles can be transferred to the criminal justice system. The legal and policy changes have worsened conditions of confinement, increased overcrowding, and created housing and programming problems in jails and prisons. Juvenile detention facilities, training schools, and jails currently are holding increasing numbers of juveniles awaiting transfer to the criminal justice system. The deterioration of the conditions of confinement in U.S. correctional facilities has reached an unprecedented level. In 1997, confinement conditions in more than 100 correctional facilities required intervention by the courts and the U.S. Department of Justice to correct them (National Conference of State Legislatures, 1999a).

One of the major changes in recent years has been the shift in policy toward the transfer of juvenile offenders to the criminal justice system. Florida leads the nation with some 5,000 juveniles transferred to criminal courts each year (Bishop, Frazier, Lanza-Kaduce, & White, 1999). Those youngsters who have the misfortune of being imprisoned in Florida are subject to further victimization in the state's adult correctional system (Bishop & Frazier, 2000). Texas is most likely to impose the death sentence on juveniles, followed by Florida and Alabama, but Texas and Virginia are most likely to execute them (Cothern, 2000). One-third of the juvenile offenders currently on death rows in the United States are incarcerated in Texas, a state where the prison system was only recently released from 19 years of federal oversight because a federal judge had ruled that the conditions of confinement there amounted to cruel and unusual punishment. Other states have disproportionately high rates of incarceration in juvenile facilities (DeComo, 1998). Juveniles in state juvenile corrections facilities have been found to be subjected to abusive conditions of confinement in Louisiana (Human Rights Watch, 1995), Georgia (Human Rights Watch, 1996b), Colorado (Human Rights Watch, 1997b), and Virginia (Joint Legislative Audit and Review Commission of the Virginia General Assembly, 1997).

Minority youth, particularly black youngsters (who have been featured in the demonic images of the new breed of juvenile superpredators), are bearing the brunt of the punitive juvenile justice reforms that the panic over juvenile violence has wrought. Thus it is not surprising that they have suffered the largest increases in arrest rates, court referrals, and rates of detention, incarceration, and transfer to the criminal justice system.

The hysteria that resulted from highly publicized random school shootings brought its own consequences for students who have been disadvantaged by zero-tolerance school policies. A major consequence of these policies has been an increase in the number of students suspended from schools. Aside from having their chances in life diminished, many suspended and expelled students, ironically, are set free to associate with delinquent and gang-involved youths on the streets during the school day. Few suspended and expelled students are referred to alternative education and other programs that work to help prevent and reduce delinquency.

Discussion Questions

1. What is the moral panic over juvenile delinquency?

2. How has the cycle of juvenile justice contributed to the current moral panic?

3. What are the main consequences of the current moral panic over juvenile delinquency for the juvenile justice system?

4. Can the overrepresentation of juvenile racial/ethnic minorities in the juvenile and criminal justice systems be explained by disproportionate involvement of these juveniles in serious and violent delinquency?

5. Why are juvenile offenders executed in the United States, even though this practice violates international law?

PART II

The Research Base on Juvenile Offenders and What Doesn't Work

This section begins with an examination of serious, violent, and chronic juvenile offenders. The discussion in Chapter 4 draws extensively on the work of OJJDP's Study Group on Serious and Violent Juvenile Offenders and Study Group on Very Young Offenders, and on the three longitudinal studies mentioned in the preface. This chapter presents developmental theories of juvenile delinquency with a view toward understanding how serious, violent, and chronic juvenile offender careers develop. Chapter 5 then reviews youth gang research, with a particular focus on the overlap of gang membership and serious, violent, and chronic juvenile offending. Chapter 6 addresses the risk and protective factors for delinquency and also examines the proportions of serious and violent juvenile offenders who experience drug problems, mental health problems, school problems, and violent victimization. Chapter 7 reviews what does not work in preventing and reducing juvenile delinquency, as revealed in prior research. The final chapter in Part II examines research on one supposed "solution" to juvenile delinquency, the transfer of juvenile offenders to the criminal justice system.

4

■

SERIOUS, VIOLENT, AND CHRONIC JUVENILE OFFENDER CAREERS

My aim in this chapter is bridge the gap between the research that has been conducted concerning juvenile offenders and the practices of the juvenile justice system. What is the value of knowledge about offender careers if this knowledge cannot be applied to the everyday operations of juvenile courts and corrections agencies? Researchers have offered developmental theories to explain the progression of offender careers, and the juvenile justice system seeks to halt offender career progression. My central purpose in this chapter is to show the value of focusing research and juvenile justice system interventions on serious, violent, and chronic juvenile offenders. In order for the juvenile justice system to target these offenders successfully, juvenile justice officials must be able to distinguish between juvenile offenders who are likely to desist from delinquency and those who are likely to persist in their delinquent careers. In this chapter, I describe the advances in research on serious, violent, and chronic juvenile offender careers that policy makers can use to improve juvenile justice system policies and practices.

I begin the chapter with an explanation of developmental theories of delinquency and then highlight important advances in these theories. I discuss in particular Loeber's three-pathways model, which describes three pathways adolescents might follow in their orderly progression through adolescent problem behaviors and delinquency. I also present empirical descriptions of serious, violent, and chronic juvenile offender careers. Throughout this chapter, I make numerous references to longitudinal studies of delinquents, principally the three ongoing longitudinal studies that make up OJJDP's Program of Research on the Causes and Correlates of Delinquency. These three studies, described in

Box 4.1, have made substantial contributions to our knowledge regarding the causes and correlates of delinquency and gang delinquency (see Chapter 5).

Developmental Theories

Current developmental theories of delinquency and crime have grown out of a unique sociological framework for examining human experiences over time that is often referred to as the *life-course perspective.*

The Life-Course Perspective

As formulated by Elder (1985a, 1985b), the life-course perspective views human development across the live span, focusing in particular on persons' progress within culturally defined roles and social transitions that are age graded. It is normal, for example, for a young person to complete his or her education, begin a career, then get married and begin a family. The terms *trajectories* and *pathways* are used to describe these long-term patterns of social development in social institutions, including families, schools, and occupations. Thus a trajectory or pathway is an avenue of development over time, such as an occupational career or delinquency involvement. *Transitions* are short-term changes in social roles within long-term trajectories, such as dropping out of school, divorce, and desistance from delinquency.

Elder conceived of the life course as being structured by a web of interlocking trajectories that generally are consistent. They are interlocking in that changes in one life domain, or pathway, may well affect other domains. On occasion, these pathways

Box 4.1
Longitudinal Studies in the Program of Research on the
Causes and Correlates of Delinquency

This OJJDP program of research consists of three studies:

- The Pittsburgh Youth Study, directed by Dr. Rolf Loeber
- The Denver Youth Survey, directed by Dr. David Huizinga
- The Rochester Youth Development Study, directed by Dr. Terence P. Thornberry

Participants in the Pittsburgh Youth Study were boys randomly selected from the first, fourth, and seventh grades of public schools. For each grade cohort, the top 30% of boys (about 250) with the highest rates of predelinquent/delinquent behavior were selected, along with an equal number of boys randomly selected from the remaining 70% for comparison purposes. This resulted in a total sample of 1,517, with approximately 500 boys from each grade. Key publications resulting from this study are Loeber, Farrington, Stouthamer-Loeber, and Van Kammen (1998); Loeber, Keenan, and Zhang (1997); Loeber, Farrington, Stouthamer-Loeber, Moffitt, and Caspi (1998); and Loeber, Wei, Stouthamer-Loeber, Huizinga, and Thornberry (1999).

Subjects in the Denver Youth Survey (1,527 children and adolescents, both boys and girls) were randomly drawn from households in high-risk Denver neighborhoods. Subjects were ages 7, 9, 11, 13, and 15 when the study began. Key publications resulting from this study are Esbensen and Huizinga (1993); Esbensen, Huizinga, and Menard (1999); Esbensen, Huizinga, and Weiher (1993); Huizinga (1995); Huizinga, Esbensen, and Weiher (1991, 1996); and Huizinga and Jakob-Chien (1998).

Participants in the Rochester Youth Development Study (1,000 boys and girls) were randomly drawn from the seventh- and eighth-grade cohorts of Rochester public schools. To maximize the number of serious, chronic offenders in the study, the sample includes more youths from high-crime areas and fewer from low-crime areas. Key publications resulting from this study are Krohn, Lizotte, Thornberry, Smith, and McDowall (1996); Krohn, Thornberry, Rivera, and Le Blanc (2001); Lizotte, Krohn, Howell, Tobin, and Howard (2000); Thornberry, Krohn, Lizotte, and Chard-Wierschem (1993); Thornberry, Krohn, Lizotte, Smith, and Tobin (2003); Thornberry, Lizotte, Krohn, Farnworth, and Jang (1994); and Thornberry and Porter (2001).

Although all of these three projects have unique features, they share several key elements:

- All three are longitudinal investigations that involve repeated contacts with the same juveniles over a substantial portion of their childhood years, throughout adolescence, and into adulthood. Thus all three are "prospective" studies (that is, causal variables were measured in advance of outcomes).
- The three sites have collaborated to use a common measurement package, collecting data on a wide range of variables that make possible cross-site comparisons of similarities and differences.
- In all three studies, researchers have conducted face-to-face interviews with adolescents in private settings. By using self-report data rather than juvenile justice records, the researchers are able to come very close to measuring actual delinquent behaviors and ascertaining the age of onset of delinquent careers.
- In all three studies, researchers obtain multiple perspectives on each child's development and behavior through interviews with the study subject, the child's primary caregiver, and the child's teachers, and by reviewing official school, police, and court records.
- In all three studies, participants are interviewed at regular and frequent intervals (6 or 12 months).
- Sample retention has been high in all three studies. The average retention rate across all interview periods is 90%.

Data collection began in all three sites in 1987 and continues; thus all study subjects are now young adults. Five publications feature cross-site comparisons of similarities and differences in the findings across sites: Huizinga, Loeber, and Thornberry (1994); Huizinga, Loeber, Thornberry, and Cothern, (2000); Kelley, Huizinga, Thornberry, and Loeber (1997); Loeber, Kalb, and Huizinga (2001); and Smith et al. (2000).

Researchers have conducted many other longitudinal studies on delinquency and related problem behaviors. For a list and descriptions of nearly 60 leading longitudinal studies on delinquency, substance use, sexual behavior, and mental health problems with childhood samples, see Kalb, Farrington, and Loeber (2001). J. D. Hawkins et al. (1998) provide a list of longitudinal studies of the predictors of youth violence.

are interrupted by life events (short-term transitions) such as being arrested, getting married, or graduating from college. "Off-age" transitions (i.e., those that are not age appropriate, such as becoming a teenage parent) can produce disorder in the life course (Thornberry, 1997). Individual adaptations to these changes are important because they may lead to different trajectories. For example, some transitions may propel individuals into pathways leading them to a life of crime, whereas others may propel persons from delinquency into a life of general compliance with legal rules (Sampson & Laub, 1993).

In the life-course perspective, childhood, adolescent, and adult experiences are viewed as a continuous process of change, depending on the consequences of earlier patterns of behavior and the influence of risk factors in several important domains (mainly the family, school, peer groups, and communities). In addition, individual characteristics (e.g., intelligence and personality traits such as resilience) affect how individuals respond to influences in these experiential domains. Studies of juvenile offenders have shown that offense onset, escalation, and desistance do not occur merely as functions of offenders' chronological age. For some, predelinquent behaviors begin in early childhood, and these children often continue offending throughout most of their lives. For others, onset of delinquent behaviors occurs in late childhood or early adolescence. Desistance takes place in childhood and adolescence for some individuals, but much later for others.

The study of how offender careers develop in relation to age is called *developmental criminology.* Many criminologists have been slow to pick up on the promise that this area of study holds for our understanding of delinquent and criminal careers. By the late 1980s, a few criminologists had formulated developmental theories of juvenile delinquency

(e.g., Becker, 1963; Hawkins & Weiss, 1985; Elliott, Huizinga, & Menard, 1989; Lemert, 1951; Thornberry, 1987, 1996). Then some developmental psychologists who crossed over to criminology gave a boost to the adoption of this perspective in the late 1980s and early 1990s. Notably, Loeber (1988) called for the use of a developmental framework in the study of crime and delinquency; he and Le Blanc later coined the term *developmental criminology* to refer to this framework (Le Blanc & Loeber, 1998; Loeber & Le Blanc, 1990). In the first of their two developmental essays, Loeber and Le Blanc (1990) document the beginnings of this theoretical orientation toward crime and delinquency. In their later essay, they summarize important contributions to developmental criminology. As Le Blanc and Loeber (1998, p. 117) explain, developmental criminology is the study of within-individual changes in offending over time—that is, the development, escalation, maintenance, and abandonment of delinquent/criminal careers. The "developmental" perspective focuses studies in two areas: first, the age links to within-individual changes in offending, and second, risk or causal factors that explain changes in offending patterns over time.

Unfortunately, the search for causes of delinquency and crime has been dominated by cross-sectional studies (a research design in which, typically, one group is studied and a single measurement is taken at one point in time) and analyses of between-individual differences found through comparisons of deviants and nondeviants. As Le Blanc and Loeber (1993) have noted, such research "has led to a near standstill in the identification of those correlates or risk factors of offending that are also most likely to be causes [and] hindered the development of new, empirically based theories and the development of another generation of much-needed innovative intervention and prevention strategies for reducing delinquency" (p. 233). A major limitation of cross-sectional measurements is that "specialization in offenses and escalation in offending often cannot be inferred from them, because the concepts refer to repeated successive offenses or to increased seriousness over time" (Le Blanc & Loeber, 1998, p. 142). Thus developmental criminology uses longitudinal studies with repeated measurements to examine within-individual changes in offending over time in relation to important dimensions of offender careers, such as activation (onset), aggravation (escalation and stability maintenance), and desistance (Le Blanc & Loeber, 1993). As will become apparent shortly, Loeber has made a seminal contribution in each of these areas by developing a model that describes three major pathways to serious and violent juvenile offending in which offense patterns are somewhat orderly and predictable.

Developmental criminology's theoretical orientation is achieving growing acceptance because of its usefulness for viewing the life course of offending over time. It involves the study of causal, or risk, factors that may explain onset, escalation, de-escalation, and desistance in individuals' delinquent and criminal careers. As Loeber and Stouthamer-Loeber (1996) observe, "In particular, a better understanding of individual differences in criminal careers can help to explain why some youths become involved in delinquency only marginally and others more deeply, and which groups of individuals start to desist in crime at which part of the life cycle" (p. 12).

Developmental criminology is spawning new theories of delinquency and crime at a rapid pace. Several of these theories have made important contributions to our understanding of juvenile delinquency. These include a social development theory (Catalano & Hawkins, 1996), a child delinquency developmental theory (Coie & Dodge, 1998; Coie & Miller-Johnson, 2001), an interactional theory (Thornberry, 1987, 1996), a developmental explanation of gang involvement (Thornberry, Krohn, Lizotte, Smith, & Tobin, 2003), an age-graded developmental theory (Sampson & Laub, 1993), a theory of developmental pathways (Loeber, 1996), an integrative theory (Farrington, 1996), and a revised strain theory (Agnew, 1999). Other scholars have also contributed to work on a developmental perspective on crime and delinquency; for example, see the contributions to two recent volumes edited by Hawkins (1996) and Thornberry (1997).

The most advanced developmental theories incorporate a life-course perspective. Three such theories are featured in this chapter: Sampson and Laub's age-graded theory; Moffitt's theory dividing offenders into two groups, "life-course-persistent offenders" and "adolescence-limited offenders"; and Loeber's theory concerning the developmental pathways to serious and violent offending. In later chapters, I describe Hawkins and Catalano's social development theory and Thornberry et al.'s (2003) gang theory.

An Age-Graded Developmental Theory

Sampson and Laub (1993) have developed an age-graded theory of informal social control that explains crime and deviance over the life span. Their main theoretical proposition is that an individual's propensity to offend is materially altered by his or her involvement in conventional activities. In other words, variations in later adolescent and adult criminality are not accounted for simply by childhood patterns. Social factors can modify childhood delinquent trajectories and decrease criminal propensities into adulthood, even among serious offenders.

Sampson and Laub use Elder's (1986) concept of "turning points" to describe the mechanisms that operate when a change occurs in the life course, when a risk pathway is recast to a more adaptive path, such as desistance from delinquency. Like Elder (1985b), they contend that individual development over the life course is a dynamic process whereby the interlocking nature of trajectories, or life paths, and life-course transitions generates turning points, or changes in the life course. In childhood, according to Sampson and Laub's theory, the main causes of delinquency are found in family dynamics such as erratic, threatening, and harsh discipline; low levels of supervision; and parental rejection. In adolescence, other causal factors become important, including lack of attachment to school, attachment to delinquent peer groups, and involvement in the juvenile justice system. In the transition to young adulthood, institutions such as labor markets, marriage, prison, and the military are particularly important.

A key proposition in Sampson and Laub's theory is that persistent delinquency and criminality over the life course are not determined solely by individual traits rooted in childhood. Although involvement in delinquent behavior makes it difficult for youngsters to establish strong positive bonds with conventional others and the community, in general, the unforseen consequences of arrest and incarceration also make important negative contributions. These experiences with the juvenile justice system and the criminal justice system reduce youths' opportunities to participate in key conventional institutional roles (e.g., jobs) and conventional lifestyles (e.g., through education). "For example, arrest and incarceration may spark failure in school, unemployment, and weak community bonds, in turn increasing adult crime" by "knifing off" future conventional opportunities (Sampson & Laub, 1993, p. 306).

Life-Course-Persistent
and Adolescence-Limited Offenders

Moffitt (1993) distinguishes between two groups of offenders: "life-course-persistent offenders" and "adolescence-limited offenders" (see also Patterson, DeBaryshe, & Ramsey, 1989; Patterson & Yoerger, 1993). Life-course-persistent offenders begin offending in childhood and adolescence-limited offenders begin their offending later (see Moffitt, 1997).

Moffitt (1993) and Patterson (Patterson, Capaldi, & Bank, 1991; Patterson, Reid, & Dishion, 1992; see also Patterson, DeBaryshe, & Ramsey, 1989; Patterson & Yoerger, 1993) both distinguish between two groups of offenders. Moffitt calls these "life-course-persistent offenders" and "adolescence-limited offenders." Life-course-persistent offenders are those who begin offending in childhood and persist in offending into adulthood (Moffitt, 1997); delinquency is limited to the adolescent period for those in the second group. Patterson proposes two groups with similar patterns: "early starters" and "late starters." Moffitt argues that the main cause of life-course-persistent offending is the interaction of "neuropsychological" deficits with adverse environmental conditions in early childhood. That is, in life-course-persistent offenders, anatomical structures and physiological processes within the central nervous system (*neurological*) produce differences in cognitive abilities (*psychological*) that are manifested in subtle cognitive deficits, difficult temperament, or hyperactivity. Such children typically suffer from inadequate parenting, disrupted family bonds, and poverty. Thus these children step off on the wrong foot. Their differences from others in childhood are perpetuated or exa

erbated by their interactions with their social environment, initially at home and later at school. They carry into adulthood the same "constellation of traits that got them into trouble as a child, such as high activity level, irritability, poor self-control, and low cognitive ability" (Moffitt, 1997, p. 21).

According to Moffitt (1993, pp. 675-679), life-course-persistent offenders make up only a small proportion (about 5%) of the entire population of juvenile offenders; she describes the offense history of a typical such offender: He engages in biting and hitting at age 4, shoplifting and truancy at age 10, selling drugs and stealing cars at age 16, robbery

and rape at age 22, and fraud and child abuse at age 30. Past age 40, the co-occurring problems of life-course-persistent offenders include drug and alcohol addiction; unsatisfactory employment; unpaid debts; normlessness; drunk driving; violent assault; multiple and unstable relationships; spouse battery; abandoned, neglected, or abused children; and psychiatric illnesses. Thus such offenders exhibit changing manifestations of antisocial behavior across the life course as age and circumstances alter their opportunities for antisocial involvement. Four characteristics distinguish life-course-persistent offenders: early onset of offending, active offending during adolescence, escalation of offense seriousness, and persistence in crime in adulthood (Howell & Hawkins, 1998).

Adolescence-limited offenders, in contrast, represent a far larger proportion of the adolescent peak in the age-crime curve. (It is well established that this peak is at about age 16 for girls and age 17 for boys; Elliott, 1994a.) These offenders do not have childhood histories of antisocial offender behavior; rather, they engage in antisocial behavior only during adolescence. As teenagers, they may show inconsistency in their behavior across situations. For example, they may shoplift while with a group of friends, but obey school and family rules. As Moffitt (1993) describes them, they "are likely to engage in antisocial behavior in situations where such responses seem profitable to them, but they are also able to abandon antisocial behavior when prosocial styles are more rewarding" (p. 686). Howell and Hawkins (1998) have noted that three characteristics distinguish adolescence-limited offenders: onset of offending after age 11-13 (Elliott, 1994a; Moffitt, 1993), a lack of progression in offense seriousness (Loeber, Keenan, & Zhang, 1997), and desistance from crime by about age 18 (Moffitt, 1993; Tracy & Kempf-Leonard, 1996). Other researchers have identified life-course-persistent and adolescence-limited groups of offenders and other adolescent groups as well (e.g., Bartusch, Lynam, Moffitt, & Silva, 1997; Dean, Brame, & Piquero, 1996; Kempf-Leonard, Tracy, & Howell, 2001; Nagin, Farrington, & Moffitt, 1995; Nagin & Land, 1993; Patterson et al., 1989; Patterson & Yoerger, 1993; Simons, Wu, Conger, & Lorenz, 1994). Actually, it has become clear that several subgroups of offenders are identifiable, and new research in Rochester, New York, shows that there may be as many as six trajectory groups (Thornberry, Krohn, McDowall, Bushway, & Lizotte, 2002).

Although few studies have followed the same participants into adulthood to see if those identified as adolescence-limited offenders do indeed desist from offending, a number have shown that the overwhelming majority do so (Farrington, 1986a; Farrington & West, 1993; Nagin et al., 1995; Shannon, 1988; Tracy & Kempf-Leonard, 1996). Unfortunately, most of the research concerning these two types of offenders has been based on studies of males. Compared with males, females usually have a later onset of delinquency and peak at a younger age, but a proportion of these late-onset females become life-course-persistent offenders (Elliott, 1994a, pp. 6, 15; Kempf-Leonard et al., 2001).

Moffitt's typology is an interesting one, and it has stimulated a number of investigations into the actual existence of the two subgroups she has identified. However, her central argument, that the main cause of life-course-persistent offending is the interaction of neuropsychological deficits with adverse environmental conditions in early childhood, has not become widely accepted. Most children with neuropsychological deficits overcome them and do not become life-course-persistent offenders (Loeber & Farrington, 2001b; Wasserman & Seracini, 2001). There is substantial empirical evidence concerning multiple-factor influences on individuals' behavior, in a developmental fashion, over the life course (J. D. Hawkins et al., 1998; Lipsey & Derzon, 1998; Loeber & Farrington, 2001a).

The criminology field is indebted to Moffitt, however, for introducing the concept of adolescence-limited offenders. Indeed, her description of this group applies to the overwhelming proportion of juveniles referred to court. This group of offenders represented about two-thirds of all juvenile court careers in Snyder's (1998) study of more than 150,000 adolescents. They never had more than three court referrals, and they never had a court referral for a serious or violent offense.

It is very important for juvenile justice officials to be able to identify adolescence-limited offenders, because such offenders need few resources allocated to them. Identifying these offenders should be of interest to prevention agencies and organizations as well, because they are ideal targets for these organizations' efforts to prevent the spread of violence in adolescence. Violence affecting adolescents spreads in three main social contexts where adolescents interact: in peer groups, at school, and in youth gangs (Howell & Hawkins, 1998). Peer group interaction has been found to be a key factor contributing to the spread of violence in adolescence in the school and youth gang contexts. Adolescent violence is characterized by group involvement (Reiss, 1988; Warr, 2002). In a recent meta-analysis, Lipsey and Derzon (1998) found that

having antisocial peers from ages 12 to 15 is one of the strongest predictors of later violent behavior, at ages 15-24.

Moffitt's conceptualization of life-course-persistent offenders needs further refinement—particularly if it is to be useful to the juvenile justice system. For example, persistent or chronic nonserious offenders need to be distinguished from chronic serious and chronic violent offenders, so that, for instance, costly interventions such as placement in residential facilities are not used for chronic non-serious offenders. A more useful typology is that suggested by Wilson and Howell (1993), which distinguishes among serious, violent, and chronic offenders. This typology captures subgroups of offenders that are excluded from Moffitt's two-part classification. As noted earlier, some offenders begin their careers in childhood and desist in adolescence. Others are chronic offenders but never become serious or violent offenders. Examination of the pathways youngsters take in their offender careers can enhance our understanding of the full panoply of offender careers—not just life-course-persistent or adolescence-limited offender careers.

Most likely, combinations of offender careers—involving serious and violent offenses, chronic and serious offenses, or chronic and violent offenses—will prove to be the most important targets for intervention. There is a great deal of evidence—in both self-report data and official records—that juvenile offenders do not specialize in particular kinds of offenses (Farrington, Snyder, & Finnegan, 1988; Loeber, DeLamatre, Keenan, & Zhang, 1998) or in either serious or violent categories of offenses (Mazerolle, Brame, Paternoster, Piquero, & Dean, 2000; Piquero, Paternoster, Brame, Mazerolle, & Dean, 1999). The propensity to offend appears to be dynamic and malleable—perhaps by juvenile court intervention early in offenders' careers (Dean, Brame, & Piquero, 1996).

Pathways to Serious, Violent, and Chronic Delinquency

This section is devoted to one of the two most debated issues concerning offender careers—stability versus change in offending patterns. I will present evidence from developmental studies to show that child delinquents do not emerge from families as full-blown life-course-persistent offenders. As Thornberry et al. (2003) put it, "Delinquent careers are not predetermined but are malleable, changing as the person's life unfolds." The developmental process that produces a juvenile delinquent is affected by numerous factors in childhood and adolescence.

How can the progression from predelinquent behaviors in childhood to serious, violent, and chronic delinquency best be characterized? A useful model for depicting this progression is one that specifies the main pathways children and adolescents take. Let us first think about the importance of this progression from the standpoint of juvenile justice system officials. The limited offense history information available in official records is of little help to these officials in distinguishing serious, violent, and chronic offenders from others. Self-report studies of delinquency involvement indicate that these records provide an incomplete picture of serious offenders' delinquent histories (Elliott, 1995; Huizinga, Esbensen, & Weiher, 1996; Stouthamer-Loeber, Loeber, Van Kammen, & Zhang, 1995). Most of the delinquent acts that youngsters commit are never brought to the attention of police or juvenile courts.

In contrast, most serious and violent offenders eventually are arrested, but not necessarily for their most serious offenses. Huizinga, Loeber, and Thornberry (1995) have reported on studies in Rochester, Denver, and Pittsburgh that found that by age 14, most chronic violent adolescents (81% in Rochester, 97% in Denver, and 74% in Pittsburgh) had begun committing violent offenses, but only relatively small proportions of the youths in these groups had been arrested (slightly more than one-third of them in Rochester and Denver, and about half in Pittsburgh). However, most chronic violent offenders are arrested at some point (two-thirds were arrested in Rochester and about three-fourths in Denver and Pittsburgh; Huizinga et al., 1995, p. 26). Examination of the self-reported delinquency histories of the Denver subjects indicated that they were not necessarily arrested for their most serious offenses, however (Huizinga et al., 1996). Only 6% of the serious violent offenders in the Denver study were arrested for the most serious violent offenses they reported having committed. About one-fourth were arrested before they committed any serious violent offenses, about one-fourth were arrested during the same year in which they committed these types of offenses, and about one-fourth were arrested after they had initiated their serious violent offending. Thus, by themselves, arrest records do not provide sufficient information to allow for accurate classification of juvenile offenders and depiction of their delinquency careers. As Elliott (1995) has observed, "To rely almost exclusively on arrest studies when describing the dynamics of criminal behavior is indefensible" (p. 21).

Loeber's Three-Pathways Model

When a young offender is first referred to juvenile court, juvenile justice system officials get a very limited view, or a "snapshot," of that individual's entire offending career in the form of the official records. This limited view makes it very difficult for officials to make distinctions between potential chronic-serious or chronic-violent offenders and adolescence-limited offenders. Risk assessment instruments are key tools for helping juvenile justice officials make such distinctions (see Chapter 12). If we can arrive at a better understanding of the pathways to serious, violent, and chronic offending, we can improve these instruments so that they can much more accurately distinguish among types of offenders. Knowledge of developmental pathways is important to the juvenile justice system because such knowledge is an important step toward identifying youth who are at risk for escalation to more serious behavior (Loeber, Wei, Stouthamer-Loeber, Huizinga, & Thornberry, 1999, p. 246).

Using a developmental model (as suggested by Loeber & Le Blanc, 1990), the study of offender careers conducted at the Pittsburgh site of the OJJDP Program of Research on the Causes and Correlates of Delinquency has produced a potential breakthrough in the specification of pathways to serious, violent, and chronic offending. Loeber prefers to use the term *pathway* to describe a segment of a delinquent or criminal career trajectory. A developmental pathway is defined as "the stages of behavior that unfold over time in a predictable order" (Loeber et al., 1997, p. 322). This is a dynamic method of classification, an empirical model for examining offenders' careers that distinguishes chronic offenders ("persisters," in Loeber's terminology) from nonchronic offenders ("experimenters"; Loeber et al., 1997). This pathways model also distinguishes among nonserious, serious, and violent offenders. Before I discuss Loeber's three-pathways model, I review below a couple of contributions to our understanding of the continuity in delinquent and criminal behavior; these are some of the conceptual underpinnings of Loeber's model.

A Stepping-Stones Model

In a major contribution to our understanding of the continuity in delinquent and criminal behavior,

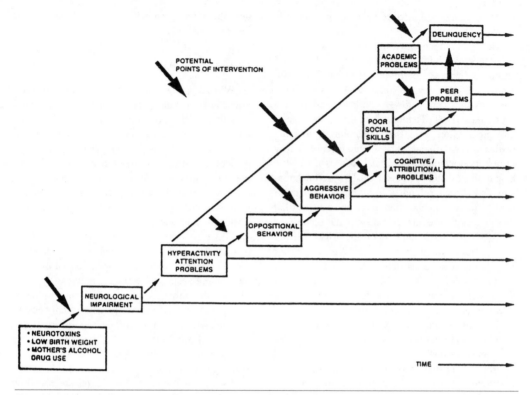

Figure 4.1   Developmental Stacking of Problem Behaviors

SOURCE: "Development and Risk Factors of Juvenile Antisocial Behavior and Delinquency," by R. Loeber (1990). © copyright 1990 by *Clinical Psychology Review,* Vol. 10 (p. 17). Reprinted with permission from Elsevier Science.

Farrington (1986b) constructed a "stepping-stones" model. He used a range of factors, measured at different points in relation to chronological aging (childhood, adolescent, and young adulthood) in the Cambridge Study in Delinquent Development (Farrington, 1995), to predict adult criminality. Two important findings resulted from Farrington's application of the stepping-stones model. First, Farrington demonstrated stepwise continuity in delinquent and criminal behavior. Troublesomeness and daring behavior at ages 8-10 predicted convictions at ages 10-13, which predicted self-reported delinquency at age 14. Self-reported delinquency with convictions at ages 14-16 predicted antisocial tendencies at age 18. In the last stage, convictions at ages 17-20 predicted convictions at ages 21-24. Second, Farrington identified a common set of predictors of offending at different ages: economic deprivation, family criminality, parental mishandling, and school failure. These indicators of a general antisocial tendency predicted adolescent aggression, offending frequency, and adult violence (Farrington, 1989).

Stacking of Problem Behaviors

Loeber's (1988, 1990) description of problem behavior "stacking" (see Figure 4.1) was a pioneering concept that predated his specification of pathways to serious and violent delinquency. Loeber theorized that new problem behaviors are added to earlier ones, which are not abandoned. He enumerated five characteristics of a developmental progression in problem behaviors: First, some behaviors have an earlier onset than others; second, there is usually escalation in the seriousness of problem behavior over time; third, early behaviors usually are retained as new ones are added; fourth, each behavior is best predicted by the developmentally adjacent behavior; and fifth, the ordering of behaviors in a pathway is sequential (Loeber, 1988).

Three Pathways

Loeber defines a "path" as that portion of a developmental trajectory that an individual travels

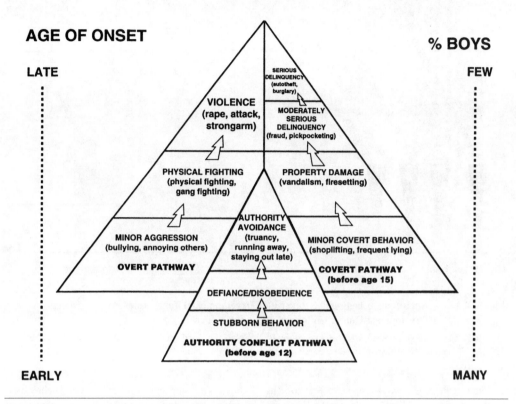

Figure 4.2   Developmental Pathways in Disruptive/Delinquent Behavior

SOURCE: "Behavioral Antecedents to Serious and Violent Offending: Joint Analyses From the Denver Youth Survey, Pittsburgh Youth Study and the Rochester Youth Development Study," by R. Loeber, E. Wei, M. Stouthamer-Loeber, D. Huizinga, & T. P. Thornberry, 1999, *Studies on Crime and Crime Prevention, 8,* p. 247. Reprinted with permission.

within a given time period (see Le Blanc & Loeber, 1998, p. 181). Analyzing data on 10- to 16-year-olds collected in the Pittsburgh Youth Study, Loeber and his colleagues discovered an empirically based set of three basic but overlapping pathways in the development of delinquency among boys from childhood to adolescence (see Loeber & Hay, 1994; Loeber et al., 1993). As shown in Figure 4.2, these are the *authority conflict pathway,* the *covert pathway,* and the *overt pathway.* The authority conflict pathway corresponds generally to predelinquent offenses, the covert pathway is related to concealing and serious property offenses, and the overt pathway corresponds to violent offenses.

The model of pathways to problem behavior and delinquency shown in this figure has three important dimensions. First, the model shows an orderly progression over time from less serious to more serious status offenses and delinquent behaviors. Second, the progressively narrowing width of the triangles in the figure illustrates the decreasing

proportion of boys (from "many" to "few") involved in particular problem behavior and delinquent offenses. Finally, the model shows the general age of onset (from "early" to "late").

Boys on the authority conflict pathway are children under age 12. Problem behavior typically begins in the authority conflict pathway with stubborn behavior, followed by defiance/disobedience, then truancy, running away, and staying out late. Persistent offenders then typically move into either the overt pathway or the covert pathway (Loeber et al., 1993). The first stage of the covert pathway is minor covert behavior (shoplifting, frequent lying); this is followed by property damage (vandalism, fire setting) and then moderately serious (fraud, pickpocketing) and serious delinquency (auto theft, burglary). The first stage of the overt pathway is minor aggression (bullying, annoying others); this is followed by physical fighting (often including gang fighting) and then more serious violence (rape, physical attacks, strong-arm robbery).

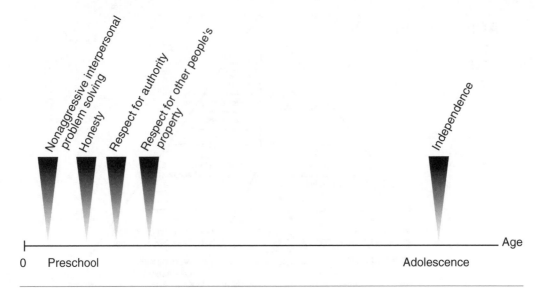

Figure 4.3   Approximate Temporal Sequence of Developmental Tasks Relevant to Prosocial
Development During Childhood and Adolescence

SOURCE: *Epidemiology of Serious Violence* (p. 4), by B. T. Kelley, D. Huizinga, T. P. Thornberry, and R. Loeber,
1997, Washington, DC: Office of Juvenile Justice and Delinquency Prevention.

Each of these pathways represents breakdowns
in the developmental tasks relevant to prosocial
development during childhood and adolescence:

- The overt pathway represents aggression as
  opposed to positive social problem solving.
- The covert pathway represents lying, vandalism, and theft as opposed to honesty and
  respect for property.
- The authority conflict pathway represents conflict as opposed to respect for authority figures.

Figure 4.3 shows the temporal sequence of
developmental tasks relevant to prosocial development during childhood and adolescence. Probably
the first such task that children encounter is learning
to solve interpersonal problems without the use of
verbal or physical aggression (Kelley, Loeber,
Keenan, & DeLamatre, 1997, p. 4). As children's
cognitive and verbal abilities increase during the
preschool period, they become ready to master the
developmental task of being honest. Somewhere
around this time, children also start to learn to
respect other people's property. Alongside these
developments, they learn to respect authority
figures, such as parents and teachers. Children
progress along the pathways to problem behavior
and delinquency when they do not successfully
accomplish these developmental tasks.

As noted above, Loeber and his colleagues use
the terms *experimenters* and *persisters* to refer to

boys who stop engaging in problem behavior or
delinquency and those who do not, respectively
(see, e.g., Loeber et al., 1997). Experimenters are
boys whose problem behaviors within a given
stage do not persist or recur at any subsequent
assessment phase. In the research on the Pittsburgh
sample of boys—on which this model is based—
persisters are boys whose problem behaviors are
acknowledged by either the boys themselves or
their primary caregivers at more than one assessment of problem behavior (Kelley, Loeber, et al.,
1997, pp. 9-10). Unlike experimenters, persisters
tend to progress from an authority conflict base.
Loeber and his colleagues have found that among
almost all of the boys they have studied, those who
persisted in either the overt or the covert pathway
had initially persisted in the authority conflict pathway. Their data suggest that among the most
chronic offenders, authority conflict generally
occurs first, followed soon by overt disruptive
behavior, then by covert behavior. Offenders do
not abandon their earlier behaviors; rather, they
add new types of offenses to their current ones in a
"stacking" pattern (Loeber, 1988, 1990). As boys
age, they continue to progress further along the
developmental pathways. Boys in the initial step of
a pathway are at less serious risk of persistence
than are those in later steps. Later progressions are
more predictable. Loeber et al. (1997) found that
all of the boys in their sample who advanced to violence in the overt pathway had progressed through

the intermediate stages of that pathway; none of the experimenters had done so.

The following are other important findings from the pathways research that Loeber and his colleagues conducted on the Pittsburgh sample of boys (see Kelley, Loeber, et al., 1997):

- Persisters were more likely than experimenters to enter a pathway at its first stage.
- Experimenters were more likely than persisters to enter a pathway at its second or third stage.
- Persisters were much more likely than experimenters to follow the sequence of stages in a pathway.
- Boys with attention deficit/hyperactivity disorder were at risk of becoming experimenters, and, even more so, of becoming persisters in one or more of the developmental pathways.
- With increasing age, the boys were more likely to persist in the more serious behaviors of multiple pathways. One of the strongest predictable occurrences was that violent boys would also engage in serious nonviolent forms of delinquency.
- About 75% of the most chronic offenders were persisters in the second or third stage of any of the pathways (Loeber, DeLamatre, et al., 1998).
- Boys who advanced in all three pathways had the highest rates of both violent and nonviolent offenses (i.e., they were serious, violent, *and* chronic offenders).
- Boys in the dual pathway of covert/overt behavior ranked second in number of offenses.
- Boys in the dual pathway of covert/authority conflict behavior ranked third in number of offenses.
- Boys in the single pathway of covert behavior ranked fourth in number of offenses.
- Boys who persisted in the advanced stages of the overt/covert pathways were most likely to have court petitions for violence.

Strong empirical support has emerged for Loeber's three-pathways model. It has been empirically supported in four other samples to date: a national sample, a Chicago study, and the Rochester and Denver longitudinal studies. Tolan and Gorman-Smith (1998) have validated Loeber's model in two other samples: the National Youth Survey and the Chicago Youth Development Study. For the vast majority of youths in both samples, the development of antisocial behavior was congruent with the sequences hypothesized by Loeber and demonstrated in the Pittsburgh sample. Most important, Tolan and Gorman-Smith discovered that, compared with general delinquents, a larger proportion of serious and violent offenders followed the pathways.

Tolan and Gorman-Smith (1998) suggest that Loeber's three-pathways model holds promise for differentiating serious, violent, and chronic juvenile offenders from others. They found that persisters in the pathways are distinguished from others by age of onset, presence of childhood behavior problems, and related aggression level. However, Tolan and Gorman-Smith caution that the model does not specify the determinants of an individual's moving from one level to another, although relative age of onset and the frequency and seriousness of prior delinquency involvement over time are important factors. Other risk factors are also important, including family functioning, peer associations, school performance, individual problems (e.g., mental health), and the type of neighborhood in which a youth resides (Loeber & Wikstrom, 1993; Wikstrom & Loeber, 2000).

Loeber's three-pathways model has been validated in the two other sites (Denver and Rochester) in OJJDP's Program of Research on the Causes and Correlates of Delinquency (Loeber, Wei, et al., 1999). As in Pittsburgh, the Denver and Rochester studies sampled inner-city, high-risk youth. The results supported the original findings at the Pittsburgh site for the three pathways (Loeber et al., 1993, 1997). In all three sites, the cumulative age of onset followed the expected pattern of pathway steps in Loeber's model—with the less serious forms of problem behavior and delinquency occurring first, and the more serious forms of delinquency occurring last. In other words, earlier problem behaviors and delinquent acts become stepping-stones for subsequent offenses.

The fit of the covert pathway was best up to age 14 (Loeber, Wei, et al., 1999, pp. 261-262). A better overall fit was found for the overt pathway than for the covert pathway. This is probably owing to the stability of aggressive tendencies over the life course—one of the most consistently documented patterns in longitudinal research (Laub & Lauritsen, 1993, p. 239).

The proportion of boys who persisted in the overt *and* covert pathways ranged from 21% to 35% in the three sites. These are serious or violent *and* chronic offenders. These percentages are much higher than those reported by Snyder (1998), Curry and Decker (2000), and Kempf-Leonard et al. (2001), for two obvious reasons. First, the Pittsburgh Study used self-reported data, whereas the other three studies used police and court data—which, as noted previously, contain less-than-complete representations of offense histories. Second, the Pittsburgh, Denver, and Rochester studies oversampled high-risk youth, who commit more offenses than low-risk youth.

However, persistence does not necessarily imply constant, high-rate, violent offending. Many youth are only intermittently involved in serious delinquency, violence, or gang membership, and involvement often lasts only a single year during adolescence (Huizinga, Loeber, Thornberry, & Cothern, 2000, p. 2; Kelley, Huizinga, et al., 1997, pp. 7-8). Among multiple-year offenders in the Denver Youth Survey, for example, there were various temporal (time-related) patterns of involvement. For careers that lasted 3 or more years, the most frequent pattern was sporadic offending. That is, well over half of these multiple-year offenders were not active every year. In fact, about 75% of those whose violence involvement spanned the full 5 years were characterized by such intermittent patterns of offending. Kelley, Huizinga, et al. (1997) note, "Clearly these offending patterns give caution to interpreting the behavior at any one given year to characterize or identify violent or non-violent individuals" (p. 8).

This research on pathways has two major program implications (Kelley, Loeber, et al., 1997). First, social service agencies must devise age-appropriate strategies for assisting children in mastering key developmental tasks. For instance, to avoid onset of the overt pathway, children must learn to control aggressive outbursts and to use words, rather than fists, to resolve problems. Second, agencies must be careful not to dismiss the warning signs of early onset of disruptive behaviors with a "this too will pass" attitude. Intervention will be more successful if the child has not already persistently performed negative behaviors or penetrated the more serious stages of a pathway. Yet early intervention is risky business, because most children who show early disruptive behaviors do not persist in them.

Thus Stouthamer-Loeber and her colleagues (1995) caution against attempting to intervene at the first sign of problem behavior, because many early problem behaviors are temporary and disappear without intervention. Rather, a developmental *pattern* should trigger concern. Factors that should be considered include early onset, how often a child is disruptive, with what intensity and provocation the child exhibits disruptive behavior, and whether the behavior occurs in multiple settings (e.g., home and school contexts) (Kelley, Huizinga, et al., 1997,

p. 17). Knowledge is still lacking regarding the best point for intervention and the specific behaviors that should be targeted.

An important question concerns the applicability of Loeber's pathways model to racial/ethnic minority and female youth. In the Pittsburgh studies, the results applied about equally well to both African American and white boys, who made up most of the sample. Tolan and Gorman-Smith's (1998) Chicago replication used a sample of high-risk inner-city youths, 57% of whom were African American and the remainder of whom were Latino. In the three-city replication described above, Loeber, Wei, et al. (1999) found that the pathway model applied about equally well to Caucasian, African American, and Hispanic populations of boys. However, the model has not yet been tested with a population of female delinquents. Only one validation included females (National Youth Survey data), but the researchers did not make any comparison between males and females (Tolan & Gorman-Smith, 1998).

In sum, as Loeber, Wei, et al. (1999) note:

"The major policy implication of the findings [on Loeber's pathways model] is that preventive and remedial interventions (i.e., primary and secondary forms of prevention) can be applied to youth who have not yet gone through one or more of the pathways. This implies a proactive approach to dealing with serious and violent forms of delinquency rather than reactively after the fact, through confinement and incarceration. (p. 262)

Intervention needs to occur earlier than typically is the case. Another analysis in the Pittsburgh Youth Study shows that the average age of boys who were referred to court for a serious or violent crime (an Index offense) was 14.5 (Rumsey, Kerr, & Allen-Hagen, 1998). For these boys, the average age of onset of minor problem behavior was 7, followed by moderately serious problem behavior at ages 9-10, then serious delinquency at ages 11-12. The 7-year gap between onset of minor problem behavior and the initial arrest for a serious or violent crime represents a window of opportunity for early intervention programming and immediate intervention by social service agencies when delinquency involvement begins.

Child Delinquents

The window of opportunity for early intervention programming must focus on child delinquents. This section addresses what is known about this very young group of offenders. The key question is this: Do we know enough about child delinquents to guide early intervention?

Before OJJDP's Study Group on Very Young Offenders was formed, the body of knowledge about child delinquents was disorganized (see Loeber & Farrington, 2001a; for summaries of this study group's work, see Loeber & Farrington, 2000, 2001c). The study group, chaired by Rolf Loeber and David Farrington, reviewed the available empirical data (and also performed a number of analyses on existing data sets) and examined studies that had been conducted concerning three categories of problematic children (up to age 12):

- Serious child delinquents (children who have committed one or more of the following acts: homicide, aggravated assault, robbery, rape, or serious arson)
- Nonserious child delinquents
- Disruptive, nondelinquent children who show persistent disruptive behavior

In this section, I summarize the findings of the Very Young Offender Study Group with respect to serious child delinquents—children who fall into the first of these three categories of problematic children. With respect to nonserious child delinquents, the study group found that, for some young children, less serious delinquency is a stepping-stone to more serious offending. Better screening devices are needed—for use in both juvenile courts and other agencies that handle child delinquents—to discriminate between children who will escalate to more serious offending and those who will not (Howell, 2001b).

With respect to disruptive children, the study group discovered that many children who become serious and violent offenders have long histories of nondelinquent, disruptive problem behavior during childhood. Typical disruptive behaviors are serious and persistent disobedience, frequent lying, aggressive behaviors, minor forms of theft, truancy during elementary school, and early substance abuse. Longitudinal studies have shown that from one-fourth to one-third of these disruptive children are at risk of becoming child delinquents (Loeber & Dishion, 1983; Tremblay, Pihl, Vitaro, & Dobkin, 1994).

The study group compiled the following list of warning signs for later problems among disruptive children during the preschool years (Loeber & Farrington, 2001b, p. xxiv):

- Disruptive behavior that is either more frequent or more severe than that of other children of the same age

- Disruptive behavior such as temper tantrums and aggression that persists beyond the first 2 to 3 years of life
- A history of aggressive, inattentive, or sensation-seeking behavior in the preschool years

What proportion of child delinquents persist in their delinquency? In an analysis of the youngest members of the Denver and Pittsburgh samples, Espiritu, Huizinga, Crawford, and Loeber (2001) found that, although the vast majority engaged in some form of aggression or minor violence (mainly throwing objects, hitting other students, and—to a much lesser extent—involvement in gang fights), only about 25% of the child delinquents persisted in minor violence, property offenses, or drug use for 5 years or more. The Denver sample included females and the Pittsburgh sample did not. Other studies have shown that about a third of all child delinquents later become serious, violent, and chronic offenders (J. D. Hawkins et al., 1998; Lipsey & Derzon, 1998; Loeber & Dishion, 1983).

A key question about child delinquents, however, is whether they are more likely to become typical juvenile delinquents or violent delinquents than are youngsters who begin their delinquent careers at older ages. All 21 of the longitudinal studies that have included child delinquents have reported a significant relationship between early onset and later crime and delinquency (for an excellent review of these studies, see Krohn, Thornberry, Rivera, & Le Blanc, 2001, pp. 74-81). The findings for females have been similar to those for males.

Rochester researchers Krohn et al. (2001) extended this line of research for the OJJDP Study Group on Very Young Offenders in a secondary analysis of data in three longitudinal studies: the Rochester Youth Development Study, a Montreal study (Le Blanc & Frechette, 1989), and the Pittsburgh Youth Study (Loeber, Farrington, Stouthamer-Loeber, Moffitt, et al., 1998). Krohn et al. explored whether offenders who begin their delinquent behavior very early (onset at age 10 or under) have more serious and violent offender careers in their adolescent and young adult years than do later-onset delinquents. Specifically, the researchers hypothesized that child delinquents' criminal careers are of greater duration, extending further into the life course; that child delinquents go on to commit more offenses and have higher individual offending rates over the life course; and that their offenses tend to be more serious and more violent than those of late-onset offenders. All three of these hypotheses were confirmed for the very youngest offenders in Krohn et al.'s analyses of data from the longitudinal studies in Rochester and Montreal, although data from the Montreal study were less consistent. The analyses included females in only the Montreal study.

In the Rochester sample, the very youngest onset group (onset at 4 to 10 years of age) had the highest prevalence rate for both serious and violent offenses during the early adult years, roughly ages 19 to 22 (Krohn et al., 2001, p. 83). More than a third (39%) of this group reported involvement in serious and violent offenses in young adulthood, compared with 20% of the youngsters with onset at ages 11-12 and 23% of those with onset at ages 13-14.

Thus it is clear that child delinquents are an identifiable group. With the development and use of appropriate screening devices, early intervention with children in this group could pay handsome dividends in terms of an impact on the rates of overall juvenile delinquency as well as serious and violent delinquency. Without intervention, child delinquents, compared with later-onset offenders, are likely to go on to commit more offenses and have higher individual offending rates, and their offenses tend to be more serious and more violent.

I now turn to a review of the Very Young Offender Study Group's findings with respect to trends in child delinquency. A comparison of national self-report studies showed that the proportion of child delinquents involved in serious and violent delinquency did not change from 1976 through 1999 (Espiritu et al., 2001), yet the study group found that the number of arrested child delinquents increased considerably from 1980 through 1996 (Snyder, 2001), and that law enforcement agencies referred a larger percentage of the child delinquents they arrested to the juvenile courts in 1997 than in 1988. Thus child delinquents came to constitute a relatively large proportion (10%) of all juvenile cases by the late 1990s (Butts & Snyder, 1997; Snyder, 2001).

Research on the Transition Between Juvenile and Adult Criminal Careers

Having described the pathways that children and adolescents take toward chronic involvement in serious and violent delinquency, I consider in this section the later segment of such serious delinquency involvement—that is, the transition to adult criminality. Little research has focused on the relationship between serious, violent, and chronic juvenile delinquency careers and adult crime. However, researchers who have examined juvenile careers have noted several key indicators that predict long-term involvement: (a) early onset and career length, (b) frequency of offending, (c) offense specialization, (d) offense seriousness, and (e) offense escalation. Studies to date have substantiated that two of these features of offender careers are related to life-course offending: early onset and frequency (chronicity) of offending. Until recently, evidence has been lacking with respect to the relationship between the remaining offender career features and continuation of juvenile offender careers into adulthood (see Loeber & Farrington, 1998c; Tolan & Gorman-Smith, 1998; Tracy & Kempf-Leonard, 1996, pp. 35-54).

In a follow-up to the 1958 Philadelphia Birth Cohort Study (see Box 4.3 on page 64), which used a sample consisting of more than 6,000 delinquents in the 1958 birth cohort, Tracy and Kempf-Leonard (1996) examined each of the above factors. A summary of their findings on each indicator follows.

Early onset and career length. Tracy and Kempf-Leonard (1996) found the age at which delinquents began to accumulate police contacts (early in the 14th year, on average) and career length to be predictors of adult offending. However, early onset, by itself, did not guarantee that the delinquent would have a lengthy delinquent career. Early onset was linked to career length in terms of the age at which the last offense was recorded. Adolescents who began accumulating offenses at age 13 and 14 had the strongest odds of becoming adult criminals (Tracy & Kempf-Leonard, 1996, p. 138). Early-onset delinquents who had their last delinquent offenses recorded between ages 15 and 18 were significantly more likely to be charged with adult crimes than were early-onset delinquents who did not have any recorded offenses in the latter part of adolescence. Tracy and Kempf-Leonard summarize the evidence: "The most basic explanation is that starting early, continuing through the delinquency years, and then being active right up to the point of becoming an adult (at age 18) are important delinquency career related precursors of adult criminality" (p. 139).

Frequency of offending. Tracy and Kempf-Leonard (1996) also found that as the delinquency level increased, "there was a substantial and consistent increase in the level of adult criminality" (p. 107). As the number of delinquent offenses increased, from none to one, to two to four offenses, and to five or more offenses, the likelihood that the delinquent became an adult offender increased significantly. Compared with "virgin" adult offenders, delinquent-to-adult criminal offenders had more offenses against persons, more offenses that resulted in personal injury, more robberies, more weapon use (including handguns and other types of firearms), and more other serious and violent offenses. Delinquent-to-criminal offenders also had significantly more drug offenses than did "virgin" adult offenders.

Offense specialization. Tracy and Kempf-Leonard (1996) found that having a police record of particular offenses increased the likelihood of a person's continuity between juvenile and adult offending. Results on this point were different for males and females. Among males, the particular offenses found to be associated with adult offending were major violence, robbery, weapons use, and being a co-offender. Significant offenses for females included major violence, major property crimes, and theft. Among chronic delinquents, being a co-offender was a significant factor for becoming an adult offender.

Offense seriousness. Tracy and Kempf-Leonard (1996, p. 185) found that delinquents with higher average offense severity across their delinquent careers were more likely than others to become adult criminals. (Involvement in status offenses did not increase the likelihood of an individual's becoming an adult offender, nor did the combination of one delinquent offense with status offenses.) "Both frequency and average severity were found to have strong, significant, and independent effects on adult crime status" (p. 184).

Offense escalation. Tracy and Kempf-Leonard (1996) found that escalation in offense severity is an important determinant of adult criminality. When offense severity occurred relatively early in the career and offense severity soon escalated, the likelihood of persistence into adult criminality was much higher.

Other longitudinal studies of the transition from juvenile delinquency to adult crime are needed to replicate Tracy and Kempf-Leonard's pioneering analysis. Such studies will help establish predictors of adult criminality among juvenile offenders that can be incorporated into risk assessment instruments for the purpose of more intensive intervention with those offenders who are highly likely to continue their criminal careers into adulthood. It appears that this research could benefit from a focus on the relative likelihood that different subgroups of juvenile offenders will become life-course persisters.

Descriptions of Serious, Violent, and Chronic Offender Careers

This section is devoted to a review of the research that has been conducted in the effort to characterize the subgroups of delinquents involved in juvenile offender careers. John J. Wilson and I have proposed the existence of three main types of delinquents that might be linked to adult criminal careers: serious, violent, and chronic juvenile offenders (Wilson & Howell, 1993). The possible combinations among these types result in six distinct subgroups: serious delinquents, violent delinquents, chronic delinquents, serious and chronic delinquents, chronic and violent delinquents, and serious and violent delinquents. An important empirical question is, Which juvenile offenders are most likely to have offense careers that expand over the course of their lives? Below, I first review some pioneering studies of chronic offenders and then examine more recent studies that have made significant contributions to our understanding of the development and maintenance of juvenile offender careers over the life course.

Early Studies of Chronic Offender Careers

Four major studies conducted in the 1970s were the first to result in descriptions of the chronic juvenile offender subgroup. These studies—the Philadelphia Birth Cohort Study (Wolfgang, Figlio, & Sellin, 1972); the Columbus, Ohio, Violent Few Study (Hamparian, Davis, Jacobson, & McGraw, 1985; Hamparian, Schuster, Dinitz, & Conrad, 1978); the Racine, Wisconsin, study (Shannon, 1988, 1991, 1998); and the Cambridge Study in Delinquent Development (Farrington, 1983)—conclusively showed that a very small proportion of juvenile offenders were responsible for the majority of delinquent acts and the vast majority of serious acts of delinquency. These studies further indicated that the youths in this small group of "chronic" delinquents began their officially recorded careers very early (by age 13 or 14), and their careers continued well into the adult years (Tracy & Kempf-Leonard, 1996). In addition to these studies, Strasburg (1977) examined this juvenile offender subgroup in the New York City juvenile justice system; he also noted the small proportion of such offenders.

Findings From OJJDP's Study Group on Serious and Violent Juvenile Offenders

OJJDP's Study Group on Serious and Violent Juvenile Offenders conducted a comprehensive review of the existing knowledge about serious, violent, and chronic juvenile offenders (Loeber & Farrington, 1998c; for summaries, see Loeber & Farrington, 1998b; Rumsey et al., 1998). The study group used as its framework for these inquiries the Comprehensive Strategy for Serious, Violent, and Chronic Juvenile Offenders (Wilson & Howell, 1993). The group's conclusions, for the most part, are limited to serious and violent offenders, because the researchers quickly discovered that varying definitions of the concept of chronic offending across studies make comparisons problematic. In the context of research on juvenile offenders, the term *chronic* usually incorporates two dimensions: frequency of offending and the length of time over which offending persists (Laub & Lauritsen, 1993). Researchers have varied in the methods they have used to measure both of these dimensions. For example, in studies using self-report measures, researchers have typically used operational definitions of chronicity that are based on relatively large numbers of offenses; in contrast, researchers conducting court studies have usually based their definitions of chronicity on referral and adjudication events.

Based on their review of serious chronic offender studies for the OJJDP study group, Loeber, Farrington, and Waschbusch (1998) offer several conclusions:

1. The proportions of chronic offenders vary considerably from study to study (from 7% to 25%).

2. The amount of crime accounted for by chronic offenders varies by ethnicity, with nonwhite male chronic offenders accounting for a larger amount of official serious delinquency.

3. There are large gender differences—that is, chronic offending is lower in females than in males.

4. The amount of crime accounted for by chronic offenders varies by cohort in the same location (see Shannon, 1988; Tracy, Wolfgang, & Figlio, 1990).

5. The amount of crime accounted for by chronic offenders varies by offense type; it is relatively low when all offenses are taken into account and somewhat higher for violent offenses, especially robbery (Tracy et al., 1990; Wolfgang et al., 1972).

It should be noted that the percentage of adolescents who have serious violent careers is very small. Lipsey and Derzon (1998) reviewed 34 prospective longitudinal studies of juveniles and found that only 8% of the juveniles were typically classified as violent or seriously delinquent on the outcome measures taken during the age period 15-25 (p. 98). The proportion of chronic violent offenders is, of course, much smaller. In the National Youth Survey, only 4% of male respondents self-reported a serious violent offense in each of 5 consecutive years (Elliott, Huizinga, & Morse, 1986, p. 497). As we have seen in Chapter 2, this percentage does not appear to have changed appreciably since the National Youth Survey was conducted (see Snyder, 1998, p. 443).

Although chronic serious and chronic violent offenders represent a small proportion of all offenders, they account for an overwhelming proportion of all such offenses committed by samples of delinquents. In the Rochester study, the chronic violent offenders constituted only 15% of the total sample; in Denver, they represented 14% (Thornberry, Huizinga, & Loeber, 1995, p. 218). Yet in Rochester the chronic violent offenders self-reported having committed 75% of all of the violent offenses reported in the entire sample. In Denver, this 14% of the study sample committed 82% of all of the self-reported violent offenses. Thus, as Thornberry et al. (1995) note, "the problem of youth violence is highly concentrated in a small proportion of the population" (p. 220). It is not possible to have much of an impact on the overall volume of adolescent violence without intervening successfully in the lives of these chronic, violent offenders. "For example, even if we were 100% successful in preventing the nonchronic violent offenders from *ever* engaging in violence, we would reduce the level of violent behavior by only 25%" (p. 220).

The OJJDP study group commissioned an empirical investigation that distinguished chronic offenders from serious and violent juvenile offenders. The group had three reasons for initiating this line of inquiry: First, the degree of overlap of chronic careers with serious and violent juvenile offender careers was of interest; second, the researchers wanted to establish an empirical foundation—a basis of comparison—for future studies of serious, violent, and chronic juvenile offenders; and third, the researchers saw that sound empirical information on these subgroups could be of enormous value to juvenile justice officials in making determinations regarding intervention in juvenile offender careers.

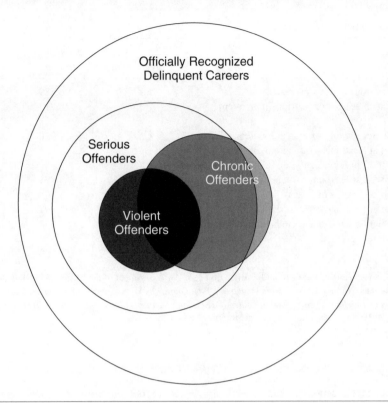

Figure 4.4   Overlap of Serious, Violent, and Chronic Offender Careers

SOURCE: "Serious, Violent, and Chronic Juvenile Offenders: An Assessment of the Extent of and Trends in Officially Recognized Serious Criminal Behavior in a Delinquent Population," by H. N. Snyder, in R. Loeber and D. P. Farrington (Eds.), *Serious and Violent Juvenile Offenders: Risk Factors and Successful Interventions* (p. 440), Thousand Oaks, CA: Sage. Copyright 1998 by Sage Publications, Inc. Reprinted with permission.

At the request of the study group, Snyder (1998) conducted an analysis of juvenile court referrals in Maricopa County, Arizona (the county that includes Phoenix as well as other, smaller cities) that resulted in the first empirical description of the parameters that distinguish serious, violent, and chronic juvenile offenders. There is a standing policy in Maricopa County that all youth arrested must be referred to juvenile court for screening. Therefore, the court records in that county actually provide complete histories of all youthful offenders' official contacts with the juvenile justice system (Snyder & Sickmund, 1999, p. 80).

Figure 4.4 illustrates the overlap of the three delinquent offender subgroups. The entire circle in the figure represents all individuals in 16 birth cohorts who were referred to juvenile courts from ages 10 through 17. Snyder (1998) found that almost two-thirds (64%) of juvenile court careers were nonchronic (fewer than four referrals) and did not

include any serious or violent offenses (see Table 4.1 for definitions of the offense categories). These offender careers are shown in the clear outer circle of Figure 4.4. Conversely, just over one-third (36%) of the delinquent careers contained serious, violent, or chronic offense histories. Nearly 18% of all careers contained serious-nonviolent referrals and were nonchronic, 8% of all careers contained violent referrals but were not chronic, and slightly over 4% of all offender careers were chronic and included serious and violent offenses. (Note that it is inappropriate to total these percentages because an individual offender can be represented in more than one career. The remaining overlapping attributes of offender careers are shown in Table 4.1.) In sum, about 18% of all careers had serious (but nonviolent) offenses, 8% included violent offenses, and 4% of the careers were serious, violent, *and* chronic. As Figure 4.4 illustrates, nearly a third (29%) of the chronic offenders were also violent offenders, about

TABLE 4.1   Frequency of Career Types

Career Type	Career Index	Number of Careers	Percentage of All Careers
Nonchronic with no serious offenses	XXX	96,589	63.9
Nonchronic with at least one serious nonviolent offense	XSX	26,717	17.7
Chronic with at least one serious nonviolent offense	CSX	11,930	7.9
Chronic with at least one serious nonviolent and one violent offense	CSV	5,027	3.3
Nonchronic with at least one violent offense	XXV	4,793	3.2
Chronic with no serious offenses	CXX	3,761	2.5
Chronic with at least one violent offense	CXV	1,397	0.9
Nonchronic with at least one serious nonviolent and one violent offense	XSV	995	0.7
Total		151,209	100.0

SOURCE: "Serious, Violent, and Chronic Juvenile Offenders: An Assessment of the Extent of and Trends in Officially Recognized Serious Criminal Behavior in a Delinquent Population," by H. N. Snyder, in R. Loeber and D. P. Farrington (Eds.), *Serious and Violent Juvenile Offenders: Risk Factors and Successful Interventions* (p. 440), Thousand Oaks, CA: Sage. Copyright 1998 by Sage Publications, Inc. Reprinted with permission.

a third (35%) of the serious offenders were also chronic offenders, and about half (53%) of the violent offenders were also chronic offenders.

Using Pittsburgh police records, Loeber, Farrington, and Waschbusch (1998) replicated Snyder's analysis. They found the overlap of career types in their sample to be similar to that found in Snyder's Arizona cohorts. In both studies, most chronic offenders did not commit violent offenses, although most violent delinquents were also chronic offenders. Further, the majority of chronic and violent offenders also were involved in nonviolent serious property crimes (pp. 18-19).

As noted previously, smaller proportions of girls than boys are serious, violent, and chronic offenders. Snyder analyzed the juvenile court careers of males and females separately in the Arizona study described above. More than two-thirds (69%) of the youths in Maricopa County with official records of delinquency were males; 31% were females. The males were nearly twice as likely as the females to be recidivists and nearly four times as likely to be chronic offenders (four or more court referrals). Smaller proportions of the females also were serious and violent offenders. Male chronic offenders accounted for a much larger proportion of all types of offenses than did females (Snyder's findings are reported in Snyder & Sickmund, 1999, pp. 80-81).

Snyder's Maricopa County data covered only the juvenile years (through age 17), therefore he could not compare male and female offender careers in adulthood. Kempf-Leonard et al. (2001) were able to make such a comparison in the Philadelphia Juvenile-Adult Career Study, which I will describe shortly. Interestingly, they found that females committed a disproportionate share of adult crime compared with their male counterparts. Thus serious, violent, and chronic female offender careers should command the attention of researchers and practitioners.

Other Empirical Descriptions of Serious, Violent, and Chronic Offender Subgroups

Three of the studies described in Box 4.2 examined the proportions of serious, violent, and chronic offenders among populations of juvenile offenders. Two of these three studies (Orange County and St. Louis) measured the size of the serious chronic juvenile offender subgroup in samples of probationers. The third one examined juvenile offenders in the Philadelphia Birth Cohort. The Orange County study was the first to examine the representation of serious and chronic juvenile offenders in juvenile court records. The staff of the Orange County Probation Department wanted to target this group of offenders in their implementation of the Comprehensive Strategy for Serious, Violent, and Chronic Juvenile Offenders (Wilson & Howell, 1993). Probation department officials used the results of this study to develop the early intervention program for potential

Box 4.2
Highlights of Studies of Serious, Violent, and Chronic Juvenile Offender Subgroups

Snyder's Maricopa County, Arizona, Study

References: Snyder (1998, 2001), Snyder and Sickmund (1999, pp. 80-81)

Sample: All persons born from 1962 through 1977 (birth cohorts) who were referred to the juvenile court in Maricopa County, Arizona, for a delinquency offense prior to their 18th birthdays. Thus the analysis focused on 16 annual birth cohort members who turned age 18 in the years 1980-1995, which generated a sample of 151,209 court careers.

Key findings:
   Almost two-thirds (64%) of juvenile court careers were nonchronic (fewer than four referrals) and did not include any serious or violent offenses; 18% of all careers had serious (but nonviolent) offenses, 8% had violent offenses, and 4% of the careers had serious, violent, *and* chronic offenses (see Table 4.1).

   Nearly a third (29%) of the chronic offenders were also serious offenders, about a third (35%) of the serious offenders were also chronic offenders, and about one-half (53%) of the violent offenders were also chronic offenders.

Note: Violent offenses included the offenses of murder and nonnegligent manslaughter, kidnapping, violent sexual assault, robbery, and aggravated assault. Serious nonviolent offenses included burglary, serious larceny, motor vehicle theft, arson, weapons offenses, and drug trafficking. Nonserious delinquent offenses included such offenses as simple assault, possession of a controlled substance, disorderly conduct, vandalism, nonviolent sex offenses, minor larceny, liquor law offenses, and all other delinquent offenses (Snyder, 1998, p. 429). Chronic offenders were classified as those with four or more court referrals.

Orange County, California, Probation Department Study

References: Kurz and Moore (1994), Orange County Probation Department (2000), Schumacher and Kurz (1999)

Samples: (a) 3,304 youths who were referred during the first 6 months of 1985 and (b) 3,164 juveniles referred in the first 6 months of 1987. Both groups were tracked in court records for 3 years, and representative subsamples were tracked for 6 years.

Key findings:
   A small proportion of both groups had four or more court referrals in the follow-up period: 10% in the 1985 group and 8% in the 1987 group.

   Nearly all members of the 8% subgroup had court referrals for at least one very serious or violent crime, or both.

   Nearly 9 out of 10 of those in the 8% subgroup (88%) subsequently were committed to juvenile correctional facilities.

   More than half (53%) of those in the 8% subgroup were arrested in early adulthood.

Washington State Study

Reference: Barnoski, Aos, and Lieb (1997)

Sample: All youths in the state of Washington who turned age 18 in 1988.

(Continued)

Box 4.2 (Continued)

Key findings:

Of the entire cohort, 18.2% were minor juvenile offenders, 2.5% were middle-risk offenders, 2.9% were chronic offenders with at least one nonviolent felony (chronic serious offenders), and less than one-half of 1% were chronic offenders with violent felony convictions (chronic violent offenders).

Only 9% of the minor juvenile offenders had adult felony convictions in criminal court—about the same proportion as among youths who had no juvenile court record (6%).

About one-fourth (23%) of the middle-risk offenders were convicted of adult felonies, as were 41% of the chronic serious offenders.

More than half (55%) of the chronic violent offenders had felony convictions in criminal court by age 25, 30% for nonviolent adult felonies and 25% for violent adult felonies.

St. Louis Study

Reference: Curry and Decker (2000)

Sample: All juvenile court referrals (ages 7 through 16) in St. Louis from 1994 through 1997. Findings listed below pertain to the court careers of 3,496 youths referred for delinquency to the St. Louis City Court at some time in 1994.

Key findings:

The group of serious, violent, and chronic offenders is small and readily identifiable.

Of the referred youth, 54% were nonchronic offenders with no serious or violent offenses, 40% were serious and violent offenders, 28% were violent offenders, and 25% were chronic offenders.

A relatively small proportion of all juveniles (14%) accounted for 41% of all court referrals.

Philadelphia Juvenile-Adult Career Study

Reference: Kempf-Leonard, Tracy, and Howell (2001)

Sample: The population of 27,160 males and females born in 1958 who resided in Philadelphia at least from ages 10 through 17 (1968-1975). Criminal records were analyzed through age 26. (See Box 4.3 for definitions used in the study.)

Key findings:

Among males with officially recorded police contacts before age 18, 51% were serious delinquents, 26% were violent delinquents, 23% were chronic delinquents, 21% were serious and chronic, and 14% were violent and chronic. Among females with officially recorded police contacts before age 18, 17% were serious delinquents, 7% were violent delinquents, 7% were chronic delinquents, 4% were serious and chronic, and 2% were violent and chronic.

Recorded police contacts as adults were reported for 48% of the serious delinquents, 53% of the violent delinquents, 59% of the chronic delinquents, 62% of the delinquents with both serious and chronic offense histories, and 63% of the violent and chronic delinquents.

Among males, the proportions who went on to have officially recorded police contacts in adulthood were 51% for serious delinquents, 56% for violent delinquents, 63% for chronic delinquents, 64% for serious and chronic, and 64% for violent and chronic delinquents.

Among females, the proportions who went on to have officially recorded police contacts in adulthood were 25% for serious delinquents, 26% for violent delinquents, 29% for chronic delinquents, 43% for serious and chronic delinquents, and 44% for violent and chronic delinquents.

Note: All of the Philadelphia Birth Cohort Study data reflect police encounters, including incidents that did not result in arrests, which serves to inflate the percentages of offenders in all categories (see Bernard & Ritti, 1991; Weitekamp, Kerner, Schindler, & Schubert, 1995).

serious chronic juvenile offenders described in Chapters 11, 12, and 13 of this volume.

Two observations are important here, considering what the three studies cited above suggest is noteworthy regarding serious, violent, and chronic offender subgroups. First, all of the studies looked at these subgroups in slightly different ways, depending on local interests. Second, one of these three studies—the St. Louis study—can be directly compared with Snyder's Arizona study, because the St. Louis researchers, Curry and Decker (2000), used the same definitions and replicated Snyder's analysis methods. Curry and Decker found that much larger percentages of delinquent careers in St. Louis contained serious and violent offenses, and the proportion of chronic offenders in their sample was also much larger than in the Arizona study. The largest difference found was in the subgroup of careers with violent offenses: 28% in St. Louis versus 8% in Snyder's study. How can these differences be explained? Snyder's Arizona sample consisted of delinquents from an entire county, whereas Curry and Decker's sample came only from one large city, St. Louis; such a difference in sample populations may account for many of the differences in findings between the two studies. In addition, it is not uncommon for the sizes of juvenile offender career subgroups to vary from one study to another (Huizinga et al., 2000; Loeber, Farrington, & Waschbusch, 1998).

The Philadelphia Juvenile-Adult Career Study

Kempf-Leonard et al. (2001) conducted the first juvenile offender career study that examined the transition of serious, violent, and chronic offenders from delinquent offenders to adult offenders (see Box 4.2). These researchers addressed the question of which subgroup of juvenile offenders is most likely to go on to be involved in adult crime. Clearly, this issue has important implications for the juvenile justice system, which should concentrate its resources on those juvenile offenders who are most likely to become adult criminals.

The intersecting circles of the Venn diagram in Figure 4.5 illustrate the proportions of male delinquents in Kempf-Leonard et al.'s sample that fell into the three career types. Areas in the figure where the circles overlap represent careers with attributes from two or more subgroups; shading denotes the percentages that also had officially recorded police contacts in adulthood. All 4,315 delinquents are included within the outer circle. Those delinquents who had no record of any serious offenses and fewer than five encounters with the police are included in the portion of the large circle outside of the other circles.

First, Kempf-Leonard and colleagues (2001) examined the size of the serious, violent, and chronic offender subgroups during the adolescent years (ages 10-18). Among delinquent males (see Box 4.2), about half were serious delinquents, one-fourth were either violent or chronic delinquents, one-fifth were serious and chronic, and 14% were violent and chronic. The proportions were much smaller among delinquent females, as shown in Box 4.2. Only 17% were serious delinquents, and less than 10% were represented in the remaining serious, violent, and chronic subgroups. It should be noted that, like the other Philadelphia Birth Cohort Studies (Box 4.3), this one also measured delinquency in terms of officially recorded police encounters, including police contacts that did not result in arrests, which serves to inflate the numbers of offenders in all categories (see Bernard & Ritti, 1991; Weitekamp, Kerner, Schindler, & Schubert, 1995). Only one-third of the police contacts resulted in an arrest; of those who were arrested, 51% of the contacts resulted in a court adjudication of delinquency (Bernard & Ritti, 1991).

Kempf-Leonard et al. (2001) found a cascading pattern of adult criminal involvement among the serious, violent, and chronic offender subgroups (see Box 4.2). Officially recorded police contacts in adulthood were reported for less than half of the serious delinquents, just over half of the violent delinquents, and nearly 6 in 10 of the chronic delinquents, and for slightly higher percentages of the delinquents with both chronic and serious offense histories and chronic and violent prior records. These increasing percentages represent a clear trend toward adult criminality as the severity and/or chronicity of the delinquency careers increased—from serious delinquents to violent delinquents, to chronic delinquents, to serious and chronic delinquents, and to delinquents who had violent and chronic offense histories.

When Kempf-Leonard et al. analyzed the data separately for both gender groups (see Box 4.2), they found that two types of delinquent careers—one including both serious and chronic delinquency and the other including both violent and chronic delinquency—were most likely to lead to adult crime, and juveniles who had these kinds of careers later committed a disproportionate share of adult crimes. Again, they found that the data on females showed lower percentages, but they observed the same trend of increasing risk with progression of the career type in seriousness and chronicity.

The general finding—that the serious-chronic and violent-chronic delinquency career types

Box 4.3
Philadelphia Birth Cohort Studies

The study subjects in the first Philadelphia Birth Cohort Study (9,945 boys) were born in that city in 1945 and resided there from ages 10 through 17 (1955-1962). This was the first criminological birth cohort study in the United States. In their book on the study, Wolfgang, Figlio, and Sellin (1972) focused on the onset, offense patterns, offense specialization, age variations, and severity and duration of juvenile careers. This study is renowned for its finding that just 6% of the cohort, and 18% of the delinquents, were responsible for 52% of all the city's officially recorded police contacts with juveniles through age 17. However, subsequent analyses of the data have raised questions about the severity of this group's offense histories (Bernard & Ritti, 1991; Weitekamp et al., 1995).

The second Philadelphia Birth Cohort Study replicated the first. In the second study, Wolfgang, Thornberry, and Figlio (1987) focused on the population of 27,160 males and females born in 1958 who resided in Philadelphia at least from ages 10 through 17 (1968-1975), and they traced the adult careers of juveniles up to age 26. This study also followed up on a subset (975) of the 1945 birth cohort to age 30.

In a third study, Tracy, Wolfgang, and Figlio (1990) compared the birth cohorts of 1958 and 1945 and found that the chronic offender effect was again quite pronounced. These delinquents represented 7.5% of the cohort members and 23% of the delinquents, and they accounted for 61% of all the officially recorded police contacts.

In a fourth study, Tracy and Kempf-Leonard (1996) traced the transition into adult crime of youths among the 6,287 delinquents in the 1958 birth cohort. The researchers collected police, court, and correctional data on offenders up to age 26. This study provides important information on the characteristics of the offense histories of juvenile offenders who continue offending into adulthood. One-third (33%) of the juvenile delinquents had officially recorded police contacts in adulthood.

In the Philadelphia Juvenile-Adult Career Study (see Box 4.2), an analysis of the second Philadelphia Birth Cohort data set, Kempf-Leonard et al. (2001) measured the relative sizes of the serious, violent, and chronic offender subgroups as well as the proportion of each of these subgroups that continued to have officially recorded police contacts in adulthood. As in previous Philadelphia Birth Cohort Study analyses, a *chronic offender* was defined as an individual having a record of five or more police encounters. A *violent offender* was defined as a person having a delinquency record that included homicide, rape, robbery, aggravated assault, or aggravated sexual assault. A *serious offender* was defined as an individual meeting all of the criteria of the violent offender, plus having a record of serious property crimes of burglary, theft, automobile theft, arson, and vandalism in excess of $500.

NOTE: A *cohort* is all persons who share a particular demographic characteristic; a birth cohort is all persons born in a given year in a particular locality.

carry increased risk of involvement in adult criminality—was also replicated for the race and socioeconomic (measured by residential location) subgroups (Kempf-Leonard et al., 2001). The researchers performed a multivariate analysis (an examination of which variables account for most of the variance in the outcome while other factors are taken into account) and found that, for males, chronic offending in the juvenile years was the strongest predictor of adult criminality, followed by major violence and then major property offenses. For females, involvement in major property offenses in the juvenile years was the strongest predictor, followed by chronic delinquency and then major violence. The socioeconomic status of the neighborhood was also a predictor of adult criminality, but racial/ethnic membership was not significant. For both males and females, offender career type was a much stronger predictor of involvement in adult criminality than socioeconomic status, gender, or race/ethnicity variables.

This study is important for several reasons. First, it was the first study to show the relative sizes of the serious, violent, and chronic offender subgroups in

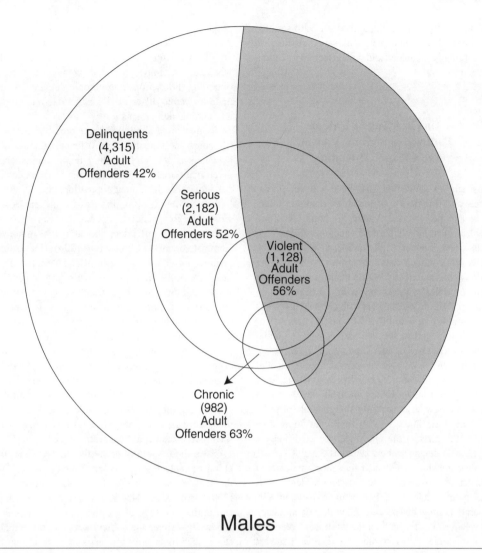

Figure 4.5   Intersections Among Delinquency Career Types for Male Delinquents
SOURCE: Data from Kempf-Leonard et al. (2001, p. 462, Table 1).

officially recorded police files. Second, the study's findings demonstrate the link between delinquent and adult criminal careers for members of these subgroups. Third, the results show differentials between males and females in these subgroups. This aspect is particularly significant because of the discovery that the effect of career type on adult criminality is more pronounced for females than for males. Fourth, this study's findings indicate that if juvenile justice system resources could be concentrated on serious *and* chronic offenders and violent *and* chronic offenders, this could have very

significant potential payoffs for adult crime reduction. Policies should be changed so that delinquents of these two offense types form the only eligible pool from which juveniles are selected for transfer to the criminal justice system; others should not be transferred, because their involvement in adult crime is negligible (see Chapter 8). Finally, this study shows that career offense patterns are stronger predictors of adult criminality than socioeconomic status, gender, or race/ethnicity variables. The juvenile justice system can use such information on offender careers to considerable advantage in matching delinquents' positions on pathways toward serious, violent, and chronic careers with sanctions that are appropriately graduated and with effective treatment programs.

Do Girls Take a Unique Pathway to Serious, Violent, and Chronic Offending?

Most studies show that girls have a lower prevalence and incidence of conduct disorders than boys (Loeber, Burke, Lahey, Winters, & Zera, 2000, p. 7), although there are exceptions (e.g., Tiet, Wasserman, Loeber, McReynolds, & Miller, 2001). However, conduct disorders appear to have more serious consequences for girls than for boys, in the form of other problem behaviors (Loeber et al., 2000, p. 7). Adolescent girls with conduct disorders are more at risk than boys for anxiety, depression, and, in turn, substance use and possibly suicidal behavior (Loeber et al., 2000, pp. 11-12). Even though girls show a lower prevalence of alcohol abuse, if they also experience depression, their level of aggression may well approach the level seen in boys. In a new large-scale Pittsburgh study of girls, Hipwell et al. (2002, p. 112) found that more than 8% of the girls in the entire sample qualified for psychiatric diagnoses between ages 5 and 8.

Research has established that more males than females are involved in serious and violent delinquency and adult crime. For example, national self-report data show that serious and violent delinquency prevalence rates throughout the adolescent years are two to three times higher for males than for females—7-8% for males, annually, compared with 2-3% for females (Elliott et al., 1986, p. 485). Over a longer period, from adolescence to young adulthood (up to age 27), 42% of males and 16% of females are involved in serious violent offenses (Elliott, 1994a, p. 8). Elliott (1994a, p. 5) summarizes the essential gender prevalence differences: The peak age in prevalence is earlier for females, the desistance rate is steeper for females, and the gender differential becomes greater over time.

Given the higher prevalence rates among males, it is obvious that male gender is a far stronger predictor of general delinquency, and also serious or violent delinquency, than female gender. In their Philadelphia study that examined continuity in offending among serious, violent, and chronic juvenile offender subgroups, Kempf-Leonard et al. (2001) found that the male-to-female differential was 3 to 1 among serious offenders (serious

property and violent offenders), 4 to 1 among violent offenders, and 3 to 1 among chronic offenders. They found even larger gender differentials when they examined repeated serious and violent offending. For serious *and* chronic delinquents the male-to-female differential was 6 to 1; for violent *and* chronic delinquents it was 7 to 1.

Some people might be tempted to conclude that life-course-persistent female offenders should not be taken as seriously as their male counterparts, given that females are less prevalent than males in the adolescent delinquent population. But when we look at the relative proportions of adult crimes for which the two genders account, we can see that female juvenile offenders should not be ignored. Kempf-Leonard and colleagues (2001) found that serious *and* chronic juvenile offenders constituted just 3.5% of the female delinquents in their sample, yet 44% of this group had officially recorded police contacts in adulthood and accounted for 16% of all police encounters with women (see p. 462, Table 1). Thus this small group of serious and chronic female delinquents was responsible for a share of adult crime 4.4 times greater than the group's size would suggest. In contrast, serious *and* chronic male delinquents made up 21% of the male offenders in the sample, but they were responsible for only 30% of the adult male criminality, just 1.4 times more than the group's size would suggest.

Even more startling is the fact that violent *and* chronic female delinquents constituted just 2% of all the female delinquents in Kempf-Leonard et al.'s (2001) sample, but 44% had adult careers in crime, accounting for 11% of the total number of police encounters. Here, the violent *and* chronic female share is 5.5 times greater than parity would suggest. Again, the males do not show the same share of adult crimes. Violent *and* chronic male delinquents represented 14% of the male delinquents but committed only 21% of the adult male crimes. This share is only 1.5 times greater than parity would suggest. This study clearly shows that males have a greater propensity to commit serious and violent crimes in their delinquency careers, but it is for females that this involvement carries the greatest risk of adult crime. This study suggests that serious, violent, and chronic female offender careers deserve far more attention in research concerning criminal careers than they have received in the past.

In sum, boys are more likely than girls to be serious, violent, and chronic juvenile offenders. However, this does not mean that the serious, violent, and chronic offender careers of girls should be taken lightly. Although the proportion of adolescent girls who become serious, violent, and chronic juvenile offenders is very small, girls in these groups go on to commit more than their share of adult crimes. Thornberry et al. (2003) have published similar findings concerning female gang members. Although female gang members represented only 16% of all girls in the Rochester sample in early adolescence, they accounted for 64% of the serious violent acts committed by all the girls. Thus developmental criminology must address gender-specific patterns in offender careers over the life course (Kempf-Leonard & Tracy, 2000). Before we can propose a possibly unique pathway to serious, violent, and chronic juvenile offender careers for girls, we first need to answer the question of whether the risk factors for delinquency are different for boys and girls.

Risk Factors

Some researchers contend that the risk factors that influence the onset and persistence of violent behavior are different for boys and girls, and that boys and girls undergo different developmental processes (Kelley, Huizinga, et al., 1997, p. 9). However, unique risk factors for female versus male delinquency have not yet been identified, and few studies have compared the two genders. In a recent review of gender differences in a wide variety of antisocial behaviors, Rutter, Giller, and Hagell (1998) found that "risk factors associated with offending in girls are generally similar to those found to apply in boys" (p. 255). Other scholars agree (e.g., Kempf-Leonard & Tracy, 2000). Indeed, a new longitudinal comparison of males and females concerning risk factors for delinquency and other antisocial behaviors, in the Dunedin Multidisciplinary Health and Development Study, strongly supports this conclusion. Moffitt, Caspi, Rutter, and Silva (2001) measured risk factors and problem behaviors over the first two decades of life and found that the same risk factors predict antisocial behaviors (conduct problems) in both males and females. The gender differences found in self-reported delinquency were accounted for by males' greater exposure to risk factors; that is, males experienced more of the risk factors that predicted serious and persistent antisocial behavior. However, this study did not measure child physical or sexual abuse. Research has shown that girls are more likely than boys to suffer physical and sexual abuse throughout childhood and adolescence (Finkelhor & Dziuba-Leatherman, 1994, p. 180) and may have more difficulty adapting socially as a result.

It also is disappointing that the Dunedin study did not separate serious and violent acts from other conduct disorders. Psychologists commonly measure "conduct disorders" as defined by the American Psychiatric Association (2000); that definition includes several serious forms of delinquency (destroying property, carrying weapons, breaking and entering, forced sex, and physical fights) and other less serious problem behaviors (running away, telling lies, truancy, stealing, bullying, setting fires, cruelty to people or animals, and staying out late). Hence the Dunedin study did not examine specifically the relationship between risk factors and serious/violent delinquency among girls. Only three longitudinal prospective studies have done so—the Rochester Youth Development Study, the Denver Youth Survey, and the Christchurch Health and Development Study. In an examination of the results of the first two of these studies, Huizinga et al. (2000) compared male and female adolescents on key predictors of serious property and serious assault offenses and found that gender differences were small in both study sites when they compared drug use, problems in school, and mental health problems (see also Loeber, Kalb, & Huizinga, 2001).

In another longitudinal study, the Christchurch Health and Development Study in New Zealand, Woodward and Fergusson (2000) found that males and females shared similar childhood risk factors (early conduct problems, childhood family environment, and adolescent lifestyle) for violence in adolescence. They note: "For both males and females, the profile of those at greatest risk was that of a young, conduct-disordered adolescent reared by physically punitive and substance-abusing parents, who upon reaching adolescence, engaged in antisocial and other risk-taking behavior" (p. 254).

Although general delinquency and other antisocial behaviors in girls and boys appear to be influenced by a common set of risk factors, the levels of certain risk factors—particularly history of physical and sexual abuse, and certain mental health problems—may be higher among girls than among boys, as I discuss below. It is possible that these particular risk factors may well have more important developmental consequences for girls than for boys. However, this possibility has not been tested; thus it remains to be seen whether girls and boys evidence different developmental processes in their progression toward serious, violent, and chronic juvenile offender careers.

A Unique Pathway

Kempf-Leonard and Tracy (2000) have called for illumination of the criminal career pathways that flow from girls' victimization in our society. In the tradition of developmental criminology, I would like to propose five stepping-stones for a subgroup of girls' pathway to serious, violent, and chronic juvenile offender careers: child physical and sexual abuse, mental health problems, running (or being thrown) away, youth gang membership, and detention/incarceration. Except for child abuse, boys and girls suffer these experiences about equally; however, the combination of all these experiences may have greater negative effects on girls than on boys, propelling a subgroup of girls toward serious, violent, and chronic juvenile offender careers. My central proposition is that the "gendered" nature (Chesney-Lind, 1997, p. 176) of these risk factors and environments may well have a greater impact on girls than on boys for the most severe delinquency outcomes—that is, serious, violent, and chronic juvenile offender careers. This, however, is an empirical question.

Child abuse is the first stepping-stone. Girls are more likely than boys to suffer physical abuse up to about age 4, and they are about twice as likely as boys to suffer sexual abuse throughout childhood and adolescence (Finkelhor & Dziuba-Leatherman, 1994, p. 180). There are similar differentials when abuse and neglect are considered together. For example, Ireland, Smith, and Thornberry (2002) found in the Rochester study that by age 18, 16% of the males and 27% of the females had substantiated cases of maltreatment.

The effects of such childhood victimization on developmental pathways may be unique for girls (Acoca, 1998b, p. 562; Chesney-Lind, 1997; Chesney-Lind & Sheldon, 1998). As we shall see in Chapter 6, research has found that a history of childhood maltreatment (abuse and neglect) significantly increases the likelihood of later self-reported juvenile involvement in moderately serious, serious, and violent delinquency for both girls and boys (Smith & Thornberry, 1995). However, Widom and Maxfield (2001) report that when they compared abused and neglected girls with girls who had not been victimized in that way, they found that the abused and neglected girls were significantly more likely to have been arrested for violence as juveniles and as adults; they did not find this pattern for males.

The second stepping-stone for girls on the pathway to delinquency is mental health problems. Adolescent females tend to have higher rates of psychiatric disorders than adolescent males (Romano, Tremblay, Vitaro, Zoccolillo, & Pagani, 2001), but this may not be true for serious and violent female offenders (Huizinga et al., 2000). Gender differentials in psychiatric disorders in general adolescent populations are mainly accounted

for by the greater frequency of internalizing disorders among females (i.e., depression, anxiety); in contrast, adolescent males tend to have a higher frequency of externalizing disorders (i.e., conduct and oppositional disorders) (Romano et al., 2001, p. 451), but, again, this pattern has not been established for serious and violent adolescent offender populations. Some research suggests a sharp rise in the onset of depression in girls in the adolescent period (Kovacs, 1996; Renouf & Harter, 1990). During childhood the depression rate is about the same in boys and girls, but after the onset of puberty, the rate among girls is about twice the rate among boys (Brent & Birmaher, 2002). This condition may contribute to the higher rate of relational aggression among girls than among boys (see Chesney-Lind & Brown, 1999; Crick & Grotpeter, 1995; Lerman & Pottick, 1995).

Boys and girls may also differ with respect to the impact of depression on violent behavior. In preliminary research for the Project on Human Development in Chicago Neighborhoods, Obeidallah and Earls (1999) found that, compared with nondepressed girls, mildly to moderately depressed girls had elevated rates of aggressive behavior and crimes against persons. Thus depression may be a central pathway through which girls' serious antisocial behavior develops, and so may be a precursor to delinquency and violence. Early pubertal maturation might be a precursor for the onset of both depression and antisocial behavior among girls (Brooks-Gunn, Graber, & Paikoff, 1994; Stattin & Magnusson, 1991), thus this may be an important screening point.

Running (or being thrown) away is the third stepping-stone. The proportion of girls (11%) who run away from home is about the same as that for boys (10%) (Hammer, Finkelhor, & Sedlak, 2002; Snyder & Sickmund, 1999, p. 58). The relationship between running away, or being thrown away, and subsequent delinquency is well established (for an excellent review of this literature, see Kaufman & Widom, 1999, pp. 349-351). Kaufman and Widom (1999) found that childhood victimization (sexual or physical abuse and neglect) increases the runaway risk, and that both childhood victimization and running away increase the likelihood of juvenile justice system involvement. They also found that running away is correlated with subsequent high-risk outcomes. Life on the streets is risky for homeless children (Hagan & McCarthy, 1997), leading to substance abuse, association with deviants, risky sexual behaviors, and violent victimization (Hoyt, Ryan, & Cauce, 1999). In a study of homeless and runaway adolescents in four midwestern states,

Whitbeck, Hoyt, and Yoder (1999) found that such street experiences also amplified the effects of early family abuse on victimization and depressive symptoms for young women. Moreover, in a subsequent analysis of only the girls in the initial study sample, Tyler, Hoyt, and Whitbeck (2000) found that girls who leave home to escape sexual abuse are often sexually victimized on the streets. Tyler and colleagues explain the pathway as follows: Exposure to dysfunctional and disorganized families early in life places youths on a trajectory of early independence; this early independence on the streets, along with the homeless/runaway lifestyle, exposes them to dangerous people and places; and this environment and the absence of conventional ties puts them at increased risk of sexual victimization (p. 238).

Youth gang involvement is the fourth stepping-stone. Child abuse, early dating, and precocious sexual activity increase the risk of gang involvement for both girls and boys (Thornberry et al., 2003). Several studies suggest that family conflict and child victimization in the home may have greater importance as risk factors for gang membership for girls than for boys (Fleisher, 1998; Maxson, Whitlock, & Klein, 1998; J. A. Miller, 2001; Moore, 1978; Moore & Hagedorn, 2001). In a study of gang girls, J. A. Miller (2001) found that girls with serious family problems—especially violence between adults in the home, parental drug or alcohol abuse, jailed family members, and physical or sexual abuse—often choose gangs as a means of avoiding chaotic family life and meeting their own social and developmental needs. For many of the young women in Miller's study, "home was not a particularly safe place" (p. 47), and these unsafe conditions helped drive them into the streets and into gangs. Unfortunately, gang involvement increases girls' risk of victimization, particularly assault and possibly sexual victimization (Fleisher, 1998; J. A. Miller, 2001). Ironically, they feel protected by older males in gender-mixed gangs, yet frequently are victimized by them (J. A. Miller, 2001).

Girls who are actively involved in gangs become the most serious, violent, and chronic juvenile offenders of all girls (Thornberry et al., 2003). As we shall see in Chapter 5, gang membership has similar detrimental long-term impacts on adolescent developmental processes for both boys and girls. Thornberry et al. (2003) have observed that, over and above increasing the "criminal embeddedness" of gang members, gangs cut youngsters off from conventional pursuits. Thus gang involvement has disruptive life-course consequences for females and males alike. According to Thornberry et al. (2003), the gang effect is particularly strong for females in the areas of early pregnancy, teen motherhood, and unstable employment. Gang membership also increases the odds of continued involvement in criminal activity throughout adolescence and into adulthood for both young men and young women.

Juvenile justice system involvement is the fifth stepping-stone on girls' pathway to delinquency. More young females (under age 14) enter the juvenile justice system via arrests for running away from home than for any other offense (Snyder, 2001, p. 37). Although only a little more than one-fourth (27%) of juveniles arrested in 1999 were girls, they represented more than half (59%) of the juvenile arrests for running away (Federal Bureau of Investigation, 2000). Once girls are placed on probation—typically for status offenses, such as running away and liquor law violations—"any subsequent offense [becomes] a vector for their greater involvement in the juvenile justice system" through probation violations and new offenses (Acoca, 1999, p. 7). Girls are far more likely than boys to be held in detention centers for minor offenses, and particularly for probation and parole violations (American Bar Association & National Bar Association, 2001). Girls are also more likely than boys to be detained for contempt of court, increasing the likelihood of their return to detention centers, providing more opportunities for further victimization.

Although intervention with treatment programs early in offender careers is beneficial (Schumacher & Kurz, 1999; Smith, Aloisi, & Goldstein, 1996; Tracy & Kempf-Leonard, 1996), incarceration in detention centers and reformatories is not. As a matter of fact, incarceration, ironically, often leads to further victimization. As Acoca (1998b) notes, "The abuses that a majority of girl offenders have experienced in their homes, in their schools, or on the streets often are mirrored and compounded by injuries they receive [in these facilities] within the juvenile justice system" (p. 562). When girls are placed in detention centers, they are often subjected to further victimization in the forms of emotional abuse; emotional distress from isolation; physical abuse, threats, and intimidation from staff; and unhealthy conditions of confinement (Acoca, 1998b). Overcrowding in such facilities is a major factor contributing to unhealthy conditions. Juvenile detention centers across the country are experiencing serious overcrowding, especially in girls' detention units (American Bar Association & National Bar Association, 2001). It is not unusual for such facilities to use common rooms with floor mats as sleeping areas. The limited resources of these detention centers are strained as they attempt to meet the basic physical and mental health needs of the girls in their custody, and the conditions of confinement are sometimes deplorable.

Girls in correctional facilities show multiple serious disorders and problem behaviors. In an examination of the records of girls held in a secure Colorado facility, Rubin (2000) found that 100% of them suffered from posttraumatic stress disorder. Other disorders in this population included substance abuse (80%), psychiatric disorders (conduct disorder, major depression, bipolar disorder, and oppositional defiant disorder; 67%), and eating disorders (50%). As Rubin states, "These behavior problems manifest themselves in poor impulse control, poor concentration, poor communication skills, poor anger expression, physical aggression, property destruction, inhibited social skills, distorted thinking, uninhibited sexual activity, low tolerance for frustration, inhibited ability to delay gratification, and, of course, low self-esteem" (p. 2). In addition, 64% had been victims of sexual abuse, 47% practiced self-harm or self-mutilation, and 14% were already mothers. In a study of all boys and girls committed to Virginia's long-term state training schools during 1993-1998, McGarvey and Waite (2000) found that 24% of the females and 5% of the males had previously attempted suicide. Nearly half of the girls (49%) and more than a third (36%) of the boys had used psychotropic medications. It is difficult to imagine how girls with problems such as these could benefit from incarceration in a reformatory.

The relevance of several of the stepping-stones described above is illustrated by Acoca's (1998b) findings from an interview study with nearly 200 girls in four California detention centers (see also Acoca & Dedel, 1998). For many of these girls, the pathway to delinquency began with childhood victimization. More than 9 out of 10 (92%) had experienced one or more forms of physical, sexual, or emotional abuse, often on multiple occasions, and 40% of them had been sexually assaulted (p. 565). More than half (53%) of them had experienced one or more forms of sexual abuse, beginning with molestation at about age 5. More than 45% had been beaten or burned by caregivers at least once, generally between the ages of 11 and 13. About 25% were victims of parental neglect.

A typical girl's story could be described as follows: At age 13 or 14 she first began risky behaviors, including running away from home, polydrug and alcohol use, school failure, and truancy, followed by expulsion from school. She became sexually active at age 13 and was a victim of sexual assault in the same year. She was first shot or stabbed at age 14, the same

age at which she delivered her first child (29% of the total sample had been pregnant, 16% while in custody). About half of the girls in this sample became affiliated with gangs at ages 13-15, and more than two-thirds of the gang members became very involved in gang life.

Because Acoca's study was cross-sectional, there is no way to specify with certainty the temporal ordering of these stepping-stones. Indeed, it is not known whether the pathways I have proposed are predominant ones for life-course serious, violent, and chronic female juvenile offenders. More research is needed on this proposed developmental pathway.

Summary

Developmental theories are of enormous value for describing and explaining offender careers. Several developmental theories of delinquency have been proffered recently (e.g., Catalano & Hawkins, 1996; Farrington, 1996; Loeber, 1996; Sampson & Laub, 1993; Thornberry, 1996; Thornberry et al., 2003). In particular, Thornberry et al.'s (2003) developmental theory of gang involvement is likely to stand for some time as the most powerfully illustrated and empirically substantiated theory of life-course consequences of adolescent deviance.

Loeber's three-pathways developmental model of adolescent problem behavior and delinquency is rapidly gaining strong empirical support, having been replicated on various adolescent samples, in different sites, and by independent investigators. This model of the orderly progression of serious, violent, and chronic offenders' careers represents a major breakthrough. It has also captured the attention of juvenile justice system practitioners. The pathways model has great practical utility; it can be used in conjunction with risk assessment instruments to help predict the likelihood of particular individuals' progressing in delinquent careers. However, risk assessment instruments need to be validated for each locality, because variations in offending patterns have been found in different localities (Loeber, Wei, et al., 1999, p. 261).

Researchers have made considerable progress in specifying risk factors that predict increases in violent delinquency in childhood and adolescence (see Chapter 5). However, more research is needed to link these predictors to stages in serious, violent, and chronic offender *careers*, or to the orderly offense progression in Loeber's pathways. Indeed, the similarities between these two models of delinquent careers are remarkable. Loeber's covert and overt pathways correspond to the serious and violent offense categories, respectively. By incorporating offense progression in the three pathways over time, his theoretical model also accounts for chronic offending. This observation explains the enormous appeal that Loeber's three-pathways model has for juvenile justice officials and practitioners. The next step in the practical application of Loeber's model is to link predictors (risk factors) with offenders who advance in the covert (serious-chronic) and overt (violent-chronic) pathways. These predictors can be incorporated into risk assessment instruments and used as a basis for offender classification and placement in graduated sanctions systems, as recommended in the Comprehensive Strategy (see Chapter 12).

Juvenile offender career studies show the value of focusing research and intervention efforts on the offender career subtypes specified in the Comprehensive Strategy for Serious, Violent, and Chronic Juvenile Offenders. We have learned a great deal about the relative concentration of offenders in the serious, violent, and chronic categories since the OJJDP's Study Group on Serious and Violent Offenders instigated studies in this area. The concentration varies by locality and degree of juvenile justice system penetration, becoming smaller as offenders move through the system.

Several studies have shown that, although chronic serious or violent offenders represent a small proportion of all offenders, they account for an overwhelming proportion of all such offenses committed by large samples of delinquents. Equally important, the small numbers of serious and violent offenders who are chronic tend to persist in their criminality into adulthood. In the Philadelphia Juvenile-Adult Career Study, Kempf-Leonard et al. (2001) found that nearly two-thirds of the serious and chronic and violent and chronic delinquents in their sample evidenced involvement in criminal activity in adulthood.

Four other very important findings have emerged from studies of serious, violent, and chronic juvenile offenders. First, the vast majority of all juvenile offender careers are nonserious, nonviolent, and nonchronic. As many as two-thirds of the youths referred to court never accumulate more than three referrals and never have one for either a serious or a violent crime. Only about one-third of chronic offenders are also violent offenders, about one-half of violent offenders are also chronic offenders, and about one-third of serious offenders also are chronic offenders. Thus a substantial proportion of serious and violent offenders are not chronic offenders. Put another way, much delinquency is concentrated in a small proportion of the adolescent population, and much of the serious and violent juvenile offending is concentrated in a small proportion of the repeat offending population (Tolan & Gorman-Smith, 1998, p. 72). Enormous amounts of juvenile justice system resources are wasted on the very large proportion of all juvenile offenders who never become serious, violent, and chronic offenders. Given the system's limited resources, juvenile justice officials and policy makers should target chronic offenders who repeatedly commit serious and violent offenses with sanctions and intensive interventions instead of confinement in facilities without rehabilitation programs or transfer to the criminal justice system. In Chapter 12, I explain how they can do this using the Comprehensive Strategy, and in Chapter 13, I provide examples of successful interventions.

Second, in their Philadelphia study, Kempf-Leonard et al. (2001) found a cascade effect in the transition from juvenile offender careers to adult criminality: from serious delinquency to violent delinquency, to chronic delinquency, and from there to serious-chronic and violent-chronic offending. Studies need to replicate this research.

Third, the offender career studies discussed above have revealed—for the first time—the significant representation of females in serious, violent, and chronic juvenile offender careers. Kempf-Leonard et al. (2001) found that although girls represent a small proportion of delinquents, they account for a much larger proportion of both juvenile delinquencies and adult crimes than their representation would suggest. A compelling empirical argument can be made for focusing juvenile justice system resources on both male and female chronic *and* serious and chronic *and* violent juvenile offenders. More research is needed on serious, violent, and chronic female offender careers. There is evidence that the career lengths of life-course-persistent female and male offenders may be similar (Elliott et al., 1986, p. 498), and it may well be that involvement in serious and violent delinquency carries a greater risk of adult crime for females than for males (Kempf-Leonard et al., 2001).

In this chapter I have suggested that a small subgroup of girls may take a unique pathway to serious, violent, and chronic offender careers. Although the research is yet scant, it appears that this may be the case. It appears that the higher level of childhood victimization suffered by girls in comparison with boys may propel them into risky behaviors. Recent research has shown that childhood victimization (sexual abuse, physical abuse, and emotional abuse) contributes to running away and mental health problems in adolescents, and these, in turn, contribute to delinquency involvement. Mental health problems, particularly depression, may be a key catalyst that accelerates girls' serious antisocial behavior development. Running away as a means of escape from abuse in chaotic families often backfires. Because girls are more likely than boys to be arrested for running away, ironically, their juvenile justice system involvement may become a stepping-stone to further violent victimization rather than a solution to their problems (Acoca, 1998b). Some girls turn to youth gangs for comfort and protection, but this may lead to further victimization, creating a vicious cycle. The importance and ordering of these stepping-stones to serious, violent, and chronic offender careers for females appear to be topics worthy of further research. Given the recent increase in arrests of females for certain violent offenses—particularly aggravated assault (Snyder, 2000, p. 4)—it has been said that "this country can ill afford to continue to downplay [the] significance [of female violence] in the full gamut of violence research, evaluation, prevention, intervention, and control" (Kelley, Huizinga, et al., 1997, p. 9; see also Weiss, Nicholson, & Cretalla, 1996).

Fourth, more research is needed concerning child delinquents. If left without treatment, about a third of all child delinquents later become serious, violent, and chronic offenders. Many children who become serious and violent offenders have long histories of nondelinquent, disruptive problem behavior during childhood. For some young children, less serious delinquency is a stepping-stone to more serious offending. In an analysis of three longitudinal databases, Albany researchers found that the very youngest onset group (onset of delinquent behavior at 4 to 10 years of age) had the highest prevalence rate for both serious and violent offenses during the early adult years. In sum, child delinquents go on to have criminal

careers of greater duration than those of later-onset delinquents, extending further into the life course; they commit more offenses and have higher individual offending rates, and their offenses tend to be more serious and more violent than those of late-onset offenders. Better screening devices are needed to discriminate between children who will escalate to more serious offending and those who will not (Howell, 2001b).

Discussion Questions

1. What is the value of a "life-course perspective" in thinking about delinquent and criminal careers?

2. What are the important differences between "life-course-persistent offenders" and "adolescence-limited offenders"?

3. What are "stepping-stones"? How are they represented in Loeber's three pathways?

4. How do Loeber's three pathways illustrate nonserious, serious, violent, and chronic offenders?

5. Describe a pathway that girls may take into serious, violent, and chronic delinquency. What do you think are the most important stepping-stones?

6. What are some of the important research findings about serious, violent, and chronic offender careers?

7. What are the implications of these important findings for juvenile justice system intervention in offender careers?

5

∎

YOUTH GANG MEMBERS AS SERIOUS, VIOLENT, AND CHRONIC OFFENDERS

Youth gangs are very prevalent in the United States. More than 3,330 jurisdictions across the country experienced youth gang activity in 2000 (Egley & Arjunan, 2002), representing 40% of all cities, suburban counties, and rural counties. Youth gangs are the most criminally active adolescent peer groups in which youths participate. In this chapter, I address how and why this is so.

The first section of the chapter is devoted to reports on youth gang trends. This is followed by a discussion of the difficult problem of defining what constitutes a youth gang and why it is important that we understand youth gangs. I then address the overlap between youth gang members and serious, violent, and chronic offenders. The final section of the chapter examines the developmental processes of gang involvement and presents a continuum of effective program options and intervention strategies.

Youth Gang Trends

The annual National Youth Gang Survey, conducted by the National Youth Gang Center (NYGC) since 1995, is the only nationally representative source of data on gang problems (Box 5.1). Findings from this survey show that the number of jurisdictions reporting youth gang problems peaked in the mid-1990s, after a new generation of youth gangs emerged in the late 1980s and early 1990s (Howell, Moore, & Egley, 2002). However, gang problems have not diminished appreciably across the entire country; this change is taking place only in localities where gang problems are relatively new—suburbs, small cities, and rural areas (Egley, 2002b).

The growth in youth gangs and the violence associated with them is the most overlooked factor in the increase in juvenile and young adult violence in the late 1980s and early 1990s. Figure 5.1 shows the cumulative growth of reported gang problems in particular segments of the United States by population category (Egley, 2002b; see also W. B. Miller, 2001). Note that the sharpest increase occurred in the late 1980s and early 1990s. This figure also shows the continuing presence of gang problems in the nation's largest cities. In a revealing analysis, Egley (2001) examined the persistence of gang problems in localities over a 5-year period following the peak in reported gang problems, in 1996. He found that the presence of youth gang problems remained unchanged from 1996 through 2000 in the nation's largest cities and receded mainly in the hinterlands—particularly in the smallest cities and rural counties. For example, in 1996, 34% of the smallest cities and towns reported gang activity versus only 13% in 2000. Similarly, 25% of rural counties reported gang activity in 1996 versus only 7% in 2000. In contrast, 100% of large cities (more than 250,000 population) reported gang activity in all 5 survey years.

The characteristics of localities' gang problems vary depending on how long youth gangs have been active. The average year of gang problem onset was 1989 for large cities, 1990 for suburban counties, 1992 for small cities, and 1993 for rural counties (Howell, Egley, & Gleason, 2002). More than half (57%) of the respondents to the National Youth Gang Survey said that their gang problems began in the 1990s. Nearly 9 out of 10 said that their gang problems began during the period 1986-1996. Thus a new generation of youth gangs has emerged, and these gangs are noticeably different from those that

---

Box 5.1
The National Youth Gang Survey

A representative sample of 3,018 law enforcement agencies across the United States have participated in the National Youth Gang Survey each year since 1996. This sample includes all police and sheriff's departments serving suburban counties and cities with populations of more than 25,000 population and a randomly selected sample of police and sheriff's departments serving rural counties and cities with populations between 2,500 and 25,000.

Highlights of the survey's findings include the following:

- From a peak in the mid-1990s, the number of localities reporting youth gangs dropped by 13%—from 53% to 40%—from 1996 through 2000 (Egley, 2002a).
- More than 24,500 youth gangs, consisting of nearly 773,000 gang members, were estimated to be active in the estimated 3,330 localities with gang problems in 2000 (Egley & Arjunan, 2002).
- Respondents reported gang activity in 4 consecutive survey years (1996-2000) as follows (Egley, 2002a):
- 100% in cities above 250,000 population
- 86% in cities between 100,000 and 250,000
- 61% in cities between 50,000 and 100,000
- 38% in cities between 25,000 and 50,000
- 13% in cities between 2,500 and 25,000
- 7% in rural counties

The following publications are the main reports of the National Youth Gang Survey:

- 1995 survey: National Youth Gang Center (1997) (This was a pilot study.)
- 1996 survey: National Youth Gang Center (1999a)
- 1997 survey: National Youth Gang Center (1999b)
- 1998 survey: National Youth Gang Center (2000)
- 1999 survey: Egley (2000)
- 2000 survey: Egley and Arjunan (2002)
- 1999-2001 surveys: Egley, Major, and Howell (2003)

The National Youth Gang Center (NYGC) has published numerous other reports as well; these are available through the NYGC Web site at www.iir.com/nygc, which also provides links to other important gang-related sites. In addition to conducting and publishing reports on the National Youth Gang Survey, the NYGC conducts literature reviews on current gang topics, compiles information on state gang legislation, identifies effective gang program strategies, operates the federal Youth Gang Consortium (including information on federal programs), and provides technical assistance on gang programming to OJJDP.

---

emerged before the mid-1980s (Howell, Moore, & Egley, 2002).

A cascading pattern is evident in the population size of localities with gang problems, with smaller and smaller jurisdictions reporting the onset of problems over time. The localities where gang problems are relatively new are most likely to be rural counties, small cities, and suburban counties with populations of fewer than 50,000 (Howell, Moore, & Egley, 2002). A general pattern of cultural diffusion of gangs among young persons occurred in these population clusters in the late 1980s and early 1990s. The population shift across the United States away from central cities and toward suburbs, small cities, and rural areas was a key factor (Egley, 2000). The relocation of gang members as they moved with their families out of the cities (Maxson, 1998b), movies glorifying youth gangs (such as *Colors*), and the popularity of "gangsta" rap music appear to have worked together to introduce large-city gang culture to youths in the suburbs and more remote areas far from central cities. This appears to be a classic case of cultural diffusion. Youth gang involvement seemingly became very faddish in the late 1980s and early 1990s, even among youngsters in small cities and rural counties.

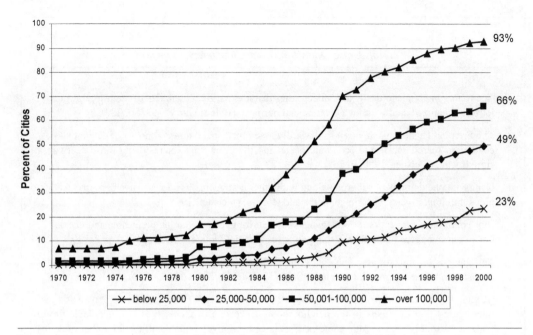

Figure 5.1   Patterns of Gang Proliferation in Cities Reporting Gang Activity in 2000

SOURCE: *Special Analysis,* by A. Egley, Jr., 2001, Tallahassee, FL: National Youth Gang Center. 2001 National Youth Gang Survey. © 2001 by the National Youth Gang Center, Institute for Intergovernmental Research. Used with permission.

As Miller (1992) has observed, gang problems in the United States as a whole historically have been characterized by an "ebb and flow pattern, [resembling] a wave that strikes with great fury at one part of the shore, recedes, strikes again at another, ebbs away, strikes once more, and so on" (p. 7). In fact, researchers have documented four distinct periods of gang growth and peak activity in the United States: in the late 1800s, the 1920s, the 1960s, and the 1990s (Curry & Decker, 1998; Howell, Moore, & Egley, 2002).

What Is a Youth Gang?

It is very difficult to define exactly what constitutes a youth gang. According to Spergel (1995, p. 79), at least 16 different sets of criteria have been used to classify gangs. One gang researcher has subsumed gangs of the late 1970s under a broad typology of 20 "law-violating youth groups" (Miller, 1992). Neither gang researchers nor law enforcement agencies can agree on a common definition (Horowitz, 1990; Miller, 1992), and a concerted national effort in the 1980s failed to reach a consensus between researchers and practitioners on what constitutes a gang, a gang member, or a gang incident (Spergel & Bobrowski, 1989).

Box 5.2 displays a variety of definitions and characterizations that gang researchers have used to describe youth gangs. These illustrate some of the many different ways in which different observers view youth gangs. Thrasher (1927), the first gang researcher, noted that "no two gangs are just alike; [gangs take] an endless variety of forms" (p. 5). Virtually every contemporary gang researcher would agree that Thrasher's observation is no less valid today than it was 75 years ago.

The terms *youth gang* and *street gang* are often used interchangeably (Howell, 1998d). To compound the definitional problem, the term *criminal street gang*—formerly used exclusively in reference to adult criminal organizations, not youth gangs—is now sometimes applied to youth gangs along with adult criminal organizations in state legislation (Klein, 1995). Some gang researchers prefer to use the term *street gang* for the purpose of emphasizing the street presence of youth gangs (Klein, 1995), but use of this label can result in the confusion of youth gangs with adult criminal street gangs. This possible confusion has prompted one experienced gang researcher to use the term *youth street gangs* to distinguish youth gangs from other criminal street gangs (Moore, 1998). Groups termed *drug gangs* are also confused with youth gangs. Gang researchers sometimes describe youthful offenders

---

Box 5.2
Youth Gang Definitions and Characterizations

The term *gang* tends to designate collectivities that are marginal members of mainstream society, loosely organized, and without a clear, social purpose. (Ball & Curry, 1995, p. 227)

The Fremont Hustlers gang was a haphazardly assembled social unit composed of deviant adolescents who shared social and economic needs and the propensity for resolving those needs in a similar way. (Fleisher, 1998, p. 264)

Gangs are one delinquent subgroup along with other homogeneous adolescent subgroups: skaters, preps, hip-hop, ravers, postgrunge, goths and stoners. (Fleisher, 1998, p. 257)

[For control and prevention efforts, gangs are] a shifting, elusive target, permeable and elastic . . . not a cohesive force but, rather, a spongelike resilience. (Klein & Maxson, 1989, p. 211)

The gang is an interstitial group (between childhood and maturity) originally formed spontaneously, and then integrated through conflict. (Thrasher, 1927, p. 18)

[A gang is] any denotable adolescent group of youngsters who a) are generally perceived as a distinct aggregation by others in the neighborhood, b) recognize themselves as a denotable group (almost invariably with a group name), and c) have been involved in a sufficient number of delinquent incidents to call forth a consistently negative response from neighborhood residents and/or law enforcement agencies. (Klein, 1971, p. 13)

A youth gang is a self-formed association of peers united by mutual interests with identifiable leadership and internal organization who act collectively or as individuals to achieve specific purposes, including the conduct of illegal activity and control of a particular territory, facility, or enterprise. (Miller, 1992, p. 21)

[Gangs are] groups that are complexly organized although sometimes diffuse, sometimes cohesive with established leadership and membership rules, operating within a framework of norms and values in respect to mutual support, conflict relations with other gangs, and a tradition often of turf, colors, signs, and symbols. (Curry & Spergel, 1988, p. 382)

[A gang is] an age-graded peer group that exhibits some permanence, engages in criminal activity, and has some symbolic representation of membership. (Decker & Van Winkle, 1996, p. 31)

Gang characteristics consist of a gang name and recognizable symbols, a geographic territory, a regular meeting pattern, and an organized, continuous course of criminality. (Chicago Police Department, 1992, p. 1)

A Criminal Street Gang is any ongoing organization, association, or group of three or more persons, whether formal or informal, having as one of its primary activities the commission of criminal acts. (Street Terrorism Enforcement and Prevention Act, 1988, California Penal Code sec. 186.22[f])

[A gang is] a self-identified group of kids who act corporately, at least sometimes, and violently, at least sometimes. (Kennedy, Piehl, & Braga, 1996, p. 158)

---

involved in drug-trafficking operations in a manner that makes them appear to be members of bona fide youth gangs (Padilla, 1992; Sanchez-Jankowski, 1991; Taylor, 1990; Williams, 1989), but these two kinds of gangs are distinguishable (Klein, 1995, p. 132; Klein & Maxson, 1994).

Some law enforcement agencies use other names, such as *crews* and *posses,* to refer to youth gangs, and they often use these descriptive terms to refer to drug gangs as well. *Taggers* (a term for youths who "tag" property such as walls with graffiti) is another term law enforcement agencies sometimes use to describe some adolescent groups, although few taggers should be considered members of youth gangs. In the 1996 National Youth Gang Survey, respondents who said that they had gang problems were asked if they had included problems with street gangs, drug gangs, juvenile gangs, stoners, satanic groups, terrorist groups, taggers, posses, or crews in their determination of whether or not they had gang problems (National Youth Gang Center, 1999a, p. 15). The overwhelming majority of these respondents said that they had included "juvenile gangs" (85%) and "street gangs" (83%), and a majority also had included "taggers" (58%) and "drug gangs" (57%). Much smaller percentages mentioned the remaining terms. The inclusion of drug gangs in any assessment of youth gang activity not only makes counting gangs difficult but also could frustrate intervention work, because strategies that are effective with drug gangs might not work with youth gangs. The latter generally are more entrenched in neighborhoods and grounded in adolescent development.

There also are significant differences in the definitions of the term *gang* used by law enforcement agencies and various state statutes (Ball & Curry, 1995; Curry, Fox, Ball, & Stone, 1992; Klein, 1995; Spergel, 1995; Spergel & Curry, 1993). For intelligence and record-keeping purposes, law enforcement agencies tend to define what constitutes a gang rather broadly. In the past 10 years, at least 20 states have passed laws explicitly defining what *gangs* and *gang members* are, chiefly so that they could "enhance" or increase the severity of penalties for criminal offenses if those offenses are committed by gang members (Howell, Moore, & Egley, 2002).

The criteria traditionally used to decide whether or not a given group is a gang include the following (Miller, 1992; Needle & Stapleton, 1983):

- The group must have a name.
- It must have a leader or several leaders.
- Its members must hang out together.
- Its members must display or wear common colors or other insignia.
- It must claim a turf or territory.
- Its members must commit crimes together.

Criteria Young People Use
to Characterize Youth Gangs

There are important differences between adolescents and law enforcement agencies in the criteria they use to characterize youth gangs (Howell & Lynch, 2000). Although adolescents often associate the groups they call gangs with violent acts, they do not apply this criterion nearly as often as do law enforcement representatives. "Committing crimes together" is the main criterion law enforcement personnel use to define a youth gang, whereas adolescents emphasize other characteristics, mainly (a) the group's having a name, (b) group members' spending time with other members, and (c) the wearing of clothing or other items to identify gang membership. This comparison suggests that school-based, or school-related, gangs may well have characteristics that distinguish them from street-based youth gangs. I will address this issue shortly.

Why Definitions Are Difficult

Several features of youth gangs make defining them particularly difficult. First, gangs are not particularly cohesive groups. They are characterized by weak friendship ties and lack the organizational characteristics commonly attributed to them by traditional gang theorists and by the print and broadcast media. The following description of the Fremont Hustlers gang in Kansas City, Missouri, illustrates how loosely organized a gang can be:

The membership boundary was open; they had no written set of rules, no membership requirements, no leader or hierarchy that might pull all 72 members into a coherent organization. The gang structure was difficult to recognize at first, because the kids didn't talk about how it was structured and operated. Fremont gang kids said they were Folks (the name of a group of loosely affiliated Chicago gangs), but they didn't know why. They just liked to draw the pitchfork symbol of the Folks. (Fleisher, 1998, p. 26)

Gangs are not particularly cohesive for another reason. Most adolescents do not remain in gangs for long periods, particularly in localities where gang problems have emerged fairly recently. Studies in Denver, Rochester, and Seattle found that from one-half to two-thirds of adolescent gang members in those cities stayed in a gang for 1 year or less; only about one-third belonged to gangs for multiple years (Thornberry, 1998). Multiple-year and intergenerational gang membership is far more common in cities with long-standing gang problems, such as Chicago (Horowitz, 1983) and Los Angeles (Moore, 1978). Adolescence is a time of changing peer relations and fleeting allegiances to both friends (Buchanan, Eccles, & Becker, 1992; Reiss, 1988; Warr, 2002) and gangs (Decker & Curry, 2000; Fleisher, 1998). Involvement in a variety of peer groups is common during the adolescent period (Warr, 2002). In many situations, it makes more sense to view youth gangs as social networks (Fleisher, 2002).

There is yet another reason gangs are not particularly cohesive: Youngsters join together in gangs largely for social reasons and to facilitate their participation in acts that are both thrilling and relatively difficult to accomplish alone. As Cohen and Vila (1996) have observed, "If it were not for gang rivalries, hostile police and neighbors, there would be little to hold these groups together save for the thrill-seeking derived from delinquent activities" (p. 133).

Few young members consider themselves to be "core" members of their gangs. In an 11-site survey of gang members who were in the eighth grade, Lynskey, Winfree, Esbensen, and Clason (2000) found that only 20% considered themselves core members. Less than half (43%) considered themselves to be either within the inner core or at the next level of the gang's membership.

Defining youth gangs is also difficult because individual gangs change over time (Hagedorn, 1994; Horowitz, 1983; Moore, 1991; Taylor, 1990). Although few studies have examined particular gangs over time, some researchers have noted how gang involvement in criminal activity changes with the passage of time. In a multiyear observational study of one gang, for example, Palacios (1996) saw the gang evolve through three stages of development. Early in its life, the gang exhibited a vertical structure; its members were all part of a homogeneous age group and lived in a common neighborhood. The gang initially was not criminally active. For the most part, the members fought with rival gangs. In the second stage, the gang took on a horizontal structure, as peripheral members were initiated into the gang. The members began to engage in criminal activities at this point, mainly armed robberies, burglaries, auto thefts, and drug dealing. In the third stage of its development, which Palacios characterizes as "familial," the gang shifted to concern for interpersonal relations among the members. Social activities within the gang took place less often, in part, because frequent arrests and incarcerations served to dampen participation by many of the members.

Another factor that makes defining youth gangs difficult is the contemporary growth of "hybrid" gangs. As Starbuck, Howell, and Lindquist (2001) have found, these gangs don't fit the mold of earlier gangs. Modern-day gangs commonly have memberships that are racially or ethnically mixed and may include both genders. Many newer gangs have such diverse characteristics that one prominent police gang investigator uses the term *hybrid gang*

culture to describe them (Starbuck et al., 2001). Contemporary hybrid gangs are characterized by a mixture of gang cultures. They often have unclear rules or codes of conduct, may use mixed symbols (e.g., colors and graffiti) to identify themselves, and may participate in criminal activities jointly with rival gangs. Members of such gangs may be members of multiple gangs, or they may have symbolic associations with more than one well-established gang. Members of contemporary gangs often "cut and paste" bits of Hollywood images and big-city gang lore into their local versions of gangs. The resulting hodgepodge of features makes classifying such gangs extremely difficult.

Starbuck et al.'s (2001) observations, which are based mainly on examination of gangs in the Midwest, have been tested nationwide by the National Youth Gang Center. In a special component of the 1999 National Youth Gang Survey, respondents who had reported gang problems were queried regarding the prevalence of "hybrid gang culture" (Howell, Moore, & Egley, 2002). They were asked if any of the gangs with which they had problems were gangs that "may have several of the following characteristics: a mixture of racial/ethnic groups, male and female members, display symbols and graffiti of different gangs, or have members who sometimes switch from one gang to another." Six out of 10 respondents answered affirmatively.

Myths about youth gangs are another factor contributing to the difficulty of developing a precise definition. There are many popular misconceptions about youth gangs (Best & Hutchinson, 1996; Decker, Bynum, & Weisel, 1998; Decker & Curry, 2000; Fleisher, 1995, 1998; Klein, 1995; Miethe & McCorkle, 1997); I review only a few of these myths here (see also Box 5.3).

The most common stereotype of youth gangs conveyed by the print and broadcast media closely resembles an image portrayed more than a decade ago in a California study conducted by Skolnick (1989; Skolnick, Correl, Navarro, & Rabb, 1988; for details on this study, see Klein, 1995, pp. 40-43, 112-135). Skolnick and his colleagues concluded that entrepreneurial youth gangs were transformed by the crack cocaine epidemic (Inciardi, 1986; Inciardi & Pottieger, 1991) into drug-trafficking organizations. The broadcast media propagated an image of these "transformed" gangs as highly structured, military-like organizations that were operating criminal enterprises. However, empirical support for this popular image of youth gangs is very limited (see Howell & Decker, 1999; Klein, 1995; Moore, 1993).

Public perceptions of youth gangs and their members are mainly influenced by popular media

Box 5.3
Myths About Youth Gangs

One widespread myth about youth gangs is that they are highly organized. Numerous studies, however, have led experts to question the extent of youth gang organization. Studies on this topic have been conducted in the following U.S. cities:

- Denver, Colorado (Esbensen, Huizinga, & Weiher, 1993)
- Cleveland and Columbus, Ohio (Huff, 1996, 1998; J. A. Miller, 2001)
- Kansas City, Missouri (Fleisher, 1998)
- Milwaukee, Wisconsin (Hagedorn, 1988)
- San Francisco, California (Waldorf, 1993)
- San Diego, California (Decker, Bynum, & Weisel, 1998; Sanders, 1994)
- Seattle, Washington (Fleisher, 1995)
- St. Louis, Missouri (Curry, Decker, & Egley, 2002; Decker & Curry, 2000; Decker & Van Winkle, 1996)
- Las Vegas and Reno, Nevada (Miethe & McCorkle, 1997)

In the most definitive study of the extent of gang organization conducted to date, Decker et al. (1998) compared two gangs in Chicago with two San Diego gangs; police had described all four gangs as the most highly organized gangs in these cities. The researchers found that the Chicago Gangster Disciples were far more organized than either the Latin Kings from Chicago or the two San Diego gangs, but that none of the gangs exhibited the extremely high level of organization attributed to them by law enforcement.

Other myths about gangs concern dramatic initiation rites, even though such rites are actually extremely rare. Some of these myths have achieved the status of urban legends; generally, these stories are without sufficient empirical basis (Best & Hutchinson, 1996; Fernandez, 1998; Fleisher, 1995, pp. 130, 140-141). The "slasher under the car" or "ankle slasher" legend involves a gangster who waits under a car until the driver returns and begins to open the car door. At that point, the gangster grabs the unsuspecting victim's ankles and assaults him or her (Best & Hutchinson, 1996, p. 387). In the "killer in the backseat" legend, the supposed gang initiation requires a youth to sneak into a woman's car while she is paying or pumping gas at a gas station and hide in the backseat until the woman gets in and drives off; the youth must then attack and rape her (Best & Hutchinson, 1996, p. 389). "Flickered headlights" refers to a legend that gang members drive after dark with their headlights turned off in order to choose victims. According to this myth, if an approaching motorist flashes his or her headlights at the gang members' car (presumably in a friendly attempt to alert the driver that the lights are off), the gangsters must chase down and kill the motorist (Fernandez, 1998).

Another myth is that youths are pressured by their peers into joining gangs. Although some gang research in the 1960s suggested that youngsters' gang friends use strong-arm tactics to persuade them to join gangs (Yablonsky, 1967), the reality is that it is not as difficult for adolescents to resist gang pressures as is commonly believed. In most instances, adolescents can refuse to join gangs without reprisal (Decker & Kempf-Leonard, 1991; Fleisher, 1995; Huff, 1998; Maxson, Whitlock, & Klein, 1998)

It is also a myth that getting out of a gang is done only with great difficulty. Studies have shown that gang members, especially marginal ones, typically can leave their gangs without facing any serious consequences (Decker et al., 1998; Decker & Lauritsen, 2002; Decker & Van Winkle, 1996; Fleisher, 1995).

images, which are based on traditional stereotypes and the picture of gangs conveyed by Skolnick et al.'s California study rather than on any scientific knowledge. Indeed, some jurisdictions may be adapting a view of the well-publicized gang problems in Los Angeles to their own jurisdictions, even though this view may be irrelevant to their situations (Miethe & McCorkle, 1997a).

The broad range in ages among youth gang members also makes defining such gangs more difficult. Youth gangs have traditionally been thought of as being made up mainly of adolescents, but this certainly is no longer the case. In 1996, law enforcement agencies responding to the National Youth Gang Survey estimated that approximately half of the gang members in their jurisdictions were juveniles (under age 18) and that half were young adults (18 and older) (National Youth Gang Center, 1999a). In 1999, respondents to this survey estimated that 63% of gang members were young adults and only 37% were juveniles (Egley, 2000). Thus the mixture had shifted from half juveniles and half young adults to a majority of young adults.

Finally, it is difficult to define youth gangs in a manner that encompasses both school-based and street-based gangs. Many gangs in which members are relatively young may be school-based gangs. In a 1995 national survey of students ages 12-19, more than one-third of the students reported that there were gangs at their schools (Howell & Lynch, 2000). Because only a fraction of student-affiliated youth gangs may be involved in multiple types of serious and violent crimes, law enforcement agencies may be reporting only a small portion of the gangs and gang members actually present in schools.

Essential Characteristics of a Youth Gang

The most important point to keep in mind in any attempt to define youth gangs is that such groups are an integral feature of the experiences of young persons during adolescence. One way of viewing gangs is along an age-graded continuum of social and criminal groups that is anchored at one end by childhood play groups and at the other by adult criminal organizations. The following groups (and more) are represented along this continuum:

- *Childhood play groups:* harmless groups of children that exist in every neighborhood
- *Troublesome youth groups:* youths who hang out together in shopping malls and other places and may be involved in minor forms of delinquency
- *Youth subculture groups:* groups with special interests, such as "goths," "straight edgers," and "anarchists," that are not gangs (Goths are not known for criminal involvement, but some members of other youth subcultures have histories of criminal activity; Arciaga, 2001.)
- *Delinquent groups:* small clusters of friends who band together to commit delinquent acts such as burglaries

- *Taggers:* graffiti vandals (Taggers are often called gang members, but they typically do nothing more than engage in graffiti contests.)
- *School-based youth gangs:* groups of adolescents that may function as gangs only at school and may not be involved in delinquent activity, although most members are involved
- *Street-based youth gangs:* semistructured groups of adolescents and young adults who engage in delinquent and criminal behavior
- *Adult criminal organizations:* groups of adults that engage in criminal activity primarily for economic reasons

Distinguishing among the many different kinds of youth groups that exist is not easy. As noted above, one researcher cataloged 20 law-violating youth groups in his 26-site gang study (Miller, 1992). Quite likely, most of these types of groups exist in major American cities. Only those groups that can be considered to be school-, community-, and street-based youth gangs should be classified as youth gangs. Yet it is often difficult to make a distinction between adolescent delinquent groups and bona fide youth gangs. The most common mistake made by individuals working in the broadcast media is the confusion of youth gangs with adult criminal organizations. The latter group—also called *criminal gangs*—should not be considered youth gangs. For convenience, the media and law enforcement agencies often refer to these groups as *gangs.* Nevertheless, they can be distinguished from youth gangs rather easily (Moore, 1990, 1998).

Because traditional definitions of what constitutes a youth gang have lost their relevance, many experienced gang researchers have updated the definitions they use. The following definition incorporates criteria now recommended by a number of gang researchers for classifying a group as a youth gang (Curry & Decker, 1998; Esbensen, 2000; Klein, 1995; Klein, Kerner, Maxson, & Weitekampf, 2001; Moore, 1998):

- The group must include three or more members.
- Members must fall within a limited age range, generally ages 12 to 24.
- Members must share some sense of identity, generally indicated by such symbols as style of clothing, graffiti, hand signs, and unique identifying gang signs or trademarks.
- Members of the group must view themselves as a gang and be recognized by others as a gang.

- The group must have some permanence and a degree of organization.
- The group must have a set of verbal and nonverbal forms of communication.
- The group must be involved in delinquent or criminal activity beyond a normal level of such involvement.

Joan W. Moore (1998), a prominent gang researcher, suggests that three characteristics distinguish the American youth street gang from other American youth groups: self-definition, street socialization, and the potential to become quasi-institutionalized in a specific local community. *Self-definition* implies not only that group members define themselves as a gang, but that the group has a social structure and group-determined norms that are not controlled by adults in any way. *Street socialization* means that unsupervised young people are socialized by each other (and by older peers in some cases) far more effectively than by conventional socializing agents such as families and schools. In regard to *quasi-institutionalization,* Moore explains that gangs "develop the capacity for reproduction—meaning that they recruit continuously, with places [in the gang] for younger members, and that they extend respect and solidarity toward older members" (p. 67). These characteristics clearly distinguish youth gangs from adult criminal organizations that consist of individuals who come together solely for the purpose of committing criminal acts.

Moore (1998) further asserts that for a youth group with these three characteristics to become established as a youth gang, certain conditions must exist. First, conventional socializing agents, such as families and schools, must be ineffective and alienating (which often is the case). Under these conditions, conventional adult supervision is largely irrelevant. Second, the adolescents must have a great deal of free time that is not consumed by other roles. Third, for the gang to become at least quasi-institutionalized—if not fully institutionalized across generations—members must have limited access to appealing conventional career lines (that is, good adult jobs). Finally, the young people must have a place to congregate—usually a well-defined neighborhood.

Other youth gang researchers have devised a way to measure adolescents' involvement in youth gangs by determining their degree of bonding to the gangs (Esbensen, Winfree, He, & Taylor, 2001; Lynskey et al., 2000). These researchers' study sample consisted of some 6,000 eighth graders (average age nearly 14) in known gang problem localities. The study measured gang bonding on a continuum in terms of five levels of involvement in progressively more serious gangs (Esbensen, Winfree, et al., 2001, pp. 115-117):

Level 1: Ever involved in a gang (17%)

Level 2: Currently a gang member (9%)

Level 3: Currently a member of a *delinquent gang* (8%)

Level 4: Currently a member of a delinquent gang that is *organized* (5%)

Level 5: Currently a *core* member of a delinquent gang that is organized (2%)

The researchers found that as each more restrictive definitional criterion was added, the proportion of qualifying gang members was reduced. The fact that nearly half of the eighth graders who claimed gang membership ("ever involved") were no longer active members confirms the point made earlier that gang membership is, indeed, short-lived for most very young members. The ingenious method that these researchers developed for gauging adolescent bonding to gangs that are *organized* and *delinquent* is potentially a very useful one for helping communities assess their gang problem (see the section of this chapter headed "Effective and Promising Gang Programs").

Why It Is Important to Understand Youth Gangs

Until recently, researchers had no idea how much of all adolescent crime committed throughout the adolescent years is accounted for by gang members. Now, longitudinal studies of large representative adolescent samples that were begun in the 1980s have made it possible for researchers to examine gang members as a subgroup among all delinquents in these samples (see Box 5.4). Thus they can compare the delinquency of gang members with the larger sample of delinquents. I cite three such studies extensively in this chapter—the Denver Youth Survey, the Rochester Youth Development Study, and the Seattle Social Development Project. A fourth longitudinal study, the Pittsburgh Youth Study, only recently began analyses of gang members because Pittsburgh officials earlier were in denial regarding gang problems. Researchers in all four sites conduct research on subgroups of gang members among the larger samples of adolescents. Research reports from the four studies are cited in Box 5.4.

Box 5.4

Longitudinal Studies of Gang Members

Currently, four longitudinal adolescent delinquency studies are examining subsamples of gang members. These studies are ongoing in Denver, Colorado; Rochester, New York; Pittsburgh, Pennsylvania; and Seattle, Washington. The first three of these studies constitute the OJJDP Program of Research on the Causes and Correlates of Delinquency (see Box 4.1 in Chapter 4). Launched in 1986, this research program represents a milestone in criminological research because the three projects constitute the largest shared-measurement approach in multiple sites ever achieved in delinquency research. The three research teams have worked together and use similar measurement techniques, thus enhancing their ability to generalize their findings. The fourth study, the Seattle Social Development Project (SSDP), is a longitudinal prospective panel study of fifth-grade students in 18 Seattle elementary schools in high-crime neighborhoods.

Studies of gang member subsamples have been embedded in these four longitudinal studies of large representative samples of children and adolescents. Gang members represent substantial proportions of all adolescents in each of these four adolescent samples—14% in Denver, 31% in Rochester, 27% in Pittsburgh, and 15% in Seattle. The following are the gang research products published to date in the four studies:

- Denver: Esbensen and Huizinga (1993); Esbensen et al. (1993); Huizinga (1997); Huizinga and Schumann (2001)
- Rochester: Bjerregaard and Lizotte (1995); Bjerregaard and Smith (1993); Lizotte, Howard, Krohn, and Thornberry (1997); Lizotte, Krohn, Howell, Tobin, and Howard (2000); Lizotte, Tesoriero, Thornberry, and Krohn (1994); Thornberry (1998); Thornberry and Burch (1997); Thornberry, Krohn, Lizotte, and Chard-Wierschem (1993); Thornberry, Krohn, Lizotte, Smith, and Tobin (2003); Thornberry and Porter (2001)
- Pittsburgh: Lahey, Gordon, Loeber, Stouthamer-Loeber, and Farrington (1999)
- Seattle: Battin, Hill, Abbott, Catalano, and Hawkins (1998); Battin-Pearson, Guo, Hill, Abbott, and Hawkins (1999); Battin-Pearson, Thornberry, Hawkins, and Krohn (1998); Hill, Howell, Hawkins, and Battin-Pearson (1999); Howell, Hill, Battin, and Hawkins (1996); Kosterman et al. (1996)

In addition, one joint analysis of gang member data collected in the Denver, Rochester, and Seattle studies has been published (Battin-Pearson et al., 1998).

The Rochester, Denver, and Seattle studies reveal several reasons an understanding of youth gangs is important for gauging the volume of serious and violent delinquency. First, the influence of gangs on levels of violence has been found to be greater than the influence of other highly delinquent peers (Battin, Hill, Abbott, Catalano, & Hawkins, 1998; Huizinga, 1997; Thornberry, 1998). Gang membership is one of the strongest predictors of individual violence in adolescence. This finding is clear in two of the longitudinal studies, in Seattle (J. D. Hawkins et al., 1998) and Rochester (Battin-Pearson, Thornberry, Hawkins, & Krohn, 1998, p. 7; Thornberry, 1998, p. 161). Thornberry, Krohn, Lizotte, Smith, and Tobin (2003), authors of the most recent report on the Rochester study, conclude, "Gang membership appears to have a more consistent and powerful impact on general delinquency and on violence than on either drug sales or drug use" (p. 112).

Second, the influence of gang membership on delinquency and violence is long lasting. Analyses in the Seattle, Rochester, and Denver studies show that youths commit many more serious and violent acts while they are gang members than they do after they leave the gang (Esbensen & Huizinga, 1993; Hill et al., 1996; Thornberry, Krohn, Lizotte, & Chard-Wierschem, 1993). Although gang members' offense rates dropped after they left the gang in all three sites, their crime rates remained fairly high (Esbensen & Huizinga, 1993; Hill et al., 1995; Thornberry et al., 1993). Rates of drug use and drug trafficking, the most notable exceptions to offense rate drops, remained nearly as high after individuals left gangs as when they were active gang members (Hill et al., 1995; Thornberry et al., 2003). Thornberry et al. (2003) note that gang involvement has a way of increasing the "criminal embeddedness" of members. Thus they suggest that membership in street gangs "may be one of the more important social environments for explaining patterns of adolescent delinquency" (p. 121).

Third, gang membership has an important negative impact on long-term adolescent developmental processes, for boys and girls alike. Over and above solidifying members' criminal involvement, the gang acts as "a powerful social network" in constraining the behavior of members, limiting access to prosocial networks, and cutting individuals off from conventional pursuits (Thornberry et al., 2003). These effects of the gang tend to produce precocious, off-time, and unsuccessful transitions that bring disorder to the life course in a cascading series of difficulties, including school dropout, early pregnancy or early impregnation, teen motherhood, and unstable employment (pp. 179-180). For some gang members, the end result of this foreclosure of future opportunities is continued involvement in criminal activity throughout adolescence and into adulthood. Thus youths should be warned about the heavy toll gang involvement is likely to take on their healthy social development and life-course experiences. In addition, the likelihood of experiencing violent victimization is much higher for gang members than it is for members of other peer groups.

Fourth, there is a high degree of overlap between gang membership and serious, violent, and chronic juvenile offending. Because of the importance of this finding for any efforts to deal with the most serious aspects of juvenile delinquency, I consider this issue in detail below.

The Overlap Between Gang Membership and Serious, Violent, and Chronic Juvenile Offending

There are two ways of examining the degree of overlap between gang membership and serious, violent, and chronic juvenile offending. The first approach is to consider the proportion of all serious, violent, and chronic juvenile offenders who are gang members. The second approach is to look at the relative proportion of all violent juvenile offenses that are committed by gang members.

Two studies have examined the proportion of all serious, violent, and chronic juvenile offenders who are gang members. In the Rochester adolescent sample, two-thirds (66%) of the chronic violent offenders were gang members (Thornberry, Huizinga, & Loeber, 1995). Similarly, about two-thirds of the high-rate serious and chronic juvenile offenders, ages 15 and younger, referred to the Orange County, California, Probation Department were significantly gang involved by the time they were in custody (Kurz, 1999). Thus the findings from these two studies suggest that about two-thirds of all serious, violent, and chronic juvenile offenders are gang members. This statement must be qualified in two respects, however: The research methods used in the Orange County study are unknown, and both studies were conducted in large urban areas.

Longitudinal studies are the best sources of data on the relative proportion of all violent juvenile offenses that are committed by gang members. The Denver, Rochester, and Seattle studies show that gang members, who make up only a small proportion of these large adolescent samples, commit the overwhelming majority of violent offenses committed by the entire samples (see Figure 5.2). In the Rochester study, the offenses committed by gang members were the more serious forms of violence (aggravated assault, robbery, and sexual assault; Thornberry et al., 2003); in the Denver site, they were "serious violent" offenses consisting of aggravated assault, robbery, gang fights, and sexual assault (Huizinga, 1997). As noted in the figure, the Seattle data displayed apply only to robberies (Battin et al., 1998). During periods of active gang membership, the Rochester gang members were responsible for, on average, four times as many offenses as their share of the total study population would suggest (Thornberry et al., 2003).

Other studies have also shown the overlap between gang membership and serious, violent, and chronic juvenile offending. For example, J. D. Hawkins et al. (1998) analyzed violence predictors in the Seattle study and found that gang membership at age 14 more than tripled the risk for involvement in violence at age 18; when subjects were members at age 16, their risk for involvement in violence at age 18 was quadrupled. The greater likelihood of involvement in violence among youths who were gang members at age 16 than among 14-year-olds probably reflects multiple-year membership among the older youths. In comparison with single-year gang members, multiple-year members have much higher serious and violent offense rates (Hill et al., 1996; Thornberry et al., 2003). In general, gang members' violent offense rates are up to seven times higher than the

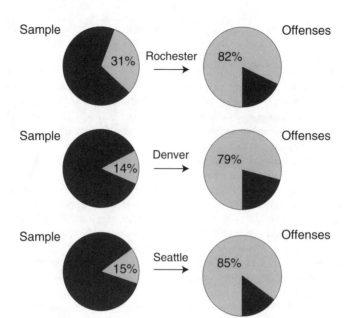

Figure 5.2   Percentages of All Serious Violent Offenses Committed by Gang Members
SOURCE: Data from Thornberry (1998).

violent crime rates of adolescents who are not in gangs (Esbensen & Huizinga, 1993; Hill et al., 1996; Thornberry et al., 1993).

Gang members have very high homicide rates. Two studies clearly illustrate the overlap between gang homicide and serious, violent, and chronic adolescent and young adult offending. In their report on a Boston study of homicides among young persons, Kennedy, Piehl, and Braga (1996) conclude: "A clear picture thus emerges. Most . . . of Boston's young homicide victims and offenders emerge from a universe of gang membership and activity; they are high-rate criminal offenders who are known to local authorities, institutionally and personally, and they move in a universe of gang membership, geography, antagonisms, and alliances" (p. 163; see also Braga, Piehl, & Kennedy, 1999). Similarly, in a Minneapolis study, Kennedy and Braga (1998) found the adolescent and young adult homicide problem to be predominantly a gang problem involving high-rate serious, violent, and chronic offenders. Among the victims age 21 and under, 63% involved gang-related motives.

It should be noted that the overlap between gang membership and serious, violent, and chronic juvenile offending described above may not be particularly high in cities, towns, and counties with recently emerging gang problems. One study in a relatively small city—Colorado Springs, Colorado—found that most of the gangs in that locality were neighborhood-based fighting gangs rather than established, criminally oriented gangs (Hughes & Duke, 1997; Stoll, Dukes, & Smith, 1997). The latter are far more likely to have high proportions of serious, violent, and chronic juvenile offenders as members. Thus it is important for individual communities to conduct careful assessments of their own gang problems, so that they avoid drawing incorrect inferences concerning the extent of involvement in serious crime of the gang members in their areas.

In sum, in localities where gang problems have existed for some time, the overlap between gang membership and serious, violent, and chronic juvenile offending is very large. As much as two-thirds of the juveniles in these three subgroups may be gang members. Below, I describe a gang assessment protocol that localities can use to assess the extent of their gang problems. Policy makers can use the results of such an assessment to develop a comprehensive continuum of interventions like the one I describe later in this chapter.

Explanations for
High Levels of Gang Violence

What are the major reasons for the current high levels of gang violence? First, we can rule out the most widely offered explanation: the connection between gangs and drug trafficking. Because the growth in youth gang violence in the period from the mid-1980s to the early 1990s coincided with the crack cocaine epidemic, these two developments were generally perceived to be interrelated (Blumstein & Rosenfeld, 1999; Skolnick, 1989; Skolnick et al., 1988). Researchers working for all levels of government conducted assessments and reached this same conclusion (Bryant, 1989; California Council on Criminal Justice, 1989; Clark, 1991; Drug Enforcement Administration, 1988; Hayeslip, 1989; McKinney, 1988; U.S. General Accounting Office, 1989). Most of their reports suggested that youth gangs were instrumental in the increase in crack cocaine sales and that their involvement in drug trafficking resulted in a growth in youth violence (Blumstein & Rosenfeld, 1999, p. 162; Fox, 1996b).

Today, most gang researchers agree that youth gang involvement in drug trafficking is mainly limited to street-level distribution, involving gang members acting on their own (Decker et al., 1998; Decker & Van Winkle, 1994, 1996; Fagan, 1989; Fleisher, 1995, 1998; Howell & Decker, 1999; Huff, 1996; Klein & Maxson, 1994; Klein, Maxson, & Cunningham, 1991). It appears that some drug distribution operations are managed by former youth gangs that transformed themselves into drug gangs or by drug gangs initially formed as such (Padilla, 1992; Sanchez-Jankowski, 1991; Taylor, 1990; Venkatesh, 1996; Williams, 1989).

However, most drug distribution systems are managed by adult drug cartels or syndicates (Eddy, Sabogal, & Walden, 1988; Gugliotta & Leen 1989; Sampson, 1985, 1988). Other groups actively involved during the crack cocaine epidemic included drug "crews" and "posses" (Fagan & Chin, 1990), traditional narcotics operatives (Klein & Maxson, 1994; Moore, 1990), and new adult criminal organizations formed to service the growing crack cocaine market (Bureau of Justice Assistance, 1997; Curtis, 1992; Fagan, 1996; Moore, 1990).

Several studies have strongly questioned the presumed connections among gangs, drug trafficking, and violence (Decker & Van Winkle, 1996; Klein et al., 1991, pp. 623-625; Moore, 1990, p. 169; Parsons & Meeker, 1999). There are exceptions, however. To be sure, as Block, Christakos, Jacob, and Przybylski (1996) have observed, some ongoing gang drug market wars have accounted for a significant number of local homicides. Block and her colleagues also point to indirect relationships among homicides, drug trafficking, and gang activity. Many gang-related homicides might not occur if drug markets did not exist to bring members of opposing gangs into frequent contact with one another. Venkatesh (1996) describes one of the worst cases of a connection between gang drug trafficking and violence, which took place in Chicago's Robert Taylor Homes, a low-income public housing development. With the advent of crack cocaine, gangs in the housing development transformed themselves from turf gangs to drug gangs, and an escalation of gang violence resulted. Other studies have documented the activities of violent drug-trafficking gangs (Sanchez-Jankowski, 1991; Taylor, 1990). An interrelationship between drug trafficking and violence is common in prison gangs, and this connection extends to the streets to some extent (Decker et al., 1998; Reiner, 1992; Schlosser, 1998; Stevens, 1997; Valdez, Alvarado, & Arcos, 2000).

Research has also shown a weak correlation between youth gang–related homicides and drug trafficking (Howell, 1999). Studies examining the possible connection have been conducted in six cities:

- Boston (Kennedy et al., 1996)
- Chicago (Block & Block, 1993; Block et al., 1996; Curry & Spergel, 1988)
- Miami (Inciardi, 1990; Sampson, 1985, 1988)
- Los Angeles (Hutson, Anglin, Kyriacou, Hart, & Spears, 1995; Klein et al., 1991; Maxson, 1995, 1998a; Meehan & O'Carroll, 1992),
- Minneapolis (Kennedy & Braga, 1998)
- St. Louis (Decker & Van Winkle, 1996; Rosenfeld, Bray, & Egley, 1999)

All of these studies consistently found a low correlation between gang-related homicides and gang-controlled drug trafficking (for a review of these studies, see Howell, 1999).

Researchers in the Rochester Youth Development Study have unraveled the connections between gang membership and involvement in drug use, drug trafficking, and violence for youngsters in that city in New York State (Thornberry et al., 2003). According to Thornberry et al. (2003), when adolescents—particularly males—join gangs, their behavior changes. Their involvement in general forms of delinquency, violence, drug selling, and—to a lesser extent—drug use increases. Gang membership also increases the likelihood of gun carrying, up to 12 times. Gang membership is the best predictor of gun carrying up to about age 16, after which involvement in drug trafficking is a stronger predictor (Lizotte, Krohn, Howell, Tobin, & Howard, 2000).

An analysis of National Youth Gang Survey data suggests that the correlation between gang drug trafficking and violence needs to be considered in the context of relationships between other crimes (Howell & Gleason, 1999). Although gang drug trafficking correlates with other serious and violent crimes, the correlations between other forms of serious and violent crime are stronger. In fact, the strongest correlations are between robbery and aggravated assault, followed by robbery and motor vehicle theft, then robbery and drug trafficking. This study suggests that gang drug trafficking may take place concurrently with other criminal activities, rather than cause other crimes. That is, when gang members are involved in one form of criminal activity, they are likely also to be involved in other types of crimes. As Klein (1995) has observed, involvement in "cafeteria-style" (widely varied) crime is typical of youth gang members. The causal sequence involved in gang violence needs to be specified. Gangs facilitate their members' involvement in a wide variety of delinquent offenses, including property crimes, auto theft, drug involvement, gun carrying, and violence.

In sum, an impressive number of sound empirical studies have established that the connections among gangs, drug trafficking, and violence are weak. There are, of course, exceptions to this general conclusion.

Other Sources of Gang Violence

If drug trafficking is not a major factor explaining gang violence, what is most gang violence all about? Research indicates that most violent crimes committed by youth gang members are related to intergang and interpersonal conflicts (Decker & Van Winkle, 1994). Most gang violence is public and participatory in nature (Rosenfeld et al., 1999). It is typically retaliatory, a response to violence—real or perceived—against the gang (Decker, 1996; Horowitz, 1983). Decker (1996) explains how the threat of attack by another group ignites the gang, increases cohesion, and produces deadly consequences. Peaks and valleys in gang violence levels appear to follow predictable patterns. These form as a result of a sequence that is initially motivated by the perceived threat that another gang poses, then instigated by a precipitating event, followed by escalation of activity, a violent event, rapid de-escalation, and, finally, retaliation.

Horowitz (1983) explains intergang violence this way: "In seeking to protect and promote their reputation, gangs often engage in prolonged 'wars,' which are kept alive between larger fights by many small incidents and threats of violence" (p. 94). For example, one of two gangs may claim precedence following a victory, and this leads to the other gang challenging the first to another fight if the second gang wants to retain its honor and reassert its reputation. As Decker and Van Winkle (1996) note, "Whatever the 'purpose' of violence, it often leads to retaliation and revenge creating a feedback loop where each killing requires a new killing" (p. 186; see also Fremon, 1995). This is the main *collective* (i.e., group dynamic) aspect of gang violence. It is contagious and spreads throughout a gang and, perhaps, from one gang to another in a community or city.

Intergang conflicts tend to be episodic. In some cases, they are prolonged, producing what have been called gang violence "spurts" (Block, 1993). These spurts are explained largely by turf disputes between warring gangs (Block & Block, 1993; Block & Christakos, 1995; Block et al., 1996). Such spurts do not generally take place citywide—they occur in specific neighborhoods and involve particular youth gangs in escalating incidents of provocation, retaliation, and revenge.

In their 2-year field study, Decker and Van Winkle (1996, pp. 171-173) observed three main reasons for violence among St. Louis gang members: First, violence is a part of their everyday lives, apart from the gang, in their neighborhoods and families; second, conflict differentiates gangs from other delinquent groups; and third, violence is endemic in gang members' individual status and role behaviors. In St. Louis gangs, "members are expected to always be ready to commit violence, to participate in violent acts, and to have engaged in some sort of violence in their initiation" into the gang (p. 173). Violence defines a gang's physical and social boundaries. As Fleisher (1995) notes, these boundaries are important, because "a threat to gang viability comes with a loss of members, loss of internal social order, and threats by outsiders" (p. 134).

In considering the nature of intragang or interpersonal gang violence, let us examine further Decker and Van Winkle's observation that violence is a part of gang members' everyday lives, apart from the gang. As Fleisher (1998) has noted regarding gang members, "Violence at home and on the street isn't new to these kids" (p. 48). The early stage of a gang member's life in the gang is but one part of a violent life course, beginning with a violent childhood and continuing through adolescence and into a violent adulthood. Fleisher (2000) explains, "A gang lifestyle is defined by drug use and sales, intra-gang and inter-gang violence, and imprisonment. These are normal expectations" (p. 90). Intragang violence (members within a gang assaulting each other) is more common than intergang violence (Fleisher, 1998, p. 50).

The use of firearms is a major feature of gang violence. Gang members are far more likely than other delinquents to carry guns and to use them. In the 2000 National Youth Gang Survey, 84% of respondents reported at least one occurrence of firearm use by one or more gang members in an assault crime (Egley & Arjunan, 2002). In the Rochester study, Thornberry et al. (2003) found that the rate of gun carrying was about 10 times higher for gang members than it was for nongang juvenile offenders. Gang members who carried guns or who owned and carried guns also committed about 10 times more violent crimes than one would expect from their numbers in the sample population. The Rochester study also found evidence that adolescent gun ownership and gun carrying facilitate involvement in a variety of crime types, not just gun crimes (Lizotte & Sheppard, 2001, p. 2). Thornberry et al. (2003) state, "If illegal gun users have been characterized as the crime problem in the United States, then gang members with guns may be at the very core of the crime problem, especially the problem of youth violence" (p. 125).

The involvement of adults in youth gangs also increases the level of gang violence. Adult members engage in more serious and violent crimes than juvenile gang members (Howell & Gleason, 1999; National Youth Gang Center, 2000; Parsons & Meeker, 1999; Wiebe, Meeker, & Vila, 1999). Wiebe et al. (1999) conducted one of the few studies that has examined this issue, using data from the Orange County, California, Gang Incident Tracking System, which compiles information on gang-related crime arrests recorded in each of the county's 22 law enforcement agencies. More than 7,500 gang arrests were made from 1995 through 1998 in Orange County, and Wiebe et al. found that of all gang-related arrests involving adults, 66% were for violent crimes; only 45% of gang-related arrests involving juveniles were for violent crimes. Stated another way, examination of the total volume of violent crimes showed that adults were involved in 46% more violent crimes than were juveniles.

Windows of Opportunity for Gang Prevention, Intervention, and Suppression

In this section I want to propose and describe a comprehensive community approach to addressing youth gang problems. Figure 5.3 illustrates the windows of opportunity that exist for intervention in the pathway children and adolescents take to gang involvement and subsequent serious and violent delinquency. This figure is organized around age periods, from about age 3 into young adulthood. The top section of the figure shows the major protective and risk factor domains—family, school, peer group, individual, and community contexts. Problem behaviors develop as a result of a preponderance of risk factors over protective factors in these five major domains (Browning & Huizinga, 1999; Catalano & Hawkins, 1996; Smith, Lizotte, Thornberry, & Krohn, 1995). These domains are organized according to their approximate relation to developmental aging of children and adolescents (Catalano & Hawkins, 1996).

The middle section of Figure 5.3 illustrates the faulty developmental process that leads to gang involvement and serious, violent, and chronic delinquency—if prevention and intervention efforts are not successful. This deviant developmental process begins with conduct problems at ages 3-4, followed by elementary school failure at ages 6-12, then child delinquency at about ages 10-12, gang membership at ages 13-15, and serious, violent, and chronic delinquency onward from mid-adolescence.

The bottom section of the figure illustrates the parallel types of interventions that would be appropriate, given youngsters' progression along the gang involvement pathway and into progressively more serious delinquency involvement. Gang suppression strategies are used when prevention and intervention efforts fail, and to prevent existing gangs from providing more opportunities for youngsters to become involved in gang life, thus repeating the cycle in communities.

Concerning activation of the risk and protective factor domains over time, the family is of primary importance as a socializing unit in the preschool period (Catalano & Hawkins, 1996). During the elementary school period, the school joins the family as an important socializing environment, with peer influences emerging toward the end of the elementary school period. In the middle/junior high school period, peers increase in importance as a socializing force. Individual risk factors can come into play at any point in the developmental process, but involvement in particular problem behaviors, such as delinquency and drug use, is especially important. Community risk and protective factors also may come into play at any point, particularly during late childhood and adolescence, and may be manifested by the presence of gangs at school or in the community. By the time youths enter high school, many of the risk and protective factors affecting drug use and delinquency have been established.

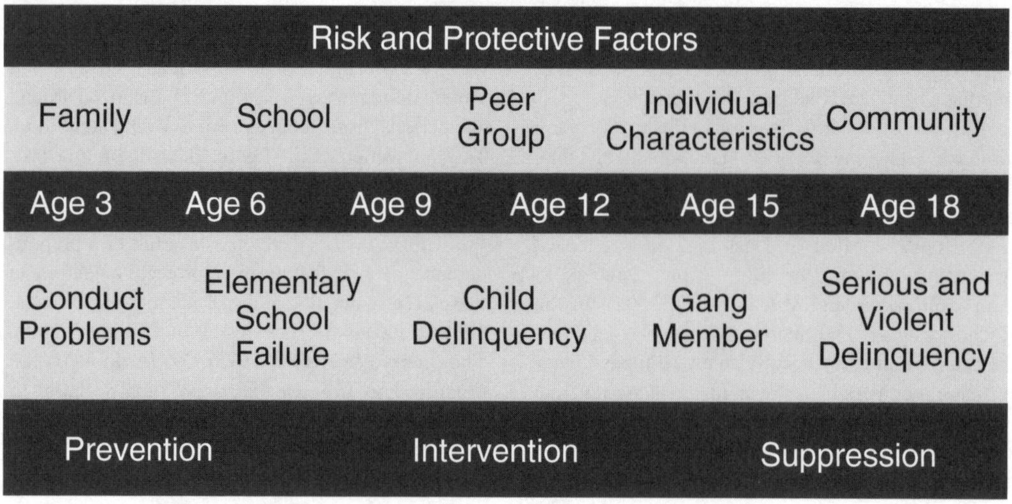

Risk and Protective Factors				
Family	School	Peer Group	Individual Characteristics	Community
Age 3	Age 6	Age 9	Age 12	Age 15	Age 18
Conduct Problems	Elementary School Failure	Child Delinquency	Gang Member	Serious and Violent Delinquency
Prevention		Intervention		Suppression

Figure 5.3   Windows of Opportunity for Gang Prevention and Intervention

The middle section of Figure 5.3 shows the progression in problem behaviors, from conduct problems in the preschool years to elementary school failure, to child delinquency by age 12, to gang membership by about age 15 for most youngsters, to chronic involvement in serious and violent delinquency by age 18. Although this pathway has not been demonstrated empirically in its entirety, there is empirical support for the stepping-stone nature of the path, from one stage of these problem behaviors to the next. If preschool conduct problems are manifest outside the home as well as in the family, the child is more likely to experience school failure in elementary school and perhaps become a delinquent in late childhood or early adolescence (see Loeber & Farrington, 2001a). School failure at the elementary level is a strong predictor of gang membership (Hill, Howell, Hawkins, & Battin-Pearson, 1999). Studies suggest that child delinquents are more likely to go on to become involved in crimes of a more serious and violent nature during adolescence (Krohn, Thornberry, Rivera, & Le Blanc, 2001). Young delinquents are at high risk for gang membership (Hill et al., 1999; Loeber & Farrington, 2001a). Youngsters on a trajectory of worsening antisocial behavior are most likely to join gangs (Lahey, Gordon, Loeber, Stouthamer-Loeber, & Farrington, 1999). Ages 14-15 are the peak ages for gang involvement (Battin et al., 1998; Esbensen & Winfree, 1998; Huff, 1998). Gang participation increases the likelihood of an individual's becoming a serious, violent, chronic juvenile offender (Thornberry et al., 2003).

Windows of opportunity for gang prevention, intervention, and suppression exist throughout the childhood-adolescent developmental period.

- *Prevention* strategies aim to prevent youth from joining gangs and engaging in gang activities. These include cognitive-behavioral approaches such as in the G.R.E.A.T. curriculum described later in this chapter.
- *Intervention* programs aim to divert gang-involved youths from gangs by providing alternatives such as after-school programs, juvenile justice system sanctions and services, employment opportunities, and other outreach efforts to gang-involved youth.
- *Suppression* activities are law enforcement tactics; they usually involve policies and procedures designed to identify, isolate, punish, and rehabilitate criminal offenders.

The prevention window of opportunity closes by about age 15, because almost all youths who join gangs have joined by that age. The intervention window of opportunity overlaps with that for prevention and extends for a longer period of time. Intervention efforts include a variety of programs and policies aimed at reducing conduct problems, school failure, child delinquency, gang membership, and serious and violent delinquency. Early interventions target children and young adolescents who evidence initial involvement in any of the problem behaviors. Treatment or rehabilitation interventions, used in combination with graduated sanctions, typically are used for adolescents who have progressed further along the pathway of gang involvement and serious and violent delinquency. A continuum of program options that includes prevention, early intervention, and sanctions (including suppression) combined with treatment is likely to have a much larger impact on a local gang problem than individual interventions, owing to the greater effect of the simultaneous implementation of multiple-level interventions. Prevention efforts reduce the number of youths who join gangs at the same time that intervention in gang careers with treatment/rehabilitation removes youths from gangs, while suppression strategies weaken gangs and thwart their recruitment efforts, serving to diminish the presence and influence of gangs in the community.

Risk Factors for Gang Membership

To have maximum impact, prevention and intervention programs need to address the major risk factors for gang involvement. I highlight below the major risk factors in each of the five risk factor domains: individual characteristics, the family, school experiences, delinquent peer groups, and community conditions. (For a review of risk factors found in longitudinal studies, see Howell, 2003; for a complete list of risk factors found in all types of studies, see Howell, 1998d, pp. 6-7.) Youths who experience multiple risk factors in multiple domains have been found to be at much higher risk of gang participation than those who do not face multiple risk factors (Thornberry et al., 2003).

Several individual characteristics predict gang membership. Studies have shown that boys with chronic histories of physical aggression commonly exhibit cognitive-behavioral problems (that is, deviant thought habits that result in inappropriate automatic reactions to situations; Tremblay & LeMarquand, 2001). Such problems may lead to school failure, which is a predictor of gang membership (Hill et al., 1999). Individual characteristics that might be linked to cognitive-behavioral problems include learning disabilities, hyperactivity, conduct problems, and low self-control (impulsiveness, risk-seeking tendencies, and physical problem-solving tendencies). Many of these individual characteristics are key risk factors for gang membership (Esbensen, Huizinga, & Weiher, 1993; Hill et al., 1999). Other individual characteristics that predict gang membership include early involvement in delinquency, alcohol/drug use, early dating and precocious sexual activity, and mental health problems (Thornberry et al., 2003). Illegal gun ownership/carrying is another strong predictor

(Bjerregaard & Lizotte, 1995; Lizotte et al., 2000; Lizotte, Tesoriero, Thornberry, & Krohn, 1994). Youngsters—particularly boys—who experience many negative/stressful life events also are more likely to join gangs (Thornberry et al., 2003). Such events include failing a course at school, being suspended from school, breaking up with a boyfriend/girlfriend, having a big fight or problem with a friend, and the death of someone close.

Key family risk factors for gang membership include the family structure (broken home) and family poverty (Hill et al., 1999; Thornberry, 1998). Poor family management—including low parental supervision, control, and monitoring of children (Hill et al., 1999; Le Blanc & Lanctot, 1998; Thornberry, 1998; Walker-Barnes & Mason, 2001a, 2001b)—and child abuse/neglect (Thornberry et al., 2003) are also relatively strong predictors. Interestingly, a high level of parental psychological (manipulative and guilt-based) control (Walker-Barnes & Mason, 2001a) may be a risk factor for gang membership. Finally, a little-researched family risk factor—gang involvement of family members, especially siblings and cousins—may be a strong predictor (Egley, 2003).

The strongest school-related risk factor for gang membership may well be low achievement in elementary school (Hill et al., 1999; Le Blanc & Lanctot, 1998). This, of course, is related to low academic aspirations (Hill et al., 1999; Thornberry, 1998) and a low degree of commitment to school (Le Blanc & Lanctot, 1998; Thornberry, 1998; Thornberry et al., 2003). In addition, negative labeling of youngsters by teachers appears to be a contributing factor to gang joining (Esbensen et al., 1993). Not surprisingly, feeling unsafe at school is also a risk factor (Gottfredson & Gottfredson, 2001). However, research has shown that large numbers of security measures in schools do not necessarily reduce gang presence (Howell & Lynch, 2000).

Association with peers who engage in delinquency is one of the strongest risk factors for gang membership, particularly for boys (Thornberry et al., 2003). Association with aggressive peers—whether or not they are involved in delinquency—during adolescence also is a strong predictor (Lahey et al., 1999; Lyon, Henggeler, & Hall, 1992). The lack of adult supervision of youngsters' time spent with friends is integrally related to the impact of negative and delinquent friends on a youngster's decision to join a gang (Le Blanc & Lanctot, 1998; Thornberry, 1998).

The strongest community or neighborhood risk factors for gang membership that have been identified in longitudinal studies are availability of drugs, the presence of many neighborhood youth who are in trouble, youngsters' feeling unsafe in the neighborhood, low neighborhood attachment, low level of neighborhood integration, area poverty, and neighborhood disorganization (Howell, 2003). Gangs tend to cluster in high-crime, socially disorganized neighborhoods (Fagan, 1996; Short & Strodtbeck, 1965; Thornberry et al., 2003; Vigil, 1988). It may well be that during adolescence, individual and family protective factors are overpowered by the influence of bad neighborhoods (Wikstrom & Loeber, 2000), and the clustering of gangs in such high-crime communities provides ample opportunity for gang involvement.

In general, youths who are on a path of worsening antisocial behavior, beginning with conduct disorders in the first grade, are most likely to join gangs (Esbensen & Huizinga, 1993; Hill et al., 1999; Le Blanc & Lanctot, 1998; Thornberry et al., 2003). Gang members evidence early development of a deviant lifestyle. Both boys and girls tend to show conduct problems early in childhood, develop delinquent beliefs, cultivate delinquent friends, begin dating early, and become involved in delinquency and drug use in late childhood and early adolescence. Sexual activity at an early age is one the strongest predictors of gang involvement for both females and males (Bjerregaard & Smith, 1993).

These behaviors are stepping-stones to gang membership (Bjerregaard & Smith, 1993; Esbensen & Huizinga, 1993; Hill et al., 1999; Lahey et al., 1999; Thornberry et al., 1993, 2003). The level of parental supervision appears to be an important family risk factor in early adolescence—but perhaps only for boys (Hill et al., 1999; Lahey et al., 1999; Thornberry, 1998). Future gang members are likely to have current gang members in their school classrooms (Curry & Spergel, 1992). They perform poorly in elementary school, and they have a low degree of commitment to and involvement in school (Hill et al., 1999; Le Blanc & Lanctot, 1998) and low attachment to teachers (Thornberry et al., 2003). They often are identified as learning disabled (Hill et al., 1999). They show higher levels of normlessness (alienation) in the family, peer group, and school contexts (Esbensen et al., 1993), and they spend a lot of unsupervised time with friends (Le Blanc & Lanctot, 1998; Thornberry, 1998). The most bonded gang members have low self-control; that is, they have tendencies toward impulsiveness, risk seeking, and physical problem solving (Lynskey et al., 2000). Many of the youngest youth gang members have few of these characteristics. These are good kids, from good families, and they

are good students; however, these youths do not remain in gangs for long.

The risk factors noted above do not necessarily apply equally to girls and boys. Only one longitudinal study to date has examined gender-specific risk factors for gang membership—the Rochester Youth Development Study (Bjerregaard & Smith, 1993; Thornberry et al., 2003). Although their analysis was hampered by the smaller number of female than male gang members, the researchers found that, when examined throughout the adolescent years, the risk factors for gang membership among girls and boys are very similar. However, more of them were statistically significant for boys. For both genders, a strong association was found between having deficits in multiple developmental domains and the likelihood of joining a gang. For girls, school variables were the most important predictors of gang membership (Thornberry et al., 2003). In addition, living in a socially disorganized neighborhood, early dating, externalizing behaviors, having delinquent beliefs, and prior delinquency appear to be particularly important risk factors for females. Although none of the family variables were statistically significant predictors for females, the odds of joining a gang were similar for females and males who were victims of child abuse. Family hostility was a stronger predictor for females than for males, although statistical significance was not reached. This study also found that gang membership during early adolescence has disruptive life-course effects for both boys and girls. The strongest risk factors for boys were early involvement in violence and general delinquency, negative life events, drug use, and peer relationships.

Factors That Protect
Against Gang Membership

Few studies have been aimed at discerning the protective factors that buffer children and adolescents from gang involvement. Research on protective factors has been slower to develop than risk factor studies, in part because of the absence of a standard for determining what constitutes protection. A related concern is confusion about whether protective factors are distinct from risk factors as developmental predictors of youth violence and gang involvement. Some protective factors may be the opposite of risk factors; for instance, low parental supervision is a risk factor, and high parental supervision is a protective factor. There also is evidence that protective factors may interact with risk factors to reduce the likelihood of gang joining (Whitlock, 2002). Although research has not established what protective factors are most likely to buffer risk factors for gang involvement, a large number of possible protective factors have been suggested in the gang literature (see especially Bjerregaard & Smith, 1993; Esbensen et al., 1993; Hill et al., 1999; Howell, 2003; Maxson, Whitlock, & Klein, 1998; Thornberry et al., 2003; Walker-Barnes & Mason, 2001a; Whitlock, 2002; Wyrick, 2000).

Other protective factors can be inferred from the well-documented risk factors for gang membership (see Howell, 2003). Durlak (1998) has identified common factors that protect youths from a wide variety of child and adolescent problems, including behavioral problems, school failure, and drug use. Because these problems are all related to risk factors for gang membership, the protective factors from Durlak's research should also apply to the gang context. The protective factors that Durlak identifies in each of the risk factor domains are as follows:

- *Individual domain:* personal and social skills; self-efficacy
- *Peer group domain:* positive peer modeling
- *Community domain:* clear and consistent social norms; effective social policies
- *Family domain:* good parent-child relationships
- *School domain:* high-quality schools
- *All domains:* social support from helping parents, peers, and teachers

It appears that self-efficacy, good parent-child relationships, and social support from helping parents, peers, and teachers may be the most important protective factors against delinquency and other problem behaviors, and possibly also against gang involvement. As Durlak (1998) notes, "Much is still to be learned about which risk and protective factors are causally related to outcomes, as opposed to correlated with them, how factors interact, the specific mechanisms through which they operate, and how the relative importance of factors differs across target populations and at the different developmental periods" (p. 519). More research also is needed on the salience of gang risk and protective factors for members of particular racial and ethnic groups and for boys versus girls. There is some evidence that risk and protective factors operate differently for members of different racial and ethnic groups (Curry & Spergel, 1992; Walker-Barnes & Mason, 2001a).

An illustration of how protective factors might work is provided by Wyrick (2000), who examined a sample of Vietnamese adolescents to identify possible protective factors against gang involvement.

This research suggests that services should focus on improving youths' attitudes about school, reducing their feelings of alienation, and modifying their perceptions that gang membership is beneficial. Furthermore, Wyrick suggests that services might prevent gang involvement if they address family conflict and buffer the influences of neighborhood gangs.

Maxson et al. (1998) also propose several such factors that might buffer adolescents from gang involvement. These include counseling for youth who experience multiple stressful events and early intervention programs that strengthen families and provide a healthy start for infants in public housing projects. Both of these categories of protective factors may serve later to insulate children from gang joining.

Effective and Promising Gang Programs

In this section I will provide examples of promising and effective gang programs that can be put into action during the three windows of opportunity—prevention, intervention, and suppression—illustrated in Figure 5.3. Programs that prevent gang joining are useful during the prevention window of opportunity. The intervention category includes early intervention and treatment/rehabilitation programs. The suppression category includes arrest and prosecution of gang members and other efforts to control the criminal activities of gangs. What follows is not intended to be an exhaustive review of all promising and effective gang intervention programs (I review others in Howell, 2000); rather, I include here descriptions of some programs that clearly fit within various sections of the "windows of opportunity" framework. Thus the programs mentioned below represent a compilation of the promising and effective program options that could be included in a comprehensive continuum of interventions. Policy makers in each community must, of course, select the interventions they wish to implement based on an assessment of the community's local gang problem.

To optimize the effectiveness of any program aimed at reducing or eliminating gang activity, a community must initiate a combination of interventions simultaneously. It is widely accepted that no single response is effective in dealing with youth gangs (Spergel & Curry, 1993). The most promising approach is a balanced, coordinated response that combines suppression and other interventions—especially social opportunities for current and future gang members—community mobilization, and crisis intervention (Fearn, Decker, & Curry, 2001).

Spergel and Curry (1990, 1993) have developed such a comprehensive gang prevention, intervention, and suppression model. This model, based on a national assessment of youth gang policies and programs, is a general framework that addresses youth gang problems through interrelated prevention, intervention, and suppression programs and strategies. It has been implemented with positive results in a number of sites (National Youth Gang Center, 2001b).

A program based on a variation on the comprehensive model designed by Spergel and colleagues was implemented in the Little Village neighborhood of Chicago, a low-income and working-class community where the population is approximately 90% Mexican American (Spergel & Grossman, 1997a, 1997b). Called the Gang Violence Reduction Program, it targeted mainly older members (ages 17 to 24) of two of the area's most violent Hispanic gangs, the Latin Kings and the Two Six. These two gangs accounted for about 70% of serious gang violence in the Little Village community. The program targeted and provided services to youth involved with these two gangs, rather than to the gangs as groups.

The Gang Violence Reduction Program integrated two coordinated strategies: graduated sanctions and intensive interventions. Violent or potentially violent youth gang offenders were targeted for graduated sanctions, which were imposed by the probation department and the police. At the same time, a wide range of social services and opportunities were provided for targeted youth, to encourage their transition to legitimate behavior through education, jobs, job training, family support, and brief counseling. The program was staffed by tactical police officers, probation officers, community youth workers from the target neighborhood, and workers from Neighbors Against Gang Violence, a new community organization established to support the project. This organization was composed of representatives from local churches, a job placement agency, youth service agencies, other community groups, the alderman's office, and local citizens. The program incorporated a comprehensive set of integrated and coordinated strategies: suppression, social intervention, provision of opportunities, and community mobilization.

The results of an evaluation of the program were positive (Spergel & Grossman, 1997a, 1997b; Spergel, Grossman, & Wa, 1998; Spergel et al., 2002; Thornberry & Burch, 1997). Favorable outcomes included a lower level of serious gang violence among the targeted gang members than among members of comparable gangs in the area, who had been exposed to a traditional approach based mainly on suppression. Specifically, there were fewer arrests for serious gang crimes (especially aggravated batteries and aggravated assaults) involving members of targeted gangs in comparison with a control group of youth from the same gangs and members of other gangs in Little Village. It appears that the coordinated project approach, using a combination of social interventions involving youth outreach workers and suppression tactics, was more effective with more violent youth, whereas the sole use of youth workers was more effective with less violent youth. Social interventions included counseling, crisis intervention, gang homicide intervention, job placement, and family, school, and special education programs and services. There also was a notable improvement in residents' perceptions of gang crime and police effectiveness in dealing with that crime. "The cohesive team approach was probably at the heart of the project's success in reducing gang crime, particularly gang violence" (Illinois Criminal Justice Information Authority, 1999, p. 4). It also appears that a more comprehensive approach, combining program elements such as social services, crisis intervention, gang suppression, and community involvement, was more effective than a one-dimensional approach (Spergel & Grossman, 1997a, 1997b; Spergel et al., 1998).

Over the past few years, the federal Office of Juvenile Justice and Delinquency Prevention has invested considerable resources in the development and testing of this model, with positive results in a number of sites (National Youth Gang Center, 2001b). (I will describe the results in one of the sites—in Mesa, Arizona—shortly.) A gang problem assessment protocol is available that any community can use to assess the seriousness and scope of the local gang problem and determine needed interventions (National Youth Gang Center, 2001a). The National Youth Gang Center has also prepared a planning and implementation guide to assist communities in developing plans to implement programs based on the comprehensive gang model (National Youth Gang Center, 2001b).

In the remainder of this chapter, I will illustrate the comprehensive gang prevention, intervention, and suppression model by describing a menu of promising and effective interventions.

Prevention

No one has yet discovered any effective strategy for preventing the formation of youth gangs (Howell, 2000). Youth gangs normally develop out of neighborhood-based child and adolescent play groups that eventually take on the characteristic features of youth gangs through conflict with other adolescent groups in the neighborhood and at school. Preventing youths from joining gangs is also a formidable task. Gangs have an enormous appeal to youths who are alienated from key social institutions such as families and schools (Moore, 1998). In addition, children and adolescents are attracted to gangs because other family members or friends are in gangs and encourage them to join; also, because of their desire for protection from personal victimization, and for the fun or social action of gang life (Thornberry et al., 2003). Nevertheless, one delinquency prevention program has proven to be effective in preventing youths from joining gangs. It is an early intervention program that targets boys who engage in problem behaviors in kindergarten. Below, I briefly describe this program and two others that appear to be effective in reducing gang involvement.

The Montreal Preventive Treatment Program was designed to prevent antisocial behavior among boys ages 7 to 9 of low socioeconomic status who had previously displayed disruptive problem behavior in kindergarten (Tremblay, Masse, Pagani, & Vitaro, 1996). This program demonstrated that a combination of parent training and childhood skills development can steer children away from gangs. The training was implemented in small groups consisting of both disruptive and nondisruptive boys; trainers used coaching, peer modeling, self-instruction, reinforcement contingencies, and role playing to build skills. An evaluation of the program showed both short- and long-term gains, including less delinquency, less substance use, and less gang involvement at age 15 (Tremblay et al., 1996). This study shows that prevention in the first window of opportunity—with children who evidence conduct problems as early as kindergarten—can be effective.

Gang Resistance Education and Training (G.R.E.A.T.) is an effective school-based gang prevention program for girls and boys. G.R.E.A.T. is a low-intensity program that is currently delivered to public middle school students in the United States (Esbensen & Osgood, 1999; Esbensen, Osgood, Taylor, Peterson, & Freng, 2001). Nearly 365,000 students received the G.R.E.A.T. curriculum in fiscal year 2002 (Special Agent Dawn F. Abrams, G.R.E.A.T., Bureau of Alcohol, Tobacco and Firearms, personal communication, November 30, 2002). The G.R.E.A.T. curriculum is taught in entire classrooms by uniformed law enforcement officers during a 13-week course. In addition to information on the dangers of gang involvement,

the lesson content places considerable emphasis on cognitive-behavioral training, social skills development, refusal skills training, and conflict resolution skills (more information about the program is available at the G.R.E.A.T Web site, at www.atf. treas.gov/great).

Esbensen, Osgood, et al. (2001) conducted an evaluation of G.R.E.A.T. and found that the program has positive long-term effects. Although the reductions in gang membership and delinquency were not statistically significant, the researchers found a "small but systematic beneficial" program effect (p. 102). The differences between treatment and control groups from the program to postprogram period were statistically significant and in the direction favorable to G.R.E.A.T. on five of the outcome measures: reduced victimization, more negative views about gangs, improved attitudes toward police, more prosocial peers, and less risk seeking (see also Esbensen, 2001).

The Gang Prevention Through Targeted Outreach program developed by the Boys & Girls Clubs of America (BGCA) also appears to be effective in reducing gang involvement (Arbreton & McClanahan, 2002). In this program, youth are identified as being at risk and recruited through direct outreach and referrals from school personnel, social service agencies, and police and probation personnel. Selected youths are recruited into local Boys & Girls Clubs to participate in all aspects of club programming. Boys & Girls Club programs are offered in five core areas: character and leadership development; education and career development; health and life skills; the arts; and sports, fitness, and recreation. The organization's life skills programs are geared toward enhancing communication skills, problem-solving techniques, and decision-making abilities (Esbensen, 2000). An evaluation of the Gang Prevention Through Targeted Outreach program showed decreases in some gang and delinquent behaviors, more positive adult and peer relationships, positive changes in participants' engagement or achievements in school, and increased engagement of participants in productive out-of-school activities (Arbreton & McClanahan, 2002).

Intervention

One study found that a youngster who joins a gang generally begins hanging out with gang members at age 12 or 13, joins the gang at 13 or 14 (from 6 months to a year after first beginning to hang out with members), and is first arrested at age 14 (Huff, 1996, 1998), typically for a property crime. The gang member's initial arrest for a violent crime occurs, on average, from 1½ to 2 years after the peak period of involvement in property crime. Other gang research suggests a much more gradual process of gang affiliation (Curry, Decker, & Egley, 2002; Decker & Van Winkle, 1996; J. A. Miller, 2001; Vigil, 1988). For example, researchers in the Denver longitudinal study observed that at least 2 years elapsed between the time of individuals' trend toward increasing involvement in delinquency and gang initiation (Esbensen & Huizinga, 1993). Regardless of the specific timing, studies suggest that there are three windows of opportunity for intervention with a young gang member. The first such point is the period in which a youngster is socially involved with gang members ("gang associates"; Curry et al., 2002) but is not yet a gang member, the second is at the point of first arrest, and the third is the time between the individual's first arrest for property crime and the beginning of involvement in violent delinquency. Decker and Lauritsen (2002) point out that a fourth unique intervention opportunity may arise when a gang member experiences a violent event (especially victimization), at which point he or she may be motivated to leave the gang.

Based on their Los Angeles studies, Vigil and Yun (2002) recommend that prevention begin in the early childhood years and extend up to age 8 or 9. Interventions, they suggest, should commence during the preteen years, at about ages 9-13, "with youths who are peripherally, but not yet deeply, connected to the streets" (p. 171). They also suggest that suppression strategies should target gang members ages 13-20.

A promising approach to preventing children and adolescents from becoming involved with gang members is to regulate their gang associations (Curry et al., 2000), especially in the "wannabe" stage, as Huff (1996, 1998) suggests. To achieve this goal, a program may need to include interventions that are designed to prevent any kind of delinquent peer associations through increased parental supervision (Walker-Barnes & Mason, 2001a) and parental monitoring of potentially negative peer relationships (Warr, 2002), provided that such interventions are not psychologically manipulative and guilt based (Walker-Barnes & Mason, 2001a). Multisystemic Therapy (Henggeler, 1997b)—a form of therapy, based on a family preservation model, that, among other things, strengthens parental control over children and adolescents—is one of the few approaches that has been shown to reduce delinquent peer group associations (Sutphen, Thyer, & Kurtz, 1995). Parental involvement is a key element of all programs that are successful in

preventing a variety of social and behavioral problems among children and adolescents (Durlak, 1997). Adult mentors also may be effective in helping youths avoid involvement with gangs in the community (Novotney, Mertinko, Lange, & Baker, 2000). Nonfamily adults rarely discourage youths from joining gangs (Maxson et al., 1998); perhaps if mentors do so, their advice may have some influence. It also appears that Boys & Girls Clubs and the G.R.E.A.T. curriculum help discourage youngsters from associating with gang members.

Intervention with youths who already are gang members is a promising strategy for reducing gang involvement and gang-related violence. Four community-based approaches to such intervention appear to be promising. Unfortunately, only one of these has been evaluated.

The BGCA's Gang Intervention Through Targeted Outreach program appears to be effective in separating youths from gangs (Arbreton & McClanahan, 2002). As noted above, the program provides alternatives to the gang lifestyle by "mainstreaming" youth into club programming. In addition, youth selected for this program are recruited to participate in a project that is staffed by BGCA but is run separately from daily club activities (either after typical club hours or on a more one-on-one case management basis). All of the intervention clubs have facilities in the worst gang areas in their communities. In their evaluation of this additional intervention project, Arbreton and McClanahan (2002) found that it had positive results that were similar to outcomes for the Gang Prevention Through Targeted Outreach program summarized above.

Homeboy Industries and Jobs for a Future are two grassroots projects developed by Father Greg Boyle, a Jesuit priest, at the Dolores Mission in the Boyle Heights neighborhood of Los Angeles (Gaouette, 1997). Community residents initially responded to gang violence by establishing an alternative school in 1988. Father Boyle then formed Jobs for a Future, a program that creates jobs for gang members—graffiti removal, landscaping, building a child-care center for the community—and places gang youths in other jobs in the community. Homeboy Industries, an enterprise that merchandises T-shirts and other silk-screened products, successfully employs workers who are members of rival gangs. These jobs provide alternatives to gang life for gang members, an escape from gangs. Gang researchers agree there is no doubt that a shift in income production for gang members from unlawful to lawful activities results in less crime and less serious crime (Fleisher, 1998). There is also research evidence that paid employment reduces recidivism among offenders who are not incarcerated (Lipsey & Wilson, 1998).

Jim Holub, also a Jesuit priest, developed a similar program in Milwaukee called Homeboyz Interactive Inc.; his purpose was to reduce gang violence by providing employment opportunities for gang members. Most of the trainees at Homeboyz Interactive have criminal records, but instead of sharing bunk space in the Milwaukee County House of Corrections, they share computer workstations. The program has designed Web sites for some big-name clients, and more than 50 of its trainees have landed e-commerce jobs in the United States and Mexico.

Violence-Free Zone programs (National Center for Neighborhood Enterprise, 1999) are based on the premise that the breakdown of the family structure is a key risk factor for gang involvement and a major contributor to destructive behavior. In many cases, gang members come from fatherless homes in which their mothers struggle to meet the economic and individual needs of their children and consequently find it difficult to provide their children with necessary guidance as well. Violence-Free Zone implementers fill this void, taking on the role of mentor and engaging in "reparenting"; that is, these adults act as parents, giving youth unconditional love, setting clear standards for behavior, and being available constantly to provide mentoring and support. Violence-Free Zone programs also provide job training and work opportunities for youths to help with their social, personal, and economic development, so that they can make the transition from gang life and criminality to violence-free lives and productive citizenship. Youth who are successful in these programs are given opportunities to collaborate with youth in other communities and cities to develop and expand Violence-Free Zone initiatives.

Communities with serious gang problems should look to the juvenile justice system for early intervention programs that use graduated sanctions in tandem with treatment programs to forestall the progression of young delinquents' careers into serious, violent, and chronic juvenile offending. The 8% Early Intervention Program in Orange County, California, has shown success with potentially serious and violent juvenile offenders, and it may be effective for gang members as well (I describe this program in detail in Chapters 11, 12, and 13). Although the impact of the program specifically for gang members has not yet been evaluated, the program has proved effective in preventing the further development of delinquent careers.

Graduated sanctions are especially important for the case management of chronic, serious (property),

and violent gang members on probation—both for public safety reasons and for the opportunity they provide to control these offenders' behavior and maximize the opportunity for treatment interventions to work. Any juvenile justice system using graduated sanctions should employ risk and needs/strengths assessment instruments to classify offenders at various risk levels (e.g., low, medium, high; examples of appropriate instruments appear in the appendix to this volume). Comprehensive treatment plans should be based on service needs assessments, and a parallel continuum of treatment programs (appropriate for offenders with low, medium, and high treatment needs) should be linked with the sanctions continuum. Periodic needs/strengths assessments should be conducted to measure offenders' progress in relation to their treatment plans. These assessments, along with reassessments of risk, should be used to move offenders up and down the levels of a graduated sanctions system.

Intensive supervision programs (ISPs) are commonly employed with serious, violent, and chronic gang members on probation. Of course, separate ISPs are not set up specifically for gang members. The TARGET program described below is an example of an ISP; in this program, existing probation officers are dedicated to handling clients. The Probation Graduated Sanctions System used in Cuyahoga County, Ohio (described in Chapter 13), is an excellent example of a program that links rehabilitation programs with graduated sanctions. A treatment program for gang members can also be linked with a court graduated sanctions system—such as the ART program described below.

As noted earlier, the point at which a gang member experiences violent victimization presents a unique intervention opportunity. An intervention program based on contact with injured victims in hospital emergency rooms could help to break the cycle of gang violence (Hutson et al., 1995). One such emergency room program, the Partnership for a Safer Cleveland, provides gang recognition seminars for hospital emergency room staff, and when gang-involved youths come into the ER, staff members refer them elsewhere for medical and psychological services (Walker & Schmidt, 1996).

Intervention with gang members who are victims of gang violence can also be accomplished outside hospital emergency rooms. The Child Development–Community Policing (CD–CP) program in New Haven, Connecticut, is an excellent example of one approach (Marans & Berkman, 1997). In this program, police refer victims of violent crimes, including gang members who are victims of gang violence, to the CD–CP program for counseling. The Gang Victim Services Program in Orange County, California, offers a full range of services and multilingual, multicultural support to all victims of gang violence, including gang members (U.S. Department of Justice, 1996). It also is important that programs aimed at intervention with gang victims include procedures for protecting victims and witnesses from gang intimidation; Finn and Healey (1996) detail some of the ways in which programs might accomplish such protection.

Little treatment programming has been developed for gang members in juvenile detention and correctional facilities (Howell, Curry, Pontius, & Roush, 2003). Interpersonal skills training appears promising for improving social skills and reducing anger and, possibly, violence among street gang youth on probation and in institutions (Goldstein, 1993). The Aggression Replacement Training (ART) program has produced impressive results using this approach with gangs in Brooklyn, New York (Goldstein & Glick, 1994; Goldstein, Glick, & Gibbs, 1998). ART also has proved to be cost-effective (Aos, Phipps, Barnoski, & Lieb, 2001). Programs based on the ART model are currently being implemented in probation departments and detention centers in 28 counties throughout the state of Washington, in a number of juvenile institutions in the state of New York, and in the Texas Department of Youth (corrections).

One correctional aftercare program has produced very positive short-term effects for gang members: the Lifeskills '95 program, which was implemented in California's San Bernardino and Riverside Counties (Josi & Sechrest, 1999). This program was designed for high-risk, chronic juvenile offenders released from the California Youth Authority. In addition to reintegrating these youths into communities, the Lifeskills '95 program aimed to reduce their need for gang participation and affiliation as a support mechanism. An evaluation of the program's results found that participating youths were far less likely to have frequent associations with former gang associates than were members of the control group (unfortunately, the evaluation covered a period of only 90 days). In addition, youths assigned to the control group were about twice as likely as program participants to have been arrested, to be unemployed, and to have abused drugs and/or alcohol frequently since their release.

Police Intervention and Suppression

Police youth gang suppression strategies have an ignominious history, beginning with "Operation Hammer," which the Los Angeles Police Department's Community Resources Against Street Hoodlums (CRASH) unit launched in South-Central Los Angeles in 1988 (Klein, 1995). This operation emphasized gang "street sweeps" (Howell, 2000, p. 22; Klein, 1995, pp. 161-165). The CRASH unit, which operated out of the LAPD's Rampart Division, was implicated in a scandalous corruption case in which alleged gang members were killed by police or framed and convicted of crimes they did not commit (Deutsch, 2000; Leinwand, 2000). Fiercely involved in fighting gangs, the police officers in the Rampart CRASH unit came to act like a gang.

Below, I describe how law enforcement and the criminal justice system can help to control gangs and gang members by using more progressive and effective intervention and suppression strategies and tactics. Targeted law enforcement actions can produce positive effects in neighborhoods where gangs are active, creating disincentives for gangs to engage in activities that will call police attention to them (Huff & Shafer, 2002). Community policing is a very promising approach for accomplishing this goal.

Community policing is a very mild form of law enforcement suppression that has grown in use over the past decade. The Columbus (Ohio) Police Department has been a leader in developing the community policing concept, an approach that is featured in a recent chapter written by Huff (a gang researcher involved in the development of the Columbus model) and Shafer (commander of the Strategic Response Bureau of the Columbus Division of Police). Huff and Shafer (2002) detail the underlying philosophy of the Columbus PD's Community-Oriented Policing (COP) program, which is based on earlier program development led by the police commander (Shafer, 1999). The problem-oriented COP program is based on a model that is grounded in three shifts in policing philosophy from traditional to community-oriented policing (Huff & Shafer, 2002, pp. 140-142). First, the police need to enlist community support. They must reach out to engage community groups and neighborhood representatives in a discussion and analysis of the gang problem. Second, the police focus must be shifted from individual gangs and crimes to the neighborhoods. "Shifting the focus to neighborhoods expands the scope of police actions to include the disorder, fear, and declining quality of life that often result from (and help sustain) the presence of gangs" (Huff & Shafer, 2002, p. 141). Third, police must recognize the importance of strategies and tactics other than what the police can provide. As Huff and Shafer (2002) put it, "The police must begin to see themselves as *part* of the solution rather than *the* solution" (p. 141).

To implement the COP program, the Columbus PD created the Strategic Response Bureau (SRB), in which community liaison officers (CLOs) are teamed with investigators and enforcement personnel (Huff & Shafer, 2002). The CLOs work with neighborhood groups to identify and assess problems; information about these problems is then passed on to investigators and street-crime officers. SRB personnel are generally assigned to geographic areas, to permit teams to collaborate on neighborhood-specific problems. The teams place strong emphasis on accurate, timely gang intelligence and on targeting habitual offenders. The SRB recently successfully targeted violent street gangs that were responsible for a large number of gang-related homicides and many other violent crimes (Huff & Shafer, 2002, p. 143). Huff and Shafer note that other COP programs that work—that is, programs based on principles similar to those guiding the Columbus COP program—exist in Dallas, Texas (Fritsch, Caeti, & Taylor, 1999); Chicago, Illinois (Higgins & Coldren, 2000); and Redlands, California (Rich, 1999).

The Tri-Agency Resource Gang Enforcement Team (TARGET) program in Orange County, California, represents a multiagency approach to targeting current gang members with suppression measures while also targeting entire gangs with police suppression. Each team in the TARGET program consists of gang investigators, a probation officer, a deputy district attorney, and a district attorney investigator (Capizzi, Cook, & Schumacher, 1995). This program aims to reduce gang crime through the use of a three-pronged strategy: (a) selective incarceration of the most violent and repeat older gang offenders in the most violent gangs, (b) enforcement of probation controls (graduated sanctions and intensive supervision) on younger, less violent gang offenders, and (c) arrests of gang leaders in "hot spots" of gang activity (Rackauckas, 1999). A major aim of the TARGET program is to reduce gang crime by selectively incarcerating the most violent and repeat gang offenders (based on their criminal records) in the most violent gangs in Orange County (Kent, Donaldson, Wyrick, & Smith, 2000). Once these offenders are identified, they are monitored closely for new offenses and undergo intensive supervision when on probation for violation of probation terms and conditions. Although the recidivism rates of gang members in the program have not been evaluated, the TARGET program has been shown to be successful in producing a sharp increase in the incarceration of gang members and a cumulative 47% decrease in gang crime over a 7-year period (Kent et al., 2000) and in reducing the overall level of gang crime in a targeted hot spot to near zero (Wiebe, 1998).

Perhaps the law enforcement suppression program that has received the most attention in the past few years is the Boston Gun Project/Operation Ceasefire. This program targeted high-rate, gang-involved offenders. It employed a strategy called "pulling levers," which involved "deterring violent behavior by chronic gang offenders by reaching out directly to gangs, setting clear standards for their behavior and backing up that message by 'pulling every lever' legally available when those standards were violated" (Kennedy, 1999, p. 3). As a result of the program, many youthful offenders received long prison sentences that federal statutes enhanced. The "pulling levers" strategy was one of two key components of the Boston Gun Project. The second was the "ceasefire" (suppression of gun use) strategy (for detailed information on the program, see Kennedy et al., 1996). A comparison of Boston's youth violence trends with other cities during the program period suggests that Operation Ceasefire may have been effective in reducing youth homicides, gun assault incidents, and "shots fired" calls for service (Braga, Kennedy, Waring, & Piehl, 2001). However, Boston recently has seen a resurgence of gang violence ("Quelling," 2001), and the program has not been evaluated for recidivism among targeted gang members once they are released from prison.

The results in Boston are typical of suppression efforts; their effectiveness generally is short-lived (Klein, 1995; Papachristos, 2001; Sherman, 1990). In the most detailed study of a suppression effort to date, Papachristos (2001) found that aggressive federal prosecution of members of Chicago's Gangster Disciples had the short-term effect of reducing this gang to a loosely arranged delinquent group in the neighborhood as members aligned themselves with other criminal gangs. The destabilization of the Gangster Disciples created a power void that was filled by competing gangs—mainly the Vice Lords and Latin Kings. Papachristos calls this long-term effect "gang succession" (p. 5). In the long run, it was almost as if nothing had changed, except the clothing of the visible gang members. Clearly, police suppression strategies need to be integrated with prevention and intervention measures if they are to have long-term effectiveness.

Programs are also needed to break the cycle followed by most gang members: moving from communities to detention to corrections and prisons and back into communities (Howell, 2000). Adult prisoners are not likely to receive rehabilitation services or job skills preparation while in prison; moreover, when released, they usually return to communities that are not well prepared to accept them (Travis & Petersilia, 2001). Ex-convicts need marketable job skills and gainful employment opportunities if they are to avoid being tempted to engage in lucrative illegal opportunities such as drug trafficking. Breaking this cycle has become all the more important as states are imprisoning younger and younger offenders who now are returning to the streets at younger ages than in the past. Effective drug treatment programs, along with schooling and legitimate jobs, would also help break the cycle.

A few other criminal justice system gang suppression programs have shown effectiveness in their immediate objectives—the arrest, prosecution, and incarceration of gang members (for descriptions of some of these programs, see Howell, 2000, pp. 21-33). The long-term impacts of such programs on local gang problems and recidivism of targeted individuals are unknown. This is an important issue because of the ineffectiveness of imprisonment (see Chapter 7). In addition, gang-involved inmates often present problems in the communities to which they return. According to 7 out of 10 of the law enforcement agencies responding to the National Youth Gang Survey, gang members returning from prison exacerbate local gang problems. Egley and Arjunan (2002) found that 30% of these agencies reported that gang members returning from prison have greatly contributed to the growth of drug trafficking in their communities, 19% reported that returning members have greatly contributed to an increase in violence among local gangs, and 12% reported that returning members have greatly increased local gang access to weapons. Thus, in order to be effective over the long term, gang suppression strategies need to be linked with rehabilitation programs.

Gang Programs for Girls

Few gang programs have been developed specifically for girls. One major federal program initiative mounted in the 1990s by the Family Youth Services Bureau provided funding for 11 gang prevention programs that exclusively targeted adolescent girls in nine cities (Curry, 1998; Curry & Decker, 1998, pp. 171-172; Moore & Hagedorn, 2001, p. 9). The central theme of the Female Gang Prevention and Intervention Program was drawn from Joan Moore's book *Going Down to the Barrio: Homeboys and Homegirls in Change* (1991), which

documents the long-term negative impacts of gangs on girls. Moore's research led to the development of 11 specialized programs to meet the needs of gang girls; the programs employed a variety of strategies to support at-risk girls and provide them with alternatives to gang involvement. Three of the programs—in Boston, Pueblo, and Seattle—were "held up as models by their respective communities, and all have received national attention" (Curry & Decker, 1998, p. 173; for case studies, see Williams, Cohen, & Curry, 1994). Boston's FORCE program was located in the city's public housing projects and focused on helping girls to build self-esteem through empowerment and assertiveness, cultural awareness, academic support, family involvement, referrals for substance abuse treatment, and community organization initiatives. The program in Pueblo, Colorado, employed a broad prevention strategy and emphasized mentoring, cultural awareness, and conflict resolution. The small program in Seattle served females referred by juvenile courts and stressed gang member counseling, positive peer support, referrals for housing, self-esteem enhancement, cultural awareness, and provision of positive role models.

Few of the prevention and intervention programs reviewed in this chapter have been evaluated specifically for effectiveness with girls. However, the Gang Prevention Through Targeted Outreach program operated by Boys and Girls Clubs of America appears to be equally effective for girls and boys (Arbreton & McClanahan, 2002). Evaluations of the G.R.E.A.T. program have not yet separated program effects for girls from those for boys; however, approximately half of the program sample is female (Esbensen, 2001). In addition, a wide variety of gender-specific services—both inside and outside the juvenile justice system—have been identified for delinquent girls (I describe these in Chapter 13). Researchers need to pay special attention to the effectiveness of youth gang programs for girls as well as for boys in future evaluations of all such programs.

Community leaders should understand that it is important to provide gang prevention and intervention programs for girls for several reasons. First, youth gang membership among girls is much more common today than was the case in the past (Curry, 1998; Moore & Hagedorn, 2001). Nationally, among 10- to 16-year-olds, the male:female ratio among youths who had ever belonged to a gang was 2:1 in 1997 (Snyder & Sickmund, 1999, pp. 58-59). Second, the sexual exploitation of female gang members within gangs should be a serious social concern (Fleisher, 1998; J. A. Miller, 2001; Moore

& Hagedorn, 2001). Third, the levels of violence perpetrated by female gang members warrant intervention. In the 11-city gang study directed by Esbensen mentioned above, 78% of the female gang members (eighth graders) reported involvement in gang fights, 65% reported carrying a weapon, and 39% reported having attacked someone with a weapon (Deschenes & Esbensen, 1999). In another study, 29% of females in the Rochester sample were gang members during the adolescent period, but they accounted for virtually all of the serious delinquencies (88%) and for nearly two-thirds (64%) of all female violent offenses (Thornberry et al., 2003). Fourth, joining a gang is a significant act for an adolescent female, and it often has important negative consequences later in life (Moore & Hagedorn, 2001; Thornberry et al., 2003). Finally, when girls become involved in the juvenile justice system, they are often further victimized. As Acoca (1998b) observes, "The abuses that a majority of girl offenders have experienced in their homes, in their schools, or on the streets often are mirrored and compounded by injuries they receive within the juvenile justice system," in detention centers and juvenile reformatories (p. 562). This implies that communities should place female delinquents in alternative facilities and programs whenever such alternatives are available.

Fleisher (1998) recommends the placement of gang girls in adult-supervised residential centers instead of in subpar detention and correctional facilities. These centers, as Fleisher envisions them, would have three specific objectives: "(1) to shelter and protect girls; (2) to provide education, job training, and job placement; and (3) to ensure a healthy start for gang girls' children" (p. 219; for detailed descriptions of how the centers could be designed to achieve these objectives, see pp. 218-225). These residential centers would be located outside high-crime inner cities but close to high schools, community colleges, and jobs. Such decentralized centers would have advantages for gang girls over traditional centralized service delivery systems in terms of access and needed services. Moreover, their young children would benefit, and this would help to break the cycle of gang involvement within families.

Integrating Comprehensive
Approaches to Prevention,
Intervention, and Suppression of Gang Crime

A variety of interventions that address delinquency as well as gang involvement can be integrated in a comprehensive approach, as illustrated by Illinois's Gang Crime Prevention Center

(GCPC) program. This program integrates five interventions, each of which I describe briefly below (more information about the program is available at the GCPC Web site: www.gcpc.state.il.us).

- The Right Track Truancy Reduction Program focuses on community decision making to address underlying risk factors for truancy by providing support to truant youth and their families while simultaneously holding parents accountable for their children's behavior.
- The Volunteer Mentoring/Tutoring Program provides at-risk elementary school children with opportunities to establish meaningful attachments to positive adult role models in school-based settings.
- The Early Intervention Probation Program (a replication of the 8% Early Intervention Program) intervenes early and intensively with those juvenile delinquents deemed most likely to reoffend at the time of their first court contact.
- The Evening Reporting Center provides a community-based sanction for juvenile offenders deemed likely to reoffend but for whom confinement is considered inappropriate. In this highly structured, supervised environment, youth engage in positive group activities designed to enrich their lives and deter reoffending.
- The Student Covenant for the Future Program provides youth with real hope for their futures as well as the resources and support necessary for them to build good futures. The program helps youth who are facing a combination of academic, social, and economic barriers to pursue higher education and gainful employment. Students who successfully complete 4 years in the program receive $10,000 toward their choice of college educational expenses or vocational training and placement.

All five of these pilot program interventions are currently being evaluated.

As noted previously, a program that integrates several complementary interventions (such as those described above) in a single community is likely to produce a much larger impact than a program that implements a single intervention. From a more general standpoint, a community's efforts to prevent and intervene in gang problems should be integrated within an overall comprehensive approach such as the Comprehensive Strategy for Serious, Violent, and Chronic Juvenile Offenders (Howell, 1995; Wilson & Howell, 1993). The comprehensive gang model (of which the GCPC program is an example) and the Comprehensive Strategy are compatible (Howell, 1998b). Both are based on research-based, data-driven, outcome-focused models. As Figure 5.3 illustrates, gang involvement is one segment in the life course of serious, violent, and chronic juvenile offenders. Thus preventing and controlling gang involvement should be part of a community's continuum of prevention, intervention, and graduated sanctions (see Chapter 12). Integration of the two strategies should produce a more effective approach to dealing with serious, violent, and chronic juvenile offenders than either strategy alone, because of the overlap between these offenders and gang members, as discussed earlier in this chapter.

Both frameworks empower communities to assess their respective problems and determine the solutions they wish to implement, and both guide communities in building programs made up of integrated interventions. By integrating the two frameworks, communities can take advantage of the juvenile justice system improvements that the Comprehensive Strategy generates. In particular, the graduated sanctions component uses risk and needs/strengths assessments as management tools to place offenders on a continuum of sanctions and treatment options, which should enhance program effectiveness by achieving a better match between offender treatment needs and available rehabilitation programs. Communities using the Comprehensive Strategy will benefit, in turn, from the increased control of chronic, violent gang offenders that programs based in the comprehensive gang model can be expected to accomplish.

There is another reason for blending the comprehensive gang model with the Comprehensive Strategy. As Thornberry et al. (2003) suggest, because there are limited numbers of gang prevention and intervention programs that have been proven effective, gang members and other at-risk youths should be steered into the large number of programs that have demonstrated effectiveness in preventing and reducing delinquency (see Chapters 9 and 10). The Comprehensive Strategy provides a framework and tools for accomplishing this (see Chapter 12). Separate rehabilitation programs are not necessarily needed for gang members, because their treatment needs are similar to those of other serious and violent offenders.

Scott Decker and David Curry (2002) made a valiant effort in St. Louis to persuade agencies to integrate programming for gang members and nongang serious, violent, and chronic juvenile offenders by implementing programs based on the comprehensive gang model and the Comprehensive Strategy simultaneously. The St. Louis SafeFutures program identified more than 500 marginally and actively involved gang youths for services. Unfortunately, the juvenile justice, youth services, and community agencies refused to cooperate with one another. At the peak of their collaboration, only one in five project youths received services from multiple agencies.

Summary

Delinquent youth gangs are prevalent in 40% of U.S. cities, suburban counties, and rural areas. Researchers and policy makers need to be careful to ensure that local definitions of youth gangs are adequate to distinguish these groups adequately from other lawful and unlawful youth groups and adult criminal organizations that are not youth gangs.

Recent gang studies have generated a large number of important findings (see Box 5.5). One of these is that youth gangs are a major source of the population of serious, violent, and chronic juvenile offenders. The overlap between gang membership and the worst juvenile offending is substantial. A longitudinal study in Rochester, New York, discovered that two-thirds of the chronic violent juvenile offenders in that study's sample were gang members. Where youth gangs are prevalent, their members account for an overwhelming majority of all serious and violent offenses that adolescents commit.

Gang violence has many sources apart from drug trafficking, which accounts for only a small portion of such violence. Violence is a part of gang members' everyday lives, apart from the gang, in their neighborhoods and families. A great deal of gang violence occurs within gangs, with members assaulting each other. Violence between gangs tends to be episodic, in a pattern of "spurts," or peaks and valleys. Gang violence is contagious; it spreads throughout a gang and, perhaps, from one gang to another in a community or city. As Decker and Van Winkle (1996) note, "It often leads to retaliation and revenge creating a feedback loop where each killing requires a new killing" (p. 186). Gun ownership and gun carrying facilitate involvement in such violence and in a variety of other crimes.

Community-specific strategies for combating youth gangs should be based on detailed assessment of local gang problems. This assessment should be an integral part of each community's larger

Box 5.5

Important Findings From Youth Gang Studies

- The number of jurisdictions reporting youth gang problems peaked in the mid-1990s.
- Gang problems have diminished only in the newer gang problem localities, not across the entire United States.
- Youth gangs are not particularly cohesive groups.
- Few young gang members consider themselves to be "core" members of their gangs.
- Youth gangs are generally not highly organized.
- Many widespread stories about gang activities lack sufficient empirical support; they are apparently no more than urban legends.
- The influence of a gang on a member's level of violence is greater than the influence of other highly delinquent peers.
- The influence of a gang on a member's delinquency and violence is long lasting.
- Gang membership has an important impact on long-term adolescent developmental processes, for boys and girls alike.
- There is a high degree of overlap between gang membership and serious, violent, and chronic juvenile offending. For example, youths commit many more serious and violent acts while they are gang members than they do after they leave a gang, and gang members' violent offense rates are up to seven times higher than those of nongang adolescents.
- Homicide and other violence rates are high in youth gangs.
- When gang members are involved in one form of criminal activity, they are likely to be involved in other types of crimes.
- The connections among gangs, drug trafficking, and violence are weak; most gang violence is related to factors other than drug trafficking.

assessment of its serious, violent, and chronic juvenile delinquency problem wherever youth gang problems exist. The National Youth Gang Center (2001a) has developed a protocol that any community can use to assess its gang problem. Resource materials are also available to assist any community in implementing programs based on the comprehensive gang model (National Youth Gang Center, 2001b).

For optimal effectiveness, a community needs a continuum of prevention, intervention, and suppression programs that parallel the developmental periods from childhood through adolescence. Human services, prevention, and child development agencies should provide programs and services designed to help prevent the onset of conduct problems and child delinquency in the early part of this developmental period. Youth development, prevention, and human service agencies should work with at-risk youth and marginally gang-involved youths. Juvenile justice agencies come into play once youth become involved in delinquency and gangs.

A number of effective and promising prevention, intervention, and suppression programs and strategies are available on the menu of options that

communities should consider in selecting the gang interventions they wish to implement. Communities should avoid the prosecution and incarceration of juvenile youth gang members in the criminal justice system whenever possible, because this strategy carries with it the unintended consequence of exacerbating local gang problems via the return of unrehabilitated gang members upon their release from incarceration.

Gang programs specifically for girls are urgently needed. Few have ever existed. Only one major federal program has ever been created for female gang members, and it no longer exists. Some 20% of the targeted youth in the sites implementing the OJJDP's Comprehensive Gang Prevention, Intervention, and Suppression program are females, but, as Moore and Hagedorn (2001) note, "much more work needs to be done to address the needs of females involved with gangs" (p. 9).

The Comprehensive Gang Prevention, Intervention, and Suppression program holds considerable promise for preventing, controlling, and reducing gang problems. In communities where gang problems exist, programs based on this model should be an integral part of the Comprehensive

Strategy for Serious, Violent, and Chronic Juvenile Offenders. When linked together in a continuum, multiple interventions hold much more promise than piecemeal approaches. Such a continuum enables localities to address multiple risk factors for gang membership and to intervene at different points in individuals' progression from minor misconduct to delinquency, to gang involvement, and to serious, violent, and chronic offender careers. In addition, a combination of prevention, intervention, and suppression approaches can simultaneously intervene with gang members and control gangs as a whole.

Discussion Questions

1. What are some of the important reasons youth gangs are difficult to define?

2. What criteria do you think best describe youth gangs?

3. What are the implications of the year of gang problem onset in a community for the extent and nature of gang problems?

4. How does gang involvement increase the criminal embeddedness of members?

5. How does gang involvement affect long-term adolescent developmental processes?

6. What evidence is there that the connections among gangs, drug trafficking, and violence are weaker than often believed?

7. What are the main contexts in which gang violence occurs? In other words, what is most gang violence all about?

8. What are the main features of the continuum of prevention, intervention, and suppression described in this chapter? Why should programs be located along this continuum?

6

■

RISK AND PROTECTIVE FACTORS
FOR SERIOUS AND VIOLENT DELINQUENCY

In this chapter, I review the research on risk and protective factors for serious and violent juvenile delinquency. Risk factors are indicators of the pathways children and adolescents take to serious, violent, and chronic juvenile delinquency. An understanding of these factors is made possible by research that has identified the major risk factor domains—families, schools, peer groups, communities, and individual characteristics. These are also potential points of intervention with at-risk youth. Thus risk factor research can help policy makers to prioritize intervention targets. Research on protective factors, of which there has been very little, unfortunately, provides guidance on the content of interventions. That is to say, the content of prevention and intervention programs should mirror the factors that research has shown to be relevant.

The chapter begins with an explanation of the risk-protection framework, followed by a review of the major risk and protective factors for serious and violent delinquency. I then summarize the findings of studies of adolescent violence predictors and present a review of childhood risk factors. The chapter then shifts to an examination of other problem behaviors that occur simultaneously with serious and violent offending. The research in this area has focused on the proportion of serious and violent juvenile offenders who also experience drug problems, mental health problems, school problems, and violent victimization.

The Risk-Protection Framework

Risk-focused approaches to the prevention of particular problems were pioneered by public health professionals and have been successful in reducing problems as diverse as cardiovascular disease and traffic-related injuries (Institute of Medicine, 1994). Risk-focused approaches to the prevention of cardiovascular disease seek to convince individuals to reduce identified risk factors in their lives, such as smoking and diets high in fat, while enhancing protective factors, such as regular exercise and balanced diet. Similarly, risk-focused approaches to prevention of other problems aim to interrupt the causal processes that are responsible for producing those problems (Coie et al., 1993; Hawkins, Catalano, & Associates, 1992). Thus risk-focused approaches to the prevention of crime, violence, and substance abuse address factors that increase young people's risk of developing these problems during adolescence and young adulthood (Hawkins, Catalano, & Brewer, 1995).

Risk factors predict increased risk for developing a problem or disorder. Protective factors, on the other hand, are conditions that counter risk factors or increase resistance to them, and thus inhibit the development of problems even in the face of risk exposure. Risk and protective factors predict increased or decreased probability of developing problem behaviors, but, just as actuarial tables do not predict any given individual's life experience, the presence or absence of particular factors does not guarantee the development or lack of development of the problem behaviors. Preventive efforts seek to reduce risk factors and promote protective factors in order to foster healthy development and avert health and behavior problems.

Researchers organize the risk factors for serious and violent delinquency according to five domains (also sometimes called risk factor levels): individual, family, school, peer group, and community. This framework is inspired by developmental psychologist Urie Bronfenbrenner's (1979) conceptualization of the different spheres of influence that affect a child's behavior, such as relations in the family, the peer group, and schools. Indeed, research shows that risk and protective factors function as predictors of violence, crime, and substance abuse at different points, as affected by risk factors in the respective spheres of influence. If risk reduction efforts address risk and protective factors at or slightly before the developmental points at which they begin to predict later delinquency or violence, it is likely they will be effective (Hawkins, Catalano, & Brewer, 1995). Research completed over the past 35 years has identified risk factors for delinquency and violence as well as protective factors that buffer against the effects of exposure to risk factors and inhibit the development of these health and behavior problems.

It is widely recognized that most problem behaviors have multiple determinants. That is, there can be many explanations for child and adolescent problems, none of which, by itself, is a complete explanation. As Durlak (1998) notes, "Rather than search for a single explanation for a particular negative outcome, it is deemed more helpful to identify multiple factors influencing adjustment and to understand the different negative developmental trajectories that can occur" (p. 512). Explaining why specific behaviors occur is very difficult, because numerous factors are involved and social interactions shape behaviors and problems over time (Kirby & Fraser, 1997).

Another important point about the dynamics of risk factors is that they are often highly interrelated, occurring together or clustering to produce added risk. Risk factors function in a cumulative fashion; that is, the greater number of risk factors, the greater the likelihood of a negative outcome. There also is evidence that problem behaviors caused by risk factors tend to cluster together. For example, adolescent delinquency and violence cluster with other adolescent problems, such as drug abuse, teen pregnancy, and school misbehavior and dropout (Hawkins, Catalano, & Miller, 1992). Figure 6.1 illustrates these principles, showing how several problem behaviors share common risk factors in the individual/peer group, school, family, and community domains. This figure also shows that multiple risk factors contribute to each problem behavior. Bullet marks in the figure denote risk factors that have been substantiated as correlates of the various problem behaviors in longitudinal studies conducted in Europe, North America, and New Zealand. The presence of each additional risk factor increases the probability of later delinquency and

crime in young adulthood (Hawkins, 1999, p. 446). Many of these factors have also been found to increase the probability of substance abuse, teenage pregnancy, and school dropout.

With the development of the criminal career paradigm in the 1970s and 1980s (see Chapter 4), researchers accumulated knowledge on the small fraction of offenders who commit a large number of offenses and have long criminal careers. This progress stimulated interest on the part of policy makers in identifying individuals with the potential to become such offenders and developing programs to prevent their likely delinquent career development. As Farrington (2000) explains, "In turn, this encouraged scholars and practitioners to search for risk and protective factors that could be changed by interventions, and hence encouraged the adoption of the risk factor prevention paradigm in the 1990s" (pp. 2-3). The risk factor prevention paradigm has been adopted for the study of delinquency in the United States (Kraemer et al., 1997; Loeber & Farrington, 1998c), and in the United Kingdom, Australia, Sweden, and the Netherlands (Farrington, 2000).

As Farrington (2000) has noted, the risk factor prevention paradigm "brought enormous benefits to criminology in the 1990s" (p. 16). He recounts how the paradigm revolutionized prevention programming, once juvenile delinquency researchers (Hawkins, Catalano, & Associates, 1992) and other preventionists imported this model into the crime and delinquency fields from medicine and public health (Mercy & O'Carroll, 1988). Prior to this development, there was little contact between criminologists and policy makers or practitioners who were implementing prevention programs.

Risk factors are those elements in an individual's life that increase his or her vulnerability to negative developmental outcomes and also increase the probability of maintenance of a problem condition or digression to a more serious state (for definitions of *risk factors* and several other important terms associated with the risk-protection framework, see Box 6.1).

As noted above, risk factors perform in a cumulative fashion; they also interact in a negative manner, as illustrated by the findings of a study conducted by Thornberry, Huizinga, and Loeber (1995). These researchers found that two risk factors—delinquency involvement and low family attachment—interact negatively (see Jang & Smith, 1997). Youth in their sample who had low levels of attachment to their families had higher rates of subsequent delinquency. And involvement in delinquency, in turn, led to subsequent reductions in attachment to parents. In other words, delinquency makes

Risk Factors

Adolescent Problem Behaviors

Risk Factors	Substance Abuse	Delinquency	Teen Pregnancy	School Drop-Out	Violence
Community					
Availability of Drugs	●				●
Availability of Firearms		●			●
Community Laws and Norms Favorable toward Drug Use, Firearms and Crime	●	●			●
Media Portrayals of Violence					●
Transitions and Mobility	●	●		●	
Low Neighborhood Attachment and Community Disorganization	●	●			●
Extreme Economic Deprivation	●	●	●	●	●
Family					
Family History of the Problem Behavior	●	●	●	●	●
Family Management Problems	●	●	●	●	●
Family Conflict	●	●	●	●	●
Favorable Parental Attitudes and Involvement in the Problem Behavior	●	●			●
School					
Academic Failure Beginning in Late Elementary School	●	●	●	●	●
Lack of Commitment to School	●	●	●	●	●
Peer and Individual					
Early and Persistent Antisocial Behavior	●	●	●	●	●
Rebelliousness	●	●		●	
Friends Who Engage in the Problem Behavior	●	●	●	●	●
Favorable Attitudes Toward the Problem Behavior	●	●	●	●	
Early Initiation of the Problem Behavior	●	●	●	●	●
Constitutional Factors	●	●			●

Figure 6.1   Risk Factors for Adolescent Problem Behaviors

SOURCE: Unpublished figure revised from "Preventing Crime and Violence Through Communities That Care," by J. D. Hawkins, 1999, *European Journal on Crime Policy and Research, 7,* p. 446. © 2002 Channing Bete Company, Inc. All rights reserved. Reproduced with permission of the publisher.

family life worse, which increases delinquency, which makes family life worse, and so on. A key element in this reciprocal process is the negative effect of delinquent behavior on parents (Stewart, Simons, Conger, & Scaramella, 2002), which can be profound (Ambert, 1999). These interactive and reciprocal effects of risk factors highlight the importance of addressing child and parent problem behaviors simultaneously, through multimodal programs.

Protective Factors

Kirby and Fraser (1997, p. 18) suggest that protective factors operate in three ways. First, they may serve to buffer risk factors, providing a cushion

---

Box 6.1
Important Terms Associated With the Risk-Protection Framework

---

Risk Factors

Risk factors may be defined generally as "individual or environmental hazards that increase an individual's vulnerability to negative developmental outcomes" (Small & Luster, 1994, p. 182), or as "any influences that increase the probability of onset, digression to a more serious state, or maintenance of a problem condition" (Kirby & Fraser, 1997, pp. 10-11). Three major types of risk factors have been identified (Kraemer et al., 1997): Risk factors that occur concurrently with problem behaviors are *correlates*; those that precede problem behaviors are called *predictive* risk factors; and risk factors that can be manipulated through experimentation or intervention and have been shown to lead to changes in behavior problems are called *causal* factors. Factors that are correlates are also sometimes called *markers*. Male gender is an example; it is a delinquency correlate or marker for other risk factors that cause or increase the risk of delinquency.

Protective Factors

Kirby and Fraser (1997) define protective factors as "the internal and external forces that help children resist or ameliorate risk" (p. 16). Garmezy (1985) describes three broad categories of protective factors:

- *Dispositional attributes:* temperamental factors, social orientation and responsiveness to change, cognitive abilities, and coping skills
- *Family milieu:* a positive relationship with at least one parent, cohesion, warmth, harmony, and the absence of neglect
- *Attributes of the extrafamilial environment:* availability of external resources and extended social supports

Some researchers call this last category *social capital* (e.g., Coleman 1988).

Resilience

Resilience is the ability to survive adverse conditions; researchers use this term to describe children who achieve positive outcomes in the face of considerable risks (Werner & Smith, 1992). Kirby and Fraser (1997, p. 14) describe three types of resilience: "overcoming the odds" (that is, achieving positive outcomes despite high-risk status), "sustained competence under stress," and "recovery from trauma." In applications within the public health model, the type of resilience referred to as "overcoming the odds" is most common.

---

against negative effects; social support is believed to operate this way. Second, protective factors may interrupt the causal processes through which risk factors operate. For example, an intervention that reduces family conflict may interrupt a chain of risks connecting the family environment with negative peer affiliations and drug use. Third, protective factors may operate by preventing the initial occurrence of a risk factor, such as child abuse. Positive temperamental characteristics, such as being easy to soothe and good-natured, may protect children from abuse in the first instance by

TABLE 6.1   Protective Factors for Eight Major Outcomes

Level of Analysis	Behavior Problems	School Failure	Poor Physical Health	Physical Injury	Physical Abuse	Pregnancy	Drug Use	AIDS
Community								
Social norms	X	X	X	X	X	X	X	X
Effective social policies	X	X	X	X	X	X	X	X
School								
High-quality schools	X	X				X	X	X
Peer								
Positive peer modeling	X	X		X		X	X	X
Family								
Good parent-child relations	X	X	X	X	X	X	X	X
Individual								
Personal and social skills	X	X	X	X	X	X	X	X
Self-efficacy	X	X				X	X	X
Other								
Social support[a]	X	X	X	X	X	X	X	X

SOURCE: "Common Risk and Protective Factors in Successful Prevention Programs," by J. A. Durlak, 1998, *American Journal of Orthopsychiatry, 68,* p. 516. ©1998 by American Journal of Orthopsychiatry. Reprinted with permission.
a. Social support can occur at all levels and help children directly or indirectly by helping parents, peers, and teachers.

enabling them to elicit positive responses from caregivers. Research is needed to identify protective factors that operate in these respective ways.

Table 6.1, which is reprinted from an article by Durlak (1998), shows protective factors for eight major child and adolescent outcomes (biological factors are excluded). The studies that Durlak reviewed suggest that all of the listed protective factors are relevant for behavior problems, school failure, poor physical health, physical injury, physical abuse, pregnancy, drug use, and acquired immune deficiency syndrome (AIDS). Each of these protective factors is worthy of further study. Note also that many of the same factors provide protection against all of the negative outcomes. Durlak suggests that self-efficacy, a good parent-child relationship, and social support from helping parents, peers, and teachers may be the most important protective factors against delinquency and other problem behaviors.

The proven-effective Seattle social development model incorporates the following protective factors for delinquency (Hawkins, 1999, p. 445):

- Positive bonding relationships with family members, teachers, or other adults
- Healthy beliefs and clear standards, including clear expectations in family, school, and neighborhood that criminal behavior is not acceptable
- Opportunities for prosocial involvement in family, school, and community
- Competencies or skills

Box 6.2 lists additional protective factors against delinquency and other problem behaviors that are supported by the research evidence. It is noteworthy that most of the listed protective factors have been demonstrated to be effective in preventing serious, violent, and chronic delinquency.

Others have emphasized the importance of social support. Psychologists Cairns and Cairns (1994) use the term *lifelines* to describe the supports that promote success in living despite the odds against it. They identify the following as the main lifelines in the context of protection against

Box 6.2
*Research-Supported Protective Factors Against Delinquency
and Other Problem Behaviors*

Individual
   High IQ (antisocial behavior)*
   Intolerant attitude toward deviance (violence, problem behavior)*
   Positive social orientation (antisocial behavior)*
   High accountability (persistent serious delinquency)**
   Ability to feel guilt (persistent serious delinquency)**
   Trustworthiness (persistent serious delinquency)**

Family
   Good relationships with parents (persistent serious delinquency)**
   Good family communication (persistent serious delinquency)**

School
   Positive commitment to school (violence, problem behavior)*
   Strong school motivation (persistent serious delinquency)**
   Academic achievement (persistent serious delinquency)**
   Positive attitude toward school (persistent serious delinquency)**

Peer Group
   Nondelinquent friends (persistent serious delinquency)**

Community
   Nondisadvantaged neighborhood (persistent serious delinquency)**
   Low neighborhood crime (persistent serious delinquency)**

NOTE: The kinds of delinquent behaviors (or general antisocial behaviors) against which the researched factors provide protection are shown in parentheses.
*U.S. Department of Health and Human Services (2001).
**Stouthamer-Loeber, Loeber, Wei, Farrington, and Wikstrom (2002). The sample in this research consisted of boys only.

adolescent problem behaviors: schools and mentors, social networks and friendships, families and neighborhoods, ethnicity and social class, individual characteristics, and new opportunities for living (pp. 258-261).

Research to date has not adequately considered other protective factors. Religiosity is a good example. Unfortunately, research on the effects of religion as a protective factor against delinquency has been very sparse (Johnson, Li, Larson, & McCullough, 2000). Some research has confirmed its importance, but suggests that the effect of religiosity may be indirect, operating through other variables such as conventional values, delinquent peers, and delinquent values (Chard-Wierschem, 1998). One major problem with this line of research is that studies typically measure religiosity in terms

of church attendance, which is not a good indicator of religiosity (Benda, 2002). The fact that a person attends church does not ensure that he or she accepts or applies key conceptual features of religion— values, beliefs, and spiritual aspects—in his or her life. The few well-designed studies that have been conducted on this topic have shown that religiosity is inversely related to delinquency (Chard-Wierschem, 1998; Jang & Johnson, 2001; Johnson et al., 2000), thus future research concerning protective factors and future enhancement initiatives should consider religiosity to be an important element.

Resilient youths overcome the odds and avoid significant involvement in delinquency in the face of considerable risk (see Box 6.1). In discussing children exposed to risk factors, Kirby and Fraser (1997) have noted: "Curiously, researchers consistently found that some children who faced stressful, high-risk situations fared well in life. . . . only about one-third of any population of at-risk children experiences a negative outcome; two-thirds appear to survive risk experiences without major developmental disruptions" (pp. 13-14). However, the proportions of youth who are resilient in extremely high-risk areas appear to be much lower than Kirby and Fraser's estimate. In a Washington, D.C., study, Chaiken (2000) found that less than 20% of a randomly selected sample of boys in census tracts with the highest rates of juvenile violence reported committing no delinquent or criminal offenses. Still, almost one in five was "resilient." This study raises an important issue: Why are some persons resilient? What protective factors serve to immunize them against risk and increase their resilience? More to the point, how do most juveniles avoid delinquency and violence in the face of seemingly overwhelming odds? The findings from two studies provide partial answers to these questions.

Problem behaviors normally develop in individuals who have a preponderance of risk factors over protective factors (Browning & Huizinga, 1999; Thornberry et al., 1995, pp. 230-232), for persistent serious delinquents (Stouthamer-Loeber et al., 2002), and even for child delinquents (Loeber & Farrington, 2001a, 2001c). However, in extremely high-risk cases, individuals need more than a simple majority of protective factors to overcome multiple risk factors (Browning & Huizinga, 1999; Smith, Lizotte, Thornberry, & Krohn, 1995). Moreover, exposure to risk domains in the relative absence of protective domains "dramatically increases the risk of later persistent serious offending" (Stouthamer-Loeber et al., 2002, p. 120).

In the first of two studies on this issue, conducted in Rochester, New York, 12 school, family, and peer protective factors were identified that buffer the effects of risk factors (Smith et al., 1995). The analysis focused on high-risk youth, those who had five or more risk factors for serious and violent delinquency. The risk factors, measured early in the children's lives, were low parental education, parental unemployment, family receipt of welfare, teenage motherhood, frequent family moves, drug-problem parents, criminogenic parents, child maltreatment, and placement of the child outside the family. Protective family factors were high levels of parental supervision and attachment; educational factors were reading ability, mathematics skills, commitment to school, doing well in school, aspirations and expectations to go to college, and parents' expectation for the child to go to college; and peer factors were association with conventional peers

and peers who were approved by the child's parents. In addition, an individual characteristic, self-esteem, was important. The main protective factors were good school performance, good parental supervision and attachment, and conventional peers (Smith et al., 1995, p. 232).

In the short run, even during the peak age of delinquency involvement, protective factors did a very good job of insulating high-risk youth—82% of the youth who had nine or more protective factors were resilient at ages 13-14 (Thornberry et al., 1995, pp. 230-232). The more protective factors youths had, the more resilient they were. The most salient protective factors for delinquency were school factors, followed by family factors and peer factors. But the positive effects did not enable the youngsters to maintain resilience for long. By ages 15-17, high-risk youth with numerous protective factors were no more likely to be resilient and to avoid delinquency than youth with fewer protective factors.

The second study, part of the Denver Youth Survey, identified key protective factors against serious delinquency; the findings also serve to illustrate the relationship between risk factors and protective factors (Browning and Huizinga, 1999). The strongest protective factors were having conventional friends, having a stable family and good parental monitoring, having positive expectations for the future, and not having delinquent friends. When the number of risk factors exceeded the number of protective factors, the chance of a successful adolescence was very small. Indeed, the chance of a successful adolescence was not high until the number of protective factors far exceeded the number of risk factors. The researchers defined a "successful adolescence" as one with minimal involvement in serious delinquency, minimal problems resulting from drug use, age-appropriate grade in school or graduation from high school, and good self-esteem/self-efficacy.

Research on protective factors has been slower to develop than research on risk factors, in part because of conceptual issues. Factors typically are designated as either "risk" or "protective"; however, some factors may have risk effects but no protective effects, and other factors may have both (Stouthamer-Loeber et al., 1993, 2002). A protective factor may be the opposite of a particular risk factor; for example, low parental supervision is a risk factor, and high parental supervision is a protective factor. Other protective factors may reside in mental (e.g., cognitive ability) and social processes (e.g., self-improvement or self-efficacy initiatives) that are not linked to risk factors (Rutter, Giller, &

Box 6.3
The Failure of Schools*

The learning problems of large proportions of students in the United States are testament to the failures of schools to educate young people properly. The annual high school dropout rate is 25%, and dropout rates are far higher for certain groups in specific locales—up to 60% for minority populations in some inner-city schools. In these areas, as much as 40% of minority youth may be functionally illiterate. About one in five students repeats at least one grade between kindergarten and eighth grade. More than 80% of students in fourth, tenth, and twelfth grades demonstrate less than adequate mathematical achievement, and half of 17-year-olds cannot perform moderately complex mathematical procedures that are commonly taught in middle schools. Some 80% are unable to summarize adequately the main point of a newspaper article or correctly calculate the change from a restaurant bill. Almost half of 13-year-olds do not understand basic scientific principles. The average writing ability of fourth and eighth graders is below the minimal competency level.

SOURCE: Durlak (1997, pp. 55-56).
*It is not my intention to imply here that schools are solely responsible for the failures of students. There are many other impediments to learning, including learning problems, health and mental health problems, lack of community support for schools, unsafe communities, lack of parental support and guidance, and the failure of parents to prepare children to enter school.

Hagell, 1998, p. 211). There also is some evidence that risk and protective effects may change during development (Stouthamer-Loeber et al., 2002). The researchers in the Pittsburgh Youth Study (Stouthamer-Loeber et al., 1993, 2002) are conducting ingenious studies of risk and "promotive" (i.e., protective) factors to explore the relative influences of risk and protective factor domains (rather than single factors) on delinquency. In this longitudinal study, Stouthamer-Loeber et al. (2002, pp. 116-117) have identified numerous protective factors for persistent serious delinquency. The factors with odds ratios greater than three are as follows: accountability, trustworthiness, ability to feel guilt, school motivation, relationships with parents, family communication, and neighborhood characteristics.

A Developmental Theory of Risk and Protection

Organizing risk factors into a sequential causal chain is problematic, because theorists and researchers disagree in this area. We can say with certainty that some risk factors are more important than others at different points as the childhood/adolescent developmental process unfolds. It is possible to organize risk factors in a causal model to explain theoretically how they operate.

The social development model (SDM) is an excellent example. Catalano and Hawkins (1996) organize their SDM (Hawkins & Weis, 1985) in relation to four developmental life-course stages: preschool, elementary school, middle school, and high school. These are distinct developmental periods organized by different socialization environments and developmentally appropriate processes that may influence youth toward either prosocial or antisocial behavior. At each stage, the behavior of youth is determined largely by a preponderance of prosocial or antisocial influences. As the social development processes begin to unfold in the preschool period, the family is of primary importance as a socializing unit, thus the constellation of family risk factors is of central importance. During the elementary school period, the school joins the family as an important socializing environment, hence this set of risk factors plays a central role. Environmental constraints begin to come into play during this period, including school policies and legal codes. Peer-related influences and risk factors emerge toward the end. By the time young people enter high school, many of the risk and protective factors for drug use and delinquency have been established. Catalano and Hawkins's theory emphasizes factors related to the maintenance of prosocial or antisocial behaviors during the high school period.

One process for building protection from risk factors is to build bonds to a prosocial unit, such as adults and nondelinquent (prosocial) peer groups who hold healthy beliefs and clear standards for behavior (Catalano & Hawkins, 1996). Hawkins, Catalano, and Brewer (1995, p. 51) describe three conditions that must be met in order for this protection process to be effective. First, children must be provided with meaningful, challenging opportunities to contribute to their families, schools, peers, and communities; this helps make them feel responsible and significant. Second, children must be taught the skills they need to take advantage of the opportunities they are provided. If they do not have the skills necessary to be successful, they will experience frustration and/or failure. Finally, children must receive recognition for their efforts; such acknowledgment gives them the incentive to continue to contribute and reinforces their skillful performance. Individual protective factors affect a child's ability to perceive opportunities, develop skills, and perceive recognition. For example, if a child has a positive social orientation, he or she is more likely to see a child-care setting as an opportunity to make new friends. A child with high intelligence may have an easier time learning to read in the classroom of a mediocre teacher than other children. These processes are illustrated in Figure 6.2, which displays Hawkins and Catalano's (1993) social development strategy.

Catalano and Hawkins's (1996) developmental model explains the reciprocal relationships among risk and protective factors across developmental periods: "If the four [periods] are laid out end to end, pro-social and antisocial influences from one period affect variables at the beginning of the causal chain in the next. In this sense, each sub-model is a phase or period, whose outcomes affect the levels of the beginning variables in the next phase or period" (p. 178). For example, children who engage in aggressive behavior in the preschool period will be less likely to perceive new encounters in the elementary period as opportunities for prosocial bonding. Transitions from one developmental period to the next "present opportunities to change behavior as old conditions of social life are replaced by new ones. These are times when the new conditions, rules, and structures are not yet clear, and the applicability of the old conditions, rules, and structures is diminished" (Catalano & Hawkins, 1996, p. 179). These transition periods present opportunities for negative influences toward delinquency.

This theoretical model illustrates very well how risk and protective factors influence behavior over the adolescent period. Indeed, it is a valid theory, having been demonstrated to explain drug use (Catalano, Kosterman, Hawkins, & Newcomb,

1996) and delinquency and violence (Herrenkohl, Huang, et al., 2001; Huang, Kosterman, Catalano, Hawkins, & Abbott, 2001).

Risk Factors for Delinquency and Violence

Figure 6.1 shows the major risk factors for adolescent violence and other problem behaviors. As noted previously, these risk factors are organized in five domains: community, family, school, peer group, and individual. My aim in this section, in addition to providing an update on important risk factors, is to familiarize readers with the contexts within which risk factors operate. Thus it is necessary to consider the relationship of these risk factors to delinquency in general and to serious delinquency as well as to violence. I highlight new research in each risk factor domain below.

Community Level

The assumption that community factors have an influence on delinquent and violent behavior stems from the common belief that offenses "arise from the interaction between an individual, with a certain antisocial tendency or crime potential, and the environment, which provides criminal opportunities" (Farrington, 1993a, p. 8). It is well-known that individual delinquency prevalence rates vary among communities or neighborhoods (Curry & Spergel, 1988; Lauritsen & White, 2001; Loeber & Wikstrom, 1993; Shannon, 1988, 1991) and that these rates are linked to community characteristics (Bursik & Grasmick, 1993, pp. 24-59; Curry & Spergel, 1988; Sampson & Laub, 1994; Shannon, 1988, 1991; Shaw & McKay, 1969). As Figure 6.1 shows, the major community risk factors for violence are availability of drugs; availability of firearms; community laws and norms favorable toward drug use, firearms, and crime; media portrayals of violence; transitions and mobility; low neighborhood attachment and community organization; and extreme economic deprivation (Hawkins, 1999; Hawkins, Catalano, & Miller, 1992).

Media portrayals of violence have been linked to real-world violence mainly through research on children's high levels of exposure to television violence (Huesmann & Miller, 1994). In the definitive study on this topic, Eron and Huesmann (1987) found that children exposed to high levels of television violence at age 8 years were more likely to behave aggressively at that age and subsequently to age 30, as measured by adult convictions for serious

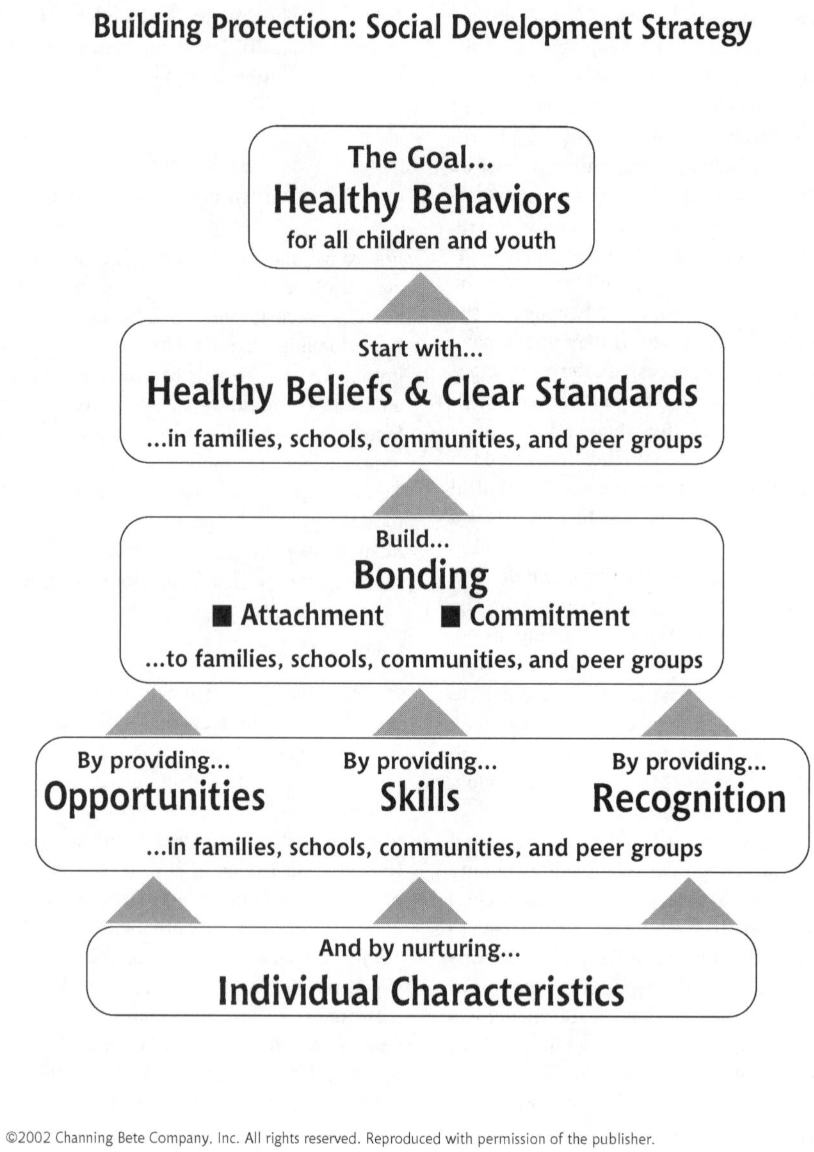
Building Protection: Social Development Strategy
The Goal...
Healthy Behaviors
for all children and youth
Start with...
Healthy Beliefs & Clear Standards
...in families, schools, communities, and peer groups
Build...
Bonding
■ Attachment ■ Commitment
...to families, schools, communities, and peer groups
By providing...
Opportunities
By providing...
Skills
By providing...
Recognition
...in families, schools, communities, and peer groups
And by nurturing...
Individual Characteristics
©2002 Channing Bete Company, Inc. All rights reserved. Reproduced with permission of the publisher.

Figure 6.2 Building Protection: Social Development Strategy

SOURCE: Unpublished figure revised from "Preventing Crime and Violence Through Communities That Care," by J. D. Hawkins, 1999, *European Journal on Crime Policy and Research, 7,* p. 449. © 2002 Channing Bete Company, Inc. All rights reserved. Reproduced with permission of the publisher.

crimes. Violent tendencies were also passed on to the children of those who themselves frequently watched violence on television and exhibited aggression.

Criminogenic neighborhoods are a major risk factor for serious and violent offending, although a substantial proportion of adolescents repeatedly commit violent acts even in neighborhoods where there is a relatively low level of disadvantage (Beyers, Loeber, Wikstrom, et al., 2001). In an examination of Pittsburgh Youth Study data on boys' progression in individual pathways to crime in different types of neighborhoods, Loeber and Wikstrom (1993) found neighborhood differences in the prevalence of boys' involvement in overt and covert behaviors, and in their progression in pathways to serious and violent offending: "Boys living in low socioeconomic neighborhoods tended to advance further into a pathway than boys living in high socioeconomic neighborhoods" (p. 200). As will be seen later in this chapter, a Seattle study found that when interviewed adolescents knew adults who were involved in criminal activities, they were significantly more likely to self-report later involvement in violence. More research is needed on the influence of adult criminal role models.

A key question concerns the effects of bad neighborhoods on adolescents with different risk and protection profiles. In an investigation of this relationship, Wikstrom and Loeber (2000) found that boys with a high number of risk factors were involved in serious offending regardless of the socioeconomic characteristics of their neighborhoods. However, juveniles in more disadvantaged neighborhoods tended to offend more than others and were more likely to engage in serious delinquency. Wikstrom and Loeber conclude, "Thus, the findings suggest that there is a significant direct effect of neighborhood disadvantage on well-adjusted children influencing them to become involved in serious offending as they reach adolescence" (pp. 1133-1134). This could well be explained by the greater prevalence of criminal opportunities in disadvantaged neighborhoods, including gang presence (Curry & Spergel, 1992); as noted in Chapter 5, gangs are more attractive to youngsters who feel unsafe in their neighborhoods (Kosterman et al., 1996).

The implication of the studies cited above is that violence prevention programs should target disadvantaged neighborhoods, not minority groups (Lauritsen & White, 2001). It also appears that bad neighborhoods have negative effects on well-adjusted youths as well as on high-risk youths.

Family Level

As Figure 6.1 shows, the major family risk factors that predict violence among adolescents are family history of the problem behavior (e.g., drug and alcohol abuse); family management problems, such as poor supervision of children; family conflict; and favorable parental attitudes and involvement in the problem behavior (e.g., parental criminality). (For a comprehensive meta-analysis of family features as related to problem behavior, aggression, criminal, and violent behavior, see Derzon & Lipsey, 1999).

Serious family problems greatly increase the risk of serious and violent delinquency involvement among adolescents. Researchers in the Rochester Youth Development Study have examined the negative impact of three major categories of family problems: multiple family problems, child abuse (also called child maltreatment), and family violence.

First, Smith et al. (1995) found that children in families with multiple problems are at a much greater risk of later involvement in serious and violent delinquency. The prevalence of serious and violent delinquency is three times higher among children experiencing five or more family-related risk factors than among children who experience none of the risks. The risk factors that Smith and her colleagues identified are as follows: low parental education, parental unemployment, family receipt of welfare, the respondent's mother having her first child before age 18, moving five or more times before the child was age 12, family members experiencing trouble with drugs, family members experiencing trouble with the law, an official record of child abuse or maltreatment, and placement of the child in care outside of the family. More than one-third of the high-risk youth (those who were exposed to five or more of these risk factors) later self-reported involvement in serious and violent delinquency.

Second, Smith and Thornberry (1995) conducted further analyses of the relationship between child maltreatment and subsequent delinquency. They found that a history of childhood maltreatment significantly increases the likelihood of later self-reported juvenile involvement in moderately serious, serious, and violent delinquency (but not minor delinquency). Maltreatment also increased significantly the child's chances of being arrested and the frequency of arrests. Both of these findings stood up when the researchers controlled for gender, race/ethnicity, social class, family structure, and mobility. Although the most egregiously maltreated youngsters (measured by frequency, severity, duration, and variety of maltreatment) exhibited the highest delinquency rates, the differences in delinquency involvement between the most severely maltreated children and others were not large. This finding led Smith and Thornberry to conclude that "having a history of childhood maltreatment serious enough to warrant official intervention by child protective services is a significant risk factor for later involvement in serious delinquency" (p. 469). It is important to note that Smith and Thornberry defined "maltreatment" very broadly, to include physical abuse, sexual abuse, emotional maltreatment, moral/legal maltreatment, educational maltreatment, physical neglect, and lack of supervision.

Other studies have shown the link between physical abuse and neglect in childhood and later violence. In a study of boys, Stouthamer-Loeber, Loeber, Homish, and Wei (2001) found that such maltreatment doubled the odds of violent behavior by age 18. In a study using official records, Widom and Maxfield (2001) found that for girls, but not for boys, abuse and neglect in childhood is a risk factor for violent arrests as juveniles and adults. However, it may be that girls' problems are better concealed from authorities. Nevertheless, about 8% of the abused and neglected girls in this sample became high-rate chronic offenders who persisted in their offending into adulthood (Richie, Tsenin, & Widom, 2000, p. 30).

Finally, the Rochester researchers found that children who experienced multiple forms of family violence in the home (child abuse, spouse abuse, and family conflict) were twice as likely to commit violent acts themselves at some later point (Thornberry, 1994). Among youths in nonviolent families, 38% reported involvement in violent delinquency. The proportion increased to 60% for youths who experienced one form of violence, to 73% for those exposed to two forms of violence, and to 78% for adolescents exposed to all three types of family violence. As many as 3.3 million children are estimated to witness spouse abuse each year in the United States, including fatal assaults with guns and/or knives as well as hitting and slapping (Osofsky & Fenichel, 1994).

Previous studies that measured only official delinquency have not shown as strong a connection to violence as that found in the self-report measures in the Rochester study (for a discussion of previous studies, see Smith & Thornberry, 1995, pp. 452-455). In a study using official records, Widom (1992) found that abuse and neglect during childhood increases the likelihood of an individual's arrest as a juvenile by 53%, arrest as an adult by 38%, and the likelihood of committing a violent crime by 38%. In a recent follow-up study examining arrest records to age 32.5, Widom and Maxfield (2001) found that, on average, those who had been abused or neglected as children were more likely to be arrested as juveniles (27% versus 17%), as adults (42% versus 33%), and for violent crimes (18% versus 14%). Interestingly, for females, but not males, abuse and neglect in childhood was a risk factor for violent arrests as juveniles and adults.

School Level

Several researchers have reviewed studies regarding school risk factors for delinquency (Gottfredson, 1981; Hawkins, Doueck, & Lishner, 1988; Hawkins & Lishner, 1987; Maguin &

Loeber, 1996; Silberberg & Silberberg, 1971). Maguin and Loeber (1996) conducted a meta-analysis of longitudinal and experimental studies and found poor academic performance to be related not only to the prevalence and onset of delinquency, but also to escalation in the frequency and seriousness of offending. Conversely, they found better academic performance to be related to desistance from offending. More specifically, they found an incremental effect: The poorer the academic performance, the higher the delinquency. Maguin and Loeber (1996, pp. 246-247) estimate that the odds of delinquency involvement are about twice as high among students with low academic performance as they are among those with high academic performance. Moreover, the studies that these researchers reviewed suggest that lower levels of academic performance are linked to a higher frequency of offenses, more serious offenses, and more violent offenses. They also found some evidence that low academic performance is related to early onset of offending. All of these findings were consistently stronger for males than for females and for white youths than for black youngsters.

The major school risk factors for adolescent violence, as shown in Figure 6.1, are early and persistent antisocial behavior at school, academic failure beginning in elementary school, and lack of commitment to school. The three projects in the OJJDP Program of Research on the Causes and Correlates of Delinquency have confirmed all three of these risk factors (Huizinga, Loeber, & Thornberry, 1995).

Bullying has received a great deal of attention recently, particularly as a school-related risk factor for violence. Bullying is a form of aggression that is linked with other predelinquent behaviors and also predicts adult offending (Farrington, 1993b). It commonly occurs during unstructured activities at school (Craig & Pepler, 1997). A large proportion of school-related victimizations escalate from peer interactions that occur in the course of routine daily activities in schools (Garofalo, Siegel, & Laub, 1987). In addition to bullying, these forms of victimization include insults and misguided mischief.

The importance of bullying as a school risk factor is not clear. Key research issues concern the relationship between bullying and/or being a victim of bullying and childhood or adolescent delinquency—particularly violence. Victimization by a bully may be linked to adjustment problems and, in turn, to delinquency, as suggested in the studies reviewed in Box 6.4. More research is needed on

Box 6.4

Bullying

Bullying is commonly defined as a specific type of aggression having three characteristics: First, the behavior is intended to harm or disturb others; second, the behavior occurs repeatedly over time; and third, the aggression involves an imbalance of power, with a more powerful person or group attacking a less powerful one (Nansel, Overpeck, Pilla, Ruan, & Simmons-Morton, 2001). Research on bullying was first undertaken in Norway by Olweus (1978, 1979, 1991, 1992, 1994), whose findings resulted in a nationwide Norwegian school program. Olweus (1991) established a relationship between adolescent bullying and adult offending, finding that more than half (60%) of the adolescent bullies in his sample were convicted of criminal offenses by age 24, and that their offending rates were four times greater than the rates among nonbullies. In the Cambridge Study in Delinquent Development, males who reported that they were bullies at age 14 were also likely to report that they were bullies at age 32 (Farrington, 1993b).

Studies have shown that bullies tend to display aggression in different settings over many years (Farrington, 1993b, 1995). They tend to be impulsive, and they tend to have low school attainment, low self-esteem, and poor social skills. Adolescent boys tend to bully others physically, whereas girls tend to bully through psychological attacks (e.g., making sexual comments and spreading rumors). Bullies of both genders tend to come from low-socioeconomic-status families in which the child-rearing techniques are poor. Adolescent bullies tend to become adult bullies, and later they tend to have children who are bullies.

Bullying is surprisingly common. In the first nationwide study of bullying prevalence in the United States, which employed a survey of nearly 16,000 students in grades 6 to 10, nearly one-third (30%) of the students reported involvement in bullying during the current school term (Nansel et al., 2001). About equal proportions self-reported bullying other students (13%), and nearly 11% said they had been the victims of repeated bullying. Only 6% said they had both been bullied and bullied others. The percentage of students who reported being bullied was highest in middle school, among sixth and seventh graders. Students in each higher grade level reported successively less bullying victimization. Students who were bullied reported poorer social and emotional adjustment and greater loneliness than did students who were not bullied. Persons who bullied others were more likely to be involved in other problem behaviors, such as drinking alcohol and smoking, and they showed poor school adjustment. However, they were not socially isolated. Students who reported both bullying others and being bullied showed poorer adjustment across both social/emotional dimensions and problem behaviors. Such young people may represent an especially high-risk group for other problem behaviors such as gang involvement—as a response to bullying victimization.

There is some evidence that bullying is related to other deviant behaviors. In a North Carolina study, Burns et al. (2001) found that three-fourths (75%) of the children ages 6 to 12 who were diagnosed with conduct disorders were involved in bullying, along with damaging property (69%) and stealing (63%). This group also had high rates of other conditions, such as attention deficit hyperactivity disorder (72%) and oppositional defiant disorder (84%). Thus bullying was strongly associated in this study with other problem behaviors. In a study of eighth-grade students in Sweden, Andershed, Kerr, and Stattin (2000) found that adolescents who bullied others in school also tended to engage in violent behavior on the streets. In addition, they found that bullying behavior in school carried with it a higher likelihood of being violently victimized on the streets. These findings held for girls as well as for boys. This research needs to be replicated in the United States.

the relationship between bullying victimization and subsequent delinquency, given the strong relationship that has been found between other forms of violent victimization and violent delinquency (Gorman-Smith & Tolan, 1998; Huizinga & Jakob-Chien, 1998; Loeber, Kalb, & Huizinga, 2001).

Peer Group Level

"One of the most stable and well-established findings in delinquency research is that the delinquent behavior of an individual is positively related to the actual or perceived delinquent behavior of that individual's friends" (Elliott & Menard, 1996, p. 29). More than 70 years ago, Shaw and McKay (1931) documented the strong relationship between delinquent peer group members and delinquent behavior; their findings are largely uncontested to this day. However, there is disagreement among researchers and delinquency theorists with respect to the causal importance of peers (Warr, 2002, pp. 39-41). The key issue is whether delinquent youngsters seek out others like them—that is, "birds of a feather flock together" (Glueck & Glueck, 1950)—or whether they become delinquent because they acquire delinquent friends. Most likely, both processes are at work. Associating with delinquent peers increases delinquency; in turn, involvement in delinquency leads to more frequent associations with delinquent peers (Thornberry, Lizotte, Krohn, Farnworth, & Jang, 1994). In his landmark book *Companions in Crime* (2002), Warr demonstrates the powerful connection between peer influence and the sharp increase and equally sharp decrease in the prevalence of criminal involvement in the adolescent years—precisely when peer relations are at their zenith.

Elliott and Menard (1996) analyzed National Youth Survey data and found that these data convincingly demonstrate that "the onset of exposure to delinquent friends typically precedes the onset of one's own illegal behavior" (p. 28). They describe the sequence as follows:

The typical progression for those who are non-delinquent and in non-delinquent peer groups is
- movement into a slightly more delinquent peer group,
- onset of minor delinquency,
- movement into a more delinquent peer group,
- onset of Index delinquency, and
- movement into a predominantly delinquent peer group. (pp. 25-26)

The sequential process that Elliott and Menard describe applies to serious and violent offending as well as to general delinquency. They found that in the vast majority of cases, exposure to delinquent friends precedes Index offending (p. 43). In fact, only 1% of the total sample self-reported Index offenses before their exposure to delinquent friends. When juveniles enter young adulthood they tend to become less involved in both delinquent peer groups and delinquent behavior (Elliott & Menard, 1996, p. 28).

The high prevalence of delinquency in groups demonstrates peer influence. Warr (1996) found that most adolescent offenses are committed by youths accompanied by two or three others (except for group fighting, in which about four others are usually involved). National victimization data also show substantial adolescent group offending (Snyder & Sickmund, 1995, p. 47). Victim reports show that more than one-half of serious violent juvenile offenses (compared with one-third of adult offenses) involve groups of offenders. These offending adolescent groups are highly unstable; Reiss (1988) describes them as "transitory," with "volatile" membership. Warr (1996) found most delinquent groups to be "demonstrably transitory" (p. 33).

"Instigators" in delinquent peer groups tend to be older offenders with longer offense histories (Warr, 1996). They play a key role in the spread of adolescent offending. "Joiners" (less experienced offenders, characteristic of adolescence-limited offenders) appear to be linked to instigators by friendship bonds. Some offenders shift frequently between these two roles as they move from group to group. Thus "instigators and joiners are the same people" (Warr, 1996, p. 31). According to Warr's study, the "mixed" offenders (those who are both instigators and joiners) constitute about half of all offenders. Pure joiners represent about a third of all offenders, and nearly half of them commit several offenses. The most common pattern is for joiners to follow an instigator who is a year or two older than they are (p. 27).

Ironically, peer rejection may be a risk factor for onset of delinquency in childhood—that is, for aggressive children (Coie & Dodge, 1998; Coie & Miller-Johnson, 2001). Social rejection by prosocial youths may serve to channel rejected-aggressive children toward deviant peer groups (Coie & Miller-Johnson, 2001, p. 204). Aggressive and antisocial youths affiliate with one another beginning in childhood (Kupersmidt, DeRosier, & Patterson, 1995), and this pattern of aggressive friendships continues through adolescence (Cairns & Cairns, 1994). In fact, aggressive elementary school–aged children tend to play with other aggressive schoolmates at home and at school, and are rarely chosen by nonaggressive peers as playmates or friends (Kupersmidt et al., 1995).

Aggressive children and aggressive young adolescents are often central members of delinquent cliques (Cairns, Cairns, Neckerman, Ferguson, & Gariepy, 1989). Antisocial youths report that their antisocial friends negatively influence them and even teach them how to do things that get them into trouble. In contrast, they report that their "conventional" friends are less likely to encourage existing deviant behavior (Sigda, Kupersmidt, & Martin, 1996).

Because gang involvement carries with it so much participation in delinquent activity, researchers are reluctant to consider it as a risk factor. Gang membership is not listed as a peer-related risk factor in Figure 6.1 for this very reason. The only peer-related factor shown in the figure is friends who engage in the problem behavior. The researchers who compiled this list of risk factors—from literature reviews—consider gang involvement to be a delinquency and violence-related outcome of the various risk factors listed in the figure. Indeed, most youths who join gangs report prior involvement in delinquency (Thornberry, 1998). Figure 5.3 in Chapter 5 illustrates that the deviant developmental process begins with conduct problems, followed by elementary school failure, then child delinquency, then gang membership, and serious, violent, and chronic delinquency onward from mid-adolescence. Nevertheless, as the discussion in Chapter 5 shows, gang involvement is a very strong risk factor for subsequent involvement in serious and violent delinquency.

There is considerable evidence that the small groups within which most delinquent acts are committed are often combinations or subsets of larger groups or cliques; Warr (2002) calls these larger groups "accomplice networks" (p. 36). This pattern is more typical of high-rate offenders than of low-rate offenders, and high-rate offenders tend to affiliate with other high-rate offenders (Reiss, 1988; Sarnecki, 1986; Warr, 2002, pp. 36-37). Gang members have the highest rates of offending of all adolescent offenders (as discussed in Chapter 5), and they tend to have gang "social networks" (Fleisher, 2002). After finding that active gang membership facilitated involvement in delinquency even when all other major risk factors were held constant, Rochester researchers concluded that gangs may be one of the more important environments for explaining adolescent delinquency (Thornberry, Krohn, Lizotte, Smith, & Tobin, 2002). Indeed, the influence of the gang on subsequent delinquency is stronger than the influence of other delinquent peers (Battin, Hill, Abbott, Catalano, & Hawkins, 1998). As seen in Chapter 5, the degree of bonding to delinquent and organized gangs (Esbensen, Winfree, He, & Taylor, 2001; Lynskey, Winfree, Esbensen, & Clason, 2000) increases the risk for subsequent delinquency.

In sum, as demonstrated in Warr's (2000) seminal work, it is peer influence that best explains the peak period of individuals' involvement in crime—during adolescence—and, as the studies reviewed in Chapter 5 show, delinquent peer influence is strongest in the gang context. That peer group relationship is stronger than the influence of other delinquent peers.

Individual Level

Figure 6.1 lists only two individual factors that longitudinal studies show to be important predictors of subsequent violence in adolescence—early initiation of problem behavior and constitutional factors. As seen earlier in this chapter, involvement in delinquency, aggressive behavior, and violence in childhood are among the main predictors of serious and violent delinquency in adolescence. Thus early initiation of problem behavior is a very important individual characteristic.

Constitutional factors that predict violence are difficult to specify. Individual violence proclivity appears to be related to a set of constitutional factors, including a fearless and uninhibited temperament, a difficult temperament, impulsiveness, cognitive impairments, and a low intelligence quotient (IQ), that can interact with other factors to produce violence (Eron & Slaby, 1994, p. 7). Genetic variation in violence-related temperament factors may also contribute to violent behaviors (Eron & Slaby, 1994). The knowledge accumulated to date indicates that the most likely linkage between children's individual traits and aggression may be a function of acquired biological deficits. These include prenatal and perinatal complications (Brennan, Mednick, & Kandel, 1991), neonatal injuries (Kolvin, Miller, Scott, Gatzanis, & Fleeting, 1990), injury to the brain and neurological dysfunction (Moffitt, 1993; Rivara, 1995), exposure to neurotoxins, and deficits in the social environment (Loeber, 1990).

I will discuss mental health as a risk factor for adolescent violence shortly, in the context of co-occurring adolescent problem behaviors. New research has demonstrated the importance of this risk factor.

Do Girls Have Unique Risk Factors
for Serious and Violent Delinquency?

Research concerning risk factors specific to girls is relatively new, owing largely to two factors: First, the incidence of serious and violent delinquency is lower among girls than among boys (e.g., the likelihood of violence among males is double that among females; J. D. Hawkins et al., 1998, p. 144), so there is less such behavior to study; and second, the lower prevalence rate means that the cost of studying serious and violent female delinquency is much higher, because researchers must draw very large samples to ensure that they contain sufficiently large numbers of females for statistical analysis. Because most studies have focused on males, there are substantial limitations in applying these study findings to females; indeed, much of what we can currently conclude about serious, violent, and chronic juvenile offenders may apply only to males (Tolan & Gorman-Smith, 1998, p. 70).

However, to date, research has not substantiated the existence of any unique risk factors for female delinquency versus male delinquency. As seen in Chapter 4, the risk factors associated with offending in girls are generally similar to those found to apply in boys (Moffitt, Caspi, Rutter, & Silva, 2001; Rutter et al., 1998). Gender differences in self-reported delinquency are accounted for by males' greater exposure to risk factors; that is, males experience more of the risk factors that predict serious and persistent antisocial behavior. However, more research is needed on child abuse as a risk factor that may account for gender differences in serious and violent delinquency. In Chapter 4, I suggested a possibly unique female pathway to serious and violent delinquency—instigated by child abuse. More longitudinal research is needed to determine whether or not certain risk factors play key roles in girls' serious and violent delinquency.

Predictors of Violent Delinquency

This section is devoted to a summary of recent reviews of longitudinal studies of adolescent violence predictors (as noted previously, a predictor is a risk factor that is measured in advance of the problem behavior, to establish predictive power). Members of the OJJDP Study Group on Serious and Violent Juvenile Offenders conducted two reviews of the literature on violence predictors during adolescence (and into early adulthood). Both make important contributions to knowledge, but curious readers will want to take note of the differences in how the two literature reviews were conducted (see Box 6.5). The main difference is that Lipsey and Derzon (1998) used "meta-analysis" statistical procedure, whereas J. D. Hawkins and colleagues (1998) conducted a narrative, study-by-study review (see Chapter 10 for a detailed explanation and comparison of the two review methods). I summarize the results of the two reviews below.

Childhood and Adolescent Risk Factors
for Serious and Violent Delinquency

Lipsey and Derzon (1998) are the first to organize risk factors and outcomes as indicated in longitudinal studies into two developmental time frames. Their review is also the first comprehensive meta-analysis of predictors of serious or violent offenses among children and adolescents. First, Lipsey and Derzon identified the main childhood (ages 6-11) predictors of serious or violent offenses

at ages 15-25. Second, they identified the main adolescent (ages 12-14) predictors of serious or violent offenses at ages 15-25. Table 6.2—which is based on their meta-analysis of longitudinal research—shows that the best predictors differ for the two age groups, because certain risk factors have different degrees of influence at various developmental stages. In general, family influences are predominant early in life, followed by school factors, then peer group influences.

Lipsey and Derzon's findings may be summarized as follows:

- At ages 6-11, the best predictors of subsequent serious or violent offenses are involvement in delinquency (general offenses) at this early age and drug use. The second-strongest group of predictors are being a male, living in a poor family (low socioeconomic status), and having antisocial parents. A history of aggression and ethnicity are in the third-strongest group of predictors.
- For the 12-14 age group, a lack of social ties and having antisocial peers are the strongest predictors of subsequent serious or violent offenses. Involvement in delinquency (general offenses) is the one predictor in the second ranking group. Several predictors are in the third-strongest group: a history of aggression, school attitude/performance, psychological condition (mental health), parent-adolescent relations, being a male, and a history of violence.
- Broken homes and abusive parents are among the weakest predictors of subsequent serious or violent offenses for both age groups.
- The significance of antisocial peers and substance abuse is reversed in the two age groups. Whereas having antisocial peers is the weakest predictor for the age 6-11 group, it is one of two very strong predictors for the 12-14 age group. Conversely, in the 6-11 age group early onset of substance use is one of two very strong predictors; it is among the weakest predictors for the age 12-14 group.

This meta-analysis is important for what it reveals about the relative strengths of predictors for the two different age groups, children (ages 6-11) and adolescents (ages 12-14). The implications are important for prevention programming priorities. Early intervention efforts, with children, should target early delinquent behaviors, including drug

Box 6.5
Technical Note on Two Important Reviews of Violence Predictors

Lipsey and Derzon (1998) reviewed violence predictors by using data drawn from an ongoing meta-analysis of prospective longitudinal studies of the development of antisocial behavior at the Vanderbilt Institute for Public Policy Studies. This meta-analysis—focused on serious delinquency as well as violent outcomes—included 66 reports on 34 independent studies that measured serious and violent outcomes when the samples were ages 15-25, when such behavior tends to peak in adolescents and young adults.

J. D. Hawkins et al. (1998) reviewed and synthesized predictors of youth violence from 33 longitudinal studies that specifically used violent acts as an outcome measure, and also measured malleable risk and protective factors. Hawkins and his colleagues also reviewed results from new analyses of the Seattle Social Development Project data set.

There are important differences between Lipsey and Derzon's study and Hawkins et al.'s study in the methods and procedures the researchers used. First, Lipsey and Derzon focused on serious delinquency as well as violent outcomes, whereas Hawkins and his colleagues focused more specifically on predictors of youth violence.

Second, Hawkins et al. summarized results at the study level, whereas Lipsey and Derzon aggregated results within risk categories. Hawkins et al.'s results are mostly descriptive, whereas Lipsey and Derzon—using meta-analysis methods—statistically controlled for methodological nuances of studies. The biggest difference between the studies may be that the Hawkins et al. review is broader in its coverage of risk factors, especially those at a social-environmental level, but Lipsey and Derzon's meta-analysis permitted more in-depth analysis within risk categories.

In addition, Lipsey and Derzon's review was more oriented toward sorting out the big picture of the comparative strengths of different categories of risk factors, with statistical controls to make those comparisons more meaningful. In contrast, Hawkins et al.'s review was more oriented toward the evidence on each risk predictor as drawn from the individual studies involving that predictor. Thus the two reviews are complementary and partially overlapping, providing different perspectives on the literature. Interested readers should also see Farrington (1998) for yet another excellent review of risk factors for adolescent violence. All of these reviews are important because they are the first comprehensive reviews of violence predictors in children and adolescents.

use and displays of aggression, family poverty, and antisocial parents. In contrast, prevention efforts with adolescents should seek to reduce young people's associations with antisocial peers and involvement in delinquency, aggression, and physical violence while strengthening their social ties, improving their relationships with parents, and improving their mental health.

This is not to say that predictors in the fourth and fifth categories should be ignored. These, too, are significant predictors. A comprehensive prevention approach that addresses predictors in more than one risk factor domain (e.g., peer group and family) is likely to have the largest impact.

Risk Factors for Adolescent Violence
as Indicated by Longitudinal Studies

The predictors that J. D. Hawkins and colleagues (1998) included in their review are

arranged in five domains: individual, family, school, peer-related, and community and neighborhood factors (for a summary of this review, see Hawkins, Herrenkohl, et al., 2000). Hawkins, Herrenkohl, et al. (2000) briefly discuss studies supporting the importance of these risk factors for adolescent violence; J. D. Hawkins et al. (1998) address these studies in greater detail. (Note that some of the risk factors listed below are not included in Figure 6.1 because the figure includes only risk factors that at least two experimental studies have confirmed. Some of the risk factors in the list below come from single studies.) The main adolescent violence predictors that J. D. Hawkins and colleagues (1998) identify are as follows:

Individual factors
- Pregnancy and delivery complications
- Low resting heart rate
- Internalizing disorders

TABLE 6.2   Ranking of Ages 6-11 and Ages 12-14 Predictors of Serious or Violent Offenses at Ages 15-25

Predictors at Ages 6-11	Predictors at Ages 12-14
Rank 1 Group	
General offenses (.38)	Social ties (.39)
Substance use (.30)	Antisocial peers (.37)
Rank 2 Group	
Gender (male) (.26)	General offenses (.26)
Family socioeconomic status (.24)	
Antisocial parents (.23)	
Rank 3 Group	
Aggression (.21)	Aggression (.19)
Ethnicity (.20)	School attitude/performance (.19)
	Psychological condition (.19)
	Parent-child relations (.19)
	Gender (male) (.19)
	Physical violence (.18)
Rank 4 Group	
Psychological condition (.15)	Antisocial parents (.16)
Parent-child relations (.15)	Person crimes (.14)
Social ties (.15)	Problem behavior (.12)
Problem behavior (.13)	IQ (.11)
School attitude/performance (.13)	
Medical/physical characteristics (.13)	
IQ (.12)	
Other family characteristics (.12)	
Rank 5 Group	
Broken home (.09)	Broken home (.10)
Abusive parents (.07)	Family socioeconomic status (.10)
Antisocial peers (.04)	Abusive parents (.09)
	Other family characteristics (.08)
	Substance abuse (.06)
	Ethnicity (.04)

SOURCE: (1998). "Predictors of Violent or Serious Delinquency in Adolescence and Early Adulthood," by M. W. Lipsey and J. H. Derzon, in R. Loeber and D. P. Farrington (Eds.), *Serious and Violent Juvenile Offenders: Risk Factors and Successful Interventions* (p. 97), Thousand Oaks, CA: Sage. Copyright 1998 by Sage Publications, Inc. Reprinted with permission.

NOTE: The values in parentheses are the mean correlations between predictors and outcomes, adjusted to equate the source studies on relevant methodological features.

- Hyperactivity, concentration problems, restlessness, and risk taking
- Aggressiveness
- Early initiation of violent behavior
- Involvement in other forms of antisocial behavior
- Beliefs and attitudes favorable to deviant or antisocial behavior

Family factors

- Parental criminality
- Child maltreatment
- Poor family management practices
- Low levels of parental involvement
- Poor family bonding and family conflict

- Parental attitudes favorable to substance abuse and violence
- Parent-child separation

School factors

- Academic failure
- Low bonding to school
- Truancy and dropping out of school
- Frequent school transitions

Peer-related factors

- Delinquent siblings
- Delinquent peers
- Gang membership

Community and neighborhood factors

- Poverty
- Community disorganization
- Availability of drugs and firearms
- Neighborhood adults involved in crime
- Exposure to violence and racial prejudice

Hawkins and colleagues (1998, pp. 142-145) also report the results of an analysis of the power of diverse violence predictors seen at ages 10, 14, and 16 in the Seattle Social Development Project. These results (also reported in Hawkins, Herrenkohl, et al., 2000, pp. 6-7) are organized into the above risk factor categories. In each case, the risk factor outcomes were measured by self-reported violence at age 18.

Individual factors

- Hyperactivity or attention deficits at age 10, 14, or 16 doubled the risk of violent behavior at age 18.
- Sensation seeking and involvement in drug selling at ages 14 and 16 more than tripled the risk of involvement in violence.

Family factors

- Parental attitudes favorable to violence when subjects were age 10 more than doubled the risk that subjects would engage in violence at age 18.
- Poor family management practices and family conflict when subjects were age 10 were not significant predictors of later violence. However, poor family management practices when subjects were age 14 doubled the risk for later involvement in violence.
- Parental criminality when subjects were age 14 (not assessed at age 10) more than doubled the risk for involvement in violence at age 18.
- Low commitment to schooling, low educational aspirations, and multiple school transitions at ages 14 and 16 predicted a

significantly increased risk for involvement in violence at age 18.

Peer-related factors

- Having delinquent friends at ages 10, 14, and 16 predicted an increased risk for later involvement in violence.
- Gang membership at age 14 more than tripled the risk for involvement in violence at age 18.
- Gang membership at age 16 more than quadrupled the risk for involvement in violence at age 18.

Community and neighborhood factors

- Community disorganization, the availability of drugs, and knowing adults who were involved in criminal activities at ages 14 and 16 all were associated with an increased risk for later involvement in violence.

Note the above finding from the Seattle project that drug selling at ages 14 and 16 more than tripled the risk of involvement in violence at age 18. This may well be a case in which a risk factor is not necessarily a causal factor (I return to this issue later in this chapter).

Childhood Risk Factors for Delinquency

The OJJDP Study Group on Very Young Offenders (see Loeber & Farrington, 2001a) found that the initial risk factors for child delinquency lie, first, within the individual child (such as impulsive behavior), and, second, within the family (such as parents' child-rearing practices; see Keenan, 2001). During the preschool years, and especially in the elementary school period and onward, the array of risk factors expands, as some children are exposed to negative peer influences outside the home. Some children are also exposed to additional risk factors situated within schools or in the community at large during this period. Compared to later-onset delinquents, child delinquents tend to come from dysfunctional families with one or more of the following characteristics: family disruption (especially a succession of different caregivers), parental antisocial behavior, parental substance abuse, mother's depression, and child abuse and neglect (Wasserman & Seracini, 2001).

Table 6.3 shows the risk factors during early childhood for child delinquency and later serious and violent delinquency. Inspired by Bronfenbrenner (1979), Loeber and Farrington (2001c) organized the risk factors in this table according to the different spheres of influence that affect child

TABLE 6.3   Childhood Risk Factors for Child Delinquency and Later Serious and Violent Juvenile Offending

Child factors
   Difficult temperament
   Impulsive behavior
   Hyperactivity (but only when co-occurring with disruptive behaviors)
   Impulsivity
   Substance use
   Aggression
   Early-onset disruptive behaviors
   Withdrawn behaviors
   Low intelligence
   Lead toxicity

Family factors
   Parental antisocial or delinquent behaviors
   Parental substance abuse
   Parents' poor child-rearing practices
   Poor supervision
   Physical punishment
   Poor communication
   Poor parent-child relations
   Parental physical and/or sexual abuse
   Parental neglect
   Maternal depression
   Mother's smoking during pregnancy
   Teenage motherhood
   Parental disagreement on child discipline
   Single parenthood
   Large family
   High turnover of caregivers
   Low socioeconomic status of family
   Unemployed parent
   Poorly educated mother
   Family members' carelessness in allowing children access to weapons (especially guns)

School factors
   Poor academic performance
   Old for grade
   Weak bonding to school
   Low educational aspirations
   Low school motivation
   Poorly organized and functioning schools

Peer factors
   Association with deviant or delinquent siblings and peers
   Rejection by peers

Neighborhood factors
   Neighborhood disadvantage and poverty
   Disorganized neighborhoods
   Availability of weapons
   Media portrayal of violence

SOURCE: "The Significance of Child Delinquency," by R. Loeber and D. P. Farrington, in R. Loeber and D. P. Farrington (Eds.), *Child Delinquents: Development, Intervention, and Service Needs* (p. 12), Thousand Oaks, CA: Sage. Copyright 2001 by Sage Publications, Inc. Reprinted with permission.
NOTE: This table is based on Chapters 5-10 in Loeber and Farrington (2001a), particularly Herrenkohl, Hawkins, Chung, Hill, and Battin-Pearson (2001), as well as on J. D. Hawkins et al. (1998), Lipsey and Derzon (1998), and Loeber, Farrington, Stouthamer-Loeber, and Van Kammen (1998).

behavior. But Loeber and Farrington go beyond the three such spheres that Bronfenbrenner suggested—family, peer group, and school relations—to specify a more distinctive development model in which certain domains of risk factors initially promote early forms of child delinquency, with subsequent development affected by additional risk factor domains. Coie and Miller-Johnson (2001) propose a developmental model that emphasizes early peer rejection as an often-overlooked factor in the onset of child delinquency. Their model applies in particular to aggressive and disruptive children. Difficulties these children face in getting along with and being accepted by conventional peers may lead to increasing aggressiveness and more disruptive behavior. This model merits further research.

Such early onset of delinquency has very important implications for individuals' life-course involvement in serious and violent crime. Rochester researchers Krohn, Thornberry, Rivera, and Le Blanc (2001) examined very early onset in several samples for the Study Group on Very Young Offenders. They found that the very youngest onset group (onset at 4 to 10 years of age) had the highest prevalence rate for both serious and violent offenses during adolescence and the early adult years, roughly ages 19 to 22 years (p. 83). More than a third (39%) of this group reported involvement in serious and violent offenses in young adulthood, compared with 20% of the youngsters with onset at ages 11-12 and 23% of the youngsters with onset at ages 13-14.

Co-Occurrence of Serious and Violent Offending and Other Problem Behaviors

Many studies have shown that several adolescent problem behaviors share a number of risk factors in the family, school, peer group, community, and individual domains (see Figure 6.1). Until recently, however, the extent of the overlap in problem behaviors among serious and violent offenders was not well researched. The key issue here is the extent to which multiple-problem youth are serious and violent offenders, and vice versa. Huizinga and Jakob-Chien (1998) reviewed evidence in the Denver Youth Survey on the co-occurrence of serious (serious nonviolent or serious violent) offending and other problem behaviors. They found a clear relationship between combinations of problems and serious/violent delinquency. In the total Denver adolescent sample, 68% of those who had drug problems, mental health problems, and school problems *and* had been victimized were serious/violent offenders.

This study prompted Huizinga, Loeber, Thornberry, and Cothern (2000), researchers in the OJJDP Program of Research on the Causes and Correlates of Delinquency, to conduct a joint analysis of problem co-occurrence in all three of the research program's longitudinal studies. I summarize the findings from this analysis below, along with other research results as appropriate. In this study, the research team—consisting of Denver, Rochester, and Pittsburgh researchers—examined multiple problem behaviors among "persistent serious delinquents," which they defined as self-reported offenders in serious assault or serious property offenses in at least 2 of the first 3 years of the respective projects.

This study shows that the relationship between persistent serious delinquency and combinations of other persistent problem behaviors was fairly consistent across the three study sites. For most male serious offenders, involvement in persistent serious delinquency and other problems go together. Yet serious delinquency does not always co-occur with other problems; that is, a youth who experiences other persistent problems is not necessarily a persistent serious delinquent.

More than half of the male serious delinquents in the Denver and Pittsburgh samples and more than half of the female serious delinquents in the Denver sample displayed other problems; in Rochester, the proportion was roughly 40% for both genders. Among those with multiple problems, as the number of problems increased, so did the chance of being a persistent serious delinquent. More than half (55-73%) of those with two or more problems were also persistent serious delinquents. For females, the relationship among combinations of persistent problems was different and varied in the two sites that sampled females, thus Huizinga et al. caution that generalizations are unwarranted. In sum, a combination of persistent drug, school, and mental health problems is a reasonably strong risk factor for persistent serious delinquency.

Of the high-risk males in the three sites, 25% were persistent serious delinquents, 15% were drug users, 7% had school problems, and 10% had mental health problems. Of the high-risk females in the two sites, about 5% were persistent serious delinquents, 11-12% were drug users, 10-21% had school problems, and 6-11% had mental health problems. Females were not studied in the Pittsburgh site. All three sites studied only high-risk children and adolescents.

The most common pattern of occurrence of persistent serious delinquency, drug use, school problems, and mental health problems was an intermittent one across the three study sites. For all sites, the most common temporal pattern of each problem behavior was that it occurred for only 1 year, followed by 2 years, then 3 years.

Persistent Serious Delinquency and Drug Use

In this analysis across the Denver, Rochester, and Pittsburgh sites, Huizinga et al. (2000) found a statistically significant relationship between persistent delinquency and persistent drug use for both males and females (across all three sites for males and in two sites for females). Indeed, persistent drug use is the problem that co-occurs most frequently with persistent serious delinquency. Smith et al. (2000) have also found that the combination of delinquency involvement and marijuana use can have serious negative consequences throughout the life course. However, Huizinga et al. found that a majority of persistent serious offenders were not persistent drug users (34-44% for males in the three sites and 46-48% for females in two sites). Thus slightly more than a third of persistent serious male delinquents, and nearly half of all persistent serious female delinquents, were drug users.

Conversely, for males, the majority of persistent drug users were persistent serious delinquents (54-70% in the three sites). This was not the case for females; only 20-23% of the persistent drug-using females were persistent serious delinquents in the two sites. Thus, among females, delinquency is a stronger indicator of drug use than drug use is an indicator of delinquency. For both genders, the majority of persistent serious offenders were not drug users.

Persistent Serious Delinquency and Mental Health Problems

Huizinga et al. (2000) found that the relationship between mental health problems (see Box 6.6) and persistent serious delinquency was statistically significant for males at all three sites. For males, the presence of mental health problems is a better indicator of serious delinquency than serious delinquency is an indicator of mental health problems. Only 13-21% of male persistent serious delinquents in the three sites displayed mental health problems. On the other hand, of those with mental health problems, almost one-third in Rochester (31%) and almost one-half at each of the other two sites (46%) were persistent serious delinquents.

The relationship was statistically significant for females in Rochester, but not in Denver. In Rochester, one-third of females (34%) who were persistent serious delinquents also had mental health problems. Conversely, only 17% of those

with mental health problems were persistent serious delinquents. This relationship is the reverse of that seen in males. Thus neither male nor female persistent serious delinquents can be characterized as having mental health problems. Conversely, it would be erroneous to characterize most adolescents with mental health problems as persistent serious delinquents.

Interestingly, in an analysis of the Denver data, Huizinga and Jakob-Chien (1998) found that low self-esteem did not appear to be related to serious/violent delinquency. Rather, consistent with a review of the link between self-esteem and violence (Baumeister, Smart, & Boden, 1996), Huizinga and Jakob-Chien suggest that high self-esteem and threats to this self-esteem may lead to violence. This finding could well apply to gang leaders.

Persistent Serious Delinquency and School Problems

Huizinga et al. (2000) found that the three sites differed substantially in the evidence they yielded about the prevalence of school problems. The sites also differed in terms of the extent of co-occurrence of persistent school problems (poor academic performance, truancy, and dropping out) and persistent serious delinquency. For example, the proportion of persistent serious male delinquents who had persistent school problems ranged from 9% in Pittsburgh to 41% in Denver. Similarly, the proportion of persistent serious female delinquents who had persistent school problems ranged from 11% in Denver to 55% in Rochester. Site differences of similar magnitude were observed in the proportions of those with school problems who are delinquents. Thus broad generalizations about the relationship between persistent serious delinquency and other persistent school problems are unwarranted. In sum, persistent serious delinquents should not be characterized as having school problems, nor should those with school problems be characterized as persistent serious delinquents. School failure problems vary by locality (see Box 6.3); these three cities may not have particularly high overall rates of school failure.

Effects of Multiple Problems

Huizinga and colleagues (2000) conclude that the degree of co-occurrence between persistent serious delinquency and other persistent problems is not overwhelming, but the size of the overlap suggests that a large number of persistent serious delinquents face additional problems that need to be addressed. It is crucial that juvenile justice system

---

Box 6.6
The Mental Health Risk Factor

Mental health as a risk factor for serious delinquency has not been well researched until recently, with publication of the seminal volume from the Pittsburgh Youth Study (Loeber, Farrington, Stouthamer-Loeber, & Van Kammen, 1998) and two federal reports (U.S. Department of Health and Human Services, 1999, 2001). About 20% of children and adolescents in the United States are estimated to have mental disorders with at least mild functional impairment (U.S. Department of Health and Human Services, 1999, p. 46). About 5-9% of all children and adolescents are estimated to have severe emotional disorders with extreme functional impairment that require treatment (Friedman, Katz-Leavy, Manderscheid, & Sondheimer, 1996). The proportion of youngsters brought into the juvenile justice system who have serious mental health problems is higher. It is estimated that at least 20% of youth who come in contact with the juvenile justice system have serious mental health disorders—that is, disorders more serious than conduct disorders (Cocozza & Skowyra, 2000, p. 6).

In a North Carolina study of a representative sample of 9- to 13-year-olds, Burns et al. (1995, p. 150) found that 20% were diagnosed with mental health problems. The most common diagnosis was for an anxiety disorder (6%); 3% had conduct disorders, nearly 3% evidenced oppositional defiant disorders, and 2% were hyperactive. Estimates of mental health problems in serious/violent juveniles were not available until Huizinga, Loeber, Thornberry, and Cothern (2000) found that from 13% to 21% of the male persistent serious (serious assault or serious property offenses) delinquents in three sites (Denver, Pittsburgh, and Rochester), and 34% of such female delinquents in Rochester, had mental health problems. In addition, the study revealed that mental health problems tend to co-occur with persistent drug and school problems.

A number of studies have suggested that antisocial behaviors are related to cognitive deficits, including deficits in social skills and social cognition, inappropriate attributions of the meanings of social contexts and interactions, failure to empathize or take the role of others in interactions, and deficits in social problem-solving thinking (Bullis & Walker, 1996). However, as Rutter (1986) suggests, several of these could be developmental problems. Other mental health links to antisocial behavior include learning disabilities (Zimmerman, Rich, Keilitz, & Broder, 1981), schizophrenia and bipolar disorders (Duchnowski & Kutash, 1996), severe emotional disturbance (Wagner, D'Amico, Marder, Newman, & Blackorby, 1992), and attention deficit hyperactivity disorder (ADHD). Although the exact relationship of ADHD to delinquency onset and escalation is not clear, a number of studies have established that there is a relationship (Loeber, Farrington, Stouthamer-Loeber, & Van Kammen, 1998; Rutter, Giller, & Hagell, 1998).

In a sample of youths in Newark, New Jersey, Lerman and Pottick (1995) found that evidence was quite strong that high scores on mental health problems are associated with behavioral problems, especially aggression. These researchers found that youths who scored high on both delinquency and aggression had the highest rates of cruel and assaultive behaviors. In this study, aggression was linked with high scores on psychological problems such as suspiciousness, feelings of worthlessness and being unloved, feeling tense, sadness or depression, and strange ideas and behaviors for both males and females. Having delinquent peers was also linked with delinquency. As Lerman and Pottick note, "Highly aggressive youth do not require the association of bad peers to be violent, but their level of cruelty and assaults are likely to increase in a high delinquent context that includes the support of bad peers" (p. 215). Youth gangs are an excellent example of such a context.

officials carefully identify the unique configurations of problems that individual youths have experienced. To do this, they need to use well-designed assessment instruments to determine the particular treatment needs of each delinquent and to help them craft an individualized treatment plan that fits those needs (see Chapter 12).

Effects of Personal
Victimization on Subsequent Violence

In the three-site study described above, Huizinga et al. (2000) did not examine the overlap of persistent serious delinquency and victimization; however, Huizinga and Jakob-Chien (1998) did in their Denver study. That analysis showed that violent victimization is a key risk factor for serious/violent delinquency. As the seriousness of offending increases, so does the probability of being violently victimized—49% of male serious, violent juvenile offenders were violently victimized, compared with 12% of nondelinquents. For males, being a victim of violence was related to seriousness of delinquent offending and especially to violent offending. For girls, being a victim of violence was related more to general delinquency than to violent offending in this study.

Loeber et al. (2001) examined risk factors for violent victimization in the Pittsburgh Youth Study and the Denver Youth Survey, and found that being a victim of violence that resulted in serious injuries was related to seriousness of delinquent offending and especially to violent offending among males and females. Across both studies and for each gender, the combination of committing assaults and carrying a weapon was particularly associated with elevated levels of victimization. Involvement in gang fights (one form of assault) was one of the strongest risky behaviors for subsequent violent victimization (p. 4). At both sites, members of minority groups, especially African American males, were more likely to have been victims.

Another longitudinal self-report study conducted by Woodward and Fergusson (2000) shows the effects of violent victimization on personal levels of violent offending (see Box 6.7). Interestingly, these researchers found that the individual and family risk factors that placed young people at risk of physical assault were the same across both gender groups. "These results suggested that the behavior and lifestyle characteristics associated with male and female assault may be the same" (p. 246). They also note, "For both males and females, the profile of those at greatest risk was that of a young, conduct-disordered adolescent reared by physically punitive and substance-abusing parents, who upon reaching late adolescence, engaged in antisocial and other risk-taking behavior" (p. 254). These results are compatible with findings on the physical assault experiences of young persons in the Dunedin longitudinal study (Martin et al., 1998), a Canadian study (Baron, 1997), and other seminal research (Lauritsen & Quinet, 1995; Lauritsen & White, 2001; Menard, 2000; Sampson & Lauritsen, 1990).

Victimized adolescents are not usually innocent bystanders, although prior victimization is a strong predictor of subsequent victimization for males (Esbensen, Huizinga, & Menard, 1999). Violent offending in adolescence is one of the strongest predictors of both violent offending and violent victimization in adulthood (Menard, 2002), as are violent victimization and marijuana use. Involvement in these offenses in adolescence also has deleterious long-term consequences. Menard (2002) examined their effects on a successful transition to adulthood, measured by employment or financial stability, conventional aspirations or beliefs, involvement in a conventional support network, and abstinence from serious criminal behavior and substance use. The strongest predictors of nonsuccess in adulthood were frequency of marijuana use and violent offending and most recent grade point average, followed closely by violent victimization in adolescence. Consistent with past research, Menard found that violent victimization in adolescence has pervasive effects on problem outcomes in adulthood (p. 14). It increases the odds that, in adulthood, a person will be a perpetrator or a victim of both violence in general and domestic violence. It nearly doubles the odds of problem drug use in adulthood, and it also increases the odds of adult property offending. Thus the establishment of problem behavior patterns in adolescence greatly increases the likelihood of the persistence of these patterns into adulthood.

It appears that the more violent altercations and risky behaviors that street youths participate in, the greater their risk of violent victimization. Deviant, risky lifestyles invite victimization and also contribute to violent offending. For example, Hoyt, Ryan, and Cauce (1999) found that adolescent victimization was predicted by street exposure—time on the streets, substance abuse, and gang involvement—in addition to prior victimization. In another analysis—of Pittsburgh Youth Study data—Loeber, DeLamatre, Tita, Stouthamer-Loeber, and Farrington (1999) found that almost all of the juveniles who were killed or wounded by guns had been highly delinquent themselves. The victims of serious violence tended to have histories of engaging in serious delinquency, gang fights, and drug selling. They also tended to carry guns. Victims tended to do poorly academically, receive less parental supervision, and have poorer communication with their parents as well as long histories of behavior problems.

Violent victimization has also been linked with gang involvement (Decker & Van Winkle, 1996; Fleisher, 1998; Thornberry, Krohn, Lizotte, et al., 2003). Student violent victimization levels are higher when gangs are present in schools. In 1995, the presence of gangs more than doubled the likelihood of violent victimization at school, according to the School Crime Supplement to the 1995 National Crime Victimization Survey (Chandler, Chapman, Rand, & Taylor, 1998). More than one-third (37%) of students surveyed have reported the presence of gangs in their schools (Howell & Lynch, 2000). Retaliation for having been violently victimized also is a risk factor for violent victimization of others, but this issue has been studied only in the gang context (Decker, 1996).

Box 6.7

Victimization in the Christchurch Health and Development Study

The Christchurch Health and Development Study has followed more than 1,200 persons from birth to age 18 thus far (Woodward & Fergusson, 2000). Nearly one in five study subjects was a physical assault victim between ages 16 and 18, and males were subject to almost twice as many assaults as females. Nearly all of the assaulted males were attacked by other males, and males typically were the perpetrators in female assault victimizations. In this study, physical assault was defined as "any form of deliberate physical harm inflicted on the respondent by another individual" (Woodward & Fergusson, 2000, p. 236).

Key predictors of physical assault were reported in two contexts: childhood predictors and current lifestyle factors. Young people who experienced physical assaults during late adolescence tended to have had more exposure to a wide range of adverse family circumstances during childhood. These included young motherhood, a lack of maternal educational qualifications, lower family income, high rates of parental criminal offending, alcohol abuse, illicit drug use, family conflict, parental change, and regular physical punishment. In addition, assault victims were reported by their parents and teachers to have higher rates of conduct problems as young adolescents. Sexual abuse prior to age 16 was a significant predictor for females but not for males.

The second set of findings from this study dealt with a series of factors relating to current risk-taking behavior and lifestyle in late adolescence. These factors included violent, property, and status offending; alcohol and illicit drug abuse; and involvement with delinquent and substance-abusing peers. The strongest predictors of physical assault were prior violent offending, status offending, and alcohol and drug abuse/dependence (Woodward & Fergusson, 2000, p. 255).

Drug Use, Drug Trafficking, and Violence

Huizinga and Jakob-Chien's (1998) analysis shows that there is a "robust" relationship between drug use and serious/violent delinquent behavior. These researchers make several observations about the literature on this connection: First, the exact levels of the relationship vary from study to study, and also by site, age, sex, and nature of the sample; second, all serious/violent drug users are not delinquents, and, conversely, not all, or even most, serious delinquents are drug users; and third, the causal relationship between drug use and crime is unknown.

In the Denver study, Huizinga et al. (1995) found that among male drug sellers, 72% self-reported having committed violent acts, compared with 24% of nonsellers, and, on the average, sellers committed 46 violent offenses per year compared with only 5 violent offenses committed by non-sellers (pp. 71-74). Huizinga and his colleagues caution that these findings do not indicate that drug selling causes violence; rather, they show that the "robust relationship" between drug sales and violence warrants further investigation.

Few studies have examined the causal relationship between adolescent drug trafficking and violence in general population samples. In a Pittsburgh study, Van Kammen, Maguin, and Loeber (1994) found evidence that drug use, serious theft, and violence precede drug selling. These researchers also found that sales of illicit drugs started significantly later in adolescence than the other three behaviors. Initiation of drug selling was strongly related to previous involvement in multiple types of delinquency. Van Kammen et al. conclude:

The present study indicated a temporal sequence between the delinquent behaviors and the onset of drug dealing. This does not mean that the relationship is causal. Instead, it is likely that drug dealing and serious forms of delinquency are expressions of similar antisocial tendencies. Whether the same etiological factors apply to each still remains to be demonstrated. (p. 240)

Van Kammen and Loeber (1994; see also Van Kammen et al., 1994) found that Pittsburgh juveniles' initiation into selling drugs was associated with a significant increase in carrying a weapon. The onset of drug use or drug dealing was associated with an increase in person-related offenses and carrying a concealed weapon. More than half of the drug sellers at age 19 were carrying a gun, and the proportion increased to almost 80% for drug traffickers selling hard drugs. From another viewpoint, of all the young men who carried a weapon at age 19, 64% were also involved in selling drugs. These findings are compatible with those from the Rochester study conducted by Lizotte, Krohn,

Howell, Tobin, and Howard (2000), which showed that gun carrying is most strongly correlated with drug trafficking among young adult offenders.

Lizotte et al. (2000) found that boys who carried hidden guns were significantly more likely to engage in serious assaults and armed robberies than those who did not carry. A high amount of drug selling (measured in terms of the dollar amount of drug sales) had a strong impact on hidden gun carrying. But this was not the strongest predictor of hidden gun carrying among adolescents. Up to about age 16, gang membership was the strongest predictor of illegal gun carrying, but the importance of gang membership diminished over time. After age 16, involvement in drug trafficking became the strongest predictor of hidden gun carrying. Those who sold high amounts of drugs had substantially increased likelihood of carrying guns because they were more likely to be selling drugs for profit.

As I have noted in Chapter 5, in the case of gangs, the connection between drug trafficking and violence for adolescents in general appears to be one of correlation, not necessarily causation. As a causal relationship, the connection between drug trafficking and violence applies much more to adults than to juveniles, because it has a stronger linkage within organized criminal enterprises than elsewhere. Juveniles are not much involved in organized criminal enterprises.

Summary

I began this chapter with an explanation of the risk-protection framework that has been imported into the juvenile justice field from medicine and public health research and prevention. This model is being used to great advantage in the juvenile justice field, in simplifying the search for causes and correlates of delinquency and violence.

I have reviewed the major risk factors for serious and violent delinquency and their categorization by domains: family, school, peer group, community, and individual. My aim in providing this review was to familiarize readers with the meaning of each risk factor and to illustrate how the factors operate with important and recent research. The influence of delinquent peers best explains the peak period of individuals' involvement in crime—during adolescence. This peer influence is strongest in the gang context, stronger than the influence of other delinquent peers. Knowledge about the developmental sequence of these risk factors (beginning with the family, then school, followed by peer groups) can help policy makers to organize the selection of interventions. All of these risk factors are important in

explaining serious and violent delinquency, because their influence is cumulative across time in the child and adolescent developmental process.

I have also reviewed studies of adolescent violence predictors in this chapter. The meta-analysis technique has enabled researchers to group the longitudinal studies in this area into those that examined predictors forward from childhood and those that examined them from early adolescence onward. Lipsey and Derzon (1998) conducted a review that showed the differential impacts of risk factors at the two developmental stages. For children (ages 6-11), the best predictors of subsequent serious or violent offenses are involvement in delinquency (general offenses) at this early age and drug use. The second-strongest group of predictors consists of being a male, living in a poor family (low socioeconomic status), and having antisocial parents. A history of aggression and ethnicity are in the third-strongest group of predictors. For the 12-14 age group, a lack of social ties and having antisocial peers are the strongest predictors of subsequent serious or violent offenses. Involvement in delinquency (general offenses) is the one predictor in the second ranking group. Several predictors are in the third-strongest group: a history of aggression, school attitude/performance, psychological condition (mental health), parent-child relations, being a male, and a history of violence.

In this chapter I have also reviewed a new area of study: the examination of risk factors for child delinquency and later serious and violent delinquency. Loeber and Farrington (2001c) have proposed a development process in which initial risk factors begin, first, within the individual child (e.g., impulsive behavior); second, within the family (e.g., parents' child-rearing practices); and third, with the preschool years and then from the elementary school period onward, the array of risk factors expands with exposure to negative risk factors in the school and community. A Rochester study confirms the critical importance of such an early onset of delinquency, not only for involvement in serious and violent offenses during adolescence, but also into young adulthood. Remarkably, more than a third of the group that initiated delinquency involvement between ages 4 and 10 reported involvement in serious and violent offenses in young adulthood. Still, it is likely that only a minority of those who become life-course-persistent offenders (Moffitt, 1997) can be identified very early in life (Loeber & Farrington, 2001c). Researchers are not in agreement as to when screening aimed at identifying such offenders should be done, and better screening devices need to be developed (Howell, 2001b). Then, too, few promising early-intervention programs for child delinquents exist (Howell, 2001a).

Child delinquents tend to come from dysfunctional families with one or more of the following characteristics: family disruption (especially a succession of different caregivers), parental antisocial behavior, parental substance abuse, mother's depression, and child abuse and neglect. The child abuse risk factor has not been well researched, but recent studies have shown that child abuse and neglect are important risk factors for early onset of delinquency (Wasserman & Seracini, 2001; Widom & Maxfield, 2001). Pioneering research in the Rochester Youth Development Study has revealed that child maltreatment (abuse and neglect) is a strong predictor of serious and violent delinquency (Smith & Thornberry, 1995; Thornberry, 1994). Moreover, this research has uncovered evidence that, when linked with other forms of family violence, child maltreatment is an even more potent risk factor for subsequent violent behavior in adolescence.

Research on protective factors and protective processes is still in its infancy, but significant progress has been made in the past few years. As Durlak (1998) has observed, "Much is still to be learned about which risk and protective factors are causally related to outcomes, as opposed to correlated with them, how factors interact, the specific mechanisms through which they operate, and how the relative importance of factors differs across target populations and at the different developmental periods" (p. 519). For example, the protective effects of religiosity have practically been ignored.

Durlak (1998) suggests that self-efficacy, a good parent-child relationship, and social support from helping parents, peers, and teachers may be the most important protective factors against delinquency and other problem behaviors. These are broadly conceived protective factors that may insulate children and youths from a broad range of undesirable outcomes. Research has demonstrated that a substantial number of factors provide protection against serious, violent, and chronic delinquency (see Box 6.2).

In the three-site study of co-occurring problems reviewed in this chapter, Huizinga and colleagues (2000) found that the degree of overlap between persistent serious delinquency and other persistent problems is substantial. Large proportions of persistent serious and violent delinquents experience other problems (drug use, school problems, mental health problems, and violent victimization) that need to be addressed. Juvenile justice system officials need to pay attention to the unique needs of individual young offenders, carefully identifying the configuration of problems facing each individual youth, particularly because these problems occur intermittently. The

obvious implication of the research findings to date is that juvenile justice system officials should use needs/strengths assessment instruments to determine the particular treatment needs of all persistent serious and violent delinquents, in order to craft individualized treatment plans that fit the needs of these offenders (see Chapter 12).

The Denver Youth Survey has produced one particularly powerful datum—that 68% of those youths who have drug problems, mental health problems, and school problems *and* have been victimized are either serious violent or serious nonviolent offenders. This finding is a clear indication of the need for a comprehensive strategy to combat the problem of juvenile offending. The high degree of co-occurrence of problem behaviors in serious, violent, and chronic juvenile offenders is evidence of the failure of social services, mental health services, child protective services, youth services, and the juvenile justice system to intervene effectively in troubled adolescents' lives. A broad interagency approach is needed that brings together drug abuse treatment agencies, mental health agencies, schools, the juvenile justice system, and others in a collaborative, integrated effort to prevent and reduce the multiple problems of troubled youths. The positive impact such an approach could have on the lives of serious, violent, and chronic juvenile offenders (and thus on crime reduction) could be substantial. I describe one such comprehensive strategy in Chapter 12 and illustrate it in Chapter 13.

Discussion Questions

1. Why do the transition periods in Catalano and Hawkins's social development model present opportunities for negative influences toward delinquency?

2. What is the strongest risk factor for serious and violent delinquency? What is the main context in which this risk factor operates?

3. What are the implications of school failure for protection of youths from risk factors?

4. Why do risk factors for violence vary by age group? That is, why are the risk factors for children different from those for adolescents?

5. What are the implications of the differences in risk factors for children versus adolescents for prevention and intervention programming?

7

■

WHAT DOESN'T WORK IN PREVENTING AND REDUCING JUVENILE DELINQUENCY

Thanks to the voluminous increase in the number of program evaluations in the past couple of decades, evidence is accumulating that some prevention and intervention strategies and programs simply do not work with juvenile offenders. I address many of the strategies and programs that do not work in the first two main sections of this chapter, and then discuss the evidence to date on many others for which the research findings are unclear, contradictory, or nonexistent. I discuss two particular ineffective strategies in some detail in later chapters: In Chapter 8, I address the failed policy of transferring juveniles to the criminal justice system, and in Chapter 11, I review some of the ineffective "collaboration" strategies that have been used in some jurisdictions for dealing with juvenile delinquency and other child and adolescent problem behaviors.

Ineffective Prevention Approaches

D.A.R.E.

I begin this section with a discussion of the delinquency prevention approach known as D.A.R.E. (Drug Abuse Resistance Education). My purpose is not to single out this well-intentioned program for criticism; rather, I believe that D.A.R.E provides an informative example of how some interventions have staying power despite their ineffectiveness.

D.A.R.E. is not effective (Durlak, 1997; Rosenbaum & Hanson, 1998); it is perhaps the most widely acclaimed "successful" intervention of all ineffective delinquency prevention programs. Launched in 1983 by the Los Angeles Police Department and the Los Angeles Unified School District, it enjoyed instant success because it fit with former First Lady Nancy Reagan's "Just Say No" to drugs campaign (Boyle, 2001). D.A.R.E. has grown into a $227-million-per-year enterprise that employs 50,000 police officers who teach the D.A.R.E. curriculum, lecturing against drug use in nearly half of the nation's elementary schools (Gottfredson & Gottfredson, 2002). Thus D.A.R.E. is the most frequently used substance abuse educational curriculum in the United States.

D.A.R.E. is one of the most poignant examples of a supposed panacea that continues to be used despite strong empirical evidence that it is not effective (Boyle, 2001). More than 20 evaluations have been made of D.A.R.E. (Gottfredson, 1997), and although some have shown small positive effects, long-term studies have found that these dissipated over time. The three most rigorous studies, which used a random assignment design, showed conclusively that D.A.R. E. is not effective (Clayton, Cattarello, & Johnstone, 1996; Rosenbaum, Flewelling, Bailey, Ringwalt, & Wilkinson, 1994; Rosenbaum & Hanson, 1998). In addition, the U.S. surgeon general has recognized that the program does not work (U.S. Department of Health and Human Services, 2001). The D.A.R.E. curriculum recently was revised to provide follow-up sessions in the later grades (Gottfredson, 1997). This version has not been evaluated.

Given the research findings, why does D.A.R.E. continue to be so popular? D.A.R.E. is a classic case study of a failed intervention that persists, in large part, because of a widespread mistaken belief in the effectiveness of deterrence (Finckenauer & Gavin, 1999), which is the underlying philosophy behind D.A.R.E. The program is based on the notion that giving youngsters instructional content on drug use that stresses consequences—with police officers serving as credible messengers—will deter them from using drugs. Finckenauer and Gavin (1999, pp. 218-219) offer several reasons for the unwavering faith of many in interventions such as D.A.R.E. despite overwhelming evidence to the contrary. First, the fundamental belief in repressive deterrence is irresistible. Second, an approach based on common sense is easier for most people to relate to than one based on scientific data. Social science is complicated; results often are difficult to interpret and sometimes contradictory. Third, some program administrators and public officials feel comfortable in going along with the sweep of public feelings and fears. Programs, like D.A.R.E., that stress consequences easily win public support despite empirical evidence that they are not effective. I discuss two other classic examples of this phenomenon below—Scared Straight programs and boot camps.

Zero-Tolerance Policies

Zero-tolerance policies are not effective. These are social control policies that, like D.A.R.E., are grounded in deterrence philosophy. Such policies promote punishment for every infraction of codes of conduct for children and adolescents. Zero-tolerance policies have also been applied to adults in some instances, such as in the "broken windows" policing philosophy (see Chapter 8) and in calls for zero tolerance of drug use (Stimmel, 1996) and gun crimes (Keen, 2001). In Chapter 8, I show how the application of zero-tolerance policies to violations of various laws has led to many cases of police abuse of individual rights.

Authorities have been especially zealous in applying zero-tolerance policies to the infractions of children and adolescents. This curious development is a product of the just desert and deterrence philosophies that filtered down to the juvenile justice system from the criminal justice system in the 1980s and 1990s and the current moral panic over the presumed "epidemic" of juvenile violence that occurred in the 1980s and 1990s (see Chapter 3). Feeling that they could no longer control children and adolescents, adults felt frustration, anger, and rage, which led them to resort to extreme control measures (Brendtro & Long, 1994). Thus zero tolerance is one of the strategies policy makers applied to youngsters, to deter them from engaging in a wide variety of delinquent behaviors. Currently, some of the best examples of zero-tolerance policies are found in schools.

There are innumerable examples of zero-tolerance policies in school systems across the

United States; most of these are aimed at drugs, weapons, violence, and speech that is deemed threatening (Leinwand, 2001). Many zero-tolerance policies have arisen from school officials' fears regarding the potential for student shootings. A sixth grader in Cobb County, Georgia, was suspended for carrying a chain that attached her Tweety Bird key ring to her wallet; the school policy banned chains that could be used as weapons. A student in Leon, Kansas, was suspended for creating an artwork that included the words, "I'll kill you all," attributed to a madman in the drawing. In another case, a 5-year-old was taken to the police station in handcuffs after rolling a pumpkin at school and hitting another student and a teacher with it (McConnaughey, 1996). In a case that received a great deal of national attention, 17-year-old Jenna Stricoff gave a friend a drink of vodka at her home before the two headed off for a day at school. She was subsequently charged with drug distribution, suspended from school, and denied entry into an alternative school. Part of the problem with this particular implementation of zero tolerance was that Jenna was a top student. In fact, she had increased her class workload so that she could graduate from high school a year early. Her father had been diagnosed with terminal cancer, and she thought her high school graduation would give him some comfort in his last days on earth. This did not matter to school officials, who remained resolute. They zealously carried out the zero-tolerance rule. The resilient Jenna overcame the poorly thought-out school action by enrolling in an independent charter school, and she did manage to graduate before her father passed away (Hui, 2001). Clearly, in cases such as Jenna's and the others cited here, zero tolerance makes zero sense.

Zero-tolerance policies are not effective because they call for immediate and severe punishment of every infraction of codes of conduct, school rules, and laws, and such an approach is not realistic. First, as Jenna Stricoff's case illustrates, rules need to be applied with some discretion. Second, every student rule violation is not brought to the attention of school authorities. Because the authorities are unable to enforce zero-tolerance policies completely and consistently, children and adolescents come to see the authorities as arbitrary and capricious in their enforcement of the rules. The authorities lose credibility, and the validity of codes of conduct, school rules, and laws is undermined. This also weakens the bonding of students to the school and teachers and undermines healthy social development, and thus may contribute to delinquency involvement. Finally, deterrence/punishment approaches in general are not effective, as I will show later in this chapter.

Aside from zero-tolerance policies and D.A.R.E., researchers have identified other ineffective school-based prevention programs (Durlak, 1997; Gottfredson, Wilson, & Najaka, 2002; U.S. Department of Health and Human Services, 2001). Most school-based programs fall short of best-practice standards (Gottfredson & Gottfredson, 2002). The effectiveness of many programs is unclear because of a lack of studies, inadequate measures of delinquency (some measure only substance use outcomes), or conflicting studies. School-based programs that are clearly ineffective include counseling regarding truancy, dropout, and antisocial or aggressive behavior (Gottfredson et al., 2002); peer-led programs (Gottfredson, 1987), including peer counseling, peer mediation, and peer leaders (U.S. Department of Health and Human Services, 2001); and nonpromotion to succeeding grades (U.S. Department of Health and Human Services, 2001). Although many substance abuse prevention programs (Orlandi, 1996) and some violence prevention programs (Powell & Hawkins, 1996) use peer leaders to train juveniles in resistance skills, peer leaders have not proven to be effective service providers. Peer leaders may eventually prove to be effective in school-based prevention programs—because peers often have higher credibility with students than teachers do—when they work in tandem with teachers who have primary responsibility for the curriculum. For example, peer leaders might effectively serve as positive role models (demonstrating refusal skills in role-playing exercises, for instance) and discussion facilitators.

Other Prevention Approaches

Many prevention approaches commonly assumed to be effective have not been tested. These include such recreational programs as Midnight Basketball, community service, and enrichment programs (Gottfredson et al., 2002; U.S. Department of Health and Human Services, 2001).

The effects of medication on childhood behavioral problems are unknown (Wasserman, Miller, & Cothern, 2000, pp. 3-4). There have been few studies of the long-term benefits of medication (Burns, Hoagwood, & Mrazek, 1999). However, positive effects have been demonstrated for some specific treatments for depression (Brent & Birmaher, 2002; Eggert, Thompson, Randell, et al., 2002), and for ADHD, especially when used with psychosocial treatment such as cognitive-behavioral therapy (Burns et al., 1999). However, as Burns et al. (1999)

note, "further replication of both psychosocial and medication interventions, separately and in combination, is seriously needed" (p. 231).

Ineffective Juvenile Justice Programs and Strategies

Punishment

Punishment is not effective for juvenile offenders. The purposes of punishment should not be confused with rehabilitation, however. Punishment serves only the purpose of "justice," to exact a penalty from one who has wronged society. Punishment does not appear to make a significant contribution to the reduction of recidivism, and studies have shown that some forms of punishment actually increase recidivism. Gendreau and colleagues conducted a meta-analysis of evaluations of programs that used a variety of "punishing smarter" techniques, including increased surveillance, home confinement, frequent drug testing, restitution, electronic monitoring, shock incarceration, and boot camps (see Gendreau, 1996b; Gendreau & Goggin, 1996). This review of 174 studies showed that these programs (both adult and juvenile) produced a slight increase in recidivism (2%). The best punishment option (restitution) reduced recidivism only 6%—in comparison with treatment programs that reduced recidivism by, on average, 25%. More severe punishments perform far more poorly. As Andrews and Bonta (1998) state: "There is no consistent evidence that variation in criminal sanctions is capable of significant reductions in criminal recidivism. The most we can say is that there is an incapacitation effect of incarceration [in the near term] but a slight increase in post-penalty criminal recidivism [in the long term]" (p. 359). Gendreau (1996) notes, "When punishment is inappropriately applied, several negative consequences can occur, such as producing unwanted emotional reactions, aggression, or withdrawal—or an increase in the behavior that is punished" (p. 129). Sanctions provide only the context for service delivery; it is the intervention within the setting that has the actual power to produce change in offenders (Andrews & Bonta, 1998; Bonta, 1996; Gendreau, Cullen, & Bonta, 1994).

Surprisingly, neither the certainty nor the severity of punishment decreases recidivism among most juveniles (Schneider, 1990; Schneider & Ervin, 1990). In her evaluation of OJJDP's national restitution program, Schneider (1990) found that adolescents who believed they were more likely to be caught committed more, rather than fewer, subsequent offenses. All of the youths had been convicted of offenses that would have been crimes if committed by adults, and many would be considered to fall into the category of serious and chronic offenders. Even those who believed they would be punished more severely if they were caught committed more, rather than fewer, subsequent offenses.

Schneider (1990, p. 109) wondered why juveniles who think they will be caught and who believe they will be punished commit more offenses, so she conducted analyses to examine several possible explanations. First, would the severity of punishment be important if the certainty of punishment was high enough? This explanation was not supported in the data. Second, would the certainty of punishment be important for persons who believed they would be punished severely if they persisted in committing offenses? This explanation was not supported. Third, would the certainty and severity of punishment be important for very-high-rate offenders? This possibility was partially supported in the data. However, this principle applied only when juveniles had six or more prior offenses. Schneider states, "This suggests that there may be a point in a juvenile career where some of the youths recognize the severity of future actions and intentionally reduce their criminal activity" (p. 109). However, most do not. Shannon (1991) found no evidence of deterrence based on severity of sanctions, but some evidence that future offense seriousness may be reduced by frequent interventions. Alternatively, we may overestimate the judgmental maturity of adolescents (Scott, 2000). They may not respond to punishment threats in the corrective manner that is often assumed. This may be attributable to the fact that they have no control over most of the risk factors that underlie their problem behaviors—especially their parents, schools, and communities.

Scared Straight Programs

Scared Straight programs are not effective. The Scared Straight approach was invented during the sixth moral panic over juvenile delinquency in the late 1970s (Finckenauer & Gavin, 1999), when a group of inmates at New Jersey's Rahway State Prison, known as the Lifers' Group, created what later became known around the world as the Scared Straight program. The program brought boys and girls into the prison and subjected them to shock therapy consisting of threats, intimidation, emotional shock, loud and angry bullying, and persuasion. The idea was to literally scare them out of

delinquency, to scare them straight. This presumed panacea was widely acclaimed and described as successful (Finckenauer & Gavin, 1999, pp. 29, 123-128). Many writers and producers for the print and broadcast media were enamored of it because of its simplicity and deterrent appeal. As many as 12,500 youths visited the Lifers each year.

However, as Finckenauer and Gavin (1999, pp. 85-93) report, empirical evidence of the effectiveness of the Rahway State Prison Scared Straight program was lacking from the beginning. Evaluations of other Scared Straight programs were mixed, but generally showed negative results (pp. 129-139). When Lipsey (1992) conducted a meta-analysis to examine the effectiveness of juvenile delinquency programs, his deterrence program category included several Scared Straight programs with other shock incarceration programs. Lipsey found that, on average, exposure to these programs increased recidivism about 12%. Remarkably, Scared Straight programs survived the negative evaluations, in part because they "reinvented" themselves by downplaying the scare tactics and emphasizing their shift in emphasis to the provision of education for youngsters about crime consequences (Finckenauer & Gavin, 1999, pp. 215-219).

Perhaps more important to the staying power of Scared Straight is the current political climate, which demands that something be done about the juvenile delinquency problem, and that this something be "rough and tough." In addition, the current media climate promoting "get tough" measures—in which programs like Scared Straight play well—helps to perpetuate the myth of their effectiveness. Various states and localities continue to replicate Scared Straight in one form or another (Finckenauer & Gavin, 1999, pp. 127-129). In 2001, middle school students in Washington, D.C., were taken on tours of the D.C. jail, where they were strip-searched; the ensuing public outcry resulted in the disciplining of several school employees (Blum, 2001).

Another version of Scared Straight in Jacksonville, Florida, is an unusually popular program that has received national attention for its "get tough" approach (Hunzeker, 1995). This program, however, puts a slightly different twist on the original Scared Straight concept described here. It exposes young delinquents to the harsh realities of adult jail (shock incarceration) and uses them as examples of youngsters gone bad to scare others, in an attempt to generate a general deterrence effect. In this program, letters are sent to county students advising them that some of their peers are doing time in the county jail. The jailed youngsters also are paraded in chains and handcuffs in front of public school students as living testimony to how serious the state is about juvenile delinquency (Hunzeker, 1995). This program has not been evaluated, but it enjoys considerable notoriety, despite the fact that programs sharing its characteristic features (shock incarceration and Scared Straight) have been shown typically to increase recidivism (Lipsey, 1992; Lipsey & Wilson, 1998). This program has staying power for the same reasons other "get tough" approaches do; in addition, the fact that it combines educational instruction with the punitive measures makes it more palatable to many people.

Boot Camps

Boot camps have not proven to be effective. Correctional boot camps—so-called because they are modeled after military induction training camps—were first established in the adult criminal justice system in 1983. They were viewed as a form of shock incarceration, following the conventional wisdom that offenders could be deterred from future criminality if they were given a taste of punishment. The first multisite evaluation of correctional boot camps was completed in 1994; the researchers concluded that recidivism rates for adults in boot camps were comparable to those for adults in traditional prisons (MacKenzie & Souryal, 1994). This conclusion has not changed (Aos, Phipps, Barnoski, & Lieb, 2001). As MacKenzie (2000) states, "There is no evidence that the correctional boot camps using the old-style military model of discipline, drill, and ceremony are effective methods of reducing recidivism" (p. 466). Nor does incarceration in boot camps reduce substance abuse (Henggeler, 1997a; Henggeler & Schoenwald, 1994). The psychological effects of the boot camp environments have long been a concern; in fact, boot camps have been shown to produce high levels of anxiety in juveniles (Gover, MacKenzie, & Armstrong, 2000). Anxiety disorders can be quite disabling (Burns et al., 1999). In a meta-analysis of predictors of juvenile recidivism from 23 studies, Cottle, Lee, and Heilbrun (2001) found that the presence of stress and symptoms of anxiety is a relatively strong predictor of recidivism.

The use of boot camps for juvenile offenders grew in popularity during the early years of the current moral panic over juvenile delinquency. The most concerted effort to develop effective boot camps for juveniles was carried out by the federal Office of Juvenile Justice and Delinquency Prevention, beginning in 1990 (Peters, Thomas, & Zamberlan, 1997). Three programs were developed in OJJDP's boot camp initiative—in Cleveland, Ohio; Denver, Colorado; and Mobile, Alabama. An evaluation of the three programs showed that boot camp participants at all three sites were slightly more likely to reoffend after release than were their control group counterparts (Peters et al., 1997).

In general, evaluations of juvenile boot camps show that recidivism rates for juveniles released from boot camps are similar to those for juveniles released from other various kinds of juvenile correctional facilities (MacKenzie, Wilson, Armstrong, & Gover, 2001). However, boot camps have the disadvantage of being far less cost-effective than other juvenile justice program alternatives (Aos et al., 2001). The cost per program participant (more than $15,000) for boot camps is greater than the benefits to taxpayers and crime benefits.

About the only positive thing that can be said about boot camps is that the inmates in them view their environment as being more therapeutic than traditional juvenile reformatories (MacKenzie et al., 2001; see also Gover et al., 2000; Styve, MacKenzie, & Gover, 2000). However, this advantage appears to be offset by the potential in boot camps for psychological, emotional, and physical abuse of youngsters—particularly for children with histories of abuse and family violence (MacKenzie et al., 2001). Staff abuses—even the deaths of several youngsters—have been reported in some juvenile boot camps (Blackwood, 2001; Krajicek, 2000). Maryland closed its boot camps after abuses were uncovered. One state—Georgia—has abandoned boot camps in response to research evidence showing their ineffectiveness (Rubin, 2000-2001). With these exceptions, the popularity of boot camps seems to continue to grow in the juvenile justice system virtually unabated. In some cases, boot camps have been made part of graduated sanctions continua—as in Texas (Briscoe, 1997) and Richmond, Virginia (Virginia Department of Criminal Justice Services, 2000). Authorities continue to find creative ways to implement the concept. In 2001, one Texas county ("New Twist," 2000) established a school-based boot camp program; it was not effective (Trulson, Triplett, & Snell, 2001).

Large Custodial Facilities

Large, congregate, custodial juvenile corrections facilities are not effective in rehabilitating juvenile offenders. Whether confinement in juvenile reformatories halts or accelerates juvenile criminal behavior is a question that has not yet been resolved; this issue has been debated since the mid-19th century (Krisberg & Howell, 1998). Postrelease recidivism rates for correctional populations range from about 55% to 90% (Austin, Elms, Krisberg, & Steele, 1991; Krisberg & Howell, 1998), and prior placement in a juvenile correctional facility is one of the strongest predictors of returning (Krisberg & Howell, 1998, p. 349; Tollett & Benda, 1999). It is clear that housing juvenile offenders in large reformatories is not an effective way to prevent or reduce juvenile offending (Bartollas & Miller, 1978; Bartollas, Miller, & Dinitz, 1976; Feld, 1977; Krisberg & Howell, 1998; Parent, Leiter, Livens, Wentworth, & Stephen, 1994; Sarri, 1981; Vinter, 1976; Visher, Lattimore, & Linster, 1991). Under the best of conditions, juvenile correctional facilities may slow down the rate of offending and—perhaps—reduce the seriousness of future offenses (Krisberg & Howell, 1998).

The most comprehensive follow-up study conducted to date of paroled youths involved inmates released from the largest complex of such facilities in the United States—the California Youth Authority. Haapanen (1990) followed parolees for approximately 15 years following their release in the 1960s. More than 90% continued to be arrested well into their adult years. In another follow-up study of youths released from the California Youth Authority, Visher et al. (1991) found that nearly 9 out of 10 youths recidivated within 3 years following their release. A main reason for the inordinately high recidivism rate in California facilities is that only 2.5% of the juveniles held in these facilities are participants in structured, long-term rehabilitative programs (Coalition for Juvenile Justice, 1999, p. 31).

Unfortunately, a large proportion of the juvenile offenders in the United States are confined in overcrowded large reformatories (Snyder & Sickmund, 1999, p. 206). Studies have shown that in large, overcrowded correctional facilities, both treatment opportunities and effectiveness of service delivery are diminished. Custodial concerns tend to override concerns about the delivery of treatment services (Sarri, 1981; Vinter, 1976), and program quality suffers (Previte, 1997). Crowding exacerbates custodial problems (Parent, Leiter, et al., 1994), making affected residential programs difficult to manage and not as safe as those operating at recommended capacities (Roush & McMillen, 2000). The result is often greater use of punitive strategies, which may increase recidivism (Andrews et al., 1990). In overcrowded juvenile facilities, violations of children's rights sometimes occur. Human Rights Watch (1995, 1996b, 1997b) has documented such violations in juvenile correctional facilities in Louisiana, Georgia, and Colorado.

Although little research has examined the negative effects of incarceration on juveniles' mental health, there is some evidence that incarcerated youths become disoriented, estranged, and alienated (McArthur, 1974), and that incarceration may produce suicidal behaviors (including attempts and self-mutilations). In the National Conditions of Confinement Study, Parent, Leiter, et al. (1994) found that in the preceding 12 months, an estimated 11,000 juveniles in reformatories and detention centers attempted 17,600 acts of suicidal behavior, and 10 suicides were completed. Several studies have shown that for juveniles, incarceration in small correctional units and placement in nonresidential programs with treatment orientations are more humane and effective than incarceration in large custodial facilities (Bakal, 1973; Bleich, 1987; Feld, 1977; Hamparian, 1987; Lerner, 1990; Lipsey & Wilson, 1998; Parent, Leiter, et al., 1994; Tollett, 1987).

Some studies seem to indicate that incarceration of juveniles further accelerates delinquency and adult criminality (Sampson & Laub, 1993; Shannon, 1991). For some youths, incarceration is but another stage in what Fleisher (1995) calls the "street life cycle." The sequence begins with a childhood stage, progresses to a teenage stage, moves to a system stage, and ends with a postsystem stage. In the system stage, chronic offenders learn to rely on juvenile corrections facilities, jails, and prisons as sanctuaries. These facilities provide safe havens from the chaos of street life for some offenders.

The cost-effectiveness of incarcerating juvenile offenders in private juvenile correctional facilities and other privately operated programs has not been determined. Pratt and Maahs (1999) note that "efforts to privatize female facilities, juvenile institutions, jails, and halfway houses have yet to be evaluated in a systematic manner" (p. 368). The costs associated with the operation of private juvenile correctional facilities have been described as "chilling," and such facilities may be inferior because of the high priority that their operators place on the profit margin (Butterfield, 1998).

Long Terms of Confinement

Sentencing juveniles to long terms of confinement is not cost-effective. Long periods of confinement do not reduce recidivism rates among juveniles, even though it might seem that they should. This is the simplistic notion behind deterrence philosophy—the longer punishment is administered, the lower the likelihood of subsequent criminality. Research has shown that this is not the case. The preponderance of evidence suggests that periods of confinement should be very brief, to minimize the negative influences of other antisocial youths in the facilities (Henggeler, Schoenwald, Borduin, Rowland, & Cunningham, 1998). These include the possibility of gang involvement (Howell, Curry, Pontius, & Roush, 2003) and the risk of violent victimization (Bishop & Frazier, 2000; Forst, Fagan, & Vivona, 1989; Parent, Leiter, et al., 1994). Juveniles should also be confined only briefly so that they can begin the process of community reintegration as early as possible (Krisberg, Neuenfeldt, Wiebush, & Rodriguez, 1994). Lipsey and Wilson's (1998) meta-analysis of institutional programs suggests that an optimal treatment program participation period is approximately 6 months; however, some confined youths view more intensive, long-term correctional programs favorably (Bishop & Frazier, 2000). In all likelihood, these youths have multiple serious problems that require long-term intensive services to ameliorate them.

Wooldredge (1988) examined the effects of length of confinement in detention centers on recidivism and found that lengthy periods of detention (more than 30 days) tended to wipe out the positive effects of court rehabilitation programs. Another study found evidence of an association between higher recidivism rates and longer detention periods as well as prior detention (Roy, 1995a).

The Special Case of
Serious and Violent Offenders

Certain juvenile justice system programs are not effective with serious and violent offenders. These include behavioral token programs—when used alone as a treatment modality (U.S. Department of Health and Human Services, 2001)—and attempts to eliminate "criminal thinking errors" with instruction and psychotherapy. The latter conception of the "criminal mind" is based on clinical work with adult criminals who were hospitalized for criminal insanity (Samenow, 1984). Studies have not demonstrated that "criminal thinking errors" are significantly more prevalent in criminals than in noncriminals. Moreover, this approach denies the importance of family, community, and other causal factors for delinquency and crime. The psychotherapy method for eliminating "criminal thinking errors" (Samenow, 1998) has not been evaluated.

For noninstitutionalized serious and violent juvenile offenders, several studies have shown that deterrence programs, as well as vocational programs that do not have educational components, actually increase recidivism. (Lipsey, 1999a;

Lipsey & Wilson, 1998). For institutionalized offenders, Lipsey and Wilson's meta-analysis shows that the weakest intervention is milieu therapy (characterized by resident involvement in decision making and day-to-day interaction for psychotherapeutic discussion).

Curfew Laws

Curfew laws do not appear to be effective in reducing serious or violent juvenile crime. Moreover, the effectiveness of curfew laws in reducing juvenile delinquency in general is questionable, as the results of three recent studies show. In a national study, McDowall, Loftin, and Wiersema (2000) examined the effects of new curfew laws in 57 large cities and found that the introduction of these laws was not followed by reductions in juvenile arrests in any serious crime category. The researchers note that "any impacts of the laws were small, and they applied only to a few offenses," such as burglary, larceny, and simple assault (pp. 88-89). These decreases occurred only for revised laws. Nighttime curfew laws appear to be no more effective than daytime laws. In a California study, Males and Macallair (1998) found that stricter curfew enforcement did not reduce juvenile crime rates. In some instances, serious crime increased at the very time officials were touting the crime reduction effects of strict curfew enforcement. Finally, in a study of four Texas cities, Adams (1997) found no consistent evidence that curfew laws reduced general rates of juvenile offending.

McDowall (2000) recently reviewed evaluations of curfew laws and concluded that these laws "have little potential to affect overall levels of crimes or victimizations involving young people" (pp. 61-62). Curfew laws cannot reasonably be expected to reduce violent juvenile crimes significantly because, ironically, most of them are imposed at a time—late at night—when few juvenile violent offenses occur. Only about one in six violent juvenile crimes occurs during curfew hours—typically between 10:00 P.M. and 6:00 A.M. (Snyder, Sickmund, & Poe-Yamagata, 1996, p. 27).

General Deterrent Policies

Policies aimed at general deterrence are not effective in reducing crime rates. This conclusion has not been altered since the 1970s (see, e.g., Blumstein, Cohen, & Nagin, 1978; Zimring & Hawkins, 1973). As Tonry (1994b) asserts, "A fair-minded survey of existing knowledge provides no grounds for believing that the War on Drugs or the harsh policies exemplified by 'three strikes and you're out' laws and evidenced by a tripling in America's prison population since 1980 could achieve their ostensible purposes" (p. 479). "Three strikes" laws do not deter crime (Kovandzic, Sloan, & Vieraitis, 2002; Shichor & Sechrest, 1996), imprisonment does not reduce recidivism (Spohn & Holleran, 2002), and there is compelling evidence that offenders sentenced to prison have higher rates of recidivism and recidivate more quickly than offenders placed on probation (Spohn & Holleran, 2002, p. 350). Interestingly, the death penalty has no deterrent effect (Cheatwood, 1993).

Unfortunately, juvenile justice policies have been becoming more and more punitive, even though increased punishments will not reduce serious and violent juvenile crime. As the research evidence reviewed above shows, most punitive general deterrence approaches are not effective with juveniles; these include detention, shock incarceration, Scared Straight programs, boot camps, incarceration in large custodial facilities, and transfer to the criminal justice system (see Chapter 8). However, there may be some delinquency reduction value to *specific* deterrence for certain types of offenses (i.e., deterrence based on an offender's personal experiences with punishment and punishment avoidance). Paternoster and Piquero (1995) found that a combination of perceived personal risk from minor forms of illegal substance use and personal experience of punishment (police apprehension, arrest, and court contact) deterred substance use in a sample of adolescents. Specific deterrence may work with serious, violent, and chronic juvenile offenders after a certain point in their careers (Schneider, 1990, p. 109).

Punishment in Adult Prisons

Punishing juveniles in adult prisons is not effective. Imprisonment of juveniles has no general deterrent effect (see Chapter 8). Confining juveniles in adult prisons appears to have only one advantage: a short-term incapacitation effect. However, there is no evidence that short-term incapacitation cannot be achieved equally effectively in juvenile reformatories. More important, the short-term incapacitation effect in adult prisons appears to be offset by detrimental long-term effects. Studies have shown that juveniles confined in adult prisons are not only more likely to recidivate than juveniles retained in juvenile reformatories, but are likely also to have increased recidivism rates and offense severity after they are released from prison (Howell, 1996). In addition, their risk of violent victimization is greater in prisons than in juvenile reformatories (see Chapter 8). Thus imprisoning juveniles in adult prisons rather than juvenile reformatories has no long-term benefit.

Out-of-Home Placements

The most restrictive out-of-home placements for mental health treatment, including psychiatric hospitalization, and placements in residential treatment centers are not effective for most child and adolescent offenders (Burns et al., 1999; Greenbaum, Dedrick, Friedman, et al., 1996; U.S. Department of Health and Human Services, 2001). Inpatient hospitalization is the least effective of all (U.S. Department of Health and Human Services, 2001, p. 171); indeed, it may do more harm than good in many cases (Weithorn, 1988). In short, "bed-driven" treatment for mental health problems is not effective. Multisystemic Therapy is recognized as an effective home-based form of treatment for delinquency, substance abuse, and mental health problems (Burns et al., 1999), and MST has demonstrated effectiveness as an alternative to psychiatric hospitalization (Henggeler, Rowland, et al., 1999).

Piecemeal Solutions

The piecemeal solutions to juvenile offending attempted by some unorganized juvenile justice systems are ineffective. In many localities, the juvenile justice systems that currently exist cannot be said to operate as "systems." Rather, they operate more like fragmented sets of subsystems that lack cohesion and integration. As Feely (2000) observes, "Each one may act with the best of intentions and totally within its guidelines, but the effect of so many agencies making individual (or at best bilateral) decisions is that a 'non-system' is formed [and] limited reforms are attempted unilaterally by one governmental branch or agency" (p. 10). Put simply, in such a "nonsystem" there is no complex whole formed by interactive, interrelated, interdependent parts—the essence of a true system. Feely illustrates the consequences with an example involving detention:

The cumulative effects of uncoordinated agency actions often have dire consequences. Youngsters are detained inappropriately, detention facilities become crowded, resources are wasted, the courts get backlogged, conditions of confinement deteriorate, and the ability of the detention agency to provide both custody and care for accused non-adjudicated youngsters is diminished. (p. 11)

Box 7.1

Common Planning Mistakes That Lead to Piecemeal Solutions

- Selection of the most popular prevention program instead of the most needed one
- Poor targeting of serious, violent, and chronic juvenile offenders
- Unbalanced emphasis on punishment versus graduated sanctions and rehabilitation
- Overreliance on detention and incarceration
- Ineffective allocation of court and correctional resources
- Failure to use risks and needs/strengths assessment instruments
- Poor matching of offenders with needed services
- Use of ineffective programs
- Failure to share information across agencies
- Failure to integrate services with other youth service systems

---

Fragmented, uncoordinated services also frustrate the mission of probation and corrections and disrupt the interface of the juvenile justice system with other child service agencies.

The "war on juveniles" mentality has undermined sound management practices, leading to such piecemeal "solutions" as boot camps, zero-tolerance policies that lead to unwarranted school suspensions and expulsions, and punitive correctional programs. Determined juvenile justice and youth service system officials can initiate system reforms that will help them to avoid some common planning mistakes that can lead to the implementation of such piecemeal solutions (see Box 7.1). In many juvenile justice systems, the planning process is encumbered by the complexity of operations and the multiple interface points among the prevention, human service, school, public safety, and social service systems. If system officials adopt sound management tools and create an interagency infrastructure that can coordinate the system parts, they can establish a comprehensive, integrated system (see Chapters 12 and 13).

Disputed Program Interventions

There is conflicting evidence about the effectiveness of several popular program interventions. These include programs that involve large groups of antisocial adolescents, gang suppression, drug/alcohol abuse treatment, drug testing and drug courts, sex offender treatment, wilderness challenge programs, restitution programs, the placement of probation officers in schools, parole, aftercare, and intensive supervision with probation. I review the research evidence on each of these interventions

below, after which I address the potential value of the "balanced and restorative justice" approach.

Programs Involving Large
Groups of Antisocial Adolescents

Programs that involve large groups of antisocial adolescents may not be effective. Research has shown that prevention programs that create intense group interactions among homogeneous groups of antisocial youths can actually increase the forms of behavior they are intended to prevent, particularly if they do not employ leaders who control the expression and rewarding of antisocial sentiments (Dishion, McCord, & Poulin, 1999). This is called the *iatrogenic effect,* meaning that the problem being addressed is inadvertently caused by the treatment procedure. Several studies have revealed this unintended consequence. In one study, Chamberlain and Reid (1998) found that children in treatment foster care homes had fewer deviant peer contacts and greater reductions in delinquency compared with children placed in group homes with other problem children. Dishion et al. (1999) found that high-risk adolescents who participated in group therapy with similar peers had more tobacco use and delinquent behavior than did adolescents in a control group at the termination of the groups, and these effects persisted through a 3-year follow-up period. Interventions that place antisocial youth together in groups may inadvertently promote friendships and alliances that undermine the very goals of the interventions and may promote further antisocial behavior rather than reduce it. (A similar dynamic may be one of the main reasons large, congregate juvenile corrections facilities are not effective; Henggeler et al., 1998.) Peer group programs such as the once-popular Positive Peer Culture (U.S. General Accounting Office, 1994) generally have had only mixed success, perhaps because they do not sufficiently counteract the negative youth culture and the helping-skills limitations of antisocial youth (Gibbs, Potter, & Barriga, 1996).

Feldman (1992) found that antisocial youths improved most in groups made up of both antisocial and conventional adolescents, with surprisingly negligible adverse effects to the conventional youth. This study suggests that an intervention that combines skilled leaders with a well-structured group context that includes a substantial proportion of conventional as well as antisocial youth can have positive effects on the antisocial youth without risking the well-being of the conventional youth.

Many prevention programs inadvertently create deviant peer groups when they form groups for activities such as anger control training, social skills training for aggressive children, and parent skills training for parents of aggressive children. This is not to say that well-managed group counseling is not an effective service intervention for reducing delinquency; it is (see Lipsey & Wilson, 1998), particularly for non-institutionalized offenders, and especially when it is integrated with other service components (Lipsey, Howell, & Tidd, 2002). A skilled therapist must manage this form of group counseling, to neutralize the negative reinforcements delinquents give each other, particularly in residential settings.

Drug Testing and Specialized Drug Courts

Drug testing is widespread in the juvenile justice system, and although there is strong professional and public support for it, under the assumption that it has a deterrent value (Crowe, 1998), to date no research has found evidence that it is an effective strategy for reducing juvenile offending. Haapanen and Britton (2002) conducted a well-designed California study in which they randomly assigned juvenile parolees to different frequencies of drug testing; they found no reductions in arrests or improved adjustment on parole in the higher test groups or for particular offender types. In fact, counter to conventional wisdom, "there was a tendency for higher testing groups to do worse" on parole (p. 232). One potential value of drug testing is the use of positive tests as a predictor of recidivism, but it appears that a history of drug use serves this purpose equally well (p. 236).

Many practitioners consider drug courts to be the panacea for substance-using delinquents. However, evaluations of juvenile drug courts are sparse, owing mainly to the relatively short history of these specialized courts. Although there are positive reports about lower rates of drug use and recidivism among juveniles handled by drug courts (Delaware Statistical Analysis Center, 1999; Shaw & Robinson, 1998, 1999), these and other studies have methodological limitations especially a lack of comparison groups (Belenko, 2001). Significant questions have been raised about the claimed success of drug courts (U.S. General Accounting Office, 1997). These specialized courts suffer from the same program limitation as programs such as D.A.R.E., boot camps, and wilderness training—failure to address the multiple determinants of delinquency, as seen in Chapter 6. Illegal substance use is a risk factor for delinquency and recidivism, but drug courts tend to ignore other risk factors and are mainly punitive in their orientation. Drug courts rarely incorporate a treatment orientation, although some do. It is possible that those that do have a much better chance of success, given Gottfredson and Exum's (2002) findings regarding a successful adult drug court that incorporated a treatment component. In addition, some of the juvenile drug court models that integrate rehabilitation with drug abuse treatment and control look promising; one example is the program currently in place in Phoenix, Arizona (Riddell, 1999).

Treatment for Alcohol and Drug Abuse

The results of the few studies that have examined drug and alcohol treatment for juvenile offenders have been mixed (Baer, MacLean, & Marlatt, 1998). Henggeler (1997a) contends that support groups, day treatment, outpatient treatment, and inpatient (residential) programs have not demonstrated effectiveness in treating children and adolescents for alcohol and drug abuse; in fact, none of these approaches appears to be more effective than no services at all (p. 262). It also is unclear whether alcohol and drug abuse treatment programs reduce delinquency. Too few well-designed studies of this topic have been conducted for us to be able to draw any conclusion (M. W. Lipsey, personal communication, October 3, 2002; Tobler, 1986).

In some cases, ineffective aftercare (relapse prevention) may negate the small positive gains achieved in drug treatment programs (Sealock, Gottfredson, & Gallagher, 1997). Some programs (e.g., group therapy) may increase juveniles' associations with problem peers, negating any positive program effects (Henggeler, 1997a, pp. 264-265). The main problem with alcohol and drug treatment programs, however, seems to be their failure to address adequately the family, school, and community problems that are strongly associated with adolescent drug use. Many of these programs have a punitive orientation. As Henggeler (1997a) observes, "It seems unrealistic to expect treatment programs (e.g., boot camps, wilderness training) that are not family- and community-based and do not address the multiple determinants of drug abuse, to be effective, and such a view is supported by the adult drug-abuse (Institute of Medicine, 1990) and delinquency (Henggeler & Schoenwald, 1994) treatment literatures" (p. 265). There are exceptions, of course, such as the use of MST for substance-abusing and substance-dependent delinquents (Henggeler, Pickrel, & Brondino, 1999).

Electronic Monitoring

The use of electronic monitoring (EM) technology for controlling offenders in North America and Europe is growing (Landreville, 1999). Begun in the United States in 1983, EM is increasingly used with juvenile offenders. What is the value of electronic monitoring? Does it help reduce recidivism? These key questions cannot be resolved at this time. Roy (1995a) has conducted some research that found low recidivism rates when EM is used in conjunction with home detention, however, as Roy notes, the low-risk offenders in the program would not have been expected to recidivate in any event. It is important to note that this study did not make use of a comparison group. Another study found higher recidivism rates among EM youths than among youths in a comparison group (Office of the Criminal Justice Coordinator, 1991). Wiebush, Wagner, Prestine, and Baird (1992) have reported on a more definitive test in which EM was used with home detention; they found no differences in recidivism between treatment and control groups. Subjects were randomly assigned to the program group or to intensive court supervision. Moreover, the EM program cost more than regular intensive court supervision.

As Wiebush and colleagues (1992) suggest, EM has a great deal of appeal. It can be—and has been—used at multiple stages of system processing, including as an alternative to detention, in conjunction with home detention, in monitoring for compliance with conditions of probation such as curfew restrictions, as an enhancement to traditional probation or parole, and as an alternative to revocation of probation or parole. Although its efficacy has not been tested in all of these environments, early studies suggest that EM contributes little, if anything, to recidivism reduction. Thus it appears that any value of EM would be for controlling offenders rather than

for any rehabilitative purpose. One study found that EM reduced juvenile offender absconding (Baumer, Maxfield, & Mendelsohn, 1993). Wiebush and colleagues (1992) found that EM had a more positive impact on serious felony offenders, although the differences were not statistically significant. EM can be used advantageously, however, as an alternative to detention (Bailey & Ballard, 2001), or as an alternative to incarceration, to reduce reliance on costly juvenile reformatories (Wood & Brown, 1989), but its potential negative psychological effects on young offenders need to be examined.

Sex Offender Treatment

As Katner (2002, p. 28) observes, most sex offender treatment programs for children and adolescents employ one or the other of the following three different treatment modalities in both residential facilities and outpatient programs:

- *Psychological therapy,* which includes sex education, victim empathy, group counseling, individual counseling, and accountability therapy
- *Biological treatment,* which includes the use of medication or drugs to suppress the male sex drive (known as chemical castration)
- *Behavior modification,* which includes social skills acquisition, modeling/role-playing therapy, individual behavioral therapy, and assertiveness training

Unfortunately, none of these specific approaches has proved to be effective (Harris, Rice, & Quinsey, 1998; Katner, 2002). There is no evidence that traditional clinical sex offender treatment reduces recidivism or converts high-risk sex offenders to individuals who are at low risk for recidivism (Katner, 2002, p. 28).

There is, however, one treatment program that has shown promise for adolescent sex offender treatment—Multisystemic Therapy (MST; Henggeler, 1997b). Unfortunately, the sample was very small ($N = 16$) in Borduin, Henggeler, Blaske, and Stein's (1990) experiment. The application of MST in programs aimed at rehabilitating sex offenders needs to be replicated in other localities with larger samples. (For a fuller discussion of MST, see Chapter 10.) It may well be that specialized clinical treatments (Romano, Tremblay, Vitaro, Zoccolillo, & Pagani, 2001) cannot succeed because sex offenders tend to have multiple other problems along with sex offending (Righthand & Welch, 2001)—including delinquency, aggressive behavior, and drug use—that need to be addressed simultaneously by programs based in multisystemic models. In addition, more studies such as Ryan, Miyoshi, Metzner, Krugman, and Fryer's (1996) examination of sex offenders are needed to build upon the scant knowledge base that exists to inform treatment.

Wilderness Challenge Programs

Wilderness challenge programs have long been promoted as a means of ameliorating delinquent behavior. As Wilson and Lipsey (2000, p. 1) note, these programs, which typically involve youth participation in a series of physically challenging activities such as rock climbing in an outdoor environment, are presumed to prevent or reduce delinquency through two interrelated dimensions of experiential learning: First, by mastering a series of incrementally challenging activities, participants realize skill mastery, which presumably builds confidence, self-esteem, and self-empowerment; and second, the group context in which the wilderness challenge program is implemented affords participants an opportunity to learn prosocial interpersonal skills that will transfer to situations outside the program.

Lipsey and Wilson's (1998) initial meta-analysis of these programs for serious and violent juvenile offenders showed that they had some weak positive effects for institutionalized youngsters but not for noninstitutionalized offenders. In a subsequent meta-analysis, Wilson and Lipsey (2000) found that wilderness challenge programs appear to be far less effective for serious and violent delinquents than for other delinquents. The researchers found that the key ingredients of more effective wilderness challenge programs appear to be (a) inclusion of a therapeutic component and (b) relatively short duration. The programs they examined that had therapeutic components employed a wide variety of techniques, including behavior management, family therapy, reality therapy, and cognitive-behavioral techniques. Wilson and Lipsey (2000) advise that, because of the small number of studies conducted to date, it is not yet "possible to draw convincing conclusions about the effectiveness of wilderness programs and how best to optimize them for reducing antisocial and delinquent behavior" (p. 8).

Restitution

Early studies of restitution programs did not show very positive effects for this approach as an independent intervention. In a multisite evaluation,

Schneider (1990) found about a 7% reduction in subsequent delinquent offenses (recidivism) in comparison with traditional probation and a lower annual offense rate of about .20 offenses per year. Her evaluation of six experimental programs showed that many restitution programs compared favorably with traditional probation, but some did not. Schneider found that restitution enjoyed an advantage when it was implemented in a programmatic fashion—that is, when offenders were assisted in finding jobs and earning money to pay restitution, as opposed to being left to their own devices to find some way to pay (which Schneider calls "ad hoc restitution"). Where restitution was slightly more effective than incarceration or traditional probation, the key ingredient seemed to be the way the program was designed. Lower recidivism rates were found when the program was not strictly punitive, but instead helped the offender to maintain a healthy self-image.

When restitution is used as a punitive measure with juvenile offenders, such as in certain kinds of community service orders, it can endanger children and adolescents. The worst recorded case is surely that of the six Las Vegas youngsters who were struck and killed by an out-of-control van as they worked on a roadside trash pickup detail; they were required to serve on the detail as part of a community service restitution requirement of their probation (Smith, 2000).

Overall, studies show that restitution has a much more positive effect when it is combined with probation and rehabilitation services (Lipsey, 1999b; Lipsey et al., 2002). Lipsey (1999b) found about a 19% reduction in recidivism when restitution is administered with probation; this reduction is nearly three times larger than Schneider found in her earlier study. Very positive effects are likely to be realized when restitution is combined with such interventions as academic enhancement and parent/family counseling, but possibly not for repeat offenders (Roy, 1995b).

In sum, punitive restitution in the form of community service does not appear to be rehabilitative in any important sense, and may put youngsters in harm's way. Use of restitution in conjunction with probation and treatment measures produces much more positive effects. In addition, it is important to note the positive effects of the restitution process on victims, in terms of victim satisfaction (Hughes & Schneider, 1989).

Probation Officers in Schools

School-based probation has become a popular strategy for immediate intervention in delinquent and predelinquent behavior. Under this model, probation officers are moved out of their traditional offices and into middle, junior high, and high school buildings (Griffin, 1999). In addition to monitoring youths on probation, school-based probation officers seek to intervene early with youths who are at risk of delinquency involvement and to facilitate improved communication between key youth services agencies and school officials. The Kern County (California) Probation Department operates what may be the oldest school-based probation program, which began in 1975. Its officers are called "prevention specialists," and they supervise probation caseloads, handle referrals for delinquency, and conduct teacher training and law-related education classes. Pennsylvania officials have established school-based probation services in 50 of that state's counties. The largest and most active program is in Allegheny County (the county that includes Pittsburgh). According to the Allegheny County Juvenile Court's policies and procedures manual, school-based probation officers are expected "to process all delinquent behavior that occurs on school grounds, before, during or after school hours, including when students are going to and from school." This program has a unique feature, the use of "behavioral assessment/referral forms," which teachers complete at the end of each class period. This admittedly crude assessment gives probation officers detailed information on each probationer's progress and school adjustment, and assists them in working with the offenders. School-based probation officers in Sacramento County, California, are involved in gang identification, truancy reduction, conflict prevention, intensive counseling, and teacher training.

Preliminary studies in Maryland and Pennsylvania suggest that school-based probation has a favorable impact on school attendance, boosts academic performance, reduces misbehavior in school, and improves the day-to-day conduct of probationers (Griffin, 1999). However, issues have been raised with respect to this program concept. Aside from the "in your face," confrontational methods used in some school-based probation programs, which are not consistent with good treatment practice, it appears that probation officers in some cases may be usurping the decision-making authority of judges by taking excessive corrective measures in the field (Griffin, 1999).

Youth Gang Suppression

Police tactics aimed at youth gang suppression include "street sweeps," the saturation of an area with police, zero-tolerance policies, and "caravanning" (cruising neighborhoods in a caravan of patrol cars) (Klein, 1995). More advanced suppression techniques include surveillance/arrest, buy/bust, and reverse sting operations; use of wiretaps; use of listening devices such as body wires; tagging of cars for electronic tracking; and use of video equipment (Bureau of Justice Assistance, 1997, pp. 62-72).

The Los Angeles Police Department (LAPD) has long been a leader in gang suppression tactics. The most notorious gang sweep, Operation Hammer, was an LAPD CRASH unit operation (Klein, 1995, pp. 162-163). It was begun in South-Central Los Angeles in 1988, when a force of a thousand police officers swept through the area on a Friday night and again on Saturday, arresting likely gang members on a wide variety of offenses, including existing warrants, new traffic citations, curfew violations, illegal gang-related behaviors, and observed criminal activities. All of the 1,453 persons arrested were taken to a mobile booking operation adjacent to the Los Angeles Memorial Coliseum. Most of the arrested youths were released without charges. Slightly more than half were gang members. There were only 60 felony arrests, and charges were filed on only 32 of them. As Klein (1995) describes it, "This remarkably inefficient process was repeated many times, although with smaller forces—more typically one hundred or two hundred officers" (p. 162).

The LAPD Rampart Division's CRASH unit polices the Rampart area, a mostly poor and Hispanic district west of downtown Los Angeles and home to the 18th Street gang. Rafael Perez, an officer in the Rampart Division, was arrested in 1998 for stealing cocaine from a police warehouse. He implicated 70 CRASH antigang officers in a variety of illegal activities: planting evidence, intimidating witnesses, beating suspects, giving false testimony, selling drugs, and covering up unjustified shootings (see Leinwand, 2000). In the end, eight cops were indicted; of these, four were cleared, three pleaded to lesser crimes, and one is awaiting trial (McCarthy, 2001).

Incredibly, the Rampart CRASH officers, who were fiercely involved in fighting gangs, came to act like gang members themselves (Deutsch, 2000; Leinwand, 2000). The line between right and wrong became fuzzy for these officers as the us-against-them ethos apparently overcame them (Deutsch, 2000). CRASH officers wore special tattoos and pledged their loyalty to the antigang unit with a code of silence. They protected their turf by intimidating Rampart-area gang members with unprovoked beatings and threats. They arrested street gang members "by the carload" (Bandes, 2000). Because of the CRASH unit's illegal activities, some 100 convictions of gang members have been overturned (McCarthy, 2001), more than 40 persons have been released from prison because of tainted convictions, and some 300 cases may be tainted and are under investigation (Leinwand, 2000). The city of Los Angeles is facing as much as $125 million in liability claims stemming from the Rampart scandal (McCarthy, 2001).

Police gang units in other cities, such as Chicago (Slater, 2000) and Las Vegas, have also been implicated in scandals arising from the use of gang suppression tactics. Gang unit police in Las Vegas conducted a drive-by shooting in a crime-infested Las Vegas neighborhood, killing one man ("Murder Case," 1998). One of the officers involved is now serving a sentence of life without the possibility of parole.

Some successes in law enforcement suppression of gangs have been reported (Braga, Kennedy, Waring, & Piehl, 2001; Orange County Chiefs' and Sheriff's Association, 1999; Wiebe, 1998), but such suppression activities typically have short-term effects. In the most detailed study of gang suppression conducted to date, Papachristos (2001) found that the aggressive federal prosecution of the Gangster Disciples had the short-term effect of reducing this gang to a loosely arranged delinquent group in the neighborhood while members aligned themselves with other criminal gangs. The destabilization of the Gangster Disciples created a power void that was quickly filled by competing gangs—mainly the Vice Lords and Latin Kings. Papachristos calls this long-term effect "gang succession" (p. 5). It was almost as if nothing had changed except the clothing of the visible gang members.

Communities typically respond to their gang problems initially with police suppression strategies (Weisel & Painter, 1997), but the tactics they use are usually of a much milder variety than those described above. Later, they tend to embrace comprehensive approaches that incorporate suppression activities with programs for prevention and intervention (see Chapter 5).

Intensive Supervision
With Probation or Parole

In their meta-analysis of institutional programs, Lipsey and Wilson (1998) did not analyze the effectiveness of intensive supervision as a separate program category for serious and violent juvenile offenders. However, Lipsey (1999b) did look at this category in his analysis of "practical" programs for delinquents in general. He found that intensive supervision programs were effective for juveniles whether they were linked with probation or with parole. In both cases the recidivism reductions were statistically significant. Lipsey's discovery of the effectiveness of practical intensive supervision programs (ISPs) in conjunction with probation contradicts the negative or neutral evaluations of ISPs that have been reported in the literature by Altschuler, Armstrong, and MacKenzie (1999) and MacKenzie (2000). Reviews of the literature on ISPs have tended to overlook certain effective probation-linked ISPs (Sametz & Hamparian, 1990) as well as the most effective parole-linked ISP (Josi & Sechrest, 1999) and the earliest ISP to be evaluated and found effective, the North Carolina Intensive Supervision Project. The North Carolina program worked effectively with status offenders who were at risk of becoming serious, violent offenders (I describe this program in Chapter 10).

It appears that most of the weak or ineffective programs reviewed by Altschuler and colleagues (1999) and MacKenzie (2000) had few of the characteristics of effective ISPs that have been identified (Sontheimer & Goodstein, 1993; Wiebush & Hamparian, 1991; see Chapter 10). The key to effective intensive supervision programs—in conjunction with either probation or parole—appears to be a strong treatment orientation. The overwhelming majority of ISPs are designed to accomplish only one thing: increase public safety through the close surveillance of offenders. By itself, this does not reduce recidivism; an ISP must be linked to a program continuum to be effective. It also should be noted that there is an important risk to offenders in intensive supervision programs: Such programs may "widen the net" of control by placing low-risk youths on intensive supervision (Barton & Butts, 1990).

Parole

As noted earlier in this chapter, follow-up studies of juveniles released from juvenile correctional facilities show high recidivism rates among these youth; this is strong evidence that juvenile parole is not effective. Corrective measures, such as reducing parole officers' caseloads, have not proved to be effective (Lipsey & Wilson, 1998).

Although the juvenile justice system has not abandoned the use of parole to the extent that the adult criminal justice system has (Travis & Petersilia, 2001), there is far less parole supervision today than in the past. In a national study of juvenile boot camps and traditional reformatories, MacKenzie et al. (2001) found that administrators in the majority of both types of facilities had no follow-up information on youths who had been released from them. Only 46% of boot camp operators and 32% of traditional juvenile reformatory administrators received follow-up information on released youth (p. 297). MacKenzie et al. comment, "We wonder how staff and administrators who view their mission as the rehabilitation of juveniles can plan and improve programs if they do not know what happens to the youth once they leave the facility" (p. 306).

Parole can be effective when it is combined with programs that help offenders make the transition from confinement to independent living. This intervention strategy, called *aftercare,* appears to be particularly effective with intensive supervision (Lipsey, 1999b), particularly in a step-up and step-down model. Effective aftercare appears to be essential for helping chronic violent offenders desist from criminal careers (Haggard, Gumpert, & Grann, 2001). However, the effectiveness of aftercare programs is disputed, as I discuss below.

Aftercare

Evaluations of aftercare programs have been sparse. Most conducted to date have been concerned with programs linked with juvenile reformatories. Altschuler et al. (1999) found that the few well-designed evaluations of aftercare programs that have been completed have shown mixed results. However, in his meta-analysis of all evaluations of "practical" (everyday) programs, Lipsey (1999b) found that aftercare programs, supplemented with intensive supervision or reduced caseload programs, produced significantly large reductions in recidivism. This discrepancy between the two reviews is difficult to explain. It appears that most of the demonstration programs Altschuler and colleagues reviewed tended to emphasize punitive measures at the expense of treatment (see Altschuler, 1998), whereas most of the practical programs Lipsey reviewed did not.

Altschuler and Armstrong (1994a, 1994b) conducted an experiment to determine whether a comprehensive aftercare model could be integrated with existing correctional programming. They implemented and tested intensive aftercare programs (IAPs) in four sites (Colorado, Nevada, New Jersey, and Virginia; for a description of the four projects, see Altschuler et al., 1999). Wiebush (2001) conducted an evaluation of the IAPs. Although it had limitations, the study found that the IAPs were not

successful in reducing recidivism. However, the IAP model was tested in states that, at that time, did not have particularly advanced procedures for matching offenders' risks and needs with the sanctions and treatment recommended in the structured decision-making model (see Chapter 12). Thus these states likely did not have suitable foundations on which to build successful aftercare programs. Jurisdictions that implement the graduated sanctions component of the Comprehensive Strategy (see Chapter 12) are in a much better position to implement effective aftercare programs than are those that mismatch offenders with programs and sanctions.

One correctional aftercare program has produced very positive short-term effects (Josi & Sechrest, 1999). The Lifeskills '95 program in California's San Bernardino and Riverside Counties is an aftercare program for youthful offenders released from the California Youth Authority. The reintegration approach of this program is based on Operation New Hope's well-developed Los Osos "lifestyles" awareness program (Degnan, 1994; Degnan & Degnan, 1993), which is grounded in William Glasser's widely acclaimed "reality therapy" approach (see Bassin, Bmatter, & Rachin, 1976).

A main objective of the interactive Lifeskills '95 program is to "reinforce the small steps of progress while addressing the fears of the real world confronted by the newly released parolee" (Degnan, 1994, p. 46). The program is based on six principles of programmatic action that address the behavioral antecedents believed to be most responsible for failure to reintegrate:

- Improve the basic socialization skills necessary for successful reintegration into the community
- Significantly reduce criminal activity in terms of amount and seriousness
- Alleviate the need for, or dependence on, alcohol or illicit drugs
- Improve overall lifestyle choices (i.e., social, education, job training, and employment)
- Reduce the individual's need for gang participation and affiliation as a support mechanism
- Reduce the high rate of short-term parole revocations

The program's treatment regimen consists of 13 counseling modules, each of which represents a 3-hour program of lecture and group discussion. Participants are exposed to a series of lifestyle choices designed to restore self-control to their lives and initiate a positive decision-making process geared toward success (Degnan, 1994).

Josi and Sechrest (1999) conducted an outcome comparison of an experimental group made up of parolees in the Lifeskills '95 program and a control group (similar parolees from a California Youth Authority reformatory who lived outside the project area), all of whom were high-risk, chronic juvenile offenders, and found considerable program success. In the 90-day follow-up, individuals assigned to the control group were about twice as likely as experimental group members to have been arrested, to be unemployed and to lack the resources necessary to gain or maintain employment, to have a poor attitude toward working, and to have abused drugs and/or alcohol frequently since release. In addition, only 8% of the Lifeskills '95 youths associated frequently with former gang associates, versus 27% of the control group members. These differences were statistically significant both at the time of the 90-day follow-up and at the time of the final comparison (which ranged from 3 months to 1 year), but the margin began to narrow over time (the researchers speculate that this might be due to the shortness of the program). Josi and Sechrest attribute the effectiveness of the program to its positive atmosphere, its individualized treatment approach, and its intensive job training element, and to the unintentional placement of many of the parolees away from their original communities in Los Angeles to outlying counties, which may have served to remove them from "the negative influences of a dysfunctional family, from renewed contact with sibling offenders, from substance-abusing associates, from negative peer gangs, and from the long-term effects of socioeconomic isolation" in Los Angeles (pp. 75-76).

In sum, Josi and Sechrest's (1999) study suggests that aftercare that incorporates principles of effective programming can produce large positive short-term effects. However, it also suggests that for aftercare to be effective, correctional agencies need to make changes in their policies and procedures. As Josi and Sechrest note: "The critical issue of re-entry itself not only concerns the offender's needs and problems during this period, but also involves the negligence of the responsible correctional agency and its service components, namely institutions and parole. These components may create many re-entry problems and take little responsibility for helping the parolees manage their reintegration" (p. 77).

Balanced and Restorative Justice

The community approach known as "balanced and restorative justice" (BARJ) is appealing to many because of its punitive orientation toward juvenile offenders and its concern for victims. BARJ has its roots in the retributive just deserts philosophy (American Friends Service Committee, 1971) and in utilitarian philosophy (Van den Haag, 1975), both of which value the concept of ensuring that offenders make things right with society (by making restitution, to restore it to its prior condition) and the concept that offenders must "pay" for having harmed society or individuals (Clear, 1994; Howell, 1997, pp. 19-20). Both of these philosophies also assume the ineffectiveness of the juvenile justice system and emphasize the value of punishment—not rehabilitation—for maintaining order in society. The adherents of utilitarian philosophy would abolish the juvenile court and have the criminal justice system adjudicate juvenile offenders, commensurate with the seriousness of their offenses. Just deserts and utilitarian philosophies influenced the shift in criminal justice system philosophy in the 1970s from rehabilitation of offenders to punishment of offenses, which filtered down to the juvenile justice system in the 1980s. Advocates of these philosophies would have the juvenile justice system focus on "doing justice" rather than on attempting to rehabilitate delinquents.

BARJ also grew out of the juvenile justice restitution and victims' rights movements in the United States (Bazemore & Umbreit, 1994). The restitution movement stresses the importance of victim satisfaction in the justice process and of having offenders repair the harm they have done to victims. The National Restitution Association was formed in the 1980s; it was renamed the National Restorative Justice Association in the early 1990s. Initially, BARJ was conceptualized as a framework for improving juvenile probation (Maloney, Romig, & Armstrong, 1988).

Advocates of BARJ state that this approach has three main purposes in regard to juvenile offenders: to promote accountability, to promote competency development, and to promote community safety. *Accountability* refers to the requirement that offenders make amends to their victims and to the community for harm caused. By *competency development*, BARJ advocates mean bringing offenders to realize that their actions are wrong and increasing their ability to empathize with the victims of their crimes. *Community protection* refers to the juvenile justice system's duty to ensure public safety. Advocates of restorative justice have embraced "community justice" and such problem-solving strategies as community policing, community prosecution, circle sentencing (in which community representatives determine punishments), and community courts. However, the essence of BARJ is its emphasis on the moral accountability of offenders to their victims and the affected community; this accountability is demonstrated through some form of reparation—that is, restorative justice (Bazemore & Umbreit, 1995).

Although they may view the restorative justice philosophy's emphasis on victims' rights and victim satisfaction with the justice process as long overdue, criminologists and practitioners are beginning to question the potential value of policies based in this philosophy, particularly because of its strong retributive focus (Herman, 1999; Levrant, Cullen, Fulton, & Wozniak, 1999; Presser & Gunnison, 1999). Many of the restorative justice policies that have been implemented are "strikingly authoritarian, retributive methods of social control" (Wakeling, Jorgensen, Michaelson, et al., 2000, p. 88). This is not to say that all restorative justice advocates embrace punishment for punishment's sake (Braithwaite, 2001). In addition, there is concern that interventions based on this philosophy will be more symbolic than substantive and that they may produce unintended punitive effects (Levrant et al., 1999).

Although the three-part BARJ framework has been used to guide intervention planning in some localities, there is no sound empirical evidence to date of the effectiveness of such approaches for reducing recidivism. However, important advances have been made in victim satisfaction as a result of increased system responsiveness to those who have been victimized and offender restitution. The BARJ model's concept of offender accountability may well make some contribution at the front end of a sanctions continuum (see Chapter 13). The three-part BARJ approach has some inherent advantages over the traditional criminal justice continuum, which has the treatment emphasis at one end and the punishment (retributive) emphasis at the other (Wilson, 2000). For BARJ to have utility for programs aimed at rehabilitating juvenile offenders, however, its concept of competency development needs to be redefined so that it addresses the specific treatment needs of offenders in the traditional, individualized justice model of juvenile courts (which works very well, as I will show in Chapter 10). As currently conceived, competency development is but a small component of the successful individualized treatment regimen of juvenile court programs concerned with the rehabilitation of serious, violent, and chronic juvenile offenders who have multiple serious treatment needs. However, the BARJ concept has some utility for structuring accountability measures at the front end of the juvenile justice system, such as in restitution programs.

Summary

Several approaches to the prevention of juvenile delinquency have been shown to be ineffective. D.A.R.E. is one of the many informational, or instructive, programs that have been shown to be ineffective. Zero-tolerance policies have also been shown to be ineffective. Drug testing does not appear to have a treatment benefit. Curfew laws do not appear to be effective in preventing delinquency—particularly not violent delinquency. Several ineffective school-based delinquency prevention programs have been identified.

Punishment is not effective in reducing recidivism. Sanctions provide only the context for service delivery; it is the intervention within the setting that has the actual power to produce change in offenders. A number of juvenile offender rehabilitation programs and strategies clearly do not work, and some of the more punitive ones may actually increase recidivism. Punishing juveniles in adult prisons is not effective. Individual deterrence programs such as shock incarceration, Scared Straight programs, and boot camps are not effective and may increase recidivism; these kinds of interventions should be abandoned. Placement of juvenile offenders in large, congregate, custodial reformatories is not effective, nor are long sentences of confinement in such facilities. In general, removal of antisocial youths from their families, schools, neighborhoods, and communities for the purpose of treatment is not effective. This includes residential drug treatment and out-of-home placements for mental health treatment and psychiatric hospitalization; the latter may do more harm than good. As a general principle, bed-driven treatment for delinquency, mental health problems, and substance abuse does not work and certainly is not cost-effective. Electronic monitoring does not appear be effective in reducing recidivism. The evidence is mixed on treatment of children for drug and alcohol abuse, and there have been too few evaluations of these treatment programs for juvenile offenders for us to be able to draw any conclusions regarding their effectiveness.

Certain juvenile justice system programs are not effective with serious and violent offenders. Several studies have shown that deterrence programs and vocational programs that do not have educational components actually increase recidivism. For institutionalized offenders, the weakest intervention is milieu therapy (characterized by resident involvement in decision making and day-to-day interaction for psychotherapeutic discussion).

Disputed interventions for delinquents in general include the use of peer leaders in prevention

---

Box 7.2

Juvenile Justice Programs and Strategies That Clearly Do Not Work

---

- D.A.R.E.
- Zero-tolerance policies
- Curfew laws
- Punishment without treatment and rehabilitation services
- Removal of antisocial youths from their families, schools, neighborhoods, and communities for treatment
- Bed-driven treatment for mental health, delinquency, and drug abuse problems
- Youth gang suppression without other interventions
- Large, congregate, custodial corrections facilities
- Shock incarceration, "scared straight" programs, and boot camps
- Programs involving large groups of antisocial adolescents
- Piecemeal solutions
- Transfer of juveniles to the criminal justice system
- Incarceration of juveniles in adult prisons

---

programs, drug testing and drug courts, electronic monitoring, drug/alcohol abuse treatment, sex offender treatment, wilderness challenge programs, programs involving large groups of delinquents, restitution, the placement of probation officers in schools, parole, police gang suppression, and intensive supervision. Two of these interventions have been shown to be effective: restitution and intensive supervision. When designed properly, intensive supervision programs that link probation with treatment interventions are effective. Finally, the popular balanced and restorative justice model appears to have little utility for the management and rehabilitation of serious, violent, and chronic juvenile offenders.

Piecemeal solutions have frustrated effective planning and service delivery in the juvenile justice system and its partner agencies. The "war on juveniles" has undermined sound management practices, leading juvenile justice officials to implement such "solutions" as boot camps, zero-tolerance policies (which have led to unwarranted school suspensions and expulsions), and punitive correctional programs. Such "easy fixes" often cause more problems than they solve. In the juvenile justice system,

as in any system, a change in policies or practices in one part affects all other parts of the system. If system officials adopt sound management tools, they can create a comprehensive, integrated, interagency system and an interagency infrastructure for coordinating the system parts. There are no magic bullets.

Discussion Questions

1. Why has the D.A.R.E. program had such staying power despite its ineffectiveness?

2. Why are zero-tolerance policies ineffective?

3. Why are there no panaceas for the problems associated with juvenile offenders?

4. Why are "bed-driven" treatment programs ineffective?

5. What are the strengths and weaknesses of the BARJ model?

6. How has the "war on juveniles" contributed to the adoption of piecemeal solutions?

8
■

TRANSFER OF JUVENILES TO THE CRIMINAL
JUSTICE SYSTEM

In this chapter, I examine the practice of transferring juveniles from the juvenile justice system to the criminal justice system. Before the juvenile justice system was created in the United States near the end of the 19th century, juveniles were handled in the criminal courts (see Box 8.1). For nearly a century, Americans accepted the juvenile justice system as society's treatment and control apparatus for virtually every juvenile offender. In the past decade, however, this acceptance has diminished (Fagan & Zimring, 2000). Transfer of juveniles to the criminal justice system is now commonplace in the United States. Legislatures have turned large numbers of juveniles over to criminal courts by increasing the role of prosecutors in transfer decisions, excluding certain offenders from the jurisdiction of the juvenile court, and lowering the age of eligibility for transfer.

With the creation of juvenile courts more than 100 years ago, Americans rejected the use of criminal courts and imprisonment to punish juveniles. Now, policy makers and legislators are embracing criminal court handling of juvenile offenders and diminishing the role of juvenile courts. Treatment and control policies concerning juvenile offenders in the United States have thus come full circle.

I begin this chapter with a brief description of juvenile justice philosophy in the United States, followed by a discussion of the principal mechanisms used to remove juveniles from the juvenile justice system and turn them over to the criminal justice system. I use the special case of one particular 11-year-old boy charged with murder as a backdrop

for considering the adequacy of the criminal justice system for handling juvenile offenders. The remainder of the chapter addresses the appropriateness of transferring juveniles to the criminal justice system.

U.S. Juvenile Justice Philosophy

Juvenile justice policy in the United States is grounded in three philosophical principles that govern how justice should be administered when the accused offenders are children and adolescents. These principles are tied to our society's views about childhood and adolescence as periods of maturation and social development. From the time juvenile courts were first established, they have recognized that "children are developmentally different from adults; they are developing emotionally and cognitively; they are impressionable; and they have different levels of understanding than adults" (National Council of Juvenile and Family Court Judges, 1998, p. 1). It has been understood that a separate court system is appropriate for children and adolescents because, by virtue of their age and immaturity, they "are not fully responsible for their antisocial behavior and can, if humanely treated in proper rehabilitation programs, become productive members of society" (Hutzler, 1982, p. 26).

These views support three clusters of philosophical principles that are central to the administration of justice in the American juvenile justice system: *diminished capacity*, *proportionality*, and *room to*

Box 8.1
The American Juvenile Justice System: A Brief History

Origins of the System

The philosophical foundations of the American system of juvenile justice are found in the concepts of "childhood" and "adolescence" developed by American social reformers (see Empey, 1978; Empey & Stafford, 1991). Before the time of the discovery of the New World, children often were discarded, ignored, and exploited. It was not uncommon in the ancient civilizations of the Middle East, Greece, Rome, and Europe for children to be thrown away. Infanticide appears to have been practiced as late as the 17th century in France and England (DeMause, 1974; Illick, 1974). Thus the English and other Europeans who established the first colonies and formed the United States inherited a disregard for children from the practices of their homelands. The modern concepts of "childhood" and "adolescence" were not developed in the United States until after the colonial era (Empey, 1978).

To define the role of the state vis-à-vis children and adolescents, Americans adopted the English concept of *parens patriae* (Latin for "parent of his country"), or government as parent. The concept originated in medieval English doctrine, where it referred to the right of the king (the state) to provide protection for any persons who did not possess full legal capacity, including insane and incompetent persons and children. The right to intervene in family matters on behalf of children and to protect property rights of the young was bestowed on the crown. The jurisdiction of English chancery courts then was extended to abused, dependent, and neglected children. In the United States, the *parens patriae* concept was expanded to include delinquent children and provided the justification for treatment and incarceration of delinquents in the new juvenile justice system.

Formation of the System

The unique American system of juvenile justice was formed of two parts: correctional facilities for children and adolescents, and juvenile courts (Finestone, 1976; Mennel, 1973; Platt, 1977; Rothman, 1971). The precedent for institutions for children originated in 16th-century European religious reform movements. These movements changed the public perception of children from "miniature adults" to immature persons whose moral and mental capacities are not fully formed. Boarding schools were established for delinquent children to help develop their mental and moral capacities through strict daily regimens (Aries, 1962).

"Gentleman reformers" created the New York House of Refuge for delinquent children and adolescents in 1825. Because they believed that the unstable urban environment in East Coast cities was corrupting to children, these reformers felt that delinquents needed to be placed in a controlled environment, in a "refuge," where they could be inculcated with the "appropriate morality" and middle-class values (Finestone, 1976). Only those children the courts believed could still be rescued from delinquency were sent to the House of Refuge; these were children who were prematurely corrupted and corrupting. Older and more serious juvenile offenders were dealt with in the adult criminal system (Fox, 1970). The House of Refuge offered food, clothing, shelter, and education to homeless and destitute children (Fox, 1970) and encouraged their reformation through a complex system of rewards and punishments.

Other houses of refuge—the original American juvenile corrections facilities—soon were built in other East Coast cities, patterned after the English bridewells (institutions for youthful beggars and vagrants) and the Elmira Reformatory for adults (Dean & Reppucci, 1974). These institutions became family substitutes, "not only for the less serious juvenile [offenders], but for other children who were defined as a problem—the runaway, the disobedient or defiant child, or the vagrant who was in danger of falling prey to loose women, taverns, gambling halls, or theaters" (Empey, 1978, p. 82). Dependent, neglected, and delinquent children were housed together, a practice that still prevails in some juvenile detention facilities.

(Continued)

Box 8.1 (Continued)

Invention of the Juvenile Court

Unlike juvenile correctional facilities, which preceded it by almost 75 years, the juvenile court is purely an American invention. In the late 1800s, the ladies of the Chicago Women's Club were finding that their efforts to improve the criminal justice system and the conditions in jails were inadequate, and they turned their reformist zeal to improving the conditions in which children were confined. They came up with the idea of establishing a special court and separate correctional procedures for children (Finestone, 1976). The members of the club believed that a separate juvenile court could be an effective instrument for the advancement of youth welfare, that it could succeed where social institutions had failed. Thus they saw the juvenile court as "the cornerstone of a comprehensive child care system" (Finestone, 1976, p. 45).

The Juvenile Court Act was passed by the Illinois State Legislature in 1899. As envisaged in the statute, the first juvenile court was to represent a radical departure in the treatment of delinquents. The juvenile court would pay less attention to the offenses themselves (in contrast to the usual practice in adult criminal court) and more attention to the general circumstances lying behind offenders' misconduct. The court was expected to protect youngsters from harmful influences and to rehabilitate them through the use of such mechanisms as probation, treatment, and incarceration, if necessary. In more serious cases, the juvenile court would rely on more restrictive measures to pursue the overall goal of remediating delinquent behavior (Maloney, Romig, & Armstrong, 1988). As Hutzler (1982) explains, "Whatever the conduct that brought the child to the court's attention, the juvenile court judge was to consider the broad range of social facts regarding the child and his family and to direct treatment 'in the child's best interests' and in accordance with his needs" (p. 27). By 1925, all but two states had established juvenile courts (Krisberg & Austin, 1993). Every one of them had juvenile reformatories in one form or another; some of them were called industrial schools or training schools (Dean & Reppucci, 1974).

Differences Between Criminal
Courts and Juvenile Courts

As in European courts, U.S. criminal court procedures were based on an accusatorial and adversarial model, in which charges are brought against the individual by the state and rebutted by the defendant's lawyer. Persons are "tried" in accordance with procedural rules and found "guilty" or "innocent." Guilty persons are sentenced to terms of community service, probation, jail, or prison, or their sentences can be conditionally set aside. The criminal courts are expected to ensure to defendants the basic protections set forth in the U.S. Constitution, including the right to an attorney, the right not to testify, the right to confront witnesses, and the right to a jury trial (Scheb & Scheb, 2002).

Juvenile courts, in contrast, are civil courts, and they do not follow criminal court procedures (Bartollas, 2002; Steinberg & Schwartz, 2000). They operate as nonadversarial, fact-finding courts. Juvenile courts consider extralegal factors that may be linked with the defendants' delinquency, especially family conditions, in deciding how to handle cases. Because these courts are designed to recognize the special needs and immature status of youngsters, they emphasize rehabilitation over punishment. Youngsters are "adjudicated" delinquent, not found guilty or innocent. "Dispositions" of cases are made instead of sentences. Socially minded judges preside over juvenile courts, hearing and adjudicating cases not according to rigid rules of law, but according to the interests of society, the interests of the child, and child development principles. Juvenile courts have no juries; instead, court staffs include sociologists, psychologists, social workers, and child-care specialists. Because juvenile courts are supposed to act "in the best interests of the child," they have no need for the formulation of legal rules of defendant rights, due process, and constitutional safeguards that, presumably, marks the adult judicial process (Maloney et al., 1988).

SOURCE: Adapted from Howell (2001a, pp. 305-307).

reform (Zimring, 1998a). Each of these principles is based in the understanding that children are not little adults, and they should not be treated as such. This view gave rise to the first juvenile court more than a century ago (see Box 8.1).

Issues grouped in the *diminished capacity* (or responsibility) category relate to the degree to which children and adolescents should be held responsible for their delinquent acts. Culpability is the key issue here—whether juvenile offenders can fully appreciate or control their actions (Grisso & Schwartz, 2000, p. 267). Although older adolescents may have adultlike capacities for reasoning, their ability to exercise sound judgment in ambiguous or stressful situations—especially while operating in a peer group context—may be limited (Scott, 2000). Historically, in the United States children below age 7 have not been deemed fully responsible for criminal acts by reason of incapacity, and those between ages 7 and 14 have been subjected to special inquiries regarding their criminal capacity. In other words, the older the adolescent, the greater the degree of responsibility. However, even youths over age 14, and perhaps beyond age 16, should not be considered fully culpable—especially from the standpoint of being able to apply the cognitive abilities that they possess uniformly across different problem-solving situations (Scott, 2000).

The logic of the concept of *proportionality* is that, "even after a youth passes the minimum threshold of competence that leads to finding capacity to commit crime, the barely competent youth is not as culpable and therefore not as deserving of a full measure of punishment as a fully qualified adult offender" (Zimring, 1998b, p. 486). This is the idea that the punishments meted out to juveniles for crimes they have committed should be graduated (i.e., made increasingly more severe) and in proportion to the offenses. Because of the malleability of youngsters, adolescence has traditionally been recognized as "a stage of developmental immaturity that rendered youths' transgressions less blameworthy than those of adults and required a special legal response" (Grisso, 1996, p. 230). Mitigation of punishments for juveniles because of their lack of development of social and mental capacity is not something new, or something that originated in the United States. This principle has its origins in ancient civilizations (Bernard, 1992, pp. 28-29), including the Code of Hammurabi (written more than 4,000 years ago), the Twelve Tables of Roman law (about 450 B.C.), Saxon law (about 500-600 A.D.), and English common law (about the mid-1300s A.D.).

The third philosophical principle is *room to reform*. Policies based on this principle "are derived from legal policies toward young persons in the process of growing up. They are the same policies as we apply to young drivers, teen pregnancy, and school dropouts" (Zimring, 1998b, p. 486). We do not ban juveniles from society for transgressions in these and other arenas. As Zimring (1998a) explains, "Room-to-reform policies address not so much the amount of punishment imposed as the kind of punishment and the kind of consequences that should be avoided" (p. 87). These policies are intended as safeguards, to reduce the permanent costs of adolescent mistakes and enable young offenders to make successful adolescence-to-adulthood transitions with their life chances intact.

These three philosophical underpinnings are the basis of the fundamental difference between the juvenile court and the adult criminal court: The juvenile court seeks to rehabilitate juvenile delinquents, thereby preventing future criminal behavior, whereas the adult criminal court seeks to induce law-abiding behavior by means of punishment for wrongdoing.

Mechanisms Used to Transfer Juveniles to the Criminal Justice System

Four primary mechanisms are used to transfer juveniles from the juvenile justice system to the criminal justice system (see Box 8.2). *Transfer* is the general term commonly used to describe this process. The term *waiver* is also used, but as a general descriptive term it can lead to some confusion, because technically *waiver* refers to the judicial form of transfer—that is, judicial waiver—which is only one of the four transfer mechanisms.

Each state has its own laws governing how juvenile offenders are handled. Adjudication of their offenses originates exclusively in juvenile courts in every state. This practice resulted from the creation of a separate juvenile justice system in the United States in the late 19th and early 20th centuries (see Box 8.1). Because the state laws give juvenile courts exclusive jurisdiction over offenders below a specific age (typically 18), other laws must be used to transfer juveniles from the juvenile justice system to the criminal justice system. Four types of laws are used for this purpose (see Box 8.2). Table 8.1 shows the application of the first three types of laws in the respective states. Originally, juvenile court judges had exclusive authority to transfer juveniles to the criminal courts. The next two mechanisms (concurrent jurisdiction, or prosecutor direct file, and statutory exclusion) have come into widespread use

---

Box 8.2

Transfer Mechanisms

Provisions for transferring juveniles to the criminal justice system fall into the following four general categories (Redding & Howell, 2000; Snyder & Sickmund, 1999, p. 102):

- *Judicial waiver:* The juvenile court judge has the authority to waive juvenile court jurisdiction and transfer the case to criminal court. In some states this process is referred to as *certification, remand,* or *binding over for criminal prosecution.* In other states, judges *transfer* or *decline* rather than waive jurisdiction.
- *Concurrent jurisdiction:* Original jurisdiction for certain cases is shared by the criminal and juvenile courts, and the prosecutor has discretion to file such cases in either court. Transfer under concurrent jurisdiction provisions is also known as *prosecutorial waiver, prosecutor discretion,* and *direct file.*
- *Statutory exclusion:* Some state statutes exclude juveniles who are accused of certain offenses from juvenile court jurisdiction. Under statutory exclusion provisions, cases originate in criminal rather than juvenile court. Statutory exclusion is also known as *legislative exclusion, automatic transfer,* and *mandatory transfer.* These statutes typically exclude from juvenile court youths who are charged with particular offenses beyond a certain age (e.g., youths age 14 and older charged with violent crimes).
- *Blended sentencing:* Some state statutes increase the sentencing options available in the juvenile court by linking juvenile and adult sentencing. The juvenile court may impose a juvenile or an adult sentence, impose both a juvenile and an adult sentence, or impose a sentence past the normal limit of juvenile court jurisdiction. Blended sentencing is also known as *blended jurisdiction.*

---

during the current moral panic over delinquency, in a wave of "get tough" juvenile legislation.

As Table 8.1 shows, most judicial waiver statutes are *discretionary* (46 states), meaning that the transfer decision is entirely within the discretion of juvenile court judges—unless there are other restrictive laws. Until recently, juvenile court judges made most of the juvenile transfer decisions. Judicial waiver is *mandatory* for certain offenses in 14 states, once the juvenile court judge determines that certain statutory criteria have been met. In 15 states, judicial waiver is *presumptive*, requiring that certain juveniles be waived to criminal court unless they can prove they are suitable for juvenile rehabilitation.

State legislatures now make transfer decisions in more than half of the states through *statutory exclusions* (28) and by allowing prosecutor concurrent jurisdiction (15). In states allowing *reverse waiver* (23 states), criminal courts are allowed to transfer a juvenile back to the juvenile justice system. *Once an adult, always an adult* means that once a juvenile has been transferred to and prosecuted in criminal court, all of his or her subsequent offenses will be

prosecuted in criminal courts. More than half (31) of the states have such provisions.

Table 8.2 shows the number of states that made existing transfer provisions tougher or enacted new ones from 1992 through 1997 as a result of the seventh moral panic over juvenile delinquency. These legislative actions brought about a sea change in transfer policies and in the number of juveniles moved into the criminal justice system. The combination of lowering the age of transfer and adding more crimes (especially less serious and less violent crimes) to the excluded offense statutes served to extract a large number of juvenile offenders from the juvenile justice system and move them into the criminal justice system. Florida alone reports an average of nearly 5,000 transfers per year (Snyder & Sickmund, 1999, p. 105). From 1992 through 1997, the age limit for transfer was lowered in 22 states, in discretionary waiver and statutory exclusion provisions (see Table 8.2). Missouri lowered the age for transfer of juvenile offenders from 14 to 12 for any felony (Torbet et al., 1996, p. 6).

A few other states lowered the age of juvenile court jurisdiction from 17 to 16, thus transferring all

TABLE 8.1   State Transfer Provisions

	Judicial waiver			Concurrent jurisdiction	Statutory exclusion	Reverse waiver	Once an adult/ always an adult
	Discretionary	Presumptive	Mandatory				
Total number of States:	46	15	14	15	28	23	31
Alabama	x				x		x
Alaska	x	x			x		
Arizona	x	x		x	x	x	x
Arkansas	x			x		x	
California	x	x					x
Colorado	x	x		x		x	
Connecticut			x			x	
Delaware	x		x		x	x	x
Dist. of Columbia	x	x		x			x
Florida	x			x	x		x
Georgia	x		x	x	x	x	
Hawaii	x						x
Idaho	x				x		x
Illinois	x	x	x		x		
Indiana	x		x		x		x
Iowa	x				x	x	
Kansas	x	x					x
Kentucky	x		x			x	
Louisiana	x		x	x	x		
Maine	x						
Maryland	x				x	x	
Massachusetts				x	x		
Michigan	x			x			x
Minnesota	x	x			x		x
Mississippi	x				x	x	x
Missouri	x						x
Montana	x			x	x		
Nebraska				x		x	
Nevada	x	x			x	x	x
New Hampshire	x	x					x
New Jersey	x	x					
New Mexico					x		
New York					x	x	
North Carolina	x		x				
North Dakota	x	x	x				x
Ohio	x		x				x
Oklahoma	x			x	x	x	x
Oregon	x				x	x	x
Pennsylvania	x	x			x	x	x
Rhode Island	x	x	x				x
South Carolina	x		x		x	x	
South Dakota	x				x	x	x
Tennessee	x					x	x
Texas	x						x
Utah	x	x			x		x
Vermont	x			x	x	x	
Virginia	x		x	x		x	x
Washington	x				x		x
West Virginia	x		x				
Wisconsin	x				x	x	x
Wyoming	x			x		x	

In States with a combination of transfer mechanisms, the exclusion, mandatory waiver, or concurrent jurisdiction provisions generally target the oldest juveniles and/or those charged with the most serious offenses, while those charged with relatively less serious offenses and/or younger juveniles may be eligible for discretionary waiver.

SOURCE: *Juvenile Offenders and Victims: 1999 National Report* (p. 102), by H. N. Snyder and M. Sickmund, 1999, Washington, DC: Office of Juvenile Justice and Delinquency Prevention. ©1999 by National Center for Juvenile Justice. Reprinted with permission.

17-year-olds accused of crimes to the criminal justice system. In addition, nearly every state enacted measures that limited the confidentiality provisions that had existed in juvenile court for juveniles accused of serious and violent offenses.

For example, states created statewide repositories of juvenile records, instituted fingerprinting and photographing of juvenile defendants, and prohibited the sealing or expunging of juvenile records; all of these changes made it easier to

TABLE 8.2   Number of States Modifying or Enacting Transfer Provisions, 1992-1997

Type of Transfer Provision	Action Taken (number)
Discretionary waiver	Added crimes (17)
	Lowered age limit (15)
	Added/modified prior record provisions (6)
Presumptive waiver	Enacted provisions (11)
Concurrent jurisdiction (prosecutor direct file)	Enacted or modified provisions (14)
Statutory exclusion	Enacted provisions (2)
	Added crimes (36)
	Lowered age limit (7)

SOURCES: Adapted from Torbet et al. (1996, p. 6) and Torbet and Szymanski (1998, p. 5).

prosecute juveniles in criminal court (Torbet & Szymanski, 1998).

More than one-third (20) of the states enacted blended sentencing provisions from 1987 through 1999 (Redding & Howell, 2000). Because of the growing popularity of this transfer mechanism, I discuss it in some detail below.

Blended Sentence Systems

Blended sentencing has been described as "a marriage of convenience between those that want to punish more and those that want to give kids one more chance" (John Stanoch, chief juvenile court judge for Hennepin County, Minnesota, quoted in Belluck, 1998, p. A26). The 20 states that have adopted some form of blended sentencing options are shown in Table 8.3.

In blended sentencing, sentences in the juvenile justice system are combined with sentences in the criminal justice system, although the adult sentence is held in abeyance. Blended sentencing is activated when an offender fails to meet the conditions of the juvenile sentence. The five basic models of blended sentencing that have emerged in recent legislation are described in Table 8.3. Three of the models are based in juvenile court; two are based in criminal court. The five models vary according to the authority vested in the respective courts.

As Tables 8.1 and 8.2 show, there are a bewildering number of transfer provisions currently in use, and the actors in transfer decisions are many and varied (Griffin, Torbet, & Szymanski, 1998; Miller, 1996; Torbet et al., 1996). Many states have multiple provisions. Blended sentencing statutes are the most confusing of all. Zimring (2000) has described the "Byzantine complexity" of blended sentencing laws (p. 215). In 6 of the 19 states using blended sentencing, juveniles ages 10 to 16 can be transferred for any criminal offense (see the state-by-state discussion of transfer provisions in Griffin

et al., 1998). Transfer of 14- to 16-year-olds is permitted in 9 states for drug offenses. The potential for net widening beyond the most serious cases is thus very great in the states using blended sentences—that is, new sanctions that are intended to serve as alternatives to given levels of system processing bring more youths into the system's net (Merlo, Benekos, & Cook, 1997).

Torbet and colleagues (1996) have observed that "confusion exists about [blended sentencing] statutes and the rules and regulations governing them, especially with respect to the juvenile's status during case processing and subsequent placement" (p. 15). They found that the selection of sentencing options is confusing "for all system actors, including offenders, judges, prosecutors, and corrections administrators" (p. 15). Thus they conclude that "blended sentencing initiatives may cause more confusion than good" (p. 15). In addition to procedural confusion, system ambivalence concerning what to do about serious and violent juvenile offenders is evident (Torbet et al., 1996). Blended sentence laws actually can result in opposing decisions being made in two courts (Miller, 1996).

The Number of Transferred Juveniles

The number of juvenile offenders currently being transferred to criminal courts in the United States is unknown. In states where the upper age limit of juvenile court jurisdiction is below age 18, of course, all juveniles between this age and 18 (the typical end of minor status for court purposes) are automatically tried in criminal courts. Snyder and Sickmund (1999) report that 13 states have 15 or 16 as an upper age limit for juvenile court jurisdiction. They found that up to 218,000 cases of 16- to 17-year-olds were tried in criminal courts in these states in 1996 (p. 106). More recent estimates are not available.

TABLE 8.3   State Blended Sentence Models

- **Juvenile—Exclusive model: The juvenile court is allowed to impose either a juvenile or an adult sentence.**
  Massachusetts
  Michigan
  New Mexico
- **Juvenile—Inclusive model: The juvenile court is allowed to impose both a juvenile and an adult sentence.**
  Connecticut
  Kansas
  Minnesota
  Montana
- **Juvenile—Contingent model: The juvenile court may impose an extended juvenile sentence until the juvenile reaches a certain age (19-21), when procedures are triggered to transfer the juvenile or to determine whether an adult sentence will be imposed.**
  Colorado
  Massachusetts
  Rhode Island
  Texas
- **Criminal—Exclusive model: The criminal court has the authority to impose either an adult or a juvenile sentence.**
  California
  Colorado
  Florida
  Idaho
  Michigan
  Oklahoma
  Virginia
  West Virginia
- **Criminal—Inclusive model: The criminal court is allowed to impose both a juvenile and an adult sentence, with the adult sentence conditionally suspended.**
  Arkansas
  Iowa
  Missouri
  Virginia

SOURCES: Redding and Howell (2000, p. 152), Torbet et al. (1996, pp. 12-13), and Torbet and Szymanski (1998, p. 6).
NOTE: Vermont has a hybrid model that allows for extended juvenile court jurisdiction and for suspended adult sentences. Colorado and Michigan have blended sentencing in both the juvenile and the criminal courts.

As noted in Chapter 3, nationally representative data are not available on the processing of juvenile offenders throughout juvenile justice systems. Thus, except for data on judicial transfers, little information is available, and data from criminal courts on their handling of juvenile offenders are conflicting (Bishop & Frazier, 2000, p. 237). The number of delinquency cases judicially waived to criminal court reached a peak in 1994 with nearly 12,000 cases (Puzzanchera, 2000). The drop since then is explained by changes in laws that have resulted in growing numbers of juvenile offenders being excluded from juvenile court handling. The largest hole in the transfer data concerns excluded offense cases and prosecutor direct files. The numbers of cases transferred to criminal court by these methods are unknown.

In the largest study of juvenile transfers to criminal court conducted to date, researchers for the organization Building Blocks for Youth (2000) found that prosecutors made most of the transfer decisions (45%), followed by state legislatures (40%), by means of laws that exclude certain juvenile offenders from juvenile court. Juvenile court judges made only 15% of the transfer decisions. The study covered the 18 jurisdictions in which the most juveniles were transferred during 1996.

Youths transferred via legislative exclusion tend not to be older chronic offenders, as might be assumed. Legislatures usually specify certain violent offenses, and chronicity often is not a determining factor. The prosecutor transfer method appears to be even less selective. Where prosecutors play an instrumental role in the transfer decision, most transferred youths tend not to be the worst offenders, and many are property offenders (Bishop & Frazier, 1991; Howell, 1996; Kempf-Leonard & White, 1999; Snyder, Sickmund, & Poe-Yamagata, 2000). In other words, the available evidence strongly suggests that the presumed targets of transfer laws—those in that small proportion of all juvenile offenders who are serious, violent, and chronic offenders—are not the juveniles most likely to be transferred by legislatures and prosecutors (although there are exceptions, of course).

There are other problems with these two transfer methods. As Feld (1998b) notes: "Prosecutorial waiver suffers from all of the vagaries of individualized discretion and without even the redeeming virtues of formal criteria, written reasons, an evidentiary record, or appellate review. Legislative offense exclusion suffers from rigidity, over-inclusiveness, and politicians' demagogic tendency to get tough" (p. 244).

Historical Developments That Led to Changes in Transfer Policies

As noted in Chapter 3, since 1987, every state has made it easier to transfer adolescents to criminal courts. Why has this happened? Four main factors account for this drastic change. Three of these are discussed in Chapter 3 in relation to their contribution to the seventh moral panic over juvenile delinquency, which brought about a wave of punitive reforms in the juvenile justice system: the enduring "cycle of juvenile justice" (Bernard, 1992), the lingering effects of the sixth moral panic, and the philosophical shift from rehabilitation to punishment stimulated by the "just deserts" philosophy that filtered down from the criminal justice system to the juvenile justice system.

The fourth factor that contributed to the increased movement of juvenile offenders into adult courts was the erroneous view that juvenile offender rehabilitation programs are not effective (for example, it has often been said that the juvenile justice system was not created to handle the "new breed" of juvenile offenders). This mistaken belief has given considerable impetus to the movement to turn presumed juvenile justice system "failures" over to the

criminal justice system. The "ineffective programs" myth has dominated the field since the mid-1970s, when a review of program evaluations in juvenile and criminal justice systems was released in which the authors largely concluded that "nothing works" in either system (Lipton, Martinson, & Wilks, 1975). More careful reviews soon proved otherwise (Cullen & Gilbert, 1982; Gendreau & Ross, 1979; Gottfredson, 1979; Lipsey, 1992, 1995; Lipsey & Wilson, 1998; Palmer, 1975, 1983), but, unfortunately, these have been all but ignored in scant literature reviews (e.g., Feld, 1998b, pp. 237-239). Thus the myth of ineffective juvenile offender rehabilitation programs persists.

The transformation of juvenile delinquents into adultlike hardened criminals (Fagan & Zimring, 2000; Singer, 1996) is an important juvenile justice consequence of the four developments. What previously were defined as "delinquent offenses" because of the age of the offenders came to be characterized as "adult crimes." The age distinction was set aside. Images of "baby-faced criminals" stimulated legislatures to take action to levy on juvenile offenders extremely punitive sanctions in the adult criminal justice system (Lyons, 1997).

In the following section, I examine the case of one baby-faced 11-year-old murderer, Nathaniel Abraham. I discuss the premises on which the juvenile court judge based his decision concerning this youngster's fate at sentencing, and then use the case as a backdrop against which to look at the relative merits of handling juveniles in the criminal justice system versus the juvenile justice system.

The Nathaniel Abraham Case

Nathaniel Abraham is believed to be the youngest child offender in American history to face murder charges as an adult (*People v. Abraham,* 234 Mich. App. 640, 599 N.W.2d 736, 740, 1999). Nathaniel, age 11 (4 feet, 9 inches tall, weighing 65 pounds) at the time of the murder, admitted firing a shot that killed an 18-year-old youth outside a convenience store in Pontiac, Michigan. He had fired the shot, using a stolen .22 caliber rifle, from a considerable distance away from the store; he denied shooting *at* anyone (Moore, 2000). He was convicted at age 13 of second-degree murder in juvenile court, under an unusual Michigan law (see Table 8.3) that allows juveniles to be tried as adults in juvenile court for certain charges, including murder.

Presiding Oakland County Juvenile Court Judge Moore had three options under the statute:

- To sentence Nathaniel as an adult, which, under the Michigan sentencing guidelines, would amount to 8 to 25 years in a state prison
- To apply a blended sentence, which would include a sentence as an adult with a delay in that sentence to follow a placement in the juvenile system, after which Nathaniel could be transferred to the adult correctional system if he were not already rehabilitated
- To sentence Nathaniel as a juvenile, which could include incarceration in a juvenile facility until his 21st birthday

Judge Moore weighed the evidence related to the three options, as required under Michigan law. He pondered several important considerations: Nathaniel was guilty of a very serious offense. His culpability in committing the offense, however, was in question. Nathaniel's teacher said that he was functioning between the 6- and 8-year-old level in terms of emotional maturity and thus unable to understand the difference between fantasy and reality. He had no prior record of delinquency, although it was noted that he had exhibited delinquent behavior for about 2 years prior to the offense. Nathaniel's mother had sought treatment for him through a community mental health agency, but he was placed on a waiting list for 6 months before any treatment was provided. He attended three treatment sessions before his mother discontinued treatment because she did not believe the therapist was helpful. Finally, Judge Moore considered the availability of future rehabilitation programs for Nathaniel in the two systems.

Facing enormous political pressure to adhere to the popular mantra of "Do adult crime, do adult time," Judge Moore made a courageous decision. On January 13, 2000, he chose the third option, to rehabilitate Nathaniel in the juvenile justice system while protecting the public by confining him in a secure juvenile facility for 8 years, until he reaches age 21. In doing so, Judge Moore placed confidence in the Michigan juvenile justice system, that it could rehabilitate the youngster.

In rejecting the adult sentencing option, Judge Moore made three poignant observations about the criminal justice system: First, he said, it successfully punishes criminals. Second, it keeps society safe from further criminal activity by a particular individual for a period of time. But, he said, we must look clearly and fully at the effects of imprisonment:

- Is the criminal rehabilitated?—The answer to this question often seems to be a clearly resounding "NO." Our adult penal system often does not rehabilitate the way it should.
- Does the criminal re-offend when released?—The answer to this question is often "YES."
- Is the public safe?—The answer to this question seems to be two-fold. The public is safe from the particular individual during the incarceration period, but the long-term effect of incarceration in our adult criminal system seems to be that we mold hardened criminals. (Moore, 2000, pp. 4-5)

Judge Moore (2000) also rejected the blended sentence option of combining a sentence in the juvenile system with one in the criminal justice system while holding in abeyance the adult sentence, reasoning that "the danger is that we won't take rehabilitation seriously" if a prison sentence is readily available (p. 9). He concluded, "We can't continue to see incarceration as a long-term solution"; although it "is a vital immediate solution to danger, it does nothing to address future criminality" (p. 9).

Thus Judge Moore accepted the third option, ruling that Nathaniel should be kept in the juvenile justice system for rehabilitation purposes until age 21. He observed that "programming is much more extensive and comprehensive in the juvenile system than in the adult system" (p. 8), and that the juvenile system "has a much higher rate of success than the adult correctional system" (p. 10). He also noted that Nathaniel had made progress toward rehabilitation in the juvenile corrections system in the 2 years that had passed since his offense.

In rejecting the option of sentencing Nathaniel to an adult prison, Judge Moore said, "If we say 'yes,' even for this heinous crime, we have given up on the juvenile justice system" (p. 8). He also noted that Nathaniel "has not failed in our juvenile programs, but rather has not been given a chance to benefit from them" (p. 9). Prison, he argued, should be considered only as a last resort—only if the juvenile justice system has failed. Moreover, he asserted that the adult criminal justice system is "a failure" and expressed concern that Nathaniel might "be subject to brutalization in prison that could destroy any hope for rehabilitation" (p. 8).

While speaking to the larger community in his decision to keep Nathaniel in the juvenile justice system, Judge Moore said: "We must do better with the thousands of juveniles we see every day in our juvenile courts. This county must be willing to pay in dollars and human energy to help prevent juvenile crime and rehabilitate juvenile offenders. . . . Children are too precious to be lost because of the system's neglect and failures" (p. 10). He urged the wider community to ensure that children and families are able to access immediately whatever services are needed for rehabilitation purposes. Such services, he insisted, must be effectively administered.

Does research support the premises on which Judge Moore based his decision to keep Nathaniel in the juvenile justice system? His decision turned on the failures of the criminal justice system in general, and in particular with juvenile offenders. Is the criminal justice system indeed a failure? The next section examines the evidence.

Is the Criminal Justice System Appropriate for Juvenile Offenders?

In this section I address the appropriateness of the use of the criminal justice system for handling juvenile offenders from several viewpoints, the first of which is recidivism. I also consider the impact of transfer to the criminal justice system on the juveniles themselves, and then examine some of the information available on the capacity of the criminal justice system to handle juvenile offenders appropriately. The chapter concludes with a discussion of the "punitive necessity" of transfer.

The Effects of Transfer on Recidivism

A review of 50 studies of juvenile transfers to the criminal justice system has revealed that recidivism rates are higher among juveniles transferred to criminal court than among those retained in the juvenile justice system. The few comparative studies available suggest that transferred juveniles are more likely to reoffend, to reoffend more quickly and at a higher rate, and perhaps to commit more serious offenses after they are released from prison than juveniles retained in the juvenile justice system (Howell, 1996). These findings support a policy of keeping juvenile offenders in the juvenile justice system. However, we must also consider the possibility that transfer of juvenile offenders to the criminal justice system has some deterrent effect.

Most transfer policies are based on the assumption that the threat of transfer to criminal justice system handling has a deterrent effect. That is, juvenile offenders' fear of being transferred to the far more punishment-oriented criminal justice system is presumed to deter future criminality. This notion stems from the popular assumption that potential juvenile offenders know that they are unlikely to draw long sentences in juvenile court. The threat of

transfer "is the quintessence of the 'scared straight' approach to crime control" (Bishop & Frazier, 2000, p. 245). Several transfer studies have shown that this assumption is without scientific basis, however, with respect to either a general deterrence effect on all juvenile offenders or a specific deterrence effect on transferred juveniles.

Four studies have examined the general deterrent effect on overall juvenile crime rates of processing juveniles in the criminal justice system. A New York study of that state's punitive Juvenile Offender Law, which lowered the age of criminal court jurisdiction to 13 for murder and four other violent offenses, found that the threat of criminal punishment had no general deterrent effect (Singer, 1996). Jensen and Metsger (1994) reached a similar conclusion in a study that examined the results of an Idaho law requiring the transfer of juveniles as young as 14 who were charged with murder and other violent crimes. They found no evidence of general deterrent effects; rather, arrests for the targeted offenses increased in Idaho following introduction of the law. In a third study, Zimring, Fagan, and Kupchik (2001) compared the arrest rates of 16- to 17-year-old youths in states that excluded them from juvenile court jurisdiction versus states that still allow these older juveniles to remain in juvenile courts, and found no deterrent effect. A fourth study in Georgia produced the same result (Risler, Sweatman, & Nackerud, 1998).

Studies that have examined the possible specific deterrent effect of transfer laws on transferred juveniles also show that these laws do not produce the intended effect. In a Florida study, Bishop, Frazier, Lanza-Kaduce, and Winner (1996) compared the recidivism of 2,738 juveniles transferred to criminal court statewide with matched youths retained in the juvenile justice system. They found that nearly a third of those in the transferred group were rearrested, compared with 19% of the nontransferred matches, and that more of the transfers who were rearrested had committed felonies. The researchers also found that transferred youths were more likely to reoffend, in a shorter period of time and with a higher offense rate, than were nontransferred juveniles. Finally, those in the nontransferred group showed a significantly greater tendency than transfers toward rearrest for lesser offenses. Bishop et al. conclude that, despite the more likely incarceration of transferred youths, and for longer periods, "overall, the results suggest that transfer in Florida has had little deterrent value. Nor has it produced any incapacitative benefits that enhance public safety" (p. 183).

In subsequent analyses over a longer follow-up period (6 years), the Florida researchers found that the differences between the two groups' recidivism likelihood disappeared after 4 years beyond release (Winner, Lanza-Kaduce, Bishop, & Frazier, 1997). This result could be anticipated, because of the long-term effects of returning parolees to their original criminogenic communities. However, the long-term follow-up confirmed the original study results with respect to individual recidivism rates: Transferred youths reoffended more quickly and with a higher frequency of rearrest.

Four other studies that tested the specific deterrent effect of transfer laws have produced similar results. In Minnesota, Podkopacz and Feld (1995, 1996) compared youth retained in the juvenile court with those waived to the criminal court and found that a significantly larger proportion of the those transferred to criminal court were convicted of new offenses compared with the youths retained in juvenile court. In another study—the only multisite study conducted to date—White (1985) compared juveniles charged with dangerous offenses in the juvenile justice system with similar young adult offenders in the criminal justice system. The data showed that the young adults recidivated 1.5 times more often than did juveniles in the juvenile justice system. Finally, in a comparison of New Jersey's juvenile system with New York's legislative transfer structure, Fagan (1995) found higher recidivism rates among criminal court cases. Reoffending occurred more quickly among juveniles transferred to criminal court, and they were more likely to be returned to confinement than juveniles not transferred. In a later replication of this study, Fagan and Liberman (2001) found no overall deterrent effect on specific offenders.

Although the studies described above need to be replicated in other jurisdictions, with more precise matching of transferred and retained youths, it is still notable that none has found lower recidivism rates among transferred juveniles in comparison with juveniles not transferred. Thus the evidence to date supports the conclusion that retaining juvenile offenders in the juvenile justice system produces lower recidivism rates. As Podkopacz and Feld (1995, p. 170) have observed, there are three possible explanations for the lower recidivism rates among juvenile justice offenders: First, by emphasizing prior records, juvenile courts appear to succeed in identifying the most chronic offenders for transfer; second, treatment in the juvenile justice system produces higher success rates; and third, the criminal justice system fails to deter juveniles from committing offenses.

Evaluations of Blended Sentencing Laws

Evaluations of the new blended sentencing arrangements are under way, but these studies are progressing slowly; researchers are experiencing a number of difficulties in conducting this research, and unexpected findings are common. The extensive evaluations of the Texas blended sentencing law that are currently in progress serve to illustrate some of the problems that researchers encounter in evaluating these unusual statutes.

The Texas Determinate Sentencing Act of 1987 is the oldest blended sentencing law in the nation (Redding & Howell, 2000). It is a good example of the effort to "criminalize" states' juvenile justice systems. Texas is one of three states that stand out for having criminalized their juvenile justice systems (Mears, 2000) by imposing on them such criminal justice procedures as determinate sentencing and adultlike trials. The other two states are Florida (Bishop & Frazier, 1996) and Minnesota (Podkopacz & Feld, 1995, 1996, 2001).

Texas legislators wanted to create a "middle ground" between the two usual alternatives of juvenile court handling or transfer of cases to adult court (Dawson, 1990). Hence the new apparatus has been characterized as "a third justice system" (Dawson, 1988)—one that is part juvenile system and part adult system. In the first phase of reforms, the state retained juvenile rehabilitation programs while introducing determinate sentencing into juvenile courts. In a strong "just deserts" approach, the law permitted juvenile sentences of up to 30 years for a short list of five very serious offenses (Dawson, 2000). Offenders convicted of these offenses served the juvenile portion of their sentences in state correctional facilities, after which they could be required to serve the remaining adult portion of their sentences in prison. The Determinate Sentencing Act also increased transfers to the criminal court, principally by lowering the transfer age (for certain excluded offenses) to age 14.

Evaluations of these changes found that this legislation did not achieve its intended goals (Dawson, 1988, 1990, 1992). Further, juvenile violence in the state continued to rise. In 1995, the Texas legislature enacted tougher measures. The list of targeted offenses was increased from 5 to 30, and the maximum length of the sentences juveniles could receive was increased from 30 to 40 years (Dawson, 2000). The state's juvenile code, then called the Family Code, was renamed the Juvenile Justice Code, for symbolic purposes (Mears & Field, 2000). Legislators also buttressed the determinate sentencing scheme with a progressive sanctions strategy in the new Juvenile Justice Code. In the progressive sanctions system, sanctions are linked with offense categories and become increasingly more restrictive, beginning with counseling and other services and progressing to probation, boot camps, and eventually secure confinement in the Texas Youth Commission.

Evaluators have struggled to make sense out of the implemented Texas laws, which have apparently had some unintended results. Transferred youths rarely serve lengthier sentences than were available in juvenile court (Fritsch, Caeti, & Hemmens, 1996). Blended sentencing channeled into the net of possible adult sentences younger juveniles who otherwise would not be subject to them under prior transfer laws (Dawson, 1990). Other unintended consequences have been uncovered, including inconsistency in sentencing (Mears, 1998) and competing interests of stakeholders (Mears, 2000)—not to mention evaluation difficulties. As Mears (1998) has observed, Texas's determinate sentencing rule "is a policy based on little information about how it is viewed or used, what criteria should be used to assess its efficacy, or what unintended effects it is having" (p. 456).

Minnesota's somewhat similar blended sentencing law has also been evaluated. In addition to the two studies described above, Podkopacz and Feld (2001) conducted a third study in Minnesota that focused on the new blended sentencing statute, which created a new intermediate category of offenders made up of individuals whom judges had previously tried and sentenced as juveniles. Offenders in the new group were called "extended jurisdiction juveniles" (EJJs). Those in this category of serious or violent offenders presumably would benefit from "one last chance" to reform. They were juveniles whom prosecutors or judges deemed no serious threat to public safety and also amenable to probation. An offender in this category would receive a blended juvenile/criminal sentence and could be kept in the juvenile justice system until age 21. Additional resources were appropriated for the rehabilitation of EJJs. Unexpectedly, the majority of them were incarcerated—in juvenile correctional facilities (Podkopacz & Feld, 2001). Despite their lower recidivism rates (new offenses) in comparison with youths transferred to criminal court, a large proportion of them had their juvenile probation sentences revoked for technical probation violations. This resulted in the unintended transfer of many of them to the criminal justice system. Thus, "the EJJ status apparently has widened-the-net and created a 'back door' to prison for youths who likely never would have been certified" (that

is, transferred to criminal court) in the absence of the new law (Podkopacz & Feld, 2001, p. 1062).

It appears that juvenile justice would be best served if juvenile courts were left alone. The blended sentencing laws that have been evaluated have apparently failed to select, transfer, and rehabilitate serious, violent, and chronic juvenile offenders. Studies have shown that juvenile court judges do the best job of selecting the worst juvenile offenders for transfer (Howell, 1996). The criteria these judges tend to use in making waiver decisions appear to explain why they do the best job. They tend to restrict transfer to older serious, violent, and chronic offenders by taking the following factors into account: gender (males are more often transferred), age (older offenders are more often transferred), number and seriousness of the instant offense(s) (including weapon use), number of prior court referrals and adjudications, and treatment history in the juvenile justice system. Application of these criteria, of course, serves to reduce the number of juveniles transferred, because only a very small proportion of juvenile offenders have serious, chronic offense histories (see Chapter 4).

Zimring (2000) makes a powerful argument for ending the linking of juvenile courts with criminal courts. He calls blended sentencing a "punitive Trojan horse," and he notes that "recent adventures with blended jurisdiction show that the flaws of a criminal justice system in the treatment of young offenders can cast long shadows over the prospects for effective juvenile justice" (p. 223). Redding and Howell (2000) make the argument that juveniles should not be moved into the criminal justice system before they have aged out of the juvenile justice system. Even then, the only juveniles eligible for criminal court should be the most serious, violent, and chronic offenders who persist in their criminal careers despite the best efforts of the juvenile system. With these policy proposals in mind, it may be instructive to examine the impact of transfer on juveniles.

The Effects of Transfer on Juveniles

Virtually every transfer study done to date has focused on either the characteristics of transferred juveniles (see Howell, 1996) or their subsequent recidivism. Florida researchers have taken the fresh approach of examining the effects of transfer on the victims—the transferred juveniles. Bishop and Frazier (2000) conducted an interview study with nearly 100 transferred and nontransferred juvenile offenders. About half of the youths in their sample had been transferred to criminal court and either confined in state prisons or placed on probation; the other half had been prosecuted in juvenile court and incarcerated in maximum-risk juvenile correctional facilities.

This is the first study to examine transfer as seen by the involved juvenile offenders. Bishop and Frazier compared the views of transferred youngsters with those of youths retained in the juvenile justice system. They asked youngsters in the respective groups about their experiences in juvenile court and criminal court, in juvenile detention/corrections facilities and adult jails and prisons. Nearly all of their respondents, including those who had been transferred, described the juvenile courts in favorable terms. Few regarded either juvenile court processes or outcomes as unfair. Most believed juvenile court judges were attempting to help them and were impressed that the judges talked with them. In contrast, few thought that criminal court judges had much interest in them or their problems. The vast majority of the transferred youths felt that the clear purpose of the criminal court proceedings and sentencing was to punish them. Many of them believed that criminal court sentencing decisions were based not on consideration of what they had done, but on judgments of them as persons, especially that they seemed "depraved" or "irredeemable." They felt unfairly vilified by these characterizations.

Bishop and Frazier's respondents viewed preadjudicatory confinement experiences in juvenile and adult institutions similarly in many respects, but there were some important differences. The youths most often described juvenile detention centers and adult jails as custodial; they saw the staff in these facilities as indifferent and viewed the confinement conditions as bleak. However, many youths confined in detention centers formed significant attachments to at least one line staff member; this did not happen in adult jails. Respondents held in jails viewed the environment there as stressful and dangerous. They found it disquieting when jail officials made no real distinction between them and the violent adult offenders with whom they were housed. Stories of older inmates preying on young boys were frequently passed along the inmate grapevine, making jailed youngsters fearful of attack by sexual predators and "crazies." Many of these youngsters felt overwhelmed, confused, and depressed.

Bishop and Frazier also found that the long-term confinement experiences of the two groups of juvenile offenders differed. Youngsters retained in the juvenile justice system described most juvenile program staff in very positive terms. For the most part, they saw staff members as caring, as understanding

of the youths' troubles, and as seeing potential in them. The researchers were impressed with the treatment orientation of the Florida juvenile facilities, as were the youngsters, who saw most of the staff as skilled rehabilitation professionals. The programs that impressed the respondents most were those that taught basic interpersonal skills and values, and enhanced self-control and self-respect. The youths viewed intensive, long-term programs as being especially valuable. They also came to recognize the importance of vocational and educational training. As Bishop and Frazier (2000) observe, it is not surprising that "the characteristics of the programs they nominated as most helpful are those that research suggests are most likely to produce reductions in recidivism" (p. 259). Indeed, these findings are consistent with the most systematic review of programs for serious and violent offenders conducted to date (Lipsey & Wilson, 1998; see Chapter 10).

The youngsters in Bishop and Frazier's sample who were held in adult prisons had quite different views of their confinement. Most of them thought the prison staff viewed them as "convicts," "criminals," or "nobodies" who would never amount to anything. They saw most correctional officers as hostile and derisive. Many of the youngsters felt physically and emotionally threatened by prison staff, who sometimes humiliated them and provoked them into conflicts that resulted in disciplinary actions against them, not the staff. Some of the juveniles became confrontational and defiant in the face of such treatment, sometimes resulting in punishment by solitary confinement. They saw that placing trust in staff was not going to help them, thus they began to spend time talking with older, more skilled and experienced offenders, who taught them how to commit crimes more effectively while avoiding detection.

The two groups of delinquents also saw their prospects for law-abiding futures differently. More than half of the juveniles confined in juvenile justice system facilities expected to remain trouble-free once they were released. Only 3% expected that they would commit further crimes. In contrast, only one-third of those in prisons expected that they would be able to be law-abiding, and 18% anticipated that they would continue in criminality.

Bishop and Frazier's findings are consistent with those of a previous study involving interviews with transferred and nontransferred juveniles conducted by Forst, Fagan, and Vivona (1989). In that study, juveniles incarcerated in training schools gave more positive evaluations of treatment and training programs, general services, and institutional personnel than did youths in prisons. Bishop and Frazier's findings also suggest that the differential socialization into crime and violence for youths in adult prisons may increase the risk of their subsequent recidivism. Spending time in prison disrupts an adolescent's development tasks (Johnson, 1978). It symbolizes community rejection, closes off opportunity, and stunts personal growth. An adolescent who survives prison time has distorted needs. The survivor must be insular, distrustful, and willing to exploit others.

Young inmates who cannot survive in adult prisons or jails have little choice but to enter protective custody, which usually means being housed in a separate, secure unit where they spend a great deal of time in isolation—a setting that is especially conducive to suicidal behavior (Parent, Dunworth, McDonald, & Rhodes, 1997, p. 5). No research has yet compared the suicide rates of youths housed in juvenile reformatories with those of youths in adult prisons, but it is well established that adolescents confined in adult jails are several times more likely to commit suicide than are those confined in juvenile detention centers (Flaherty, 1983; Library Information Specialists, 1983; Memory, 1989).

Juveniles are also far more likely to be violently victimized in adult prisons than in juvenile correctional facilities (Forst et al., 1989). Sexual assault is five times more likely in prison, beatings by staff nearly twice as likely, and attacks with weapons almost 50% more common. Research on the effects of incarceration of juveniles in adult facilities in Texas has shown that juveniles pose more discipline problems and are more often in restrictive custody (McShane & Williams, 1989). Young inmates are more likely than older ones to respond to threats with aggression (McCorkle, 1992); in contrast, fearful older inmates primarily use more passive avoidance behaviors to reduce the threat of victimization.

As with all generalizations about the juvenile and criminal justice systems, there are exceptions to the findings noted above. Some criminal justice courts handle accused juvenile offenders in a fair and just manner—those most likely to do so are courts that use risk-based sentencing (Tonry, 1999b). Courts using risk-based sentencing can effectively prosecute targeted juvenile offenders through a problem-oriented strategy that links courts with law enforcement and prosecutor offices in a multiagency team, such as the TARGET program described in Chapter 5. However, criminal courts have great difficulty controlling career criminals on their caseloads (Chaiken & Chaiken, 1991).

Some correctional treatment in adult prisons has been shown to be effective in reducing recidivism (Aos, Phipps, Barnoski, & Lieb, 2001; Gaes, Flanagan, & Motiuk, 1999). Effective interventions include therapeutic communities; intensive, in-prison drug treatment; basic education; and vocational training. In addition, prison labor programs appear to have modest effects on the reduction of recidivism, and they can increase inmates' positive behavior while they are in prison (Gaes et al., 1999). However, the provision of such rehabilitation programs in adult prisons is extremely rare (Petersilia, 2001; Travis & Petersilia, 2001).

The Capacity of the Criminal Justice System to Handle Juvenile Offenders

Critics of juvenile courts who favor transferring juvenile offenders to criminal courts have vilified the juvenile justice system. Among other criticisms, they cite the system's lack of due process procedures to protect individual rights; they also point out the problems of "justice by geography" (glaring inconsistencies in treatment of offenders by the courts from one geographic area to another) and disproportionate minority representation. Some of these critics go so far as to call for the abolition of juvenile courts (Ainsworth, 1991, 1995; Feld, 1993, 1998a, 1998b, 1999; Schwartz, 1999; Wolfgang, 1982), although others have responded that this proposal amounts to "nonsense" (Arthur, 1998; Howell, 1998a; Rosenberg, 1993; Zimring, 2000, 2002). Nevertheless, many critics contend that juvenile offenses should be adjudicated in criminal courts.

Responding to the outspoken critics of the juvenile court system, Geraghty (1997) gives several important reasons the criminal courts should not be entrusted with the adjudication of juvenile offenders. First, Geraghty asserts, the operations of criminal courts, especially those in large urban areas, fall short of the requisite level of performance to take on complex juvenile delinquency matters. He points out that many of the criminal courts in large urban areas are in a state of crisis:

> There are too many cases, too few lawyers representing too many defendants, and too few resources to support probation and correctional services. . . . Overburdened courts and correctional agencies are simply not prepared to absorb the number and character of the cases, which, if juvenile courts were abolished, would flood criminal systems. (p. 217)

Second, Geraghty notes, children are second-class citizens in criminal court. Even in juvenile court, children have no social or economic power:

The status of the special needs of children within a criminal court system would be even lower. . . . We should not make matters worse for children and for society by subjecting children to a criminal justice system that has no incentives to take their special needs into account. (p. 218)

Third, in criminal court, children are subjected to the influence of adults charged with crimes. Geraghty (1997, p. 219) points out that lawyers who defend adolescents have noted the powerful influences that adult codefendants and gang leaders can have on adolescents. Adult criminals often pressure youngsters into criminal behavior.

Fourth, Geraghty (1997, pp. 221-222) asserts that jury trials conducted in criminal courts are incomprehensible and intimidating to children. The incomprehensible nature of criminal court procedures is but one basis for questioning the competency of juveniles to defend themselves in these courts (Bonnie & Grisso, 2000; Grisso & Schwartz, 2000). Adjudicative competence standards for adults include the ability to understand their legal rights and the legal proceedings affecting them, the capacity to consult with counsel, and the possession of rational decision-making capacity about their cases (Redding & Howell, 2000, pp. 158-159). For juveniles, the competency standard may implicitly include additional factors, such as developmental maturity, and enhanced procedural protections may be necessary.

Actually, most criminal court cases are disposed of by judges, without the benefit of jury trials and other due process protections. Only 5-10% of all criminal cases go to trial in criminal court (Levin, Langan, & Brown, 2000; Roberts & Stratton, 2000; Schmalleger, 1999, p. 335). In 1996, an astounding 91% of defendants in criminal cases pled guilty; the proportion of cases that were plea-bargained is unknown (Levin et al., 2000). Thus only a small fraction of juvenile defendants are likely to benefit from the constitutional and procedural protections that Feld (1998a, 1999) and Ainsworth (1991, 1995) claim are available to juveniles in criminal courts. Most of these never come into play when cases don't go to trial—including the right to confront witnesses and the right to a jury trial itself. The 6th Amendment right to a trial by jury in the criminal justice system is one of the most basic rights preserved by the U.S. Constitution, one of the "fundamental" liberties embodied in the Bill of Rights that the due process clause of the 14th Amendment makes applicable to the states.

Criminal court judges typically dispose of cases in rapid-fire succession in crowded courtrooms in front of mystified plaintiffs, giving virtually no attention to the vagaries of each case. The facts of cases that are plea-bargained typically are not thoroughly investigated. Sentencing of defendants to "treatment" programs in these courts is a rarity. The judge typically directs the defendant to go to jail, to enter a drug treatment program (on his own), to get a job (on his own, without adequate job skill development), and/or to "keep his nose clean." This process is best described as cookie-cutter justice. The arbitrariness of juvenile court dispositions pales in comparison with criminal court case handling (Roberts & Stratton, 2000). Further, unlike in juvenile courts, victims rarely are heard in criminal courts.

Geraghty's (1997) fifth point is that the legal culture of criminal courts is damaging to children. He notes: "The greater degree of adversariness in criminal court often far exceeds the contentiousness found in juvenile court. . . . [There is] a greater degree of aggressiveness, of inflexibility, and retributivist motivation" in criminal court than in juvenile court (p. 225). As Rosenberg (1993) observes: "For the most part, the typical criminal court in urban areas is a harsh, tough, mean institution cranking out pleas. It is not a place for an adult defendant to be, much less a child" (p. 174).

Sixth, Geraghty (1997, pp. 226-227) asserts, plea bargaining in criminal court is unfair to children. Many child defendants do not understand the consequences of the decision to go to trial or to accept a negotiated plea bargain, and they have little if any ability to gauge the probability of conviction. Worse yet, young people in criminal courts may receive longer sentences just because they ask for jury trials (this is commonly recognized as a "tax" for refusing a plea offer; Geraghty, 1997, p. 226). Moreover, they cannot comprehend the impact of a short or lengthy sentence in their lives (p. 226). It is not certain that adults, much less children, have the requisite capacity to understand the ramifications of the complex blended sentence transfer laws in Texas (see Mears, 2000) and Minnesota (see Redding & Howell, 2000).

Seventh, Geraghty (1997, pp. 227-228) notes, the sentences juveniles receive in criminal court are too harsh. Juveniles transferred to criminal courts and admitted to adult prisons in 1996 (the most recent data available) received longer average maximum sentence lengths than adults for all violent offenses (murder, robbery, aggravated assault, and other violent offenses) except for sexual assault (Levin et al., 2000). Juveniles also received longer sentences than adults for weapons offenses. Adults received longer sentences than juveniles only for property offenses and drug offenses. In a report written for the federal Bureau of Justice Statistics, Brown and Langan (1998) show that transferred juveniles convicted of felonies were handed longer prison sentences than adults. Transferred juveniles were sentenced to prison, on average, for a maximum of 9 years, versus 7 years for adults under 18 (as defined by state statutes) and 5 years for adults 18 and older (for a summary of the BJS report, see Snyder & Sickmund, 1999, p. 178). These inequities demonstrate the inability of the criminal justice system to treat juvenile offenders fairly and apply a reasonable measure of proportionality to their cases.

Finally, Geraghty (1997, pp. 228-229) points out that adult court judges, prosecutors, and defenders are not child specialists. Criminal court judges and their staffs are not trained in the developmental needs of children and adolescents, thus they lack the ability to work with children, their parents, schools, and others in the community to resolve problems associated with adolescence. The disposition of cases in criminal court does not require that the court build a network of services and supports around a child, the family, and other societal institutions. Criminal courts are about punishment, not rehabilitation. As Geraghty notes, "Placing children in adult court will make them indistinguishable from adults and may lead to the stifling of initiatives and learning" (p. 228). Indeed, transferred juvenile offenders are practically "invisible" on crowded criminal court dockets (Young, 2000).

Other Problems of the Criminal Justice System for Juvenile Offenders

Recidivism rates are high among offenders whose cases are adjudicated in criminal courts. A recent review published by the Manhattan Institute (1999) shows that about two-thirds of adult probationers commit other crimes within 3 years of their sentences, and many of these crimes are serious. In an earlier review of adult probation evaluations, Geerken and Hayes (1993) found that from one-third to two-thirds of all probationers are rearrested, thus probation recidivism rates may have worsened since the studies they reviewed were completed.

The main reason recidivism rates are so high in criminal courts is that, unlike the courts in other countries, U.S. criminal courts seldom use community corrections options and other advanced rehabilitation techniques (Tonry, 1999a, 1999c). Day fines, very popular in European countries for punishment of minor or moderate crimes, are seldom used in the United States (Tonry, 1999c).

Prosecutorial fines are widely used in Germany and Holland, but not in the United States. Many other countries use sentences of community service, scaled to the seriousness of the crime, as an alternative to incarceration; in the United States, only minor offenders are given such sentences. In contrast, sentencing guidelines, including mandatory minimums and "truth in sentencing" rules, are unique to the United States.

Prison recidivism rates are even higher than failure rates in criminal courts (Petersilia, Turner, & Peterson, 1986). Approximately 67% of released prisoners are rearrested within 3 years, and more than half of released prisoners are returned to prison (Langan & Levin, 2002). High prison recidivism rates are found in research dating back to the 19th century (Chambliss, 1995, p. 255).

Recidivism rates are not higher in juvenile courts than in criminal courts, although they should be, because of the age-crime curve (Farrington, 1986a). Juvenile courts handle persons who are in the peak years of criminal activity (age 17 is the peak year of involvement in serious violent crime; Elliott, 1994a). Further, comparisons of juvenile and adult treatment and correctional interventions show that juvenile justice system programs and intervention strategies are far more cost-effective (Aos et al., 2001).

Criminal Justice System Handling of Capital Murder Cases

Recently, research has revealed gross inequities in the criminal justice system's handling of capital murder cases. Columbia University Law School researchers Liebman, Fagan, and West (2000) found that of the more than 4,500 U.S.-appealed state capital murder cases in the period 1973-1995, two-thirds of the convictions were overturned on appeal because they were flawed by serious, reversible error. Liebman et al. characterize the criminal court process for handling capital murder cases as "irrational" and as a "broken system." In another study, Radelet, Bedau, and Putnam (1992) documented more than 400 U.S. cases in which persons were wrongly convicted of criminal homicide and sentenced to death. Even in capital cases, where the criminal justice system should be on its best behavior, the adult courts operate in a woefully inconsistent manner.

The criminal justice system does not appear to perform any better in handling juvenile capital murder cases (Cothern, 2000). Several studies have found that the majority of cases in which juvenile offenders were put to death had flaws in the criminal court procedures that resulted in the executions (Amnesty International, 1998a, 1998b; Lewis et al., 1988; Robinson & Stephens, 1992). In one of these studies, Robinson and Stephens (1992) found that two-thirds of the 91 juveniles sentenced to death across the country shared varying combinations of the kinds of mitigating circumstances that the U.S. Supreme Court (in *Gregg v. Georgia*) has said the courts must take into account to avoid cruel and unusual punishment—which is prohibited by the 8th and 14th Amendments to the U.S. Constitution. In addition to the defendants' being "youths," which the Supreme Court (in *Eddings v. Oklahoma*) has said is an important consideration, two-thirds of the 91 juvenile cases evidenced such mitigating factors as psychological disturbances, troubled family history and social background, mental disability, substance abuse, and indigence. These factors typically are not placed in evidence at the time of trial or sentencing (Amnesty International, 1998a, 1998b; Lewis et al., 1988).

In addition, juveniles sentenced to death are often represented by public defenders or other appointed counsel who often do not have the time or resources to investigate adequately the possible existence of mitigating factors, such as their clients' psychiatric history, family issues, and mental capacity. Based on the scant evidence used to justify putting them to death, it appears that the overwhelming majority of the juveniles in these studies were wrongfully executed even under the protections of the U.S. Constitution and applicable case law. Equally shameful is the fact that, every single one of them was put to death in violation of international law (Amnesty International, 1998b). In August 2000, the U.N. Sub-Commission on the Promotion and Protection of Human Rights resolved that the execution of people who were under the age of 18 at the time they committed crimes is contrary to what is termed "customary international law." A principle of customary international law is a general practice accepted as law. Such a law is binding on all countries, regardless of any treaties they have or have not ratified (more information on this subject is available at the Amnesty International Web site, at www. amnesty.org).

As noted in Chapter 3, the United States violates two international laws whenever juveniles are executed or sentenced to life without the possibility of parole (Amnesty International, 1998a); these laws are the International Covenant on Civil and Political Rights (ICCPR) and the U.N. Convention on the Rights of the Child (CRC). Article 6(5) of the ICCPR states that the death penalty must not be imposed for crimes committed by people when they were under 18 years of age. Article 37(a) of the CRC states that "neither capital punishment nor life imprisonment without the possibility of release shall be imposed for offenses committed by persons below eighteen years of age."

Concern about wrongful executions, of any offenders, increased in the late 1990s, beginning with the American Bar Association's call for a halt to the death penalty (Coleman, 1998). Momentum picked up in 2000 following the Columbia University Law School study cited above (Liebman et al., 2000) and the statewide moratorium on executions put in place in Illinois by Governor George Ryan. Since then, more than 30 cities across the country have passed similar resolutions calling for statewide moratoriums, according to the Quixote Center in Maryland (for information, visit the center's Web site at www.quixote.org). These moratoriums are intended to allow time for the states to review the procedures of their criminal courts, in hopes of making them more reliable and thus reducing the likelihood of the execution of innocent persons.

A key issue in the moratorium debate is the lingering notion that public executions deter potential offenders from committing crimes, despite the fact that several studies have shown convincingly that they do not (e.g., Cheatwood, 1993; Harries & Cheatwood, 1997). As Zimring (1999) has noted:

> Executions in the 20th century have never reached a level that is even one percent of our current rates of criminal homicide, and executions have averaged less than one-fifth of one percent of homicides in the 1990s. To expect punishment so limited to make a major dent in crime would make the miracle of the loaves and fishes seem modest. (p. 140)

Other Evidence of a
Flawed Criminal Justice System

The criminal justice system has many other flaws in addition to those noted above. Widespread problems render the system unsuitable for handling juvenile cases in a fair and just manner. Criminal justice system practices are, in general, discriminatory, arbitrary, and capricious (Liebman et al., 2000; Roberts & Stratton, 2000; Tonry, 1994a, 1994b, 1999b; Uviller, 1999).

A number of studies conducted over the past quarter century have shown that these problems are common and widespread. For example, discrimination based on defendants' race or ethnicity occurs at all stages of the criminal justice system: arrest

---

Box 8.3

International Human Rights Organizations

Two international human rights organizations are actively involved in juvenile justice issues worldwide: Amnesty International and Human Rights Watch.

Amnesty International

Amnesty International (AI) is a worldwide movement that campaigns to promote all the human rights enshrined in the Universal Declaration of Human Rights and other international standards. AI currently has approximately a million members and supporters in 162 countries and territories. The organization's activities range from public demonstrations to letter writing campaigns, from human rights education to fund-raising concerts, from individual appeals on particular cases to global campaigns on particular issues. In particular, Amnesty International campaigns to free all prisoners of conscience; to ensure fair and prompt trials for political prisoners; to abolish the death penalty, torture, and other cruel treatment of prisoners; to end political killings and "disappearances"; and to end human rights abuses by opposition groups. With respect to juveniles, AI's efforts have been focused mainly on protesting wrongful executions and sentences of life without parole (Amnesty International, 1998a, 1998b). Amnesty International is impartial and independent of any government, political persuasion, or religious creed. (More information about Amnesty International is available on the organization's Web site at www.amnesty.org.)

Human Rights Watch

Human Rights Watch (HRW) is dedicated to protecting the human rights of people around the world. HRW investigates and exposes human rights violations and holds abusers accountable. It challenges governments and those who hold power to end abusive practices and respect international human rights law. HRW's Children's Rights Division monitors human rights abuses against children around the world and campaigns to end them. It sends fact-finding missions to places where abuses are occurring to interview child victims, parents, human rights activists, lawyers, child-care workers, government officials, and others, working closely with local human rights groups to identify specific abuses and strategies for change. The division then writes objective, factual reports and presents them to governments, international organizations, nongovernmental organizations, policy makers, and the media (Human Rights Watch, 1995, 1996b, 1997b, 1999, 2002a, 2002b). It also devises campaigns and works in coalitions with other groups to expose abuses of children's rights and to put a stop to them. HRW's Children's Rights Division calls on the international community to join in the effort to encourage governments and civil society to take stronger action to implement the provisions of the U.N. Convention on the Rights of the Child, strengthen protections for children, and fulfill the promises made to the children of the world. Of particular concern are sentences for juvenile offenders that violate the international principle that deprivation of liberty should be a measure of last resort and for the shortest appropriate period of time or that constitute torture or cruel, inhuman, or degrading treatment. (More information about Human Rights Watch is available on the organization's Web site at www.hrw.org.)

(Mann, 1993; Sampson & Lauritsen, 1997), pretrial release (Bridges, 1997), federal pretrial release (bail) practices, prosecutor decision making (LaFree, 1980; Radelet, 1989; Spohn, Gruhl, & Welch, 1987; Uviller, 1999), sentencing (Mauer, 1997; McDonald & Carlson, 1992; Tonry, 1999b; Wooldredge, 1998), imprisonment (Austin, Marino, Carroll, McCall, & Richards, 2000; Chiricos & Crawford, 1995; Petersilia & Turner, 1985), and prison release decision making (Carroll & Mondrick, 1976; Petersilia, 1983). In addition, the poor and indigent are systematically discriminated against in criminal courts (Katz, 1970; Weston, 1969).

Research has also found that the criminal justice system routinely practices "justice by geography." This is most evident in arrests (Shannon, 1988; Smith, Visher, & Davidson, 1984), sentencing (Tonry, 1999c), imprisonment (Bridges, Crutchfield, & Simpson, 1987; Chiricos & Crawford, 1995; Crutchfield, Bridges, & Pitchford, 1994), and imposition of the death penalty (Willing & Fields, 1999). Imprisonment rates and the overrepresentation of minorities in prison vary widely from state to state (Austin et al., 2000).

The disparate handling that minority youths face in the juvenile justice system pales in comparison to the inequitable treatment they receive in the criminal justice system. In a California study, Males and Macallair (2000) found that youths of color were more than eight times as likely as white youths to be incarcerated by adult courts for equally serious crimes. The criminal justice system inequities in Cook County, Illinois, are worse yet. There, 99% of the juvenile offenders transferred to adult court for drug crimes in 1999-2000 were African American or Latino (Ziedenberg, 2001), despite the fact that white youth use and sell drugs at rates that are similar to or higher than those of young people of color (National Institute on Drug Abuse, 2000).

Gross disparities are also found in the numbers of white youths versus youths of color among juveniles transferred to criminal courts (Bortner, Zatz, & Hawkins, 2000; Howell, 1996; U.S. General Accounting Office, 1995). In 1997, of some 7,400 juvenile admissions to adult prisons, 3 out of 4 were minorities (Poe-Yamagata & Jones, 2000).

The Revolving Door of State Prisons

As noted above, of the persons released from adult prisons, two-thirds (66%) are rearrested within 3 years, nearly half (47%) are convicted of new crimes, and more than half (52%) are returned to prison, either for new crimes or for technical violations of the terms of their release (Langan & Levin, 2002). These proportions have increased slightly from those found in prior studies (Beck, 2000; Beck & Shipley, 1989). Interestingly, Langan and Levin (2002) found no evidence that longer prison sentences reduce recidivism; in fact, they found that imprisonment is even less effective with juvenile offenders than with older inmates. In their sample, more than 8 out of 10 released juveniles were rearrested, versus nearly 7 out of 10 overall. In general, recidivism varied inversely with age.

Other developments suggest that this revolving-door situation could worsen. First, the growth in imprisonment rates has been enormous, with state prison populations nearly doubling from 1990 to 2001 (Beck, Karberg, & Harrison, 2002). State prisons now house almost 1.2 million people, an additional 631,000 persons are held in local jails, and another 141,000 are confined in federal prisons, for a total of nearly 2 million. Second, sentencing policy has become "fragmented," to use Tonry's (1999b) term. By fragmentation, Tonry means that there is no standard approach. There was a standard approach 30 years ago, in indeterminate sentencing policies, but this has given way to a wide variety of sentencing options, including mandatory minimum sentences, three-strikes laws (designed to increase prison terms for multiple offenders), and "truth in sentencing" laws (which require that offenders serve some specified proportion of their sentences). The result, as Travis and Petersilia (2001) put it, is "a national crazy quilt made up of piecemeal sentencing reforms—without a public rationale that would explain the relationship between imprisonment and release" (p. 296). Third, the system of parole has been weakened. More and more inmates are being released unconditionally, without formal supervision. Travis and Petersilia (2001) suggest that, "taken together, these three developments paint a picture of a system that has lost its way" (p. 299). Indeed it has.

Today, most prisons in the United States are operating at well over 100% capacity, and, as Riveland (1999) notes, "this crowding, aggravated by the increase in street gang members, drug offenders, mentally ill, and youthful offenders, has stressed the prisons and corrections systems" (p. 5). With the exception of violent street gang members and dangerous drug traffickers, most of the offenders in prisons today, especially juveniles and those who are mentally ill, do not belong in prison. Critics contend that confinement in these facilities amounts to cruel and unusual punishment, because inmates have severely limited access to programs, exercise, staff, and other inmates (Human Rights Watch, 1997c). Little is known about the psychological effects of prison isolation and solitary confinement in these facilities, especially on juveniles. Unfortunately, "supermax" prisons and intensive management units often are used to confine juvenile offenders (Lovell, Cloyes, Allen, & Rhodes, 2000; Riveland, 1999). Few of these youngsters are dangerous, violent offenders. Most of them fall into the "nuisance inmate" category—the label given to troublemakers in the prison inmate population, not hardened criminals (Riveland, 1999, p. 7).

More people are leaving prison today than at any time in history, and large proportions of those released are unprepared for life on the outside

(Johnson, 2000; Travis & Petersilia, 2001). This trend is expected to continue for several years. Juvenile offenders are now added to the growing number of inmates who are streaming out of prisons each year, unrehabilitated and totally unprepared for their freedom (Johnson, 2000). Prison officials estimate that 78% of juveniles admitted to prison will be released by age 21, and 93% will be released by age 28, still in the crime-prone age range (Strom, 2000). Because of the shift in philosophy from rehabilitation to punishment, few of them will have job skills. Travis and Petersilia (2001) lament "the prisoners moving through the high-volume, poorly designed [prison] assembly line that has, in many respects, lost a focus on reintegration, are less well prepared individually for their return to the community and are returning to communities that are not well prepared to accept them" (pp. 300-301).

The infrastructure supporting the growth in rates of imprisonment in the United States and the accompanying prison-building binge has been described as the "prison-industrial complex" (Schlosser, 1998). Criminologists have begun to take a stand against the inequities in this system. Normally silent on public crime policy, the American Society of Criminology's National Policy Committee (2001) recently issued a national policy white paper that exposes the gross inequities in the uses of imprisonment. The paper states unequivocally:

A major reason for the dramatic increase in the U.S. prison population and associated increases in the number of Blacks, Hispanics, and women, has been substantial increases in the numbers of persons sentenced to prison for drug crimes. . . . African Americans and Hispanics are grossly over represented in the prisoner population, and this over representation has increased over the past two decades in concert with the selective enforcement of certain forms of drugs which are associated with race and ethnicity. (p. 15)

The growth in the use of imprisonment is a product of the U.S. "wars" on drugs and crime (see Box 8.4).

Given the disturbing state of American imprisonment policies, it is difficult to understand why politicians and corrections officials continue to call for the imprisonment of more persons and for longer periods of time (Beckett & Sasson, 2000). William Chambliss (1995), one of the most respected criminologists in the United States, has observed that "the criminal justice system is demonstrably the least effective and arguably the most counterproductive of all social policies designed to reduce crime . . . [yet] it is the one

institution that receives more public funding the more it fails" (p. 255).

In 1996, the *Economist* (a British journal) published a review of American crime and imprisonment trends titled "Violent and Irrational—and That's Just the Policy." As Weitekamp (2001) has noted, other European observers see the United States as a country that "has the highest incarceration rate in the Western industrialized world, applies . . . the most repressive criminal justice policies, still has the death penalty, executes record numbers, has almost more weapons in the streets than it has inhabitants, and fights 'wars' against crime and drugs" (p. 314). In 2001, the United States achieved the highest reported incarceration rate in the world (690 inmates per 100,000 population)—even higher than Russia's (676 per 100,000) (Sentencing Project, 2002).

Punitive Necessity Versus Rehabilitation

Given all of the considerations that make the transfer of juveniles to criminal courts inadvisable, why are juveniles increasingly being transferred? Zimring (2000) refers to the main rationale behind this trend as the "punitive necessity." That is, the demand for punishment of juveniles exceeds the capacity of the juvenile justice system. When older adolescents are accused of conduct that punishment advocates contend cannot be sufficiently punished in the juvenile justice system, pressure is brought to bear to transfer them to the adult system, which is guided by a strong punitive philosophy.

Political support for the transfer of juveniles to criminal court, however, appears to have other bases. Zimring (2002) contends that a gap developed between incarceration policies in the juvenile and adult systems during the 1970s and 1980s. Juvenile justice incarceration rates for offenders ages 14 through 17 did not change substantially, but the incarceration rates for 18- to 24-year-olds in the criminal justice system doubled. The gap in the amount of punishment between the two systems caught the attention of "get tough" policy advocates. Zimring asserts that it is this gap, and not juvenile crime rates, that drives juvenile justice policy. Otherwise, with juvenile crime rates currently dropping, legislators would already be reversing their get-tough policies.

Summary

The seventh moral panic over juvenile delinquency and several historical developments that preceded it brought the most important juvenile justice policy of all—the venue for adjudicating juvenile

Box 8.4

A Brief History of the U.S. Wars on Drugs and Crime

Legislators and policy makers in the United States have a tendency to "declare war" on social problems, thus their actions in response to such problems are often characterized by aggression (Zimring, 1998a). The "war on crime" begun by the Nixon administration and the "war on drugs" fought by the Reagan administration and both Bush administrations (both of which were continued in full force by the Clinton administration) are the results of events that made crime a prominent public policy issue.

Crime first became an important public policy issue in modern times when presidential candidate Barry Goldwater, looking for a message to grab the public's attention, made frightening pronouncements about crime and demanded "law and order," so women and children would be safe on the streets (Chambliss, 1995). The media and the public responded with alarm, and a "moral panic" was created. Congress soon got on the bandwagon, passing the Omnibus Crime Control and Safe Streets Act of 1968, which legalized wiretapping and "bugging" by federal agents and local police without a court order. The act also authorized $3 billion for prison construction. In that same year, presidential candidate Richard Nixon was hammering away at the issue of law and order. By the time he was elected president, surveys showed that Americans placed "crime, lawlessness, looting and rioting" as their second main concern, behind the Vietnam War (Chambliss, 1995, p. 247). In 1970, President Nixon signed into law the Organized Crime Control Act, which contained "some revolutionary changes in the administration of criminal law" (Chambliss, 1995, p. 249). These included changes in the requirements of the evidence-gathering process, new federal sanctions and punishments, and the creation of a powerful investigative federal grand jury. In addition, the act allowed the courts to compel witnesses to testify if they were granted immunity and expanded conditions under which witnesses could be charged with perjury.

President Ronald Reagan appointed a "drug czar" to lead the "war on drugs," and his administration as well as the administrations of every president since that time have spent billions of dollars fighting the "war," yet there is no evidence that this spending has had any significant impact. The total cost of the U.S. war on drugs is about $40 billion per year (Caulkins, Rydell, Everingham, Chiesa, & Bushway, 1999, p. 1).

"Asset forfeiture" laws soon were made an instrument of the war on drugs. These laws allowed federal agents to seize and dispose of a person's car, house, or other property if there was "probable cause" that the property had been used in relation to drug trafficking—even if the owner was never arrested or convicted of any crime (Bovard, 1999). Without any due process of law, agents seized cars, boats, homes, and other properties presumably used in some connection with criminal drug trafficking.

In one of the most notorious asset forfeiture cases, the U.S. Supreme Court upheld the constitutionality of these laws (Biskupic, 1996). The defendant, Guy Jerome Ursery, was arrested for growing marijuana on his land. Law enforcement agencies seized his home. He argued that this violated his constitutional protection against double jeopardy, contending that he was punished twice for the same offense: by being arrested and by losing his home. The Supreme Court ruled against him in a vote of eight to one. Speaking for the majority, Chief Justice William H. Rehnquist reasoned that the government did not violate Ursery's constitutional right against double jeopardy because the civil action was taken against his home, not against him. His house was deemed guilty.

In another case, Florida police seized the automobile of Tyvessel White, a citizen who was arrested for an offense unrelated to drug trafficking. However, police suspected that White had used his car to deliver illegal drugs, and they seized it under the state's asset forfeiture law. Although White was never charged with drug trafficking, the U.S. Supreme Court upheld the car seizure, simply on the grounds that the automobile was suspected of being involved in a crime (Bovard, 1999).

More than $5.9 billion was deposited in the U.S. Justice Department's Asset Forfeiture Fund between 1985 (when federal authority to seize property was expanded) and 1999 (Fields, 1999). The Civil Asset Forfeiture Reform Act of 2000 amended the federal law to require that the government show a "preponderance of the evidence," not just "probable cause," in order to seize personal property; the new law also provides some recourse for falsely accused citizens. The new act was opposed by the Clinton administration, the U.S. Justice and Treasury Departments, and law enforcement organizations, on the grounds that it would unreasonably restrict their use of the 1985 law (Fields, 1999). Nevertheless, the act was passed in Congress, and President Clinton signed it into law on August 23, 2000.

(Continued)

Box 8.4 (Continued)

In recent years, the "war on crime" has taken on a new dimension inspired by the "broken windows" philosophy of policing (Kelling & Coles, 1996; Wilson & Kelling, 1982), which is based on the notion that small crimes lead inevitably to bigger ones. The idea is that just as unrepaired broken windows on buildings in a neighborhood often lead to further deterioration of the area, ignored minor offenses and other public disorderly behavior frighten citizens and lead to more serious crimes (Greene, 1999). Beginning in 1993, New York City led the way in implementing a zero-tolerance policing strategy based on this concept, strictly enforcing laws concerning disorderly behavior in public places. William Bratton, then the new commissioner of the New York Police Department, "took the handcuffs off" the police (Bratton, 1998). Patrol officers were "unleashed" and directed by Commissioner Bratton to "stop and search citizens who were violating the most minor laws on the books (e.g., drinking a beer or urinating in public), to run warrant checks on them, or just pull them in for questioning about criminal activity in their neighborhood" (Greene, 1999, p. 175).

Commissioner Bratton and New York's mayor, Rudy Giuliani, attributed a drop in serious and violent crime rates in the city to these zero-tolerance policing strategies (Bratton, 1998). However, the connection was overstated—if not purely coincidental (Greene, 1999). In fact, certain forms of violence had been declining substantially in New York City for 8 years prior to the implementation of "broken windows" policing, and the declines could not plausibly be explained by these later events (Zimring & Fagan, 2000). As Sampson and Raudenbush (2001) observe, "It is the structural characteristics of neighborhoods, as well as neighborhood cohesion and informal social control—not levels of disorder—that most affect crime" (p. 4). Serious and violent crime rates were dropping sharply at the same time across the country in cities where no such strategies were implemented. Moreover, reports of police brutality increased in New York City during this period (Amnesty International, 1996). Nevertheless, other cities emulated New York's zero-tolerance approach and, generally, more aggressive policing. Boston's Gun Project/Operation Ceasefire is a case in point (see Chapter 5). Richmond's Project Exile—based on zero tolerance for gun violations—served as another popular model that many other jurisdictions replicated (Keen, 2001). However, the legal changes giving police broader investigative and arrest authority probably had a far greater impact than widely publicized models of zero-tolerance policing. Now, excessive use of force by police is commonplace (Bureau of Justice Statistics, 2001).

The public's attention has been called to only a few high-profile cases in which police have been accused of using excessive force. Abuses in the New York City Police Department probably have received the most attention—particularly the cases of Haitian immigrant Abner Louima, who was sodomized with a broom handle by New York cops in 1997 (Jones, 2001), and Amadou Diallo, who died in a torrent of gunfire from four white police officers in 1999 (McWhorter, 1999). The Los Angeles police beating of Rodney King may have horrified the public more than these New York cases, however, because it was televised, thanks to a citizen's videotape (Jacobs, 2001).

In recent years, drug-related police corruption scandals have surfaced in many large cities, such as Atlanta, Chicago, Cleveland, Detroit, Los Angeles, Miami, New Orleans, New York, and Philadelphia (see U.S. General Accounting Office, 1998). At last count, 14 city police departments have come under investigation by the U.S. Department of Justice for patterns of illegal conduct by officers (Locy, 2001). Other Department of Justice investigations (of police departments in Pittsburgh, Pennsylvania; Steubenville, Ohio; and Los Angeles; and of the New Jersey State Police) have led to consent decrees that provide guidelines for police activity. DWB, or "driving while black (or brown)," is now a popular label for the kinds of discriminatory police practices that affect minorities (Austin, Marino, Carroll, McCall, & Richards, 2000). The Los Angeles Police Department's Rampart Division corruption case (see Chapter 7) is probably the most disturbing police corruption case to date, because citizens were killed by police and others were framed and convicted of crimes they did not commit.

The International Association of Chiefs of Police (IACP, 2000) has called upon President George W. Bush to create a national commission, like the 1967 President's Commission on Law Enforcement and the Administration of Justice (called the Crime Commission, established in 1965), to examine the widespread and deeply rooted problems existing in the U.S. criminal justice system today. Concerned in particular about police corruption, racial profiling, and criminal court proceedings (Fields, 2000), the IACP hopes that a comprehensive review of law enforcement and the administration of justice in the United States will prompt changes in the system that will lead to more measured responses to crime.

Amnesty International (1999) has noted that U.S. police abuses violate international human rights laws aimed at providing protection against torture, degrading treatment, and racial discrimination, and has called upon federal officials to keep better track of police abuse cases and to recognize that these abuses of individuals are no less egregious than human rights abuses in other countries.

offenders—full circle, with juvenile offenders back in the criminal courts from which they were rescued when the American juvenile justice system was created. Once again, juveniles are the "victims of change" (Finestone, 1976).

Juvenile offenders are victimized when they are transferred to the criminal justice system because it fails to apply three accepted philosophical principles in the administration of justice for juveniles: diminished capacity, room to reform, and proportionality in sentencing. Rather than making allowances for youthful mistakes, criminal courts punish juveniles more severely than adults for the same serious crimes. Inexplicably, transferred juveniles convicted of felonies in criminal courts receive longer sentences than adults for the same offenses. In addition, juveniles placed in adult prisons and jails are at risk of violent victimization. Worst of all, the criminal justice system, in effect, violates international law when it sentences juveniles to death or to life without parole.

Legislators have taken large categories of juvenile cases away from the juvenile courts and turned them over to the criminal justice system. They have done so in three main ways. First, they have passed into law excluded offense statutes. Under these statutes, when juveniles are charged with certain offenses, they are automatically excluded from the juvenile system and handled in criminal courts. Second, legislators have passed laws lowering the transfer age for specific offenses. And third, they have passed laws that increase the role of prosecutors in making transfer decisions. In addition, the legislatures in a few states have lowered the upper age limit for juvenile court jurisdiction. This means that all juveniles over a certain age who are accused of crimes are automatically handled in criminal courts, even youngsters who could benefit from the treatment options available in the juvenile system.

We have seen in this chapter that transferring juveniles to the criminal justice system is not a solution to juvenile delinquency. The case of Nathaniel Abraham illustrates the dilemma that judges and other decision makers face in handling of serious and violent delinquents. In Nathaniel's case, a juvenile court judge courageously made the decision to keep the boy in the juvenile justice system, for rehabilitation and accountability purposes. In making this decision, Judge Moore observed that the criminal justice system is not effective and that adult prisons do not rehabilitate offenders.

The review of the evidence presented above confirms Judge Moore's judgment. The criminal justice system is the wrong place for any juvenile offender. The system itself is a failure on many grounds: It is ineffective in rehabilitating offenders, it operates in an arbitrary and capricious manner, and it discriminates against minorities. In addition, criminal justice court programs are largely ineffective, and the prison system operates like a revolving door. Both have all but abandoned rehabilitation in favor of punishment. The criminal justice system has "lost its way" (Travis & Petersilia, 2001).

The criminal justice system that promised to protect the rights of juveniles (Ainsworth, 1991, 1995; Feld, 1998a, 1999) is like a fairy tale that never came true. Constitutional protections of individual rights for at least 9 out of 10 cases in criminal court are a myth, because only about 5-10% of all criminal court cases go to trial, even though the 6th Amendment to the U.S. Constitution guarantees all individuals the right to a speedy and public trial before an impartial jury. Thus important constitutional protections are available for only a small fraction of alleged offenders.

In short, it appears that juveniles' constitutional rights are more likely to be violated in criminal courts than in juvenile courts. Justice is most likely to be served for juveniles in juvenile courts. Equally important, youngsters are far more likely to receive treatment and rehabilitation services in the juvenile justice system.

Given the negative and unintended results of transfer laws, it appears that juvenile justice would be best served if juvenile courts were left alone. The criminal justice system lacks the capacity to handle juvenile cases effectively. Transferred juveniles are more likely to reoffend, and to do so more quickly and at higher rates, and perhaps to commit more serious offenses after they are released from prison than juveniles retained in the juvenile justice system. Thus juveniles should not be transferred to the criminal justice system. Juvenile offenders should be graduated to the criminal justice system only when their criminal careers continue into their adulthood.

Zimring (2000) suggests the implementation of three policies aimed at bringing about consistency in juvenile transfer policies. The first is that the level of punishment imposed on a young offender in any court should be reduced when it is evident that the offender's immaturity is such that he or she has diminished responsibility. Second, age-appropriate institutions, programs, and protections should be part of any justice policy toward young offenders. And third, courts should make an effort "to avoid punishments that seriously impinge on the life chances of young offenders" (p. 222). Uniform federal standards to prevent the transfer of juveniles with rehabilitative potential would help (Ullman, 2000). Juvenile justice officials must use appropriate risk and needs assessment instruments (Beyer, Grisso, & Young, 1997) to help determine the likelihood of offenders' future recidivism as well as their treatment needs (Chapter 12).

In addition, future transfer policies need to address public opinion. Currently, most members of the general public are not well-informed regarding the consequences of transfer for juveniles, and it is unclear what the public wants with respect to this issue. Although a majority of surveyed Americans say they want juveniles transferred to criminal courts, most also say they don't want juvenile prisoners mixed with adults (Cullen, Golden, & Cullen, 1983; Mears, 2000, 2001; Wu, 2000). It appears that people in general are unaware that most transferred juveniles are very likely to be mixed with adult criminals, because, once transferred, they are transformed into "adults." Public support for transfer also is linked with support for rehabilitation of juvenile offenders, which is highly unlikely in the criminal justice system. The two goals are incompatible.

The United States needs to ratify the U.N. Convention on the Rights of the Child and end the practice of transferring juveniles to the criminal justice system, where they can receive death sentences and sentences of life without parole. Our country needs to be a world leader on such human rights issues, but it is increasingly difficult for the United States to speak out on human rights issues internationally because of its dismal record in ratifying human rights treaties (Human Rights Watch, 2001a). According to Human Rights Watch, when the United States has ratified such treaties, it has typically carved away any new protections for those in the United States by adding reservations, declarations, and understandings on such issues as stopping ongoing execution of juvenile offenders and providing enhanced protection from invidious discriminatory treatment.

Discussion Questions

1. If you had been the presiding juvenile court judge handling the Nathaniel Abraham case, what would your decision have been on the transfer issue? Why?

2. Is our society better served when juveniles are prosecuted in criminal courts or when they are prosecuted in juvenile courts? Why?

3. Why is the criminal court system unsuitable for handling juvenile offenders?

4. As noted in this chapter, juveniles receive longer prison sentences than adults for the same offenses. How might this be explained?

PART III

Effective Prevention and Rehabilitation Programs in a Comprehensive Framework

The framework described in the chapters that make up Part III is represented in the Comprehensive Strategy for Serious, Violent, and Chronic Juvenile Offenders (Howell, 1995; Wilson & Howell, 1993). As shown in Figure III.1, the Comprehensive Strategy consists of two main components, delinquency prevention and graduated sanctions, that are linked by a seamless continuum of services and sanctions. The prevention component targets at-risk youth, and the graduated sanctions component targets delinquent youth in the juvenile justice system. Note that the

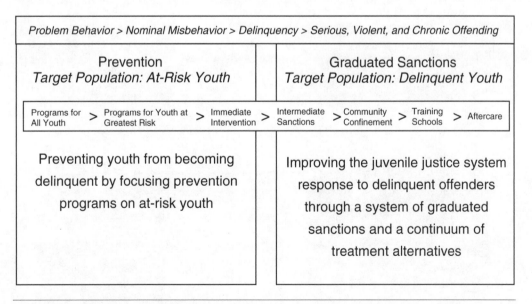

Figure III.1   The Comprehensive Strategy Framework: A Seamless Continuum of Services and Sanctions
SOURCE: Wilson and Howell (1993).

continuum of services and sanctions (beginning with programs for all youth and ending with aftercare) parallels the offender career (which begins with problem behavior and ends with serious, violent, and chronic delinquency). Once a community puts in place an integrated continuum of delinquency prevention, graduated sanctions, and parallel programs, it will have a complete array of program options for addressing delinquent careers at every stage.

Effective prevention and early intervention programs are described in Chapter 9. Early intervention is the bridge between the prevention and graduated sanctions components of the Comprehensive Strategy. Chapter 10 then reviews effective rehabilitation programs—especially principles and characteristics of effective programs—that any community should consider in building a continuum of programs that parallel the system of graduated sanctions. Chapter 10 also features a practical, research-based approach to improving existing programs. The intellectual foundation of the Comprehensive Strategy framework is examined in Chapter 11, which traces the development of comprehensive juvenile justice approaches. Chapter 12 then describes in detail the Comprehensive Strategy framework, including the "linchpins" and practical tools that facilitate its implementation. Chapter 13 illustrates implementation of the Comprehensive Strategy with real-world programs and strategies.

9
■

EFFECTIVE PREVENTION AND EARLY INTERVENTION APPROACHES

In this chapter I present a review of the research on effective prevention and early intervention programs. In the following pages I identify a wide array of program options that any community should consider including in a comprehensive delinquency prevention action plan using the framework of the Comprehensive Strategy for Serious, Violent, and Chronic Juvenile Offenders (see Chapters 12 and 13). Box 9.1 presents a brief discussion of the potential value of effective prevention and early intervention programs for reducing the monetary costs to society of adolescent victimization.

Prevention of juvenile delinquency is no longer the "fugitive utopia" described in the early 1970s (Empey, 1974). Some readers may find it surprising that prevention programs directed at the behavioral problems of children and adolescents are at least as effective as, and perhaps more effective than, medical treatments (Durlak & Wells, 1997; Lipsey & Wilson, 1993). Equally important, very few delinquency prevention programs have been shown to produce negative effects, and most of those that have been found are negligible (Durlak & Wells, 1997).

I begin this chapter with a review of delinquency prevention science (Coie et al., 1993). The risk and protective factor model described in Chapter 6 has evolved into a scientific approach to the prevention of delinquency that is research based, data driven, and outcome focused. Before delinquency prevention evolved into a science, community leaders—in the absence of data on the risk factors for delinquency that were most prevalent in their communities—made their "best guesses" about the major risk factors for delinquency in their areas. Based on

their guesses, they would select their favorites (not necessarily the most effective) among the programs available; typically the programs implemented were those that the most powerful community leader(s) presumed would be most effective. This could be called the "guesswork" or "hit or miss" approach to delinquency prevention. Fortunately, communities can now abandon this wasteful and ineffective approach. Delinquency prevention science—consisting of knowledge of the major risk factors for delinquency, a method for measuring them, and knowledge of effective programs—now empowers communities to engage systematically in effective prevention programming.

As Tonry and Farrington (1995b) have stated, "Developmental prevention is the new frontier of crime prevention efforts" (p. 10). Developmental theory suggests the feasibility of linking a continuum of prevention programs to infant, child, and adolescent stages of development (such a continuum is illustrated in this chapter). Another implication of developmental theory is that prevention programs may be more effective when they are aimed at more than one risk factor that affects developmental processes. A large number of the programs reviewed in this chapter demonstrate this effectiveness. Developmental prevention is the most comprehensive approach, because entire communities (Catalano, Arthur, Hawkins, Berglund, & Olson, 1998; Tonry & Farrington, 1995a) and larger jurisdictions, such as states and counties, can be mobilized to implement risk- and protection-focused prevention (Farrington, 2000). Later in this chapter, I review promising and effective early intervention and delinquency prevention programs.

Box 9.1

The Monetary Costs of Adolescent Victimization

Macmillan (2000) used a life-course sequence model to calculate the monetary costs of violent victimization of young persons during the adolescent period, linking these events to diminished earnings later in life. His analysis shows that, because violent victimization during adolescence decreases the victims' commitment to education and the effort they put into schoolwork, it has an indirect negative effect on educational performance. These diminished educational investments and performance undermine overall educational attainment. As a result, individuals who have been victims in adolescence have lower occupational status in early adulthood. Those who reach only low occupational status in adulthood, in turn, have lower personal incomes. Macmillan (2000, p. 574) estimates that the expected lifetime income loss for a person who has been subject to any violent victimization in adolescence is $237,200; for sexual assault in adolescence, the loss is $241,600; for robbery, $262,400; and for other forms of assault, $212,800. This research indicates the high cost to U.S. society of the failure to protect young people against exposure to violence.

(Delinquency prevention programs that target youths age 12 and under are commonly called *early intervention* programs; generally, any prevention programs not specifically described as early intervention programs are aimed at older youths.)

One of my aims in this chapter is to show the variety of ways in which delinquency prevention programs are classified. Understanding how various researchers have organized prevention programs in undertaking their literature reviews is important to an appreciation of the many potential applications of promising and effective programs.

Another of my aims in this chapter is to demonstrate that delinquency prevention programs also prevent violence. Both serious and violent delinquency are predicted by similar sets of risk factors (see Figure 6.1 in Chapter 6). Frequent and serious/violent offending also are dependent on the same risk factors (Tolan & Gorman-Smith, 1998, p. 71). Therefore, prevention programs need not be tailored especially to chronic serious and violent delinquency to prevent it (Capaldi & Patterson, 1996). Some adolescent violence can be prevented through the implementation of general prevention programs. Later in this chapter I also discuss some prevention programs specifically designed to prevent violence in childhood and adolescence.

Positive Youth Development and Delinquency Prevention

As a first step in this discussion, I want to make a distinction between the field of delinquency prevention and the broader field of "youth development." Professionals in the latter field focus on the improvement of the general well-being of youth—that is, helping children and adolescents grow up healthy in every respect. The general indicators of well-being include good mental health, good school performance, good peer relations, good problem-solving skills, and very low levels (or the absence) of involvement in a variety of problem behaviors, such as delinquency, gang membership, drug and alcohol use, school dropout, and early pregnancy (National Research Council & Institute of Medicine, 2002). Indicators of positive development during late adolescence and adulthood include completion of high school, completion of higher education, adequate transition into the labor market, avoidance of drug and alcohol abuse, participation in stable and supportive intimate relationships, involvement in civic and community activities, and the absence of any stays in juvenile correctional facilities, jails, or prisons (National Research Council & Institute of Medicine, 2002, pp. 82-83).

In contrast, professionals in the field of delinquency prevention in the past have tended to focus mainly on one undesirable developmental outcome, delinquency, but they recently have begun to focus on related problem behaviors. It is well documented that several behavior problems are related to delinquency, including school dropout, teen pregnancy, illegal substance use, and violence (see Figure 6.1 in Chapter 6). Adolescents seem to have a "behavior proneness" in which risky problems cluster together (Jessor & Jessor, 1977); that is, such problems come in "packages" (Kazdin, 1994). The Comprehensive Strategy thus urges collaboration between delinquency preventionists and youth development advocates to prevent a wide variety of problem behaviors.

Box 9.2

Positive Youth Development

The following are the main personal and social assets that facilitate positive youth development:

- Physical development
- Intellectual development
- Psychological and emotional development
- Social development

Program settings that promote positive development have the following distinctive features:

- Physical and psychological safety
- Appropriate structure
- Supportive relationships
- Opportunities to belong
- Positive social norms
- Support for efficacy and mattering
- Opportunities for skill building
- Integration of family, school, and community

SOURCE: National Research Council & Institute of Medicine (2002, pp. 6-10).

Some youth development advocates urge a shift from risk- and protection-focused delinquency prevention to an emphasis on only the protection side of the equation, what they prefer to call *positive youth development.* They promote the use of what is sometimes called strengths-based training, resilience strengthening, or assets building (Brendtro & Ness, 1995; Leffert, Saito, Blyth, & Kroenke, 1996). This is a narrow view of youth development; as noted in Chapter 6, studies have shown that multiple risk factors decrease the likelihood of positive outcomes. Therefore, communities must reduce the causal risk factors to achieve significant reductions in delinquency.

Unfortunately, the idea of risk reduction is sometimes misinterpreted as something negative, as though it involves blaming youths for being at risk. Risk- and protection-focused prevention does *not* entail blaming youths for their risk factors. Four of the five major risk factors for delinquency (community, family, school, and individual problems) are largely beyond the control of affected youths (Howell, 1997). Children do not choose the families into which they are born, the communities where they live, the schools they attend, or many of the individual problems they develop, such as mental illness. They do choose their peer associations and make choices that lead to certain individual problems, such as drug and alcohol use. Hence risk

reduction involves changing the conditions to which youth are exposed that negatively affect their life chances.

Although incomplete, the evidence suggests that the more positive features present in a community program (see Box 9.2), the greater the contribution the program will make to positive development (National Research Council & Institute of Medicine, 2002, p. 112). In other words, effective youth development programs tend to have certain distinctive features. Youth development programs that have been shown to be most effective in preventing delinquency employ two general program strategies: (a) social or cognitive skill building and (b) environmental and organizational change programs that focus on peer social norms or on influencing teacher classroom practices (Catalano, Berglund, Ryan, Lonczak, & Hawkins, 1999). Almost all of the 25 successful youth development programs identified by the National Research Council and the Institute of Medicine (2002) not only contributed to youth development but also showed significant reduction in certain problem behaviors, including drug and alcohol use, school misbehavior, aggressive behavior, violence, truancy, high-risk sexual behavior, and smoking (pp. 150-165). Given this evidence showing that youth development programs also prevent delinquency, it is important for delinquency preventionists

Table 9.1   Risk Factors for Eight Major Outcomes

Level of Analysis	Behavior Problems	School Failure	Poor Physical Health	Physical Injury	Physical Abuse	Pregnancy	Drug Use	AIDS
Community								
Impoverished neighborhood	X	X	X	X	X	X	X	
Ineffective social policies	X	X	X		X	X	X	
School								
Poor-quality schools	X	X	X			X	X	X
Peer								
Negative peer pressure/modeling	X	X	X			X	X	X
Peer rejection	X				X			
Family								
Low SES	X	X	X	X	X	X	X	X
Parental psychopathology	X	X	X	X	X	X	X	X
Marital discord	X	X			X	X	X	
Punitive childrearing	X	X	X	X	X		X	
Individual								
Early onset of target problem	X	X	X	X	X	X	X	X[a]
Problems in other areas	X	X	X	X	X	X	X	X
Other								
Stress[b]	X	X	X	X	X	X	X	X

SOURCE: "Common Risk and Protective Factors in Successful Prevention Programs," by J. A. Durlak, 1998, *American Journal of Orthopsychiatry, 68,* p. 514. ©1998 by American Journal of Orthopsychiatry. Reprinted with permission.
a. Early sexual activity is a risk factor.
b. Stress can occur at all levels and affect children directly or indirectly through parents, peers, and teachers.

and youth developers to work together in collaborative community efforts. The Community Change for Youth Development (CCYD) program is an operational system for engaging communities in youth development that is similar in many respects to the Communities That Care system, which I discuss later in this chapter; Walker, Watson, and Jucovy (1999) have evaluated CCYD.

Table 9.1 displays Durlak's (1997, 1998) risk factors for eight major outcomes, showing the interrelationships among risk factors for behavior problems, which include delinquency, and other undesirable youth problems. Durlak identifies both the risk factors and undesirable outcomes in his review of some 1,200 prevention program evaluations. These are common areas in which delinquency preventionists and youth developers can work together to reduce risk factors for delinquency and other problem behaviors. Similarly, Durlak's table of protective factors for the eight major outcomes (Table 6.1 in Chapter 6) shows common areas in

which the two groups of scientists and practitioners can work together to increase protection against delinquency and other problem behaviors.

Categorizing Prevention Programs

Delinquency prevention programs can be categorized in many different ways. The oldest way is according to the primary, secondary, and tertiary classification schema (Brantingham & Faust, 1976). Primary delinquency prevention programs aim to prevent the occurrence of delinquency by modifying conditions in the environment (such as high-crime communities) that contribute to delinquency involvement. Secondary delinquency prevention is concerned with intervention with children and adolescents who are in the early stages of delinquency involvement (hence programs in this category are also called early intervention programs). Tertiary delinquency prevention involves the prevention of recidivism and the promotion of rehabilitation. *Intervention* is the term more commonly used to describe these kinds of programs. The Center for the Study and Prevention of Violence (CSVP) has conducted a review of a wide range of "violence prevention" programs for children and adolescents that illustrates this program classification approach (Elliott, 1998; see also CSVP, 1998; Mihalic, Irwin, Elliott, Fagan, & Hansen, 2001). Actually, the CSVP review was not limited to either prevention or violence. Drug-use prevention programs and nonviolent delinquency reduction programs were also included (see Chapter 10 for a complete list). In other words, this review covered primary, secondary, and tertiary prevention programs.

The second schema for classifying programs—the one common to public health research—is according to program targets: universal, selected, and indicated. Universal (general population) prevention programs are provided to all individuals in a given population irrespective of possible differences in risk. Selected (high-risk population) programs operate from a secondary prevention approach, attempting to reduce the prevalence of delinquency cases. Indicated (in-crisis population) programs, like tertiary ones, seek to lessen the seriousness, chronicity, or continuation of delinquency involvement. Programs in this last category are normally called intervention programs. Tolan and Guerra's (1994) review of adolescent violence prevention programs provides an excellent example of this classification method.

The third way of classifying prevention programs is in relation to the major risk factor domains (Hawkins, Catalano, & Miller, 1992). Program reviews have recently been made in each of these domains: family (Kumpfer & Alvarado, 1998), peer group (Coie & Miller-Johnson, 2001), community (Catalano et al., 1998; Catalano, Berglund, et al., 1999), school (Gottfredson, 1997; Gottfredson & Gottfredson, 2002; Gottfredson, Wilson, & Najaka, 2002; Gottfredson et al., 2000; Hawkins, Farrington, & Catalano, 1999), and individual (Tremblay & Craig, 1995; Tremblay & LeMarquand, 2001). It should be noted that some of the authors of these reviews also use one of the classification schemes described above. For example, Kumpfer and Alvarado (1998) use the universal, selected, and indicated schema to classify family-strengthening prevention programs.

A fourth way of classifying prevention programs is in relation to particular topics of interest. For example, because of the few high-profile student firearm attacks at schools in the past decade, there currently is enormous interest in school violence prevention programs. In the recently completed National Study of Delinquency Prevention in Schools, Gottfredson et al. (2000; see also Gottfredson & Gottfredson, 2002) examined the effectiveness of such programs in a nationally representative sample of more than a thousand schools, comparing current school programs with "best practices." Gottfredson and Gottfredson (2002) suggest that "the effectiveness of prevention practices would be improved if schools increased the intensity of the activities they are conducting and incorporated more of the content and especially the methods that have been shown to be related to positive outcomes" (p. 27).

None of the ways of organizing information on promising and effective prevention programs reviewed above is particularly user-friendly for professionals working in the delinquency prevention field. For these practitioners, there is a more practical way of organizing and presenting this information, which I describe in the next section.

Effective Early Intervention and Prevention Programs

The most practical way of categorizing delinquency prevention programs is in relation to the developmental periods of childhood and adolescence. This method of classification is especially useful to any community that wants to build a continuum of effective prevention programs. The interventions discussed below are organized developmentally, from the prenatal period through adolescence. Programs for children under age 13 are classified as *early interventions;* those for older youth are called *delinquency prevention* programs.

Space limitations do not permit me to provide a fully comprehensive review of all effective programs for the prevention of general juvenile delinquency. Unfortunately, researchers have not yet conducted comprehensive meta-analyses of existing evaluations of delinquency prevention programs; therefore, I have no choice but to review programs one by one in the absence of knowledge of the general principles of effective delinquency prevention programs. Meta-analysts have so far tended to concentrate on the results of juvenile rehabilitation programs, but they are beginning to move into the prevention arena. Dr. Mark Lipsey and his colleagues are currently conducting a comprehensive meta-analytic review of delinquency prevention programs (information is available on the Web site of the Center for Evaluation Research and Methodology at Vanderbilt University, at www.vanderbilt.edu/cerm/articles.htm). I describe the recent reviews

---

Box 9.3

Reviews of Effective Delinquency Prevention Programs

Two reviews of promising and effective delinquency prevention programs conducted in the mid-1990s by Brewer, Hawkins, Catalano, and Neckerman (1995) and Hawkins, Catalano, and Brewer (1995) still stand as the most comprehensive reviews of these programs. The excellence of these reviews is owed to the fact that they are part of an ongoing review of delinquency prevention programs that began some 20 years ago. In these two literature reviews, Brewer, Hawkins, and their colleagues reviewed the prevention program literature to identify effective strategies from conception to age 6 as well as evaluations of selected strategies in childhood and adolescence. Both reviews were conducted in conjunction with refinement of the Comprehensive Strategy for Serious, Violent, and Chronic Juvenile Offenders (Wilson & Howell, 1993), and both are summarized in the practitioner's *Guide for Implementing the Comprehensive Strategy* (Howell, 1995) and in the *A Sourcebook: Serious, Violent, and Chronic Juvenile Offenders* (Howell, Krisberg, Hawkins, & Wilson, 1995).

These initial comprehensive reviews of promising and effective delinquency prevention programs by Hawkins, Brewer, and colleagues were updated by the work of the Study Group on Serious and Violent Juvenile Offenders, which has been published in a volume edited by Loeber and Farrington (1998c). This volume contains a literature review of community- and school-based interventions to prevent serious and violent delinquency (Catalano, Arthur, Hawkins, Berglund, & Olson, 1998; for a summary, see Catalano, Loeber, & McKinney, 1999). Another review by this study group that was broader in scope covered programs that target risk factors for serious and violent offending (Wasserman & Miller, 1998; for a summary, see Wasserman, Miller, & Cothern, 2000).

Yet another update of this literature focused on prevention programs for child delinquents was conducted in conjunction with the second Comprehensive Strategy study group—the Study Group on Very Young Offenders (Loeber & Farrington, 2001a). This review, undertaken by Herrenkohl, Hawkins, Chung, Hill, and Battin-Pearson, (2001), covered school and community risk factors and interventions for child delinquents (under age 13). In another review, Howell and Hawkins (1998) specifically identified effective violence prevention programs for adolescence-limited and life-course-persistent offenders.

Other researchers have identified many more promising and effective delinquency and violence prevention programs; for example, see Durlak (1995, 1997); Durlak and Wells (1997); Gottfredson (2001); Gottfredson, Wilson, and Najaka (2002); and U.S. Department of Health and Human Services (2001).

---

upon which I draw in Box 9.3. I have chosen the programs included here based on their effectiveness in preventing delinquency, particularly serious and violent delinquency; their practical program approaches; and/or their utility for the formation of a continuum of prevention programs. A community can form such a continuum in relation to age groups to address risk factors in the family, school, peer group, community, and individual domains.

A number of programs have shown effectiveness in preventing child or adolescent delinquency and violence. In addition to preventing delinquency, several of these programs are considered "violence prevention" programs, although some of them have demonstrated effectiveness only in preventing aggressive behavior or anger, not actual violence (e.g., hitting, assault). I include programs that prevent aggression in this discussion because aggression is considered a minor form of violence.

Consistent with a public health model (Institute of Medicine, 1994), to be most effective, interventions need to address the major risk factors for delinquency (see Chapter 6). For maximum impact, these programs should provide protection or increase juveniles' resilience to counter the negative effects of risk factors. As noted in Chapter 6, programs that address risk and protective factors at or slightly before the developmental points at which those factors begin to cause later delinquency or violence are most likely to be effective (Hawkins, Catalano, & Brewer, 1995).

Effective Early Intervention Programs

A key feature of some effective early intervention programs is a multimodal approach in which the needs of children (early education) and parents (parental training, family strengthening, and parental support) are addressed simultaneously. The OJJDP's Study Group on Very Young Offenders recommends that very early intervention programs optimize their effectiveness by targeting persistently disruptive children and child delinquents and doing the following (Loeber & Farrington, 2001a):

- Address multiple problems of the child, where necessary.
- Apply a multimodal model of interventions that addresses more than one domain of risk factors (e.g., the individual child and the family, the family and the school).
- Integrate services across human service delivery agencies. No single agency is best equipped to reduce child delinquency; integrated interagency efforts are most likely to be effective.
- Use nonlegal sanctions for children; in particular, detention and incarceration of children should be avoided.

The study group also strongly urges a shift in human services agencies' "early intervention" time frame, from elementary school to the toddler period—and even infancy. In some cases, disruptive behavior problems that occur as early as age 3 may predict delinquency at a very young age (Loeber & Farrington, 2001a). As noted in Chapter 4, when disruptive behavior problems are evident in families *and* school settings, there is a much greater likelihood that these conduct problems may lead to delinquency.

Below, I describe some effective early intervention programs in relation to two developmental periods: prenatal and during infancy, and ages 2 to 6.

Prenatal and Infancy

Home visitation by health professionals during pregnancy is an effective early intervention strategy. This approach includes intensive health education for high-risk mothers (e.g., teens) and improves their health-related behaviors; it also reduces the rates of preterm deliveries and low-birth-weight babies (Olds & Kitzman, 1993).

Home visitation with high-risk families by nurses has been shown to be a cost-effective form of intervention (Karoly, Greenwood, & Everingham,

1998; Olds & Kitzman, 1993). For example, the Prenatal/Early Infancy Project targeted a geographic area with high rates of poverty and child abuse in the semirural Appalachian region of New York State (Olds, Henderson, Tatelbaum, & Chamberlin, 1986). A subsample of mothers were unmarried and from the lowest socioeconomic group, and nearly half were teenagers. One group received only prenatal home visitation, and a second group received home visitation by a nurse during pregnancy and until the child was 2 years old. The nurse home visitors followed a comprehensive intervention plan that focused on the mother's personal health, environmental health, quality of caregiving for the infant and toddler, and the mother's own personal development, such as preventing unintended subsequent pregnancies and finding work. The nurse home visitors also were expected to involve family members and friends in the program and to help families use other needed community health and human services. In a 15-year follow-up, Olds et al. (1998) found that home visitation through infancy significantly reduced running away, arrests and convictions, and violations of probation.

Ages 2 to 6

Parent training combined with early child care has proved to be an effective form of early intervention for this age group. Four programs that provided both of these interventions have demonstrated positive effects on antisocial behavior and delinquency (Yoshikawa, 1995; see also Yoshikawa, 1994); these are the High/Scope Perry Preschool Project (Schweinhart, Barnes, & Weikart, 1993), the Syracuse University Family Development Research Program (Lally, Mangione, & Honig, 1988), the Yale Child Welfare Project (Seitz & Apfel, 1994), and the Houston Parent Child Development Center (Johnson & Walker, 1987). Each of these programs focused on improving children's individual capacity (cognitive ability) and family functioning through a combination of early childhood education and family support services. The programs offered both home visits (parent training) and center-based educational child care (aimed at improving cognitive skills). All four programs focused on early childhood and served urban, low-income families. These programs have been widely recognized for their effectiveness (Smith, Fairchild, & Groginsky, 1997), and they have served as models for programs in many states (National Conference of State Legislatures, 1999a).

Remarkably, two of these programs—Perry Preschool and Syracuse University Family

Development—have proven effective in reducing serious and chronic delinquency in long-term follow-ups. The Perry Preschool Project was designed to prevent delinquency by targeting preschoolers. The follow-up of experimental groups at age 27 showed that significantly fewer program group members than no-program group members were frequent offenders—that is, arrested five or more times in their lifetimes (7% versus 35%) or as adults (7% versus 31%) (Schweinhart et al., 1993). The program group also had noticeably fewer juvenile arrests and significantly fewer arrests for drug manufacturing and drug distribution offenses (7% versus 25%). The Syracuse program also produced a decrease in the total number, severity, and chronicity of later involvement in officially recorded offenses (Lally et al., 1988). Yoshikawa (1995) found that the combination of early education for the child and family support produced the strongest long-term effects on antisocial behavior and delinquency. He also attributes the success of these programs to their effects on multiple risks for serious delinquency. Such early interventions are also cost-effective. However, there is a long wait for the payback, because early intervention programs with infants and children have lagged or long-term effects (Berrueta-Clement, Schweinhart, Barnett, Epstein, & Weikart, 1984; Esbensen, Osgood, Taylor, Peterson, & Freng, 2001; Hawkins, Hill, Battin-Pearson, & Abbott, 2000; Olds et al., 2001; Tremblay et al., 2001).

The Interpersonal Cognitive Problem-Solving (ICPS) curriculum is an effective social skill development program for preschool students (Herrenkohl, Hawkins, et al., 2001). The ICPS curriculum was tested with a sample of 4- to 5-year-old African American children drawn from 10 federally funded Head Start programs (Shure & Spivack, 1988). Overall, the researchers found that the ICPS curriculum improved children's problem-solving skills and behavioral adjustment. Decreases in behavior problems and aggressive and socially inappropriate behavior were observed. Other evaluations of the curriculum confirm the effectiveness of ICPS as a social competence enhancement/behavior modification program (Shure & Spivack, 1988).

The Incredible Years Training Series (Webster-Stratton, 1999) is an effective intervention for the prevention of aggression in preschool children. This intervention combines parent training, teacher training, and child training in its multimodal approach. An evaluated program that targeted 4- to 8-year-olds diagnosed with oppositional defiance disorder or conduct disorder (defined as high rates of aggression, noncompliance, and defiance) had significantly fewer students who were misbehaving, disruptive, or aggressive with peers and teachers (Webster-Stratton, 2000).

Effective Prevention Programs

Delinquency prevention agencies commonly think of programs for children and adolescents age 6 through 17 as prevention programs rather than early intervention programs. Programs for the younger subgroup (6 to 12) in this age range aim to prevent the onset of delinquency in childhood, and programs for the older subgroup (13-17) aim to prevent the spread of delinquency and violence during adolescence. Most prevention programs are based either in the community or in schools. Gang involvement is an important context in which delinquency and violence spread in adolescence. Schools represent another important context, in part because of the opportunities they provide for adolescents to associate with delinquent peers.

Ages 6 to 12

Parent training. One means of reducing the onset of delinquent and violent childhood behavior is through reducing abuse and neglect (Smith & Thornberry, 1995). Parent training using Multisystemic Therapy (MST; see Henggeler, 1997b) has been successfully applied to abusive and neglectful parents of elementary school–age children (Brunk, Henggeler, & Whelan, 1987). Parents exposed to MST controlled their children's behavior more effectively, maltreated children exhibited less passive noncompliance, and neglecting parents became more responsive to their children's behavior.

The Montreal Preventive Treatment Program (described in Chapter 5) was an effective violence prevention program that incorporated school- and family-based components in an early intervention with boys who had displayed disruptive behavior in kindergarten (Herrenkohl, Hawkins, et al., 2001). The program focused on families and individual children living in low socioeconomic areas of Montreal. The most disruptive boys at age 6—as assessed by their kindergarten teachers—were recruited to take part in the program. An evaluation of the program demonstrated its effectiveness (Tremblay, Masse, Pagani, & Vitaro, 1996). Boys who participated in the treatment group showed decreases in aggressive behavior, serious school adjustment problems, and minor delinquency (fighting, trespassing, theft, and burglary) (Herrenkohl, Hawkins, et al., 2001, p. 227).

Behavior management. A second major strategy for reducing behavior problems during the elementary period (ages 6-12) is the use of behavior management methods in school classrooms and on playgrounds. Two examples follow.

A behavioral classroom management technique called the Good Behavior Game was designed to prevent disruptive and aggressive behavior. Program teachers measured students' levels of aggression and disruption during a baseline period and then assigned students to one of three heterogeneous teams that included equally aggressive/disruptive children. When the Good Behavior Game was in progress, the teachers assigned check marks on the chalkboard to a team when a student in that team engaged in a disruptive behavior. At the end of a particular game period, teams with fewer than five check marks earned rewards. During the beginning of the program, game periods were announced and tangible rewards, such as stickers, were immediately distributed to team members. As the program progressed, the teachers began the game unannounced and provided less tangible rewards that were delayed until the end of the day or week; for example, students might be given the privilege of participating in an upcoming activity (e.g., extra recess or class privileges). Teams that had the fewest check marks received a special reward on Friday. The program reduced antisocial and aggressive behavior (Dolan et al., 1993; Kellam, Rebok, Ialongo, & Mayer, 1994).

In Tallahassee, Florida, a school program for boys and girls in kindergarten through second grade effectively reduced aggressive behavior on the playground (Catalano et al., 1998; Catalano, Berglund, et al., 1999; Herrenkohl, Hawkins, et al., 2001). The program offered organized games, such as jump rope and races, to children who arrived at the school playground before the school day began. Before the program was established, school staff regarded students' disruptive and aggressive behavior on the playground as a problem during this morning period. Three aides supervised the program activities and used a time-out procedure to discipline students whose behavior was particularly unruly. During a time-out, the disruptive student was required to sit quietly on a bench for 2 minutes. The program showed a significant reduction in aggression as a result of the structured activities (Murphy, Hutchinson, & Bailey, 1983).

Promoting school functioning. Promoting academic adjustment and school achievement is another effective approach to reducing risks (for antisocial behavior) in children ages 6-12. Academic failure is

a risk factor for the onset of delinquency and the escalation of serious offending (see Chapter 6), and interventions that improve children's academic performance have been shown to reduce delinquency (Maguin & Loeber, 1996). Interventions aimed at promoting school functioning need to address low academic performance; weak bonds to school, low educational aspirations, and low school motivation; truancy; poorly defined rules and expectations for behavior; and inadequate enforcement of rules against antisocial behavior (Herrenkohl, Hawkins, et al., 2001, p. 217). All of these are proven risk factors for delinquency.

Three comprehensive approaches for addressing multiple risks and enhancing achievement and protection during the elementary school period have been evaluated and found to be effective: the Fast Track program, the Seattle Social Development Project, and the Child Development Project.

Fast Track is a comprehensive, multisite intervention that effectively prevents serious and chronic antisocial behavior among kindergarten children (Herrenkohl, Hawkins, et al., 2001). The program targets kindergarten children in low-income, high-crime communities who have shown conduct problems at school and at home. The first of six Fast Track components is a teacher-led classroom curriculum, called PATHS (Promoting Alternative THinking Strategies), that is directed toward emotional and relationship development as well as the development of problem-solving skills and self-control. The curriculum is designed to build children's interpersonal and problem-solving skills, including their ability to use positive conflict resolution strategies (Greenberg & Kusche, 1993). Other program components are parent training, home visitation, child social skills training, child tutoring in reading, and peer pairing. Evaluation of the program involved schools that were randomly assigned to treatment and control groups. At the end of the first grade, children in the Fast Track program showed improvements in prosocial behavior, social cognitive skills, peer liking, and positive expression of feelings. In addition, the treatment classes evidenced decreases in aggression and hyperactivity, aggressive-disruptive behavior at school, and conduct problems at home (Conduct Problems Prevention Research Group, 1999a, 1999b).

The Seattle Social Development Project is a proven-effective adolescent violence prevention program (U.S. Department of Health and Human Services, 2001). The project, which consisted of multiple components, provided social competence training for children while training teachers and parents in how to encourage young children's interest in school and help them learn to interact with others. The interventions took place in elementary schools (grades 1 to 6) in Seattle's most crime-ridden neighborhoods. In the initial evaluation, this program proved to be effective in reducing aggressive behavior in boys and self-destructive behavior in girls (Hawkins, Von Cleve, & Catalano, 1991).

Hawkins, Catalano, Kosterman, Abbott, and Hill (1999) conducted a study of the long-term effects of the Seattle project and found improved academic achievement, greater commitment and attachment to school, and reduced school misbehavior among participants 6 years after the interventions. The researchers also found that the interventions successfully reduced violent behavior, heavy drinking, and sexual activity among adolescents who had participated in the program. The project appears to have been particularly effective with poor children.

Along with Fast Track and the Seattle Social Development Project, the Child Development Project has demonstrated that the teaching of academic and social/emotional skills can be integrated into the classroom, with the effect of preventing violence among children and adolescents (Herrenkohl, Hawkins, et al., 2001). The Child Development Project uses cooperative learning and proactive classroom management methods to foster responsibility, establish prosocial norms, and strengthen conflict resolution skills. The program, which spans a 3-year period during the elementary grades, also offers classroom and schoolwide community-building activities, activities for students and parents to do at home together, and a reading and multicultural language arts program that emphasizes students' critical thinking about relevant social and ethical issues. Evaluations of the program have found significant increases in student attachment and commitment to school and academic achievement, and decreases in weapon carrying, interpersonal aggression, and vehicle theft among students in a high-implementation subgroup (Battistich, Schaps, Watson, & Solomon, 1996; Battistich, Solomon, Watson, & Schaps, 1997).

Violence prevention curricula. The best evidence regarding the effectiveness of a violence prevention curriculum in the classroom comes from one designed for use in elementary grades 2 and 3 (Herrenkohl, Hawkins, et al., 2001). The Second Step violence prevention curriculum uses 30 specific lessons to teach skills related to anger management, impulse control, and empathy. It promotes prosocial behavior by increasing children's competence in peer interactions and friendships, and

teaches interpersonal conflict resolution skills to help them avoid and resolve interpersonal disputes. In an evaluation of the program, Grossman et al. (1997) found increases in prosocial behavior and empathy; increases in interpersonal problem-solving, anger management, and behavioral-social skills; and decreases in aggressive playground and lunchroom behavior (Herrenkohl, Hawkins, et al., 2001, p. 229).

Altering school climate and culture. PeaceBuilders is a schoolwide program for children in kindergarten through grade 5 that has been deemed effective in reducing injuries. The program was intended to alter the climate and culture of the entire school, generally promoting prosocial behavior and changing characteristics of the setting that trigger aggressive, hostile behavior. Activities were designed to improve daily interactions among students, teachers, administrators, support staff, and parents. The program was purposely woven into the school's everyday routine to make it "a way of life," not just a curriculum activity (Krug, Brener, Dahlberg, Ryan, & Powell, 1997). Children were taught five simple principles: Praise people, avoid put-downs, seek wise people as advisers and friends, notice and correct hurts, and right wrongs. These principles were taught using several methods, including models of positive behavior, environmental cues to signal this behavior, opportunities to rehearse it, and rewards for practicing it. The evaluation found positive effects on fighting-related injuries, as indicated in a significant reduction in injury-related visits to the school nurse and in confirmed fighting episodes (Krug et al., 1997).

Reducing risk and increasing protection. The Children at Risk (CAR) program—now called Striving Together to Achieve Rewarding Tomorrows, or START—demonstrated some effectiveness in reducing risk factors and increasing protective factors for delinquency and drug use among very high-risk youth. The program targeted such youth in distressed neighborhoods in five cities: Austin, Texas; Bridgeport, Connecticut; Memphis, Tennessee; Savannah, Georgia; and Seattle, Washington. Participants were ages 11-13, lived in the target neighborhoods, attended school and were in the sixth or seventh grade, and exhibited risk in one of four domains: family, neighborhood, school, or personal factors. Case managers collaborated closely with staff from criminal justice agencies, schools, and other community organizations to provide comprehensive, individualized, and intensive services that targeted the risk factors. The program's aim was to offset the negative effects of these risk factors (Harrell, 1996; see also Hirota, 1994a, 1994b; Tapper, 1996).

In a 1-year follow-up evaluation of the CAR program, Harrell, Cavanagh, and Sridharan (1999; see also Tapper, 1996) found that it had been successful in significantly reducing drug use (both using and selling drugs) and self-reported violent delinquency, but not property offenses. Other problem behaviors were not reduced; these included sexual activity, running away, dropping out of school, early pregnancy or parenthood, and gang membership. Risk factors were reduced and protective factors were increased in only one of the four targeted domains: the peer group. Risk and protective factors were not affected significantly in the family, neighborhood, and individual risk factor domains. However, the evaluators speculated that the program may have a more positive impact in the longer term by virtue of having helped troubled youngsters through some difficult crises during the crucial developmental stage of early adolescence (Harrell et al., 1999, p. 9).

What are the implications of the limited effectiveness of this program? First, the program goal—to prevent delinquency by building resilience in the major risk factor domains—was laudable. However, this proved to be problematic except in the peer group domain. We need to understand the reasons for this program's failure in the other domains in order to improve future programming of this type. Second, the program targeted relatively high-risk youths, but the "distressed" nature of the communities meant that few resources and services were available. Moreover, distressed communities produce distressed families (National Research Council, 1993). Indeed, Harrell et al. (1999) found that "engaging the parents themselves in sponsored activities was one of the most difficult aspects of the program to implement successfully" (p. 5). Most of the parents did not participate in parenting classes, a core CAR component intended to reduce the family risk factor. Parents commonly failed to show up for mental health services and substance abuse treatment and other core program services designed to help families and adult caregivers function better. Given these difficulties, it is surprising that the program was as successful as it was. Very intense and prolonged interventions are usually needed under such circumstances. A "wraparound" model might be required for many of the targeted clients and their families (see Chapter 11).

Ages 13-17

Community programs. Two community-based prevention program strategies have been shown to be particularly effective. The first of these, mentoring, is one of the prevention program strategies that communities should consider using in their array of prevention programs. The second strategy is community-based gang prevention programming.

Big Brothers Big Sisters of America (BBBSA) is the oldest and best-known mentoring program in the United States, and research shows that it is effective. Local Big Brothers and Big Sisters programs are autonomously funded affiliates of the national organization. The more than 500 affiliates oversee in excess of 100,000 one-to-one relationships between a volunteer adult and a youth. Matches are carefully made using established procedures and criteria. Although the program serves children ages 6-18, most participants are 10-14 years old, and a significant proportion of them are from disadvantaged single-parent households. A mentor meets with his or her youth partner at least three times a month for 3 to 5 hours per visit. These visits encourage the development of a caring relationship between mentor and youth.

The BBBSA mentoring program has been shown to be effective in preventing truancy, drug and alcohol use, and some aggressive or violent behavior (Grossman & Garry, 1997; Tierney & Grossman, 1995). Evaluations have found that youth in the mentoring program, compared with youth in a control group, have improved school attendance, attitudes toward school, and school performance as well as improved peer and family relationships. In addition, the mentored youths are less likely to start using drugs and alcohol and less likely to hit someone. Other studies have also shown the effectiveness of adult mentoring of at-risk youth, in middle school (McPartland & Nettles, 1991) and with high-risk male offenders (Moore, 1987). The multisite Juvenile Mentoring Program (JUMP) is currently being evaluated (Novotney, Mertinko, Lange, & Baker, 2000). As I will discuss in more detail in Chapter 10, mentoring has been found to be one of the most effective interventions with juvenile offenders (Lipsey, Howell, & Tidd, 2002). A common situation is adult mentoring of youths diverted from juvenile court (Davidson, Redner, & Amdur, 1990). The effectiveness of mentoring has also been noted in an evaluation of youth with mental health problems receiving family-based residential treatment in lieu of hospitalization (Mikkelsen, Bereika, & McKenzie, 1993).

Mentoring adults serve as one of the "lifelines" that can provide protection against risk factors in adolescence (Cairns & Cairns, 1994, pp. 258-261). Studies of resilient high-risk children show that those who do well almost invariably have had long-term

---

Box 9.4

Costs and Benefits of Early Childhood Interventions

RAND researchers Karoly, Greenwood, and Everingham (1998) conducted a cost-benefit study of 10 early childhood interventions, examining the program effects on parents as well as participating children. They found that "in some situations, carefully targeted early childhood interventions can yield measurable benefits in the short run and that some benefits persist long after the program has ended" (p. 61). Specifically, Karoly et al. draw four main conclusions (pp. 107-108):

- For high-risk children, early intervention may lower the chance that they will become chronic or violent criminals or fall behind in schoolwork, and may raise the likelihood that they achieve economic self-sufficiency.
- For high-risk mothers, early intervention programs may improve their quality of life not only by improving their children's well-being and achievement, but also by giving them such benefits as increased employment and reduced drug dependency.
- For individual states and communities, providing early intervention programs may be a means of reducing the escalating costs of corrections, welfare, and special education.
- For the economy as a whole, early intervention may be a way to improve overall social welfare while reducing the pain and suffering associated with criminal victimization.

The RAND research team concludes that three key factors make a difference in terms of whether an early childhood program generates savings to government:

- *Targeting:* "Programs that target children and families who will benefit most from the services offered have the highest chance of repaying their costs. In most cases, more disadvantaged children are likely to realize the greatest benefits" (p. 106).
- *The time required for the payback of program costs:* Most cost savings are not realized for several years, because they accumulate over the lifetimes of the children and mothers in these programs. "The longer the time period permitted for the payback, the greater the chance that the savings generated by program benefits will outweigh the program's costs" (p. 107).
- *The evaluation's inclusion or exclusion of outcome measures for the mother:* "Improvements in mothers' outcomes may generate savings to government that are as large or larger than the savings generated by improvements in the children's outcomes" (p. 107).

---

relationships with caring adults outside the immediate family to provide support and guidance (Werner & Smith, 1982). This principle applies equally to troubled children (Vance & Sanchez, 1998). Most high-risk children say they prefer informal and personal attachments to impersonal interactions with agencies (Werner & Smith, 1992). With proper clinical supervision and specific strategies for promoting protective factors, trusting adult-child relationships can be maximized to deliver treatment in a way that is acceptable to this population (Vance & Sanchez, 1998). Experienced practitioners contend that wraparound systems of service delivery can be designed to use mentoring adults, along with teachers, clinicians, and others, as effective vehicles for change. In fact, the wraparound process itself is conducive to mentoring relationships (see Chapter 11).

I have reviewed promising and effective gang prevention programs in Chapter 5. As noted there, of the many programs that have been designed to prevent gang involvement among adolescents (Howell, 2000), few have been evaluated. The school-based Gang Resistance Education and Training (G.R.E.A.T.) program and the Boys & Girls Clubs of America's Gang Prevention Through Targeted Outreach program hold considerable promise. (For more these two programs, see Chapter 5.)

Prevention of gang membership should be a priority in the Comprehensive Strategy for Serious, Violent, and Chronic Juvenile Offenders in any community where assessments of delinquency indicate that gang problems exist. As the discussion in Chapter 5 shows, child delinquents are at high risk for gang membership, thus prevention of delinquency in the first instance will help prevent gang involvement.

There is another intersection between general delinquency and gang involvement that can be addressed in delinquency prevention and early intervention programs. Curry, Decker, and Egley (2002) discovered this intersection recently in a St. Louis study of middle school students. They found that youths need not be members of gangs to be negatively affected by gang members. Youths who associated with gang members ("gang associates," in Curry et al.'s terminology) evidenced the delinquency-enhancing effects of gang membership even though they were not actual members. Early-adolescent gang associates were less delinquent than current gang members, but significantly more delinquent than youngsters not involved with gang members. As Curry et al. observe, "This finding supports the need for early prevention and intervention programs with youths and families, especially in neighborhoods with high levels of gang membership or in families with older siblings who belong to gangs" (pp. 289-290). Prevention programs that intervene with families containing predelinquent youths can lessen gang involvement. The Montreal Preventive Treatment Program, which was designed to prevent delinquency among disruptive, low-socioeconomic-status kindergartners, is a good example—it also prevented gang involvement (see Chapter 5).

School-based programs. A variety of school-based delinquency prevention programs have been shown to be effective in preventing delinquency and violence among children and adolescents. Several of these programs have used social competence training to help students learn positive social behaviors (e.g., behavioral control strategies and refusal skills) and to improve social-cognitive processes (e.g., problem solving and anger management).

The Program Development Evaluation (PDE) method is a multicomponent middle school organizational intervention carried out by School Improvement Teams made up of teachers, parents, and school officials (Gottfredson, 1986; Gottfredson, Gottfredson, & Hybl, 1993). PDE is an effective method of improving school discipline and classroom management. It has been shown to result in significant decreases in classroom disruption, better classroom organization, and increased clarity of rules (Gottfredson et al., 1993).

Responding in Peaceful and Positive Ways (RIPP) is an example of an effective violence prevention curriculum for middle school students (Herrenkohl, Hawkins, et al., 2001). RIPP, which is part of the Richmond Youth Against Violence Project (Farrell & Meyer, 1997; Meyer & Farrell, 1998), seeks to build knowledge, change attitudes, and enhance skills to act against violence. It also teaches children about the nature of violence and its consequences. The curriculum, consisting of 18 sessions over the course of one semester, teaches urban sixth-grade students strategies for negotiating interpersonal conflicts nonviolently. Adult role models trained in the curriculum administer the weekly sessions. Peer mediation, team-building activities, small group work, and role playing are used regularly. Differences in intervention effects of the program for males and females were examined in the Richmond project. Boys, but not girls, showed decreases in violent behavior (e.g., fighting, threatening to hurt, carrying weapons), suppression of anger, frequency of hitting teachers, and schools suspensions; girls showed differences in problem solving (Herrenkohl, Hawkins, et al., 2001, p. 229).

Safe Dates, a program designed to prevent dating violence, consists of school and community interventions targeting eighth and ninth graders. In an evaluation of the program, Foshee et al. (1998) randomly assigned 14 public schools to treatment (school activities and community activities) and control (community activities only) groups. The program's school activities consisted of changing norms associated with partner violence, decreasing gender stereotyping, improving conflict management skills, and help-seeking training. Community activities consisted of special services for adolescents in violent relationships and community service provider training. At follow-up—1 month after the program ended—the researchers found that, compared with students in control schools, students in treatment schools exhibited less psychological abuse perpetration, less sexual violence perpetration, and less violence perpetrated against the current dating partner. In a subsample of adolescents reporting no preprogram dating violence, there was less initiation of psychological abuse in treatment schools than in control schools. Most of the program effects were explained by the school activities, not the community activities. Few victims of dating violence sought help from traditional community agencies. Foshee et al. (1998) describe Safe Dates as a promising intervention for preventing dating violence among adolescents.

The Social Competence Promotion Program for Young Adolescents (Weissberg & Greenberg, 1997) is an effective individually targeted violence prevention program (Herrenkohl, Hawkins, et al., 2001) that teaches cognitive, behavioral, and affective skills to middle school students (grades 5 through 8) through classroom instruction. The program seeks to promote social competency (self-control, stress management, responsible decision making, social problem solving, and communication skills), improve communication between school personnel and students, and prevent antisocial behavior, such as aggression and substance use, as well as high-risk sexual behavior. In the program, children are taught how to respond effectively to daily problems. In an evaluation, Weissberg and Caplan (1998) found that children exposed to the intervention demonstrated improved problem-solving and conflict resolution skills. Compared to controls, they were more adjusted to school and also engaged in less minor delinquent behavior (stealing, getting sent out of the classroom, starting fights, vandalism, going out at night without permission, skipping school, and getting suspended).

The Social Relations Intervention Program is an effective prevention approach that provides training in social skills, problem solving, and anger management for children in fourth grade who are rated by peers as poorly behaved and rejected (Herrenkohl, Hawkins, et al., 2001). The program has four components: training in social problem solving, positive play training, group-entry skills training, and training in dealing effectively with strong negative feelings. Lochman, Coie, Underwood, and Terry (1993) conducted an evaluation of the program with a sample of children in inner-city schools who had been rated negatively by their peers at pretest on indicators of social acceptance and behavior. The majority of children were African American and from low-income families. Lochman et al. assigned children randomly to experimental and control conditions, and comparisons between the two groups revealed positive effects of the intervention at its completion and a year later. Children who received the intervention were less aggressive and exhibited more prosocial behavior than those who did not receive the intervention.

The Anger-Coping Intervention is an effective individually targeted violence prevention program (Gottfredson et al., 2002). In his pioneering cognitive-behavioral work with highly aggressive boys, Lochman targeted specific cognitive skills using behavioral techniques (operant conditioning) to increase compliance with group rules. His Anger-Coping Intervention targets boys in grades 4 through 6 who have been identified by teachers as aggressive and disruptive. In an evaluation of the intervention, Lochman, Burch, Curry, and Lampron (1984) found that, compared with aggressive boys who received no treatment or minimal treatment, the boys who received treatment reduced their disruptive-aggressive off-task behavior in school and their overall aggressive behavior, as rated by parents and teachers. Feindler, Marriott, and Iwata (1984) found another cognitive-behavioral program of anger management training for disruptive boys in school to be effective for minor verbal and physical violence (see Gottfredson et al., 2002).

Law-Related Education (LRE) programs provide K-12 classroom instruction designed to educate children and adolescents about the origins and roles of law in key social systems (e.g., family, community, and school) and the juvenile and criminal justice systems. Some forms of LRE have broader application, such as in street law, which draws practical connections between the everyday lives of young people and the law, human rights, and democratic values (for more information, see Street Law Online at www.streetlaw.org). LRE programs have been shown to be effective in improving academic performance and as a practical approach for preventing delinquency in general (Gottfredson et al., 2002; Lipsey, 1999b; Maguin & Loeber, 1996). In addition, there is some evidence that LRE prevents aggressive behavior (Gottfredson, 1990; Johnson & Hunter, 1985).

The Midwestern Prevention Project (MPP) is a successful program for preventing one form of delinquency: gateway drug (alcohol, cigarette, and marijuana) use among both low- and high-risk seventh and eighth graders (Johnson et al., 1990). MPP is unique in that the program has components that address all five of the risk factor domains. Individual skill training is provided for all of the students, and their parents are provided with training as well as opportunities for direct involvement with their children and the schools. Peers are involved in positive modeling. In MPP, the school is the central component for drug prevention programming, including a variety of social learning techniques, and the program works to modify policies to discourage drug use. Lastly, the program seeks to modify and clarify community policies and social norms about drug use, to set and reinforce clear behavioral standards.

Crisis Intervention Programs

Crisis intervention programs are not normally included in reviews of prevention and early intervention programs. They should be included, however, because many of them involve predelinquent or delinquent children with serious emotional problems. "Couch kids" are a case in point (Stack, 2002). These are young people who walk away from unpleasant situations in their homes and spend a few days—perhaps longer—on the couches of friends, relatives, or acquaintances. This behavior creates a crisis situation for parents, because of their legal responsibility to provide food, clothing, shelter, and a nurturing environment for their children. Police actions in these cases are limited, because simply walking away from home is not a crime. "Couch kids" put themselves at risk of victimization and possible development of emotional problems.

Three types of crisis intervention programs have been evaluated (U.S. Department of Health and Human Services, 1999, pp. 178-79): a program using a mobile crisis team, programs using short-term residential services, and programs using intensive in-home service. Youth Emergency Services (YES) in New York City sends clinicians directly to the scene of a crisis. A number of programs provide short-term residential services (Kumpfer & Alvarado, 1998). The use of in-home crisis intervention services was initiated by Homebuilders in the state of Washington in the 1970s (Sondheimer, Schoenwald, & Rowland, 1994). A family preservation program, Homebuilders is an intervention designed for families whose children otherwise face imminent removal to foster care. The intervention begins when the family is determined to be in crisis.

Two variants of the Homebuilders approach have been developed (Evans & Boothroyd, 1997). One version consists of home-based crisis intervention; the other adds an intensive case management approach. Both versions include cognitive-behavioral approaches to behavior management and problem solving as well as a variety of support services. Programs based on the Homebuilders model are now used to avert psychiatric placement of seriously emotionally disturbed youth.

In the next section, I discuss the possible prevention of the most serious form of delinquency: violent shootings. As noted in Chapter 3, despite the fact that the numbers of such events are relatively small, that they occur at all raises the important issue of how they can be prevented.

The Problem of School
Shootings: Is Prevention Possible?

Schools are among the safest places children and adolescents can be; only about 10% of schools report any serious violent crimes to police each year (Snyder & Hoffman, 2001). Some 95% of the crimes reported in U.S. public schools in 1996-1997 did not involve serious or violent acts (Donohue, Schiraldi, & Ziedenberg, 1999). About 80% of all schools reported five or fewer crimes of any kind

(serious or petty) on school property during the 1996-1997 school year. Moreover, serious violent juvenile crimes cluster in the hours immediately after the close of school (Snyder & Sickmund, 1999, p. 65). Nevertheless, the few highly publicized school shootings that have taken place in recent years (see Chapters 2 and 3) prompted the U.S. Secret Service to undertake an assessment of ways to prevent school shootings (National Threat Assessment Center, 2000). The assessment was based on 37 school shootings involving 41 attackers. The study's findings (displayed in Box 9.5) provide little encouragement that school shootings can be prevented in any way except through the elimination of youngsters' access to guns. The prospects are better for intervention with troubled students who are having difficulty coping with major losses or perceived failures, particularly when feelings of desperation and hopelessness are involved (National Institute of Justice, 2002). School-based intervention programs that identify and assess problems and sources of help for troubled students offer the best prospects. One example is the school-based Norfolk, Virginia, Assessment Center, which I discuss in some detail in Chapters 11 and 13.

The use of metal detectors to reduce violence by making firearms unavailable within school buildings is another promising school shooting prevention strategy (Catalano, Berglund, et al., 1999). One survey of a representative sample of New York City high school students found that juveniles who attended schools with metal detectors were half as likely as students who attended schools without metal detectors to carry guns, knives, or other weapons to or from school or inside a school building (Ginsberg & Loffredo, 1993). Other advanced techniques for ensuring school safety are available that can be incorporated in a more comprehensive approach (Green, 1999; Trump, 1998).

The Safe Schools Unit of the San Diego County (California) Office of Education operates an impressive comprehensive school safety program that is a promising approach for preventing school violence (Sakamoto, 1996). The school safety activities in this program extend beyond school security and address staff training and development needs, mainly through the program's Violence Prevention/Intervention (VPI) Team. This team operates the education office's Rapid Response Unit, which assists any school during a crisis situation. Reported crimes in San Diego County schools are significantly lower than the statewide averages.

The Family Educational Rights and Privacy Act (FERPA; 20 U.S.C. Sec. 1232g) governs the disclosure of information from education records of

---

Box 9.5

Findings From the National Threat Assessment Center's Study of School Shootings

---

- Prior to most incidents, the attacker told someone about the idea or plan.
- Incidents of targeted violence at school are rarely impulsive.
- There is no accurate or useful profile of "the school shooter."
- Most attackers had used guns previously and had access to guns.
- Most shooting incidents were not resolved by law enforcement intervention.
- In many cases, other students were involved with the attacker in some capacity.
- In a number of cases, bullying played a key role in the decision to attack.
- Most attackers engaged in some behavior prior to the incident that caused concern or indicated a need for help.

SOURCES: National Institute of Justice (2002) and National Threat Assessment Center (2000).
NOTE: More information on this topic is available at the National Threat Assessment Center's Web site at www.treas.gov/usss/ntac.

---

public elementary and secondary schools (Medaris, Campbell, & James, 1997). FERPA provisions allow schools to play a vital role in partnership with juvenile courts and law enforcement, in both prevention and follow-up, to ensure school safety. The sharing of relevant information on students between schools and law enforcement units is permitted for the purpose of maintaining safe schools. When a safety emergency exists, schools may share relevant information about students involved in the emergency with appropriate parties to protect the safety of students and others. These procedures may help prevent violent episodes such as school shootings in the future.

A school-based bullying prevention program developed in Norway shows some promise for preventing delinquency and violence at school that may lead to shootings. This program aimed to increase awareness of and knowledge about bullying among teachers, parents, and students. Booklets summarizing the knowledge about bullying and suggesting some steps that can be taken to reduce it were distributed to teachers and students in schools and to the parents of students. Students completed anonymous self-report questionnaires about the prevalence of bullies and victims in their schools during a specially arranged school conference day. Teachers were encouraged to develop explicit rules about bullying (e.g., Bullying will not be tolerated; Tell someone when bullying happens; Try to help victims) and to discuss bullying in their classes, using a video and role-playing exercises. Also, teachers were encouraged to improve their

monitoring and supervision of students, especially on the playground.

This program model may need strengthening to be considered effective (see Chapter 10). In an exhaustive review of bullying prevention programs in the United States, Farrington (1993b, pp. 425-426) identified key elements of a promising antibullying program. In addition, some program models designed to target other problem behaviors may prevent or reduce bullying (Coie & Miller-Johnson, 2001).

Community-Oriented Policing

Community-oriented policing (COP) is a popular practice with prevention potential. From 1994 through 1999, the use of COP tactics swept the country, fueled in part by nearly $9 billion in grants awarded to police departments by the federal Community Oriented Policing Services (COPS) office. The new federal program had twin goals: to put 100,000 additional cops on the streets and to increase the use of community-oriented policing methods. Although most of the funds supported the hiring of additional police, COP programs flourished (Roth et al., 2000). The fastest-spreading programs were citizen-police academies, cooperative school truancy programs, structured problem-solving initiatives, and programs in which police patrol on foot, bike, or other transportation modes that offer greater potential for interacting with citizens than the use of patrol cars. At the same time, traditional police support for such ineffective programs as D.A.R.E. continued, subsumed under the community policing label, along with zero-tolerance policies and practices.

The term *community-oriented policing* is commonly used to refer to situations in which police departments, other government agencies, and members of the community work together to solve crime problems. However, three essential features distinguish true COP from traditional policing (Adams, Rohe, & Arcury, 2002). *Shared responsibility* on the part of police and the community is the first one. The second essential feature is *prevention*. Working with citizens, COP officers are expected to identify the underlying conditions that lead to crime and then organize efforts to modify those conditions. Third, COP officers are expected to exercise *police discretion* in addressing community problems without making arrests.

Numerous COP programs have been evaluated (Adams et al., 2002; Lurigio & Rosenbaum, 1994). A few of these studies have shown a reduction in disorder, and others have reported positive effects on resident satisfaction in areas using community policing, but actual reductions in citizen victimization rates as a result of community-oriented policing are rare. In general, COP programs result in decreases in residents' perceptions of and fear of crime and, in many cases, result in more positive evaluations of police by residents.

Evaluating COP programs is a difficult enterprise, and the effectiveness of programs is understandably uneven (Weisel & Eck, 1994). The most thoroughly evaluated COP program meeting the criteria of a true community-oriented policing program is the Chicago Alternative Policing Strategy (CAPS). In the CAPS program, officers in all districts and on all beats were instructed to work with neighborhood residents to identify chronic local crime problems and to devise solutions for them. The views of the local communities were expressed through district-level advisory committees and monthly public meetings for residents. To evaluate the program, Skogan et al. (1999) obtained data on 15 police beats from observations and ride-alongs, agency files, attendance at public meetings, interviews with community leaders, and surveys of local residents. The evaluators gave an "excellent" rating to 4 of the 15 beats. Another 5 were found to be mounting reasonable programs, 2 were struggling, and 4 received failing grades. The ratings were based on success in problem-solving practices, efforts to involve the community, and adherence to a clear plan of action. Some of the best practices were developed in some of the poorest neighborhoods, but at least 5 beats in ethnically diverse or primarily African American neighborhoods did not receive very good service. Skogan et al. (2000) have developed a manual that other communities can use in implementing programs based on the CAPS model.

Two other COP programs are noteworthy for their innovative approaches. One of these, implemented in Columbus, Ohio, I have described in Chapter 5. In Redlands, California, the police department has taken the community-oriented policing concept even further in the prevention direction by instituting "risk-focused policing" (Rich, 1999). The Redlands PD's COP strategy is influenced by the application of the risk- and protection-focused Communities That Care system. Information about community risk factors and existing programs (protection) is entered into a database, and mapping software is used to display the results by census block. To improve the effectiveness of delinquency prevention, the police department focuses existing resources on those areas that most need risk reduction and protection enhancements. This is a promising approach.

Although it appears that community-oriented policing has not realized its potential, the concept shows a great deal of promise, and it is fair to say that it is too early to pass judgment on this approach. Preventing delinquency, however, seems to be a less likely outcome of COP programs than preventing crime in general. The New Haven CD–CP program described in Chapter 5 may prove to be effective for preventing delinquency because of the innovative way in which it involves multiple agencies in interrupting the cycle of interpersonal violence.

Comprehensive Delinquency Prevention Approaches

Large data sets have confirmed the relationship between delinquency and certain risk and protective factors. Data from statewide probability samples of secondary students in the states of Kansas, Maine, Oregon, South Carolina, and Washington show that increased risk exposure is associated with an increase in the prevalence of arrests and of self-reported violent behavior among adolescents (Pollard, Hawkins, & Arthur, 2000). These data also show that greater protection against delinquency and violence is associated with lower prevalence of these indicators of delinquency at any level of risk exposure. In other words, consistent with the public health model, risk exposure increases negative outcomes, and protection against risk exposure reduces negative outcomes.

The efficacy of individual prevention programs that reduce specific risk factors and increase protective factors has been demonstrated in several experimental and quasi-experimental studies (Brewer, Hawkins, Catalano, & Neckerman, 1995; Catalano et al., 1998; Durlak, 1998; Hawkins, Arthur, & Catalano, 1995). However, the long-term effectiveness of communitywide delinquency prevention programs has not been demonstrated. A major obstacle faced by researchers in this field is that it is often difficult to convince communities to use effective programs (Arthur, Glaser, & Hawkins, 2001). Many communities expend their resources on supposedly effective prevention approaches for which there is little or no evidence of effectiveness. The unwarranted popularity of the D.A.R.E. program is a case in point (see Chapter 7). Relatively little is known about the best ways to disseminate information on effective prevention programs and to implement science-based prevention in communities (Arthur et al., 2001; Walker et al., 1999). This common problem of translating research findings into practice pervades the delinquency prevention, juvenile justice, and criminal justice fields.

Progress has been made on the delinquency prevention front with the pioneering Communities That Care (CTC) operating system (Hawkins, Catalano, & Associates, 1992). Experiences with CTC implementation demonstrate that prevention advocates can successfully promote research-based prevention activities by providing community members with training and technical assistance in the areas of needs assessment and strategic prevention planning (Arthur, Ayers, Graham, & Hawkins, in press; Arthur et al., 2001; Feinberg, Greenberg, & Osgood, 2001).

Communities That Care is an effective community mobilization strategy that empowers communities to engage in risk- and protection-focused prevention. Although the first experimental evaluation of CTC has not yet been completed, studies have shown that, with adequate training in CTC, community key leaders and prevention planning boards generally are successful in doing the following (Hawkins, 1999, pp. 455-456):

- Adopting a research-based approach to prevention planning
- Collecting and analyzing risk and protective factor data from their communities
- Using these data to make decisions to select research-based policies and programs to address their unique profiles of risk and protection (Arthur et al., in press; Harachi, Abbott, Catalano, & Haggerty, 1996)

Several studies have reported the following positive outcomes in communities using the CTC strategy (Jenson, Hartman, & Smith, 1997; Office of Juvenile Justice and Delinquency Prevention, 1997; U.S. General Accounting Office, 1996):

- Improved interagency collaboration
- Reduced duplication of services
- Coordinated allocation of resources
- Strategic targeting of prevention activities to priority risk and protective factors
- Increased use of research-based approaches with demonstrated effectiveness
- Increased involvement of professionals, citizens, and youth in community prevention activities

Of course, risk- and protection-focused prevention programming can be effectively guided by other operating systems, provided they are based in developmental theory.

A 5-year study is currently under way in 41 communities in 7 states that will be a definitive test of CTC's risk- and protection-focused approach to the prevention of alcohol and drug abuse (Arthur et al., 2001). Preliminary results indicate that there are two keys to successful implementation: the training of community representatives in science-based prevention and the development of a written action plan based on community studies of risk and protective factors. It remains to be seen whether communities that are guided by the CTC operating system wind up funding continuums of prevention programs that actually prevent delinquency. Creating such a continuum involves community change, which is a far more complex enterprise than establishing a single program intervention.

Summary

In its broadest sense, delinquency prevention is a form of positive youth development. The interventions that will have the greatest effects will likely be those that reduce the risk factors that put children in the most danger of developing delinquent or violent behavior and increase protection at the same time. Prevention programs should address the highest-priority risk factors to which youth in the community are exposed. Efforts to change a community to reduce risk and enhance protection need to be guided by analyses of both the most noxious risk factors and the existing strengths of the community. When a community takes this approach, it will move away from funding discrete, piecemeal programs that do not address the specific factors contributing to delinquency and violence in that community.

When a community develops a continuum of prevention programs, it is likely to prevent other problem behaviors of youth aside from delinquency and violence—including teenage pregnancy, drug use and abuse, school dropout and school performance problems, mental health problems, and gang involvement—because of the risk factors these various problem behaviors have in common (see Chapter 6). To be comprehensive, the continuum also needs to include violence prevention programs. As the descriptions of effective violence prevention programs in this chapter indicate, these programs typically provide social competence training for youth, teaching them positive social behaviors and behavioral control strategies.

A community's prevention continuum also needs to include early intervention programs, such as family-focused programs for preschoolers and school-based programs for youngsters in kindergarten and elementary school. Crisis intervention services are a very important part of early intervention in predelinquent and delinquent behavior. I have identified some effective crisis intervention models in this chapter; such programs need to be a part of any community's continuum of prevention programs.

Early intervention with high-risk children and their parents has been shown to be cost-effective, but most cost savings are not realized for several years, because they accumulate over the lifetimes of the children and mothers in these programs (Karoly et al., 1998). Effective interventions include home nurse visitation with pregnant teenagers, parent training, preschool intellectual enrichment programs, cognitive-behavioral training, and interpersonal skills training.

The specific interventions that a community selects are important. The strongest interventions have effects simultaneously at multiple levels (e.g., family, school, and peer group). Exemplary prevention programs are capable of intervening with multiple risk factors. A comprehensive framework of prevention programming that employs a multifaceted, integrated approach is quite likely to be successful. As Catalano et al. (1998) observe, "Multiple prevention strategies crossing multiple domains that are mutually reinforcing and that are maintained for several years produce the greatest impact" (p. 277).

Discussion Questions

1. What is positive youth development? How does delinquency prevention contribute to this outcome?

2. What is the meaning of the term *developmental prevention*? How does developmental prevention work?

3. What are the characteristic features of effective early intervention programs?

4. Why are programs that connect adults with children and adolescents in one-on-one mentoring relationships effective in preventing delinquency?

5. What is the most obvious way to prevent school shootings?

6. What is involved when a community undertakes to build a continuum of early intervention and prevention programs? What benefits can such a continuum produce aside from delinquency and violence prevention?

10

■

EFFECTIVE REHABILITATION
PROGRAMS FOR JUVENILE OFFENDERS

In this chapter, I present a review of programs that effectively rehabilitate juvenile offenders, programs that any community should consider in building a continuum of programs that can be linked with a system of graduated sanctions (I discuss the continuum-building process in Chapter 12). Few programs are described here; rather, the discussion is devoted mainly to the characteristics of effective programs. In the last section of the chapter, I describe a new procedure that communities can use to assess existing programs and improve them before they select new programs.

I begin this chapter with a discussion of four key myths about juvenile justice programs: that nothing works, that the juvenile justice system is not effective, that the juvenile justice system is not effective with serious and violent juvenile offenders, and that community-based programs don't work. The discussion of these myths also highlights effective juvenile justice system programs. I then address the characteristics of effective programs for serious and violent juvenile offenders, followed by a review of new research on the cost-benefit value of juvenile justice programs. I also present some new evidence regarding the effectiveness of practical (everyday) juvenile justice system programs. The chapter concludes with a brief illustration of how communities can make use of the growing knowledge base concerning the most effective juvenile justice interventions to improve their juvenile justice system programs.

The findings and observations of the OJJDP Study Group on Serious and Violent Juvenile Offenders (Loeber & Farrington, 1998b, 1998c)

provide excellent background material for this chapter. As Loeber and Farrington (1998b) note, the study group established a key principle: that it is "never too early and it is never too late" to intervene with serious, violent, and chronic juvenile offenders (pp. 28-29). This means that communities need to begin prevention efforts as early as possible with high-risk youth and also intervene effectively with those who are already serious violent juvenile offenders, regardless of how old they are or how long they have been offending.

It is never too early:

- Early intervention in childhood and adolescence can reduce the likelihood that young "at-risk" juveniles will become serious violent offenders.
- Youth gang involvement can be prevented.
- Preventive interventions should be based on public health approaches and should target known risk factors for serious and violent delinquency.
- The best preventive interventions integrate the varied services provided by prevention agencies, schools, mental health agencies, social service agencies, youth development programs, child protection agencies, religious institutions, and the juvenile justice system.
- Early prevention or intervention is important. It can take many forms, including home visitation for pregnant women and teenage parents, parent training, preschool intellectual

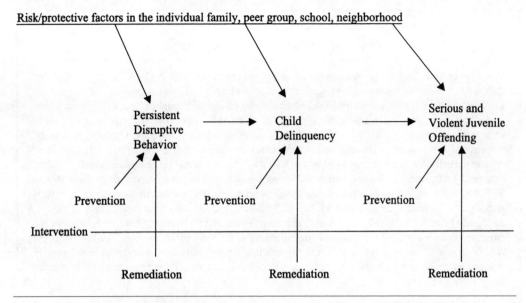

Figure 10.1   Relationships Among Risk/Protective Factors, Development of Child Problem Behavior, and Interventions

SOURCE: "The Significance of Child Delinquency," by R. Loeber and D. P. Farrington, in R. Loeber and
D. P. Farrington (Eds.), *Child Delinquents: Development, Intervention, and Service Needs* (p. 18), Thousand Oaks, CA:
Sage. Copyright 2001 by Sage Publications, Inc. Reprinted with permission.

enrichment programs, and interpersonal skills training.

It is never too late:

- The use of appropriate interventions, particularly interpersonal skills training and cognitive-behavioral treatment, can reduce the reoffending of serious violent offenders.
- The use of appropriate risk assessment tools to distinguish between life-course persistent offenders and others at the time of their referrals to the juvenile justice system could greatly enhance the effectiveness of that system.
- The use of well-designed needs assessment instruments could help court juvenile staff to achieve appropriate matches between offenders' treatment needs and available programs.
- The use of graduated sanctions in tandem with rehabilitation programs that match offender behavior problems with suitable treatments can produce lower rates of reoffending.
- Interventions should be multimodal, so that they address multiple problems—including

lawbreaking, substance use and abuse, academic problems, and family problems—across the juvenile justice system, mental health system, schools, and child welfare agencies. (The administration of such multimodal programs requires integration of the services provided by these agencies.)
- The implementation of aftercare (relapse prevention) programs is essential to reduce the likelihood of reoffending.

Figure 10.1 illustrates the "never too early, never too late" principle. This figure, which is a representation of the Comprehensive Strategy framework, shows prevention and intervention options for juveniles displaying a range of problem behaviors, from nondelinquent disruptive behavior to serious and violent offending. The top line in the figure shows that risk factors operating throughout the developmental process, from less serious nondelinquent problem behavior to serious delinquency, need to be addressed through a continuum of program options. The bottom line shows that rehabilitative options need to be applied throughout the developmental process as well.

Box 10.1

The Monetary Value of Saving a High-Risk Youth

The costs of juvenile delinquency careers to society are enormous. Cohen (1998) has calculated that the cost of a career in delinquency ranges between $1.7 and $2.3 million, depending on whether the youth is involved in multiple forms of delinquency over an active criminal career of about 10 years. According to Cohen's calculations, the typical career criminal in the United States creates costs to society of between $1.3 million and $1.5 million (and these costs are borne by people other than the perpetrator—victims, other citizens, taxpayers). If the delinquent is a heavy drug user, this costs society and the offender an additional $150,000 to $360,000 over a lifetime (in reduced productivity, drug treatment costs, criminal justice costs, and so on), and a high school dropout costs $243,000 to $388,000 more (in lost wage productivity, fringe benefits, and nonmarket losses). Thus Cohen estimates that we would need to invest $1.7 to $2.3 million today to cover the future costs of youths' delinquent behavior, school dropout, and drug abuse. Snyder and Sickmund (1999, p. 82) illustrate the monetary costs associated with juvenile delinquency in the form of an "invoice" addressed to the American public, the message of which is pay less now or pay more later. Prevention and intervention programs focused on high-risk youth that succeed at least some of the time are likely to pay for themselves many times over.

Myths Versus Research Evidence

Four key myths currently dominate public opinion about juvenile justice programs. The first one—that "nothing works"—has been predominant for more than two decades. I address this myth below, as well as the other three key myths: that the juvenile courts are not effective, that the juvenile justice system is not effective with serious and violent juvenile offenders, and that community-based programs that serve as alternatives to incarceration for serious and violent juveniles are ineffective. These myths are central to the debate over the future role of the juvenile court.

I do not frame the discussion that follows in terms of whether or not the juvenile court should exist, because such an argument is specious. Those who suggest that the juvenile court should be abolished (see Chapter 8) fail to recognize four important realities. First, this institution is society's official means of holding itself accountable for the well-being of children and the family unit; it does not exist only to reduce delinquency (Arthur, 1998; Howell, 1998a). Indeed, juvenile delinquency cases probably do not constitute a majority of the juvenile court caseload. Dependency cases (including cases concerning child abuse and neglect) may represent more than half of the workload of juvenile courts (National Council of Juvenile and Family Court Judges, 1998). Juvenile court judges must ultimately decide whether families in crisis will be broken apart and the children placed in foster care or whether out-of-home placement can be safely prevented through the reasonable efforts of the human service system. The juvenile court is society's legal mechanism for resolving these difficult cases. This is a main reason that many juvenile courts are called "juvenile and family courts," that is, unified courts. Those who would abolish the juvenile court fail to take into account all of this institution's vital roles.

Second, three-fourths of all juvenile offenses are not criminal offenses (Snyder, 2000) and thus do not come under the jurisdiction of the criminal justice system. In the absence of juvenile courts, there would be no legal entity to be responsible for these cases, save for social service agencies, which do not have a good track record with the cases they currently handle. Third, criminal courts have neither the capacity nor the requisite expertise to handle juvenile delinquency cases (see Chapter 8). And fourth, the majority of juvenile justice programs reduce recidivism, as I will show in this chapter. Juvenile courts are, however, severely limited by a lack of resources (Humes, 1996). The median time needed to move delinquency cases through juvenile courts increased 24% from 1985 to 1994 (Butts & Halemba, 1996). Growing numbers of youths are being referred to juvenile courts, and the system needs more resources to handle the added workload. Juvenile courts typically have limited numbers of program options available to them, and those they have are rarely adequately funded

(National Council of Juvenile and Family Court Judges, 1998). Because juvenile reformatories are better funded in most states than alternative programs, many low-risk offenders wind up in reformatories—an expensive option, given that the construction cost per resident can be as much as $150,000, and operational costs may be as high as $50,000 per year (Roush & McMillen, 2000, p. 15). As I will show in this chapter, many rehabilitation programs offer far less costly and more effective alternatives.

Myth: Nothing Works With Juvenile Offenders

The "nothing works" myth has dominated the field since the mid-1970s, when a review of program evaluations in juvenile and criminal justice systems was released (Lipton, Martinson, & Wilks, 1975; Martinson, 1974). The most-quoted conclusion from this review is Martinson's (1974) statement that "with few isolated exceptions, the rehabilitative efforts that have been reported so far have no appreciable effect on recidivism" (p. 25). Although Martinson (1979) later recanted this overstated conclusion, and the findings of the entire review were challenged on methodological grounds (Gendreau, 1981; Palmer, 1975) and for the researchers' failure to document the amount of change associated with treatment (Garrett, 1985), the "nothing works" myth persisted. Curiously, two National Academy of Sciences reviews supported Lipton and colleagues' review (Martin, Sechrest, & Redner, 1981; Sechrest, White, & Brown, 1979), as did other reviews in the 1970s that reached similar negative conclusions (for a list, see Lipsey, 1999b, p. 612). However, critics contend that many of the program evaluations conducted up to that point were flawed, that there was convincing evidence that some programs were effective, and that negative conclusions of reviewers were guided more by ideology than by research evidence (Cullen & Gilbert, 1982; Gendreau & Ross, 1979; Gottfredson, 1979; Lipsey, 1999a, p. 143; Palmer, 1975, 1983).

Studies of the relative effectiveness of juvenile justice programs have consistently been positive since the early 1980s, for two main reasons. First, the program evaluation base has expanded significantly, providing a deeper and more detailed body of empirical evidence about the effects of rehabilitative programs for juvenile offenders (Lipsey, 1999b, p. 613). Second, the new quantitative technique of meta-analysis emerged; this technique allows researchers to analyze and synthesize data so that they can summarize program evaluation results. It also enables them to examine a wider range of program evaluations in a more systematic manner than was possible in the past (Lipsey & Wilson, 2000; see Box 10.2 for a discussion of meta-analysis).

There are two fundamentally different approaches to summarizing the body of knowledge from program evaluations. The traditional method is the study-by-study review of individual program evaluations. In such a review, the evaluations are summarized in narrative form. Researchers using this approach apply rigorous scientific criteria to limit the number of program evaluations reviewed, based on the scientific merits of the evaluations' research designs. This approach is exemplified by the Blueprints Project (Mihalic, Irwin, Elliott, Fagan, & Hansen, 2001) and the University of Maryland's "what works" project (Sherman et al., 1997). There is much to be said for giving greater weight to the findings of evaluations that have used strong research designs (preferably random assignment of subjects to treatment and control groups). However, the meta-analysis technique also allows for differential weighting of evaluation results.

More than a dozen meta-analyses have been conducted on evaluations of the effects of rehabilitative programs on recidivism, especially for juvenile offenders (for a list, see Lipsey, 1999b, p. 613). As Lipsey (1999b) notes, these are important because "it is no exaggeration to say that meta-analysis of research on the effectiveness of rehabilitative programming has reversed the conclusion of the prior generation of [program-by-program] reviews on this topic" (p. 614). This is particularly true with respect to juvenile offender programs. Nevertheless, the myth of ineffective juvenile justice programs continues to be perpetuated in the juvenile justice literature (Feld, 1998b; Hsia & Beyer, 2000; Schwartz, 1999).

Lipsey's (1992; see also Lipsey, 1995) meta-analyses have been instrumental in debunking the "nothing works" myth with respect to juvenile rehabilitation programs. His initial meta-analysis included nearly 400 experimentally designed studies of general delinquency treatment published since 1950. Contrary to the myth, Lipsey found that juveniles in treatment groups had recidivism rates about 10% lower than those of untreated juveniles. The best intervention programs produced up to a 37% reduction in recidivism rates and similar improvements in other outcomes. These treatment programs typically focused on changing overt behavior through structured training or behavior modification interventions designed to improve interpersonal relations, self-control, school achievement, and specific job skills. Treatment programs

---

Box 10.2

Meta-Analysis

Originally developed in the field of education (Glass, McGaw, & Smith, 1981), meta-analysis is a quantitative technique for coding, analyzing, and summarizing research evidence. In conducting a meta-analysis, a researcher uses statistical procedures to synthesize and compare clusters of studies on a given topic. Meta-analysis enables a researcher to examine a wider range of program evaluations in a more systematic manner than is possible in a conventional program-by-program review. This procedure is now widely accepted "as a sophisticated way to extract, analyze, and summarize the empirical findings of a collection of related research studies" (Lipsey, 1999b, p. 616). The methods used to conduct meta-analyses are very similar to those employed in good survey research (Lipsey, 1999b, pp. 617-618). In a meta-analysis, the database is developed by trained coders who are guided in their review of existing research by questionnaires concerning data elements and program characteristics. Depending on the subject matter of the inquiry, a population of research studies is defined for the analysis, and a sample of relevant studies is drawn—or the entire universe of studies in a given field may be retrieved for review and synthesis. Once the data are extracted, they are analyzed and synthesized through the use of statistical methods.

In the case of program evaluations, meta-analysts standardize program intervention effects (known as the *effect sizes*) to permit comparisons across studies. The effect size is the magnitude of the difference between the mean value on the outcome variable (recidivism) for the individuals receiving intervention (the treatment group) and the mean value for a comparable group (the control group) (Lipsey, 1999b, pp. 616-617). "The result is a rather complete statement of currently available research evidence about the effects of rehabilitative interventions on [in this instance] the recidivism of juvenile offenders" (Lipsey, 1999a, p. 162). Two common criticisms of meta-analysis are that this review technique "cannot overcome problems of poor research design" (McCord, Widom, & Crowell, 2001, p. 191) and that summarizing studies with different methodological features creates an "apples and oranges" problem (Sharpe, 1997). These are not insurmountable problems. Meta-analysts can handle research design nuances quite adequately with multivariate analyses that permit method adjustments in effect sizes to control for between-study differences, although better multivariate analysis techniques are needed (Lipsey & Wilson, 1998, 2000). There are many other program evaluation particulars that may have far more important influences on outcomes than broad design quality ratings (Durlak & Lipsey, 1991; Lipsey, 2000a). These include attrition, type of delinquency outcome measure, sample size, statistical power (Lipsey & Wilson, 1998, 2001), and the involvement of researchers in the design, delivery, and supervision of treatment in demonstration programs (Lipsey, 1999b). Nevertheless, these influences on outcomes can be identified and assessed in meta-analyses (Lipsey & Wilson, 2000)—something that cannot be done in conventional narrative reviews.

Meta-analysis has many other advantages as well. As Lipsey (1999b) notes, "Most striking, perhaps, is the power of meta-analysis to identify intervention effects not clearly visible to traditional reviewers" (p. 619; see also Lipsey & Wilson, 1993; Schmidt, 1992). Lipsey's (1999b) discovery of the delinquency reduction potential of "practical" juvenile justice program interventions is an excellent example. Another advantage of meta-analysis is that this technique enables users to assess program effectiveness easily on a number of other dimensions, such as the types of offenders with which program interventions work best, gender effects of different interventions, and supplementary program interventions that work well with particular interventions. These are program features that cannot be assessed comprehensively in program-by-program reviews. Thus the narrative review method lacks the scope and depth of meta-analysis procedures (Redondo, Sanchez-Meca, & Garrido, 1999). In addition, meta-analysis study results are far easier to translate into practice than are narrative review results—as will be seen later in this chapter.

---

found to be most effective were "more structured and focused treatments (e.g., behavioral, skill-oriented) and multi-modal treatments seem to be more effective than the less structured and unfocused treatments (e.g., counseling)" (Lipsey, 1992,

p. 123). After completing his review, Lipsey (1995) observed:

It is no longer constructive for researchers, practitioners, and policymakers to argue about whether delinquency treatment and related rehabilitative approaches "work," as if that were a question that could be answered with a simple "yes" or "no." As a generality, treatment clearly works. We must get on with the business of developing and identifying the treatment models that will be most effective and providing them to the juveniles they will benefit. (p. 78)

To be more useful to communities, intervention research needs to focus less on what works and more on determining what works for whom, when (in the careers of offenders), and in what settings.

Myth: Juvenile Courts Are Not Effective

Lipsey's work has also helped to debunk the myth that juvenile courts are not effective. In a meta-analysis of more than 500 juvenile justice programs—the overwhelming majority of which were juvenile court programs—Lipsey (2000b) found that most of them reduce recidivism. Certain juvenile courts are more effective than others, and more recent studies suggest that juvenile court effectiveness may have increased in the past decade or so. For example, one of the earliest comprehensive studies, carried out in Arizona and Utah juvenile courts (Snyder, 1988; see also Snyder & Sickmund, 1995, p. 158), found that 56% of all juveniles receiving court referrals returned for new offenses. More recent studies indicate greater juvenile court effectiveness. In a St. Louis study, Curry and Decker (2000) found that only 38% of more than 1,300 children referred to the juvenile court in 1994 were referred again for a delinquent offense over the next 3 years. In a Washington State study of 8,000 probationers, Barnoski (1997) found that only 27% recidivated (measured by subsequent court referrals) with felony offenses. In a Missouri study of 475 first-time referrals to juvenile court, Minor, Hartmann, and Terry (1997) found that 33% recidivated (subsequent court referrals), and 84% of these juveniles were diverted in response to the second referral. These studies are fairly representative of recent juvenile court recidivism studies, which often show fairly low recidivism rates—somewhat lower than for criminal courts, as seen in Chapter 8.

Juvenile court recidivism studies also suggest that the combination of probation and treatment programs produces low recidivism rates. In a study of more than 2,000 petitioned juvenile offenders, Wooldredge (1988) found that the most effective of 12 combinations of interventions for reducing recidivism rates was a lengthy period of probation (about 2 years) combined with community treatment. In a study of the New Jersey Early Court

Intervention Project, which targeted youths at high risk of becoming chronic offenders, Smith, Aloisi, and Goldstein (1996) found that probation and treatment interventions were consistently related to lower levels of reoffending. Tracy and Kempf-Leonard (1996) have reported that the timing of probation in relation to delinquent career progression makes a very significant difference. They found that early intervention with probation mutes career offending.

Other studies have shown that early juvenile court intervention in offender career paths produces lower recidivism rates (Brown, Miller, & Jenkins, 1991; Land, McCall, & Williams, 1990; Schumacher & Kurz, 2000; Smith et al., 1996). Interestingly, one study indicates that early juvenile court intervention can have very long-term impacts. In this North Carolina study, Dean, Brame, and Piquero (1996) found lower recidivism rates among previously incarcerated juvenile offenders who had been adjudicated delinquent at an early age in juvenile court. In a 6-year follow-up of more than 800 juveniles released from state training schools, these researchers found that an increased number of prior adjudications had a restraining effect on recidivism (measured by arrests following release from the correctional facility) among those who were first adjudicated at very young ages. For those who experienced a later first adjudication, exactly the opposite result was found. Early intervention with juvenile court probation makes a big difference in juvenile rehabilitation.

Even minimal court intervention appears to show positive effects when intervention occurs early in the offender's career (Tracy & Kempf-Leonard, 1996). As McCord (1985) notes: "Perhaps, . . . in providing ceremonial condemnation, the courts clarify boundaries for acceptable behavior. Conversely, diversion from the courts may [contribute] to crime by blurring the boundaries between acceptable and unacceptable behavior" (p. 81).

A major reason for the effectiveness of juvenile courts is the multisystemic approach that is fundamental to the intervention philosophy of these courts (Howell, 1997). Developers of the original juvenile court system recognized that failures of core social institutions, such as families and schools, and negative peer groups, crime-ridden communities, and individual characteristics contribute directly to delinquency involvement. To this day, juvenile court staffs employ multiple prevention and intervention programs to negate the harmful influences of these environments on troubled youths.

Myth: The Juvenile Justice System Is Ineffective
With Serious, Violent, and Chronic Offenders

The myth that the juvenile justice system cannot
handle serious, violent, and chronic juvenile offenders
has emanated mainly from the general public's
acceptance of the "superpredator" image of juvenile
offenders. As described in Chapter 2, a number of
observers have disseminated the myth of this hypo-
thetical "new breed" of juvenile offenders who are
beyond redemption (and so presumably cannot be
rehabilitated). In addition, this supposed new generation of juvenile offenders presumably includes a
larger proportion of serious and violent offenders
than earlier generations; these offenders are said to
commit more crimes and to begin committing violent and serious offenses at younger ages than their
predecessors. But, as I have also noted in Chapter 2,
the research evidence does not support these pre-
sumptions (Snyder, 1998; Snyder & Sickmund,
2000; Zimring, 1998a).

Several studies have shown that the juvenile
justice system is effective with violent and chronic
offenders. In an Arizona study, Snyder (1988)
found that only 17% of the offenders initially
referred to court for violent offenses returned for
second violent offenses. Thus these courts prevented the overwhelming majority of violent
offenders from becoming repeat violent offenders.
In a Philadelphia study, Tracy, Wolfgang, and
Figlio (1990, p. 291) found that juvenile court intervention reduced recidivism substantially for three-
time recidivists.

More generally, the myth that the juvenile justice
system is ineffective with serious, violent, and
chronic juvenile offenders was debunked by Lipsey
and Wilson's (1998) meta-analysis of 200 programs
for serious and violent juvenile offenders. This
analysis showed that the average juvenile justice
system program serving serious and violent juveniles reduced recidivism about 12% in comparison
with control groups, a slightly larger effect than programs for delinquents in general, which an earlier
meta-analysis found to be about 10% (Lipsey, 1992,
1995). The best programs for serious and violent
delinquents were capable of reducing recidivism
rates by as much as 49%, a 12% larger reduction
than the best programs for delinquents in general
(up to 37%; Lipsey, 1995). Programs with greater
concentrations of serious offenders in them showed
larger intervention effects. As Lipsey and Wilson
observe, "If anything, then, it would appear that
the typical intervention in these studies is more effective with serious offenders than with less serious
offenders" (p. 332)—just the opposite of the myth.

Myth: Community-Based Programs
for Juveniles Are Ineffective

The history of the juvenile justice system is
distinctive for its vacillation between policies
supporting incarceration and the use of community-
based alternatives to confinement (Bernard, 1992;
Finestone, 1976). Increased use of incarceration
typically follows moral panics (Bernard, 1992). As
I have shown in Chapter 3, more use of confinement
has been a predominant response to the current
moral panic over juvenile delinquency.

The promise of alternatives to incarceration for
juvenile offenders has changed dramatically over the
past 25 years. The early reviews of alternative juvenile justice program evaluations found very few
effective programs (Romig, 1978). This dismal state
of the art was owing to two main factors: poor evaluation designs and poor program implementation.
There are notable exceptions to the negative results,
however. The success of the Silverlake program
(community treatment of seriously delinquent boys;
Empey & Lubeck, 1971) and the Provo experiment
(intensive supervision for a group of delinquents who
would otherwise have been incarcerated; Empey &
Erickson, 1972) indicated the promise of alternatives
to incarceration. These results encouraged a grand
reformation of the Massachusetts youth corrections
system. In 1971, that state's director of youth services, Jerome Miller, abruptly closed the state's
reformatories and replaced them with a network of
decentralized community-based services and a few
small secure-care units for violent juvenile offenders
(Miller, 1973, 1991). The Massachusetts changes
constituted the most sweeping reforms in youth corrections in the United States since the establishment
of juvenile reformatories in the 19th century
and juvenile courts in the 20th century (Bakal,
1973, 1998; Miller, 1991). Other states followed
Massachusetts's lead, closing large youth training
schools and replacing them with small community-
based facilities and programs—these states included
Pennsylvania, Utah, and Maryland (Lerner, 1990),
although the effect was not positive in Maryland's
case (Gottfredson & Barton, 1997). This reformation
of juvenile corrections did not last, however (Bakal,
1998). Many community correctional policies were
reversed in the late 1980s and early 1990s as a result
of the seventh moral panic over delinquency, and
reliance on juvenile reformatories again increased.

A major issue remained unresolved, however:
Are community-based alternatives more effective
than juvenile reformatories, particularly with serious and violent offenders? For about a decade following the "nothing works" report (Lipton et al.,

1975), the conclusion that prevailed was that community-based programs are only about equally effective as—although less costly than—juvenile correctional programs (Altschuler & Armstrong, 1984; Krisberg, Currie, Onek, & Wiebush, 1995). This conclusion has been revised now that Lipsey and Wilson's (1998) meta-analysis has shown the greater effectiveness of noninstitutional programs, even for serious and violent offenders. In addition, Aos, Phipps, Barnoski, and Lieb (2001) have conducted a comprehensive cost-benefit study, and their results indicate that community-based programs are far more cost-beneficial than institution-based treatment.

Early Intervention With Juvenile Offenders

Juvenile justice programs have employed two major kinds of approaches to intervene early in the careers of juvenile offenders. The first is early intervention with child delinquents, and the second is intervention with young delinquents who have the potential to become serious and violent juvenile offenders.

Early Intervention With Child Delinquents

Few juvenile justice programs have been developed for child delinquents (Howell, 2001a). Program development in this area has been limited because deinstitutionalization and diversion policies of the past 25 years have turned child delinquents away from juvenile courts. Now, the presumed greater prevalence of very young violent offenders has stimulated support for the development of programs for children who might fall into this group. Although such young offenders are in reality no more prevalent today than in the past (see Chapter 3), this development is good for the field and for society, because early intervention with child delinquents can make a significant contribution to reducing the future number of serious, violent, and chronic adolescent offenders.

Two very promising program models for child delinquents have been developed (Howell, 2001a). One is the result of a 1995 study conducted by the Hennepin County (Minnesota) Attorney's Office (1995), which led to the creation of a new program in the county designed to provide services to child delinquents and their families. This program, called Delinquents Under 10, is a joint undertaking of several Hennepin County departments, led by the Hennepin County Attorney's Office. The program's Screening Team, which is made up of interagency

representatives, reviews police reports on child delinquents and determines an appropriate disposition for each child. Interventions range from an admonishment letter to parents from the county attorney to referrals to child protective services and other agencies, diversion programs, petitions for children in need of protection or services (known as CHIPS petitions), and targeted early intervention (TEI) for the children deemed at highest risk for future delinquency. The Screening Team determines the level of intervention based on three considerations: the alleged delinquent act or indicated problem behavior, the degree of the child's volition, and the number and nature of risk factors that each child presents, as determined by a standardized risk factor checklist.

For each child the Screening Team determines to be in need of TEI, the Delinquents Under 10 program strives to create a wraparound network consisting of a primary organization (for more in-depth assessment and coordination of service delivery), an Integrated Service Delivery Team (co-located staff who deliver and help access services), a critical support person (mentor), secondary network organizations (which provide extracurricular activities), and a corporate sponsor (which mainly funds extracurricular activities). In their report on Phase I of an independent evaluation of the program, Stevens, Owen, and Lahti-Johnson (1999) describe Delinquents Under 10's progress to date and some implementation experiences, focusing in particular on the TEI element. Outcome data are not yet available.

The process evaluation of the Delinquents Under 10 program has documented serious obstacles to working with the program's target group and their families. Stevens et al. (1999) found that these early-onset offenders often live in homeless families and in extremely high-risk environments: "High rates of exposure to domestic violence, child maltreatment, crime, chemical dependency and mental health issues are particularly striking" (p. 70). When project staff "began to directly assess the families and their histories, it was apparent that the initial paper screening vastly under-represented the extent of these problems" (Hennepin County Attorney's Office, 1998, p. 21). Moreover, the plethora of county services these families had received had "done little to solve these problems on a long-term basis" (pp. 19-20). Thus this program has shown that it can be very difficult to ameliorate the many problems of very young offenders, which may include mental health deficiencies, learning problems, and other disabilities that are nested in these problematic families. The lack of human service agency effectiveness and the presence of such family obstacles are major reasons that adolescent treatment models need to encompass the family as well as the child or adolescent.

Two important lessons are apparent from this program experience. First, juvenile court authority is sometimes necessary to require effective social service intervention with problem parents. Second, parent training is not sufficient for correcting these complex problems. Short-term parent training programs are unlikely to succeed with families that are characterized by low stability and high conflict and plagued by unemployment, poverty, illness, and other crises. Thus a child-focused and family-centered wraparound approach is most promising.

The most fully developed intervention to date for child delinquents is a Canadian program, the Earlscourt Child and Family Centre's Under 12 Outreach Project (ORP) (for detailed information on the program, see Augimeri, Koegl, & Goldberg, 2001). In Canada, children under 12 who commit offenses fall under the authority of provincial child welfare agencies, rather than the juvenile justice system. ORP serves children ages 6-12 who have been contacted by police. The program's screening and assessment procedures involve two interviews at intake—one with the child, another with the parent—using the Early Assessment Risk List for Boys (EARL-20B; Augimeri, Webster, Koegl, & Levene, 1998). ORP employs a multisystemic approach, combining interventions that target the child, the family, and the child-in-the-community. The program uses a variety of established interventions: skills training; training in cognitive problem solving, self-control strategies, and cognitive self-instruction; family management skills training; and parent training. Two preliminary program evaluations have shown ORP to be somewhat effective, although the study samples were small, no comparison group was used in either study, and the follow-up periods were short in both experiments. ORP has been expanded to include a gender-specific program for girls exhibiting behavior problems.

Early Intervention With Potential Serious, Violent, and Chronic Juvenile Offenders

The first known evaluated program that targeted potential serious, violent, and chronic juvenile offenders at court intake is the North Carolina Intensive Protective Supervision Project (IPSP), which operated in four sites in the state during the late 1980s. Youth referred to the program were status offenders deemed to be at risk of becoming serious, violent offenders, who were randomly assigned to either IPSP or ordinary probation services.

Caseloads in IPSP were small—no more than 10 per youth counselor. IPSP counselors, who received training in counseling, supervision, and therapeutic techniques, maintained frequent contacts with clients and worked intensively with them and their families. Clients also underwent mental health assessments. The program developed an individualized treatment plan for each client, and for up to a year, the counselor, along with contracted service providers, made regular home visits in carrying out the treatment plan.

Land et al. (1990) evaluated IPSP and found it to be very effective in keeping participants from moving from status offenses to delinquency. Participation in the program reduced the likelihood of a delinquent offense during the course of the program by about 60% compared with the regular probation control group. The program effect was not significant, however, for IPSP youth with prior referrals for delinquency. Nevertheless, this experiment had a lasting impact on juvenile offender programming in North Carolina (K. Dudley, personal communication, December 17, 2001). Early court intervention with potential serious offenders became statewide policy thereafter.

Any program designed to intervene with child delinquents needs to be linked to a juvenile justice graduated sanctions system, to facilitate further processing of child delinquents who do not desist from delinquent careers. Although it does not specifically target child delinquents, the 8% Early Intervention Program in Orange County, California, illustrates how this can be done (Schumacher & Kurz, 2000). This program is an excellent example of early intervention with child delinquents and young adolescents ages 15 and under who are at risk of becoming serious, violent, and chronic juvenile offenders. About 25% of the youths served in the program thus far have been age 13 or younger (S. Hunt, personal communication, June 10, 2002).

The development of the 8% Early Intervention Program stemmed from an analysis of court referrals that found that 8% of referred adolescents account for more than half of all repeat offenses among juveniles on probation. Thus the program targets young offenders (under age 15) who are deemed to be at risk of becoming chronic, serious, and violent juvenile offenders. Those who are potential "8% cases" are identified during screening at court intake through the use of a comprehensive risk assessment instrument (see Howell, 2001b) that was validated on a sample of previous court referrals (see Chapter 4). The criteria that characterize 8% cases are as follows: chronic family dysfunction (abuse/neglect, criminal family members, lack of parental supervision and control), significant school problems (truancy, failing multiple courses, and/or recent suspension or expulsion), a pattern of individual problems (drug and/or alcohol use), and predelinquent behavior patterns (youth gang involvement, chronic running away, and/or stealing). Youngsters with first-time court referrals who score high in three of these four risk domains are admitted to the 8% Early Intervention Program.

The same study that led to the establishment of the 8% Early Intervention Program also led to development of a model continuum of graduated sanctions and services managed by the Orange County Probation Department. I describe this continuum, which includes prevention, intervention, secure corrections, and transitional aftercare components (Kurz, 1999; Schumacher & Kurz, 2000), in Chapter 13.

A long-term follow-up study of the 8% Early Intervention Program is currently under way. Offenders in the 8% group are randomly assigned either to the Repeat Offender Prevention Program (experimental group) or to the Intensive Intervention Program (control group). Preliminary results show that the experimental program youth are committing fewer crimes and less serious crimes than their nonprogram counterparts (Orange County Probation Department, 2000). In a 2-year follow-up, compared with the control group, the 8% Early Intervention Program group has had significantly fewer petitions filed for new law violations, a lower overall number of petitions filed, and a lower average number of days in custody (S. Hunt, personal communication, June 10, 2002).

These results are not surprising. First, the program uses a statistically validated risk assessment instrument to identify potentially serious, violent, and chronic juvenile offenders. Second, it combines graduated sanctions with early intervention services (as indicated by needs/strengths assessments) to interrupt young offenders' further progression in life-course persistent pathways. Third, the program employs a highly structured wraparound model of service delivery. Fourth, it uses a multimodal approach that encompasses the child, family, school, peer group, and community contexts. And fifth, the program employs proven-effective cognitive-behavioral interventions.

Effective Interventions for Serious and Violent Juvenile Offenders

As noted earlier in this chapter, Lipsey and Wilson's (1998) meta-analysis dispelled the myth that juvenile justice system programs are ineffective with serious and violent offenders. In addition, Lipsey and Wilson's study showed that the best programs for serious and violent delinquents are capable of producing large reductions in recidivism rates—reductions as large as 49%. In this section, I address the specific types of interventions that are effective with the worst offenders.

Lipsey and Wilson's (1998) meta-analysis included 200 evaluations of programs for serious and violent offenders (for summaries, see Lipsey, 1999a; Lipsey, Wilson, & Cothern, 2000). These were selected from Lipsey's database of some 500 evaluations of juvenile justice programs published in the United States and other English-speaking countries since 1950. Because this meta-analysis was conducted as part of the work of the OJJDP Study Group on Serious and Violent Juvenile Offenders, Lipsey and Wilson were careful to select evaluated programs that had serious and violent juvenile offenders in them. Because very few programs serve only serious or violent juvenile offenders (Montgomery et al., 1994), Lipsey and Wilson selected those programs that had the highest representations of such offenders. The great majority (all in some programs) of the juveniles in the evaluated programs were adjudicated delinquents. In addition, most (or all) of the juveniles in these programs had records of prior offenses. Finally, their offense histories involved more person or property crimes and few substance abuse, status, or traffic offenses.

Lipsey and Wilson (1998) classified program types into categories according to degree of effectiveness with institutionalized and noninstitutionalized juvenile offenders (see Table 10.1). The results show that interpersonal skills training is particularly effective in either setting. Otherwise, there are important differences in the kinds of interventions that are effective in the respective settings. Three main types of treatment showed the most positive effects in noninstitutionalized offenders: individual counseling, interpersonal skills training, and behavioral programs. These were followed closely by multiple services (Lipsey & Wilson, 1998, p. 332). In contrast, teaching family homes, behavioral programs, community residential programs, and multiple services showed the most positive effects in institutionalized offenders, along with interpersonal skills training (see Table 10.1). Lipsey and Wilson (1998) caution that "many more studies of intervention with institutionalized serious offenders will be needed before strong conclusions can be reached," because few of these programs have been evaluated (p. 328).

It is common to think about program effectiveness strictly in terms of the choice of interventions.

TABLE 10.1   Effectiveness of Interventions for Serious and Violent Juvenile Offenders

Type of Treatment Used With Noninstitutionalized Offenders	Type of Treatment Used With Institutionalized Offenders
Positive effects, consistent evidence	
Individual counseling (.46)	Interpersonal skills (.39)
Interpersonal skills (.44)	Teaching family homes (.34)
Behavioral programs (.42)	
Positive effects, less consistent evidence	
Multiple services (.29)	Behavioral programs (.33)
Restitution with probation/parole (.15)	Community residential (.28)
	Multiple services (.20)
Mixed but generally positive effects, inconsistent evidence	
Employment related (.22)	Individual counseling (.15)
Academic programs (.20)	Guided group counseling (.09)
Advocacy/casework (.19)	Group counseling (.05)
Family counseling (.19)	
Group counseling (.10)	
Weak or no effects, inconsistent evidence	
Reduced caseload, probation/parole (−.04)	Employment related (.15)
	Drug abstinence (.08)
	Wilderness/challenge (.07)
Weak or no effects, consistent evidence	
Wilderness challenge (.12)	Milieu therapy (.08)
Early release, probation/parole (.03)	
Deterrence programs (−.06)	
Vocational programs (−.18)	

SOURCE: Adapted from Lipsey, M. W., & Wilson, D. B. (1998). Effective Interventions With Serious Juvenile Offenders: A Synthesis of Research. In R. Loeber and D. P. Farrington (Eds.), *Serious and Violent Juvenile Offenders: Risk Factors and Successful Interventions* (p. 332). Thousand Oaks, CA: Sage. © 1998 by Sage Publications, Inc. Adapted with permission.
NOTE: The midpoints of estimated effect sizes are shown in parentheses.

Interestingly, Lipsey and Wilson's (1998) meta-analysis showed that the type of intervention is not necessarily the strongest predictor of program success for serious and violent offenders. In the case of programs for noninstitutionalized offenders, the factors that made up the most effective programs were as follows (listed here in descending order of importance):

1. Certain characteristics of the juveniles served in them (when a larger proportion of the program clients had prior offenses, more serious

prior offenses, and more aggression in their offense histories and were older males, with an ethnic mix)

2. Type of treatment (as shown in Table 10.1)

3. Amount of treatment (total weeks of treatment, frequency of treatment, mean hours/week, mean hours of total contact, rated amount of meaningful contact, rated intensity of treatment event, integrity of treatment implementation, and difficulties in treatment delivery)

4. General program characteristics (program age, demonstration program, juvenile justice agency program, juvenile justice facility, juvenile justice treatment personnel, mental health treatment personnel, juvenile justice authority for the program, voluntary versus mandatory participation, and researcher's role)

The analysis showed that the relative importance of these factors was different in the case of programs for institutionalized offenders:

1. General program characteristics

2. Amount of treatment

3. Type of treatment

4. Characteristics of the juveniles

It is interesting that the type of treatment was not the strongest predictor of program effectiveness for either group; it was the second-strongest predictor of program effectiveness in the case of noninstitutional programs and the third-strongest predictor for institutional programs. Other important program characteristics associated with greater program effectiveness were the amount of service provided (longer duration), the quality of service delivery, well-designed treatment protocols, thorough training of treatment personnel, close monitoring of treatment delivery, and careful selection of clients to make sure they are appropriate (Lipsey & Wilson, 1998).

As noted earlier in this chapter, Lipsey and Wilson (1998) found that positive treatment effects tended to be larger for samples containing more serious offenders. Otherwise, they found little differentiation in program effectiveness with respect to other characteristics of the juvenile samples, including extent of aggressive history, gender, age, and ethnic mix (p. 332). In other words, this is evidence that juvenile justice programs appear to be about equally effective with very aggressive and minimally aggressive offenders, females as well as males, all age groups, and all racial/ethnic groups.

Effectiveness of Graduated Sanctions With Serious and Violent Juvenile Offenders

The effectiveness of graduated sanctions used in conjunction with treatment programs is supported by research on violent juvenile offenders (Hamparian, Schuster, Dinitz, & Conrad, 1978; Mahoney, 1987), nationwide program assessments (Altschuler & Armstrong, 1984; Parent, Wentworth, & Burk, 1994; Petersilia & Turner, 1993), and a number of state and local program and policy studies (Burke & Pennell, 2001; Butts & DeMuro, 1989; Holsinger & Latessa, 1999; LeClair, 1983; Pennell, Curtis, & Scheck, 1990; Sametz & Hamparian, 1990; Wiebush & Hamparian, 1986). I discuss four effective graduated sanctions programs in this chapter: the 8% Early Intervention Program (reviewed above), the Cuyahoga County (Ohio) Probation Graduated Sanctions System, San Diego's Breaking Cycles program, and the Illinois Unified Delinquency Intervention Services program. Each of these programs has been evaluated and found to be effective.

The Cuyahoga County Probation Graduated Sanctions System may well have been the most elaborate graduated sanctions system developed to date (see Chapter 13 for details). The main component of the system was an intensive probation supervision (IPS) program that used a unit team approach. Each team consisted of three surveillance officers, one senior probation counselor, and one probation manager (for a full description of the program, see Cuyahoga County Juvenile Court, 1996). The senior probation counselor played a critical role, providing administrative supervision of the team members and coordinating the services that the client received. The services provided to each probationer were determined by a comprehensive needs assessment. An individual behavior contract set expectations for each probationer, defined the responsibilities of all parties to the contract, and focused the interventions of team members. The program consisted of three phases during which the intensity of supervision and surveillance decreased; the phases culminated in the formation of an aftercare support group and discharge. The IPS component of this program had several important features (Wiebush & Hamparian, 1991):

- Reduced caseload for probation officers (not more than one-half the normal caseload)
- Increased frequency of officer-client contact
- Use of team supervision
- Balanced use of control and treatment
- Use of needs assessments to determine treatment needs
- Use of individualized interventions
- Management of the program by a skilled coordinator

The evaluation of the Cuyahoga County Juvenile Court's intensive probation supervision program found that it produced a large reduction in recidivism: 29% (Sametz & Hamparian, 1990; Wiebush & Hamparian, 1991). Moreover, less than one-third of the serious felony offenders in the program were subsequently committed to the Ohio Department of Youth Services correctional system. These impressive results seem to be attributable to four key factors. First, the Probation Graduated Sanctions System was driven by an empirically validated risk assessment instrument that classified offenders according to their degree of risk for recidivism. Only high-risk offenders were admitted to the IPS program. Second, intensive services were delivered along with intensive supervision. Third, the program used a needs assessment instrument to identify priority treatment needs and to develop and implement treatment plans. Fourth, the senior probation counselor on each unit team played a critical role in ensuring that probation officers abided by the classification system in making placement decisions and handling IPS probationers in a manner consistent with the IPS program guidelines (Cuyahoga County Juvenile Court, 1996).

The graduated sanctions program in San Diego County, California, is part of the county's Comprehensive Strategy (for a full description, see Chapter 13). Briefly, this program, called Breaking Cycles, is operated by the probation department; it handles court-ordered placements of youth, assigning referred offenders to one of three graduated options (home placement, a community-based program, or a juvenile correctional institution) for variable lengths of time. A multiagency team of professionals conducts a comprehensive assessment of each case to evaluate both the child's and the family's risk and resilience, and to develop a Breaking Cycles case plan. The family-centered, strengths-based case plan is designed to promote accountability, rehabilitation, and community protection. Each of the intervention levels is linked with community programs and resources that are needed to carry out the comprehensive treatment plan. Most of the youths in this program begin their rehabilitative process in a highly structured institutional setting and are stepped down to lower levels of program structure and supervision (i.e., community-based programs and home placement, as shown above) as reassessments are made. Youths may also be stepped up from initial less restrictive placements or after having been stepped down to lower levels—again, depending on reassessment results.

In an evaluation of the Breaking Cycles program, Burke and Pennell (2001) used a matched comparison group design to examine the impact of the prevention component. They also used a retrospective quasi-experimental design to evaluate the impact of the graduated sanctions component. A random sample of cases assigned to probation prior to the initiation of the Breaking Cycles program served as the comparison group. The experimental sample was randomly chosen from cases assigned to the Breaking Cycles program in 1999.

Burke and Pennell found that the graduated sanctions component was effective in keeping offenders from progressing to more serious delinquency. Regardless of commitment length, youths in the Breaking Cycles program were less likely than preprogram youths either to have court referrals for felony offenses or to be adjudicated for felony offenses during the 18-month follow-up period. Breaking Cycles youths also were less likely to be committed to long-term state correctional facilities. Moreover, at follow-up, Breaking Cycles youths were more likely to be enrolled in school and less likely to be using alcohol or drugs.

Murray and Cox's (1979) evaluation of the Illinois Unified Delinquency Intervention Services (UDIS) program for chronic inner-city juveniles showed the effectiveness of this graduated sanctions system through comparisons of the various levels of intervention. Level I sanctions consisted of arrest and release. At Level II, offenders were subject to a series of graduated sanctions; Level II sanctions were reserved for those who recidivated in Level I. Those who failed at Level II were transferred to Level III, where the sanctions consisted of placement in juvenile correctional facilities. Murray and Cox's analysis showed that more crimes were "suppressed" at each subsequent level of sanctions. Youngsters placed on probation (in Level II) also showed suppression effects, but these were of much smaller magnitude than among the incarcerated juveniles. However, the suppression effects were highest for an intensive care program that was based in a hospital and in residential settings, using positive peer programs, individual counseling, and academic work. Out-of-town residential camps featuring vocational activities, schooling, recreation, counseling, and aftercare produced the second-highest suppression effects. Imprisonment was next in effectiveness, followed by group homes, nonresidential services, and wilderness programs. Thus this study suggests that graduated sanctions programs may suppress some offenses, but they are likely to be far more effective when sanctions are combined with treatment.

Lipsey and Wilson (1998) identify numerous other effective programs incorporating graduated sanctions in their review of institutional and noninstitutional programs. These include contingency contracting programs (Jessness, Allison, McCormic, Wedge, & Young, 1975), Achievement Place (Kirigin, Braukmank, Atwater, & Worl, 1982), programs that include training for parents (Wolf, Phillips, & Fixson, 1974), and the Planned Re-Entry Program (Seckel & Turner, 1985). An important key to the effectiveness of graduated sanctions is how well the sanctions are linked to effective programs.

Programs for Serious
Violent Juvenile Offenders

Many programs have demonstrated success in rehabilitating serious and violent juvenile offenders (Lipsey & Wilson, 1998). I feature three here that serve as good examples of the kinds of program structures that work effectively with such juveniles, particularly violent offenders. Each of the programs described below is (or was) operated in a secure juvenile correctional setting. One of them—Florida's "Last Chance Ranch"—is located in a swamp. I have also chosen the programs described here for the uniqueness of their approaches.

Violent Juvenile Offender
Research and Development Program

The OJJDP Violent Juvenile Offender (VJO) Research and Development Program provided treatment for both violent and property felony offenders. The program emphasized the reintegration of the offenders into their communities, to which they were returned after fairly brief incarceration periods in small secure juvenile correctional institutions (Fagan, Rudman, & Hartstone, 1984). To do this, the VJO program created a continuum of sanctions and services, beginning with small secure facilities, followed by gradual reintegration into the community via community-based residential programs, then a period of intensive neighborhood supervision. This model proved to be effective in localities where it was implemented thoroughly (Fagan, 1990). VJO youths in these sites had significantly lower recidivism rates and less serious subsequent offenses, and they recidivated less quickly than did youths in the control group.

Florida Environmental Institute

The Florida Environmental Institute (FEI), also known as the "Last Chance Ranch," serves some of Florida's most serious and violent juvenile offenders. Almost two-thirds of FEI youths are committed for violent crimes; the remainder, for chronic property or drug offenses (Krisberg et al., 1995). Located in a swamp in a remote area of the state, FEI is a highly structured, environmentally secure program that consists of several phases. In the FEI facility, where there is a low staff-to-client ratio, clients spend about a year in a program that includes presumably therapeutic physical labor, educational and vocational training, a restitution component, and reintegration programming. Clients are then assisted with community living in an extensive aftercare phase. Evaluations of the program have shown quite promising results (see Krisberg et al., 1995, pp. 164-165). FEI has produced much lower recidivism rates than other Florida correctional programs, and the state has replicated the program in other localities.

Capital Offender Program

Even juvenile murderers can be rehabilitated. Begun in 1988, the Capital Offender Program (COP) at Giddings State Home and School in Texas is an innovative group treatment program for juveniles committed for homicide. It is a highly structured, intensive, 16-week empathy-training program for small groups of juveniles aimed at teaching them to manage their emotions. A residential treatment component recently was added to COP; the students live together in the same cottage until their release. Most program participants are incarcerated at Giddings for an average of 2 to 3 years. Youths must meet four criteria to be eligible for COP:

- They must be committed for homicide (capital murder, murder, or voluntary manslaughter).
- They must have been at Giddings for at least 12 months and have at least 6 months remaining on their sentences.
- They must be at either a senior or prerelease level at Giddings.
- They cannot be diagnosed as psychotic or mentally retarded, or have a pervasive developmental disorder.

The primary goals of the COP treatment regimen are to promote verbal expression of feelings, to foster empathy for victims, to create a sense of personal responsibility, and to decrease feelings of hostility and aggression. The program uses group psychotherapy, with an emphasis on role playing. Participants role-play their life stories as well as their homicidal offenses, reenacting their crimes first from their own perspectives and then from the perspectives of their victims. An evaluation of COP by the Texas Youth Commission (Briscoe, 1997; see also Krisberg et al., 1995, pp. 165-166) found that, while in the program, youths displayed significant changes in levels of hostility and aggression, in extent of internal control and ability to assume responsibility, and in the degree of empathy for their victims. To assess the program impact on recidivism, the evaluators compared COP participants' rearrest and reconviction rates at 1- and 3-year intervals after release with those of a control group of untreated capital offenders (Briscoe, 1997). They found that the program reduced by 53% the likelihood of capital offenders' being arrested for violent offenses within 1 year of release (Briscoe, 1997, p. 12). After 3 years, however, these differences disappeared. Still, both the in-program changes and the short-term impact on recidivism suggest that COP should be considered a promising strategy for violent offenders.

Gender-Specific Programs

The program evaluation literature supports two important observations about the effectiveness of juvenile justice programs for girls versus boys. First, programs for serious and violent juvenile offenders appear to be as effective with girls as they are with boys (Lipsey & Wilson, 1998, p. 332). Second, as I will show later in this chapter, everyday, practical juvenile justice system programs appear to be equally effective for both genders in reducing general delinquency (Lipsey, 1999b, p. 631). Nevertheless, there appears to be a small proportion of high-rate female offenders who present a special challenge to those who operate rehabilitation programs (Acoca, 1998a, 1999; Acoca & Dedel, 1998; Richie, Tsenin, & Widom, 2000). As noted in Chapter 4, a small subgroup of female offenders appear to follow a unique pathway to serious and violent delinquency, and those in this special group may have unique treatment needs that program designers should take into account. Only a handful of gender-specific programs nationwide have been recognized for effectiveness in dealing with the most difficult female offenders (Acoca, 1999; see Chapter 13 for a

discussion of some specific kinds of interventions that are needed for these girls). To maximize the effectiveness of existing programs with girls, jurisdictions need to use risk and needs/strengths assessments that can help them to place female offenders at the appropriate places in the graduated sanctions system and to get the best matches between treatment needs and available programs. I explain this process in Chapter 12.

Cost-Beneficial Programs for Adolescent Offenders

Before I describe some cost-beneficial programs for adolescent offenders, I want to make a clear distinction between the analysis of cost-effectiveness and cost-benefit analysis. An analysis that is concerned with a program's cost-effectiveness compares only program costs per client with crime reduction per client. In contrast, a cost-benefit analysis goes further, taking into account such benefits to society as taxpayer benefits (e.g., criminal justice system costs) and crime victim benefits (victim costs that are saved as a result of crime reduction per client). Thus a cost-benefit analysis is far more complex than an analysis of cost-effectiveness, and it produces a more comprehensive measure of program benefits.

The most comprehensive cost-benefit study of juvenile justice programs to date is that produced by the Washington State Institute for Public Policy (WSIPP) in its review of juvenile justice and adult programs in Washington. When the Washington State Legislature issued a mandate that only effective programs are to be funded and implemented in the state, it also commissioned WSIPP to undertake an exhaustive review of existing programs. The WSIPP researchers, Aos et al. (2001), reviewed nine program clusters. Inspired by Lipsey's pioneering meta-analyses, Aos and colleagues used meta-analytic techniques to determine the average sizes of the crime reduction effects of the various programs within the nine program clusters. Box 10.3 shows the results of their review.

Aos et al. (2001) place programs into four broad categories in the WSIPP review: early childhood programs, middle childhood and adolescent programs for nonoffenders, juvenile offender programs, and adult offender programs. It is readily apparent that the most cost-beneficial programs are juvenile offender programs. Few adult offender programs are particularly cost-beneficial, whereas several of the juvenile justice programs produce large taxpayer and crime victim benefits. Aos et al. found that Multisystemic Therapy (MST) is most cost-beneficial of all (Henggeler, 1997b; Henggeler, Schoenwald, Borduin, Rowland, & Cunningham, 1998; see Chapter 11 for a detailed description of MST). It can produce taxpayer and crime victim benefits of nearly $132,000 per participant at a direct cost of only $4,743 per participant. MST has been demonstrated to be an effective treatment for multiple problems of serious and violent juvenile offenders in different settings (Borduin et al., 1995; Henggeler, 1999; Henggeler, Cunningham, Pickrel, Schoenwald, & Brondino, 1996; Henggeler, Melton, & Smith, 1992; Henggeler, Melton, Smith, Schoenwald, & Hanley, 1993). It also has been proven effective with abusive and neglectful families (Brunk, Henggeler, & Whelan, 1987; Henggeler et al., 1998), with adolescent sexual offenders (Borduin, Henggeler, Blaske, & Stein, 1990), with substance-abusing and -dependent delinquents (Henggeler, Pickrel, & Brondino, 1999). A study supported by the National Institute of Mental Health is currently examining whether the impressive MST outcomes to date are comparable in sites where MST is not administered by its developers (Burns, Schoenwald, Burchard, Faw, & Santos, 2000). (MST training manuals and other teaching resources are available; see the MST Services Web site at www.mstservices.com. For access information about the wraparound process, see Burns et al., 2000, p. 309.)

Two other kinds of "off the shelf" programs for juvenile offenders are rather cost-beneficial: Functional Family Therapy (FFT; Barton, Alexander, Waldron, Turner, & Warburton, 1985; Hannson, 1998) and Multidimensional Treatment Foster Care (MTFC; Chamberlain, 1998; Chamberlain & Reid, 1998) (see Box 10.3). This is owed mainly to the fact that the these two forms of interventions (and MST) are research demonstration programs; I will explain how these differ from other programs shortly.

Box 10.3

Washington State Institute for Public Policy Cost-Benefit Study

---

The table below shows the results of a literature review and cost-benefit analysis of selected programs conducted by the Washington State Institute for Public Policy (WSIPP) to examine what would happen if the programs were implemented in the state of Washington (Aos, Phipps, Barnoski, & Lieb, 2001). In the table, program effectiveness is expressed in terms of the average "effect size" of the program (see column 2), which is roughly equivalent to the percentage of reduction in crime rates. The "standard error" is shown in parentheses in column 2. This is the range of the confidence that can be placed in the average effect size; the larger the standard error relative to the effect size, the less confidence that the average effect size is the true effect size (Aos et al., 2001, p. 9). The net direct cost of the program (column 3) is the best estimate of what the program typically costs per participant, and the net benefits per participant are shown in columns 4 and 5. These are the benefits that a program is expected to produce in terms of future crime reduction, less the costs of the program as shown in column 3. Column 4 shows only taxpayer benefits (crime reduction minus costs)—the lower end of the range of net benefits. For the taxpayer view, the question is whether spending a taxpayer dollar now on a program will save more than a taxpayer dollar in the years ahead (Aos et al., 2001, p. 9). Column 5 combines crime victim benefits with taxpayer benefits to show the upper end of the range of net benefits. This column adds the crime victim view: If a program can reduce rates of future criminal offending, not only will taxpayers receive benefits but there will also be fewer crime victims. The first column shows the number of studies reviewed for the analysis. Note that the criminal justice costs, crime victim benefits (personal and property losses), and program costs shown in this table are specific to Washington State; all of these costs and benefits may vary for other states.

(Continued)

Box 10.3 (Continued)

Table 1: Summary of Program Economics (All Monetary Values in 2000 Dollars)

	Number of Program Effects in the Statistical Summary	Average Size of the Crime Reduction Effect* & (Standard Error) note that a negative effect size means lower crime	Net Direct Cost of the Program, Per Participant	Net Benefits Per Participant (i.e., Benefits minus Costs)	
				Lower End of Range: Includes Taxpayer Benefits Only	Upper End of Range: Includes Taxpayer and Crime Victim Benefits
	(1)	(2)	(3)	(4)	(5)
Early Childhood Programs					
Nurse Home Visitation (for low income single mothers)	2	-0.29 (0.21)	$7,733	-$2,067 to	$15,918
Early Childhood Education for Disadvantaged Youth	6	-0.10 (0.04)	$8,936	-$4,754 to	$6,972
Middle Childhood & Adolescent (Non-Juvenile Offender) Programs					
Seattle Social Development Project	1	-0.13 (0.11)	$4,355	-$456 to	$14,169
Quantum Opportunities Program	1	-0.31 (0.20)	$18,964	-$8,855 to	$16,428
Mentoring	2	-0.04 (0.05)	$1,054	$225 to	$4,524
National Job Corps	1	-0.08 (0.03)	$6,123	-$3,818 to	$1,719
Job Training Partnership Act	1	0.10 (0.05)	$1,431	-$4,562 to	-$12,082
Juvenile Offender Programs					
Specific "Off the Shelf" Programs					
Multi-Systemic Therapy	3	-0.31 (0.10)	$4,743	$31,661 to	$131,918
Functional Family Therapy	7	-0.25 (0.10)	$2,161	$14,149 to	$59,067
Aggression Replacement Training	4	-0.18 (0.14)	$738	$8,287 to	$33,143
Multidimensional Treatment Foster Care	2	-0.37 (0.19)	$2,052	$21,836 to	$87,622
Adolescent Diversion Project	5	-0.27 (0.07)	$1,138	$5,720 to	$27,212
General Types of Treatment Programs					
Diversion with Services (vs. regular juvenile court processing)	13	-0.05 (0.02)	-$127	$1,470 to	$5,679
Intensive Probation (vs. regular probation caseloads)	7	-0.05 (0.06)	$2,234	$176 to	$6,812
Intensive Probation (as alternative to incarceration)	6	0.00 (0.05)	-$18,478	$18,586 to	$18,854
Intensive Parole Supervision (vs. regular parole caseloads)	7	-0.04 (0.06)	$2,635	-$117 to	$6,128
Coordinated Services	4	-0.14 (0.10)	$603	$3,131 to	$14,831
Scared Straight Type Programs	8	0.13 (0.06)	$51	-$6,572 to	-$24,531
Other Family-Based Therapy Approaches	6	-0.17 (0.04)	$1,537	$7,113 to	$30,936
Juvenile Sex Offender Treatment	5	-0.12 (0.10)	$9,920	-$3,119 to	$23,602
Juvenile Boot Camps	10	0.10 (0.04)	-$15,424	$10,360 to	-$3,587
Adult Offender Programs					
Adult Offender Drug Treatment Programs (compared to no treatment)					
In-Prison Therapeutic Community, No Community Aftercare	5	-0.05 (0.05)	$2,604	-$899 to	$2,365
In-Prison Therapeutic Community, With Community Aftercare	11	-0.08 (0.02)	$3,100	-$243 to	$5,230
Non-Prison TC (as addition to an existing community residential facility)	2	-0.17 (0.10)	$2,013	$4,110 to	$15,836
In-Prison Non-Residential Substance Abuse Treatment	5	-0.09 (0.03)	$1,500	$1,672 to	$7,748
Drug Courts	27	-0.08 (0.02)	$2,562	-$109 to	$4,691
Case Management Substance Abuse Programs	12	-0.03 (0.03)	$2,204	-$1,050 to	$1,230
Community-Based Substance Abuse Treatment	3	-0.07 (0.05)	$2,198	$237 to	$5,048
Drug Treatment Programs in Jails	7	-0.05 (0.05)	$1,172	$373 to	$3,361
Adult Sex-Offender Treatment Programs (compared to no treatment)					
Cognitive-Behavioral Sex Offender Treatment	7	-0.11 (0.05)	$6,246	-$778 to	$19,534
Adult Offender Intermediate Sanctions (compared to regular programs)					
Intensive Supervision (Surveillance-Oriented)	19	-0.03 (0.03)	$3,296	-$2,250 to	-$384
Intensive Supervision (Treatment-Oriented)	6	-0.10 (0.06)	$3,811	-$459 to	$5,520
Intensive Supervision: Diversion from Prison	3	0.00 (0.08)	-$5,925	$6,083 to	$6,386
Adult Boot Camps	11	0.00 (0.03)	-$9,725	$9,822 to	$10,011
Adult Boot Camps--As partial diversion from prison	11	0.00 (0.03)	-$3,380	$3,477 to	$3,666
Cognitive-Behavioral Programs (compared to no treatment)					
Moral Reconation Therapy	8	-0.08 (0.04)	$310	$2,471 to	$7,797
Reasoning and Rehabilitation	6	-0.07 (0.04)	$308	$2,202 to	$7,104
Other Programs (compared to no treatment or regular programs)					
Work Release Programs (vs. in-prison incarceration)	2	-0.03 (0.11)	$456	$507 to	$2,351
Job Counseling/Search for Inmates Leaving Prison	6	-0.04 (0.02)	$772	$625 to	$3,300
In-Prison Adult Basic Education	3	-0.11 (0.05)	$1,972	$1,852 to	$9,176
In-Prison Vocational Education	2	-0.13 (0.04)	$1,960	$2,835 to	$12,017
Correctional Industries Programs	3	-0.08 (0.02)	$1,800	$1,147 to	$9,413

* The summary effect size shown on this table for each area is the weighted average standardized mean difference effect size. For those studies with bi-variate outcome measures, the mean difference effect sizes are approximated using the arcsine transformation as described in Lipsey & Wilson(2000), Table B10, Formula 22. The individual study effect sizes are adjusted using the Hedges correction for small sample sizes as described in Lipsey & Wilson(2000), page 49, Equation 3.22. The weights are the inverse variance weights as described in Lipsey & Wilson(2000), page 49, Equations 3.23 and 3.24.

SOURCE: *The Comparative Costs and Benefits of Programs to Reduce Crime* (p. 8), by S. Aos, P. Phipps, R. Barnoski, and R. Lieb, 2001, Olympia: Washington State Institute for Public Policy. Copyright 2001 by Washington State Institute for Public Policy. Reprinted with permission.

Functional Family Therapy is a cognitive-behavioral intervention that has been applied successfully to a wide range of problem youth and their families in various contexts (e.g., rural, urban, and multicultural) and treatment systems (e.g., clinics, home-based programs, juvenile courts, independent providers) (for a summary of FFT and its effectiveness, see Mihalic et al., 2001, p. 9). Clinicians are trained to work with parents and children simultaneously to deliver the intervention. FFT uses such behavioral change techniques as clear specification of rules and consequences, contingency contracting, use of social reinforcement, and more cognitively based interventions in adolescent problem solving, in three treatment phases. Phase 1 involves engagement and motivation of targeted youths and their families. In Phase 2, clinicians develop and implement behavior change plans. Phase 3 involves applications of family change to various contexts.

Multidimensional Treatment Foster Care was initially developed as an alternative to residential group care placement for adolescents who evidence serious and chronic delinquency (Chamberlain, 1994). It later was adapted to youth with severe emotional and behavioral problems who were leaving the state psychiatric hospital. In MTFC, foster parents act as mentoring adults and are trained to provide home-based treatment that extends into the school and community. They are well trained in the MTFC intervention approach and are closely supervised while they provide youngsters with cognitive-behavioral therapy—with intensive supervision, positive reinforcement for appropriate behavior, and disincentives for inappropriate behavior and association with delinquent peers. Other key objectives of the MTFC intervention approach are to encourage youth to develop academic skills and positive work habits, to encourage family members to improve communication skills, and to decrease conflict between family members. In the latest application of the model, MTFC is being used in work with adolescents who have developmental disabilities and histories of sexual problems. Chamberlain (1998) summarizes the successful use of MTFC in three cost-beneficial juvenile justice programs, all of which share two features: They are multisystemic (addressing, at a minimum, individual and family problems) and multimodal (applying more than one intervention).

The WSIPP study also shows that a number of general types of treatment programs are somewhat cost-beneficial, and some are not. The three family-based therapy approaches highlighted above—MST, FFT, and MTFC—show large cost savings, up to nearly $31,000 per participant. Other impressive interventions are in the "coordinated services"

category. The most successful programs in this category provide integrated services. A more current example of these would be the 8% Early Intervention Program, which has wraparound features (see Chapters 11 and 13). The use of intensive probation as an alternative to incarceration is another cost-beneficial program strategy. As Aos and colleagues (2001) explain, even when recidivism rates are about the same for intensive probation as they are for incarceration, communities can realize considerable cost savings (nearly $19,000 per participant) by using this strategy as an alternative to incarceration.

This rigorous cost-benefit study is also revealing in that it shows that not all "effective" programs are cost-beneficial. Consider, for example, the Quantum Opportunities Program. In their evaluation of this program, Hahn, Leavitt, and Aaron (1994) found a delinquency reduction of 31% (see column 2 in the table displayed in Box 10.3). However, owing to the very high cost of this program per client ($18,964; column 3), it is not cost-beneficial when we consider only taxpayer benefits: The taxpayer loss is $8,855 per participant (column 4). However, if we add long-term victim benefits to the estimated benefits (column 5), the program is cost-beneficial (a savings of as much as $16,428 per participant). Therefore, this program would not be cost-beneficial in the short term, but it may represent a good long-term investment.

Finally, some programs simply are not cost-beneficial. Scared Straight programs increase recidivism about 13% and thus accrue costs to taxpayers and victims of more than $24,000 per participant (see column 5 in the table in Box 10.3). Juvenile boot camps also are ineffective: They increase recidivism about 10%. But because they sometimes are used as alternatives to incarceration, they are not nearly as wasteful of resources as Scared Straight programs.

Although incarcerating juveniles in large reformatories has been shown to be ineffective (see Chapter 7), some treatment components have been found to be effective in residential facilities—such as interpersonal skills training, behavioral programs, and multiple services (Lipsey & Wilson, 1998). Aggression Replacement Training (ART) is one intervention that the WSIPP researchers found to be effective in correctional facilities (see Box 10.3). Other correctional programs hold a great deal of promise (see Chapter 13).

Other states can use the results of the impressive WSIPP cost-benefit study as a guide to the types of programs that are likely to be cost-beneficial or to waste public resources. This study suggests that some interventions clearly should not be used, such as Scared Straight programs and boot camps. Others can be used to considerable advantage. Many of these are practical, everyday programs, which I discuss later in this chapter. Before turning to that topic, however, I next consider the principles of effective intervention.

Principles of Effective Intervention

Canadian criminologists—particularly Andrews, Bonta, Gendreau, and Ross—and their American colleagues (especially Cullen and Latessa) have successfully challenged the "nothing works" myth with respect to adult criminal justice programs (Bonta & Gendreau, 1990; Cullen & Gendreau, 1989; Cullen & Gilbert, 1982; Gendreau, 1981; Gendreau & Andrews, 1990; Gendreau & Ross, 1979, 1987; Gerber & Fritsch, 1995). Because the Canadian researchers typically include juvenile programs in their reviews of program outcomes, their meta-analyses and traditional program reviews have made an enormous contribution to debunking the "nothing works" myth with respect to juvenile offenders. They have also contributed to debunking the myth that treatment programs are not effective with serious and violent offenders. Whereas Lipsey and colleagues have identified characteristics of clusters of effective programs that are grouped for meta-analysis, the Canadian scholars have identified principles of effective (and ineffective) interventions based on program-by-program reviews and in selected meta-analyses.

The following summary of the literature on the principles of effective intervention draws upon a large volume of mainly Canadian/American reviews of adult criminal and juvenile delinquent intervention programs (Andrews, 1995, 1996; Andrews & Bonta, 1998; Andrews, Dowden, & Gendreau, 1999; Andrews & Hoge, 1995; Antonowicz & Ross, 1994; Bonta, 1996; Cullen & Applegate, 1997; Cullen, Gendreau, Jarjoura, & Wright, 1997; Cullen & Gilbert, 1982; Gendreau, 1996a, 1996b; Gendreau, Cullen, & Bonta, 1994; Gendreau & Goggin, 1997; Gendreau, Goggin, & Paparozzi, 1996; Gendreau, Little, & Goggin, 1996; Gendreau & Ross, 1987; Lipsey, 1992, 1995; Losel, 1995; Pearson, Lipton, & Cleland, 1996). The main focus of the Canadian researchers has been on using correctional outcome studies to develop a "best practices" model that integrates clinical and management practices in corrections (Kiessling & Andrews, 1980). These "best practices" are stated as principles of effective correctional intervention (Andrews & Bonta, 1998; Andrews et al., 1990; Cullen & Gendreau, 2000). The Canadian psychologists' theory of correctional rehabilitation is based on four major principles, each of which I address in turn below.

Principle 1: Interventions should target the known predictors of crime and recidivism for change. The predictors that place offenders at risk for criminal involvement are of two types: *Static* risk factors are those that cannot be changed, such as an offender's criminal history; *dynamic* risk factors are those that can be changed, such as antisocial values. The most salient predictors are dynamic. These include the following:

- Antisocial/procriminal attitudes, values, beliefs, and cognitive-emotional states
- Procriminal associates and isolation from prosocial others
- Antisocial personality factors, such as impulsiveness, risk taking, and low self-control

Some personality factors, such as low self-esteem, are not strong predictors and thus should not be targeted. Changing these particular personality defects is not likely to reduce crime.

Principle 2: The treatment services should be behavioral in nature. The most effective interventions involve behavioral, social learning, and cognitive-behavioral strategies (Andrews & Bonta, 1998, p. 245). Cognitive-behavioral problems—also called *cognitive distortions*—are those deficiencies that compromise a youth's ability to develop, choose, and implement solutions to interpersonal problems (Henggeler et al., 1998, pp. 194-207). Thus cognitive-behavioral interventions—also called *behavior therapy, social learning, social cognition, reality therapy,* and the like—involve assisting youths in thinking through and behaviorally practicing solutions to specific interpersonal problems that are targeted for change.

Cognitive-behavioral programs fall into two categories (Lester & Van Voorhis, 1997): *Cognitive restructuring* programs attempt to change the content of what offenders believe, such as prodelinquency attitudes; *cognitive skills* programs attempt to change the way that offenders reason, such as coping with anger and control of negative impulses. Cognitions—what and how an individual thinks—govern behavioral choices, such as delinquency involvement.

Therapists in juvenile treatment programs use four types of strategies to accomplish cognitive-behavioral restructuring (Henggeler et al., 1998, p. 195): modeling, role-play exercises, behavioral contingencies, and self-monitoring and self-instruction. The most effective cognitive-behavioral therapy for delinquency involvement, called *problem-solving training,* combines all four of the above strategies in Henggeler's Multisystemic Therapy model. In this approach, parents and teachers are actively involved in the process of helping youths to solve problems that arise in social interactions, monitoring and reinforcing the changes initiated in individual sessions with youths using behavioral contingencies and praise (Henggeler et al., 1998, pp. 194-207). The use of problem-solving training in real-world situations appears to be a key to the success of this approach.

Principle 3: Treatment should be delivered in a style and mode that is consistent with, or matched to, the learning styles of the offender. This is what the Canadian criminologists call the *responsivity principle* (see Andrews 1995; Andrews & Bonta, 1998; Andrews et al., 1990; Gendreau, 1996b). It is derived "from the fact that offenders differ in motivation, personality, and emotional and cognitive abilities, and these characteristics can influence the offender's responsiveness to various therapists and treatment modalities" (Bonta, 1996, p. 31). Bonta (1996) gives this example:

> An agency may deal with high-risk offenders who have the same criminogenic needs (substance abuse treatment), but within that group there are individuals differing along such dimensions as anxiety, intelligence, self-esteem, and so on. These factors affect how well the client responds to the style and modes of therapy and necessitate a matching of client characteristics with treatment. It is quite possible that withdrawn and shy clients may respond best when treatment is given on an individual basis, whereas extroverted, self-confident clients may respond well to a group therapy format. (pp. 31-32)

Cullen and colleagues (1997) outline another example:

> Offenders who have low IQs would perform more effectively than higher functioning offenders in an instructional format that requires less verbal and written fluency, and abstract conceptualizations. In addition, they would likely profit from a more extensive use of tangible reinforcers and from repeated, graduated behavioral rehearsal and shaping of skills. Moreover, therapists should be selected who relate optimally to offenders' styles of intellectual functioning and to the content of the treatment modality. (p. 403)

Unfortunately, risk and needs/strengths assessment instruments currently are not capable of this level of precision matching. This is a challenge for future work in the development of such instruments (Andrews & Bonta, 1998, p. 248). An instrument that can be used to measure offender responsivity to different treatment modalities would be of great benefit to the juvenile justice system.

Principle 4: Treatment interventions should be delivered mainly to higher-risk (as opposed to lower-risk) offenders. This is what the Canadian/American scholars call the *risk principle* (Andrews, Kiessling, Robinson, & Mickus, 1986), meaning that programs are most effective with high-risk offenders. Low-risk juvenile offenders generally require no or very little intervention because they are unlikely to recidivate. Scarce resources are wasted on offenders with a low likelihood of recidivism (Schumacher & Kurz, 2000). Moreover, the imposition of structured, intrusive sanctions on low-risk offenders may actually increase their likelihood of recidivism (Andrews & Bonta, 1998).

Andrews and colleagues (1990) tested the principles of effective treatment in a meta-analysis of 80 juvenile and adult program evaluations. They organized treatment interventions into three categories: appropriate (consistent with the main principles of effective programs), inappropriate (inconsistent with the main principles), and unspecified (could not be categorized for lack of information). Programs that were judged consistent with the principles of effective programs produced large reductions (about 30%) in recidivism. Programs that employed inappropriate interventions produced increases in recidivism, and programs that used unspecified intervention techniques produced modest reductions in recidivism (about 13%). This study was later replicated by another team of investigators (Pearson et al., 1996).

In a subsequent meta-analysis on a larger database of program evaluations, Andrews et al. (1999) examined the effects of programs that employed one or more of the key principles of effective programs. They found that when a program incorporated only one of the principles, it barely reduced recidivism. Programs that adhered to two of the principles showed modest reductions in recidivism, and programs that followed all of the key principles showed substantial recidivism reductions.

Antonowicz and Ross (1994) produced consistent findings in a similarly designed meta-analysis. They found that the most successful rehabilitation programs were more likely to have these characteristics: (a) a sound conceptual model, (b) multifaceted programming, (c) the targeting of "criminogenic needs," (d) the responsivity principle, (e) role playing, and (f) social cognitive skills training.

Box 10.4

Practical Features of Effective Juvenile and Adult Rehabilitation Programs

---

Effective rehabilitation programs tend to share the following features:

- They train workers thoroughly in the delivery of the specific treatment protocol.
- They employ enthusiastic and caring workers who serve as advocates for the offenders.
- They ensure that workers demonstrate and reinforce clear alternatives to antisocial styles of thinking, feeling, and acting.
- They ensure that workers engage in and demonstrate concrete problem solving and skill building.
- They provide clinical supervision to service delivery agents.
- They monitor service delivery and intermediate gains.
- They reassess clients at regular intervals.
- They exercise authority in firm and fair ways.
- They make training/program manuals available to workers.

SOURCE: Andrews and Bonta (1998, p. 360).

In sum, the Canadian/American criminologists cited above have made an important contribution to development of the theory of rehabilitation: the application of research-based principles to correctional treatment in the criminal justice system. Their contributions have helped considerably to move correctional practices away from extremely punitive measures and toward more effective treatment and rehabilitation (Latessa, Cullen, & Gendreau, 2002). Progress in this area of adult corrections has been much more impressive in Canada than in the United States (Motiuk, McGuire, & Gendreau, 2000).

Other Reviews of Juvenile Offender Programs

Program-by-program reviews that focus on research and development programs are useful for identifying the characteristics of the most effective ones. Two reviews that are characteristic of this type have recently been conducted. The University of Maryland conducted a congressionally mandated review of juvenile and adult programs for the U.S. Department of Justice (Sherman et al., 1997; see also MacKenzie, 2000). The overall effort of the Maryland group is commendable, given the time and resource constraints under which the researchers operated. Their report had to be completed in a matter of months. Unfortunately, because they had to give priority to the adult arena, they performed only a cursory review of the juvenile justice field. They missed a large number of effective juvenile justice programs, mainly because

they virtually ignored meta-analyses of juvenile justice system programs. The most valuable part of the Maryland review is Gottfredson's (1997) examination of school-based delinquency prevention programs, which has been updated and expanded (Gottfredson, 2001; Gottfredson, Wilson, & Najaka, 2002).

The Center for the Study and Prevention of Violence (CSPV) conducted a program-by-program review of a wide range of prevention and rehabilitation programs for children and adolescents (Mihalic et al., 2001). As I noted earlier in this chapter, although the acclaimed effective programs were called "violence prevention" programs, the list (see Table 10.2) was not limited to prevention or violence. Drug use prevention programs and delinquency reduction programs were also included. The researchers used rigorous scientific criteria to identify effective programs in a literature review. A program had to meet the following criteria to be declared "effective": use of an experimental evaluation design, evidence of a statistically significant deterrent (or marginal deterrent) effect, replication in at least one additional site with an experimental design and demonstrated effects, and evidence that the deterrent effect was sustained for at least 1 year posttreatment. These criteria served to exclude from consideration most evaluated juvenile justice system programs. Only well-funded research and development programs have the resources for replication in other sites. Their financial backing also makes it possible for them to use more rigorous—and expensive—evaluation designs. However, most research and development programs are evaluated

TABLE 10.2   "Blueprint" Programs

Effective programs

    Midwestern Prevention Project (MPP)
    Big Brothers Big Sisters of America (BBBSA)
    Functional Family Therapy (FFT)
    Quantum Opportunities Program
    Programs employing Life Skills Training (LST)
    Multisystemic Therapy (MST)
    Nurse-Family Partnership (NFP)
    Multidimensional Treatment Foster Care (MTFC)
    Bullying Prevention Program (BPP)
    Promoting Alternative THinking Strategies (PATHS)
    The Incredible Years: Parent, Teacher, and Child Training Series (IYS)

Promising programs

    Good Behavior Game (GBG)
    FAST (Families and Schools Together) Track
    Intensive Protective Supervision Project (IPSP)
    Iowa Strengthening Families Program (ISFP)
    Parent Child Development Center Programs (PCDCP)
    Perry Preschool Program (PPP)
    Preventive Intervention (PI)
    Preventive Treatment Program (PTP)
    Project Northland
    Project PATHE
    Project STATUS
    School Transitional Environmental Program (STEP)
    Seattle Social Development Project (SSDP)
    Syracuse Family Development Research Program (FDRP)
    Yale Child Welfare Project (YCWP)
    I Can Problem Solve (ICPS)
    Preparing for the Drug-Free Years (PDFY)
    Striving Together to Achieve Rewarding Tomorrows (START)
    Linking the Interests of Families and Teachers (LIFT)
    Brief Strategic Family Therapy (BSFT)
    Athletes Training and Learning to Avoid Steroids (ATLAS)

SOURCES: Elliott (1998) and Mihalic, Irwin, Elliott, Fagan, and Hansen (2001).

NOTE: Information on all of the programs listed in this table can be accessed online at www.colorado.edu/csvp/blueprints.

by the developers, which raises some skepticism regarding the outcomes.

The CSPV study identified 11 programs that meet the above criteria (see Table 10.2), and 19 other programs were found to be promising. The 11 designated-effective programs have been written up in the form of "blueprints" for jurisdictions interested in replicating them (see Mihalic et al., 2001). The federal Office of Juvenile Justice and Delinquency Prevention has provided training and technical assistance to jurisdictions wishing to implement one of the 11 exemplary projects. The successes or failures of these replication efforts have not yet been reported. Such a piecemeal approach does not hold much promise for building a cost-effective juvenile justice system, unless a state has large sums of money for extensive training and technical assistance. For maximum effectiveness, selected programs need to fit into a jurisdiction's continuum of program options and be consistent with the characteristics and principles of effective programs summarized above. It is likely that success with these programs would be limited, because it is very difficult to replicate research demonstration programs, for reasons that I will discuss shortly.

I must attach several caveats to the CSPV's list of effective programs. First, the review team overlooked the effectiveness of the Seattle Social Development Project. One of the eligibility criteria (that the program had to be replicated in at least a second site) unfortunately excluded large-scale experiments in which programs were implemented simultaneously in multiple sites. Thus the Seattle Social Development Project (Hawkins, Catalano, Kosterman, Abbott, & Hill, 1999) was excluded from the effective category even though it was replicated in 18 Seattle schools. This effective program has also been shown to be cost-beneficial (Aos et al., 2001; see the discussion of the program in Chapter 9). Two of the programs on CSPV's "promising" list have been shown to be cost-effective: the High/Scope Perry Preschool Program (Karoly, Greenwood, & Everingham, 1998) and the Syracuse Family Development Research Program (Aos et al., 2001). The program employing prenatal and infancy home visitation by a nurse has been shown to be cost-effective only for high-risk families, not for low-risk families (Karoly et al., 1998). Another program that the CSPV declared effective, the Bullying Prevention Program, actually has had mixed results. Although it has shown effectiveness in Norway (Olweus, 1991) and England (Eslea & Smith, 1998), neither of these evaluations was particularly rigorous (Gottfredson et al., 2002; Herrenkohl, Hawkins, Chung, Hill, & Battin-Pearson, 2001), and the program was not found to be effective in a U.S. replication (Melton et al., 2000). And finally, the Quantum Opportunities Program has not been shown to be effective in preventing violence (Gottfredson et al., 2002).

The CSVP replication approach to improving juvenile justice system programs also has important limitations. Most of the 11 programs are research demonstration programs (Lipsey, 1999b) that are very costly and difficult to replicate—particularly in small towns and rural areas—and may not be compatible with other existing programs. MST may be an exception; it has been successfully replicated in a large number of sites. Other exceptions are single-component programs, which can be replicated without great difficulty. A school curriculum add-on is a good example.

In the remainder of this chapter and in Chapters 12 and 13, I describe a systematic approach to juvenile justice system improvement, as an alternative to piecemeal changes. It may well be that communities can strengthen everyday juvenile justice system programs so that they produce large reductions in recidivism—and even emulate the features of research demonstration programs—without having to import costly intervention models that may not meet a large number of their needs. I explore this prospect next.

Effective Practical Juvenile Justice System Programs

Programs that are designed specifically to demonstrate the effectiveness of particular interventions—called *research demonstration programs*—typically produce the largest positive program effects (Lipsey, 1992, 1995). This is because the interventions in such programs are tested under optimal conditions. A distinguishing feature of research demonstration programs is active research team involvement in planning and implementing the program. In addition, research demonstration programs are typically highly structured around specific and systematically administered treatment protocols. Service providers in such programs are usually well trained in service delivery, and treatments are closely monitored. Because practical juvenile justice system programs typically do not have these costly features, research demonstration programs are more effective; they normally reduce recidivism about twice as much as practical programs (Lipsey, 1999b, p. 640).

These kinds of programs are well represented in the shaded portions of Figure 10.2, which denote statistically significant recidivism reductions. Note first, however, that of the 556 juvenile justice system outcome studies in Lipsey's (2000b) database, the majority (57%) reduced recidivism. Thus it can be said that *most* juvenile justice system programs reduce recidivism. This is an important point that counters the myth of ineffective juvenile justice system programs discussed in the beginning of this chapter.

Lipsey (1999b) recently conducted a meta-analysis to determine whether effective "practical" juvenile justice programs (routine programs designed and managed by system professionals) are worthwhile. From his database of juvenile justice program evaluations (Lipsey, 1992, 1995), he selected for this analysis programs that had a rehabilitative orientation, did not involve researchers directly, were sponsored by public or private agencies, and had clients that came to the programs through public or private agencies, rather than being recruited by researchers. In other words, these were programs that had a rehabilitation orientation but were not costly research and demonstration programs.

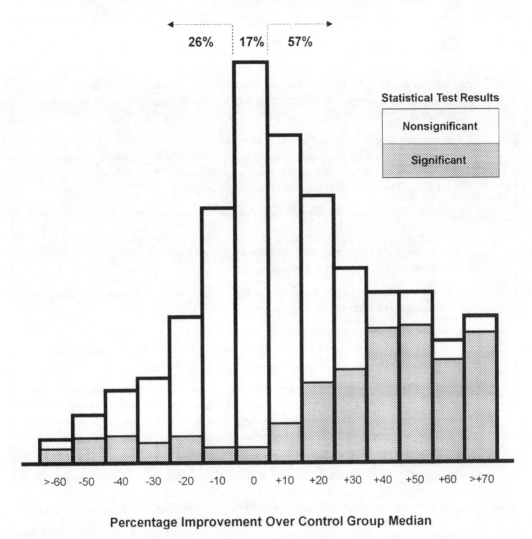

Percentage Improvement Over Control Group Median

Figure 10.2   Recidivism Results of 556 Delinquency Outcome Studies

SOURCE: *What 500 Intervention Studies Show About the Effects of Intervention on the Recidivism of Juvenile Offenders* (p. 10), by M. W. Lipsey, 2000. © 2000 by Mark W. Lipsey. Reprinted with permission.

Lipsey (1999b, 2000b) analyzed these 196 evaluations of practical juvenile justice system programs and found that 93% of the programs with favorable characteristics reduced recidivism and that nearly half (44%) of them reduced recidivism between 10% and 24%. He also found that some practical programs (about 17% of the nearly 200 programs) produced very worthwhile reductions in recidivism rates, about 20-25%. Lipsey (1999b) found that four main program characteristics were associated with the largest recidivism reductions: the provision of certain services, a distinct role for

the juvenile justice system, a sufficient amount of service, and administration of services to the most appropriate juvenile subpopulation.

In addition, comparable positive program effects were found for samples in which all the juveniles had prior offenses and/or high proportions were adjudicated or institutionalized delinquents and high proportions were reported to have histories of aggressive or violent behavior. This research shows that practical juvenile justice system programs can be effective with more chronic, serious, and violent offenders (Lipsey, 1999a). The success of practical

---

Box 10.5

Ten Principles of Effective Juvenile Justice System Programming

---

1. Communities can make existing programs for most juvenile delinquents more effective by configuring them around the features of practical programs that produce large recidivism reductions.

2. Communities should select cost-effective interventions that will produce the largest recidivism reductions per program dollar spent. Even highly effective research demonstration programs may not be cost-effective; some are too expensive to be cost-effective in many jurisdictions, especially small cities and towns and rural areas.

3. Community-based treatment services are more effective than programs operated inside correctional facilities.

4. On average, intervention programs are somewhat more effective with serious and violent delinquents than with less serious offenders.

5. Juvenile justice system programs are about as likely to be effective with more aggressive juveniles, females, and minority offenders as with other offenders.

6. Some research demonstration programs have been shown to reduce recidivism about twice as much as practical (routine) programs, but they are far more expensive to implement than practical programs.

7. Features of highly effective research demonstration programs can be emulated in juvenile justice and youth service agencies. Communities can achieve significant reductions in recidivism without having to fund costly demonstration programs or import whole programs. For example, a community can make incremental improvements by adding to routine probation one of the "best" interventions, coupled with very good program implementation (Lipsey, 1999a).

8. The most effective programs for serious and violent delinquents are those that have program designs and treatment protocols that are relatively highly structured; those that focus on developing skills (interpersonal skills, academic and employment skills); those that use behavioral and cognitive-behavioral methods (with follow-up reinforcements), including social learning techniques such as modeling, role playing, and graduated practice; and those that use multiple components to address offenders' problems in multiple domains (e.g., individual, family, school, peer group, and community).

9. A graduated sanctions system offers the most cost-effective way of protecting the public and matching offenders with appropriate programs and sanctions.

10. It is never too early and it is never too late to intervene with serious, violent, and chronic juvenile offenders (Loeber & Farrington, 1998b).

---

programs with older offenders may reflect some natural social maturation among offenders—that is, the process of "aging out" of delinquency.

Lipsey's discovery of the effectiveness of practical intensive supervision programs—whether linked with probation or with parole—deserves special attention. This finding refutes the previous negative findings of program-by-program reviews of intensive supervision programs (see Chapter 7). In addition, several studies have shown that intensive supervision programs can be effective with serious, violent, and chronic juvenile offenders (Josi & Sechrest, 1999; Sametz & Hamparian, 1990; Sontheimer & Goodstein, 1993) and also

TABLE 10.3   Proportion of Practical Programs With Different Numbers of Favorable Characteristics and Associated Improvement in Recidivism Rates Relative to Control

Number of Favorable Characteristics	Distribution of Programs (%)	Percentage Reduction in Recidivism
0	7	+12
1	50	−2
2	27	−10
3	15	−20
4	2	−24

SOURCE: *What 500 Intervention Studies Show About the Effects of Intervention on the Recidivism of Juvenile Offenders* (p. 10), by M. W. Lipsey, 2000. © 2000 by Mark W. Lipsey. Reprinted with permission.
NOTE: Favorable program characteristics are as follows: uses one of the more effective types of service; juvenile justice–administered program conducted in non–juvenile justice facility; good program implementation with high amount of service; juveniles' ages 15+; and mixed prior offenses.

with potential serious, violent, and chronic offenders (Burke & Pennell, 2001; Land et al., 1990; Schumacher & Kurz, 2000; Smith et al., 1996).

The Cumulative Impacts of Practical Programs With Effective Characteristics

To examine the cumulative impact of these more effective program characteristics, Lipsey (1999b) analyzed their impacts in tandem, by separating programs in the database into categories according to whether they scored high on none, one, or more of the four program characteristics described above (see Table 10.3). Programs that had none of the four characteristics (7% of the programs) *increased* recidivism somewhat. Those that had only one of the four characteristics (50% of the programs) reduced recidivism insignificantly (only 2%). However, those that had two of the four characteristics (27% of the programs) reduced recidivism 10%, those with three of the four characteristics (15% of the programs) reduced recidivism 21%, and those with all four of the highly effective program characteristics (2% of the programs) reduced recidivism 25%. Thus the presence of three or four of the desired program characteristics produced a very substantial impact on recidivism.

Table 10.3 also shows that the overwhelming majority of practical juvenile justice system programs reduce recidivism. Only programs that had none of the characteristics of effective programs (7%) failed to produce some recidivism reduction. However, half of the programs reduced recidivism insignificantly (only 2%).

Programs with additional features of effective programs reduce recidivism more. Figure 10.3 illustrates the incremental gains in expected recidivism for practical programs with various numbers of favorable intervention characteristics. It shows that programs with none of the favorable intervention characteristics had a 56% recidivism rate (versus 50% for the average control group). In other words, these programs increased recidivism. Lower recidivism rates were produced with each addition of a favorable program characteristic, from 49% for those programs with only one characteristic to only 38% for those with all four favorable program characteristics. In short, the more favorable characteristics a program has, the more it reduces recidivism.

Now that we can identify the characteristics of the most effective juvenile justice system programs, the key issue is how we can use this knowledge to strengthen existing programs. Lipsey (1999a) has issued this challenge to juvenile justice practitioners: "A focused effort must be made to establish effective types of programs and deliver the associated services at a consistently high level for a wide range of eligible offenders" (p. 164). Indeed, the majority (57%) of practical programs are not configured with sufficient regard for the program characteristics that are strongly associated with greater recidivism reduction, and thus did not produce meaningful effects on recidivism (Lipsey, 1999b, p. 636). About one-fourth (27%) fell into the middle range, producing modest effects, and 17% fell into the upper category, producing large recidivism reductions (20-24%).

Lipsey (1999a, p. 154) has shown the incremental benefits in recidivism reduction that can be achieved with program improvements, using probation as an example. Assume that the recidivism rate for offenders on routine juvenile probation in a

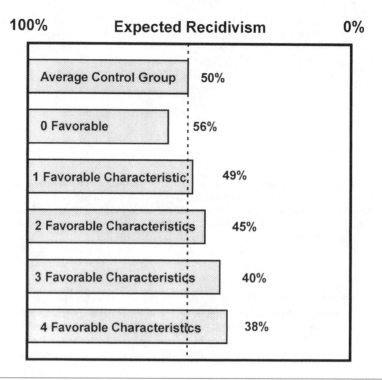

Figure 10.3   Expected Recidivism for Practical Programs With Various Numbers of Favorable
Intervention Characteristics

SOURCE: *What 500 Intervention Studies Show About the Effects of Intervention on the Recidivism of Juvenile
Offenders* (p. 10), by M. W. Lipsey, 2000. © 2000 by Mark W. Lipsey. Reprinted with permission.

given community is about 50%. By adding a minimal
program to routine probation, the community can
reduce recidivism to 46%. By adding a "best"
known intervention to routine probation, the community can expect to reduce recidivism to 40%. By
adding one of the "best" interventions to routine
probation and implementing the intervention well,
the community can reduce recidivism to 35%. By
extending the duration of that well-implemented
"best" intervention that has been added to routine
probation, the community can reduce recidivism to
32%. In this way, a community can achieve considerable reductions in recidivism without having to
fund a costly demonstration program or import a
whole program from another locale. Incremental
improvements can add up to an overall significant
recidivism reduction. This is an innovative
approach to program improvement that has a great
deal of practical application.

The lessons from Lipsey's meta-analysis of practical juvenile justice programs are both obvious and
important. First, communities can make existing

programs more effective by configuring them around
the program features that produce large recidivism
reductions. Second, older juveniles can be rehabilitated in the juvenile justice system with practical programs. It has long been assumed that the juvenile
justice system does not have the capacity to rehabilitate many older juvenile offenders; thus they are considered to be good candidates for transfer to the
criminal justice system. This assumption has proved
to be wrong. Third, both programs for serious and
violent juvenile offenders and practical programs for
all delinquents appear to be as effective with females
and minority youths as with other offenders (Lipsey,
1999b, p. 631). Fourth, features of research demonstration programs can be emulated in juvenile justice
and youth service agencies. However, Lipsey
(1999b) cautions that "such beneficial effects do not
come automatically. A concerted effort must be
made to configure the programs in the most favorable manner and to provide the types of services that
have been shown to be effective, and avoid those
shown to be ineffective" (p. 641).

Moving Knowledge of
Effective Programs Into Practice

There are three kinds of approaches that communities can take to move knowledge of effective programs into practice. The first is to import effective prevention and intervention programs that have shown very positive results in research demonstration (R&D) experiments. This is being done in selected sites in the "blueprints project" (Mihalic et al., 2001) and statewide by legislative mandate in the state of Washington (Aos et al., 2002).

The second kind of approach involves the mounting of experimental evaluations of existing programs in a community. This route is cost-prohibitive. The third kind of approach is a more cost-effective alternative; it involves the extraction of program principles and guidelines for effective interventions from previous evaluations through meta-analysis. In this approach, the community is engaged in emulating the features of the most effective program interventions (often called evidence-based practices or best practices) and uses this information in program development. This is the most practical approach.

It is commonly assumed that the juvenile justice system treatment enterprise is organized in a series of rather large-scale "programs." In reality, this is not the case. Rather, communities typically tie multiple interventions together in myriad combinations. For example, in a study conducted by the Center for Evaluation Research and Methodology (2002), the average evaluated "program" was found to comprise 5.5 treatment elements. Thus, from a practical standpoint, efforts to improve juvenile treatment and rehabilitation programs necessarily must focus on the application of individual interventions and combinations of them. This is not to say that communities should abandon the idea of implementing effective R&D programs, although replication and implementation of R&D program "blueprints" is proving to be very difficult (D. S. Elliott & S. Aos, personal communications, September 26, 2002). Equally important, it is unrealistic for some communities—such as rural communities where there are few clients and few program resources—to attempt to replicate most R&D models. However, it may be possible for some communities to achieve positive results, provided they have access to detailed implementation manuals and extensive training and technical assistance to ensure fidelity to the program model. Given the obvious expense and difficulty of such an enterprise, it seems more practical for most communities to make improvements in existing programs before they attempt to import R&D program models.

Meta-analysis allows communities to apply the existing knowledge about effective interventions more widely and more cost-effectively than they have been able to in the past. The concept of best practices does not refer to a set of program models to be emulated. Rather, it refers to a differentiated set of program characteristics, many combinations of which are known to be associated with positive outcomes (Lipsey, 1992, 1995; Lipsey & Wilson, 1998). In his most recent meta-analysis of nearly 400 juvenile delinquency treatment programs, Lipsey identified four major features of effective juvenile delinquency treatment programs (Center for Evaluation Research and Methodology, 2002):

- *Primary intervention:* The primary intervention is effective, independent of its use with another intervention.
- *Supplementary services:* Adding another service component to an intervention typically increases its effectiveness.
- *Service delivery:* The amount of service provided is sufficient, as indicated by service frequency, program duration, and extent of implementation.
- *Characteristics of the juvenile clients:* Some programs are more effective for high-risk juveniles than for low-risk offenders and vice versa; others are more effective for older or younger offenders.

It seems feasible to evaluate existing interventions against this knowledge base. Lipsey and his colleagues at Vanderbilt University are developing a program evaluation protocol that includes the evaluation of these features of effective programs. A prototype instrument has been developed specifically for North Carolina programs; I describe it in Chapter 12. The next step should be to engage local practitioners in a process of using this instrumentation to assess and improve existing programs so that they correspond more closely with evidence-based practices.

Canadian/American studies concerning the principles of effective rehabilitation have moved the adult and juvenile correctional fields forward along the same lines. The theory of correctional rehabilitation stemming from these studies has invigorated correctional programming with a progressive approach based on the risk principle: that programs should target high-risk offenders and focus on offender characteristics that can be changed. In addition, the American contingent at the University of Cincinnati (led by Latessa) has developed a methodology (called the Correctional Program Assessment Inventory) for assessing existing programs against the principles of effective rehabilitation and engaging practitioners in making program improvements (Latessa & Holsinger, 1998; Matthews, Hubbard, & Latessa, 2001).

Summary

I began this chapter by examining several commonly repeated myths about juvenile rehabilitation. To sum up that discussion: It is no longer accurate to say that "nothing works," and the presumption that juvenile courts are ineffective is without foundation. In addition, it may come as a surprise to many, but the juvenile justice system is effective even with serious and violent juvenile offenders. Equally important, community-based programs are more effective with juvenile offenders—even serious and violent offenders—than incarceration.

Several remarkable research advances—most significantly the use of meta-analytic techniques in reviewing program evaluations—have changed the thinking in the field about juvenile offender rehabilitation and treatment. Lipsey's (1992, 1995) meta-analyses of programs for delinquents in general corrected earlier negative conclusions about the overall effectiveness of juvenile justice programs. Lipsey and Wilson's (1998) later meta-analysis of programs for serious and violent offenders reversed assumptions about the ineffectiveness of programs for these offenders. Then, Lipsey's (1999b) meta-analyses of practical programs opened eyes to the effectiveness of everyday juvenile justice programs. Lipsey's work also shows that juvenile justice system programs are about equally effective with both genders and with minority and nonminority youths. In their comprehensive Washington State cost-benefit study, Aos et al. (2001) showed, for the first time, that a number of juvenile justice programs are remarkably cost-beneficial, and that they are more cost-beneficial than criminal justice system programs.

Lipsey and Wilson's (1998) meta-analysis of programs for serious and violent juvenile offenders is important for two significant discoveries. First, it revealed that juvenile justice system programs are even more effective with these categories of offenders than with delinquents in general, and that community-based programs are most effective with them. Second, it showed that the treatment components are not necessarily the most important features of effective programs, and that the

distinguishing features vary, depending on the treatment setting.

The clear implication is that factors other than the type of service intervention play an important role in making programs effective. In general, the most effective treatment programs for serious and violent delinquents may be described as follows (Lipsey & Wilson, 1998):

- They are programs in which the program designs and treatment protocols are relatively highly structured.
- They are programs that focus on developing skills (interpersonal skills, academic and employment skills).
- They are programs that use behavioral and cognitive-behavioral methods (with reinforcements), including social learning techniques such as modeling, role playing, and graduated practice.
- They are programs that use multiple components to address offenders' problems in multiple domains (e.g., individual, family, school, peer group, and the community).

For noninstitutionalized offenders, the most effective types of interventions are interpersonal skills training, individual counseling, and behavioral programs, followed closely by multiple services. For institutionalized offenders, the most effective types of interventions are interpersonal skills training, teaching family homes, behavioral programs, community residential programs, and multiple services. Communities need to link these effective interventions in program structures to form a continuum of effective programs (see Chapter 12).

Lipsey's meta-analysis of "practical" programs provided the rationale for development of an innovative way of increasing the effectiveness of juvenile justice system programs. He discovered that most such programs at least minimally reduce recidivism, but that the overwhelming majority of everyday juvenile justice system programs have few of the characteristics of the most effective programs, leaving much room for improvement. The question that remained to be answered was how communities could go about improving their existing programs. The answer lies in the results of Lipsey's continuing meta-analyses (Center for Evaluation Research and Methodology, 2002). These findings suggest the feasibility of the development of a brief instrument that would contain the characteristics of the most effective programs and could be used like a template to assess existing programs.

Heretofore, it was not feasible for communities to attempt to improve existing programs to emulate the most effective ones because there was a lack of available knowledge about the specific features of the most effective interventions. Instead, localities have been encouraged to import programs from elsewhere that are purported to be models that will work anywhere. But there are no panaceas, no magic bullets. Many of the programs communities might try to import are very costly and difficult to implement successfully. Most cannot be implemented at all in rural areas where there are few juvenile offenders. It makes much more practical and economic sense for communities to try to improve their existing programs before they decide to import new program models.

The state of North Carolina is currently using the available knowledge about effective programs to improve existing ones. The North Carolina project (which I describe in more detail in Chapter 13) entails the assessment of existing juvenile justice system programs against the knowledge base about effective programs, the identification of weak programs, and the application of existing knowledge of best practices to improve current programs. This approach holds a great deal of promise for building a continuum of effective juvenile rehabilitation programs that can be linked with a system of graduated sanctions.

Discussion Questions

1. What are the major myths about juvenile justice programs? Which of these myths are you most surprised to see debunked?

2. Which of the four major principles of the Canadian/American psychologists' theory of rehabilitation seems most important to you? Why?

3. What are some of the advantages of meta-analysis? Why is this method of reviewing rehabilitation programs superior to program-by-program reviews?

4. How have Lipsey's meta-analyses produced a breakthrough in juvenile justice program development?

11

THE DEVELOPMENT OF COMPREHENSIVE
JUVENILE JUSTICE APPROACHES

The fragmentation of services to children and families is widespread (National Research Council, 1993; Nelson, Rutherford, & Wolford, 1996; Roush, 1996b; Soler & Shauffer, 1990; U.S. Department of Health and Human Services, 1999). As Roush (1996b) has observed, "Services fail because they are too crisis-oriented, too rigid in their classification of problems, too specialized, too isolated from other services, too inflexible to craft comprehensive solutions, too insufficiently funded, and they are mismanaged" (p. 29). He asserts that this fragmentation of services "is at the core of the failure to address the problems of youth by each of the child-serving systems" (p. 29). In addition, public sector services are overly reliant on institutional care (Burns et al., 2001; Henggeler, Schoenwald, Borduin, Rowland, & Cunningham, 1998; U.S. Department of Health and Human Services, 1999).

Any given problem child is generally known to more than one child service agency, yet any one of these agencies is not likely to be aware that the child is also being serviced by other agencies. In a Sacramento study, Brooks and Petit (1997) found that 50% of the 9- to 12-year-old youths arrested in Sacramento County were known to child welfare authorities. However, child delinquents known to social service agencies are not likely to be known to juvenile courts (Burns et al., 2001). The youngest offenders with multiple problems are most likely to be dealt with by other agencies (Burns et al., 1995).

This is appropriate for the youngest children, because they most likely are predelinquents in need of child development-enhancing and protective services. Intervention with these youngsters is most appropriately handled by social service agencies. However, juvenile courts need to be more active participants with other agencies in early intervention efforts with older child delinquents, and other agencies need to join the juvenile courts in early intervention with potential serious, violent, and chronic delinquents (Howell, 2001a).

Unfortunately, the juvenile court has long served as a "dumping ground" for children who display a wide variety of problem behaviors and are inadequately served by our society's institutions (Kupperstein, 1971; Office of Juvenile Justice and Delinquency Prevention, 1995). Many of these children represent failures of child and family service agencies, including child welfare agencies, social service agencies, child protective services, mental health agencies, and public schools.

It is essential that communities be able to link troubled youths with programs that are intended to serve them. Currently, in many cases youths' access to services is involuntary, after problems have worsened and authorities are brought into play; this occurs because parents and adolescents often do not know where to turn for help before problems escalate to that level (Lerman & Pottick, 1995). In their study of youths referred to the Newark Family

Crisis Intervention Unit and community mental health centers, Lerman and Pottick (1995) found that most parents had relied on their own efforts in working with their children; they had tried behavior modification techniques, systems of rewards and punishments, and other forms of discipline, but to no avail. More than one-third had tried counseling or had contacted hospitals, doctors, or psychiatrists to get help—again, to no avail. Parents' talks with teachers were least likely to result in specific suggestions concerning agencies that likely could provide help. Contacts with police and court officials were most productive, followed by contacts with state youth workers and family workers. Remarkably, the parents in Lerman and Pottick's study sample said that none of the help sources they contacted appeared to understand the mental health problems experienced by their problem children, and professionals often made inappropriate suggestions for help.

In a Washington, D.C., study, Chaiken (2000) found that only 4% of boys in census tracts with the highest rates of juvenile violence could name a single community center or other city youth service organization. Chaiken also found that few local government agencies in Washington were involved in coordinated efforts to address the problems of juvenile delinquency, crime, and violence. Few surveyed administrators of local programs were aware of more than one of the citywide coalitions that were supposed to be effecting collaboration among local programs (p. 11). Conversely, staff in the citywide coalitions were frustrated that local agencies were unwilling to cooperate in collaborative efforts. This situation, which is typical of most cities, illustrates why a community needs an integrated strategy for dealing with the needs of children and families. Needless to say, it also suggests how difficult it might be to achieve this goal in some cities.

Whether they are young children or teenagers, youth who come into the juvenile justice system typically have multiple problems that need addressing. More than half of youngsters with two or more problems are also persistent serious delinquents (Huizinga, Loeber, Thornberry, & Cothern, 2000). A wide range of conduct problems—and sometimes serious emotional disturbance—typically manifest early in child delinquents (Burns et al., 2001). Many older serious violent juvenile offenders have developed serious academic problems, mental health problems, and drug problems, and many may well have been victimized (Huizinga et al., 2000). The period between the onset of minor problem behavior (in childhood) and the time when violent offenses are first committed (in adolescence) is

when multiple social services are needed to prevent the development of serious and violent delinquent careers and other serious problem behaviors. Even earlier intervention would be preferred (see Chapter 10)—as early as age 3—for the small proportion of very young starters (Loeber & Farrington, 2001a).

There is a large window of opportunity for intervention between the onset of delinquency and the point at which juvenile court intervention occurs. Stouthamer-Loeber, Loeber, Van Kammen, and Zhang (1995) found that by the time a youngster got to court for an Index offense in Pittsburgh, his or her parents had likely coped for several years with the child's problem behavior. By the eighth grade (about age 14), 20% of boys in the Pittsburgh sample had committed delinquent acts and had been referred to juvenile court. Only 41% of these boys' parents had ever sought help from anyone. The average interval between the time of initial problem behaviors and court contact was 4 years. For youths who exhibited more serious problem behaviors, the average interval was 2 years. More than half of the juveniles in this latter group had exhibited problem behaviors for 5 years or more, and in 16% of the cases the child's problems had been occurring for more than 10 years. Professional help had been sought for less than 30% of all delinquents. However, the court-referred delinquents had received more intensive professional help (much of which appeared to have been court initiated) than the nonreferred youths. The numbers of attempts to get help that the youngsters' caregivers had made were astonishing. Among the court group, youngsters received a mean number of 25 help contacts, 13 of which were from professional sources. In contrast, the no-court group received 14 help contacts, half of which were from professional sources. Hence this study suggests that juvenile courts are most capable of commanding multiple services.

The development of comprehensive, integrated systems of care has focused mainly on children with "serious emotional disturbances." The application of this legal term to a child's case triggers a host of mandated services from the education, child welfare, mental health, social services, and juvenile justice systems. *Serious emotional disturbance* refers to a diagnosed mental health problem that substantially disrupts a child's ability to function socially, academically, and emotionally (U.S. Department of Health and Human Services, 1999, p. 172). As noted in Chapter 6, some 20% of youth who come in contact with the juvenile justice system have serious mental health disorders—that is, more serious than conduct disorders (Cocozza & Skowyra, 2000, p. 6).

In this chapter, I review the history of comprehensive juvenile justice approaches, examining how the field has moved toward integrated and comprehensive strategies for serving the needs of children, adolescents, and their families. *Collaboration* is the most commonly used model in communities that attempt to develop comprehensive juvenile justice and youth services. The first federal model for coordinating interagency efforts took the form of Youth Services Bureaus. The next development in the evolution of comprehensive, integrated strategies was the "system of care" service delivery concept. This was followed by the development of the "wraparound" model for planning and coordinating the provision of both formal and informal services in the community. Finally, the Comprehensive Strategy for Serious, Violent, and Chronic Juvenile Offenders (see Chapters 12 and 13) was developed; this is a framework for the integration of child and adolescent services programming that links the juvenile justice system with human service and other related agencies, such as schools, child welfare services, mental health agencies, and social services. The door through which children and adolescents enter these systems should not matter; all young people should receive integrated services from all providers.

Collaboration Models

Integration of services differs from *collaboration among service providers* in two important ways. First, in an integrated service delivery model, multiple services are provided to the individual child or adolescent. Second, in such a model, multiple services are administered to the child or adolescent and his or her family simultaneously. Thus, as I will show in this chapter, *integration of services* encompasses more than *collaboration among systems.* Collaboration (defined as interagency cooperation) is the currently popular strategy for coordinating program activities. This form of collaboration is also referred to as *partnering.*

There are numerous examples of collaborative attempts that failed to achieve established objectives. In the Annie E. Casey Foundation's New Futures Initiative, 10 midsize cities—all of which had high poverty levels, high rates of school dropout, and large minority populations—were awarded $5-12.5 million over 5 years to improve the life chances of disadvantaged youths in their communities (Center for the Study of Social Policy, 1995). The cities were to use the grant money to restructure and realign existing institutions to be more responsive to the needs of at-risk youths and their families, with the aim of accomplishing four objectives: reduce the school dropout rate, improve students' academic performance, prevent teen pregnancies and births, and increase the number of college entrants. The cities were to accomplish these objectives through the formation of new local governance bodies, called collaboratives, made up of representatives of local agencies, parents, community representatives, business representatives., and elected officials. They were to devise new policies and practices for meeting the needs of at-risk youth while requiring accountability for positive outcomes.

The results of an evaluation of this program by the Center for the Study of Social Policy (1995) were disappointing. None of the sites achieved the stated objectives, and little change was seen in the four target problems. The researchers found that, "for the most part, the collaboratives were largely unable to define a comprehensive action plan that cut across multiple organizations. Instead, they reverted to what they knew best: funding discrete interventions" (p. xiii). They conclude, "Our collective rhetoric about cross-system change is far ahead of any operational knowledge about how to get there from here" (p. xiii).

It is not my purpose here to single out this well-intentioned program for criticism. Other community change initiatives have encountered serious difficulties as well, such as the Community Change for Youth Development program (Walker, Watson, & Jucovy, 1999). Many of the federal, foundation, and state initiatives aimed at preventing various childhood and adolescent problem behaviors that have been funded over the past two decades have had the same limitations as the New Futures Initiative.

OJJDP modeled the SafeFutures program after the Annie E. Casey Foundation's New Futures Initiative. This multisite program provided six sites with approximately $1.4 million per year for 5 years (the sites were in Boston, Massachusetts; Contra Costa County, California; Seattle, Washington; St. Louis, Missouri; Imperial County, California; and Fort Belknap in Harlem, Montana). The main goal of the program was to reduce youth violence and delinquency by improving service delivery systems and building on existing collaborative efforts (Morley, Rossman, Kopczynski, Buck, & Gouvis, 2000). A specific objective of the program was to help each community form a "continuum of care" in which prevention, intervention, and treatment services were well integrated. Unfortunately, OJJDP determined the discrete interventions to be implemented in advance of funding: mentoring, family strengthening, after-school activities, treatment alternatives for female offenders, mental health services, day treatment, and interventions for gang-involved youth. The program provided separate funding for these services.

Two years after the projects were funded, OJJDP encouraged the program sites to use the strategic planning process in the Comprehensive Strategy framework (see Chapter 12), but, at this point, the participating agencies were not interested in objective and systematic problem assessment and integration of services (Rossman, 2001). All of the SafeFutures sites fell far short of achieving the main goals of the program. Their refusal to use Comprehensive Strategy tools left them to their normal program-planning devices—determining priority problems without objective data and selecting popular rather than proven-effective programs to address them. The fact that OJJDP had presumed to identify the interventions the various sites would need even prior to funding them made matters worse. In the end, program sites did little more than fund discrete interventions.

As noted in Chapter 5, the local evaluators of the SafeFutures program, Professors Decker and Curry (2002), recommended to St. Louis officials the establishment of integrated programming for youths; the juvenile justice, social service, and community agencies refused, however. Decker and Curry's evaluation of the St. Louis project shows that, instead of a well-integrated web of interventions, the St. Louis SafeFutures site more closely resembled a series of unrelated services. The project was plagued by implementation problems, uneven matches between clients and services, the involved agencies' refusal to create a continuum of integrated services and sanctions, "program drift" away from established goals and objectives, organizational disorganization, and budgetary management problems. The greatest failure of the St. Louis SafeFutures program, however, may have been the unwillingness of the participating agencies to "share" clients across agencies.

Another limitation of collaborative efforts—and one that explains why they are not likely to result in comprehensive, integrated service delivery systems—is that they often do not use service delivery approaches that have been demonstrated to be essential for the development of truly comprehensive and integrated systems. However, some federal initiatives represent a move in this direction. In 1992, the U.S. Congress funded the Comprehensive Community Mental Health Services for Children and Their Families Program (information on this program is available at the Center for Mental Health Services Web site at www.mentalhealth.org/cmhs/ childrenscampaign). Congress appropriated $60 million in 1995 for grants under this program to improve the delivery of mental health services through "systems of care." The program supports 45 sites across the country in implementing, enhancing, and evaluating local systems of care. It is based on the recognition that the multiple problems associated with mental health problems and delinquency in children and adolescents are best addressed through a system of care approach, in which multiple service sectors work in an integrated manner (U.S. Department of Health and Human Services, 1999, pp. 190-193). Private foundations also have played a leadership role in this arena. Notably, the Robert Wood Johnson Foundation has funded the Children's Initiative in North Carolina, which is directed toward improving mental health service systems (Morrissey, Johnson, & Calloway, 1997).

In sum, the use of collaborative approaches in child and adolescent services has not produced impressive results (Burns et al., 2001; Lerman & Pottick, 1995; Nelson et al., 1996; Stouthamer-Loeber et al., 1995). As VanDenBerg (1999, pp. 1-2) has observed, in many communities it is as if the juvenile justice system and social services agencies are working in grain silos: They exist and function in the same vertical sphere, but they don't mix services even when the children and families they serve have needs that cut across the boundaries of service categories. Agencies tend to be protective of their budgets and clientele, and this works against the establishment of integrated service delivery (Morrissey et al., 1997). When the juvenile justice system, mental health services, social services, child welfare agencies, and education systems have the same child and family clients, they may be working at cross-purposes or duplicating services. In the remainder of this chapter, I review the developments in child and adolescent programming for seriously disturbed children and delinquents that have led to the more comprehensive, integrated systems of services that exist in some communities today.

Youth Services Bureaus

The first national effort to encourage comprehensive service delivery for children and adolescents in juvenile justice and other human services occurred in the 1960s. The President's Commission on Law Enforcement and Administration of Justice (1967) recommended that instead of handling minor offenders in the juvenile courts, communities should establish neighborhood youth-serving agencies, called Youth Services Bureaus (YSBs), which would be located in comprehensive neighborhood community centers. The YSBs would receive juveniles (delinquent and nondelinquent) referred by the police, the juvenile court, parents, schools, and other agencies. The YSBs would act as brokers of all community services for young people and would also fill service gaps, especially for less seriously delinquent juveniles. Congress placed federal responsibility for the YSBs in the new Youth

Development and Delinquency Prevention Administration (YDDPA) in the U.S. Department of Health, Education, and Welfare. In the early 1970s, Congress found that the YDDPA was a failure and created the Office of Juvenile Justice and Delinquency Prevention (OJJDP) in the U.S. Department of Justice. The Juvenile Justice and Delinquency Prevention Act of 1974 (P.L. 93-415) did not mandate further development of YSBs. Rather, it emphasized the coordination of all federal juvenile justice and delinquency prevention programs and the use of a joint funding mechanism to achieve more comprehensive local juvenile justice programming. A federal Coordinating Council was created to ensure federal collaboration. Although this mandate generated a number of jointly funded programs, none of these achieved the level of integration Congress had intended. However, the seeds were planted at OJJDP for development of a comprehensive, integrated approach that would be formulated some 20 years later. In the meantime, other important developments in the integration of service delivery occurred that contributed to its formulation.

System of Care

The system of care concept was developed in the early 1980s (Duchnowski & Kutash, 1996). A *system of care* came to be defined as "a comprehensive spectrum of mental health and other necessary services which are organized into a coordinated network to meet the multiple and changing needs of severely emotionally disturbed children and adolescents" (Stroul & Friedman, 1986, p. iv). This concept was stimulated by a study that exposed the lack of public responsibility for children in need of mental health services (Knitzer, 1982). This pioneering study led to the development of a 1984 initiative at the National Institute of Mental Health called the Child and Adolescent Service System Program (CASSP; Lourie & Katz-Leavy, 1987; Stroul & Friedman, 1988). The program's aims were to develop leadership in addressing the mental health service needs of adolescents and children, to establish mechanisms for interagency collaboration, to increase family participation at all levels of planning and treatment, and to develop a culturally competent system of care. As a result of the CASSP initiative, the public mental health system became oriented toward a holistic, child- and family-centered, and integrated approach (Duchnowski & Kutash, 1996).

The best-known multiagency system of care was established in 1984 in Ventura County, California: the Children's Demonstration Project. Created by the California State Legislature, this program implemented a community-based system of care that aimed to integrate four child-serving systems: juvenile justice, education, child welfare, and mental health. Although a rigorous evaluation of the project was never conducted, Goldman (1992) has reported that it produced numerous positive results, including reductions in the rates of admissions to state psychiatric hospitals, group home placement rates, reincarceration rates for juvenile offenders, and total days of incarceration.

In the next stage of development, CASSP stimulated the creation of a broader community-based system of care that integrated family services with child services. Stroul and Friedman (1986) identified six types of community-based services that should be integrated in a system of care framework: mental health, social, recreational, vocational, health, and educational. They emphasized, however, that the system of care concept represents more than a network of services; it also calls for child-centered and family-focused service systems. This philosophy spawned the Virginia Council on Community Services for Youth and Families, which applied the CASSP model at the local community level (MacBeth, 1993). A statewide model is now in place in Virginia, embodied in state legislation, the Community Services Act. It grew out of the CASSP philosophy, from one of its pilot projects in Norfolk (Lourie & Katz-Leavy, 1987; Stroul, 1996; Stroul & Friedman, 1986).

The early successes of the CASSP model later supported new federal legislation, the Comprehensive Community Mental Health and Services Act of 1992 (Duchnowski & Kutash, 1996), to develop the model further. Yet more progress was needed in the development of the system of care concept (Burns, 1991). Indeed, a 1993 study conducted by the National Mental Health Association was aptly titled *All Systems Failure* (Koyanagi & Gaines, 1993). This study brought home the reality that a comprehensive system of care was still far from a reality (Duchnowski & Kutash, 1996).

In perhaps the most rigorous test of a system of care model, the Continuum of Care Demonstration Project in Fort Bragg, North Carolina, was found to be ineffective in terms of individual-level mental health outcomes (Bickman, 1995; Bickman, Guthrie, & Foster, 1995). This project created a system of care, funded and operated by mental health agencies, that provided a package of nonresidential, innovative services and allocated them in a planned, coordinated manner using case managers. However, the Fort Bragg evaluation has been challenged on methodological grounds (Mordock, 1997; for a rejoinder, see Bickman et al., 1998) and regarding the interpretation of the results (Friedman & Burns,

1996). A subsequent evaluation of a similar program in Stark County, Ohio, produced similar results (U.S. Department of Health and Human Services, 1999, p. 193).

A main lesson learned from the Fort Bragg and Stark County system of care programs—both of which improved *access* to mental health services through better coordination—was that both systems of care lacked two important ingredients. First, these programs apparently did not improve the *quality* of mental health services delivered in the community (effective services are, of course, imperative). Second, although each program offered a continuum of program options, neither apparently *integrated* these options in a manner consistent with the principles of the wraparound model that was to follow. The organization of coordinated, collaborative services in a system of care, or in a continuum of care, does not guarantee that services will be effective. The organizers of systems of care need to pay attention to the effectiveness of the services delivered within these systems, not only to the organization of the systems themselves (U.S. Department of Health and Human Services, 1999, p. 193).

It is widely recognized that systems of care have not yet produced impressive results in terms of client rehabilitation (U.S. Department of Health and Human Services, 1999, 2001). However, studies to date have consistently shown improvements across a range of outcomes, such as reduced reliance on ineffective residential treatment, fewer arrests and better school grades, and improved mental health (U.S. Department of Health and Human Services, 1999, p. 191). Further evaluation of this model is needed. In particular, the relationship between changes at the system level and clinical outcomes is unclear. The Children's Services Program component of the Comprehensive Community Mental Health Services for Children and Their Families Program provides continued support for operation and evaluation of systems of care for emotionally disturbed children in 45 sites across the country (U.S. Department of Health and Human Services, 1999, p. 191). For program interventions to be effective, they need to (a) use principles of effective intervention, (b) be well matched to client treatment needs as determined by objective risk and needs assessments, and (c) employ "wraparound" principles.

Wraparound Philosophy

The next generation of comprehensive child and youth service programs was strengthened through the incorporation of the wraparound concept. As VanDenBerg (1999) notes, "As the national CASSP effort was beginning to take root as a systems change movement, the wraparound approach became a major underpinning of how to apply system of care principles to individual children and families" (p. 3). The term *wraparound* refers to a service delivery system that has as its main purpose the integration of service delivery for individual children and their families who require services from multiple service providers.

The wraparound philosophy appears to have been implemented independently in the United States and in Canada at about the same time—during the early 1980s. But development of the concept began earlier in the United States, pioneered by Dr. Lenore Behar, then chief of Child Mental Health Services in the North Carolina Department of Human Resources. It appears that she was the first to use the term *wraparound* (Behar, 1986).

A class action lawsuit filed against the state of North Carolina in October 1979 on behalf of Willie M. (a child) and three other children gave Behar the opportunity to implement the wraparound philosophy she had begun developing in the late 1970s (Soler & Warboys, 1990, p. 78). These children had a history of violent behavior and mental or emotional handicaps. The plaintiffs sought the right to receive treatment and educational services that had repeatedly been denied them, because no existing programs were designed to meet their needs. The innovative Willie M. Program, which Behar developed—now called the Special Populations Program—provides community-based treatment for children and adolescents with serious mental, neurological, or emotional disabilities, accompanied by violent or aggressive behavior (Behar, 1985). To be eligible for the program, clients must also be institutionalized or at risk of confinement. An independent committee reviews each case and determines eligibility.

Successful demonstration of this program model is due, in large part, to the "integrated system of services" approach Behar developed for the Willie M. Program. The model wraps individualized services around the adolescents and their families using a case manager approach, with services delivered mainly by local mental health service providers (see Box 11.1).

In the course of implementing this wraparound system, Behar quickly made three important discoveries. First, "a troubled child is a child needing an individualized treatment approach, regardless of the agency that last served him or her" (Behar, 1986, p. 19). Second, children who come into the Willie M. Program "usually do not require different services than those who come into [it] via special

---

Box 11.1

Philosophical Principles of the Willie M. Program

- A system of services ranging from highly restrictive settings to settings that approximate normal family living is needed to rehabilitate the youngsters eligible for the program.
- Children are best served close to their own communities, to maximize the possibility of family involvement and to allow for reintegration of each child into his or her natural environment.
- To deal effectively with these children, a full continuum of care must be in place; discrete components standing alone, whether of the more intensive or the less intensive variety, will fail.
- The system must provide for linkages among the various components within the system, as well as services from other child-caring systems.
- There must be flexibility in funding and decision making to allow the movement of children through the system as their needs change, and backup services and respite services must be available on a 24-hour basis.
- The management structure must be flexible, so that shifts can be made in funds and staff to allow for the movement of children, and there can be no admissions criteria delayed to program components.
- Individualized treatment and educational planning, with broadly defined case management as the backbone, is essential.

SOURCE: Behar (1986, p. 16).

---

education or mental health routes" (p. 19). And third, treatment plans developed within the context of a program are limited to what that particular program can provide. Thus for an individualized treatment plan to be effective, it must be developed outside of any one treatment or service program. Case management, Behar suggests, is "perhaps the most unifying factor in service delivery" (p. 19).

Even though the Willie M. Program has not been evaluated using an experimental research design, there is considerable evidence of its success (North Carolina Department of Health and Human Services, 2000; Weisz, Walter, Weiss, Fernandez, & Mikow, 1990). It has succeeded in moving violent and seriously emotionally disturbed youngsters to less restrictive residential settings, in reducing their violent and aggressive behavior, and in keeping them in school. It has also reduced arrests: One study found that two-thirds of the children who had been arrested prior to entering the program remained arrest-free, and four-fifths of the children who had not been arrested prior to entering the program remained arrest-free (North Carolina Department of Health and Human Services, 2000, p. 56). Thus the Willie M. Program provides a model for the successful delivery of a well-coordinated system of mental health care and other services for the treatment of extremely violent youths (Lewis, 1984; Weisz, Martin, Walter,

et al., 1991; Weisz et al., 1990). Moreover, this program appears to be most successful with violent children who have the worst problems: "These were the clients most likely to be hurting others or themselves, living in locked facilities, with no social support, failing at school, or getting into trouble with the law" (North Carolina Department of Health and Human Services, 2000, p. 48).

The wraparound approach also was pioneered in the early 1980s in Canada by John Brown, who developed the idea of placing children with emotional problems in small group homes with individualized care and flexible programming in lieu of confinement in large facilities or institutions (VanDenBerg, 1999). Brown's concepts were adapted by the founders of the Kaleidoscope Program in Bloomfield and Chicago, Illinois, and later in the Alaska Child and Adolescent Service System Program, and by others in Vermont, Washington State, and elsewhere (VanDenBerg, 1999).

Burns, Schoenwald, Burchard, Faw, and Santos (2000) describe the wraparound philosophy as "a philosophy of care that includes a definable planning process involving the child and family and results in a unique set of community services and natural supports that are individualized for the child and family to achieve a positive set of outcomes" (p. 295). The theoretical foundation of

---

Box 11.2

Ten Essential Elements of the Wraparound Process

- Wraparound efforts must be based in the community.
- Services and supports must be individualized and built on strengths, and they must meet the needs of children and families across the life domains in order to promote success, safety, and permanency in home, school, and community.
- The process must be culturally competent.
- Families must be full and active partners in every level of the wraparound process.
- The wraparound process must be team driven, involving the family, the child, natural supports, agencies, and community services working together to develop, implement, and evaluate the individualized service plan.
- Wraparound teams must use flexible approaches supported by adequate and flexible funding.
- The wraparound plan must include a balance of formal services and informal community and family resources.
- The service/support plan should be developed and implemented based on an interagency, community/neighborhood collaborative process.
- Outcomes must be determined and measured for each goal established with the child and family as well as for those goals established at the program and system levels.

SOURCE: Goldman (1999, p. 11). See also Burns and Goldman (1999); Burns, Hoagwood, and Mrazek (1999); Goldman and Faw (1999); and VanDenBerg and Grealish (1996).

---

this philosophy is found mainly in "environmental ecology" (Munger, 1998)—the notion that "a child will function best when the larger service system surrounding him/her coordinates most efficiently with the microsystem of his immediate home and family environment" (Burns et al., 2000, p. 296). Wraparound is, in other words, a developmental model. As Burns et al. note, the model includes "the assumption that effective wraparound programs change the surrounding environment of the child and thus foster lasting changes that occur in the individuals, families, and communities" (p. 296).

The wraparound philosophy embodies several important treatment values that underscore this theory of change. These include parental and child involvement in determining needed services; service provider compassion for children and families; integration of services and delivery systems; flexibility in the funding and provision of services; safety, success, and permanence in home, school, and the community; unconditional care that is individualized, strengths based, family and community centered, and culturally competent; and the provision of services close to home and in natural environmental settings (Burns et al., 2000, p. 297).

Wraparound also has legal roots (VanDenBerg, 1999, p. 2). In addition to the Willie M. litigation, a Massachusetts court decision (*Brewster v. Dukakis,*

C.A. No 76-4423-F, E.D. Mass. December 16, 1978) encouraged client involvement in the planning and implementation of services. Further, the principle of delivering services "in the least restrictive setting appropriate for the child's specific needs" is well established in case law (see VanDenBerg, 1999).

Wraparound also is grounded in the core treatment values of the system of care model developed and later revised by Stroul and Friedman (1986):

- The system of care should be child centered and family focused, with the needs of the child and family dictating the types and mix of services provided.
- The system of care should be community based, with the locus of services as well as management and decision-making responsibility resting at the community level.
- The system of care should be culturally competent, with agencies, programs, and services that are responsive to the cultural, racial, and ethnic differences of the populations they serve.

Box 11.2 lists 10 essential elements of the wraparound process that have been identified by proponents of this model; these elements are based on the core treatment values listed above.

By 1995, the number of sites using variations of the wraparound process was growing "by leaps and bounds" (VanDenBerg, 1999, p. 5), spurred by demonstration grants provided by the federal Center for Mental Health Services. In a 1998 survey, Faw (1999) found that wraparound programs were in existence in 47 of the 55 U.S. states and territories.

Juvenile or Community Assessment Centers

The first "juvenile assessment center" (JAC) opened in Hillsborough County, Florida, in 1993 (Dembo & Rivers, 1996). It was created in response to the recognized need for centralized intake of arrested juveniles, whose numbers were rapidly growing in Florida, and to increase collaboration among agencies involved in working with these clients. The Hillsborough County JAC was designed for initial treatment of drug-using arrested juveniles. The basic elements and functions of the model include the following:

- Centralized location of relevant agencies serving at-risk youths and their families; screening, diagnosis, and, if indicated, linkage of arrested and other high-risk juveniles with community-based service providers
- Case management of juveniles assigned to justice system diversion programs
- Tracking of arrested juveniles (usually limited to the determination of referral disposition)

Dembo and Rivers (1996) have reported that there is evidence that the Hillsborough JAC "increased coordination among various stakeholder agencies, and resulted in improved efficiency in the processing of arrested youths" (pp. 142-143). The success of the Hillsborough JAC prompted the development of similar centers in many other communities in Florida and elsewhere (Oldenettel & Wordes, 2000; Rivers & Anwyl, 2000; Rivers, Dembo, & Anwyl, 1998). Dembo and Rivers suggest that the next step is to expand the JAC model to create a juvenile health services center that "would more creatively identify and effectively respond to the multiple problems of high-risk youth and their families and would more efficiently coordinate and integrate substance abuse, other mental health, medical and social services" (p. 143). Indeed, this appears to be happening in the development of what is called the *community assessment center* (CAC) model, in which several kinds of agencies are linked, including law enforcement, juvenile justice, mental health, and child welfare agencies (Oldenettel & Wordes, 2000, p. 5). Box 11.3 lists some of the typical functions of existing CACs.

Most large communities could benefit from having a 24-hour centralized point of intake and assessment for juveniles who have come into contact, or are likely to come into contact, with the juvenile justice system. All communities need better integration of prevention and early intervention activities with local police, social services, child welfare, school, and family preservation programs. As Oldenettel and Wordes (2000) explain: "By providing a single point of entry, a CAC can reduce duplication of services, promote system efficiency, and facilitate access to services for youth and families. The CAC's one-stop shop could better serve youth and families by eliminating the systems' current maze of caseworkers and improving system efficiency" (p. 4).

It may not be practical for some communities, particularly smaller ones, to maintain a single physical point of entry for assessments and intakes to various agencies, but these communities may be able to establish a "virtual" single point of entry through coordinated assessment and referral activities. Procedures and policies can ensure that all youth receive the same assessment and case management protocols from the same or different agencies at several locations. Information gathered by one service provider would be shared with other service providers via an integrated management information system. In addition, consistent assessment and case management services would be provided to youth, but could be conducted by the same or a different agency (Oldenettel & Wordes, 2000, p. 4).

A number of observers have raised some important concerns regarding the operations of CACs, especially regarding such issues as due process, "net widening," stigmatizing of youth, and overrepresentation of minorities (Oldenettel & Wordes, 2000, pp. 10-11; Puritz, Burrell, Schwartz, Soler, & Warboys, 1995). In addition, CACs could become "dumping grounds" for law enforcement—that is, police might take youths who ordinarily would not be arrested to the centers unjustifiably. If these issues can be resolved satisfactorily, the CAC mechanism seems to hold a great deal of potential as an initial entry point to the juvenile justice system and to other affiliated agencies. CACs should be capable of conducting comprehensive risk and needs assessments—or at least initial screening for risk and treatment needs—and could possibly begin the process of developing comprehensive treatment plans that need to involve multiple agencies in

Box 11.3

Common Community Assessment Center Functions

Most of the community assessment centers currently operating aim to perform rather limited functions, including the following:

- Reduce the law enforcement time devoted to juveniles by creating a central booking and receiving facility specifically for juvenile offenders
- Provide a single point of entry for the assessment and referral of juveniles
- Provide a facility to hold dependency juveniles awaiting placement
- Conduct comprehensive risk and needs assessments immediately
- Expedite the processing of juveniles through the system
- Expedite court proceedings by providing needed information to defense attorneys and prosecutors
- Provide referrals for parents and children
- Accelerate juveniles' access to treatment
- Pool resources from different agencies
- Provide early intervention services for troubled juveniles and problem families
- Facilitate cooperation and communication among agencies
- Streamline the current fragmented service delivery system

SOURCE: Oldenettel and Wordes (2000).

addressing the multiple problems of juvenile offenders. It remains to be seen whether the CAC model can be implemented effectively. The National Council on Crime and Delinquency is currently conducting an evaluation.

In an innovative implementation of the assessment center concept, the Norfolk, Virginia, Community Services Board (a mental health agency) created the school-based Norfolk Assessment Center to identify and assess children and youth at risk for delinquent behavior. The center is staffed by several agencies, including the Community Services Board, public schools, the court services unit, the Department of Human Services, and the Boys and Girls Club. Each of these agencies makes referrals of at-risk youths—youths who are experiencing mild to moderate emotional and/or behavioral difficulties—to the center. Each referred youth first receives a comprehensive mental health assessment, after which center personnel develop an individual service plan for the youth to address his or her needs in the areas of mental health, substance abuse, medical attention, education, human services, court services, recreation, and employment. The center also provides follow-up and case management services for the youth and family. The case managers facilitate interagency service delivery, empower clients, offer emotional support, arrange appointments, monitor

compliance, make home/school visits, and perform other needed services. An evaluation has shown the effectiveness of the Norfolk Assessment Center in terms of recidivism reduction (Pindur & Elliker, 1999). This is an effective mechanism for linking at-risk children and adolescents with comprehensive services.

Wraparound Service Delivery Versus the Multisystemic Therapy Treatment Model

As noted, above, the term *wraparound* is commonly used to refer to a unique method of service delivery; wraparound is not a treatment method. Burns and colleagues (2000) compare and contrast the wraparound process with the best-known home-based treatment modality—Multisystemic Therapy (MST)—in considerable detail in an article devoted exclusively to this objective. The following summary of their excellent review of the two models illustrates the similarities and differences between the two concepts (see Table 11.1).

Before I comment on this comparison, I need to provide a brief introduction to the MST intervention. Developed by Henggeler and colleagues, MST

TABLE 11.1   Comparison of Multisystemic Therapy and the Wraparound Process

Category	Multisystemic Therapy	Wraparound
Theory	Social ecology and systems theory	Environmental ecology
Approach to treatment	Clinical treatment in home; families seldom linked to existing services	Plan and coordinate treatment and services provided by community organizations
Major treatment modalities	Behavioral, cognitive-behavioral, and pragmatic family therapy	Not specified (varies with availability in the community)
Treatment site	Home primarily, school, peers, neighborhood, community	Clinic, home, school, community
Value placed on individualized care, family participation, and cultural competence	Important	Important
Clinical staff:client ratio	1:4-6	1:6
Duration of intervention	3 to 5 months in most cases	Long-term, no limit
Availability of services	24 hours/7 days a week	24 hours/7 days a week
Frequency of family contact	Daily or less often	Weekly or less often
Flexible funds	Occasionally	Yes
Team leader qualifications	Usually a master's-level clinician	Usually a bachelor's degree for resource coordinators
Responsibility for outcomes	Clinician	Shared by team, including family and child
Expectations of outcomes	Rapid behavioral change in the child, family, school, peers, and neighborhood	Gradual change in child, family, and community to facilitate adjustment and reduce risk of placement
Training	One week, weekly on-site supervision, phone consultation, and quarterly booster sessions	Workshops by national leaders and local follow-up
Training materials	Comprehensive manual	Introductory manual and videotapes
Fidelity monitoring	Adolescent, parent, clinician self-report; factor scores correlated with outcomes	An observation form with interrater reliability
Research base by design	Randomized trials: 7 Quasi-experimental: 1 Pre-post: 1	Randomized trials: 2 Quasi-experimental: 1 Pre-post: 9 Case studies: 2

SOURCE: "Comprehensive Community-Based Interventions for Youth With Severe Emotional Disorders: Multisystemic Therapy and the Wraparound Process," by B. J. Burns, S. K. Schoenwald, J. D. Burchard, L. Faw, and A. B. Santos, 2000, *Journal of Child and Family Studies, 9,* p. 306. © 2000 by Human Sciences Press, Inc. Reprinted with permission.

views each youth as being nested within a complex of interconnected systems that encompass individual, family, and extrafamilial (peer, school, neighborhood) factors (see Henggeler, 1997b, 1999; Henggeler, Melton, & Smith, 1992; Henggeler et al., 1998). Behavior problems can be maintained by problematic transactions within or between any one or a combination of these systems. MST targets the specific factors in each youth's and family's ecology (family, peer, school, neighborhood, support network) that are contributing to antisocial behavior. MST interventions are pragmatic and goal oriented, and they emphasize the development of family strengths. The overriding purpose of MST is to help parents to deal effectively with their child's behavior problems, including disengagement from deviant peers and poor school performance. To accomplish the goal of family empowerment, MST also addresses identified barriers to effective parenting (e.g., parental drug abuse, parental mental health problems) and helps family members to build an indigenous social support network (e.g., with friends, extended family, neighbors, fellow church members). MST is typically provided in the home by a master's degree–level counselor who carries a low caseload and is available 24 hours a day, 7 days a week. The average duration of treatment is about 4 months, which includes approximately 50 hours of face-to-face therapist-family contact.

MST incorporates the following nine treatment principles, several of which evidence wraparound philosophy (particularly Principles 7-9):

Principle 1: The primary purpose of assessment is to understand the fit between the problems identified and their broader systemic context.

Principle 2: Therapeutic contacts emphasize the positive and use systemic strengths as levers for change.

Principle 3: Interventions are designed to promote responsible behavior and decrease irresponsible behavior among family members.

Principle 4: Interventions are present focused and action oriented, targeting specific and well-defined problems.

Principle 5: Interventions target sequences of behavior within and between multiple systems that maintain the identified problems.

Principle 6: Interventions are developmentally appropriate and fit the developmental needs of the youth.

Principle 7: Interventions are designed to require daily or weekly effort by family members.

Principle 8: Intervention effectiveness is evaluated continuously from multiple perspectives, with providers assuming accountability for overcoming barriers to successful outcomes.

Principle 9: Interventions are designed to promote treatment generalization and long-term maintenance of therapeutic change by empowering

caregivers to address family members' needs across multiple systemic contexts.

Thus MST is a child- and family-centered intervention in which treatment is individualized and delivered within a family preservation model of service delivery (Sondheimer, Schoenwald, & Rowland, 1994). Indeed, a major goal of the MST treatment approach is to empower the family to implement cognitive-behavioral training of the child or adolescent. This treatment is provided mainly in the home and in other natural environments, using a strengths-based approach, wrapping other community supports and services around the child and family.

Burns and colleagues (2000) note a number of similarities between the wraparound process and MST. The main goal of both interventions is to keep youths in their home communities and with their biological families whenever possible. Both MST and wraparound require a shift in the role of families in the intervention process toward greater participation—in terms of "access, voice, and choice" (Burns & Goldman, 1999). Both are individualized, community-based interventions that target seriously emotionally disturbed youth and their families. Both MST and wraparound employ a team approach— MST uses a clinician and a supervisor, whereas wraparound uses multiple agency providers and community supports. Both interventions draw upon resources from the surrounding environment for each family they serve. Natural support groups (neighbors, teachers, church members, extended family members) are tapped in both interventions to maintain emphasis on the natural environment of the child and family in the treatment process. Both employ strengths-based service plans; indeed, families are seen as full collaborators in both interventions. The goals of the treatment plan are driven by the input of family members, and family members are actively involved in the treatment process—to avoid isolating the youth for treatment. Both interventions make every effort to avoid blaming parents. Instead, they focus on the parents' strengths—and build on those strengths in the intervention work—while involving the parents in the process of altering the environment around the family and child.

Despite all these similarities, there are also important differences between the wraparound process and MST (see Table 11.1). For example, although the main goal of both interventions is to keep youths in their home communities, this is accomplished in different ways. As Burns et al. (2000) observe: "The major difference between the two interventions is the approach to service provision. MST primarily provides direct treatment, utilizing ancillary services as required, whereas wraparound is oriented towards coordinating (and creating if necessary) a range of professional services and community supports" (p. 307). Wraparound programs are organized to integrate the services of multiple child and adolescent service agencies in the community. In MST, a team made up of three to four clinicians and a clinical supervisor develops and coordinates the treatment plan, which is carried out by a therapist (clinician) in collaboration with the young client's parents. In wraparound, a larger team—consisting of agency professionals—develops the treatment plan, guided by a resource coordinator; therapeutic services are then provided by a therapist, who ordinarily is a member of the wraparound team.

The community relationships of these models also differ (Burns et al., 2000). Wraparound intervenes at the community level. The concept of wraparound services arose from a need to decrease the fragmentation of child and family services for children in the mental health, education, juvenile justice, and child welfare sectors—mainly in the area of institutionalized care for seriously emotionally disturbed youth. MST arose from a recognition of the failure of institution-based treatment, thus it intervenes at the family level to alter the child's behavior and interactions among multiple systems—the family and the child's peer group, school, and neighborhood. It is based on the findings of risk factor research, which show that the major causes and correlates of adolescent behavior problems reside in these domains. The MST intervention is grounded in a clinical team's assessment of problem areas. Thus MST focuses on changing the functioning of the child in the family and in other social systems, whereas wraparound focuses on changing the community as a means of improving the functioning of the child and family. The MST therapist helps parents to implement interventions that are designed to achieve the objectives of the comprehensive treatment plan (see Chapter 13 for more details). The MST intervention period is short—typically 3-5 months. Wraparound has set no time period. It takes much longer to change the structure and operation of services in a community than it takes to change the functioning of the child in the family, school, peer group, and community.

Effectiveness of Wraparound and MST

Studies of programs employing the wraparound model show considerable evidence of success. Burns, Goldman, Faw, and Burchard (1999, pp. 79-81) report on studies conducted in nine states: Alaska, Vermont (three programs), Kentucky, Maryland (two programs), Illinois (three programs), Wisconsin (Wraparound Milwaukee), Indiana (the Dawn Project), New York, and Florida. In addition, a Virginia wraparound model, the Norfolk Interagency Consortium, has shown positive results (Pindur & Elliker, 1999; Wilt, 1996). Further evaluations of programs based on wraparound models are needed, using experimental research designs. As noted in Chapter 10, MST has been rigorously evaluated, and programs using MST have shown the highest level of cost-effectiveness among all evaluated juvenile offender rehabilitation programs—representing a cost savings to taxpayers of more than $31,000 per program participant (Aos, Phipps, Barnoski, & Lieb, 2001).

Applications of Wraparound and MST

Most wraparound initiatives have focused on children with serious emotional and behavioral problems who are at risk of out-of-home placement; however, wraparound is also being used as an early intervention model with children at risk of involvement in delinquency and other problem behaviors. The wraparound concept is also being employed in programs aimed at youths on probation and incarcerated youths.

Wraparound Milwaukee is an effective wraparound service delivery program that integrates the mental health, juvenile justice, and other systems to address the mental health needs of juvenile justice system clientele and parental problems at the same time (Burns, Goldman, et al., 1999; Kamradt, 2000). It began by successfully providing services to youth and their families in the mental health system. Now, it is a county-operated collaborative that provides comprehensive care to youth referred from both the child welfare and juvenile justice systems and their families (Kamradt, 2000; see also Goldman & Faw, 1999). Wraparound Milwaukee serves as the hub of a comprehensive system linking several human service agencies, thus forming a managed-care continuum of treatment options.

The program components deemed essential to the success of the Wraparound Milwaukee program are as follows (Kamradt, 2000, pp. 17-18):

- Care coordination (the "cornerstone" of the system)
- The child and family team (wraparound plans are family driven)
- The Mobile Urgent Treatment Team (a mobile crisis team that is available to meet

the needs of youth and families when a care coordinator might not be available)

- The provider network (consisting of more than 170 agencies that respond to the multiple needs of youth and families)
- Blended funding (to break down barriers to service delivery that can arise when multiple agencies are involved)

The use of blended funding has been particularly important to the success of the Wraparound Milwaukee program (Kamradt, 2000). The project is sustained by pooled funds that come from the system partners in this integrated, multiservice approach to meeting the needs of youth and their families. The fact that the involved agencies share the expenses of the program helps enormously to break down barriers to system integration. The program receives a flat monthly fee for each client and must pay for all treatment services, including incarceration and residential care. In 1999 the program received more than $26 million in pooled funds. After all funds are pooled and decategorized, the program can use them to cover any services that families need, in a mix of formal and informal services. This approach helps ensure that the most appropriate services are purchased. Project staff thus have an incentive to keep as many youth as possible in their homes.

The Dawn Project in Indianapolis is an excellent example of a wraparound program that links the juvenile justice system with other agencies (Burns, Goldman, et al., 1999, pp. 91-92). This ongoing project, an interagency consortium, is outcomes driven and based mainly on family, functional, and fiscal incentives. Participants are required to be county residents between 5 and 18 years of age (most clients to date are ages 11-14). They also must qualify for the services of two or more consortium members (such as child welfare, mental health, social services, and juvenile justice), be at risk of separation (or already separated) from their families, have a mental health problem diagnosis, and have functional impairment in at least two of four specified areas (self-care, interpersonal relationships, emotional, and self-direction). At program intake, each participant family is assigned a service coordinator who leads the treatment planning team. Services include therapeutic mentoring, recreation mentoring, and parent mentors. A special feature of the Dawn Project is a crisis support component called Youth Emergency Service (YES), which consists of a team made up of one case manager from child protective services and one YES counselor who provide mobile, community-based services and crisis support around the clock. Positive outcomes to date from an ongoing evaluation of the Dawn Project include improved mental health, reduced placement in residential treatment facilities, and lower individual service costs (Burns, Goldman, et al., 1999).

The wraparound process has also been applied to a juvenile probation population. The 8% Early Intervention Program in Orange County, California, provides wraparound services, linked with a continuum of sanctions, for this small proportion of potentially serious and chronic juvenile offenders. The program employs an approach that combines the wraparound service delivery model with family-centered treatment. This combination is implemented mainly in the Repeat Offender Prevention Program (ROPP) component of the 8% Early Intervention Program continuum (see Chapter 13 for descriptions of the continuum components). The treatment intervention is much like MST, in that family-centered cognitive-behavioral therapy is employed in working with ROPP clients, parents, and siblings in Youth and Family Resource Centers (Schumacher & Kurz, 2000). In the wraparound process, staff members from participating agencies—including education, mental health, social services, drug/alcohol abuse, employment, and health care—work as a team at these centers to assess the problems of each high-risk youth and implement a comprehensive treatment plan.

The wraparound approach for ROPP clients also envelops parents and siblings. The action plan for parents focuses mainly on family strengthening, by reducing or eliminating problems that impede parents' ability to provide adequate supervision and control. This may include addressing such issues as parental criminal involvement, potential family violence, and sources of family stress—substance abuse, unemployment, illness, marital discord, and other factors. The action plan for siblings typically focuses on health, mental health, and education deficits. Preliminary evaluation results of this wraparound model are positive.

Virginia's Norfolk Interagency Consortium (NIC) targets institutionalized youths and those at risk of placement in residential facilities. As noted earlier, it grew out of a pilot CASSP project, thus it embraces the wraparound philosophy. Formation of the Norfolk NIC was given impetus when a juvenile court judge became frustrated by a case in which the same social service and juvenile justice agency representatives reappeared before him several times with the same youngster, who evidenced growing problems. The judge ordered the agency representatives to go away, conduct a comprehensive assessment of the child's and family's treatment needs, and not return to court until they had developed a comprehensive treatment plan, or else he would find them in contempt of court. Of course, the agency representatives acted on the judge's order; in doing so, they found the approach rewarding, and they have gone on to make it common practice in Norfolk.

The NIC uses a wraparound process to ensure that clients have access to services. Community Assessment Teams make comprehensive risk-needs assessments of youths (and their families) at risk of residential placement. These are interagency teams of juvenile justice, public health, mental health, social services, child welfare, education, parent, and private provider representatives. The result of each assessment is a long-term treatment plan (supported by nine combined funding streams); as treatment progresses, it is monitored by the Community Assessment Team (Wilt, 1996). Two factors contribute greatly to the success of this wraparound model. First, the initial risk-needs assessment is very comprehensive and thorough, owing to the fact that the joint nature of the assessment team brings into consideration all information on each referred youth that exists in various agency files. Second, pooled funding streams facilitate a seamless continuum of wraparound services for the youths and their families. These policies help greatly to break down the barriers between agencies and serve to reduce individual agencies' urges to protect their turf. A process evaluation concluded that the NIC is effective in its collaboration and in providing comprehensive, community-centered treatment (Wilt, 1996), and another study suggests that the NIC process reduces recidivism (Pindur & Elliker, 1999). One indication of the success of the Norfolk model is that in its first 3 years of operation, the number of youths in Virginia state psychiatric facilities was reduced from 70 to just 2 (Pratt, 1994). Youths who might otherwise have been placed in these facilities were instead provided family- and community-based mental health services combined with other treatment interventions.

The Indianapolis interagency consortium (the Dawn Project) and the Norfolk Interagency Consortium provide two models of the wraparound process that other communities can easily replicate. In the Dawn Project, youths must qualify for the services of two or more consortium members (such as child welfare, mental health, social services, and juvenile justice). This kind of requirement is implicit in the NIC as well. The main difference between these two programs is that the latter limits services to youths who are manifestly at risk of placement or

are already in residential facilities. Either program, however, could accommodate the other's scope and objectives. The Dawn Project was created with early intervention objectives in mind, whereas the Norfolk Interagency Consortium's creators aimed to provide community-based mental health treatment for youths in long-term psychiatric facilities.

Integration of Wraparound in a System of Care

The next step in implementing comprehensive service delivery is to integrate services in a continuum of treatment options. A major purpose of the Comprehensive Strategy framework is to integrate treatment services for juvenile offenders that are provided in the juvenile justice system and by various social service agencies (Wilson & Howell, 1993). The wraparound service delivery model is ideal for integrating the services that make up the continuum of care that the Comprehensive Strategy guides communities to develop.

As Burns and colleagues (2000) suggest, communities are likely to be more successful at rehabilitating juvenile offenders and reducing other problem behaviors of youths, including serious emotional problems and mental illness, if they integrate the wraparound process with effective, evidence-based treatment service delivery, such as MST. This would enable communities to decrease their reliance on ineffective institution-based service delivery in favor of community-based and family-centered treatment, using the wraparound process, and increase the effectiveness of rehabilitation efforts, using effective service components. A number of different interventions have been shown to be effective for youths with mental disorders (Burns, Hoagwood, & Mrazek, 1999). Certain other service components have proved to be effective treatments for juvenile offenders (Lipsey, Howell, & Tidd, 2002).

As noted earlier in this chapter, North Carolina has pioneered the development of the system of care concept, beginning with the initiation of the wraparound concept in the Willie M. Program in the early 1980s. A number of CASSP and Center for Mental Health Services projects have been implemented in the state since then that have contributed to further development of a system of care in the state. This work recently culminated in the establishment of the North Carolina Collaborative System of Care, a system designed to provide services to children and adolescents with a wide range of problems (see Box 11.4). It is based on a core set of values that embrace the wraparound philosophy:

Box 11.4
North Carolina Collaborative System of Care

The North Carolina Collaborative System of Care consists of three levels: a State Collaborative, Community Collaboratives, and Child and Family Teams. The Child and Family Teams work at the point of service, led by a case manager. Teams of agency representatives and other supporters provide wraparound services. Community Collaboratives build community resources for comprehensive care and ensure that local public, private, and community decision makers work together as a team to ensure the success of the Child and Family Teams. These collaboratives also identify service gaps and troubleshoot service access problems. Finally, the State Collaborative brings state agency decision makers together as a team to promote or develop policies that support local community collaboratives and the Child and Family Teams.

SOURCE: North Carolina Division of Mental Health, Developmental Disabilities and Substance Abuse Services (2000).

- The system is family centered and inclusive of family members. It recognizes and respects the family as the single greatest influence on their children, and that parents are the constant, guiding relationship, and the experts on their children, their culture, and their strengths and needs.
- The system is strengths based, building on the unique strengths of each child and family, and their neighborhood and community, to achieve success.
- The system is culturally competent, recognizing that each child and family is unique in experiences, preferences, strengths, and needs.
- The system is holistic, recognizing that formal agency services and informal neighborhood and community resources must unify their efforts on behalf of children and families—that is, one family, one team, one intervention plan, with individualized services supported by "braided funding and blended services."

Each eligible child and family in this system of care has an individualized Child and Family Team that is responsible for the planning and delivery of services that are appropriate to meet their unique needs. In 2001, the North Carolina legislature funded the Comprehensive Treatment Services Program (CTSP), which makes a wide array of community-based, outpatient, and other services readily available through the Collaborative System of Care for participating children and families (North Carolina Department of Health and Human

Services, 2002). More than 3,500 children were served in the first year of the program. Preliminary assessments indicate that a number of positive outcomes for children and families have resulted from the CTSP services delivered in the new Collaborative System of Care. Further progress remains to be seen. This is an enormous (statewide) undertaking—the first of its kind—in a state that is somewhat large, consisting of 100 counties.

Summary

The fragmentation of public sector services for problem children and adolescents is a common problem that speaks to the failure of the agencies providing these services to address effectively the multiple problems of youths. Integration of the necessary services is problematic because both public and private agencies are overly reliant on residential care. Dr. David Roush's (1996b) observation bears repeating: "They are too crisis-oriented, too rigid in their classification of problems, too specialized, too isolated from other services, too inflexible to craft comprehensive solutions, too insufficiently funded, and they are mismanaged" (p. 29).

There is an important lesson to be learned about the limitations of collaboration efforts to solve these problems. The collaboration models reviewed at the beginning of this chapter are very limited in their capacity to build bridges to connect the human service agency silos. The state of the art of child and adolescent service delivery has moved beyond simple collaboration or partnering. Collaboration is but the first step in the attempt to design comprehensive, integrated systems to deliver services for children and families. A collaborative or cooperative process is necessary to bring agencies, family representatives, and other community stakeholders together to begin developing a comprehensive, integrated system that addresses child and adolescent problem behaviors, but integration of the programs and services offered by various agencies is a different matter.

The integration of services into what might be called a seamless continuum is a major goal of the Comprehensive Strategy for Serious, Violent, and Chronic Juvenile Offenders (Wilson & Howell, 1993). Such integration would mean that youths and their families would not be bounced around from one agency to another to receive services. Uninterrupted services would be provided simultaneously by participating agencies, as appropriate. In a seamless system of services, a child or family may be unaware of organizational distinctions in the referral path (Morrissey et al., 1997). The service delivery agencies would be linked together through individual comprehensive prevention or treatment plans based on comprehensive assessments of risk factors and treatment needs. Several studies have shown the effectiveness of such an integrated approach, in Norfolk, Virginia (Wilt, 1996); Orange County, California (Schumacher & Kurz, 2000); and San Diego, California (Burke & Pennell, 2001).

Programs should be linked with the juvenile justice system, so that sanctions can be combined with effective programs for delinquents, thereby diminishing the likelihood of continuing delinquency in the adolescent years and criminal involvement into adulthood. Networked and integrated service delivery is essential for child delinquents who are at risk of becoming chronic, serious, violent delinquents, because children with serious emotional disturbances need multiple services simultaneously, in a continuum of accessible services. Such a system needs to have multiple screening and multiple entry points for services (Howell, 2001a; Loeber, Dishion, & Patterson, 1984). Community assessment centers could serve as central intake points. These centers could perform initial screening for risk and needed services, make referrals to appropriate agencies for more in-depth assessment, and expedite emergency services. For maximum effectiveness, CACs should create continuums of program options while integrating and coordinating the many agencies and organizations that typically intervene, at one time or another, with troubled families that produce child delinquents.

The Comprehensive Strategy framework facilitates development of an integrated seamless continuum of services. To help form such a continuum, a Community Planning Team, with outside technical assistance and training, can develop a long-term strategic plan. To implement the plan, the Community Planning Team would negotiate an Interagency Teamwork Protocol for information exchange and cross-agency client referrals—which is critical to integrated services (Rivard, Johnsen, Morrissey, & Starrett, 1999)—and build an infrastructure to support the continuum. An effective infrastructure might consist of three levels, as in the case of the North Carolina Collaborative System of Care (see Box 11.4): Child and Family Treatment Teams (led by case managers), a Community Collaborative (or an Interagency Council), and, ideally, a State Collaborative. Such an infrastructure ensures that the door through which clients enter the service delivery system does not limit service access.

Even this ideal kind of system will not necessarily solve the problem of ensuring parents and troubled youngsters immediate access to services. Lerman and Pottick (1995) make several recommendations for improving the responsiveness of agency systems, helping parents to become more effective help seekers, and encouraging youths to become their own help seekers. Much work remains to be done in these areas. Little is known about help seeking. Facilitating immediate service access would help greatly to intervene early in problem behaviors, when treatment is likely to be more effective and less costly.

Discussion Questions

1. Why have simple collaboration initiatives failed? Give examples.

2. Compare and contrast collaborative and integrated services.

3. What are some key features of the wraparound process?

4. What are some important differences between MST services and the wraparound process?

5. Describe some examples of successful wraparound implementation.

12

■

THE COMPREHENSIVE
STRATEGY FRAMEWORK

In this chapter, I describe the structure and operational tools of the Comprehensive Strategy for Serious, Violent, and Chronic Juvenile Offenders (shown in Figure III.1). Resources for implementing the Comprehensive Strategy are listed in Box 12.1. In the pages that follow, I explain the general principles of the Comprehensive Strategy, its theoretical foundations, and tools that are used in its implementation. I use the case of North Carolina to illustrate how these tools can be used to build a comprehensive plan. I do not discuss any particular prevention or rehabilitation programs in this chapter; I reserve that discussion for Chapter 13, in which I address implementation of the Comprehensive Strategy. In this chapter, I highlight juvenile justice system structures to clarify the key features of the Comprehensive Strategy framework.

General Principles of
the Comprehensive Strategy

The Comprehensive Strategy calls for a proactive and balanced approach that integrates prevention and control. It is based on the following five general principles:

- We must strengthen the family in its primary responsibility to instill moral values and provide guidance and support to children. Where there is no functional family unit, we must establish a family surrogate and assist that entity to guide and nurture the child.

- We must support "core" social institutions such as schools, religious institutions, and community organizations in their roles of developing capable, mature, and responsible youth. A goal of each of these societal institutions should be to ensure that children have the opportunity and support to mature into productive, law-abiding citizens. In a nurturing community environment, core social institutions are actively involved in the lives of youth.

- We must promote delinquency prevention as the most cost-effective approach to reducing juvenile delinquency. Families, schools, religious institutions, and community organizations, including citizen volunteers and the private sector, must be enlisted in the nation's delinquency prevention efforts. These core socializing institutions must be strengthened and assisted in their efforts to ensure that children have the opportunity to become capable and responsible citizens. When children engage in acting-out behavior, such as status offenses, the family and community, in concert with child welfare agencies, must respond with appropriate treatment and support services. Communities must take the lead in designing and building comprehensive prevention approaches that address known risk factors and target other youth at risk of delinquency.

- We must intervene immediately and effectively when delinquent behavior occurs to

---

Box 12.1

Resources for Implementing the Comprehensive Strategy

The original published version of the Comprehensive Strategy for Serious, Violent, and Chronic Juvenile Offenders (Wilson & Howell, 1993, pp. 9-24) is but 16 pages in length. It is reprinted in *Guide for Implementing the Comprehensive Strategy for Serious, Violent, and Chronic Juvenile Offenders* (Howell, 1995, pp. 7-15), which is available online at www.ncjrs.org/pdffiles/guide.pdf.

Three books have been published on the Comprehensive Strategy. The *Guide* (Howell, 1995) summarizes the first book:

J. C. Howell, B. Krisberg, J. D. Hawkins, and J. J. Wilson (Eds.). (1995). *A Sourcebook: Serious, Violent, and Chronic Juvenile Offenders*. Thousand Oaks, CA: Sage.

This is the academic version of the national review of prevention and juvenile rehabilitation programs for juvenile delinquency that are summarized in the *Guide*.

The second book was published in 1998:

R. Loeber and D. P. Farrington (Eds.). (1998). *Serious and Violent Juvenile Offenders: Risk Factors and Successful Interventions*. Thousand Oaks, CA: Sage.

This book contains the results of the work conducted by the OJJDP Study Group on Serious and Violent Juvenile Offenders, a detailed assessment of research-based knowledge about and programs for serious and violent offenders. The chapters in this volume update the national assessment of promising and effective programs for juvenile offenders that was published in the 1995 *Guide* and in the *Sourcebook* (Howell et al., 1995). This study group report presents the results of a thorough review of effective rehabilitation programs specifically for serious and violent offenders; in conducting this review, the researchers applied more rigorous scientific standards than had been used in the past.

Two published works summarize the findings that appear in the study group book:

*E. Rumsey, C. A. Kerr, and B. Allen-Hagen (1998). *Serious and Violent Juvenile Offenders* (Juvenile Justice Bulletin). Washington, DC: Office of Juvenile Justice and Delinquency Prevention.

R. Loeber and D. P. Farrington (1998). "Never Too Early, Never Too Late: Risk Factors and Successful Interventions With Serious and Violent Juvenile Offenders." *Studies on Crime and Crime Prevention* (published by the Swedish National Council for Crime Prevention), *7*, 7-30.

Several OJJDP Juvenile Justice Bulletins have been devoted to specific chapters in the study group volume:

*R. F. Catalano, R. Loeber, and K. McKinney (1999). *School and Community Interventions to Prevent Serious and Violent Offending* (Juvenile Justice Bulletin). Washington, DC: Office of Juvenile Justice and Delinquency Prevention.

This bulletin summarizes the chapter on promising and effective school- and community-focused interventions. All of the reviewed programs address multiple risk factors in a variety of settings.

*J. D. Hawkins, T. I. Herrenkohl, D. P. Farrington, D. D. Brewer, R. F. Catalano, T. W. Harachi, and L. Cothern (2000). *Predictors of Youth Violence* (Juvenile Justice Bulletin). Washington, DC: Office of Juvenile Justice and Delinquency Prevention.

This bulletin summarizes the chapter on predictors of youth violence that have been identified in longitudinal studies.

*G. A. Wasserman, L. S. Miller, and L. Cothern (2000) *Prevention of Serious and Violent Juvenile Offending* (Juvenile Justice Bulletin). Washington, DC: Office of Juvenile Justice and Delinquency Prevention.

This bulletin summarizes the chapter on prevention programs that address risk factors for serious and violent juvenile offending.

*M. W. Lipsey, D. B. Wilson, and L. Cothern (2000). *Effective Interventions for Serious and Violent Juvenile Offenders* (Juvenile Justice Bulletin). Washington, DC: Office of Juvenile Justice and Delinquency Prevention.

This bulletin summarizes the chapter on a meta-analysis of 200 evaluations of programs for serious and violent juvenile offenders, which found that many of them are effective with this population.

The third book on the Comprehensive Strategy was published in 2001:
R. Loeber and D. P. Farrington (Eds.). (2001). *Child Delinquents: Development, Intervention, and Service Needs.* Thousand Oaks, CA: Sage.

This book is devoted to the results of the work of the OJJDP Study Group on Very Young Offenders, a detailed assessment of research and programs on/for offenders up to age 12. The study group's work was guided by the Comprehensive Strategy. This volume is, in a sense, a sequel to the original book on the work of the OJJDP Study Group on Serious and Violent Juvenile Offenders. The major focus of the Study Group on Very Young Offenders was on potential serious, violent, and chronic juvenile offenders.

The work of the Study Group on Very Young Offenders is also summarized in the following article:
R. Loeber and D. P. Farrington (2000). "Young Children Who Commit Crime: Epidemiology, Developmental Origins, Risk Factors, Early Interventions, and Policy Implications." *Development and Psychopathology, 12,* 737-762.

The following bulletin describes the experiences of the people who were involved in the three OJJDP pilot Comprehensive Strategy sites: in Lee and Duval Counties, Florida, and in San Diego County, California. The authors provide an overview of the three sites and discuss the lessons learned there in relation to critical success factors, challenges and obstacles, and accomplishments and outcomes.
*K. Coolbaugh and C. J. Hansel (2000). *The Comprehensive Strategy: Lessons Learned From the Pilot Sites* (Juvenile Justice Bulletin). Washington, DC: Office of Juvenile Justice and Delinquency Prevention.

*These documents are available free of charge from the Juvenile Justice Clearinghouse: order by phone at (800) 638-8736 or by e-mail at puborder@ncjrs.org.

prevent delinquent offenders from becoming chronic offenders or committing progressively more serious and violent crimes. Initial intervention efforts, under an umbrella of system authorities (police, intake, and probation), should be centered in the family and other core societal institutions. Juvenile justice system authorities should ensure that an appropriate response occurs and act quickly and firmly if the need for formal system adjudication and sanctions is demonstrated.

- We must identify and control the small group of serious, violent, and chronic juvenile offenders who have committed felony offenses or have failed to respond to intervention and nonsecure community-based treatment and rehabilitation services offered by the juvenile justice system. Measures to address delinquent offenders who are a threat to community safety may include placement in secure community-based facilities, training schools, and other secure juvenile facilities. Even the most violent or intractable juveniles should not be moved into the criminal justice

system before they graduate from the jurisdiction of the juvenile justice system.

The Comprehensive Strategy is a two-tiered system for responding proactively to juvenile delinquency and crime. In the first tier, delinquency prevention and early intervention programs are relied upon to prevent and reduce the onset of delinquency. If these efforts fail, then the juvenile justice system, the second tier, needs to make proactive responses to juvenile delinquency by addressing the risk factors for recidivism and associated treatment needs of delinquents, particularly those with a high likelihood of becoming serious, violent, and chronic juvenile offenders. To reduce this likelihood, a continuum of sanctions and services for juvenile offenders needs to be in place.

Thus the Comprehensive Strategy is based on two principal goals: (a) preventing youth from becoming delinquent by focusing prevention programs on at-risk youth, and (b) improving the juvenile justice system's response to delinquent offenders through a system of graduated sanctions and parallel programs. Both of these goals are addressed through an integrated or "seamless" continuum of prevention, early intervention, and treatment options linked with graduated sanctions.

The Comprehensive Strategy is research based, data driven, and outcome focused. It is a blueprint or framework that is based on the findings of a decade of reviews and syntheses of research and program evaluation results. It empowers communities to assess their own delinquency problems and needs, and guides them in how to use these data to design and develop their own comprehensive strategies, because local ownership of programs and strategies breeds success (Tolan, Perry, & Jones, 1987). Finally, the Comprehensive Strategy is outcome focused in that it guides communities in the development of action plans that specify measurable outcomes.

The Comprehensive Strategy is comprehensive in four respects:

1. It encompasses the entire juvenile justice enterprise—prevention, early intervention, and the juvenile justice system.

2. Although it specifically targets serious, violent, and chronic juvenile offenders, it provides a framework for dealing with all juvenile offenders as well as other problem children and adolescents.

3. It calls for an integrated multiagency response to childhood and adolescent problems, bringing the juvenile justice system together with the mental health, child welfare, education, and law enforcement systems, and community organizations as well, to address multiple youth, family, and community problems.

4. It links the resources of all juvenile justice system components in an interactive manner. Comprehensive juvenile justice is not a zero-sum game. Resources are shared, and so are decisions as to the allocation of resources. An ideal mantra for participating agency officials is "Put your money on the table and take your hands away."

The Comprehensive Strategy guides jurisdictions in developing continuums of responses that parallel offender careers, beginning with early intervention and followed by prevention and graduated sanctions. By building such a continuum, a community can organize an array of programs that correspond with further development of offender careers. The collective effect of these programs is likely to be much greater than the impact of a single program, as illustrated in a RAND cost-benefit study of juvenile delinquency prevention and treatment programs (Greenwood, Model, Rydell, & Chiesa, 1996). The researchers found that, if implemented statewide, a combination of four delinquency prevention and treatment programs could achieve the same level of serious crime reduction as California's "three strikes" law, which mandated imprisonment for the third strike. The RAND researchers projected that the four juvenile delinquency prevention and treatment programs would cost less than $1 billion per year to implement throughout California, compared with about $5.5 billion per year for "three strikes." Thus, at less than one-fifth the cost, the state could fund the four programs and prevent more serious crimes rather than fund imprisonment. As the RAND researchers note, "Based on current best estimates of program costs and benefits, investments in some interventions for high-risk youth may be several times more cost-effective in reducing serious crime than mandatory sentences for repeat offenders" (Greenwood et al., 1996, p. 40).

Offender careers develop over time, thus a continuum of programs aimed at different points along the life course have a much better chance of succeeding than a single intervention. As noted in Chapter 6, certain risk factors operate at particular times in individuals' lives. Early on, programs are needed that address family risk factors. A few years later, in childhood, preschool- and elementary school-focused programs are needed, along with family support programs. Then, in adolescence, peer influences are predominant, and programs are needed that buffer the effects of exposure to delinquent peer influences and the spread of delinquency and violence in adolescence. Interventions that counter individual (e.g., mental health problems) and community risk factors are needed all along the life course.

Target Populations

The initial target population for prevention programs is juveniles at risk of involvement in delinquent activity. Although primary delinquency prevention programs provide services to all youth wishing to participate, communities can achieve maximum impact on future delinquent conduct by seeking to identify and involve in prevention programs those youth at greatest risk of involvement in delinquent activity. This includes youth who exhibit known risk factors for future delinquency (see Chapter 6)—in the family, school, peer group, individual, and community domains. It includes youth who have had contact with the juvenile justice system as nonoffenders (neglected, abused, and dependent), status offenders (runaways, truants, alcohol offenders, and

---

Box 12.2
Benefits of Using the Comprehensive Strategy

- Increased prevention of delinquency (and thus fewer young people enter the juvenile justice systems)
- Enhanced responsiveness from the juvenile justice system
- Greater accountability on the part of youth
- Decreased costs of juvenile corrections
- A more responsible juvenile justice system
- More effective juvenile justice programs
- Less delinquency
- Fewer delinquents become serious, violent, and chronic offenders
- Fewer delinquents become adult offenders

SOURCE: Wilson and Howell (1993).

---

incorrigibles), or minor delinquent offenders (e.g., child delinquents). Finally, it includes youth who have had contact with other social service systems—mental health, child welfare, social services, child protective services, and education—and evidence potential delinquency involvement.

The next target population is youth, both male and female, who have committed delinquent (criminal) acts, including juvenile offenders who evidence a high likelihood of becoming, or who already are, serious, violent, and chronic offenders. Interventions should target the highest-risk offenders, in keeping with what Canadian/American criminologists call the risk principle (see Chapter 10). Lipsey and Wilson's (1998) meta-analysis has shown that treatment programs reduce recidivism most among serious and violent juvenile offenders. Perhaps this is because they possess the highest level of risks and needs, and also have the most room to improve their behavior. In any event, a key Comprehensive Strategy principle is that the most intensive services and sanctions should be used for the most serious, violent, and chronic offenders. Treatment is likely to be effective for them, recidivism is most likely to be reduced, and public safety is most likely to be enhanced when they are targeted.

Comprehensive Strategy Rationale

What can communities and the juvenile justice system do to prevent the development of and interrupt the progression of delinquent and criminal careers? Juvenile justice agencies and programs are one part of a larger picture that involves many other local agencies and programs that are responsible for working with at-risk youth and their families. It is important that juvenile delinquency prevention and intervention programs are integrated with graduated sanctions and a continuum of rehabilitation programs. All programs must reflect those problems and program priorities that the local community has determined to be most pressing.

Comprehensive approaches to delinquency prevention and intervention require the integration of efforts between the juvenile justice system and other service provision systems, including mental health, health, child welfare, and education. Developing mechanisms that effectively link these different service providers at the program level will strengthen treatment programs because of the multiple problems that serious and violent offenders exhibit.

Theoretical Foundations of the Comprehensive Strategy

Developmental criminology (see Chapter 4) and the public health model (see Chapter 6) are the two overarching theoretical models on which the Comprehensive Strategy is based. Developmental criminology organizes the research base with respect to identifying the risk and causal factors for development of delinquent behavior over the periods of childhood and adolescence (see, e.g., Le Blanc & Loeber, 1998; Loeber & Le Blanc, 1990). This theoretical framework also focuses attention on the development of offender careers—from childhood disorders to involvement in serious, violent, and chronic delinquency.

As noted in Chapter 9, application of the public health model in prevention programming involves preventing delinquency by reducing risk factors and increasing protective factors (Institute of Medicine, 1994). A focus on risk and protective factors in delinquency prevention is supported theoretically by the social development model (Catalano & Hawkins, 1996), a developmental theory that integrates learning theory (Akers, Krohn, Lanza-Kaduce, & Radosevich, 1979; Bandura, 1977) and control theory (Hirschi, 1969). The social development model hypothesizes that youths commit offenses across developmental periods because they encounter antisocial influences in the family, peer group, school, and community domains that reinforce (learning) offending (Bronfenbrenner, 1979). Conversely, they resist or desist from offending if they encounter prosocial influences that inhibit (control) offending. If risk and protective factors are addressed at or slightly before the developmental points at which they begin to predict later delinquency or violence, it is likely that risk reduction efforts will be effective (Hawkins, Catalano, & Brewer, 1995).

Both learning theories and control theories are reflected in the key principles of the Comprehensive Strategy, which advocates strengthening the family and other core social institutions—such as schools, religious institutions, and community organizations—in their roles of developing capable, mature, and responsible youth. In contrast, control theory is reflected in the emphasis on controlling serious, violent, and chronic juvenile offenders with graduated sanctions.

Like the prevention component, the graduated sanctions component of the Comprehensive Strategy is grounded in developmental theory (see Chapter 4). From its inception, the juvenile justice system has employed a developmental perspective in responding to child and adolescent delinquency (Krisberg & Austin, 1993). A central premise in juvenile court jurisprudence is that children are not developmentally mature, and hence should be treated differently from adults. Children often need protection from unhealthy situations. They should not be held as fully responsible for their acts as adults, because their behavior is shaped by risk factors that, for the most part, are beyond their control (Howell, 1997).

The concept of graduated sanctions also has a theoretical basis in learning theory (Bandura, 1973, 1986, 1999; Sutherland, 1973). As Bandura (1999) explains, individuals repeat reinforced behaviors, especially in situations akin to those in which the behaviors were previously reinforced. Conversely, individuals avoid behaviors that elicit negative reactions from others. Thus cognitive-behavioral treatment approaches should be effective in a graduated sanctions context.

The graduated sanctions component also integrates *positivist criminology* (use of rehabilitation) and *classical criminology* (use of sanctions) in a balanced approach to recidivism reduction. We did not use the word *punishment* in the original formulation of the Comprehensive Strategy (Wilson & Howell, 1993) because it is well established that punishment does not reduce recidivism (see Chapter 7). Instead, we chose the term *sanctions*. Although sanctions that restrict freedom may help bring antisocial behavior under control and may restrain offenders from committing delinquent acts in the short term, severe sanctions (punishment) may increase recidivism in the long term (Gendreau, 1996b; Gendreau & Goggin, 1996). Hence sanctions should be viewed as providing only the setting for service delivery; it is the intervention within the setting that has the actual power to produce change in offenders (Andrews & Bonta, 1998; Bonta, 1996; Gendreau, Cullen, & Bonta, 1994). Sanctions themselves do not address the treatment needs of offenders.

Components of the Comprehensive Strategy

The Comprehensive Strategy for Serious, Violent, and Chronic Juvenile Offenders consists of two principal components (Figure III.1):

- *Prevention and early intervention:* The Comprehensive Strategy empowers communities to prevent juvenile delinquency by conducting risk- and protection-focused prevention and selecting needed prevention and early intervention programs from a menu of effective program options.
- *A system of graduated sanctions and a parallel continuum of treatment alternatives:* The elements in this system include immediate intervention, intermediate sanctions, intensive supervision, community-based correctional programs, secure corrections, and aftercare.

The Prevention and Early Intervention Component

An understanding of the evidence on risk and protective factors for serious and violent delinquency (see Chapter 6) suggests a set of principles that should guide prevention programming (Hawkins, Catalano, & Brewer, 1995, pp. 51-52):

- To be effective, prevention efforts must address known risk factors for delinquency, violence, and substance abuse.

Box 12.3

The Planning Process

Training and technical assistance providers use the Comprehensive Strategy curriculum to guide communities through the system reform process. The Comprehensive Strategy planning process consists of the following four phases:

- *Mobilization:* Community leaders are enlisted and organized to participate in the Comprehensive Strategy planning process. A formal Community Planning Team is created to receive training and technical assistance and to develop a 5-Year Strategic Plan. Representatives of all sectors of the community are engaged in the planning process, including youth development agencies, citizen volunteers, private organizations, schools, law enforcement agencies, prosecutors, courts, corrections agencies, social service agencies, civic organizations, religious groups, parents, and teens.
- *Assessment:* Quantitative data are gathered and analyzed for use in the development of a baseline profile of the community's risk and need factors and a comprehensive juvenile justice profile. The data can guide decision making regarding long-term program planning, coordination, and optimum resource allocation.
- *Planning:* A 5-Year Strategic Plan is created for building a continuum of services to address the community's priority risk and need factors, based on best practices. The plan clearly articulates the community's vision, mission, goals, and objectives.
- *Implementation and evaluation:* Systems and programs are developed according to the 5-Year Strategic Plan; these include a seamless continuum of prevention, intervention, and graduated sanctions and programs. Evaluation mechanisms and procedures are established.

SOURCE: Developmental Research and Programs, Inc., and National Council on Crime and Delinquency (2000).

- Prevention efforts must make clear connections between program activities and the goal of risk reduction. For example, family management problems have been identified as a risk factor for health and behavior problems in children. These problems may emerge from different sources. If it appears that family management problems are occurring in a particular community because parents who work need more effective ways to monitor their children's behavior, child-care centers, schools, and latchkey programs could supervise children's daily behavior for parents, to assist them in monitoring their children's behavior when they are not present. Alternatively, if a community's family management problems arise from parents' lack of knowledge of effective discipline techniques, programs that provide parents with opportunities to learn and practice a variety of discipline techniques may be effective.
- The link between prevention activities and the risk reduction objective should be clearly specified.

- Prevention programs should seek to strengthen protective factors while reducing risk.
- Risk reduction activities should address risks at or before the time they become predictive of later problems. Intervening early to reduce risk is likely to minimize the effort needed and maximize the outcome. For example, interventions aimed at improving family management practices that are implemented very early (e.g., with expectant mothers and parents of infants) are likely to be more effective than interventions that are not initiated until after referrals for abuse and neglect.
- Interventions should target individuals and communities that are exposed to multiple risk factors. Given the evidence that those exposed to multiple risks are at elevated risk, efforts to prevent chronic and serious problems of crime, violence, and substance abuse are most likely to be effective if they are focused on these populations. Targeting high-risk communities is particularly advantageous in that it can prevent individual

children in these communities from being labeled as potential problems at very early ages. Families at risk include those headed by single, poor, and/or teenage mothers. Communities at risk include poor and disorganized neighborhoods with high levels of crime, violence, and substance abuse. A communitywide approach allows higher- and lower-risk families in a neighborhood to work and learn together, modeling, supporting, and reinforcing efforts to strengthen protective factors and processes.

- Because the presence of multiple risks in multiple domains is a predictor of serious crime, violence, and substance abuse, prevention approaches should be multifaceted, addressing the key risk factors affecting the neighborhood or community.
- Prevention programs must be designed and implemented so that they will reach and be acceptable to members of all the diverse racial, cultural, and socioeconomic groups to be included.

Recent advances in prevention science and health epidemiology have resulted in new tools that communities can use to plan and implement strategic, outcome-focused plans for reducing the prevalence of antisocial behavior among adolescents and young adults. Enormous progress has been made in the past 20 years in the development of the research base for prevention science (Hawkins, 1999). A fundamental principle of this research is that increased exposure to risk factors increases delinquency involvement and other problem behaviors, whereas an increase in protective factors decreases delinquency and associated problems (Durlak, 1998). Longitudinal studies under way in Europe, North America, and New Zealand have identified the major factors associated with communities, families, school experiences, peer groups, and individuals themselves that increase the probability of delinquency in adolescence and criminality in early adulthood. Figure 6.1 in Chapter 6 shows that many of these factors have been found to increase the probability of substance abuse, teen pregnancy, and dropping out of school as well as delinquency and violence.

A second major breakthrough in prevention science is related to the remarkable advances that have been made in the past decade in the development and testing of effective prevention interventions (Hawkins, 1999). Numerous studies have shown that prevention actions that reduce risk and enhance protection can prevent later delinquency and violence (see Chapter 9). As Hawkins (1999) notes, "It is possible now to move to outcome focused prevention, that is, to design systems for risk reduction and protective factor enhancement to achieve specified prevention outcomes" (p. 449).

Adoption of the public health model in the delinquency prevention enterprise serves to provide a structured approach to prevention—using the tools of prevention science. As noted in Chapter 9, most communities take a "hit or miss" approach to delinquency prevention. Use of the public health model to engage communities will help to align prevention programs with science-based risk and protective factors.

The approach most clearly proven to be effective for engaging entire communities in risk- and protection-focused prevention is the Communities That Care (CTC) operating system (Hawkins, 1999). It contains research-based tools to help communities promote the positive development of children and adolescents and prevent adolescent substance abuse, delinquency, teen pregnancy, school dropout, and violence.

The Graduated Sanctions Component

The juvenile justice system has always had a rudimentary system of graduated sanctions, ranging from police apprehension and arrest to informal handling at court intake, adjudication and probation, and secure confinement (Bernard, 1992). Figure 12.1 illustrates a continuum of graduated sanctions that cover the entire juvenile justice system. This model shows how offenders are stepped up and stepped down in a graduated sanctions system. Youth first enter the system with police contact, which in the first or second instance may result in their being counseled and released or their being arrested. The severest sanction (at the top of the figure) is confinement in a secure correctional institution. Although aftercare programs are less common today than in the past, the downward steps in the continuum of graduated sanctions ideally consist of decreasing restrictions and services.

To be most effective, the components in a graduated sanctions system need to match the developmental history of the delinquent career and the risk of recidivism. When offenders persist in serious and violent delinquency, their position in a graduated sanctions system should be advanced. As offenders progress in the graduated sanctions system, linked rehabilitation programs must become more structured and intensive, to deal effectively with the intractable problems that more difficult and dangerous offenders present, while reserving secure confinement for the much smaller number of serious, chronic, and violent juvenile offenders. To accomplish these twin goals, the graduated sanctions component of the Comprehensive Strategy framework consists of five

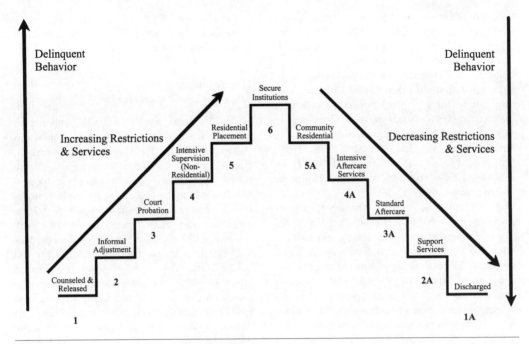

Figure 12.1   Example of Graduated Sanctions

SOURCE: *Risk and Needs Assessment for Juvenile Justice,* by D. Wagner, 2001. © 2001 by National Council on Crime and Delinquency. Reprinted with permission.

levels of sanctions, moving from least to most restrictive (Figure III.1):

1. Immediate intervention with first-time delinquent offenders (misdemeanors and nonviolent felonies) and nonserious repeat offenders

2. Intermediate sanctions for first-time serious or violent offenders, including intensive supervision for chronic and serious/violent offenders

3. Community confinement

4. Secure corrections for the most serious, violent, chronic offenders

5. Aftercare

These gradations—and the sublevels that can be created within them—form a continuum of intervention options that should be paralleled by a continuum of treatment options, which should include an array of referral and disposition resources for law enforcement, juvenile courts, and juvenile corrections officials. Intensive aftercare programs are critical to the success of juveniles once they complete treatment, for reinforcement, and when they return to their families, neighborhoods, and communities following confinement.

In many jurisdictions, juvenile justice systems need to be reformed so that system interventions parallel more exactly the progression in offenders' careers. The linking of graduated sanctions with a continuum of rehabilitation options is intended to interrupt offender career progression. Communities can greatly reduce their likelihood of implementing "hit or miss" rehabilitation practices by applying the current research-based knowledge of effective treatment programs, including effective practical, everyday rehabilitation programs. Below, I describe the tools that juvenile justice system agencies can use to align sanctions and treatment programs more closely with the stages in offenders' delinquent careers.

Linchpins of the Comprehensive Strategy

The Comprehensive Strategy is activated by two processes that are considered linchpins in the process of developing comprehensive juvenile justice models. First, the community must conduct a comprehensive assessment of risk and protective factors for delinquency in that specific jurisdiction, instead of arbitrarily selecting prevention programs that may miss the mark. The best system for scientific yet community-controlled prevention is the Communities That Care process (Hawkins, Catalano, & Associates, 1992). Each community is different from all other communities, with its own combination of predominant risk factors, therefore this assessment process is critical to successful prevention programming (Catalano, Arthur, Hawkins, Berglund, & Olson, 1998; Catalano, Loeber, & McKinney, 1999; J. D. Hawkins, 1995, 1999). I will describe this process in more detail shortly.

Second, juvenile justice system agencies must assess the community's delinquent population for risk and treatment needs, to classify and position offenders within a structured system of graduated sanctions. To develop comprehensive juvenile justice systems, many communities need to change their thinking about how to manage the operations of these systems. Instead of relying on "magic bullets," juvenile justice systems need to make use of available tools to improve the management of juvenile delinquent populations in the various parts of the juvenile justice system. If communities make the management and control of serious, violent, and chronic offenders the top priority in their juvenile justice systems, then management of the remainder of the delinquent offender population will be easier and more cost-effective.

Three tools are used in this process; these tools make up what has been called a *structured decision-making model* (Wiebush, Baird, Krisberg, & Onek, 1995). First, juvenile justice officials use risk assessment to determine the level of sanctions needed to protect the public from a particular offender. They next use needs assessment to determine the offender's treatment needs. Then, to find the best match between offender and program, which is critical for effective rehabilitation (Bonta, 1996; Gendreau, 1996b; Jones, 1996), they use the results of the offender's needs assessment in tandem with those of his or her risk assessment to place the offender in a particular supervision level and then in a program within that supervision level; to accomplish this step, they use a matrix that organizes sanctions and programs by risk level and offense severity. I present an example of this process in the next section.

How to Build a Comprehensive Juvenile Justice Plan

In this section, I describe the necessary tools for implementing the prevention component of the Comprehensive Strategy, and then use North Carolina's experience to illustrate the graduated sanctions component.

How to Build a
Comprehensive Prevention Plan

The Communities That Care prevention planning system (Hawkins, 1999; Hawkins, Catalano, & Associates, 1992) effectively empowers communities to organize themselves to engage in outcome-focused prevention planning using the tools of prevention science. CTC must be implemented at the community level, because profiles of risk and protection vary from community to community (Hawkins, 1999, p. 450). The CTC prevention planning system is based on the theoretical framework of the social development model (Catalano & Hawkins, 1996). As noted above, this integrated theory combines control and social learning theories. The social development model has been demonstrated to be a valid theory for explaining adolescence drug use, delinquency, and violence (see Chapter 6).

The implementation of CTC involves five phases (Hawkins, 1999, pp. 451-455). In the first, called the Readiness Phase, key community stakeholders assess their community's readiness to engage in risk- and protection-focused prevention. In the second phase, key community stakeholders are educated about prevention science and involved in the CTC planning process. This necessitates the formation of a structure—a community planning board or coalition—to move the community toward its vision for the future of its children. This coalition or planning board of key leaders must have broad community representation. Community assessments are conducted in the third phase. Using CTC's validated archival indicators of risk and outcomes and CTC's Youth Survey, the coalition develops a profile of the community based on community-specific data on levels of risk factors, protective factors, delinquency, and crime in the community's neighborhoods. In the fourth phase, the coalition drafts the community's strategic youth development and prevention plan after using the results of the preceding assessments to arrive at a baseline assessment of risk and protective factors and a prioritized subset of two to five risk factors that are most prevalent. The strategic plan is based on an inventory of community resources that already address priority risk factors and are designed to enhance protective factors. It builds on existing community resources, avoids duplication of effort, and fills gaps in existing policies and

---

Box 12.4

Common Juvenile Justice System Conditions

- Unbalanced emphasis on prevention versus graduated sanctions
- Overreliance on detention, incarceration, and residential programs
- Poor targeting of serious, violent, and chronic juvenile offenders
- Poor matching of offenders with appropriate levels of supervision, sanctions, and programs
- Use of ineffective programs
- Poor program planning
- Lack of continuity between juvenile court and corrections system operations
- Underdeveloped parole supervision/aftercare and transitional services
- Ineffective allocation of court and correctional resources
- Lack of a clear focus on the use of and objectives for confinement resources (often demonstrated in poor classification systems and excessive numbers of lengthy placements)
- Inadequate data collection on offenders in the system, management information systems, and information sharing
- Lack of good policy guidance in the development of institutional classification, length of commitment, and release criteria
- Lack of good policy guidance for state executive, legislative, and judicial stakeholders in the development of legislation, standards, and other policy directives that create data-driven, outcome-based, and results-oriented juvenile justice policy reforms

---

programs. Coalition members select new programs from a menu of promising programs that have been tested and shown to be effective in changing selected risk and protective factors and preventing delinquency, violence, or other problem behaviors (Hawkins, 1999). In the fifth phase, the coalition implements and evaluates the strategic plan.

During the fourth phase of the CTC process, CTC managers guide the community coalition members in the selection of promising and effective prevention programs, using the community's risk and protective factor profiles to develop clear, measurable outcomes. This involves reviewing programs and activities that have been tested and shown to be effective in reducing specific risk factors and enhancing protective factors, and selecting the approaches the coalition members wish to include in the community's continuum. The product is a written action plan for implementing new programs and strategies, enhancing/expanding existing resources, and planning for evaluation. Some 400 communities across the United States have implemented CTC, as have communities in the United Kingdom (Scotland, England, and Wales) and the Netherlands (Hawkins, 1999). CTC is now a commercial product of the Channing Bete Company, Inc.

It is possible, of course, for a community to organize and implement risk- and protection-focused prevention without using the CTC process. For a community to be successful in preventing delinquency, it must use a process that is research based, data driven, and outcome focused. In addition, to be effective, communitywide delinquency prevention needs to adhere to the risk- and protection-focused framework of the public health model (Institute of Medicine, 1994) and be grounded in developmental theory (see Chapter 4). In order to have the most comprehensive impact on child and adolescent problem behaviors, prevention programs and strategies must target the broad array of risk factors (see Table 9.1 in Chapter 9) and protective factors (see Table 6.1 in Chapter 6) that are linked to intersecting positive and negative outcomes for children and adolescents. For the largest impact on delinquency, it also is crucial that prevention strategies and programs be meshed with existing community resources and linked with the juvenile justice system and other child-serving/development agencies, as prescribed in the Comprehensive Strategy.

How to Build a Graduated Sanctions System

Because of the seventh moral panic over juvenile delinquency, some states have had difficulty maintaining a good balance between public safety considerations and rehabilitation. One of these goals need not be sacrificed for the other. North

	Risk Level		
Offense	Low	Medium	High
Violent	Level 2 or 3	Level 3	Level 3
Serious	Level 1 or 2	Level 2	Level 2 or 3
Minor	Level 1	Level 1 or 2	Level 2
Level 1 Community			
Level 2 Intermediate			
Level 3 Commitment to Youth Development Center			

Figure 12.2   North Carolina Offender Classification Matrix

Carolina is a case in point. In the mid-1990s, the juvenile justice system in North Carolina was experiencing the consequences of "get tough" policies. Some of the state's juvenile reformatories—called Youth Development Centers (YDCs)—were overcrowded and overpopulated with minor offenders. Admissions were increasing at a rate of approximately 10% per year (Lubitz, 2001). In 1996, only one-fifth of the juveniles confined in YDCs were violent felony offenders; the majority (nearly 60%) were moderately serious offenders (Lubitz, 2001), and about one-fifth were misdemeanant offenders. The growth in admissions had been driven by the increased confinement of misdemeanant and moderately serious offenders, not by any increase in the numbers of violent offenders.

Influenced by the Comprehensive Strategy for Serious, Violent, and Chronic Juvenile Offenders (Wilson & Howell, 1993), North Carolina state officials and legislators saw a way to address two policy concerns. First, they wanted to increase public safety by targeting the most serious, violent, *and* chronic juvenile offenders for more restrictive sanctions, particularly confinement in the YDCs. Second, they wanted to preserve the futures of the state's young people by increasing early intervention efforts with community treatment programs. North Carolina's 1998 Juvenile Justice Reform Act incorporated the Comprehensive Strategy framework and addressed both of these policy goals by incorporating the graduated sanctions scheme recommended in the Comprehensive Strategy. The act mandated the use of the structured decision-making model recommended in the *Guide for Implementing the Comprehensive Strategy* (Howell, 1995),

consisting of risk and needs assessments and an offender classification matrix to place offenders along a continuum of programs and sanctions.

The North Carolina classification matrix, shown in Figure 12.2, uses two factors to determine the placement of adjudicated juvenile offenders: current offense and risk level. A complex formula—factoring in chronic offending and whether or not the current offense was committed while the offender was on probation—guides determination of the risk level. The intersection of the risk level and current offense governs placement of an offender at Level 1, 2, or 3. For example, an offender with a serious and chronic offense history (i.e., high risk) who has been adjudicated for a violent offense would earn a Level 3 disposition, commitment to a Youth Development Center. Level 2 is an intermediate disposition, and Level 1 is a community disposition.

The continuum of sanctions and services, which the act mixed for each disposition level, is shown in Table 12.1. Only three of the possible Level 1 disposition alternatives require removal from the home: residential placement with a relative or in a group home, intermittent confinement, and placement in Eckerd Wilderness Camp. In contrast, several of the Level 2 disposition alternatives remove the child from the home, and only one disposition alternative is possible for Level 3, placement in a YDC. Note also that regular probation is a disposition option in Level 1, and intensive supervision probation is prescribed in Level 2. Thus the disposition alternatives in the three levels clearly demonstrate the graduated sanctions concept. The legislature made an attempt to permit flexibility in the choice of sanctions and

TABLE 12.1   North Carolina Disposition Levels[a]

Level 1 Community	Level 2 Intermediate (may also include Level 1 dispositions)	Level 3 Commitment
Community-based program	Eckerd Wilderness Camp	Commitment to training school
Victim-offender reconciliation program	Structured day program	
Community service (up to 100 hours)	Community service (up to 200 hours)	
Restitution (up to $500)	Restitution ($500 and over)	
Suspension of driver's license	Regimented training program	
Curfew	Intensive supervision probation	
Counseling, including intensive substance abuse treatment	House arrest with or without electronic monitoring	
Vocational or educational program	Multipurpose group home	
Regular probation	Residential placement in treatment facility or group home	
Residential placement with relative or group home	Placement in an intensive nonresidential treatment program or intensive substance abuse program	
Intermittent confinement (up to 5 days)	Short-term secure confinement (up to 14 days)	
Fine		
Eckerd Wilderness Camp		

SOURCE: *Fiscal Year 1999 Juvenile Justice Statistics for North Carolina: Juveniles Adjudicated Delinquent* (p. 4), by D. M. Dawes and P. Ross, 2000, Raleigh: North Carolina Sentencing and Policy Advisory Commission. Copyright 2000 by North Carolina Sentencing and Policy Advisory Commission. Reprinted with permission.
a. See N.C.G.S. §§ 7B-2506, 7B-2508.

services by permitting use of Level 1 disposition alternatives for Level 2 cases.

Where the matrix indicates alternative disposition options at a given risk level, court officials are expected to make the final determination using risk and needs assessment results. For example, if an offender's risk assessment score indicates that he or she does not warrant a higher-level disposition, and the needs assessment instrument indicates that the youth would benefit from a program that is available for lower-risk offenders, then the youth should be placed in the lower disposition level in order to access the needed service.

The North Carolina Department of Juvenile Justice and Delinquency Prevention (DJJDP) has blended these dispositions with early intervention, prevention, community-based intervention, residential, and secure residential programs to form a continuum of programs and sanctions (see the annual reports: North Carolina DJJDP, 2001a, 2002). This continuum will be refined as the state learns more about program effectiveness from the North Carolina project, which I will describe shortly.

With the assistance of the National Council on Crime and Delinquency (NCCD), the DJJDP developed, by committee, an instrument to assess juveniles' risks of future offending as well as an instrument to assess juveniles' and families' strengths and treatment needs. Both of these instruments were developed through the consensus approach described later in this chapter (the two resulting instruments appear in the appendix to this volume). The risk assessment instrument incorporates the major

TABLE 12.2   Risk Level by Disposition (North Carolina)

| | Risk Level | | | | | | | |
| | Low | | Medium | | High | | Total | |
Dispositional Level	N	%	N	%	N	%	N	%
Level 1: Community	718	65	346	31	37	3	1,101	100
Level 2: Intermediate	160	27	278	47	152	26	590	100
Level 3: Commitment	7	7	25	23	76	70	108	100
Protective supervision	112	47	117	49	9	4	238	100
Other	12	43	12	43	4	14	28	100
Total	1,009	49	778	38	278	14	2,065	100

SOURCE: Adapted from *North Carolina Department of Juvenile Justice Risk Assessment Profile* (p. 2), by D. Wagner and S. Connell, 2002, Madison, WI: National Council on Crime and Delinquency. © 2002 by National Council on Crime and Delinquency. Adapted with permission.
NOTE: Percentages may not add to 100 because of rounding.

research-based predictors of juvenile offender recidivism. It is used to classify offenders as low, medium, or high risk, depending on how many points they accumulate.

The needs assessment instrument is more detailed than most such instruments, because it was designed to provide very explicit information on treatment needs for future development of comprehensive treatment plans. Unlike some needs assessment instruments, it assigns a "total needs score" that is useful for the immediate task at hand—assisting court officials in determining proper placement of the assessed offender in the disposition matrix.

We now turn to an examination of data on how the Comprehensive Strategy has affected the processing of juvenile offenders in North Carolina. Preliminary results are available on the functioning of the state's structured decision-making model (Wagner & Connell, 2002). These data are based on all juvenile court referrals throughout the state during the last quarter of 2001—a total of more than 2,000 delinquent and "undisciplined" youths. (The latter are status offenders who could have had prior delinquency referrals.) The data for both groups are combined in Table 12.2, which shows that 49% of the referrals were classified as low risk, 38% were medium risk, and only 14% were classified as high risk. It should be noted that North Carolina would be expected to have a relatively small proportion of high-risk offenders because the upper age limit for juvenile court jurisdiction ends at age 15; older juveniles are handled in the state's criminal justice system. Thus the excluded 16- and 17-year-olds

would have more time to accumulate offenses and thus would be classified as being at higher risk than many of the youths age 15 and younger.

In a validation study, Fraser, Day, and Schwalbe (2002) found that the risk assessment instrument and the current offense reliably classified youths in the three placement levels, as the disposition data in Table 12.2 suggest. However, they found that the use of current offenses to establish classification in the disposition matrix (Figure 12.2) was a determining factor in the placement of youths in different levels. Nevertheless, Fraser et al. found that the risk assessment instrument predicted low, medium, and high recidivism rates reasonably well at these respective risk levels. Whereas only 20% of the low-risk offenders recidivated with new offenses, 34% of the medium-risk offenders recidivated, and 45% of the high-risk offenders had new offenses. The DJJDP has implemented court services policies and procedures to ensure more consistency in court services and to enhance court effectiveness (see North Carolina DJJDP, 2001b).

The data displayed in Table 12.2 suggest that North Carolina's structured decision-making model is functioning very much as intended. Nearly two-thirds (65%) of the low-risk offenders received a Level 1 (community) disposition, and 70% of the high-risk offenders received a Level 3 (commitment) disposition. Thus the classification matrix and risk assessment instrument appear to be functioning quite well in guiding disposition decisions. Table 12.2 also displays additional evidence to support this observation. Notice the large differences in the proportions of high-risk offenders who received

Level 1 (3%), Level 2 (26%), and Level 3 (70%) dispositions. These differences are a good indication of the discriminatory power of the classification scheme.

Further, there is evidence that the structured decision-making model is helping North Carolina achieve its objective of targeting serious, violent, and chronic juvenile offenders for more restrictive sanctions. Table 12.3 shows dispositions by offense. Note, first of all, that only 5% of all of the referred youngsters were committed to the state's Youth Development Centers. The highest proportion of commitments (38%) came from the violent offender category. Overall, most violent and serious offenders (56% and 58%, respectively) received intermediate sanctions (Level 2). An independent study in one of the state's juvenile courts revealed that court staff go to great lengths to avoid confining youths (Howell, 2002). Believing that community-based programs are more effective, they showed a tendency to use these programs extensively in concert with graduated sanctions, keeping the child in the home whenever possible. Consistent with the emphasis on rehabilitation in the Comprehensive Strategy, staff showed a tendency to increase the intensity of services as youths continued to engage in problem behavior. They displayed a "never give up" treatment philosophy. If this philosophy is pervasive across the state, this may be a key factor explaining declining training school commitments, along with the effectiveness of the structured decision-making model.

In a separate study of admissions to Youth Development Centers, Lubitz (2001) found that admissions for violent offenses increased sharply following enactment of the new law in 1998. Since then, admissions to YDCs have dropped 58% (North Carolina Department of Juvenile Justice and Delinquency Prevention, 2002), even though the drop in arrests during this period was small (15% for violent juvenile offenses and 7% for serious property offenses) (Snyder, 1999; see also OJJDP Statistical Briefing Book online at ojjdp.ncjrs.org). However, extensive use of detention in the state is a cause for concern.

The North Carolina experience shows how a state or community can use risk assessment and classification instruments to improve the efficiency, consistency, and fairness of the juvenile justice system. In addition, it shows that the policy goal of reserving costly long-term confinement for the most dangerous offenders is achievable. In other words, these data demonstrate the reliability of the classification matrix and the risk and needs assessment instruments for placing offenders at the proper level of risk. It is

apparent that the Comprehensive Strategy tools have helped ensure that North Carolina's juvenile reformatories are reserved for the most serious, violent, and chronic juvenile offenders.

The current work in building the North Carolina continuum of graduated sanctions and services involves development of a method for assessing the effectiveness of existing programs and improving them to optimize their potential to reduce recidivism. In the course of this work, the state of North Carolina has begun an experiment in which knowledge of the most effective interventions is used to improve existing programs. Jurisdictions are commonly encouraged to import effective intervention programs that have shown very positive results in research and demonstration experiments (Mihalic, Irwin, Elliott, Fagan, & Hansen, 2001). As noted in Chapter 10, this can be very costly, and it is unrealistic for small-town and rural jurisdictions to attempt to replicate these models. North Carolina is a case in point; 92 of the state's 100 counties are primarily rural. Before considering the possibility of importing such programs, North Carolina juvenile justice officials chose to attempt to make improvements in existing programs by using the broad knowledge base of effective interventions that Lipsey developed.

The statewide North Carolina project (the Standardized Evaluation of North Carolina's Juvenile Justice System Programs) entails the assessment of existing juvenile justice system programs against best practices, the identification of weak programs, and the application of knowledge of the characteristics of effective programs to improve current ones. Very detailed information has been gathered on the variety of service components that are in use across the state. This detailed information on types of service components enabled Lipsey to apply his database of some 400 juvenile justice program evaluations in a unique manner (Lipsey, Howell, & Tidd, 2002). He matched the North Carolina service components with similar service components of effective programs that had been evaluated—including research demonstration programs. This comparison identified effective features of 13 service components that are commonly used in the state (see Table 12.4). In addition to the type of treatment (e.g., the service component), Lipsey found that three other program characteristics boost the effectiveness of interventions (Lipsey et al., 2002):

- *Supplementary services:* In some cases, adding another service component to a program increases its effectiveness.
- *Service delivery:* This refers to the amount of service provided, as indicated by service

TABLE 12.3   Disposition by Offense (North Carolina)

| | Disposition | | | | | | | | | | |
| Offense | Level 1 | | Level 2 | | Level 3 | | Protective Supervision | | Other | | Total | |
	N	%	N	%	N	%	N	%	N	%	N	%
Violent	2	4	27	56	18	38	0	0	1	2	48	100
Serious	159	28	329	58	76	13	0	0	3	1	567	100
Minor	938	78	233	20	14	1	1	0	11	1	1,197	100
Undisciplined	1	0	0	0	0	0	235	96	10	4	246	100
Other	1	14	1	14	0	0	2	29	3	43	7	100
Total	1,101	53	590	29	108	5	238	12	28	1	2,065	100

SOURCE: *North Carolina Department of Juvenile Justice Risk Assessment Profile* (p. 3), by D. Wagner and S. Connell, 2002, Madison, WI: National Council on Crime and Delinquency. © 2002 by National Council on Crime and Delinquency. Reprinted with permission.
NOTE: Percentages may not add to 100 because of rounding.

frequency, program duration, and extent of implementation.

- *Characteristics of the juveniles:* Some programs are more effective for higher-risk juveniles; others are more effective for older or younger offenders.

All of the interventions listed in Table 12.4 are effective, even those on the lowest tier. Intensive supervision, for example, is an effective intervention, but it can be improved by being supplemented with another service component, such as interpersonal skills training. The most effective interventions are interpersonal skills training, behavior management, cognitive/behavioral treatment, parent/family training, mentoring, and drug/health education or counseling.

Lipsey then designed a prototype instrument, the Standardized Program Evaluation Protocol (SPEP; Lipsey et al., 2002), that contains the characteristics of the most effective evaluated programs. The SPEP is currently under development in North Carolina. In this preliminary version, the instrument's rating scheme assigns points for different program characteristics according to their relationship to recidivism outcomes in the available research. Juvenile justice officials can use the rating scheme to assess their existing programs and select options for improving them, such as by supplementing a program with another effective service component, improving service delivery, or changing the client target group. Although it has not yet

been validated, this process can dramatically change the way a community goes about building a continuum of effective programs. It moves decision makers away from chasing "magic bullets" and toward building on existing programs by changing the way they operate or by adding effective service components.

Figure 12.3 shows the preliminary SPEP template used to assess interpersonal skills training services. Because interpersonal skills training is a particularly effective service intervention (see Table 12.4), it is worth 60 points as a stand-alone intervention. Programs being assessed using the SPEP earn extra points, up to a total of 100, if they have other features of the most effective interpersonal skills training programs that have been evaluated. These features, as shown in Figure 12.3, cover three categories of program effectiveness: supplementary services, service delivery, and characteristics of the juveniles. This SPEP prototype is likely to be revised following pilot testing; nevertheless, it shows the direction in which this effort to translate research into practice is moving. In the next phase of the project, localities will be trained in how to improve current programs when those programs do not score high on the SPEP. One immediate option for strengthening an existing program would be to add a supplementary service component to it. Alternatively, a locality could opt to discard a weak program in favor of a stronger one. In short, the instrument allows for a number of options for optimizing program effectiveness.

TABLE 12.4   Effective Juvenile Justice
System Interventions

Highest tier

Interpersonal skills training
Behavioral contracting/contingency
management
Cognitive/behavioral
(e.g., cognitive restructuring)
Parent/family training or counseling
Mentoring
Drug/health education (e.g., drug/alcohol and
pregnancy counseling, and STD prevention)

Middle tier

Individual counseling
Group counseling
Restitution
Academic enhancement
(e.g., tutoring, teaching study skills)

Lowest tier

Intensive supervision
Multimodal (e.g., service brokerage,
case management)
Employment training

SOURCE: Adapted from Lipsey, Howell, and Tidd
(2002).

Compared with usual practices, this is a fundamentally different way of going about developing a continuum of juvenile justice programs. Jurisdictions engaged in strategic planning typically review their existing programs, identify gaps in the continuum formed by those programs, and fill the gaps with new programs that they import from elsewhere. However, they could instead take far less costly steps to improve their existing programs. Communities can improve weak programs at relatively low cost by applying the existing research-based knowledge of the characteristics of effective programs. This process also can enable juvenile courts and corrections agencies to achieve better matches between offender risks/needs and effective programs, and thereby achieve larger recidivism reductions than current programs are yielding.

A future goal of North Carolina's comprehensive plan is the integration of prevention, early intervention, and treatment programs. The focal point of this work is at the local level. The 1998 Juvenile Justice Reform Act established Juvenile Crime Prevention Councils (JCPCs) in every county across the state. Each council has a membership of not more than 25 persons, all of whom are appointed by county boards of commissioners. The councils are made up of representatives of the full array of county governmental, social service, and education agencies, as well as youth representatives and representatives of the juvenile justice system, the faith community, and the business sector. The JCPCs are charged with developing comprehensive delinquency prevention and graduated sanctions plans; they also manage the funding process, ensuring that a wide variety of services and dispositional options are available. Council members have been trained in a modified version of the Communities That Care model described above. Having assessed risk and protective factors in each county, every one of the 100 JCPCs in the state has developed a comprehensive prevention and early intervention plan. The JCPCs are now developing the graduated sanctions components of their strategic plans.

North Carolina will soon be positioned to integrate the prevention and graduated sanctions components in its comprehensive strategy. This will be done at the county level, led by the JCPCs. Virtually all prevention and treatment programs linked with graduated sanctions are funded through the JCPCs. They will need to ensure that funded programs serve children and families in need regardless of whether the main purpose of a particular program is prevention, early intervention, or rehabilitation. For example, a comprehensive treatment plan for a youth referred to court for delinquency involvement could include—as an immediate intervention—participation in a prevention program. Simultaneously, the youngster's parents might receive parent training through a family-strengthening component of an immediate intervention program.

In the remainder of this section, I describe how the specific levels of the graduated sanctions component of the Comprehensive Strategy can be implemented.

Early Intervention With
Delinquent Children and Their Families

Social services, child protective services, the education system, child welfare agencies, and mental health agencies need to do a better job of addressing the risk factors and precursor behaviors that lead to delinquency. Many of the children who need effective services in these systems—particularly children with mental health problems—end up being dumped into the juvenile justice system (Teplin, 2001). This inappropriate response may further exacerbate the problems of these youngsters,

Interpersonal Skills Training [Social skill building, communication, interpersonal problem solving, conflict resolution, assertion training]	**Points**
This is an upper tier program	60

Supplementary Services [check if applicable]

- ☐ Drug-health education [10 pts]
- ☐ Individual counseling [5 pts]

☐

Frequency of Service [check one]

- ☐ < 1 session/hour per week [0 pts]   ☐ 3-4+ sessions/hours per week [2 pts]
- ☐ 1-2 sessions/hours per week [3 pts]

☐

Duration of Service [check one]

- ☐ 0-3 weeks [0 pts]   ☐ 14-26 weeks [10 pts]
- ☐ 4-13 weeks [7 pts]   ☐ 27-52+ weeks [3 pts]

☐

Implementation [check one]

- ☐ 90-100% completion [10 pts]   ☐ 60-69% completion [2 pts]
- ☐ 80-89% completion [7 pts]   ☐ < 60% completion [0 pts]
- ☐ 70-79% completion [4 pts]

☐

Risk Level for Majority of Juveniles [check one]

- ☐ Minor first offenders or at-risk; minor property, etc. offenses; no aggressive/violent history [4 pts]
- ☐ Delinquent; adjudicated, community supervision; most with priors; less that half with aggressive/violent history [2 pt]
- ☐ Institutionalized or appropriate for confinement; all have priors; many or most with aggressive/violent history [0 pts]

☐

Age of Juveniles [check one]

- ☐ Average 13 years old or under [2 pts]   ☐ Average 15 years old [0 pts]
- ☐ Average 14 years old [1 pts]

☐

| | **Total Points** | ☐ |

Figure 12.3   Interpersonal Skills Training Template in the Standardized Program Evaluation Protocol for North Carolina's Juvenile Justice System Programs

SOURCE: *A Standardized Program Evaluation Protocol for North Carolina's Juvenile Justice System Programs* (p. 20), by M. W. Lipsey, J. C. Howell, and S. T. Tidd, 2002, Nashville, TN: Center for Evaluation Research and Methodology. © 2002 by Vanderbilt University, Center for Evaluation Research and Methodology, and the North Carolina Department of Juvenile Justice and Delinquency Prevention. Reprinted with permission.

because the juvenile justice system is not equipped to meet their mental health treatment needs.

Early intervention programs aim to ameliorate risky conditions and, simultaneously, build resilience to them in hopes of preventing progression of early problem behavior into full-blown delinquency. The Delinquents Under 10 program described in Chapter 10 is a promising intervention (see also Howell, 2001a). Juveniles who continue delinquency involvement move into the juvenile justice system, into graduated sanctions and treatment programs. Even earlier identification of potential serious, violent, and chronic juvenile offenders may be possible, at multiple points, using multiple informants, multiple variables, and multiple screening tools (Howell, 2001a).

In Chapter 13, I describe a model continuum of juvenile justice services that illustrates early intervention with delinquents who are very likely to become serious, violent, and chronic juvenile offenders. A key feature of this model continuum is early intervention with young, first-time juvenile court referrals. The model illustrates how juvenile justice officials can use risk and needs assessments at court intake to group offenders into one of three classifications: low, medium, and high risk. The last of these categories is likely to contain most potentially serious, violent, and chronic juvenile offenders.

Community assessment centers (described in Chapter 11) may constitute an effective early intervention mechanism for integrating service delivery for youths with multiple problems that cut across several social service agencies. Such centers can help to integrate the services of several agencies by conducting comprehensive assessments of at-risk youth and providing case management of comprehensive treatment plans. School-based centers are one viable option.

If risk and needs assessments cannot be made at a single physical point of entry, then all agencies and organizations evaluating youth should use uniform assessment procedures, tools, and training. In either event, a two-step assessment process should be employed. First, each youth should receive an initial broad-based screening to determine whether more in-depth assessments are needed. Then, if a problem is revealed, a more comprehensive assessment pertaining to that specific area should be conducted. Objective risk and needs assessments should be driven by public safety concerns and youths' needs, not by funding streams or the agendas of individual agencies.

Immediate Intervention

First-time delinquent offenders (misdemeanors and nonviolent felonies) and nonserious repeat offenders (generally misdemeanor repeat offenses) make up the appropriate target group for immediate intervention. As noted in Chapter 4, the overwhelming majority of these offenders will not become serious, violent, and chronic juvenile offenders. For those in this group, nonintrusive sanctions are most appropriate.

However, there is a subgroup of offenders within this category who score high on risk assessment instruments, and these offenders must be provided more intensive services based on their multiple problem behaviors and high probability of becoming more serious, violent, and chronic in their delinquent activities (Wilson & Howell, 1993). Nonresidential community-based programs, including prevention programs for at-risk youth, may be appropriate for many of these offenders. Such programs are small and open, located in or near the juveniles' homes, and maintain community participation in program planning, operation, and evaluation. Other offenders may require sanctions tailored to their offenses and their needs to help control them so that they do not commit additional crimes and to provide the necessary program structure for treatment to work.

Early juvenile court intervention with these kinds of offenders can be very effective. Tracy and Kempf-Leonard (1996) found that use of court adjustment and probation early in the offender career, particularly in the case of the most chronic offenders, reduced subsequent offenses, including continuation into adulthood. The earlier in chronic offender careers that probation and informal court handling were applied, as opposed to police lecture and release, the lower the recidivism rates among serious offenders. Compared with delinquents who received late-career probation, delinquents who received informal court adjustment, early probation, or mid-career probation had significantly lower odds of continuing their recidivism and becoming adult offenders. Tracy and Kempf-Leonard's analysis showed that as the frequency of delinquency increased, and probation occurred later in the delinquent career, the more likely the offender was to become an adult criminal. When probation was administered later and later, especially for high-rate delinquents, the probability of adult crime escalated dramatically.

Other studies have shown that early juvenile court intervention in offender career paths, especially combining treatment with probation, produces lower recidivism rates (Brown, Miller, & Jenkins, 1991; Land, McCall, & Williams, 1990; Smith, Aloisi, & Goldstein, 1996). One of the programs that has produced such findings is Orange County's 8% Early Intervention Program (Schumacher & Kurz, 2000), which I review in Chapter 13. In a North Carolina study, Dean, Brame, and Piquero (1996) found lower recidivism rates among incarcerated juvenile offenders who had been adjudicated delinquent at an early age in juvenile court. In a 6-year follow up with more than 800 juveniles released from state training schools, the researchers found that an increased number of prior adjudications had a restraining effect on recidivism—measured by arrests following release—among those who were first adjudicated at very young ages. For those who experienced a later first adjudication, exactly the opposite result was found. Early intervention with juvenile court probation makes a big difference in the success of juvenile rehabilitation with chronic offenders.

Intermediate Sanctions

Intermediate sanctions programs are appropriate for first-time serious or violent offenders and for chronic offenders who have not yet committed serious or violent offenses. These generally are moderate-risk offenders. Intermediate sanctions include programs such as probation, day reporting centers, and electronic monitoring. Intensive supervision is an appropriate level of sanction for such offenders who score at the upper extreme of the moderate-risk category. However, these sanctions are more effective when they are coupled with treatment programs, such as the programs Lipsey has identified as falling within the highest effectiveness tier (see Table 12.4). Multisystemic Therapy is an excellent intermediate sanction that serves as an alternative to incarceration. Alternatives to confinement can now safely be used far more widely than they have been used in the past. As noted in Chapter 10, alternatives to incarceration are more effective than confinement. Jurisdictions need a structured way of ensuring that intermediate sanctions are used for most juvenile offenders; placing them in training schools is both needlessly expensive and not particularly effective.

Only a small number of juvenile offenders require secure confinement. At the other end of the risk continuum, there is another relatively large group of offenders for whom secure confinement should never be used. For the large middle portion of the juvenile offender population, however, the decision as to whether to use confinement is not obvious. It is a complex, uncertain, and sometimes highly contentious process involving a wide assortment of policy makers, practitioners, and even members of the community (Butts & Adams, 2001).

At this stage, it would be appropriate to place many serious and violent offenders in intensive supervision programs as an alternative to secure incarceration. Lipsey's (1999b) meta-analysis of "practical" juvenile justice programs has shown that intensive supervision programs (ISPs) nested in probation and parole/aftercare sanctions effectively reduce recidivism. In addition, intensive probation supervision has been found to be a cost-beneficial alternative to incarceration (Aos, Phipps, Barnoski, & Lieb, 2001). I discuss one such program that has been demonstrated to be effective, the Ohio Intensive Probation Services Program, in Chapter 13.

Residential or Secure Corrections for Serious, Violent, and Chronic Offenders

The criminal behavior of many serious, violent, *and* chronic juvenile offenders requires the application of secure sanctions to ensure public safety and to provide a structured treatment environment. Large congregate-care juvenile facilities have not proven to be effective in rehabilitating juvenile offenders. In those cases where secure confinement of juveniles is necessary to protect the public, small secure facilities work best. Small community-based facilities that provide intensive services in a secure environment offer the best hope for successful treatment. Secure sanctions are most effective in changing future conduct when they are coupled with comprehensive treatment and rehabilitation services. Two graduated sanctions strategies are proposed within the secure corrections option: community confinement and incarceration in secure correctional facilities.

Community Confinement

Offenders whose presenting offenses are sufficiently serious (such as violent felonies) or who fail to respond to intermediate sanctions, as evidenced by continued reoffending, may be appropriate for community confinement. Offenders at this level represent the more serious (such as repeat felony drug trafficking or property offenders) and violent offenders among the juvenile justice system correctional population. In addition to having been adjudicated for serious or violent offenses, candidates for community confinement should also have chronic offense histories.

Community confinement refers to secure confinement in small community-based facilities that offer intensive treatment and rehabilitation services. These services include individual and group counseling, educational programs, medical services, and intensive staff supervision. The proximity of such facilities to the offenders' community enables direct and regular family involvement with the treatment process as well as a phased reentry into the community that draws upon community resources and services.

Incarceration in Training Schools, Camps, and Ranches

The very few juveniles who cannot be confined safely in the community, who constitute an ongoing threat to community safety, or who have failed to respond to high-quality community-based correctional programs may require placement in training schools, camps, ranches, or other secure care options that are not community based. These facilities should offer comprehensive treatment programs for these youth, with a focus on interpersonal skills development, cognitive-behavioral treatment, education, and vocational or employment training. Juveniles convicted and sentenced in the criminal justice system should be provided rehabilitation services in these juvenile facilities until they reach the age at which they are no longer eligible to remain in the juvenile justice system.

Transfer to the Criminal Justice System

The original Comprehensive Strategy (Wilson & Howell, 1993) permitted transfer of the most violent or intractable juveniles to the criminal justice system. This is no longer recommended. As noted in Chapter 8, the criminal justice system has neither the capacity to handle juveniles in a fair and just manner that can ensure their health and safety nor the necessary programs to rehabilitate them. If punishment is the aim, juveniles can be confined more safely and humanely in the juvenile justice system. Moreover, as seen in Chapter 10, the juvenile justice system is effective even with serious and violent juvenile offenders. Thus there is no longer any justification for transferring juveniles to the criminal justice system. In states that permit transfer, only judicial waiver, which requires constitutional safeguards, should be statutorily permitted.

Aftercare

Effective aftercare is an important component of residential programs for serious, violent, and chronic juvenile offenders. Standard parole practices, particularly those that have a primary focus on social control, have not been effective in normalizing the behavior of high-risk juvenile parolees over the long term. Consequently, there is growing interest in intensive aftercare programs that provide high levels of social control and treatment services. Aftercare program components must be highly structured, must begin prior to release, and must combine treatment programming with stepped-down controls as the offender is reintegrated into the community. Two models of aftercare programs have been developed that incorporate these principles: the intensive supervision program and the intensive aftercare program. Such programs can be implemented in any community.

Aftercare can be conceptualized in a number of ways. The term *aftercare* is generally used in reference to "reintegrative" services that aim to link newly released incarcerated youths with their communities, families, schools, and/or employment. However, the term also has a much broader application, including relapse prevention (booster training following participation in a treatment program) and the transitional services provided in the course of moving a client from one treatment program to another. Thus aftercare services need to be provided at every major transition throughout a graduated sanctions system. Aftercare also should be provided at any point in the juvenile justice system for youths returning to the community from any type of secure program or facility.

Aftercare programs are not likely to be very successful for offenders in the deep end of a juvenile correctional system that does not have a structure of graduated sanctions. In the absence of a well-structured system, it is unlikely that any treatment and rehabilitation programs preceding an inmate's release would have been effective, because there probably would have been a poor match between the offender's risks and needs and the sanctions and treatment the offender has received. A foundation needs to be laid for aftercare to build upon. Thus jurisdictions that implement the graduated sanctions component of the Comprehensive Strategy are in a much better position to implement effective aftercare programs than others that mismatch offenders with programs and sanctions.

There are a number of obstacles to developing effective aftercare programs for juveniles who have been held in corrections facilities. First, incarcerated youngsters have serious, multiple problems of (Acoca, 1998a, 1998b, 1999; Acoca & Dedel, 1998; McGarvey & Waite, 2000). Second, as Josi and Sechrest (1999) note, "institutional confinement does not prepare youths for return to the community" (p. 58). There are good reasons this is so in some juvenile correctional systems. Unhealthy and dangerous conditions of confinement (Parent, Leiter, Livens, Wentworth, & Stephen, 1994), the growing emphasis on punishment at the expense of treatment (Torbet, Griffin, Hurst, & MacKenzie, 2000), overcrowding (Roush & McMillen, 2000), and the deleterious effects of gangs in facilities (Howell, Curry, Pontius, & Roush, 2003) all militate against positive outcomes. These circumstances point to potential serious mental health damages to juveniles as a result of long-term secure confinement. Despite such obstacles, one aftercare program has proved to be effective: Lifeskills '95 (see Chapter 7).

Tools for Building a Comprehensive Juvenile Justice System

The Comprehensive Strategy guides jurisdictions in the development of integrated and coordinated systems that link prevention and early intervention programs with the juvenile justice system. By using the science-based framework of risk and protective factors found in the public health model, communities can structure the delinquency prevention enterprise. In the remainder of this chapter, I describe the tools that communities need to use to optimize the effectiveness of their juvenile justice systems.

Basic Comprehensive Strategy Tools

Over the past 20 years or so, many tools have been developed for building a comprehensive juvenile justice system. Below, I discuss a number of these tools in relation to the two main components of the Comprehensive Strategy: prevention and graduated sanctions linked with a program continuum.

Delinquency Prevention

Delinquency prevention is a haphazard enterprise in most communities. Despite the efforts of many researchers to disseminate information about science-based prevention practices and effective programs, many communities still use prevention approaches that show little or no evidence of effectiveness (Arthur, Glaser, & Hawkins, 2001). It is quite common for community leaders to design prevention strategies without first assessing the risk factors for delinquency that exist in their particular communities (for example, drug use is often presumed to be the main cause of delinquency, when, in fact, several other risk factors generally are

present; see Chapter 6). Then the leaders select their favorite programs—typically, these are the programs that the most powerful community leader(s) presume are most effective (leaders who presume drug use is the main cause of delinquency often select the ineffective D.A.R.E. program; see Chapter 7). This might be called the "shotgun" approach to delinquency prevention planning. In addition, these problems—of community leaders not engaging in systematic problem assessment and not selecting effective programs—are often compounded by the ineffective implementation of the programs that are selected (Gottfredson & Gottfredson, 2002).

Delinquency prevention science incorporates the risk- and protection-focused prevention model that initially was pioneered in public health research. The public health model demonstrated that certain health conditions, such as cardiovascular disease, can be prevented through a reduction of the risk factors for those conditions and an increase of the protective factors that buffer or counter those risk factors (Institute of Medicine, 1994). Similarly, the aim of risk- and protection-focused prevention is to interrupt the causal processes that lead to problem behaviors (see Chapter 6).

Because several factors put children at risk of becoming juvenile offenders, multiple-component programs are needed, and priority should be given to preventive actions that reduce risk factors in multiple domains. This is important because, at this point, it is difficult to disentangle risk factors from correlates of serious and violent juvenile offending (Farrington, 2000, p. 7). Moreover, many of the risk factors that predict delinquency and violence also predict other adolescent problem behaviors, including substance abuse, school dropout, early sexual involvement, and teen pregnancy (see Figure 6.1 in Chapter 6). Thus the community benefits of early intervention and prevention programs can be wide-ranging.

The public health approach can be effective with serious and violent juvenile offenders because preventive actions work best when they are implemented at the community level (Catalano et al., 1998). For example, school-based strategies are useful, especially those focused on school organization or classroom-based curricula emphasizing the reinforcement of prosocial and academic skills. The community can intervene by reducing the availability of firearms and drugs and by encouraging norms and laws favorable to prosocial behaviors. Fear of crime is likely to remain high in a community unless local crime conditions are directly addressed (Lane & Meeker, 2000).

A community that takes a data-driven approach to delinquency prevention gathers data to identify and prioritize elevated risk factors in the community; the data, in turn, guide the selection of prevention programs that reduce risk factors and increase protective factors (Arthur et al., 2001). For example, Mahoning County, Ohio, was guided by the Communities That Care operating system in developing a comprehensive prevention plan. The Mahoning County experience, which I describe in Chapter 13, shows how effectively the CTC process works. Hundreds of communities have used it in a similar manner.

Juvenile Justice System

The juvenile justice system needs tools that help minimize the wasteful use of resources on low-risk offenders and maximize allocation of resources to high-risk offenders. This problem is particularly acute at the present time because of the overload of offenders, especially minor ones, in juvenile justice systems across the country. Police, juvenile courts, and correctional systems tend to ignore minor delinquent offenders several times and then crack down on them, pushing them deep into the system to no avail. Conversely, they often fail to recognize potentially serious, violent, and chronic delinquents, and these youths do not receive the necessary sanctions and services. The findings of three studies illustrate these system shortcomings.

In an Oklahoma offender classification study, Wiebush, Wagner, Prestine, and Van Gheem (1993) examined the relationship between the assigned level of supervision (determined informally by the probation officer and the supervisor) and the level of supervision indicated by the results of a structured risk assessment. They found that under current practices, only 2% of the community-supervised youth were assigned to the intensive supervision level; 73% were assigned to the low level of supervision. In contrast, the formal risk assessment results indicated that 27% of the youth were high risk (and therefore should have received intensive supervision) and just 29% were low risk. These extraordinary discrepancies between presumed levels of risk and the levels indicated by formal risk assessments clearly show that the use of informal methods resulted in a significant degree of underclassification. In turn, this finding raises important public safety issues, given that such a small proportion of high-risk offenders were actually receiving the highest level of supervision (Wiebush, 2000).

The second study involved an analysis of offense histories and risk characteristics of training school populations in 14 different states. In each state, Krisberg, Onek, Jones, and Schwartz (1993) applied a structured risk assessment tool to the current training school population to determine the proportion of incarcerated youth who, according to the risk assessment guidelines, required long-term placement in a secure facility, required only short-term secure care, or could be directly placed in a community-based setting. The researchers found that an average of one-third of the training school population in the 14 states scored at low or medium risk on the scales; that is, these youths did not require confinement. It is clear that states do not reserve the use of juvenile corrections facilities for the dangerous few; rather, many have sizable populations of relatively less serious juvenile offenders (Wiebush, 2000).

In the third study, Austin et al. (1994) examined the offenses for which youths were admitted to states' juvenile reformatories in 1993. About half (51%) of the juvenile offenders were not committed for serious or violent offenses, nor had they previously been confined. Only 14% of them were admitted for serious or violent offenses. Unfortunately, these are the most recent national data on youths admitted to states' juvenile reformatories. As noted in Chapter 3, the federal government no longer collects these data (Howell & Krisberg, 1998).

A state or community cannot know for sure whether it is properly protecting the public from juvenile offenders and using its juvenile justice resources in the most cost-effective manner unless it performs formal risk assessments. In addition, without the information that such assessments provide, it has little chance of effectively targeting serious, violent, and chronic delinquents. Better screening of court-referred youth to identify those with multiple risk factors for recidivism can provide a basis for early intervention, which is likely to impede their progression to more serious and violent behavior. Multiple-problem youth—those experiencing a combination of mental health and school problems along with drug use and victimization—are at greatest risk for continued and escalating offending (Huizinga & Jakob-Chien, 1998; Huizinga, Loeber, Thornberry, & Cothern, 2000).

Organizational constraints limit how many juveniles a particular jurisdiction can screen to identify subsets of chronic offenders who can be targeted for special interventions, such as more intensive supervision and more intensive treatment (Smith & Aloisi, 1999). Each jurisdiction needs to set priorities with respect to which subgroups of offenders it wishes to address in a concerted manner, given limited resources. Many jurisdictions choose to assess correctional populations first, because of the high daily costs of confinement. Others choose to assess juvenile court populations first, in a strategy aimed at reducing correctional populations in the future. The next threshold issue is, Which juvenile court subpopulation should be screened? One option is to screen first-time court referrals and allocate additional resources to potential serious, violent, and chronic offenders. This would be an immediate intervention strategy. Another option is to screen repeat offenders and allocate additional resources to them, using intensive probation supervision in a delinquency reduction strategy.

Several studies have shown that when a community has a variety of sanction options, it is likely to use them in a fashion that results in a system somewhat resembling a continuum (Burke & Pennell, 2001; Holsinger & Latessa, 1999; Sametz & Hamparian, 1990; Virginia Department of Criminal Justice Services, 2000; Wagner & Connell, 2002). In general, as offender seriousness increases, so does the level of sanctions. There is some evidence, for example, that criminal activity among high-risk youths may be reduced substantially if the youths are provided more active supervision in the form of more frequent contact with probation officers (Baird, Heinz, & Bemus, 1979; Eisenberg & Markley, 1987). Wiebush and Hamparian (1991) have identified the best practices of probation intensive supervision programs (see Chapter 10).

One recently developed program illustrates the value of using risk and needs assessment instruments to structure juvenile court intervention levels. The Early Court Intervention Project (ECIP), a research and demonstration project, used a risk assessment instrument to identify youths at high risk of becoming chronic offenders and to provide more targeted and appropriate responses within the program. Smith et al. (1996) evaluated ECIP in two New Jersey counties. They assigned cases randomly to an experimental group, in which assessment and interview results were shared with intake personnel, juvenile referees, and judges; and a control group, in which no additional information was shared with court personnel. Some services were provided for the youth in the experimental group, matched with risk level and identified treatment needs. These probation and treatment interventions were consistently related to lower levels of reoffending than were shown by the youth in the control group, who received regular probation.

It should be noted that there are arguments both pro and con regarding the legal and moral fairness of graduated sanctions systems in which sanctions are based on risk assessments (Jones, 1996; Le Blanc, 1998; Smith & Aloisi, 1999; Taxman, Soule, & Gelb, 1999). The main issue is that the risk of harm to society must be balanced against the constraints on liberty associated with juvenile justice system intervention (Smith & Aloisi, 1999). Constraints on individual liberties are unfair when assessments result in "false positives" (that is, juveniles who are not high risk are classified as high risk) and sanctions are wrongly imposed. In addition, excessive punishment may increase recidivism. Conversely, there are higher costs to society when assessments result in "false negatives" (that is, juveniles who are high risk are misclassified as low risk); uncontrolled high-risk juveniles may pose a threat to public safety.

However, whether or not graduated sanctions and risk assessments are used, juvenile justice system staff routinely make judgment calls that result in intrusions in juvenile offenders' lives; for example, they often rely on official records of arrests, which may have little correspondence to the individuals' actual prior behavior (Elliott, 1995). Thus a risk-based classification process that is validated with recidivism data stands a very good chance of increasing the fairness of a system that in the past has often arrived at decisions based on subjective judgments (Wiebush, 2002). In addition, fairness is enhanced by increased consistency in the decisions made in similar cases.

Development of a Structured Decision-Making Model

To improve the administration of juvenile justice, many state and local juvenile justice systems need more structured decision-making systems, driven by risk and needs assessments, governed by individual case management principles, and supported by management information systems. Indeed, in a recent national survey of juvenile probation departments, Torbet (1999) found that this is the general area in which they most need technical assistance. More than one-third of the respondents said that they need help in developing and validating risk and needs assessment instruments, in developing or enhancing their automation capability, and in conducting systemwide assessments of offenders for classification.

These management tools permit juvenile justice system staff to classify offenders based on risk assessments and match offenders with appropriate treatment interventions based on needs assessments. Because all offenders are not the same, jurisdictions need to make concerted efforts to identify subgroups of like offenders who can be dealt with

Box 12.5

Rationale for Using Formal Assessment and Classification Procedures

Programs for juvenile offenders should use formal systems for the assessment and classification of participants for the following reasons (Wiebush, 2002):

- To provide greater validity, structure, and consistency to the assessment and decision-making processes
- To make the allocation of limited system resources more efficient by directing the most intensive and intrusive interventions to the most serious, violent, and chronic offenders
- To promote effective case management practices by providing sound information for the development of detailed treatment plans

Objective classification systems have distinct advantages over informal, discretionary assessments (Office of State Courts Administrator, 2002) because they do the following:

- Promote consistent decisions regarding level of supervision, treatment planning, and program placement
- Reduce threats to public safety by (a) ensuring that those offenders who present unacceptable risks to society are confined in secure settings and/or placed under intensive supervision and (b) reducing the likelihood of future delinquency
- Reduce inequities in case handling by ensuring that individuals with similar histories and patterns of behavior are not treated differently
- Minimize resource waste and inefficiency
- Serve as a basis for determining types and amounts of community services

The following are some of the potential negative consequences of not using formal assessment and classification procedures (Wiebush, 2002):

- Increased risk to public safety, because high-risk and/or violent youths may be placed in settings that are not sufficiently restrictive to control their behavior
- Inefficient use of resources resulting from the placement of nonviolent or low-risk youths in overly restrictive settings
- Inequities resulting from the placement of youths with similar offense, risk, and need characteristics at different levels of intervention
- Negative or inconclusive evaluation of the system and/or individual interventions because of net widening or other evidence of failure to serve intended target populations

---

using a similar management approach, thus facilitating individualized treatment. Jurisdictions will not only be able to target serious, violent, and chronic juvenile offenders more effectively using these tools, their overall effectiveness will be improved by the allocation of scarce resources in the most cost-beneficial manner. However, in addition to being trained in the use of risk and needs assessment instruments, state and local professionals need to be educated concerning the value of using these assessments in a structured decision-making model (see Box 12.5). When such training is not provided, professionals are not apt to see the

utility of these instruments; instead, they are likely to see the work of conducting assessments as burdensome and a waste of time and resources (Mears & Kelly, 1999). Local professionals also need training that addresses a number of legal and process issues (Mears & Kelly, 1999; see also Beyer, Grisso, & Young, 1997).

Objective classification systems are superior to informal, discretionary assessments in that they promote consistent decisions and improve the efficiency of court operations (Office of State Courts Administrator, 2002). A number of negative consequences may result when assessment and

---

Box 12.6

Four Components of the NCCD Structured Decision-Making Model

Structured case assessments:

- Detention screening instrument (to determine eligibility of placements)
- Research-based risk assessment
- Objective assessment of child and family strengths and needs
- Placement matrix for recommending court dispositions
- Standardized case plans
- Routine assessment of case plan progress

Differentiated service standards based on risk, severity, and the youth's need for treatment intervention

A workload accounting system to support agency staff allocation, service planning, and budgeting

A management information system to provide case data for service delivery quality assurance, planning, and evaluation

---

SOURCE: Wiebush (2002).

---

classification procedures consistently fail to link youth with the interventions designed for them (Wiebush, 2002) (see Box 12.5).

The National Council on Crime and Delinquency has developed a structured decision-making model (Wiebush, 2002; see also Baird, 1981, 1984, 1991; Baird, Wagner, & Neuenfeldt, 1992; Howell, 1995; Wiebush et al., 1995) that includes risk assessment, strengths and needs assessment, offender classification, and other management functions (see Box 12.6). Needs assessments are used in tandem with risk assessments to place offenders in different supervision levels, and in programs within various supervision levels, using an offender classification matrix that is organized by risk level and offense severity. Strengths/needs assessments are then used to ensure the best matches between offenders' treatment needs and available programs. In the remainder of this section, I describe the three essential tools of a structured decision-making model: a risk assessment instrument, a needs assessment instrument, and an offender classification matrix.

Risk Assessment and Classification of Offenders

Risk assessment is a statistical procedure for estimating the likelihood that a "critical" event will occur at some time in the future (Wiebush, 2002). In the automobile insurance industry, for example, a critical event is an accident involving an insured driver. In the juvenile justice system, a critical event is generally a new offense committed by a juvenile offender who is on probation or parole. A critical event could also be a new adjudication (finding of guilt) for a new offense or a subsequent commitment (sentencing to placement) to a juvenile reformatory.

Figure 12.4 illustrates the risk assessment concept in terms of the likelihood of a future offense or juvenile court adjudication (Wagner, 2001). This likelihood ranges from no chance (0%) to absolute certainty (100%). However, the most that can be expected of any risk assessment instrument is an *estimate* of this likelihood—for example, an estimate that the probability is "very low," "low," "medium," or "high." Like automobile insurance industry actuarial tables, a juvenile offender risk assessment instrument does not yield infallible predictions for single individuals, only for groups of offenders with similar characteristics (see Box 12.7).

Risk assessments serve to accomplish two important juvenile justice system objectives: the objective of predicting recidivism (a public safety consideration) and the objective of placing offenders in programs that will increase the likelihood of successful rehabilitation (thus serving probation

Box 12.7

Risk Assessment Instrument Development

From the time of their creation, juvenile courts and correctional agencies have used some means of assessing offenders' risk levels. There are four basic approaches to risk assessment: staff judgments, clinical or psychological assessments, consensus-based assessments, and assessments using "actuarial" (research-based) instruments (Wiebush, 2000). Two of these are not reliable at all: Informal staff judgments result in "overclassification" (that is, too many false positives) (Gilliland, Hanke, & Liedka, 1996; Krisberg & Howell, 1998; Krisberg, Onek, Jones, & Schwartz, 1993; Schneider, Ervin, & Snyder, 1996), and clinical predictions have been shown to be significantly less accurate than assessments based on the use of empirically derived tools. In a comparison of clinical judgments with actuarial approaches, actuarial methods performed better than clinical procedures in 46% of the studies, and equally well in 48%, whereas clinical judgments outperformed actuarial prediction in only 6% of the studies (Grove et al., 1990; for a summary of this study, see Grove & Meehl, 1996). Consensus-based risk assessments (i.e., assessments using structured tools that incorporate items agreed upon by a group of agency staff) are also less accurate than assessments made using actuarial instruments (Wiebush, Johnson, & Wagner 1997; Wiebush & Wagner, 1995), but most jurisdictions have no choice but to begin with consensus-based assessments, because they do not have the necessary historical data to develop actuarial instruments.

The actuarial approach to risk assessment is similar to that used by the automobile insurance industry to determine insurance rates. Insurance companies analyze historical data on driver characteristics and outcomes (accidents) to determine the set of driver characteristics most closely correlated with accidents. After those characteristics are identified, all new clients are assessed to determine the extent to which their characteristics are similar to those who have had low, medium, or high failure rates in the past. In other words, the individual's future behavior is estimated based on the known outcomes of a group of individuals with similar characteristics (Baird, 1984).

Similarly, actuarial juvenile offender risk assessment instruments are based on the statistical relationship between youth characteristics (risk factors) and recidivism rates (Wiebush, 2002; see also Baird, 1984; for a discussion of the essential properties of assessment and classification systems, see Wiebush, Baird, Krisberg, & Onek, 1995, pp. 181-183). These instruments are designed to estimate the likelihood of an individual's reoffending within a given time period—generally, 18-24 months. Thus risk assessment instruments are used to separate offenders into risk levels, a practice sometimes called *risk-level classification*. Ideally, offenders would be placed at various levels within a graduated sanctions system based on their likelihood of recidivism.

A *valid* risk assessment instrument is one that does what it purports to do—that is, accurately distinguishes among subgroups of youth according to the probability that they will engage in delinquent behavior (Wagner, 2001). A *reliable* instrument is one that successfully ensures that similar cases receive similar placements and similar recommendations for interventions and services. Research results supporting the validity of risk assessments "have increased dramatically in recent years" (Andrews, 1996, p. 43). One reason is that, with the growth of automated court and correctional records systems, large databases are now available to researchers who want to conduct risk assessment studies.

Recent studies have examined the validity and reliability of risk assessment instruments for probation and parole populations in the juvenile field in Georgia (Risler, Sutphen, & Shields, 2000); Maryland (Wiebush et al., 1997); Missouri (Johnson, Wagner, & Matthews, 2001; Kempf-Leonard, 1998); Nebraska (National Council on Crime and Delinquency, 1996a); North Carolina (Fraser, Day, & Schwalbe, 2002); Oklahoma (Wiebush, Wagner, Prestine, & Van Gheem, 1993); Oakland, California (Ebner, 2001); Rhode Island (Wagner & Wiebush, 1996; Wiebush & Wagner, 1995); Travis County, Texas (National Council on Crime and Delinquency, 1996b); and Virginia (Wiebush, Wagner, & Ehrlich, 1999; Wiebush, Wagner, Healy, & Baird, 1996).

(Continued)

Box 12.7 (Continued)

The predictive validity of juvenile risk assessment instruments has been established in a number of other studies (Holt, 1997; Jung & Rawana, 1999; Krysik & LeCroy, 2002; Sawicki, Schaeffer, & Thies, 1999; Schumacher & Kurz, 2000; for references to other validations, see Bonta, 1996, p. 23; Wiebush, 2002). Risk assessment instruments recently have been validated for several serious and violent juvenile offender subgroups, including felony recidivists (Barnoski, 1998), and first-time referrals versus second- and third-time referrals (LeCroy, Krysik, & Palumbo, 1998), and also for potential chronic offenders among second-time offenders (Smith & Aloisi, 1999). In this last risk assessment instrument validation, which was done on a sample of juvenile court cases in New Jersey, Smith and Aloisi (1999) found that the most efficient prediction method would be to screen second-time offenders, because their likelihood of continuing to offend is very high. They also found that both prospective and retrospective risk instruments predicted chronic delinquent behavior well for second-time juvenile offenders. One instrument has been validated specifically for females (Funk, 1999).

and correctional rehabilitation goals). To fulfill the latter objective, jurisdictions must conduct needs assessments (which I discuss shortly) in conjunction with risk assessments in order to make the best matches between offender treatment needs and intervention options.

Risk assessment instruments are composed of predetermined sets of scale items that research has shown to be statistically related to recidivism. Offenders' scores on these instruments are used to sort them into groups with differing probabilities of reoffending. A set of core variables have been identified repeatedly as recidivism predictors for juvenile offenders. In an examination of 13 research-based risk assessment instruments that NCCD had developed, Wiebush (2002) found that substance abuse and peer relations appeared on all 13 instruments, and that age at first referral to court intake and school discipline/attendance appeared on 12 of the 13 scales. Other common items include total referrals for violent/assaultive offenses, parent/sibling criminality, parental supervision, victim of child abuse or neglect, number of out-of-home placements, and total number of court referrals. These 10 items make up the NCCD Model Risk Assessment Instrument (Wiebush, 2002). Wiebush (2000) found that some items increase the classification power of the scales in some jurisdictions but not in others. This finding suggests that there are site-specific factors that influence either recidivism or the measurement of it. Therefore, it is essential that each jurisdiction validate its own risk assessment instrument.

Until recently, risk assessment instruments could not reliably predict violent recidivism, because of the low base rate. Numerous risk assessment validation studies have indicated that only about 10% of juvenile offenders who recidivate do so by committing violent offenses (Wiebush, 2000). This low base rate makes it difficult to identify with statistical confidence those characteristics that discriminate between youth who do and do not subsequently commit violent offenses (Clear, 1988). However, the recent availability of large, statewide databases has made such a discrimination possible. Three risk assessment instruments have been validated that successfully classified youth based on their likelihood of committing subsequent violent offenses—in Maryland (Wiebush et al., 1997), Missouri (Johnson, Wagner, & Matthews, 2001), and Virginia (Wiebush et al., 1999). Juveniles classified as high risk using the Virginia scale were found to be three times more likely than low-risk offenders to have subsequent violent offenses. The Missouri risk assessment instrument is even stronger: High-risk youth had a subsequent violent offense referral rate that was six times greater than that of low-risk youth (Johnson et al., 2001).

Canadian/American researchers are incorporating needs assessment items with risk factors in an attempt to strengthen the predictive power of assessment instruments. Their studies suggest that needs assessment also has predictive validity for recidivism (Andrews & Bonta, 1998; Bonta, 1996; Holsinger & Latessa, 1999). Thus treatment needs are viewed as a subset of risk factors in the Canadian/American prediction studies.

Many American experts in juvenile risk assessment contend that combining risk and need items on a single scale only serves to undermine the risk classification process, because such a scale includes

Risk Continuum
(Risk of New Arrest or Adjudication)

Risk Assessment Classifications

Very Low	Low	Moderate	High

Figure 12.4   Elements of Risk Assessment

SOURCE: *Risk and Needs Assessment for Juvenile Justice,* by D. Wagner, 2001. © 2001 by National Council on Crime and Delinquency. Reprinted with permission.

items that are not related to recidivism (Wiebush, 2000). Smith et al. (1996) conducted a study to compare such a combination instrument with an instrument designed to assess risk alone. They first combined risk and need factors into one scale of six items that were statistically significant predictors of recidivism: poor school performance, behavior problems in school, lack of parental control, negative peer influences, substance abuse, and lack of a sense of mastery. They found that a seven-item risk scale was more successful in identifying high-risk juvenile offenders than the combined risk and needs scale. Items on this scale were poor school performance, poor school behavior, parental reports of juvenile behavioral problems, juvenile self-reported drug use, lack of a sense of mastery, lawbreaking of juvenile peers, and a reading comprehension test. Smith et al. also examined legal and neurological risk instruments, but neither predicted recidivism as well as the seven-item risk scale.

Needs Assessments

Needs assessments are used to determine the specific program interventions to be delivered within the designated custody/supervision level (Wiebush et al., 1995, p. 181). A needs assessment is intended to do the following:

- Provide an overview of the level of seriousness of the juvenile offender's treatment needs
- Provide information that can assist professionals in developing a treatment plan to address the juvenile's needs
- Provide a baseline for monitoring the juvenile's progress
- Provide a basis for establishing workload priorities
- Aid agency administrators in evaluating resource availability throughout the jurisdiction and determining program gaps that need to be filled

The use of formal needs assessment instruments to identify critical treatment needs of offenders is rare (Latessa, Cullen, & Gendreau, 2002), but rapidly gaining in popularity. Unlike risk assessments, needs assessments do not predict future behavior, thus they are not developed through empirical research. Instead, jurisdictions employ a consensus approach to identify and set priorities for the most important service issues. Local professionals are responsible for selecting the items to include in the needs assessment instrument. They are guided in this effort by existing state and federal laws (e.g., laws addressing special education services), research identifying effective and promising programs, and local philosophies about effective rehabilitation services. In the structured decision-making model, needs assessment results are used to adjust the placement of offenders in various risk levels (as recommended by risk assessment results). For example, a juvenile offender who is determined to be at medium risk and has a very high treatment needs score might be placed in a program for high-risk juveniles to take advantage of the relatively intensive treatment services offered by the program.

Needs assessment instruments typically include items concerning offender needs in areas that correspond with risk factors for delinquency, including family functioning or relationships, school attendance and behavior, peer relationships (e.g., negative peer associations and gang involvement), and individual problems (e.g., substance abuse and emotional stability) (Wiebush et al., 1995, p. 183). Many instruments also include measures of health and hygiene, intellectual ability, and learning disabilities. For an example of one such instrument, see the North Carolina Assessment of Juvenile Needs, which is included in the appendix to this volume.

A structured needs assessment serves several purposes in addition to its usefulness for program selection and case planning. It ensures that all staff examine certain treatment issues consistently for all youth. It provides a simple, easy-to-use overview of an individual's problems for the case manager, program staff, and service providers. Needs assessment scores also provide additional measures that can be used in setting priorities; that is, more time can be devoted to cases with higher scores. Periodic reassessments of treatment needs also help case managers monitor client progress and can indicate when adjustments might be needed in individual treatment regimens. Finally, aggregated information derived from needs assessments provides a database for agency planning and evaluation, especially for determining whether there are sufficient treatment resources in the community to meet current client treatment needs.

A third type of assessment tool frequently used in the juvenile justice system is the *placement assessment* or *custody assessment* instrument (Wiebush et al., 1995, pp. 179-180). Although such instruments may include predictive items, they generally are driven by policy considerations (issues of public safety) rather than by recidivism results. They may be used in several different ways: as screening tools to determine whether youths should be placed in detention pending their adjudication hearings, as guides for corrections officials to use in determining youths' appropriate placement or level of security, or as methods for determining the custody needs of incarcerated youths (Roush, 1996a). Because public safety is the main consideration in the use of these instruments, they typically include measures of current and prior offense severity.

Classification Matrices

Figure 12.1 illustrates the continuum of graduated sanctions in the NCCD graduated sanctions model. Classification matrices simply group such sanctions according to the risk levels of offenders for which certain sanctions are appropriate. A simple classification matrix—the one currently used in North Carolina—is shown in Figure 12.2, and the continuum of options for that matrix is shown in Table 12.1. There are alternative ways of representing options in a graduated sanctions continuum. Figure 12.5 shows the juvenile court classification matrix used in Travis County, Texas. Note the dispositions that juvenile offenders are expected to receive at the different classification levels. Level 1 cases receive 3 to 6 months of probation. Level 2 cases are assigned to probation plus curfew restrictions. Offenders classified in Level 3 are assigned to the ISP or residential treatment. Finally, offenders classified in Level 4 are committed to the Texas Youth Commission, which likely means placement in a long-term residential correctional facility.

Figure 12.6 is yet another classification matrix. It was developed for the classification of juvenile offenders in the Indiana Department of Corrections. Note the more elaborate disposition options in this matrix for offenders placed in each classification level. I should insert one caveat here: A classification matrix merely suggests possible disposition options; judges are not bound to order specific dispositions. Classification matrices serve as guidelines to help increase the consistency of dispositions. Each community that develops a classification matrix decides which treatment options it wishes to include in its continuum of program options. Use of a classification matrix helps to improve case management of juvenile offenders.

A hallmark of the juvenile justice system is individualized treatment of offenders. By using risk and needs assessments and a classification matrix, a community can facilitate better matching of offenders' risk profiles with the appropriate sanction levels to protect the public and better matching of offender treatment needs with interventions. The next frontier in this work is assessment of offender responsivity to treatment (see Chapter 10). Offenders differ in their motivations, personalities, and

Risk Level

Offense Severity Class	High	Medium	Low
Aggravated Felony 1	Level 4	Level 4	Level 4
Non-Aggravated Felony 1	Level 4	Level 3	Level 2
Felony 2	Level 3	Level 3	Level 2
Felony 3 or 4/Misd. Weapon	Level 3	Level 2	Level 1
Misdemeanor—No Weapon	Level 2	Level 1	Level 1
Status	Level 1	Level 1	Level 1

Level 1 = Probation 3-6 months
Level 2 = Probation/Curfew
Level 3 = ISP or Residential Treatment
Level 4 = Texas Youth Commission

Figure 12.5   Travis County Juvenile Court Draft Presumptive Placement Matrix for Juvenile Adjudications

SOURCE: *Risk and Needs Assessment for Juvenile Justice,* by D. Wagner, 2001. © 2001 by National Council on Crime and Delinquency. Reprinted with permission.

emotional and cognitive abilities, and these characteristics can influence their responsiveness to various therapies and treatment modalities (Bonta, 1996, p. 31). Tools also are needed that will help jurisdictions reduce minority overrepresentation in juvenile justice systems. Use of objective risk and needs assessment instruments will help (Box 12.8).

Information Systems

Jurisdictions need automated information systems to help them carry out the essential functions of a juvenile justice case management system. Missouri has developed the J-TRAC system, which is an ideal automated information system that is compatible with the state's Juvenile Offender Risk and Need Assessment and Classification System (Office of State Courts Administrator, 2002). J-TRAC allows users to complete risk and needs assessments, assign dispositions for delinquency cases, and collect case management information on juvenile offenders and victims of neglect and abuse online. As the acronym suggests, J-TRAC automates the four basic functions of the full classification strategy:

• *Tracking:* Information on juvenile offenders is stored in J-TRAC's central repository.

This secure system is accessible to juvenile and family court professionals and fully documents official activities involving the offender.

• *Referral:* Demographic, offense, and disposition information is collected and warehoused in J-TRAC for use in future case management decision making and administrative planning.

• *Assessment:* J-TRAC provides for interactive, online risk and needs assessment of juvenile offenders.

• *Classification:* J-TRAC selects from the classification matrix a set of graduated sanctions for a given risk classification and offense severity level.

(More information about J-TRAC is available on the Web site of Missouri's Office of State Courts Administrator, at www.osca.state.mo.us/osca/index.nsf.)

The Missouri Juvenile and Adult Court Programs Division is currently integrating the classification system (risk and needs) with sanctions and programs within the juvenile case management automated information system. This will provide a full profile—across the state—of offender risk levels, sanctions that are used for them, treatment

Risk

Offense Severity	High	Medium	Low
I. Violent offenses	Violent offender program, assaultive sex offender program, staff secure residential	Violent offender program, assaultive sex offender program, staff secure residential	Boot camp, intermediate sanction program
II. Serious offenses	Boot camp, intermediate sanction program, Ecology/Job Corps	Intermediate sanction program	Intermediate sanction program, day treatment, specialized group homes
III. Less serious offenses	Intermediate sanction program, day treatment, specialized group homes	Tracking, proctor program, community service	Community service, community supervision, mentors
IV. Minor offenses	Proctor program, tracking, community supervision	Community supervision, mentors	Mentors

Figure 12.6   Indiana Department of Corrections Placement Matrix (proposed)

SOURCE: *Risk Assessment and Classification for Serious, Violent, and Chronic Juvenile Offenders* (p. 197), by R. G. Wiebush, C. Baird, B. Krisberg, and D. Onek, 1995, Thousand Oaks, CA: Sage. Copyright 1995 by Sage Publications, Inc. Reprinted with permission.

needs, and programs that are provided, by risk and treatment need levels. Juvenile justice staff will then be able to identify gaps in sanctions and services without any guesswork.

Detention Reform

As noted in Chapter 3, over the past decade, the numbers of youths who are being detained have grown, largely because of increases in the numbers of juvenile court cases. A majority of these youths are held in overcrowded facilities. Because of the overuse of detention and the unacceptable conditions in many detention centers (Burrell, 2000), in 1992 the Annie E. Casey Foundation launched the Juvenile Detention Alternatives Initiative (JADI), a multimillion-dollar 5-year, five-site experiment designed "to streamline and rationalize local juvenile detention systems" (Stanfield, 2000, p. 1). This very successful initiative provides a blueprint for detention reform that any jurisdiction experiencing common detention problems can follow (see Box 12.9 for a list of some widespread problems).

Confining juvenile offenders in detention centers is very expensive. The cost of constructing a detention center averages $100,000 per bed, and operating costs hover around $100 per bed per day (Steinhart, 2000a, p. 54). These combined costs amount to as much as a half million dollars for one bed over a 10-year period. Steinhart (2000a) describes in detail the major milestones in a comprehensive juvenile detention planning strategy:

Stage 1: Document and describe the current juvenile detention system (Steinhart, 2000a, pp. 20-36). Step 1 should consist of a quantitative analysis of current detention use and characteristics of detained youth. Step 2 is a "systems analysis," a review of detention policies and procedures. Step 3 is an analysis of the conditions of confinement (Burrell, 2000), to meet legal standards of care and to ensure the protection of children and staff. Step 4 is a cost analysis, including the cost per day per detention bed, alternative program cost per day, proposed cost of new facilities, case processing costs, and policy-related costs.

Box 12.8

Addressing Minority Overrepresentation With Risk and Needs Assessments

---

The use of objective risk and needs assessment and placement instruments can help greatly to reduce minority overrepresentation in the juvenile justice system. When agencies do not use objective instruments, they have a tendency to make disposition decisions strictly on the basis of juveniles' official offense histories. Because minorities are more likely than nonminorities to be arrested, they tend to have longer arrest records. This means that minority youths are more likely to receive harsher dispositions. The use of objective instruments to assess risk and needs and to determine placement can help to level the playing field by taking other factors into consideration. For example, objective risk assessment instruments measure the level of risk to public safety that minority youths *actually* present, and objective needs assessment instruments show their *actual* treatment needs. When placement decisions are based on such assessments, there is an increased likelihood that minorities will be placed in community-based treatment programs rather than in correctional facilities, where there are fewer treatment programs.

All jurisdictions should use an established methodology to assess whether minorities are overrepresented in the juvenile justice system (Pope, 1995). Where children of color are overrepresented, jurisdictions should: (a) implement training workshops focusing on race and juvenile processing, (b) establish systems of "checks and balances" with regard to juvenile processing decisions, and (c) develop guidelines to aid decision makers in reaching outcome decisions. They should also develop ways to fill existing program gaps so that the programs address the specific needs of children of color (National Council of Juvenile and Family Court Judges, 1990). Austin (1995) suggests several other specific steps communities can take to alleviate disproportionate minority representation in the juvenile justice system:

- Provide cultural sensitivity training for police, probation officers and judges.
- Provide family counseling and support services to minority clients in community-based agencies.
- Use social workers and case advocates to help minority youths and families navigate the juvenile justice system and to develop alternative-to-institution dispositions.
- Provide mentoring programs to link positive role models to high-risk youths and to build self-esteem and responsibility among these youths.
- Provide voucher systems for purchases of services by minority families.
- Provide job training and placement programs for minority youths.
- Provide police diversion and other preadjudication diversion programs, funded in proportion to local minority representation in the juvenile justice system.
- Dedicate assets captured in the "war on drugs" to minority programs, in proportion to current rates of minority representation in the juvenile justice system.

Stage 2: Identify local juvenile detention goals, which constitute the essential framework for local detention policy (Steinhart, 2000a, pp. 37-39). Secure pretrial detention is justified by state and federal laws as a means to protect the public and ensure a minor's court appearance. The U.S. Constitution bars the use of pretrial detention for the purpose of punishment (Burrell, 2000).

Stage 3: Define the reformed system. Key reform strategies should include (a) developing objective screening criteria and risk assessment instruments, (b) addressing unnecessary case

processing delays, (c) developing alternatives to secure detention, (d) dealing with minors in postdisposition detention, (e) addressing conditions of confinement, (f) dealing with disproportionate minority and female confinement, and (g) deciding to build or not to build additional detention capacity (Steinhart, 2000a, pp. 40-57).

Stage 4: Identify the cost of reforms, resources needed, and barriers to reform (Steinhart, 2000a, pp. 58-62). These are important considerations in the development of a realistic plan.

Box 12.9
Common Detention Problems

- Overcrowding in the detention facility
- No screening criteria applied at intake
- Proposed construction of new facilities or additional detention capacity
- High detention rates for status offenders and misdemeanor property/drug cases
- High rates of disproportionate minority confinement
- High detention rates for children with failures to appear, technical probation violators
- Many postdisposition youths (e.g., placement failures) in custody
- Detention beds filled with adult court cases (i.e., transfers)
- Deteriorating facilities, substandard conditions of confinement
- Children locked down for long periods of time during the day
- Physical or chemical restraints employed to control children
- High rate of AWOLs (absent without leave) or escapes
- Few or no alternatives to secure detention available
- Hostile relations and poor communication between agencies with juvenile detention roles and responsibilities

---

SOURCE: Steinhart (2000a, p. 15).

Stage 5: Finalize and draft the action plan. The following are important considerations in setting priorities (Steinhart, 2000a, pp. 63-67):

- Comprehensive reform is best.
- Front-gate controls (objective risk screens) are a vital first step.
- Reduction of overcrowding must be a priority.
- Facility or program defects affecting the health and safety of children must be addressed.
- A continuum of alternatives to secure custody should be established (DeMuro, 2000).
- Priority should be assigned to reforms that are likely to address the problems causing the highest detention loads.
- Projections of future detention populations must be made.
- Management information system improvements are important, especially to increase accountability and improve operations.

A similar prescriptive guide is needed for the reform of juvenile reformatories, but such reform is more difficult because rehabilitation programs are involved, whereas detention—because of the short stays—involves few treatment programs. In addition, detention facilities typically are locally controlled, whereas reformatories are usually state controlled. Nevertheless, the use of Comprehensive Strategy tools will take states a long way toward reforming juvenile corrections. For example, use of tools in the structured decision-making model will reduce reliance on long-term confinement, because few low- and medium-risk offenders will be placed in long-term facilities. This would be a major first step toward reform, but improvements in many other areas are also needed.

Observations on System
Reform and Evaluation

Many states are not ready to undertake the kinds of broad-scale system reforms and attendant improvements that North Carolina and other states have achieved (see Chapter 13). Juvenile justice and youth service officials in many states are content with the status quo. Many allow egregious youth service and juvenile justice system problems, such as misuse and overuse of detention, to go unattended. In many cases, they do so because they feel that the resources they would need to change the situation simply are not available. Reforming juvenile justice systems for the better currently is not a priority in most state legislatures. It is as difficult for many legislators to foresee the long-term benefits of system reform as it is for them to foresee the long-term negative consequences of punishment-oriented systems.

Other states and localities are enticed by piecemeal approaches, such as importing a single highly touted program that they are led to believe will magically improve their overall system. Simplistic solutions for oversimplified delinquency problems are very appealing. Boot camps are a current example. In an era almost, but not completely, gone by, Scared Straight programs represented a panacea. Jurisdictions that opt for risky, simplistic solutions can easily get "caught with [their] panacea down around [their] ankles" (Miller, 1996, p. 77). As noted in Chapter 7, several lawsuits have been filed to challenge the conditions of confinement in boot camps, and the deaths of several youngsters sentenced to boot camps have been reported (Blackwood, 2001; Krajicek, 2000).

States go through cycles in which attitudes shift from liberal to conservative, or from rehabilitation to punishment in juvenile justice policies, just as the entire nation does (Bernard, 1992). States and localities that get a grip on the management of their juvenile justice systems by using a structured decision-making model driven by research and by formal risk and needs assessment and placement instruments are much more likely to sustain comprehensive system reforms. In contrast, states that do not systematically use these tools tend to drift back and forth between progressive and business-as-usual policies and practices.

Implementation of the Comprehensive Strategy is a long-term system reform process. Complete implementation of the prevention, early intervention, and graduated sanctions components may take as long as 4 or 5 years. Approximately a year is required to complete the "linchpin" assessment in the prevention component. Development and implementation of the tools for the structured decision-making model (risk and needs assessment instruments and a classification matrix) and validation studies of the risk assessment instruments may take 3 to 4 years. Then, the development of a continuum of program responses takes time. For example, development of the graduated sanctions component of San Diego's Comprehensive Strategy—Breaking Cycles—took approximately 2 years from start-up to stabilization of services. Thus, as a first step in redesigning its juvenile justice system, a community needs to develop a 5-year strategic plan that lays out the multiple steps involved in establishing a comprehensive framework that integrates prevention, early intervention, and graduated sanctions components.

Thus the Comprehensive Strategy needs to be evaluated in a long-term context. Several process evaluations have been completed on pilot implementation sites (Coolbaugh & Hansel, 2000). Evaluation of the San Diego Breaking Cycles program has been completed. The other three pilot sites were not evaluated. Preliminary results are available from the Orange County, California, implementation. Another evaluation, in Richmond, Virginia, assessed the implementation of the city's graduated sanctions continuum (Virginia Department of Criminal Justice Services, 2000). Evaluation of the Baton Rouge implementation is under way. I discuss each of these programs in Chapter 13.

Some evaluation tools are built into the Comprehensive Strategy framework. A well-developed prevention plan is based on a baseline of risk and protective factors. Programs selected to address these factors are expected to change the baseline risk and protective factors. If they do not, they are not effective and should be either improved or discarded.

Similarly, a structured decision-making model that includes reassessments of risks and needs makes evaluation of a continuum of programs possible at two levels. Evaluation at the first level involves determining whether or not programs and services are successfully reducing risks and meeting the treatment needs of offenders. An automated management information system that includes risk-needs assessments and reassessments will facilitate this level of program evaluation. Evaluation at the second level involves determining whether or not programs and services are reducing recidivism, which also can be tracked using the automated management information system. The structured decision-making model used statewide in Missouri has both of these evaluation capabilities, as I show in Chapter 13. Communities should arrange for periodic independent experimental evaluations of programs to verify whether or not the tracked outcomes are actually the result of programs in the graduated sanctions continuum.

If the Standardized Program Evaluation Protocol development work currently under way in North Carolina is successful, it may be feasible for researchers to develop a protocol of sufficient scope that it will have general applicability elsewhere. Such a protocol might enable the evaluation of the entire continuum of juvenile justice programs in a given jurisdiction and, collectively, statewide. Independent evaluation is needed to measure the extent to which risk and needs assessments, and the use of a structured decision-making model, produce better matches between offenders' risk and needs and particular sanctions and program interventions. This is a key principle of the Comprehensive

Strategy. The extent to which the Comprehensive Strategy provides a context within which the wraparound process can be more effective also needs to be evaluated.

Summary

In this chapter, I have described the Comprehensive Strategy for Serious, Violent, and Chronic Juvenile Offenders (Wilson & Howell, 1993). I have discussed the general principles of the Comprehensive Strategy framework, the strategy's theoretical foundations, and its major components. I have also cited some of the research supporting the Comprehensive Strategy, referring back to discussions in earlier chapters. In addition, I have defined and explained the major tools that are used in the implementation of the Comprehensive Strategy.

A major goal of the Comprehensive Strategy is juvenile justice system improvement. This goal is activated by two processes that are considered to be linchpins in comprehensive juvenile justice strategy development. First, a community must conduct a comprehensive assessment of the risk and protective factors for delinquency in its specific jurisdiction, instead of arbitrarily selecting interventions that may miss the mark. Communities are different from one another. Because each has a distinct combination of predominant risk factors, this assessment process is critical to successful prevention programming.

Second, juvenile justice system agencies must assess the delinquent populations in their jurisdictions for risk and treatment needs, to classify and position offenders within a structured system of graduated sanctions. Comprehensive risk and needs assessments are needed to get the best matches between offenders and programs (Bonta, 1996; Gendreau, 1996b; Jones, 1996). Good matches cannot be achieved until risk assessments are done to determine which offenders belong in various classification levels of the juvenile justice system. In the structured decision-making model developed by the National Council on Crime and Delinquency, juvenile justice officials use needs assessments in tandem with risk assessments to place offenders in different supervision levels, then in programs within various supervision levels, by consulting a matrix that organizes sanctions and programs by risk level and offense severity (Howell, 1995; Wiebush, 2002; Wiebush et al., 1995).

The overall goal of a graduated sanctions system is to achieve a good fit between the positions of delinquents in pathways toward serious, violent, and chronic careers and interventions that are graduated in concert with progression in delinquent pathways. Offenders can be stepped up through the levels of sanctions as they progress in delinquent careers and stepped down as they decelerate or desist from delinquent activity. Aftercare is a critical component of a comprehensive system, because it constitutes step-down interventions and continuous treatment.

The prevention and early intervention component of the Comprehensive Strategy uses a risk and protection assessment process that is grounded in the public health model. In this chapter, I have used the Communities That Care system to illustrate how communities can better focus prevention programs on priority risk factors. I have also described a structured decision-making model that employs the tools of risk and needs assessment instruments and an offender classification matrix to place offenders along a continuum of graduated sanctions and programs. The structured decision-making model should be combined with other tools—especially an automated management information system—for cost-effective operation of the juvenile justice system.

To maximize the cost-effectiveness of their juvenile justice systems, communities and states need integrated, multidisciplinary, multiagency wraparound service delivery systems that can simultaneously address multiple child and adolescent problem behaviors and ensure public safety. Adoption of this framework for system reform will enable communities to address effectively most of the juvenile justice system problems outlined at the beginning of this chapter, particularly the following:

- Poor targeting of serious, violent, and chronic juvenile offenders
- Poor matching of offenders with appropriate levels of supervision, sanctions, and programs
- Overreliance on detention, incarceration, and residential programs
- Inadequate data collection on offenders in the system, management information systems, and information sharing
- Lack of good policy guidance for state executive, legislative, and judicial stakeholders in the development of legislation, standards, and other policy directives that create data-driven, outcome-based, and results-oriented juvenile justice policy reforms

Because the Comprehensive Strategy is a research-based, data-driven, and outcome-focused process, participating communities use the data gathered in these initial steps to determine needed system reforms and improvements. In the North Carolina example, a sharp reduction in training school admissions was achieved using risk and needs assessments in a structured decision-making model. An $11 million reduction in training school costs was realized in just 3 years.

In Chapter 13, I illustrate the Comprehensive Strategy components described above by providing examples from actual programs.

Discussion Questions

1. What is the philosophy of the Comprehensive Strategy?

2. How does the Comprehensive Strategy work?

3. What are the two linchpins for successful implementation of the Comprehensive Strategy? What are the tools that are used to carry out the linchpin functions?

4. What is the structured decision-making model? What are the benefits of this model?

5. What is unique about the way North Carolina is going about implementing the graduated sanctions component of the Comprehensive Strategy?

13

■

AN ILLUSTRATION OF THE
COMPREHENSIVE STRATEGY FRAMEWORK

In Chapter 12, I described and explained the components of the Comprehensive Strategy and the tools used to implement those components. I also described North Carolina's experience in the use of Comprehensive Strategy tools to illustrate how these advanced techniques are applied. In this chapter, I describe a number of programs that can be used all along the continuum of prevention and graduated sanctions. I feature the experiences of states and communities that are in the process of implementing the Comprehensive Strategy.

Comprehensive Strategy Components

As noted in Chapter 12, the Comprehensive Strategy consists of two main components: prevention and early intervention, and graduated sanctions.

The prevention and early intervention component is based on a risk- and protection-focused model that was initially developed in the public health arena. A continuum of prevention strategies is needed to address each of the major risk factor domains (individual, family, peer group, school, and community).

The graduated sanctions component consists of five levels of sanctions, moving from least to most restrictive (see Figure III.1):

- Immediate intervention with first-time delinquent offenders (misdemeanors and non-violent felonies) and nonserious repeat offenders
- Intermediate sanctions for first-time serious or violent offenders, including intensive

supervision for chronic and serious/violent offenders
- Community confinement in small community-based facilities or programs for offenders who require intensive services in a staff-secure environment
- Secure corrections for the most serious, violent, and chronic offenders
- Aftercare for confined youths, including step-down interventions coupled with decreasing services

In this chapter, I show how a community can use the linchpin tools of the Comprehensive Strategy to build an infrastructure in each of the two principal components: to link a continuum of proven-effective program options with community profiles in the prevention component and with offender profiles in the graduated sanctions component.

Delinquency Prevention
and Early Intervention

The delinquency prevention component of the Comprehensive Strategy also includes early intervention with disruptive children and child delinquents. Early intervention is included with prevention (for all youths) because the programs that intervene early with child delinquents and disruptive children (at-risk children) who may become child delinquents normally are outside the juvenile justice system.

Box 13.1
Comprehensive Strategy Continuum

Delinquency prevention and early intervention

    Delinquency prevention with all youth
    Early intervention with disruptive children and child delinquents

Graduated sanctions

    Immediate intervention
    Intermediate sanctions
    Community confinement
    Secure care
    Aftercare

SOURCES: Wilson and Howell (1993); Howell (1995).

Delinquency Prevention

Mahoning County, Ohio, is currently implementing the prevention/intervention and graduated sanctions components of the Comprehensive Strategy. The entire Mahoning County Strategic Plan for Youth and Families is posted on the county's Web site devoted to the Comprehensive Strategy at www.compstrat.org. The development of this prevention/intervention plan was guided by the Communities That Care prevention planning system. Information on the Web site succinctly describes the planning process, in which the community engaged a 120-member team of representatives from every sector of the community (click on "Community Planning Team") in assessing research-based risk factors for delinquency and other problem behaviors as shown in Figure 6.1 in Chapter 6 of this book. In fact, this figure appears on the Mahoning County Web site in the condensed version of the Strategic Plan. Once the members of the Community Planning Team completed their assessment of risk factors for delinquency and other problem behaviors, they identified four as having high priority: extreme economic deprivation, favorable parental attitudes toward crime and involvement in the problem behavior, early and persistent antisocial behavior, and alienation and rebelliousness. (Information on the data collection and analysis is also available on the Web site; click on "Data Collection Work Group Pages" in the full version of the Strategic Plan). The Planning Team then assessed existing community resources (i.e., prevention

programs) in terms of the extent to which these address risk factors and protective factors, identified gaps, and crafted a program development plan to address the priority risk factors. The Planning Team also identified actions that can be taken to increase protective factors that are specified in the social development strategy (Hawkins & Catalano, 1993) shown in Figure 6.2 in Chapter 6 of this book (which also appears in the condensed version of Mahoning County's Strategic Plan). Finally, the Planning Team developed a detailed set of recommendations that currently are being implemented to carry out Mahoning County's comprehensive strategy, a program called the Mahoning County Strategic Plan for Youth and Families, developed "for the community by the community."

Mahoning County's experience is an excellent example of how communities can be engaged in research-based risk- and protection-focused prevention. It shows how the Communities That Care process empowered the county leaders to assess *their own area's* risk factors, prioritize them, and then assess existing programs, identify gaps, and select strategies and programs *this community* wishes to implement. This is what is meant by the expression *implementing prevention science.*

Another example, one that shows the linkage between prioritized risk factors and selected *programs* more explicitly, is the case of the application of the CTC prevention planning system in Galveston, Texas (Comprehensive Youth Strategies Project, 2000). Information about Galveston's experience can be accessed online (at 129.109.4.55/resource/compstrat/compstrat.htm). Other examples of community-level implementation of risk- and protection-focused prevention are found in OJJDP reports on the Title V prevention program, which used the CTC prevention planning system for several years (Office of Juvenile Justice and Delinquency Prevention, 2002).

Early Intervention With
Disruptive Children and Child Delinquents

As noted in Chapter 4, from one-fourth to one-third of disruptive children become child delinquents, and about a third of all child delinquents later become serious, violent, and chronic offenders. Yet, as Loeber and Farrington (2000) observe, "we know less about [the numbers and characteristics of such] children in the United States than about farm animals" (p. 756). There are no annual surveys concerning the numbers of persistent disruptive children in elementary schools, or in child welfare/protection agencies. Police referral data are scant, and juvenile courts have not been expected to handle them for a quarter of a century (Howell, 2001a). Policy makers are more likely to fund programs for adolescents and costly residential corrections for older juveniles rather than they are to fund programs for child delinquents (Loeber & Farrington, 2000).

There are four fundamental strategies for early intervention with child delinquents. The first is to intervene with at-risk children, particularly disruptive children. This has proven to be an effective early intervention strategy. The Montreal Preventive Treatment Program combined parent training with training in individual social skills for disruptive 7- to 9-year-old boys. In an evaluation of the program, Tremblay, Masse, Pagani, and Vitaro (1996) found both short- and long-term gains, including decreases in aggressive behavior, serious school adjustment problems, and minor delinquency (fighting, trespassing, theft, and burglary). I have identified a number of other effective programs for disruptive children in Chapter 9, including the Child Development Project, Fast Track, the Good Behavior Game, the Second Step curriculum, and the Responding in Peaceful and Positive Ways curriculum.

In the second strategy, programs intervene with high-risk families that are most likely to produce child delinquents. A combination of parent training and early childhood education is the most effective approach with these families (Karoly, Greenwood, & Everingham, 1998; Yoshikawa, 1994, 1995). In Chapter 9, I have identified four programs that improve children's individual capacities (cognitive abilities) with center-based educational child care or preschool and improve family functioning with home visits (parent training). A number of other promising or proven-effective family-strengthening interventions are available (Kumpfer & Alvarado, 1998). It should be noted, however, that early intervention is a long-term investment, and legislators and juvenile justice policy makers are often reluctant to support it.

The third early intervention strategy involves intervention with high-risk children and their families. The Children at Risk (CAR) prevention program (see Chapter 9) prevented delinquency among high-risk adolescents who lived in distressed neighborhoods by reducing risk factors and increasing protective factors for delinquency and drug use.

Child abuse and neglect are strong risk factors for child delinquency (Chapter 6). Parents at high risk for abuse and neglect of their children, or who already are abusing or neglecting them, can also be targeted with interventions. These forms of maltreatment are risk factors for the more serious and violent forms of delinquency, and the risk increases as the seriousness of the maltreatment increases (Kelley, Thornberry, & Smith, 1997). Studies have also shown that a relatively small group of "high-risk" families accounts for a disproportionately large percentage of subsequent abuse/neglect referrals, serious maltreatment, and out-of-home child placements (Wiebush, Baird, Krisberg, & Onek, 1995). The Children's Research Center (CRC, 1993) has developed an innovative method of identifying the relative degree of risk for continued abuse or neglect among families that already have substantiated abuse or neglect referrals. CRC uses risk assessment instruments to classify cases into risk levels. A validation study showed that the recidivism rate for families classified as high risk was 10 times higher than that for low-risk families (Wiebush et al., 1995). Multisystemic Therapy has also demonstrated effectiveness in intervening with abusive and neglectful families (Brunk, Henggeler, & Whelan, 1987; Henggeler, Schoenwald, Borduin, Rowland, & Cunningham, 1998). Rather than waiting for child delinquents to emerge from abusive families and reach the juvenile justice system, it is preferable to undertake strategic early intervention with such families.

The fourth strategy involves intervening with juveniles early in their delinquent careers. Because of noticeable early misbehavior and the tendency of seriously troubled families to come to the attention of social service agencies, child delinquents often are seen by a greater variety of agencies than older delinquents. These agencies include child welfare and child protection agencies, schools, mental health clinics, and juvenile courts—especially in the case of families brought to court on charges involving dependency and neglect.

There is a pressing need for juvenile justice systems to coordinate and integrate service delivery for child delinquents and their families. Three possible models have been identified (Howell, 2001a; Loeber & Farrington, 2000). First, an interagency mechanism could be set up that comprises representatives of all the involved agencies; the Norfolk Interagency Council and the wraparound process (see Chapter 11) are examples of such mechanisms.

Second, a single agency could be established to integrate the provision of services from different agencies, so that there is a single point of entry for all children in an integrated case management system. Two very promising programs following this model have been created specifically to work with child delinquents and their families: the Minnesota Delinquents Under 10 program and the Toronto Under 12 Outreach Project (Howell, 2001a). In an alternative version of this strategy, the Norfolk Assessment Center (see Chapter 11), which is staffed by multiple agencies, helps at-risk children and adolescents who display problem behaviors and evidence mental health problems (Norfolk Community Services Board, 1999). The mean age of the center's clients is slightly under 12 years. Incorporating core wraparound values—providing child-centered, family-focused, and community-based services—the Norfolk Assessment Center provides comprehensive mental health and substance abuse assessments, develops child- and family-centered service plans, and provides case management services. Many communities could benefit from similar centers, because of the high cost and ineffectiveness of psychiatric hospitalization for treatment of mental health problems (Burns, 1991; Burns, Hoagwood, & Mrazek, 1999; Henggeler et al., 1998).

Third, every community's Comprehensive Strategy plan needs to focus on child delinquents. It is particularly important that a community tie together its prevention, early intervention, and graduated sanctions continuum with child delinquents in mind. This will ensure that the continuum includes programs that (a) prevent disruptive children from becoming delinquents; (b) prevent child delinquents from becoming serious, violent, and chronic offenders; and (c) use graduated sanctions and linked programs to rehabilitate juvenile offenders.

A central purpose of the Comprehensive Strategy is to integrate the various disciplines and human service agencies that come into play in serving troubled children and their families at any point during childhood and adolescence. Agency efforts need to be integrated for maximum effectiveness, because child delinquents often have multiple problems that result in multiple needs for services. In addition, family problems (e.g., parental drug and alcohol abuse,

child abuse and neglect, and lack of effective parental supervision) often need to be addressed because of their contribution to child delinquency. Services need to be "wrapped around" problem children and their families. I discuss this service delivery model next, before I address graduated sanctions, because the wraparound model of service delivery can effectively integrate services for all clients of the juvenile justice system and allied agencies that deal with problem youths and their families.

The Wraparound Model of Service Delivery

The Comprehensive Strategy embraces the wraparound model of service delivery for the integration of juvenile justice functions with mental health, health, child welfare, and social services, as well as other services for children and adolescents. As noted in Chapter 11, this is an ideal model for breaking down the "silo" mentalities of such agencies. Grounded in an "unconditional care" commitment, the wraparound service delivery model reflects the rehabilitation potential of juvenile justice and other human service agencies. This model also embodies ideal principles of service planning and delivery that should be reflected in every juvenile justice and human service agency. These include parental and child involvement in determining needed services, integration of services and delivery systems, flexibility in the funding and provision of services, individualization of services, and provision of community-based services close to home and in natural environmental settings that are culturally competent, strengths based, and family and community centered. The team-driven process of wraparound treatment plan development and implementation is central to the Comprehensive Strategy philosophy.

Wraparound Milwaukee is the best example of a proven-effective wraparound service delivery model that integrates mental health, juvenile justice, and other systems in addressing the multiple needs of juvenile justice system clientele and their families (Burns, Hoagwood, & Mrazek, 1999; Kamradt, 2000). Because of the program's successes (Kamradt, 2000), the Milwaukee community has adopted the wraparound model for early intervention services for abused and neglected children in the child welfare system. This is an interagency model that other jurisdictions can use to build comprehensive front-end systems of service delivery. Another wraparound program, the Dawn Project in Indianapolis, also serves as a model for linking the juvenile justice system with other agencies (Burns, Goldman, Faw, & Burchard, 1999, pp. 91-92). The result is integrated—*seamless,* to use the popular term—service delivery for multiple treatment needs. The wraparound model also fosters development of an integrated information system for tracking clients, managing treatment delivery, and evaluating outcomes.

Wraparound Milwaukee and the Dawn Project are excellent examples of programs based on the wraparound service delivery model. In both cases, the juvenile justice system is integrated with other social service agencies, including mental health and child welfare. Blended, pooled, or "braided" funding is key to the success of the wraparound model. Another key is the assignment of a single service coordinator to lead the assessment and treatment planning team. This responsibility can be rotated among individuals from participating agencies.

Obviously, every juvenile justice system case is not a candidate for wraparound service delivery. Some two-thirds of all juvenile court referrals are very-low-risk or low-risk offenders who are not likely to commit serious or violent crimes. The remaining one-third of offenders are good candidates for possible wraparound service delivery. Wraparound programs should select the juveniles who will receive their services by applying three criteria. First, they should select those juveniles who have both relatively high risk of recidivism and multiple treatment needs, as indicated by their risk and needs assessments. Second, they should give priority to youths who are at risk of residential placement in child-care facilities or juvenile corrections facilities. And third, they should select youths who are eligible for services from two or more of the participating agencies.

The wraparound model should be applied at the child delinquency intervention level of the prevention component of the Comprehensive Strategy as well as in the graduated sanctions component. The youngest child delinquents—approximately age 10 and under—are best handled in social service and youth service agencies. Because of their age and emotional immaturity, they should not, under any circumstances, be confined in detention centers or juvenile reformatories.

As noted in Chapter 11, the mental health system has led the way in providing integrated services, with its emphasis on community-based mental health treatment in lieu of residential services. Yet the mental health system—along with child welfare, social services, child protective services, and public schools—often uses the juvenile justice system as a "dumping ground" for its failures. As Roush (1996b) has noted, service fragmentation "is at the core of the failure to address the problems of youth by each of the child-serving systems" (p. 29). Many juvenile offenders and their families are besieged by multiple problems and needs. Youths often enter the same system

repeatedly, but through different doors, such as child welfare organizations, juvenile justice agencies, and various treatment programs. Rather than providing a system of coordinated care, however, service providers often operate independent of one another, unaware of the involvement of their clients and their clients' families with other services. Programs based on the wraparound model avoid the needless waste and ineffectiveness of such duplication of services.

The community assessment center (CAC) also holds promise as a mechanism for interagency service integration at the front door of the juvenile justice system—generally police arrest or custody of a youth (see Chapter 11). The CAC approach has four key elements (Oldenettel & Wordes, 2000, pp. 1-2):

- Single point of entry
- Immediate and comprehensive assessments
- Management information system
- Integrated case management

Any sizable community could profitably use a CAC as a single point of entry to the juvenile justice and other service systems *and* a wraparound service delivery model for integration of services for youths who become enmeshed in the various systems.

Graduated Sanctions

For maximum and sustained impact, delinquency prevention and early intervention programs need to be linked with graduated sanctions and rehabilitation services; this is the second component of the Comprehensive Strategy (Wilson & Howell, 1993). Public safety is the first objective. Society is protected from dangerous offenders when they are controlled through restrictive sanctions. A major premise of the Comprehensive Strategy is that graduated sanctions provide a stable context that gives treatment a chance to work. The worst offenders tend to have multiple risk factors and multiple problem behaviors. When a community applies the tools of the structured decision-making model (see Chapter 12), it can build a well-structured graduated sanctions system that is cost-effective, allocating most resources to the highest-rate offenders.

In most of the remainder of this chapter, I will illustrate the graduated sanctions component of the Comprehensive Strategy by featuring programs that structure the handling of offenders in the juvenile justice system in an efficient and cost-effective manner. Before a community can begin to select programs from a menu of program options, it must establish a system of graduated sanctions. Plenty of available programs have been shown to be effective for treatment and rehabilitation (see Chapter 10).

Immediate Intervention

Immediate intervention is one of the weakest components of most juvenile justice systems. This is especially unfortunate at this time when juvenile justice systems are being flooded with offenders— many of whom do not belong there (see Chapter 3). Therefore, in a system of graduated sanctions and program options for first-time minor delinquent offenders and nonserious repeat offenders, detailed attention should be given to the role of immediate interventions. Such interventions can be structured in many ways. I discuss seven possibilities below: crisis intervention, immediate intervention with advocacy services, mental health screening, mental health court, alternatives to detention, youth courts, and community-oriented policing.

Crisis Intervention

Many young people who enter the mental health and juvenile justice systems are at a point of crisis (U.S. Department of Health and Human Services, 1999, p. 178), either because of the severity of their personal problems—particularly emotional and mental health problems—or because their parents need help in addressing their children's problems. Currently, more than a dozen promising or proven-effective programs provide services for youths in crisis (Evans & Boothroyd, 1997; Kumpfer & Alvarado, 1998). Crisis services should be available in every community to help youth access needed services and to help families with short-term management of out-of-control adolescents. Yet few communities have family crisis centers or family-stabilizing facilities; most have only crisis hot lines for adolescents, and these programs provide little parental support. Some have shelter-care facilities that serve as temporary alternatives to detention and are useful in helping to resolve family conflicts, but animal shelters are more commonly seen than youth shelters in most communities. Several of the crisis intervention programs reviewed in Chapter 9 can be replicated in other communities, including programs that provide mobile crisis teams, short-term residential services, and intensive in-home services. Homebuilders has been providing crisis in-home intervention support services since the 1970s (Sondheimer, Schoenwald, & Rowland, 1994), particularly for families in which there is imminent risk that the children may be removed and placed in foster care.

Programs employing community assessment centers and offering wraparound service delivery are also appropriate for addressing family crisis intervention needs. The Dawn Project in Indianapolis is an excellent example; it incorporates New York City's Youth Emergency Service (YES) team concept of providing mobile, community-based services and crisis support around the clock.

Immediate Intervention With Advocacy Services

Children and adolescents need, and are entitled to, effective legal representation at first contact with the juvenile justice system (Puritz & Shang, 1998). However, in many states, public defenders are prohibited from representing clients until the clients have made their initial appearance in court to determine indigence. Thus the interests of juveniles who have been arrested are often seriously compromised, and "many juvenile defendants [are left] literally defenseless" (Puritz & Shang, 1998, p. 1). Children with severe mental health problems are especially vulnerable. Improvement is needed in both the availability and the quality of legal representation by public defenders for children in trouble (Puritz, Burrell, Schwartz, Soler, & Warboys, 1995).

Several promising approaches to juvenile indigent defense have been shown to be worthy of replication (Puritz & Shang, 1998). The First Defense Legal Aid program in Cook County, Illinois, bridges this gap by providing fast, free legal advice to juveniles at the police station, immediately after arrest and until a public defender is assigned.

The Neighborhood Defender Service (NDS) in Harlem, New York, operates in the neighborhood it serves (Puritz & Shang, 1998). In New York City, every child who is arrested and under the jurisdiction of the family court is interviewed by a probation officer. NDS's early intervention program provides attorneys to accompany children and their families to these probation interviews to advise them. Court-appointed attorneys cannot engage in this practice because probation interviews typically occur before the appointment of counsel. NDS also sees to it that social workers address the social needs that frequently overshadow juvenile clients' legal problems. In addition, NDS attorneys are able to represent their clients in school expulsion or subsequent hearings.

Project TeamChild in King County, Washington, is a resource for public defenders, who can refer their clients to the project for advocacy on such issues as access to education, mental and medical health benefits, and safe living conditions

(Puritz & Shang, 1998). For example, the project seeks readmission to school and other educational alternatives for expelled students and obtains specialized assessments and services for disabled youth. Project TeamChild has often secured the help of representatives of educational, mental health, and social services to persuade judges to give youths community sentences. Volunteer tutors and mentors also play a critical role in Project TeamChild's success. In an evaluation of Project TeamChild clients, Ezell (1997) found that they showed better stability and direction in their school, mental health, family, and employment status, and that they were unlikely to be rearrested, to violate probation, or to be convicted of new crimes.

Mental Health Screening

All youth who come into the juvenile justice system should be screened for mental health disorders at their earliest point of contact with the system (Cocozza & Skowyra, 2000). One standardized screening tool that has been developed for this purpose is the Massachusetts Youth Screening Instrument (MAYSI; Grisso, Barnum, Fletcher, Cauffman, & Peuschold, 2001), which appears to hold promise for use in juvenile justice settings, including court intake, probation, detention, and correctional facilities (Cocozza & Skowyra, 2000). The Center for the Promotion of Mental Health in Juvenile Justice at Columbia University has developed a computerized screening protocol for diagnosing specific mental health problems: the Diagnostic Instrument Schedule for Children (DISC-4; information is available online at www.promotementalhealth.org). In addition, the center has designed a template specifically to assist mental health staff in community agencies in locating appropriate services for youth who have been diagnosed with psychiatric disorders (Wasserman, Ko, & Jensen, 2002).

Juvenile Mental Health Court

The Santa Clara County Juvenile Court, which operates in San Jose, California, has implemented an innovative juvenile mental health court called the Court for the Individualized Treatment of Adolescents (CITA) (Arredondo et al., 2001). It uses the MAYSI to screen all minors who are brought into custody and remain in the juvenile detention center. Children deemed eligible for the CITA receive comprehensive assessments using other psychological instruments. Those youth with substance abuse disorders are referred to concurrent diversion and treatment for drug abuse. A multidisciplinary team develops a comprehensive treatment plan for each eligible juvenile that integrates the wraparound philosophy of the county's mental health system with the graduated sanctions system of the juvenile court. An elaborate set of protocols has been developed for CITA program operations (Arredondo et al., 2001).

Alternatives to Detention

Communities use detention all too often as a crisis management option when they should instead use alternatives to detention for youths who have not committed delinquent acts and do not present threats to themselves or others. The Jefferson County, Kentucky, Juvenile Services Division operates a program that offers one of the most effective alternatives to detention (Roush, 1996b, pp. 43-44). Juveniles in the program are placed in a group home called the Phoenix House, where the primary goal is to keep residents safe and secure while managing their behavior during the court process (New Jersey Juvenile Justice Commission, 1999, p. 95). The program, which is obligated to take any court-ordered youth, serves as a predisposition option that allows residents to attend their own schools and earn weekend passes. The program also has a strong behavior management component.

Foster care has long been known to be an effective alternative to detention (Young & Pappenfort, 1977), and a wide variety of other alternatives are also effective (Land, McCall, Williams, & Ezell, 1998). The strongest alternative model is Multidimensional Treatment Foster Care (see Chapter 10). San Francisco's Detention Diversion Advocacy Program (DDAP) is another effective alternative to detention. It uses case management techniques to integrate a wide range of alternative services for youths and their families who are identified through a formal risk assessment as good candidates for the program (Shelden, 1999). DDAP has been shown to reduce recidivism and subsequent court referrals.

Other effective alternatives to detention (including the Phoenix House group home) are described in detail in the New Jersey Juvenile Justice Commission's publication *National Directory of Juvenile Detention Alternative Programs* (1999). This valuable resource is the product of a national search for such programs that began with a survey of detention center administrators in which they were asked to identify model programs. The researchers then sent profile forms to the alternative

---

Box 13.2
Youth Courts

The terms *youth court* and *teen court* usually refer to courts that involve young people in the sentencing of their peers who are diverted from juvenile courts. Youth courts operate using one of four main case-processing models: adult judge, youth judge, tribunal, or peer jury (for detailed descriptions of these models, see Fisher, 2002; see also Goodwin, 2000; Goodwin, Steinhart, & Fulton, 1996). Youth courts were established with the expectation that they would be able to reduce delinquency by bringing peer pressure to bear on youngsters involved in minor delinquent acts (Williamson, Chalk, & Knepper, 1993). Butts, Buck, and Coggeshall (2002) evaluated four youth courts for the Urban Institute and found that recidivism rates among teen court youth were lower than those of youth in the regular juvenile justice system in all four sites; the rates were significantly lower in two of the four sites. Butts et al. conclude that youth courts appear to be a cost-effective alternative in localities that do not, or cannot, provide a meaningful response for every young, first-time nonviolent offender. In another evaluation of a single "teen court," Harrison, Maupin, and Mays (2000) found an acceptable recidivism rate (25%), but the reoffense rate was higher among youths with prior offenses. Thus youth courts may be most effective with first-time offenders, and community service may be a more effective disposition than punitive sanctions, such as curfew (Minor, Wells, Soderstrom, et al., 1999).

As of early in 2002, at least 811 youth courts were operating in the United States (National Youth Court Center, 2002); half of the states have enacted legislation supporting such courts (Heward, 2002). The National Youth Court Center manages an information clearinghouse on youth courts; see this organization's Web site at www.youthcourt.net. In addition, Fisher (2002) has developed a manual to guide communities in developing, implementing, and operating youth courts.

---

programs named and reviewed the submitted information. The resulting directory provides very detailed information on 139 model programs. Remarkably, 38 (27%) of the programs listed in the directory serve as alternatives to detention for serious offenders as well as other youths.

A well-managed detention center incorporates graduated levels of supervision. The Multnomah County (Oregon) community detention program specifies contact requirements using hourly workers from a private agency (Volunteers of America) to provide face-to-face supervision at four levels (DeMuro, 2000, p. 16). Detainees' compliance with detention center rules and behavioral expectations affects their movement from one level of restrictiveness to another in this scheme.

Youth Courts

Youth courts serve as immediate intervention with minor offenders who can be diverted from the juvenile justice system (see Box 13.2). These courts fill an intervention gap in many jurisdictions where heavy caseloads and the need to focus on more serious offenders result in a low priority for the enforcement of misdemeanor charges (Goodwin, 2000). Youth courts provide immediate sanctions,

holding young persons accountable for minor delinquent acts in a positive manner, while extending that accountability to the community (Fisher, 2002). Thus they hold considerable promise as an immediate intervention in a graduated sanctions system.

Community-Oriented Policing

Community-oriented policing can effectively involve police in immediate intervention. Children do not choose where they live; they are dependent on parents, schools, neighbors, and police to provide a safe and secure environment in which to play, go to school, and develop socially. Community-oriented policing can play an important role in creating a safer environment for children. Community police officers can not only help to reduce criminal activity but also become positive role models and establish caring relationships with the youth and families in a community.

Unfortunately, the term *community-oriented policing* is used to refer to a wide variety of policing methods, including innovative methods that bring police into cooperative problem-solving approaches in concert with community representatives (Goldstein, 1990; see also Goldstein, 1979).

The U.S. Department of Justice's Office of Community Oriented Policing Services (COPS) describes community policing as a new concept in police reform in which close, mutually beneficial ties between police and community members form the foundation for a successful policing strategy.

Police can work closely with mental health professionals in providing immediate intervention in situations involving violent victimization, as they do in the Child Development–Community Policing (CD–CP) program in New Haven, Connecticut. This program combines community-oriented policing with child development principles in a multicomponent community intervention. It brings police officers and mental health professionals together to provide direct interdisciplinary intervention for children who are victims, witnesses, or perpetrators of violent crime in incidents that police investigate. While investigating crimes, police have direct, around-the-clock access to clinicians at the project's Child Study Center, who can make referrals to mental health and social services or later provide direct services to affected children and their families to interrupt the cycle of violence. This is a promising model for preventing violent victimization and possible subsequent violent offenses through intermediate intervention and services, although it has received little evaluation (Marans & Berkman, 1997).

Intermediate Sanctions

Typically, intermediate sanctions are not used effectively with first-time serious or violent offenders or with chronic and serious/violent offenders. A major reason is that such sanctions emphasize offender surveillance and control at the expense of treatment and rehabilitation (Altschuler, 1998; Byrne & Pattavina, 1992). Drug and alcohol testing, electronic monitoring, curfews, boot camps, and strict revocation policies are commonly used at the intermediate level, whereas treatment and other services related to substance abuse, employment, and family problems are minimized (see Chapter 7). There is considerable evidence that the deterrence approaches do not reduce recidivism (Lipsey & Wilson, 1998).

Juvenile probation can be an effective intermediate sanction when linked with certain community-based programs. In his meta-analysis of practical (everyday) programs, Lipsey (1999b) found that probation combined with certain types of intensive supervision/reduced caseload requirements, or supplemented with certain types of counseling programs and restitution programs, produces

TABLE 13.1   Cuyahoga County Probation Graduated Sanctions System

Intensive probation supervision (4 to 8 months)
- "High" score on risk assessment
- Three phases (as depicted in Table 13.2)

Medium supervision (3 to 6 months)
- "Medium" score on risk assessment
- 1 face-to-face contact per month
- Parent and school supervision as needed

Low supervision (3 to 6 months)
- "Low" score on risk assessment
- 1 face-to-face contact per 2 months
- Parent and school supervision as needed
- Use of volunteers in supervision

SOURCE: Cuyahoga County Juvenile Court (1996).

significant reductions in recidivism. Less effective interventions linked with probation can be improved if they are organized around the program features that produce large recidivism reductions.

The most effective types of interventions for serious and violent offenders in community programs are interpersonal skills training, individual counseling, and behavioral programs, followed closely by multiple services (Lipsey & Wilson, 1998). Communities can use these types of interventions more often as intermediate sanctions when they use risk assessments to assess objectively and realistically the dangers that offenders present to public safety.

A Probation Graduated Sanctions System Using Intermediate Sanctions

The Cuyahoga County Probation Graduated Sanctions System (Sametz & Hamparian, 1990; Wiebush & Hamparian, 1986) provides an excellent illustration of the use of risk and needs assessments in a graduated sanctions system. Unfortunately, this system no longer exists; it was operational in the 1980s but was disbanded in the mid-1990s for political reasons having nothing to do with the program itself. This ideal graduated sanctions system consisted of three levels of supervision: intensive, medium, and low. Table 13.1 shows the structure of the Cuyahoga County system.

In Cuyahoga County, juvenile offenders' risk levels were reassessed every 90 days or when there was a significant change in a youth's behavior, a probation violation occurred, there was a violation of a court order, or an offender committed a new offense. These risk reassessments were used to

TABLE 13.2   Phases of the Ohio Intensive
Probation Supervision (IPS)
Program

Phase 1 (3 to 4 months)

- Probation agreement (behavior contract)
- Three contacts at random by surveillance officer per week
- Biweekly counseling sessions by probation counselor
- Team assessment—probation officer, probation counselor, surveillance officer—using risk and needs assessment
- Service delivery

Phase 2 (2 to 3 months)

- Two contacts at random by surveillance officer per week
- Service delivery—increasing parental responsibility

Phase 3 (1 to 2 months)

- One contact at random by surveillance officer per week
- Compliance with rules and conditions of probation
- Completion of service delivery
- Complete formation of support group (parents and significant others)
- Discharge

SOURCE: Adapted from Cuyahoga County Juvenile Court (1996).

move the offenders up or down the Probation Graduated Sanctions System.

For youth at the highest level of intermediate sanctions, serious and violent offenders who often qualify for secure confinement, the most cost-effective alternative to incarceration is Multisystemic Therapy (MST) (Aos, Phipps, Barnoski, & Lieb, 2001), which has been shown to produce cost savings to taxpayers of more than $31,000 per program participant. MST is an effective treatment for serious, violent, and chronic juvenile offenders (see Chapter 11).

Intensive Supervision
as an Intermediate Sanction

As noted in Chapter 7, few intensive supervision programs have produced positive results. The Ohio Intensive Probation Supervision (IPS) program is a major exception; an evaluation of this program found that it was very effective (Sametz & Hamparian, 1990; Wiebush & Hamparian, 1991).

The IPS was nested within the Cuyahoga County Probation Graduated Sanctions System described above. The program was designed to handle probationers from the time they were placed on probation for a period of 6 to 8 months. High-risk offenders were placed in the IPS program, which consisted of three phases: Phase 1 lasted 3-4 months, Phase 2 lasted 2-3 months, and Phase 3 lasted 1-2 months. Table 13.2 shows the expected number of contacts per month in each phase and the type of service delivery. Offenders were moved up and down the levels of the IPS program depending on their performance.

When linked with probation, such an intensive supervision program can be an excellent alternative to incarceration. Had just six of the major metropolitan Ohio counties diverted a reasonable proportion of lower-risk incarcerated offenders to the IPS program, the state could have realized a 20% reduction in the Ohio institutional population (Wiebush, 1993, pp. 85-86). In a manual written for the American Probation and Parole Association, Fulton, Stone, and Gendreau (1994) provide guidelines for developing a prototypical intensive supervision program that incorporates lessons learned from research and practical program experience.

Linking Probation Violators
With Graduated Sanctions

The use of intermediate sanctions for probation violators is a good example of the application of graduated sanctions. In Cook County, Illinois, sanctions for probation violators are determined through a four-step classification procedure (Steinhart, 2000b, pp. 26-28). First, a caseworker screens the offender for level of public safety risk. Second, the caseworker determines the severity of the probation violation by using a table of offenses and behaviors. Third, the caseworker cross-references the offender's risk score and violation severity on a grid to arrive at a level of sanctions. And finally, the caseworker selects sanctions from a "sanction severity table" (see Table 13.3).

The Cook County system uses several intermediate sanctions for offenders—whether or not they are on probation—including intensive home supervision (house arrest or home detention), day and evening reporting, day treatment, restitution, weekend detention, and electronic monitoring. Preference is given to these alternatives over committing probation violators to juvenile reformatories. In fact, the Cook County system could be used to reduce such confinement in many communities. For example, in North Carolina about one-third of

TABLE 13.3   Sanctions Severity Table: Cook County Administrative Sanctions Program

Level 1 (low risk)
- Admonishment by probation officer
- Impose curfew
- Minor to contact probation officer weekly by phone
- Require minor to attend a special program
- Require minor to seek employment
- Other sanctions

Level 2 (medium risk)
- Require attendance in counseling or group therapy
- Order community service
- Minor to contact probation officer weekly in person
- School detention where available, or teachers to sign class attendance sheet
- Limit minor's freedom of travel
- Other sanctions

Level 3 (high risk)
- Judicial admonishment
- House arrest after school
- More frequent personal reporting to probation officer
- Participate in "personal enrichment program" sponsored by probation department

SOURCE: "Special Detention Cases: Strategies for Handling Difficult Populations," by D. Steinhart, in Annie E. Casey Foundation (Ed.), *Pathways to Juvenile Detention Reform* (Vol. 9, p. 27), Baltimore: Annie E. Casey Foundation. © 2000 by the Annie E. Casey Foundation. Reprinted with permission.

all offenders admitted to juvenile reformatories in the latter half of 2001 were placed there for probation violations, and about 30% of these offenders were charged with only misdemeanor offenses (Lubitz, 2001). If most states were to use a system for probation violators like that employed in Cook County, many of them could achieve significant reductions in training school confinement.

Community Confinement

Aside from small secure facilities, there are other program alternatives to incarceration. I feature two examples below: an unfenced, community-based facility in Maryland and Ohio's "community

correctional facilities." These alternatives illustrate the effectiveness of well-developed community-based programs.

Community-Based Residential Treatment

The Thomas O'Farrell Youth Center is an excellent example of a community-based intermediate sanction that serves as an alternative to incarceration (Krisberg, Currie, Onek, & Wiebush, 1995). It is a 38-bed, unlocked, staff-secure residential program for male youths committed to the Maryland Department of Juvenile Services. The typical O'Farrell juvenile has numerous prior court referrals, generally for property crimes and drug offenses. Graduated sanctions are built into the O'Farrell treatment program. The program begins with an orientation period of about a month. Then, in Phase 1, which lasts about 60 days, youths acquire more knowledge about O'Farrell and its normative system. To move to Phase 2, residents must demonstrate consistent and positive behavior in all aspects of O'Farrell life, including school attendance, work details, and group meetings. In this phase, youths must also demonstrate high levels of success in on-campus jobs and are encouraged to find part-time employment in the community. Phase 3, aftercare, lasts for 6 months and includes assistance in reentering school, vocational counseling, crisis intervention, family counseling, transportation, and mentoring. An evaluation of the O'Farrell program yielded positive results (Krisberg et al., 1995, p. 163).

RECLAIM Ohio

Ohio has also developed effective community-based alternatives to incarceration for juvenile offenders. In 1991, Ohio's juvenile facilities were operating at 150% of capacity. State officials saw a way of meeting the twin needs of protecting the public by incarcerating serious and violent juvenile offenders and reducing institutional populations. Recognizing the overcrowded conditions in the state's juvenile corrections facilities, Ohio officials developed the Reasoned and Equitable Community and Local Alternatives to the Incarceration of Minors (RECLAIM Ohio) program. The program provides financial incentives for local courts to keep most of the less serious juvenile offenders in the community for treatment. Each county receives a monthly allocation of funds based on the number of juvenile felony adjudications. Judges can use that money to purchase long-term confinement from the Department of Youth Services or to develop, expand, or purchase community-based alternatives locally. Judges can incarcerate serious, violent offenders free of charge (for murder, aggravated murder, and rape).

In a single year, counties were able to keep more than $18 million from RECLAIM to serve more than 8,600 delinquent youths in local programs. In a study in pilot Ohio counties, Moon, Applegate, and Latessa (1997) found that the program achieved its objective of decreasing admissions to juvenile reformatories for less serious offenses and increasing admissions for more serious felony offenses. Nearly all of the pilot counties increased the number of community-based services offered. A recent evaluation of the new local programs, called "community correctional facilities," found most of them to be effective (Latessa & Holsinger, 1999).

Other Alternatives to Confinement

Alternatives to confinement are also needed for the treatment of juveniles with mental health and alcohol/drug abuse problems. As noted in Chapter 3, both the mental health system and the juvenile justice system rely excessively on the most costly of all placement options: residential treatment. This overreliance on deep-end solutions often results in the placement of the wrong youngsters in long-term residential care. Ironically, officials in these two systems may wind up compounding each other's problems. Many juvenile justice system clients are placed in residential psychiatric facilities to no avail (see Chapter 7). Conversely, many seriously emotionally disturbed youngsters are placed in state juvenile correctional facilities, a large proportion of which are unable to meet their needs (Roush & McMillen, 2000). Thus these two systems should join together to provide more effective family- and community-based programming.

Indeed, in a national survey, probation department officials in urban and suburban areas have identified residential and nonresidential mental health services and residential drug and alcohol abuse treatment as their top program expansion need (Torbet, 1999). These survey results are difficult to interpret, however, because respondents also put these services at the top of their list of least effective programs. The safest interpretation is that probation officials across the country want more residential and nonresidential services that are more effective in the treatment of both mental health and alcohol/drug abuse problems.

It is unfortunate that probation department officials believe they need more *residential* services for treatment of mental health and alcohol/drug abuse

problems. As noted in Chapter 7, research has found that residential and outpatient treatment programs are not effective in the treatment of either mental health problems or drug/alcohol abuse. Instead, treatment of youths for these problems needs to be approached differently. Effective treatment interventions should be employed in collaborative efforts involving multiple agencies. Jurisdictions that have not created such systems of care must rely on particular treatment programs.

Only a few treatment programs for drug abuse have been shown to be effective; numerous others are considered promising (Center for Substance Abuse Treatment, 1999). As noted in Chapter 7, the results of substance abuse treatment programs have been mixed (Baer, MacLean, & Marlatt, 1998). One correctional treatment program, the Chemical Dependency Treatment Program, incorporates key principles of effective intervention and has shown good results, even with serious offenders, in localities that have implemented it well (Mears & Kelly, 2002). In addition, MST has shown positive results in preliminary research (Henggeler et al., 1998; Henggeler, Pickrel, & Brondino, 1999). According to the principles of MST, drug abuse treatment programs can be effective only when the communities in which they operate make the following system-level changes (Henggeler, 1997a, pp. 266, 268):

- Reduce the use of restrictive services
- Increase the availability of community-based services
- Increase provider accountability
- Increase service integration
- Reform mechanisms for financing services
- Train providers in the delivery of clinically effective and cost-effective services

Treatment for adolescent substance abuse is most successful when it is part of a continuum of interventions designed to support the youth's overall development. These interventions will be most effective when they are integrated into the juvenile and family court process. To achieve the needed level of integration, communities must provide youth workers, social workers, and probation professionals with comprehensive training in substance abuse treatment.

Secure Care

In an ideal world, states would use only small facilities to confine their most dangerous juvenile offenders, because large congregate facilities have been shown to be ineffective in reducing recidivism with these offenders (Henggeler et al., 1998; Krisberg & Howell, 1998; Parent, Leiter, Livens, Wentworth, & Stephen, 1994). As noted in Chapter 7, small correctional units and nonresidential programs with treatment orientations are more effective as well as more humane. Unfortunately, nearly two-thirds of youth confined in public reformatories are housed in facilities with more than 100 residents; only 12% are confined in facilities with fewer than 31 residents (Snyder & Sickmund, 1999, p. 206). However, several states use small secure facilities and community-based programs successfully in lieu of large juvenile reformatories; these include Massachusetts, Kentucky, Pennsylvania, and Missouri (Guarino-Ghezzi & Loughran, 1996; Krisberg & Austin, 1993; Lerner, 1990; Mendel, 2001). For example, in Massachusetts, juvenile offenders are housed in a few 15-bed secure facilities. Missouri closed its only large juvenile reformatory in 1983 and subsequently converted it into an adult prison (Mendel, 2001, p. 9). Kentucky houses youthful offenders in small campus settings with capacities ranging from 30 to 45 per center (Commonwealth of Kentucky, 2002). Youths confined in these residential facilities often "step down" to less restrictive placements such as group homes or therapeutic foster care prior to returning home. This process eases their transition back to their homes while allowing them to continue working on their treatment goals.

The state of California, in contrast, relies mostly on large juvenile correctional facilities that hold more than 1,000 youthful offenders. Recidivism rates for offenders held in California Youth Authority facilities are perhaps the highest in the country (Krisberg & Howell, 1998; Visher, Lattimore, & Linster, 1991). Juvenile correctional recidivism studies show that, although there is some evidence that sound juvenile justice system programs reduce the rate of subsequent criminal offending, there is not much support for the thesis that traditional incarceration reduces the likelihood of subsequent offending or recommitments. Research indicates that intensive community-based options are more effective (Lipsey & Wilson, 1998).

When placement in a secure facility is a jurisdiction's primary or only treatment option, it becomes an expensive catchall, one that replaces less restrictive and equally (or more) appropriate options (Dunlap & Roush, 1995). The result is that minor offenders are likely to be placed in secure correctional facilities, even though research has shown that as much as one-third of the juvenile training school population could be placed in less secure settings at much lower cost (Krisberg, Onek, Jones, &

Schwartz, 1993). State departments of corrections need to employ risk assessments to ensure that they use secure facilities only for the most dangerous juvenile offenders. These facilities should also hold juveniles who are currently being incarcerated in adult correctional facilities. At the same time, juvenile justice officials need to address overcrowding problems in juvenile corrections facilities.

The National Juvenile Detention Association (NJDA) provides training for detention and training school staff and administrative personnel that can help jurisdictions to reduce overcrowding in their juvenile correctional facilities. NJDA training has transformed the Kentucky juvenile justice system (Alexander, 2000-2001). Through its academy at Eastern Kentucky University's Training Resource Center, NJDA trains all direct-care staff at the state's 35 residential treatment facilities and 3 detention facilities. This training is important not only because it supports the Kentucky Department of Juvenile Justice's "solution-focused" and individually tailored balance of sanctions and services, but because it reduces staff assaults on juvenile residents and offender assaults on staff. Overcrowding has been shown to increase the likelihood of both of these tragic events (Roush, 1996a; Roush & McMillen, 2000). In a national study, Alexander (2000-2001, p. 16) found that undertrained staff in detention and corrections facilities are more likely than well-trained staff members to assault their charges and to be assaulted themselves.

Aftercare

Aftercare should be provided for all youths returning to the community from any type of secure program or facility, but, unfortunately, this is rare. Aftercare is a part of the Orange County Model Juvenile Justice Continuum described shortly (see Figure 13.1); the Transitional Program in this graduated sanctions continuum serves high-risk offenders who receive services from the Youth and Family Resource Center and also older first-time wards who are held in custody for 90 days or more. Transitional Program services are provided for periods of from 90 days to 6 months. This is an economical way of providing aftercare services to youths released from long-term state care, rather than creating separate services in correctional departments and agencies.

However, there is a relatively simple way for jurisdictions to construct aftercare services in long-term juvenile corrections agencies: They can build these services into a graduated sanctions system as it is being constructed. A jurisdiction that builds a well-structured graduated sanctions system—one that is based on a structured decision-making model, containing stepped-up and stepped-down services and sanctions—will find it much less difficult to develop aftercare services than will a jurisdiction that attempts to append these services to an existing, poorly structured correctional system. This approach is illustrated in the National Council on Crime and Delinquency's graduated sanctions model (see Figure 12.1 in Chapter 12). The stepped-down services and sanctions constitute aftercare, following secure confinement in a long-term state correctional facility.

NCCD has designed an aftercare model, called the Intensive Supervision Program (ISP; Krisberg, Neuenfeldt, Wiebush, & Rodriguez, 1994), that can be integrated into a graduated sanctions system as it is being developed. The ISP is a well-structured, continuously monitored, individualized plan that consists of five phases with decreasing levels of restrictiveness:

1. Short-term placement in secure confinement

2. Day treatment

3. Outreach and tracking

4. Routine supervision

5. Discharge and follow-up

The ISP model incorporates a wide range of treatment interventions in the first four phases, in a continuation of correctional treatment. Phases 2-5 of the ISP constitute what traditionally has been called *reintegration* and is now more commonly known as *aftercare* or *step-down services*. Phase 2, the first step toward community reintegration, allows youth's to function in a highly controlled environment, assuming greater responsibility and accountability, while remediation of skills deficits continues and development of a prosocial network begins. During Phase 3, juveniles are expected to demonstrate that they can function productively and responsibly in a community setting. Programming focuses on the youth and on interactions with parents, peers, persons at school or work, and the persons and agencies in the community involved with the youth's reintegration. Phase 4 is a transition phase, preparing the juvenile for discharge from correctional supervision. The client should have a stable living environment; be in school, employed, or completing job training/educational objectives; and be involved in prosocial networks. The youth is discharged (Phase 5) when a community-based support system is in place.

Another aftercare model, the Intensive Aftercare Program (IAP), has five primary components (Altschuler & Armstrong, 1994a, 1994b):

1. Progressively increased responsibility and freedom

2. Facilitation of client-community interaction and involvement

3. Work with both the client and targeted community support systems

4. Development of new resources, supports, and opportunities

5. Monitoring and testing

The three main program elements in the IAP are organizational and structural characteristics, overarching case management (consisting of assessment and classification, individual case planning, a mix of surveillance and services, incentives and graduated consequences, service brokerage, and links with social networks), and management information and program evaluation. As noted in Chapter 7, the IAP did not show recidivism reductions in a three-site demonstration program (Wiebush, 2001); however, the importance of this finding is tempered by the facts that two of the three sites had small sample sizes and there was contamination of the control group in one of the sites (i.e., the control group received some of the treatment intended exclusively for the treatment group). Development of the IAP model continues (Altschuler & Armstrong, 2002).

Another aftercare program has produced very positive short-term effects (Josi & Sechrest, 1999): the Lifeskills '95 program (see Chapter 7 for a description of this program and a discussion of the reasons for its success). I next discuss four successful examples of Comprehensive Strategy implementation that are illustrative of several of the strategy's key principles. The first, the San Diego County Breaking Cycles program, provides an illustration of how a community can integrate the prevention and graduated components of the Comprehensive Strategy. The second example, the Orange County, California, 8% Early Intervention Program, illustrates how a community can effectively target potential serious and chronic juvenile offenders with a model continuum of sanctions and services. The third example, the Baton Rouge Partnership for the Prevention of Juvenile Gun Violence, illustrates a unique use of the Comprehensive Strategy to target the most chronic violent offenders in the community. Finally, Missouri's statewide graduated sanctions approach illustrates the effective use of structured decision-making tools.

A Comprehensive Continuum of Prevention and Graduated Sanctions

San Diego County used the Comprehensive Strategy guide (Howell, 1995) to develop its Comprehensive Strategy for Youth, Family, and Community. San Diego was the first site to implement the entire Comprehensive Strategy. The county began development of the strategy in 1996 and commenced implementation in 1997. The strategy was developed and implemented under the leadership of the Juvenile Justice Coordinating Council, part of the Children's Initiative of San Diego County, which provides coordination and staff support (more information about this organization is available online at thechildrensinitiative.org/ JJjuvenilejustice.htm).

San Diego's Comprehensive Strategy consists of two main components: prevention and graduated sanctions. These components are linked in an overall program called Breaking Cycles (Burke & Pennell, 2001). The prevention component targets youths who have not yet entered the juvenile justice system but evidence problem behaviors (chronic disobedience to parents, curfew violations, repeated truancy, running away from home, drug and alcohol use, and other serious behavior problems). This secondary prevention approach is different from that of most community prevention strategies, which typically focus primary prevention programs on all youth. San Diego's program concentrates on youths in the early steps of Loeber's pathways to serious and violent offending (see Chapter 4). San Diego County's assessment of community risk factors identified poor school attendance and substance abuse as the two most prevalent risk factors for youth at high risk of juvenile justice system involvement. Five Community Assessment Teams (CATs) provide referrals and services to at-risk youths and their families throughout the county.

The overall Breaking Cycles program has three specific goals (Burke & Pennell, 2001, p. 27):

- To reduce the number of at-risk minors who become delinquent by involving them in a prevention program
- To improve the juvenile justice system through the implementation of a system of graduated sanctions with a focus on community-based treatment

- To break the cycle of substance abuse and family problems that fosters crime and violence

The CATs address the Breaking Cycles prevention goal by providing direct services to high-risk youth and by linking youths with social supports in the community through five CATs that are strategically located—for easy access—across the county. Youths at risk of referral to the juvenile justice system are referred to the CATs. For each such youth, a team composed of a coordinator, probation officers, case managers, and other experts conduct a comprehensive youth and family assessment. The results of this assessment guide the development of either a case management plan (for a long-term case) or referral to community agencies (for a short-term case).

Youths in the second target group—those in juvenile court for delinquency involvement—access the graduated sanctions component of Breaking Cycles only through a valid juvenile court commitment decision. Eligibility for the graduated sanctions component is determined, in part, by a Probation Department screening committee. This determination is based on the offender's current offense and prior criminal history as well as the results of a risk assessment.

A Breaking Cycles case plan is developed for each youth. The case plan is family centered, strengths based, and designed to promote accountability, rehabilitation, and community protection. Youths are assigned for variable lengths of program participation—90, 150, 240, or 365 days—depending on risk severity and treatment needs. The following continuum of placement options is used:

- Institutional placement (e.g., minimum-security custody)
- Community-based placement (e.g., day treatment in the Reflections Program)
- Home placement (e.g., the Community Unit)

Each of these intervention levels is linked with community programs and resources that are needed to carry out the comprehensive treatment plan. Most juvenile offenders begin their rehabilitative process in highly structured institutional settings and are stepped down to lower levels of program structure and supervision (i.e., community-based and home placement, as shown above) as reassessments are made. They may also be stepped up from initial less restrictive placements or after having been stepped down to lower levels—again, depending on reassessment results. Services are linked to each of the three placement levels to provide youths and their families "with a fluid and seamless system of service delivery" (Burke & Pennell, 2001, p. 31).

Burke and Pennell (2001) recently conducted an experimental and comprehensive process and outcome evaluation of the San Diego Comprehensive Strategy that encompassed both the secondary prevention component and the graduated sanctions component. They found that the prevention component succeeded in keeping most at-risk youths out of the juvenile justice system. Remarkably, less than 20% of the long-term CAT cases were referred to court, and only 7% of all long-term CAT cases subsequently were adjudicated delinquent (p. 6). Compared with other at-risk juveniles in the comparison group, long-term CAT clients were less likely to use alcohol and drugs after program participation, and they were more likely to perform better in school in the year following program participation.

Burke and Pennell also found that the graduated sanctions component was effective in keeping offenders from progressing to more serious delinquency. Regardless of commitment length, youth in the Breaking Cycles program were less likely than preprogram cases either to have a court referral for a felony offense or to be adjudicated for a felony offense during the 18-month follow-up period. Breaking Cycles youths also were less likely to be committed to long-term state correctional facilities. Moreover, the Breaking Cycles youths were more likely to be enrolled in school during follow-up and less likely to be using alcohol or drugs.

In addition, Burke and Pennell (2001, p. 11) report that the San Diego juvenile justice system is more cost-efficient as a result of Comprehensive Strategy implementation. First, the Breaking Cycles program targets appropriate youth for intervention. Second, in addition to reducing juvenile delinquency, the program uses resources wisely by aiming to prevent delinquency involvement of potential offenders in the prevention component and to reduce serious and violent juvenile delinquency in the graduated sanctions component. Finally, the San Diego County Probation Department has succeeded in intervening with offenders at earlier points in their delinquent careers and also in holding them accountable when their offending has continued.

A Model Probation Continuum Combining Immediate and Intermediate Sanctions

The Orange County, California, Probation Department has used the Comprehensive Strategy

TABLE 13.4   Orange County "8% Problem" Risk Factors

- **School behavior/performance**
  Attendance
  Behavior
  Poor grades

- **Family problem**
  Poor parental supervision
  Significant family problems
  Criminal family members
  Documented child abuse and neglect

- **Delinquency/peer group**
  Stealing pattern
  Runaway pattern
  Gang member/associate

- **Individual problem**
  Drugs and alcohol

SOURCE: Schumacher and Kurz (2000, pp. 6-8).

to develop a unique system of graduated sanctions and a parallel continuum of program options. The 8% Early Intervention Program is the first known implementation of the Comprehensive Strategy's graduated sanctions framework (Schumacher & Kurz, 2000). The building of this graduated sanctions system began with development of a program for potential serious and chronic juvenile offenders. As noted in Chapter 4, this program was based on the research finding that 8% of court referrals are the most chronic offenders. These offenders typically have at least five prior arrests. In the 8% Early Intervention Program, potential "8% cases" are identified at court intake through the use of a risk assessment instrument made up of items based on the characteristics of the original 8% study group. Table 13.4 lists the profile factors incorporated into the risk assessment instrument. Court wards who are 15.5 years old or younger at the time of their first or second court referral and who have three or more of the four profile risk factors (which places them at greatest risk of becoming serious chronic offenders) are admitted to the 8% Early Intervention Repeat Offender Program.

The Orange County juvenile probation study also identified two other groups of offenders: a medium-risk group (22% of the total sample) and a low-risk group (the remaining 70%). The 22% group had one or two of the four profile risk factors, which placed them at medium risk of becoming

---

Box 13.3

Washington State's Juvenile Justice System Improvements

A unique experiment is currently taking place in the state of Washington. As discussed in Chapter 10, the Washington State Institute for Public Policy has conducted a review of juvenile justice programs for the purpose of identifying effective juvenile rehabilitation programs (Aos, Phipps, Barnoski, & Lieb, 2001). This work was undertaken because the Washington State Legislature had issued a mandate that only cost-beneficial programs be funded in Washington's juvenile courts. As a result of the WSIPP review, the state chose to implement three programs that the researchers had found to be cost-beneficial: Functional Family Therapy, Aggression Replacement Training (ART), and Multisystemic Therapy. The state also took steps to increase interagency collaboration based on a mental health collaboration effort (Tolan, Perry, & Jones, 1987). One of the three treatment programs has been evaluated thus far; preliminary results show that ART, which was implemented in 20 of Washington's juvenile courts, significantly reduced recidivism when well implemented (Washington State Institute for Public Policy, 2002).

Overall, successful implementation of the three programs is likely to be uneven (S. Aos, personal communication, September 26, 2002), because of the difficulties associated with transferring research and demonstration models (Chapter 10). The ART model may be the least complex model to implement, it has been placed in 20 of the state's juvenile courts, and it likely benefits from the fact that Washington State already has in place two key tools of the structured decision-making model: risk assessment and needs assessments.

The Back on Track risk assessment and case management information system, created by Allvest Information Services, Inc. (see this organization's Web site at www.allvest.com), is an advanced automated system that enables juvenile courts to routinize risk and needs (called protective factors in this system) assessments and track cases in a continuum of services and sanctions. Back on Track consists of risk and needs assessment software and a database that enable court administrators and probation officers to classify offenders and craft dispositions that address offenders' specific risks and needs. It is in place in all of Washington's 39 counties. Using this system, juvenile justice staff can monitor individual client progress, using reassessments of risks and needs, and compare the effectiveness of individual programs in terms of the extent to which they reduce risks and successfully meet the treatment needs of offenders.

---

serious chronic offenders. The low-risk group had none or only one of the four profile risk factors.

An interdisciplinary team of practitioners from throughout the county then developed a model continuum of juvenile justice services to manage all three groups simultaneously (see Figure 13.1). The team used the Comprehensive Strategy to guide their development of the intervention approach. Youths who are found, through risk assessment, to be in the 70% group are assigned to the Immediate Accountability Program, those in the 22% group are assigned to the Intensive Intervention Program, and those in the 8% group are admitted to the 8% Early Intervention Youth and Family Resource Center's (YFRC) Repeat Offender Prevention Program. In addition, court-referred youths age 15.5 or older who are placed in custody for 90 days or more are placed in the Challenge Program at the YFRC, along with

youths with active cases who receive similar court dispositions in custody. The final component of the model continuum is transitional aftercare (the Transitional Program).

Figure 13.2 shows an overview of the Orange County program model, depicted as a program matrix. It shows the components of the model continuum to which offenders are assigned, depending on their risk classifications, which are governed by the number of 8% risk factors they possess, their degree of criminal sophistication, offense severity, and so on.

Youths in the low-risk group (70% of first-time court referrals, assigned to the Immediate Accountability Program) are supervised by volunteer probation officers, who link them with community-based programs and ensure that they meet accountability (sanction) requirements. These offenders do not present any significant needs for

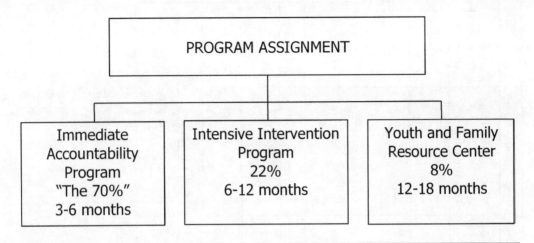

Figure 13.1   Orange County Model Juvenile Justice Continuum

SOURCE: Modified from Orange County (California) Probation Department, *Model Continuum of Juvenile Justice Services* (personal communication, July 21, 2000).

intervention services. Their program period is longer if they are 15 years of age or younger (6 months) than if they are 16 years of age or older (only 3 months).

Youths in the medium-risk group (22%) are assigned to the Intensive Intervention Program for a period of 6-12 months. Because these moderate-risk youth can quickly escalate to a higher risk status, they receive intensive, wraparound intervention and accountability services immediately upon program assignment. They are also subject to intensive supervision probation sanctions, along with a continuum of multiagency intervention services for them and their families at the YFRC. Intensive Intervention Program officers also supervise wards who are transitioning back to the community from commitments of less than 90 days as well as "8% potential" cases for whom YFRC program space currently is not available.

Youths in the high-risk group (8%) are assigned to the Repeat Offender Prevention Program (ROPP) at the YFRC for a period of 12-18 months. Like those in the medium-risk group, they receive intensive wraparound interventions and intensive supervision sanctions. However, they and their families also receive a wide array of services at the YFRC, including the following:

- Intensive in-home family services
- Health screening, health education, and basic health services
- Substance abuse services

- Mental health services
- A full spectrum of on-grounds educational services

In addition, a Community Resource Collaborative provides restorative justice (Pranis, 1998), enrichment activities, parent education, and teen parenting programming. With the exception of intensive in-home family services, the above services are made available to older wards who go into the Challenge Program. Transitional Program (aftercare) services are provided to youths in both groups upon completion of the programs.

The Orange County program represents an impressive probation graduated sanctions system that combines immediate and intermediate sanctions with a continuum of treatment programs (Schumacher & Kurz, 2000, pp. 43-46). All wards of the court receive appropriate sanctions and services, based mainly on the results of risk and needs assessments. Offenders can be moved up and down the continuum of sanctions and program levels, depending on their progress in staying out of trouble and success in treatment programs. The YFRC component of the program has proved to be a valuable asset. Many of the 8% wards and their family members have such serious problems that they require brief periods of residential treatment. Such wraparound, center-based services are also needed for family members, particularly younger siblings, who may become 8% group members without this early intervention (Schumacher & Kurz, 2000).

Target Population Characteristics	Immediate Accountability	Intensive Intervention	Youth and Family Resource Center		
			Repeat Offender Prevention Program (ROPP)	Opportunities	Transitional Aftercare*
Risk clarification	Low to medium	Medium to high	High	High	Medium to high
Number of "8%" risk factors	N/A (Problems identified are in normal adolescent range.)	0–2	3–4	3–4	3–4**
Degree of criminal sophistication (minor)	Low	Low to medium	Medium	Medium	Medium
Offense severity	Nonviolent	All types	All types	All types	All types
Institutional commitment	< 90 days	Full range	Full range	Full range	90 days or more**
Age at wardship declaration	All ages (mostly 16 and older)	All ages (more 16 and older)	15 and under	16 and older	All ages
Other	Supportive family; primary casework issue: complete accountability requirements.	Risk factors not chronic; amenable to short-term intensive intervention.	(Family)	**Chronic Risk Factors** (Drugs/Gangs)	

*This component will not serve first-time wards.

**Exceptions will be policy overrides based on community protection issues.

Note: Range of Graduated Sanctions available to all program participants:
1. Community-based sanctions.
2. Juvenile court work program.
3. Institutional commitments.

Figure 13.2 Orange County Program Model Overview (Program Components for First-Time Wards)

SOURCE: Modified from Orange County (California) Probation Department, *Model Continuum of Juvenile Justice Services* (personal communication, July 21, 2000).

Parental problems such as child abuse, substance abuse, and criminal involvement are addressed.

The Orange County system is a premier example of how jurisdictions should apply the Comprehensive Strategy's graduated sanctions framework. This system goes beyond most applications of the structured decision-making model by formally organizing distinct program structures for low-, medium-, and high-risk offenders. Any large jurisdiction would benefit from building a similar structure.

A Comprehensive Approach to Targeting Chronic Young Violent Offenders

Baton Rouge, Louisiana, has used the Comprehensive Strategy to guide the development of a continuum of prevention, intervention, and suppression activities targeting adolescents and young adults involved in gun violence. The Baton Rouge Partnership for the Prevention of Juvenile Gun Violence targets the most chronic violent youths up to age 21 from two high-crime zip code areas (Sheppard, Grant, Rowe, & Jacobs, 2000). Juveniles and young adults on probation for gun-related offenses are designated as "Eigers," named after the Swiss mountain, one of the world's most difficult to climb. This concept has helped enormously to mobilize the community to contribute in myriad ways to the program, to help Eigers overcome their problems. Nearly 300 community agencies and citizens are involved in some way.

"Operation Eiger" has developed three linked prevention, intervention, and suppression strategies, as shown in Figure 13.3. Intensive supervision and strict enforcement of conditions of probation (suppression) by police-probation teams form one key component. The probation conditions are linked to risk factors associated with each youth's violent behaviors, which are addressed with program interventions. A comprehensive treatment plan (intervention) is developed for each Eiger that includes services for family members. A Life Skills Academy, pioneered by the Partnership for the Prevention of Juvenile Gun Violence and conducted in local churches, offers a wide variety of education, training, and rehabilitation options for Eigers. Prevention is the third main Operation Eiger component; the program works to build youths' resilience in the community by addressing existing risk factors and thus prevent the spawning of future Eigers. With this comprehensive continuum of program options, Operation Eiger stands in sharp contrast to most highly publicized youth violence control programs, such as the Boston Gun Project/Operation Ceasefire, which typically focus only on deterrence (Kennedy, 1999). Operation Eiger is likely to have a much greater long-term impact than single-component programs because of the Comprehensive Strategy in which it is based.

An evaluation of the effectiveness of the Baton Rouge program is currently under way (Sheppard et al., 2000). Lizotte and Sheppard (2001, pp. 8-9) have found that gun-related homicides, as a percentage of all homicides in the program's target area, decreased from 91% in 1996 to 63% in 1999. In addition, preliminary results from individual monitoring activity indicate that the percentage of contacts with Eigers by police-probation teams for which probation violations were reported decreased from 44% when the program began in 1997 to 26% in 1999.

A Continuum of Graduated Sanctions and Services

In Chapter 12, I described the Comprehensive Strategy tools for building and operating a continuum of graduated sanctions and services. These include—at a minimum—a risk assessment instrument, a needs assessment instrument, and a classification matrix. Risk and needs assessments should be standardized, but classification (or disposition) matrices may be designed and used in a variety of ways. Similarly, there is a great deal of variation in how states and localities structure and use graduated sanctions. Such variations are matters of local preferences. Flexibility is one of the unique features of the Comprehensive Strategy.

Missouri's statewide development of a continuum of graduated sanctions and services is an example of Comprehensive Strategy implementation that sets a very high standard for other states to follow. Guided by the Comprehensive Strategy, Missouri developed a structured decision-making model that uses risk and needs assessments and a classification matrix: the Missouri Juvenile Offender Risk and Need Assessment and Classification System (Office of State Courts Administrator, 2002). A major goal of the state in establishing this classification system is to promote statewide consistency in the classification and supervision of juvenile offenders. The three tools of the system are as follows:

- An actuarial risk assessment tool, completed before court adjudication, classifies youth into three categories: high, moderate, or low probability of reoffending. The risk

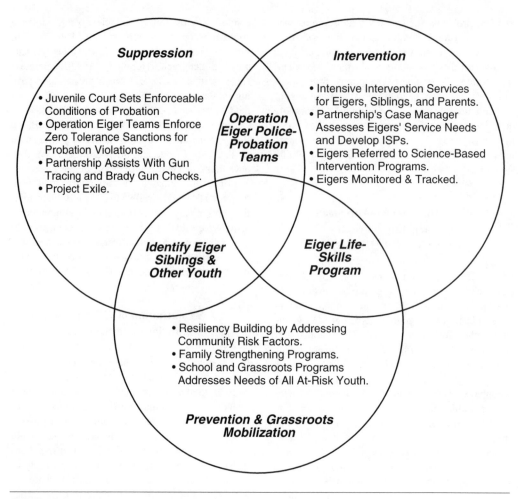

Figure 13.3   Operation Eiger's Linked Strategies

SOURCE: *Gun Use by Male Juveniles: Research and Prevention* (p. 9), by A. J. Lizotte and D. Sheppard, 2001, Washington, DC: Office of Juvenile Justice and Delinquency Prevention.

assessment instrument has been validated (Johnson, Wagner, & Matthews, 2001).

- A classification matrix recommends sanctions and service interventions appropriate to the youth's risk level and his or her most serious adjudicated offense.
- A needs assessment instrument recommends services that will reduce the likelihood of a youth's reoffending by reducing risk factors that are linked to recidivism.

In addition, Missouri has developed a set of standards—Performance Standards for the Administration of Juvenile Justice (Office of State Courts Administrator, 2000)—that help balance individual rights and treatment needs with public

protection. These standards establish a common framework within which juvenile justice personnel can understand and assess the work of juvenile and family courts and enhance the courts' performance. They are "premised on the notion that court performance should be driven by core values of equity, integrity, fairness, and justice" (Office of State Courts Administrator, 2000, p. 2). The standards also include contact guidelines for high, medium, and low levels of supervision, based on the placement of offenders in the classification matrix. Lastly, Missouri conducted a workload study to determine whether juvenile court staff were meeting intake and supervision performance standards (Johnson & Wagner, 2001). Overall, court staff met expected standards in 93% of the cases tracked.

A user's manual for the classification system contains guidelines and instructions for completing the risk and needs assessments and for placing juveniles within the parameters of the classification matrix. The efficiency of Missouri's classification system is enhanced by the use of Juvenile Tracking Referral Assessment and Classification (J-TRAC) software. As noted in Chapter 12, this is an automated system for collecting and storing demographic, referral, assessment, classification, and disposition information on juvenile offenders. It is currently being implemented in several of the state's circuit courts. A recent report of Missouri's Office of State Courts Administrator (2001) profiles the risk levels and treatment needs of youths in the state, illustrating the value of the Juvenile Offender Risk and Need Assessment and Classification System. Juvenile justice officials can assess these data, along with information on available programs, to identify gaps in services. Thanks to J-TRAC, officials statewide will soon be able to determine their budgetary needs while sitting at a computer, using actual juvenile justice system processing and outcome data. Recidivism data soon will be added to the system, which will permit improved matching of offenders who have certain risk-need profiles with the most effective programs. This Missouri system represents a remarkable advancement in juvenile justice system management.

Statewide Comprehensive Strategy Implementation

Several other states have used the Comprehensive Strategy as a framework to guide their development of comprehensive juvenile justice systems. Interestingly, these states have all gone about pursuing this objective in different ways. I begin this brief review with California, because the Comprehensive Strategy was first implemented there.

The first Comprehensive Strategy implementation commenced in Orange County, California, in 1994 (Schumacher & Kurz, 2000), just 1 year after the Comprehensive Strategy was first published (Wilson & Howell, 1993), although planning for the pioneering 8% Early Intervention Program began earlier, using a draft of the Comprehensive Strategy. In addition to describing this program in detail above, I have mentioned it in Chapter 11 in relation to the wraparound model of service delivery, and I have highlighted its research origins in Chapter 4.

The early success of the 8% Early Intervention Program led to a statewide California initiative that replicates it. The statewide program is named after the intensive wraparound component of the 8% Early Intervention Program: the Repeat Offender Prevention Program (ROPP). In late 1994, the California State Legislature created ROPP (Chapter 730, Statutes of 1994). Through this program, the legislature has funded the Orange County ROPP and replicated it in seven other counties: Fresno, Humboldt, Los Angles, San Francisco, San Diego, San Mateo, and Solano (California Board of Corrections, 2001). More than $14 million in awards were made to the eight programs from 1995 through 2001. Each county must conduct an evaluation that addresses outcomes specific to its project. For the statewide evaluation, all programs are using a common database that contains background, service, and outcome information for juveniles participating in the project. Positive preliminary results are available in a report published by the California Board of Corrections (2001).

The Comprehensive Strategy is also being implemented statewide, without any federal assistance, in other states. I have highlighted Missouri's successful graduated sanctions work in this chapter. In addition, as I have discussed in Chapter 12, North Carolina is implementing both components of the Comprehensive Strategy. Connecticut, Virginia, and Oklahoma have also begun implementing the Comprehensive Strategy.

Oklahoma made considerable progress in implementing the Comprehensive Strategy in the absence of statewide legislation. The initiative was spearheaded by the Oklahoma Office of Juvenile Affairs (OJA), which was headed by Jerry Regier, a former OJJDP administrator. Under Regier, the OJA has formulated the Promise Approach, a Comprehensive Strategy that is built around a "FutureFocus" model (Office of Juvenile Affairs, 2000). It consists of four key components: prevention (parental responsibility), protection (public safety), accountability (graduated sanctions), and promise (individual development). A continuum of programs supports each of these components. The graduated sanctions component, including risk and needs assessments, was piloted in several counties and now is being expanded statewide.

Kansas has implemented both components of the Comprehensive Strategy by law (Juvenile Justice Reform Act of 1995; Kan. Stat. Ann. § 75-7001 et seq.). This is an excellent example of a research-based, data-driven, outcome-focused Comprehensive Strategy implementation. The prevention component uses the Communities That Care prevention planning system. In 1998, Community Planning Teams in every judicial district developed Comprehensive Strategic Plans based on community assessments of risk and protective factors for delinquency. These plans also assessed existing graduated sanctions, identified barriers/gaps in services and resources, and called for a balanced system of sanctions and services (see the Kansas Juvenile Justice Authority's Web site at jja.state.ks.us/reform.htm). Each judicial district is implementing a continuum of graduated sanctions, including immediate, intermediate, secure, and aftercare sanctions. A graduated sanctions matrix was implemented in 1999. Statewide outcomes were established for the prevention and graduated sanctions components. The state will soon be measuring progress against the established objectives.

The Comprehensive Strategy is also being implemented in localities in 15 other states (Florida, Hawaii, Iowa, Kentucky, Louisiana, Maryland, Michigan, Minnesota, New Jersey, New Mexico, Ohio, Oregon, Rhode Island, Texas, and Wisconsin). Each state's governor was required to select several localities to receive OJJDP technical assistance. It would have been advisable for the states to have attempted to mobilize communities before they made their selections. Many of these attempts at implementation will not succeed now that OJJDP has terminated the supporting program of training and technical assistance in favor of a piecemeal approach to system improvement. Training and technical assistance are essential to successful implementation (Coolbaugh & Hansel, 2000).

Progress is often slow in states that have not incorporated the Comprehensive Strategy in any juvenile justice reform legislation or provided implementation funds. This factor accounts, in part, for the rapid progress North Carolina has made. The National Conference of State Legislatures (1999a) has developed a guide for lawmakers to use in legislating "comprehensive juvenile justice." This excellent guide summarizes the research foundation of the Comprehensive Strategy, explains the rationale behind it, and describes its components while highlighting a plethora of examples of comprehensive juvenile justice initiatives that have been legislated across the United States. Most of these are independent of the Comprehensive Strategy, but can serve as a foundation for the development of statewide comprehensive strategies. State collaborative councils (described in Box 13.5) made up of the heads of various human service agencies can facilitate collaboration on such matters as early childhood development and welfare, mental heath, and juvenile justice. Such councils could serve as excellent cornerstones in statewide comprehensive strategies.

In the remainder of this chapter, I discuss two key aspects of successful Comprehensive Strategy implementation that I have not addressed thus far: the importance of community involvement and the necessity of building a continuum of effective services for girls.

Community Involvement

Community organizations and individual citizens who are not part of any public or private youth-serving agencies need to be active participants in their community's comprehensive strategy to reduce juvenile delinquency. Indigenous neighborhood groups, community-based youth development organizations, schools, civic organizations, religious groups, parents, teens, and business and commercial organizations all need to be actively involved in the prevention component of the comprehensive strategy. In addition, they should be active participants in the graduated sanctions component. For example, community agencies and organizations provide many of the services that are made available in the Orange County 8% Early Intervention Program. These contributions amount to half of the costs of all services in that program.

In the comprehensive continuum of juvenile justice services developed in Tarrant County, Texas, community residents serve as advocates, mentors, and monitors of youth in the Tarrant County Advocate Program (TCAP). These residents play a key role in bringing together a support network to surround troubled youths—a child/family team that includes family members, neighbors, child welfare workers, clinical social workers, and community volunteers (Mendel, 2001). Advocates do intensive work with the youth, in their families and communities, for up to 30 hours per week over a 6-month period. This supportive TCAP network has enabled the county to reduce dramatically the number of commitments to secure-care juvenile corrections facilities. The success rate for keeping youth out of these facilities is 78%. Tarrant County's experience demonstrates the enormous contribution that community residents can make to juvenile rehabilitation programs. Involved residents need to be trained, however. Training for TCAP participants was provided by Youth Advocate Programs, Inc., in Harrisburg, Pennsylvania (TCAP is based on a model developed by Youth Advocate Programs).

A Continuum of Services for Girls

Because of the growing number of girls in the juvenile justice system and worsening conditions of

Box 13.4
Juvenile Justice Reform in Louisiana

The state of Louisiana provides a case study of how the Comprehensive Strategy can guide statewide juvenile justice system reform. Louisiana has been plagued by juvenile justice system problems for a number of years. In the 1990s, an investigation by Human Rights Watch (1995) revealed abuses of juveniles and violations of their individual rights in the state's juvenile correctional facilities. The privately operated Tallulah Correctional Center had the distinction of being the worst such facility in the nation (Soler, 2001). In 1998, the U.S. Justice Department sued the state of Louisiana for violating the civil rights of youth held in state custody, marking the first time the federal government actively sued a state over the conditions of its juvenile facilities (Soler, 2001). Shortly thereafter, management of the Tallulah facility was returned to the state (Coalition for Juvenile Justice, 1999). A comprehensive approach to improving the Louisiana juvenile justice system was soon recommended by the Louisiana State Supreme Court's chief justice, Pascal Calogero. He appealed to all three branches of government to examine the current state of Louisiana's juvenile justice system, "to re-envision, restructure, and reform the juvenile justice system" (quoted in Louisiana Juvenile Justice Commission, 2001-2002b). He urged the state to use the Comprehensive Strategy framework in this process. The Louisiana State Legislature responded to Calogero's recommendation by creating the Juvenile Justice Commission (House Concurrent Resolution No. 94). The goals of the Juvenile Justice Commission are as follows:

- To develop, organize, maintain, and make readily accessible to decision-makers and the general public accurate, up-to-date, information on the juvenile justice system of Louisiana;
- To analyze and report on the strengths, weaknesses, opportunities and threats affecting the juvenile justice system of Louisiana;
- To analyze, assess, and report on the feasibility of developing and implementing a comprehensive strategy that would create a true system of outcome-based services linked to the specific needs of each target population; and
- To develop specific short- and long-term strategies for improving the juvenile justice system of Louisiana based on the principles of the comprehensive strategy; and to make recommendations to the executive, legislative, and judicial branches of state government, and possibly local governments and the private sector, regarding the various strategies. (Louisiana Juvenile Justice Commission, 2001-2002a)

To guide the development of a comprehensive juvenile justice system, the commission adapted the basic principles of the Comprehensive Strategy as a framework for system reform. These principles include the following:

- The Louisiana juvenile justice system should support core institutions, including schools, churches, and other community organizations, so that they can reduce risk factors and help children develop their potential.
- The Louisiana juvenile justice system should promote prevention strategies that enhance protective factors and reduce the impact of negative risk factors affecting the lives of young people at high risk for delinquency.
- The Louisiana juvenile justice system should intervene immediately and constructively when delinquent behavior first occurs.
- The Louisiana juvenile justice system should identify and control the small segment of serious juvenile offenders who repeatedly victimize the community and who account for the vast majority of serious and violent delinquent acts.
- The Louisiana juvenile justice system should establish a continuum of services to meet the specific needs of the state's children and families; and it should establish a system of graduated sanctions that will hold offenders accountable, that will protect public safety, and that will provide programs and services to meet identified educational and treatment needs. (Louisiana Juvenile Justice Commission, 2001-2002c)

(Continued)

Box 13.4 (Continued)

The interbranch Juvenile Justice Commission consists of a Planning Team and an Advisory Board. The Planning Team is composed of representatives from the executive, legislative, and judicial branches of Louisiana government. In addition, Mary Fairchild, program director, Children and Families, of the National Conference of State Legislatures, served as a resource provider. In the first phase of work, the Advisory Board, made up of state and local experts, gathered information and conducted research on the state's juvenile justice system. In addition, public hearings were held around the state. The Advisory Board will use this information in the second phase of the work to draft findings and make recommendations to the commission. The approved recommendations will be the focus of a second round of hearings in 2003. The results of these hearings and additional suggestions by the Advisory Board will enable the commission to propose action to implement Louisiana's system reforms.

---

confinement (as described in Chapter 3), it is imperative that priority be given to the treatment needs of female offenders. It is particularly important that juvenile justice system services be linked with services from other providers in a continuum of program options. There are numerous system impediments to collaborative efforts between dependence and delinquency agencies that lead to inadequate services for young female clients. As the authors of a joint publication by the American Bar Association and the National Bar Association (2001) have observed, "Cross-system designs for girls' services, protocols for transitioning girls into communities, and advocacy models for girls that cross systems and provide ancillary legal services must be developed" (p. 38). They also state that "communities with increasing populations of delinquent girls need to develop and provide appropriate prevention, intervention, and treatment alternatives that address the root causes of girls' delinquent behavior and promote safe and healthy communities" for them (p. 20).

Gender-Specific Programs

The best window of opportunity for intervention with problem girls is in early adolescence. For most of them, the pathway to serious problem behaviors commences between ages 12 and 15. The vast majority of delinquent girls can be served in the existing effective juvenile justice system programs that are offered across the country, as noted in Chapter 10. Even programs for serious and violent juvenile offenders appear to be as effective for girls as for boys (Lipsey & Wilson, 1998, p. 332). However, programs are needed that take into account the developmental differences between girls and boys and the possible unique developmental pathway to delinquency for girls (see Chapter 4). Researchers have recommended the development of several types of female-specific programs (Acoca, 1998b;

Acoca & Dedel, 1998; Kempf-Leonard, 1997; Loper, 2000; National Council of Juvenile and Family Court Judges, 1998):

- Programs that include treatment for neglect and sexual and physical victimization
- Crisis intervention programs that provide short-term shelter, family mediation, and conflict resolution
- Programs that engage girls in healthy relationships and provide social skills training
- Programs that provide medical care for pregnant teens
- Programs for unwed teenage mothers, including parent training and child-care relief time
- Programs that build and preserve the teen mother-child bond
- Programs for sexually active females (and males)
- Programs that include peer mediation to deal with conflicts concerning boyfriends and peer status

More community-based treatment options are also needed for girls, as alternatives to detention and long-term incarceration. It is highly unlikely that long-term incarceration in a typical juvenile correctional facility will correct the sources of girls' underlying problems—such as physical and sexual abuse early in childhood—and reverse the causal processes that result in serious and violent delinquency. Foster care is a viable alternative. The cost-effective Multidimensional Treatment Foster Care (MTFC) model (Chamberlain, 1998) serves girls as well as boys, and a new replication of this model addresses the specific needs of adolescent females with delinquent histories and severe emotional and behavioral difficulties. The MTFC model has been modified to address the specific needs of female delinquents. Another replication, the Early

---

Box 13.5

Collaborative Councils

Collaborative councils are bodies of state representatives that address key issues in collaborative child, youth, and juvenile justice policies and programs. To date, four types of collaborative councils have been created in 27 states, grouped according to two important structural distinctions: whether the council has members from outside the executive branch of government (stakeholders) and whether the council interacts with local interagency collaboratives. The four types of councils are as follows:

- *Cabinet councils:* Members are cabinet officials, and their work is focused at the state level. The states with cabinet councils are Alaska, Delaware, Louisiana, Maine, Michigan, and Rhode Island.
- *Networked cabinet councils:* Members are cabinet officials, and their work is locally oriented. The states with networked cabinet councils are Maryland, Minnesota, North Dakota, Ohio, Utah, Vermont, and West Virginia.
- *Stakeholder councils:* Members are stakeholders, and their work is focused at the state level. The states with stakeholder councils are Connecticut, Iowa, Montana, New York, Pennsylvania, and Tennessee.
- *Networked stakeholder councils:* Members are stakeholders who are networked at the local level. The states with networked stakeholder councils are Colorado, Georgia, Hawaii, Illinois, Kentucky, Missouri, Oregon, and Washington.

North Carolina's Collaborative System of Care (see Chapter 11) includes a State Collaborative that is made up of state agency policy decision makers who work together as a team to promote and develop policies that further integrated local services. This collaboration model—which is something of a hybrid—is unique in its organizational linkage with local programming through Community Collaboratives and Child and Family Teams.

Intervention Treatment Foster Care program, applies the TFC model to severely abused and neglected 3- to 7-year-old boys and girls in state foster homes. Oregon is the only state that requires agencies serving adolescents to ensure that girls and boys have equal access to appropriate services, treatment, and facilities (Morgan & Patton, 2002). Agencies in the state are required to implement plans ensuring that girls receive *equity* in access to social, juvenile justice, and community services statewide. Guidelines and an accompanying manual for implementing gender-responsive programming in the state have been developed (see Morgan & Patton, 2002, pp. 58-64).

Only a handful of gender-specific programs nationwide have been recognized for their potential effectiveness. These include PACE Center for Girls in Jacksonville, Florida; the Female Intervention Team in Baltimore, Maryland; and Reaffirming Young Sisters' Excellence (RYSA) in Oakland, California (Acoca, 1999, p. 9). Two nationwide initiatives will identify others: Girls Incorporated (1996) has conducted a national assessment of juvenile justice system programs for females, and the

Juvenile Justice Center at the American Bar Association has launched the Girls' Justice Initiative for the purpose of improving policies, practices, and programs for girls in the juvenile justice system (American Bar Association & National Bar Association, 2001).

The Alameda County, California, Department of Juvenile Probation, with the assistance of the National Council on Crime and Delinquency, has developed a girls' unit that serves girls at all levels of the juvenile justice system (Acoca, 1998a). The unit provides a comprehensive array of gender-specific services, including health, mental health, and developmentally sequenced services for teen mothers and their children. The NCCD is evaluating the program.

Summary

In remarks he made at a roundtable discussion in 2000, John J. Wilson described the rationale behind the Comprehensive Strategy:

The Comprehensive Strategy is based on a fairly simple formula that works. If you catch delinquency early and address the source of the problem, you are much less likely to be dealing with a crime and a criminal later. Achieving this formula requires a coordinated effort at critical times in a child's life with a range of services, supports, and opportunities in a continuum of care.

In this chapter, I have illustrated the Comprehensive Strategy's continuum of juvenile justice interventions, which empowers communities and states to develop the following segments in the two main Comprehensive Strategy components, prevention/early intervention and graduated sanctions:

- Delinquency prevention
- Early intervention with problem children and their families
- Immediate intervention with first-time and nonserious delinquent offenders
- Intermediate sanctions for first-time serious or violent offenders
- Community confinement
- Secure corrections for the most serious, violent, and chronic offenders
- Aftercare

I have illustrated each of these parts of the Comprehensive Strategy continuum with specific program examples. I have also featured four broad examples of adaptations of the Comprehensive Strategy framework developed by three localities (San Diego and Orange Counties in California and Baton Rouge, Louisiana) and one state (Missouri). Each of the three localities tailored the Comprehensive Strategy framework to its particular circumstances. San Diego County wanted to achieve two specific objectives: to prevent high-risk youth from coming into the juvenile justice system and to impede further development of delinquent careers among youths who already were in the juvenile justice system. The county accomplished both

of these goals with the Breaking Cycles program, which integrated prevention with graduated sanctions. Orange County set out to prevent youths at high risk of becoming serious chronic offenders from doing so by bringing them into an early intervention program that featured a graduated sanctions scheme. The county's pursuit of this objective led to the creation of a three-part probation department framework that allocated fewer resources to medium- and low-risk offenders, respectively, thus forming an impressive continuum. In the third case, Baton Rouge targeted a specific group of offenders, violent youths, and fashioned a comprehensive strategy of prevention, intervention, and suppression (sanctions) around them and their families. In sharp contrast, Missouri officials have proceeded in somewhat of a textbook fashion in implementing—statewide—the graduated sanctions component of the Comprehensive Strategy framework. All of these cases illustrate the flexibility of the Comprehensive Strategy.

Discussion Questions

1. How did Mahoning County, Ohio, implement risk- and protection-focused prevention?

2. What are some ways in which early intervention works to prevent child delinquency?

3. What is the value of the wraparound model of service delivery in the implementation of the Comprehensive Strategy?

4. How did the Orange County Probation Department identify three groups of offenders and structure a three-part continuum to deal with each of them?

5. What do you think of the crisis intervention approaches that have been developed? Would they work in all situations?

6. Which example of the implementation of the Comprehensive Strategy impresses you the most? Why?

CONCLUDING OBSERVATIONS

We must get the right service to the right kid at the right time.

—John J. Wilson, coauthor of the Comprehensive Strategy

The past 20 years have been a tumultuous period for the American juvenile justice system. Although many have claimed that a general "epidemic" of juvenile violence occurred in the United States from the mid-1980s through the early 1990s, research has shown that this did not actually happen. Rather, during that period violence increased in all age groups, and the rate of increase was larger among 30- to 49-year-olds than among any other age group, including teenagers (Males, 1997). It could be said, however, that a gun epidemic occurred, as indicated by both homicides and suicides among young persons. From 1973 through 1994, the number of guns in private ownership in the United States rose by 87 million (Malcom, 2002), to an estimated 200 million (Reich, Culross, & Behrman, 2002), of which approximately 60 million are handguns (Zimring, 1998a). The largest absolute increase in the homicide rate was among young adult black males, ages 18-24 (Cook & Laub, 1998). For every two murdered youths (ages 0-19), one commits suicide; between 1979 and 1994, juvenile suicide rates involving firearms increased by one-third among young white males while almost tripling among young black males—the very group that DiIulio singled out as fearless, "stone-cold predators." With the exception of the homicide rate, only a small increase occurred in serious forms of juvenile violence, with slightly more juveniles involved in violence; juveniles were not offending at a higher rate. Nevertheless, the widely presumed general epidemic of juvenile violence contributed to the seventh moral panic over juvenile delinquency.

This most recent moral panic over juvenile delinquency and the myths associated with it—such as that an epidemic of youth violence was taking place and that a new breed of juvenile superpredators was emerging—led to dramatic changes in juvenile justice policies and practices in the 1980s and 1990s, and their influence is still in evidence. Once again, juveniles are "victims of change" (Finestone, 1976). Significant changes have occurred in the boundaries of the juvenile justice system and in policies and procedures for handling juvenile offenders within it. Large numbers of juvenile offenders have been removed from the juvenile justice system and placed in the criminal justice system. Rehabilitation is emphasized far less, and punitive measures are used more widely, than ever before. New laws have designated more juveniles as serious offenders, brought more minor offenders into the system, and extended periods of confinement in juvenile correctional facilities. One comparison illustrates the overall trend. From 1990 through 1999, the total number of juvenile arrests for violent offenses *decreased* by 55% and juvenile arrests for serious property offenses *decreased* by 23% (Snyder, 2000). Nevertheless, during approximately the same period, the total number of referrals to juvenile court *increased* by 44% (Stahl, 2001). Juvenile court intake and probation caseloads are overwhelming, and detention centers and juvenile reformatories have become and remain overcrowded, particularly with minor offenders. Minority youth, particularly black youngsters, are bearing the brunt of the punitive juvenile justice reforms that the panic over juvenile violence has wrought—although Latino and Latina youth are catching up (Villarruel & Walker, 2002). This is the general context within which juvenile justice systems across the United States currently operate.

Overloaded juvenile courts are confronted with the particularly difficult task of distinguishing offenders who will not persist in delinquency if returned to the community from those who will. The research and management tools reviewed in this book can increase the certainty with which juvenile justice officials select the correct offenders for more intensive services and sanctions. Risk assessment instruments make the risk classification task more manageable, and needs/strengths assessments help link offenders with appropriate services.

Enormous strides have been made recently in research on disruptive children and child delinquents and the development of programs to serve them. Left without services, from one-fourth to one-third of disruptive children will become child delinquents, and about a third of all child delinquents will later become serious, violent, and chronic offenders. To disrupt this progression, communities must serve these children outside the juvenile justice system—enlisting social service agencies, mental health agencies, and educational institutions—when their disruptive behaviors are first identified. Services need to be "wrapped around" these problem children and their families.

When John Wilson and I first developed the Comprehensive Strategy, we proposed that the juvenile justice system needed to give priority to serious, violent, *and* chronic offenders in order to have the largest impact in terms of delinquency reduction (Wilson & Howell, 1993). This position represented a departure from common knowledge at that time, because the field was focused only on the chronic offender subgroup as a result of the Philadelphia Birth Cohort Study (Tracy, Wolfgang, & Figlio, 1990; Wolfgang, Figlio, & Sellin, 1972; Wolfgang, Thornberry, & Figlio, 1987), which equated chronic offenders with serious offenders. Subsequent research in juvenile offender careers has shown that much of the serious and violent juvenile offending is concentrated in a small proportion of the repeat offender population. The proportion of high-rate serious or violent offenders ranges from about 4% to 14% in the population of juvenile offenders referred to court.

More research on the serious, violent, and chronic offender subtypes would provide information useful for the development of risk assessment instruments and would help communities to prioritize treatment and graduated sanctions while achieving better matches between offenders and programs. Once better information on these subtypes is incorporated into risk assessment instruments, longitudinal research on offender careers should help court officials to estimate offenders' position on the pathways to serious, violent, and chronic offending. The next step in the practical application of Loeber's pathways model (see Chapter 4) is to identify predictors (risk factors) for groups of offenders that advance in the covert (serious-chronic) and overt (violent-chronic) pathways. When the best predictors have been isolated, these can be incorporated into risk assessment instruments, along with currently known recidivism predictors, and used as a basis for offender classification and placement in graduated sanctions systems, as recommended in the Comprehensive Strategy. Much more work is needed to refine risk assessment instruments to this level of application.

Several studies have documented the overlap between serious, violent, and chronic juvenile offending and gang membership, as well as the devastating effects of gang involvement on an individual's life course. These discoveries are seminal products of gang member studies that were embedded within longitudinal adolescent studies in Denver, Pittsburgh, Rochester, and Seattle. In their report on the landmark Rochester gang study, *Gangs and Delinquency in Developmental Perspective,* Thornberry, Krohn, Lizotte, Smith, and Tobin (2003) suggest that membership in street gangs "may be one of the more important social environments for explaining patterns of adolescent delinquency." They found that the more a person was exposed to the gang, the more that individual's life course experiences was turned toward deviance and away from conformity. The contribution of gang members and gangs to violence among adolescents and young adults is probably the most overlooked factor in explanations of violence in these age groups (Howell, 1999; Thornberry et al., 2003).

The National Youth Gang Center (2001b) has developed a manual for implementing the comprehensive gang model for preventing and controlling gang members and gangs that consists of a continuum of prevention, intervention, and suppression strategies. In any given community, specific strategies for combating youth gangs should be based on a detailed assessment of the community's own local gang problems. This assessment should be an integral part of the community's assessment of its serious, violent, and chronic juvenile delinquency problem wherever youth gang problems exist. The National Youth Gang Center (2001a) has also developed an assessment protocol that any community can use to assess its gang problem as well as resource materials to assist communities in implementing the comprehensive gang model. The elements of this model can be integrated with the components of the Comprehensive Strategy.

In the chapters in Part III of this volume, I have used the Comprehensive Strategy framework to guide a review of prevention, early intervention, and rehabilitation programs that can be linked with graduated sanctions. I have reviewed the history of efforts to coordinate and integrate services to prevent delinquency and rehabilitate delinquents, and in doing so I have endorsed the wraparound model of service delivery for integrating the services offered by the wide variety of public and private agencies that serve troubled children, adolescents, and their families—often simultaneously. I have described the advanced tools and techniques that are available to help communities take advantage of the latest findings in delinquency prevention science as well as the tools of the structured decision-making model, which can improve juvenile justice system operations and optimize program effectiveness. These are the tools of the Comprehensive Strategy framework for preventing and reducing juvenile delinquency.

A community attempting to build a continuum of program options has plenty of cost-effective juvenile justice programs to choose from. One of the surprising findings from Lipsey's comprehensive meta-analyses is his discovery that most everyday juvenile justice programs ("practical programs," Lipsey calls them) reduce recidivism, although a large proportion of them do not produce significant reductions. This discovery led Lipsey to conclude that many everyday programs could be improved so that they emulate many of the features of the most effective programs, and this would serve communities' continuum-building purposes.

Lipsey's pioneering meta-analyses may well produce a major breakthrough, simplifying the procedures a community needs to undertake to build a continuum of effective juvenile justice programs. Lipsey's practical new method of assessing current programs by using a template of the features of the most effective programs (as evidenced in prior evaluations) has great promise. This approach simplifies the continuum-building process by moving the field away from reliance on importing whole program models to replace weak programs. It may be possible to train professionals to assess and strengthen existing programs, and even to improve

weak programs, to achieve larger recidivism reductions. This process will be enhanced where risk and needs assessments are being used to facilitate better matching of offenders with programs. The North Carolina experiment using this approach bears close watch.

In the final two chapters of this book I have described and illustrated a comprehensive framework for integrating the various segments of the juvenile delinquency prevention field and juvenile justice systems. Delinquency prevention, effective early intervention, and a continuum of graduated sanctions linked with rehabilitation programs in the juvenile justice system are the key main components of the Comprehensive Strategy. In the first level, delinquency prevention and early intervention programs are promoted as the most cost-effective approaches to dealing with juvenile delinquency. Emphasis is placed on intervening early with disruptive children and their families, and immediately when delinquency first occurs, to prevent child delinquents from becoming serious, violent, and chronic offenders. When other institutions fail to prevent delinquency, the juvenile justice system intervenes, at the second level, working with other agencies to reduce delinquency.

This is a research-based framework that is grounded on information presented in Parts I and II of the book and on best practices and advanced management techniques that have been developed in the juvenile justice field over the past 25 years or more. In Chapter 13, I have described examples of the implementation of the Comprehensive Strategy in several localities and states across the country. I have used examples to illustrate the flexibility of the Comprehensive Strategy framework in several adaptations.

Implementation of the Comprehensive Strategy remains in its infancy. Although few sites have completed long-term implementation, refinement, and evaluation, early results are highly encouraging. To give but a few examples: Orange County (California) Probation Department officials have successfully implemented the graduated sanctions component. San Diego County has integrated the prevention and graduated sanctions components in its successful implementation. Missouri has implemented the graduated sanctions component. North Carolina is implementing both components, and has seen promising results with graduated sanctions. Baton Rouge used the Comprehensive Strategy to develop a continuum of prevention, intervention, and suppression activities targeting adolescents and young adults involved in gun violence. Results are not yet in on other implementations.

The effectiveness of a state's or locality's Comprehensive Strategy ultimately hinges on the effectiveness of the continuum of prevention, early intervention, and juvenile offender rehabilitation programs; the last of which must parallel a system of graduated sanctions. I have described a continuum of effective prevention and early intervention programs in Chapter 9 (for many others, see Loeber & Farrington, 1998c, 2001a). I have described few whole-cloth treatment programs in Chapter 10 because advanced work on the principles of effective rehabilitation (by Canadian/American criminologists) and meta-analyses (by Lipsey) have provided a foundation for simplifying the juvenile justice system program development enterprise. Lipsey's pioneering meta-analyses appear to be leading to the development of what promises to be a very practical method for assessing existing program interventions against evidence-based practices, and then engaging localities in improving current programs to emulate best practices.

Washington State is engaged in a unique experiment that also bears close watch. Although this effort is not expressly guided by the Comprehensive Strategy, it employs many of the tools recommended in the strategy. The Washington program employs a structured decision-making model, including risk and needs assessments, in an impressive automated system. The Washington State Legislature has mandated that only effective programs will be funded in the state and has provided communities with the resources they need to replicate several cost-beneficial "blueprint" programs that were identified in a rigorous cost-benefits study at the Washington State Institute for Public Policy (Aos, Phipps, Barnoski, & Lieb, 2001).

Many states and localities are finding that the Comprehensive Strategy framework is very user-friendly. It is flexible in that communities can begin wherever they wish in implementing it. Some start with prevention; others begin with graduated sanctions. Should a community choose to initiate better management and control in the latter component, it can begin work at the front end (as Orange County did), or it can begin at the back end, with training schools, as other localities have done. It is not imperative that risk and needs assessment instruments be put in place before implementation of graduated sanctions begins. The existing juvenile corrections population can be assessed and reassigned to programs in a very short period of time, instead of waiting for the development and testing of assessment instruments. In short, it is up to each community to decide how it wishes to begin implementing its own Comprehensive Strategy.

The Comprehensive Strategy empowers local professionals and citizens to conduct an assessment of their community's delinquency problem, select solutions they wish to implement to address identified problems, and integrate the selected programs in an overall continuum of prevention and rehabilitation programs and strategies. This research-based, data-driven, and outcome-focused strategy is more likely to be effective than piecemeal approaches. For one thing, this strategy brings multiple interventions into play that address risk factors (for prevention purposes) in each of the developmental domains—family, school, peer group, community, and individual characteristics. Similarly, programs address treatment needs in each of these developmental domains.

The OJJDP Study Group on Very Young Offenders built a bridge between the prevention and graduated sanctions components of the Comprehensive Strategy with its documentation of the importance of intervening very early with at-risk children and child delinquents. Delinquency progresses from disruptive behavior in early childhood to child delinquency, and then to serious, violent, and chronic delinquency. A continuum of prevention and remediation programs is needed to address risk and protective factors at all stages of predelinquent and delinquent career development. These represent a combination of prevention, early intervention, and graduated sanctions. Prevention and early intervention programs aim to shore up these social institutions and increase protective factors, both to prevent the onset of delinquency and other problem behaviors and to intervene early in disruptive behaviors and minor forms of child delinquency before they become serious. Then the juvenile justice system must intervene with older child and adolescent delinquents. This is a useful model for building a continuum of prevention and early intervention programs.

The juvenile justice system naturally employs a developmental perspective in interventions with children or adolescents and their families, schools, and delinquent peer groups. It intervenes, out of necessity, when other social institutions fail. The juvenile justice system views adolescents as being in a developmental transition between childhood and adulthood, and as having diminished responsibility for delinquency because of their lack of maturity and also because of the failure of social institutions. This diminished responsibility standard holds young offenders accountable while acknowledging that their behavior choices are less blameworthy than those of adults (Scott, 2000). A continuum of graduated sanctions, linked to progression in serious, violent, and chronic delinquency, holds them accountable and protects the public, and a continuum of rehabilitation programs addresses treatment needs they have in the family, school, peer group, and individual problem arenas. Adolescent problem behaviors come in bundles, often stacked on top of one another (Loeber, 1990), thus multiple social service agencies must be involved in addressing them. Juvenile courts cannot solve these multiple problems alone; other agencies need to bring their resources and services to the table, joined with juvenile court services in a wraparound service delivery model. Nondelinquent youth should be served by social service agencies; they should not be handled in the juvenile justice system.

Eight Policy Change Proposals

Enormous amounts of juvenile justice system resources are wasted on the very large proportion of all juvenile offenders who will never become serious, violent, and chronic offenders. Lawmakers have gotten it backward in cracking down on first-time offenders, and this policy has overloaded juvenile courts, probation departments, and detention centers. We now know, from several offender career studies, that as many as two-thirds of all juvenile offenders will *never* become serious, violent, or chronic offenders. The necessary risk assessment technology is available today to sort these low-risk offenders out from the remainder so that they can receive the immediate sanctions and short-term program interventions that have proven effective with such juveniles.

More gender-specific programming is needed in the juvenile justice system. Although most girls who become juvenile offenders take pathways to serious and violent delinquency that are similar to those taken by boys, it appears that a small proportion of girls may take a unique pathway to serious, violent, and chronic offender careers (see Chapter 4). Even though programs for serious and violent juvenile offenders appear to be as effective for girls as for boys (Lipsey & Wilson, 1998, p. 332), girls can benefit from gender-specific programs such as the following:

- Programs that provide treatment for neglect and sexual and physical victimization
- Programs that provide medical care for pregnant teens
- Programs for unwed teenage mothers, including parent training and child-care relief time

- Programs that build and preserve the teen mother-child bond
- Programs for sexually active females (and males)
- Programs that include peer mediation to deal with conflicts concerning boyfriends and peer status

Ideally, all state policies that allow the transfer of juveniles to the criminal justice system for criminal conviction and adult punishment should be ended. Aside from the fact that such policies are not the mark of a civilized society, the practice of exposing adolescents to adult courts and prisons is neither effective in reducing crime nor cost-beneficial. The criminal justice system does not have the capacity to treat or protect juveniles, and incarcerating juveniles in adult facilities is not effective in deterring future crime. Transferring juveniles from the juvenile justice system to the criminal justice system and confinement in prisons, where developmental and treatment programs are a rarity, drastically reduces their life chances, and this is simply morally wrong.

At best, imprisonment results in only short-term incapacitation. Transferred juveniles are more likely to reoffend, more quickly, and at a higher rate, and perhaps commit more serious offenses, after they are released from prison than juveniles retained in the juvenile justice system (Howell, 1996). Those who have criticized the juvenile justice system for its alleged lack of due process have claimed that juveniles' constitutional rights would be better protected in the criminal justice system (Feld, 1998a, 1999), but this has never proven to be true. Only about 5-10% of all criminal court cases proceed to trial, thus only a small fraction of alleged offenders—less than 1 in 10—are afforded their full constitutional protections. Juveniles' constitutional rights are far more likely to be irrelevant in criminal courts than they are in juvenile courts. More than one-third of all cases referred to juvenile courts are adjudicated, at which point almost all constitutional protections afforded to adults apply to juveniles (Snyder & Sickmund, 1999, pp. 90-92).

State legislatures should immediately take several steps to limit the practice of transferring juveniles to criminal courts. By injecting common sense, laypersons often make points more simply and clearly than do academics. This observation made by the Reverend Thomas Masters is a case in point: "There's no way in the world you can receive a fair trial in an adult arena where you're looked upon as an adult when you have the mind of a child" (quoted in Zaczor, 2002, p. 7A). The developmental immaturity of adolescents is both obvious and well documented (Scott, 2000), thus several legal and policy changes need to occur. First, in 13 states, the upper age limit of juvenile court jurisdiction is less than 18; it is time for these states (perhaps with the help of the courts) to establish 18 as the minimum age of full adult criminal responsibility (J. J. Wilson, personal communication, July 19, 2002). Second, all excluded offense and concurrent jurisdiction (prosecutorial discretion) statutes should be eliminated. Only judicial waiver, which requires constitutional safeguards, should be statutorily permitted. In addition, all juvenile offenders waived to the criminal justice system should remain in juvenile justice system facilities and programs at least until they are 18 years old.

Other ineffective programs and practices should be abandoned as well (see Chapter 7). The use of detention for punishment purposes is one of these. Sometimes called "a quick dip," this practice accomplishes nothing positive (i.e., it does not motivate youths to receive treatment), and research suggests that excessive use of detention may wipe out the positive effects of treatment programs. Generally, punitive detention includes the broad category of "shock incarceration" and programs such as Scared Straight and boot camps, which do not have the intended deterrence effect and may actually *increase* recidivism. Zero-tolerance policies are also ineffective and often make zero sense; for example, youths who are suspended or expelled from school for minor rule infractions often end up on the streets, where they are exposed to harmful influences and persons. Large, congregate, custodial juvenile corrections facilities are not effective in rehabilitating juvenile offenders. New research shows that curfew laws are not effective in reducing serious or violent juvenile crime. Neither the hospitalization of youths with mental health problems nor bed-driven drug treatment is effective. There currently is no research to support the assumption that drug testing, by itself, is effective in reducing drug use. I have discussed these and other disputed interventions in Chapter 7.

The United States must work to eliminate the disproportionate representation and confinement of minorities in the juvenile justice system, a situation for which there is no empirical justification. There are no substantive differences among racial or ethnic groups in age-specific prevalence rates nationwide for self-reported serious and violent offenses during the early to mid-adolescent period (Elliott, 1994b). When differences do appear, they are linked to neighborhoods, not to ethnicity (Peeples & Loeber, 1994). That is, white youths and

black youths have similar rates in the same underclass neighborhoods. The International Convention on the Elimination of All Forms of Racial Discrimination (CERD), to which the United States is a party, defines race discrimination as conduct that has the "purpose or effect" of restricting rights on the basis of race (Human Rights Watch, 2000b). Under CERD, governments may not engage in "benign neglect"; that is, they may not ignore the need to secure equal treatment of all racial and ethnic groups, but rather must act affirmatively to prevent or end policies that have unjustified discriminatory impacts. Although the United States has made significant progress through OJJDP's Disproportionate Minority Confinement Initiative, much more work needs to be done to achieve the overall goal. I have detailed some of the steps communities can take to eliminate disproportionate minority representation in the juvenile justice system in general, and in confinement in particular, in Chapter 12. By using objective risk and needs assessment instruments and placement instruments, communities can help greatly to reduce minority overrepresentation in the juvenile justice system.

The United States should stop executing minors (individuals under age 18) and sentencing minors to life without the possibility of parole, both of which practices violate international law. The International Covenant on Civil and Political Rights states that the death penalty must not be imposed for crimes committed by people when they were below 18 years of age. The United States ratified the ICCPR in 1992, but reserved the right to impose the death penalty for crimes committed by those under age 18. Article 37(a) of the U.N. Convention on the Rights of the Child states that "neither capital punishment nor life imprisonment without the possibility of release shall be imposed for offenses committed by persons below eighteen years of age." The United States has not ratified this convention. In the past 3 years, only two other countries, the Democratic Republic of Congo and Iran, are known to have executed individuals for offenses they committed when they were under age 18. Both now explicitly repudiate the practice, making the United States the only country that continues to claim the legal authority to execute such offenders (Human Rights Watch, 2002). Currently, 22 U.S. states authorize the death penalty for minors, and 15 of them have such offenders on death row. Statutory laws in only a handful of states expressly prohibit courts from sentencing individuals under age 16 to life without the possibility of parole; the overwhelming majority of states appear to permit such sentences or even make them mandatory upon conviction of certain crimes in criminal court (Logan, 1998). Given that the federal government is not likely to bring the United States into compliance with international law on these two matters in the foreseeable future, state legislatures should act. One mark of a civilized society is the humane and just treatment of the young.

The systems used for counting youths in all forms of confinement in the United States (in mental health, substance abuse, child welfare, juvenile corrections, and adult corrections facilities) need to be improved (Lerman, 2002). The data generated by existing information systems typically are 3 to 5 years behind current usage of the facilities and yield deficient resident and admissions data (Lerman, 1991). Admissions data are not even collected for juvenile justice system detention and long-term correctional facilities. Only a modest investment of fiscal resources would be required to improve these systems so that they yield more timely reports, fuller coverage of facilities, improved demographic enumeration, and unduplicated counts of intersystem trends (Lerman, 1991). It is shameful that we know so little about the numbers, characteristics, presenting problems, and outcomes of many of the children and adolescents in confinement in the United States today.

State legislatures should mandate use of the tools of the Comprehensive Strategy framework by state juvenile justice systems. Several state legislatures already have done so (National Conference of State Legislatures, 1999a). Many communities will never implement the Comprehensive Strategy of their own volition. Legislatures that take a punitive approach to juvenile delinquency have overloaded their systems to the point of crisis, and juvenile justice system managers have difficulty employing good system management practices under these circumstances. In other cases, managers are resigned to punishment-based policies and practices; they believe "That's just the way it is." As a general observation, the entire spectrum of public sector services is overly reliant on institutional care. Service fragmentation is a main factor in the failure of child-serving systems to address the problems of youth. As Roush (1996b) sums it up, "Services fail because they are too crisis-oriented, too rigid in their classification of problems, too specialized, too isolated from other services, too inflexible to craft comprehensive solutions, too insufficiently funded, and they are mismanaged" (p. 29). By applying the principles and the management tools of the Comprehensive Strategy, communities can resolve these problems. Orlando L. Martinez, commissioner of the Georgia Department of Juvenile Justice, recently stated, "The best way to predict a young person's future is to help create it" (quoted in Rubin, 2000-2001, p. 15). As John Wilson (2000) has observed, preventing and reducing delinquency "requires a coordinated effort at critical times in a child's life with a range of services, supports, and opportunities in a continuum of care."

APPENDIX

The North Carolina Assessment of Juvenile Risk of Future Offending and the North Carolina Assessment of Juvenile Needs

SOURCE: Wagner, D., & Connell, S. (2002). *North Carolina Department of Juvenile Justice Risk Assessment Profile* (pp. 3-9). Madison, WI: National Council on Crime and Delinquency.

NORTH CAROLINA ASSESSMENT OF JUVENILE RISK OF FUTURE OFFENDING

Juvenile Name (F, M, L)		DOB:
SS#:	County of Residence:	
Juvenile Race: ☐White ☐ Black ☐ Native American ☐ Latino ☐ Asian ☐ Multi-racial ☐ Other		
Juvenile Gender: ☐ Male ☐ Female		
Date Assessment Completed:	Completed by:	

Instructions: Complete each assessment item R1 to R9 using the best available information. Circle the numeric score associated with each item response and enter it on the line to the right of the item. Total the item scores to determine the level of risk and check the appropriate risk level in R10. Identify the most serious current offense in R11. Assessment items R1-R5 are historical in nature and should be answered based on the juvenile's lifetime. Items R6 and R7 should be evaluated over the 12 months prior to the assessment. R7-R9 should be evaluated as of the time of the assessment. Use the Comments section at the end as needed for additional information or clarification.

R1.   **Age when first delinquent offense alleged in a complaint:** Circle appropriate   **Score**
score and enter the actual age.

a. Age 12 or over or no delinquent complaint	0	
b. Under age 12	2	
Actual age:		

R2.   **Number of undisciplined or delinquent referrals to Intake** (Referrals are instances of complaints coming through the Intake process. A referral may include multiple complaints; for example, breaking or entering and larceny, or multiple larcenies or other offenses that occur at one time.)

a. Current referral only	0
b. 1 Prior referral	1
c. 2-3 Prior referrals	2
d. 4+ Prior referrals	3

R3.   **Most serious prior adjudication(s).** Enter the actual number of prior adjudications for each class of offense shown in b through e then circle the score for <u>only</u> the **most serious** offense for which there has been a prior adjudication. **The maximum possible score for this item is 4.**

a. No Prior Adjudications		0
b. Prior Undisciplined	# of adjudications:	1
c. Prior Class 1-3 misdemeanors	# of adjudications:	2
d. Prior Class F-I felonies or A1misdemeanors	#of adjudications:	3
e. Prior Class A-E felonies	#of adjudications:	4

R4   **Prior Assaults:** "Assault" is defined as any assaultive behavior, whether physical or sexual, with or without a weapon as evidenced by a prior delinquent complaint. Record the number of complaints for each assault category shown. Then circle the score for the assault category with the highest numerical score. **The maximum possible score for this item is 5.**

a. No assaults		0
b. Involvement in an affray	# of complaints:	1
c. Yes, without a weapon	# of complaints:	2
d. Yes, without a weapon, inflicting serious injury	# of complaints	3
e. Yes, with a weapon	# of complaints:	4
f. Yes, with a weapon inflicting serious injury	# of complaints:	5

R5.   **Runaways (from home or placement):** "Runaway" is defined as absconding from home or any placement and not voluntarily returning within twenty-four (24) hours as evidenced by a complaint, motion for review, or from reliable information. Circle appropriate score.

a. No	0	
b. Yes	2	
Actual number of runaway incidents		

R6.   **Known use of alcohol or illegal drugs during past 12 months:** Do not include tobacco in scoring this item. Circle appropriate score.

a. No known substance use	0
b. Some substance use, need for further assessment	1
c. Substance abuse, assessment and/or treatment needed	3

R7.   **School behavior problems during the prior 12 months:** Circle appropriate score.

a.	No problems (Enrolled, attending regularly)	0
b.	Minor problems (attending with problems handled by teacher/school personnel, **or** 1-3 unexcused absences/truancy)	1
c.	Moderate problems (4 to 10 unexcused absences /truancy, **or** 1 or more in-school suspensions **or** 1 short-term suspension – up to 10 days)	2
d.	Serious problems (more than 1 short-term suspension, **or** 1 or more long-term suspension, **or** more than 10 unexcused absences **or** expelled/dropped out.)	3

R8.   **Peer relationships:** Circle appropriate score. Put check in the line following appropriate information.

a.	Peers usually provide good support and influence	0
b.	Youth is rejected by pro-social peers ____, **or** youth sometimes associates with others who have been involved in delinquent/criminal activity but is not primary peer group _____	1
c.	Youth regularly associates with others who are involved in delinquent/criminal activity	3
d.	Youth is a gang member ____ **or** associates with a gang ____	5

R9.   **Parental supervision:** (Score the current responsible parental authority) Circle appropriate score.

a.	Parent, guardian or custodian willing and able to supervise	0
b.	Parent, guardian or custodian willing but unable to supervise	2
c.	Parent, guardian or custodian unwilling to supervise	3

R10.

TOTAL RISK SCORE	

Check Risk Level: ☐ Low risk (0-7)   ☐ Medium Risk (8-14)   ☐ High Risk (15+)

R11. Completed before or after adjudication: (check) before____ after____

Most serious offense alleged /adjudicated in current complaint/petition	
Statute number	

Class offense: ☐ A-E Felony   ☐ F-I Felony, A1 Misdemeanor   ☐ Class 1-3 Misdemeanor   ☐ Undisciplined

Note: Risk level is to be considered along with the current offense.

NORTH CAROLINA ASSESSMENT OF JUVENILE NEEDS

Juvenile Name (F, M, L)		DOB:
SS#:	County of Residence:	
Juvenile Race: ☐White ☐ Black ☐ Native American ☐ Latino ☐ Asian ☐ Multi-racial ☐ Other		
Juvenile Gender: ☐ Male ☐ Female		
Date Assessment Completed:	Completed by:	

Instructions: Complete each needs assessment item using the best available information. Circle the score associated with the most appropriate item choice and enter the number on the line to the left of the item. Items that are of a current nature should be considered as of the time of the assessment unless a time period for consideration is noted. Assessment items that are historical in nature (Y6 and F5) should be answered based on the juvenile or family member's lifetime. Total the points for all items to determine the total need score and then check the appropriate needs level (low, medium or high). Complete the information source checklist. Finally, identify at least three priority needs for constructing a case plan and appropriate service interventions. Give additional information as needed in the Comments section.

YOUTH NEEDS
Score

Y1. Peer Relationships

_____

0   a.   Peers usually provide good support and influence.

2   b.   Youth is rejected by pro-social peers.

3   c.   Youth sometimes associates with others who have been involved in delinquent/criminal activity but this is not a primary peer group.

4   d.   Youth regularly associates with others who are involved in delinquent/criminal activity.

5   e.   Youth is a gang member _____ or associates with a gang _____.
         Name of gang _____

Y2. School Behavior/Adjustment

_____

0   a.   No problems. Youth is attending regularly _____, graduated _____, or has GED _____.

1   b.   Minor problems. Work effort _____, or disciplinary problems _____ that were handled by classroom teacher/school personnel or 1-3 unexcused absences/truancy _____.

3   c.   Moderate problems. Youth has 4 to 10 unexcused absences _____, or received 1 or more in-school suspensions _____, or 1 short-term suspension (i.e. less than 10 days)_____.

4   d.   Serious problems. Youth has dropped out of school _____, or been expelled _____, or received more than one short-term suspension _____, or one long-term suspension (10 days or more) _____, or has more than10 unexcused absences _____.

Y3. General Academic Functioning

_____

0   a.   Generally functioning above or at grade level _____ , or is placed in appropriate Exceptional Children's program _____.

3   b.   Generally functioning below grade level. Needs an educational evaluation _____, or has identified Exceptional Children's needs that are unserved _____.

         Check Assessed Exceptional Children's needs: Autism _____, Behaviorally Emotionally Disabled _____, Deaf/Blind _____, Gifted/Talented _____, Hearing Impaired _____, Mentally Disabled _____, Multi-handicapped _____, Orthopedically Impaired _____, Other Health Impaired _____, Pregnant Student _____, Specific Learning Disabled _____, Speech/Language Impaired _____, Traumatic Brain Injury _____, Visually Impaired _____

Y4. Substance Abuse Within Past 12 months (Do not consider tobacco in this item.)

_____

0   a.   No known substance use.

1   b.   Some substance use, need for further assessment.

3   c.   Substance abuse, assessment and/or treatment needed.
         Check all that apply: Denial _____   Refusal of treatment _____
         Unmet need for treatment _____   Prior treatment failures _____   Currently in treatment _____
         Describe substance abuse noted above by type: (check all that apply, leave blank if none)
         Cocaine_____   Amphetamines _____   Opiates _____   Inhalants _____
         Alcohol _____   Cannabinoids _____   Other _____

Y5. Juvenile Parent Status

0   a.   Juvenile is not a parent.

1   b.   Juvenile is a parent, but does *not* have custody of child.

2   c.   Juvenile is a parent _____ or an expectant parent _____ but has adequate childcare support.

4   d.   Juvenile is a parent _____ or an expectant parent _____ but inadequate childcare support. Number of children _____

Y6. History of Victimization by Caregiver or Others

0   a.   No history or evidence of physical, sexual, or emotional abuse or neglect or other criminal victimization.

2   b.   Victimization with appropriate support. History or evidence of physical, sexual, or emotional abuse or neglect or other criminal victimization with appropriate response to protect against subsequent victimization.

3   c.   Victimization without support. One or more incidents of victimization; failure to protect against subsequent victimization.

Check all that apply to the youth: physical abuse _____, sexual abuse _____, emotional abuse _____, neglect _____, criminal victimization _____, other _____

Y7. Sexual Behavior During Past 12 Months

0   a.   No apparent problem.

2   b.   Behavior that needs further assessment such as use of pornography _____, obscene phone calls _____, voyeurism _____, uses sexually explicit language or gestures_____ or other _____.

3   c.   Engages in sexual practices that are potentially dangerous to self or others _____.

4   d.   Youth's sexual adjustment/behavior results in victimization of others _____. May use sexual expression/behavior to attain power and control over others _____.

Y8. Mental Health

0   a.   No need for mental health care indicated.

1   b.   Has mental health needs that are being addressed.

3   c.   Behavior indicates a need for additional mental health assessment _____or treatment _____.

Check all behaviors that apply:

Withdrawn _____	Self mutilation _____	Sad _____	Runs away _____
Confused _____	Hallucinations _____	Anxious _____	Fights _____
Sleep problems _____	Eating problems _____	Angry _____	Restless _____
Risk-taking/impulsive _____	Other _____		

Diagnosis (from MH professional) _____

Y9. Basic Physical Needs/Independent Living

0   a.   Youth is living with parents, guardian or custodian. Basic needs for food, shelter and protection are met.

1   b.   Youth is in temporary residential care or shelter _____or living independently with basic needs for food, shelter and protection being met _____.

2   c.   Youth is living with parents, guardian or custodian. Basic needs are not being met. Food needs not met_____, shelter needs not met _____, protection needs not met _____.

3   d.   Youth is living independently. Basic needs are not being met.   Food needs not met_____, shelter needs not met _____, protection needs not met _____.

Y10. Health & Hygiene (exclude Mental Health Conditions)

0   a.   No apparent problem.

1   b.   Youth has medical, _____dental _____, health/ hygiene education _____needs which do not impair functioning. **Youth uses tobacco products _____.**

2   c.   Youth has physical handicap _____or chronic illness _____that limits functioning and the condition is being treated.

3   d.   Youth has physical handicap _____or chronic illness _____ that limits functioning and the condition is not being treated. Youth does not comply with prescribed medication _____ or has an unmet need for prescribed medication _____.

Juvenile Name (F, M, L) _____   **DOB:** _____

FAMILY NEEDS: Answer the following questions about the juvenile's primary family. The primary family is the juvenile's natural family or the family unit that the juvenile is living with on a permanent basis. If the juvenile is placed away from home, the questions should be answered about the "family" to which the juvenile will be returning. Make any needed clarifying comments in the comment section.

_____ **F1. Conflict in the Home Within Past 12 Months**

0   a.   The home environment is relatively supportive; there are no problems that require outside intervention.

2   b.   Marital or domestic discord resulting in emotional or physical conflict (without serious injury) with spouse, partner, and/or child(ren) _____. Family members avoid contact with each other _____.

4   c.   Domestic violence resulting in injury or the involvement of law enforcement and/or domestic violence programs ____. Restraining orders/criminal complaints ____ substantiated abuse ____.

Check if there is a history of domestic discord _____ or domestic violence _____.

_____ **F2. Supervision Skills**

0   a.   Adequate skills. Parent makes rules for youth and generally enforces them; parent attempts to keep track of the child's activities and uses discipline when needed; youth respects parent for the most part.

2   b.   Marginal skills. Parent may make rules, but has difficulty enforcing them ____ or youth often engages in inappropriate activities without parent's knowledge ____ or parent does not react with necessary sanctions when rules are broken ____ or parents say they are having difficulty controlling the juvenile ____.

4   c.   Inadequate. Parent supports juvenile's delinquency/independence or excuses it ____ or parent refuses responsibility for youth ____ or abandons youth ____.

_____ **F3. Disabilities of Parent, Guardian or Custodian**

0   a.   Parent, guardian or custodian has no known disabilities that interfere with parenting.

2   b.   Parent, guardian or custodian's ability to provide for youth is impaired by serious mental health disorder _____ or a serious health problem _____ or other disability _____.

_____ **F4. Substance Abuse Within the Past 3 Years By Household Members** (Do not include juvenile.)

0   a.   No evidence of alcohol or drug abuse.

3   b.   One or more household members abuse alcohol or drugs.

Indicate all that apply: Parent is abuser _____   Sibling is abuser _____
Other household member is abuser ____   Unmet need for treatment _____   Denial _____
Refusal of treatment _____   Prior treatment failures _____   Job loss _____
DWI _____   Other conflict with the law _____   Abusive/destructive behavior_____
Describe substance use/abuse noted above by type (check all that apply, leave blank if none)
       Cocaine_____   Amphetamines _____   Opiates _____
       Alcohol _____   Cannabinoids _____   Other _____

_____ **F5. Family Criminality**

0   a.   No family member (including siblings) has been convicted/adjudicated for criminal acts.

1   b.   Parents, guardian or custodian and/or siblings have record of convictions/adjudications.
Parent, guardian or custodian conviction _____   Sibling conviction/adjudication _____

3   c.   Parent, guardian or custodian and/or siblings are currently incarcerated, or are on probation or parole (give relationship and status) _____
_____ or are known gang members ____.

_____ **Total Needs Score**

_____ **Check Needs Level:**   □ Low (0-12)   □ Medium (13-22)   □ High (23+)

Sources of information: Check all that apply

Juvenile _____	Mother _____	Father _____	Other Caregiver _____
Sibling _____	Other relative _____	School _____	Victim _____
Neighbor _____	Law Enforcement _____	DSS _____	Mental Health _____
Others _____	_____	_____	_____

REFERENCES

Acoca, L. (1998a). Defusing the time bomb: Understanding and meeting the health care needs of incarcerated women in America. *Crime & Delinquency, 44,* 49-69.

Acoca, L. (1998b). Outside/inside: The violation of American girls at home, on the streets, and in the juvenile justice system. *Crime & Delinquency, 44,* 561-589.

Acoca, L. (1999). Investing in girls: A 21st-century strategy. *Juvenile Justice, 6*(1), 3-13.

Acoca, L., & Dedel, K. (1998). *No place to hide: Understanding and meeting the needs of girls in the California juvenile justice system.* San Francisco: National Council on Crime and Delinquency.

Adams, K. (1997, November). *Juvenile curfew as crime prevention.* Paper presented at the annual meeting of the American Society of Criminology, San Diego.

Adams, R. E., Rohe, W. M., & Arcury, T. A. (2002). Implementing community-oriented policing: Organizational change and street officer attitudes. *Crime & Delinquency, 48,* 399-430.

Adult treatment of juvenile offenders may aggravate recidivism. (1996, May 15). *Law Enforcement News,* p. 8.

Agnew, R. (1999). A general strain theory of community differences in crime rates. *Journal of Research in Crime and Delinquency, 36,* 123-155.

Ainsworth, J. E. (1991). Re-imagining childhood and re-constructing the legal order: The case for abolishing the juvenile court. *North Carolina Law Review, 69,* 1083-1133.

Ainsworth, J. E. (1995). Youth justice in a unified court: Response to critics of juvenile court abolition. *Boston College Law Review, 36,* 927-951.

Akers, R. L., Krohn, M. D., Lanza-Kaduce, L., & Radosevich, M. (1979). Social learning and deviant behavior: A specific test of a general theory. *American Sociological Review, 44,* 636-655.

Albert, R. L. (1998). *Juvenile Accountability Incentive Block Grants program* (Fact Sheet No. 1998-76). Washington, DC: Office of Juvenile Justice and Delinquency Prevention.

Alexander, B. (2000-2001, December-January). Once lame juvenile justice system jockeys to the lead. *Youth Today,* pp. 1, 16-17.

Altschuler, D. M. (1998). Intermediate sanctions and community treatment for serious and violent juvenile offenders. In R. Loeber & D. P. Farrington (Eds.), *Serious and violent juvenile offenders: Risk factors and successful interventions* (pp. 367-385). Thousand Oaks, CA: Sage.

Altschuler, D. M., & Armstrong, T. L. (1984). Intervening with serious juvenile offenders: A summary of a study on community-based programs. In R. A. Mathias, P. DeMuro, & R. S. Allinson (Eds.), *Violent juvenile offenders: An anthology* (pp. 187-206). San Francisco: National Council on Crime and Delinquency.

Altschuler, D. M., & Armstrong, T. L. (1994a). *Intensive aftercare for high-risk juveniles: An assessment.* Washington, DC: Office of Juvenile Justice and Delinquency Prevention.

Altschuler, D. M., & Armstrong, T. L. (1994b). *Intensive aftercare for high-risk juveniles: A community care model.* Washington, DC: Office of Juvenile Justice and Delinquency Prevention.

Altschuler, D. M., & Armstrong, T. L. (2002). Juvenile corrections and continuity of care in a community context: The evidence and promising directions. *Federal Probation, 66*(2), 72-77.

Altschuler, D. M., Armstrong, T. L., & MacKenzie, D. L. (1999). *Reintegration, supervised release, and intensive aftercare* (Juvenile Justice Bulletin). Washington, DC: Office of Juvenile Justice and Delinquency Prevention.

Ambert, A. (1999). The effect of male delinquency on mothers and fathers: A heuristic study. *Sociological Inquiry, 69,* 621-640.

American Bar Association & National Bar Association. (2001). *Justice by gender: The lack of appropriate prevention, diversion and treatment alternatives for girls in the juvenile justice system.* Washington, DC: Authors.

American Friends Service Committee. (1971). *Struggle for justice: A report on crime and punishment in America.* New York: Hill & Wang.

American Psychiatric Association. (2000). *Diagnostic and statistical manual of mental disorders* (4th ed., rev.). Washington, DC: Author.

American Society of Criminology, National Policy Committee. (2001). The use of incarceration in the United States. *Criminologist, 26*(3), 14-16.

Amnesty International. (1996). *Police brutality and excessive force in the New York City Police Department.* New York: Author.

Amnesty International. (1998a). *Betraying the young: Human rights violations against children in the US justice system.* New York: Author.

Amnesty International. (1998b). *On the wrong side of history: Children and the death penalty in the USA.* New York: Author.

Amnesty International. (1999). *Race, rights, and brutality: Portraits of abuse in the USA.* New York: Author.

Amnesty International. (2002). *Amnesty International report 2002.* New York: Author.

Andershed, H., Kerr, M., & Stattin, H. (2001). Bullying in school and violence on the streets: Are the same people involved? *Journal of Scandinavian Studies in Criminology and Crime Prevention, 2,* 31-49.

Andrews, D. A. (1995). The psychology of criminal conduct and effective treatment. In J. McGuire (Ed.), *What works: Reducing reoffending* (pp. 35-62). New York: John Wiley.

Andrews, D. A. (1996). Criminal recidivism is predictable and can be influenced: An update. *Forum on Corrections Research, 8,* 42-44.

Andrews, D. A., & Bonta, J. (1998). *The psychology of criminal conduct* (2nd ed.). Cincinnati, OH: Anderson.

Andrews, D. A., Dowden, C., & Gendreau, P. (1999). *Clinically relevant and psychologically informed approaches to reduced reoffending: A meta-analytic study of human service, risk, need, responsivity, and other concerns in justice contexts.* Unpublished manuscript, Carleton University, Ottawa, ON.

Andrews, D. A., & Hoge, R. D. (1995). The psychology of criminal conduct and principles of effective prevention and rehabilitation. *Forum on Corrections Research, 7*(1), 34-36.

Andrews, D. A., Kiessling, J. J., Robinson, D., & Mickus, S. (1986). The risk principle of case classification: An outcome evaluation with young adult probationers. *Canadian Journal of Criminology, 28,* 377-384.

Andrews, D. A., Zinger, I., Hoge, R. D., Bonta, J., Gendreau, P., & Cullen, F. T. (1990). Does correctional treatment work? A clinically-relevant and psychologically informed meta-analysis. *Criminology, 28,* 369-404.

Antonowicz, D. H., & Ross, R. R. (1994). Essential components of successful rehabilitation programs for offenders. *International Journal of Offender Therapy and Comparative Criminology, 38,* 97-104.

Aos, S., Phipps, P., Barnoski, R., & Lieb, R. (2001). *The comparative costs and benefits of programs to reduce crime* (Version 4.0). Olympia: Washington State Institute for Public Policy. Retrieved from http://www.wsipp.wa.gov/crime/costben.html

Arbreton, A. J. A., & McClanahan, W. (2002). *Targeted outreach: Boys and Girls Clubs of America's approach to gang prevention and intervention.* Philadelphia: Public/Private Ventures.

Arciaga, M. (2001). *Evolution of prominent youth subcultures in America.* Tallahassee, FL: Institute for Intergovernmental Research, National Youth Gang Center.

Aries, P. (1962). *Centuries of childhood.* New York: Alfred A. Knopf.

Arredondo, D. E., Kumli, K., Soto, L., Colin, E., Ornellas, J., Vavilla, R. J., et al. (2001). Juvenile mental health court: Rationale and protocols. *Juvenile and Family Court Journal, 52*(4), 1-19.

Arthur, L. G. (1998). Abolish the juvenile court? *Juvenile and Family Court Journal, 49*(1), 51-58.

Arthur, M. W., Ayers, C. D., Graham, K. A., & Hawkins, J. D. (in press). Mobilizing communities to reduce risks for substance abuse: A comparison of two strategies. In W. J. Buoski & Z. Sloboda (Eds.), *Handbook of drug abuse theory, science, and practice.* New York: Plenum.

Arthur, M. W., Glaser, R. R., & Hawkins, J. D. (2001). *Community implementation of science-based prevention programming.* Seattle: University of Washington, Social Development Research Group.

Associated Press. (1996b, February 18). Expert warns of US "bloodbath" (AP wire story).

Augimeri, L. K., Koegl, C. J., & Goldberg, K. (2001). Children under age 12 years who commit offenses: Canadian legal and treatment approaches. In R. Loeber & D. P. Farrington (Eds.), *Child delinquents: Development, intervention, and service needs* (pp. 405-414). Thousand Oaks, CA: Sage.

Augimeri, L. K., Webster, C. D., Koegl, C. J., & Levene, K. S. (1998). *Early Assessment Risk List for Boys: EARL-20B, Version 1* (Consultation ed.). Toronto: Earlscourt Child and Family Centre.

Austin, J. (1995). The overrepresentation of minority youths in the California juvenile justice system. In K. Kempf-Leonard, C. E. Pope, & W. H. Feyerherm (Eds.), *Minorities in juvenile justice* (pp. 153-178). Thousand Oaks, CA: Sage.

Austin, J., Clark, J., Hardyman, P., & Henry, D. A. (1999). The impact of "three strikes and you're out." *Punishment and Society, 1*(2), 131-162.

Austin, J., Elms, W., Krisberg, B., & Steele, P. (1991). *Unlocking juvenile corrections: Evaluating the Massachusetts Department of Youth Services.* San Francisco: National Council on Crime and Delinquency.

Austin, J., Krisberg, B., DeComo, R., Del Rosario, D., Rudenstine, S., & Elms, W. (1994). *Juveniles taken into custody research program: FY 1993 annual report.* Oakland, CA: National Council on Crime and Delinquency.

Austin, J., Marino, A. B., Carroll, L., McCall, P. L., & Richards, S. C. (2000, November). *The use of incarceration in the United States: National policy white paper for the American Society of Criminology, National Policy Committee.* Paper presented at the annual meeting of the American Society of Criminology, San Francisco.

Baer, J. S., MacLean, M. G., & Marlatt, G. A. (1998). Linking etiology and treatment for adolescent substance abuse: Toward a better match. In R. Jessor (Ed.), *New perspectives on adolescent risk behavior* (pp. 182-220). New York: Cambridge University Press.

Bailey, K. A., & Ballard, J. D. (2001). Community programs for juveniles and the use of electronic monitoring. *Journal of Offender Monitoring, 14*(3-4), 19, 29.

Baird, C. (1981). Probation and parole classifications: The Wisconsin model. *Corrections Today, 43*(3), 36-41.

Baird, C. (1984). *Classification of juveniles in corrections: A model systems approach.* Washington, DC: Arthur D. Little.

Baird, C. (1991). *Validating risk assessment instruments used in community corrections.* Madison, WI: National Council on Crime and Delinquency.

Baird, C., Heinz, R. C., & Bemus, B. J. (1979). *The Wisconsin Case Classification/Staff Deployment Project: A two-year follow-up report.* Madison: Wisconsin Health and Social Services Department.

Baird, C., Wagner, D., & Neuenfeldt, D. (1992). *Using risk assessment to structure decisions about services—Protecting children: The Michigan model.* Oakland, CA: National Council on Crime and Delinquency.

Bakal, Y. (Ed.). (1973). *Closing correctional institutions.* Lexington, MA: D. C. Health.

Bakal, Y. (1998). Reflections: A quarter-century of reform in Massachusetts youth corrections. *Crime & Delinquency, 44,* 110-116.

Baker, H. (1910). Procedures of the Boston Juvenile Court. *Survey, 23,* 643-652.

Ball, R. A., & Curry, G. D. (1995). The logic of definition in criminology: Purposes and methods for defining "gangs." *Criminology, 33,* 225-245.

Bandes, S. (2000, November 19). To reform the LAPD, more civilian pressure is necessary. *Los Angeles Times,* p. M6.

Bandura, A. (1973). *Aggression: A social learning analysis.* Englewood Cliffs, NJ: Prentice Hall.

Bandura, A. (1977). Self-efficacy: Toward a unifying theory of behavioral change. *Psychological Review, 84,* 191-215.

Bandura, A. (1986). *Social foundations of thought and action: A social cognitive theory.* Englewood Cliffs, NJ: Prentice Hall.

Bandura, A. (1999). Social learning and aggression. In F. T. Cullen & R. Agnew (Eds.), *Criminological theory: Past to present* (pp. 21-32). Los Angeles: Roxbury.

Barnoski, R. (1997). *A study of recidivism of serious and persistent offenders among adolescents: Washington State juvenile court recidivism estimates—fiscal year 1994 youth.* Olympia: Washington State Institute for Public Policy.

Barnoski, R. (1998). *Juvenile Rehabilitation Administration assessments: Validity review and recommendations.* Olympia: Washington State Institute for Public Policy.

Barnoski, R. (1999). *Juvenile Rehabilitation Administration intensive parole: Program evaluation design.* Olympia: Washington State Institute for Public Policy.

Barnoski, R., Aos, S., & Lieb, R. (1997). *The class of 1988, seven years later.* Olympia: Washington State Institute for Public Policy.

Baron, S. W. (1997). Risky lifestyles and the link between offending and victimization. *Studies on Crime and Crime Prevention, 6,* 53-72.

Bartollas, C. (2002). *Juvenile delinquency* (6th ed.). Boston: Allyn & Bacon.

Bartollas, C., & Miller, S. J. (1978). *The juvenile offender: Control, correction, and treatment.* Boston: Holbrook.

Bartollas, C., Miller, S. J., & Dinitz, S. (1976). *Juvenile victimization: The institutional paradox.* New York: John Wiley.

Barton, C., Alexander, J. F., Waldron, H., Turner, C. W., & Warburton, J. (1985). Generalizing treatment effects of Functional Family Therapy: Three replications. *American Journal of Family Therapy, 13,* 16-26.

Barton, W. H., & Butts, J. A. (1990). Viable options: Intensive supervision programs for juvenile delinquents. *Crime & Delinquency, 36,* 238-256.

Bartusch, D. R. J., Lynam, D. R., Moffitt, T. E., & Silva, P. A. (1997). Is age important? Testing a general versus a developmental theory of antisocial behavior. *Criminology, 35,* 13-48.

Bassin, A., Bmatter, T. E., & Rachin, R. L. (Eds.). (1976). *The reality therapy reader: A survey of the work of William Glasser, M.D.* New York: Harper & Row.

Battin, S. R., Hill, K. G., Abbott, R. D., Catalano, R. F., & Hawkins, J. D. (1998). The contribution of gang membership to delinquency beyond delinquent friends. *Criminology, 36,* 93-115.

Battin-Pearson, S. R., Guo, J., Hill, K. G., Abbott, R. D., & Hawkins, J. D. (1999). *Early predictors of sustained adolescent gang membership.* Seattle: University of Washington, Social Development Research Group.

Battin-Pearson S. R., Thornberry, T. P., Hawkins, J. D., & Krohn, M. D. (1998). *Gang membership, delinquent peers, and delinquent behavior* (Juvenile Justice Bulletin, Youth Gang Series). Washington, DC: Office of Juvenile Justice and Delinquency Prevention.

Battistich, V., Schaps, E., Watson, M., & Solomon, D. (1996). Prevention effects of the Child Development Project: Early findings from an ongoing multisite demonstration trial. *Journal of Adolescent Research, 11,* 12-35.

Battistich, V., Solomon, D., Watson, M., & Schaps, E. (1997). Caring school communities. *Educational Psychologist, 32,* 137-151.

Baumeister, R. F., Smart, L., & Boden, J. W. (1996). Relation of threatened egotism to violence and aggression: The dark side of high self-esteem. *Psychological Review, 103,* 5-33.

Baumer, T. L., Maxfield, M. G., & Mendelsohn, R. I. (1993). A comparative analysis of three electronically monitored home detention programs. *Justice Quarterly, 10,* 121-142.

Bazemore, G., & Umbreit, M. S. (1994). *Balanced and restorative justice.* Washington, DC: Office of Juvenile Justice and Delinquency Prevention.

Bazemore, G., & Umbreit, M. S. (1995). Rethinking the sanctioning function in juvenile court: Retributive or restorative responses to juvenile crime. *Crime & Delinquency, 41,* 296-313.

Beck, A. J. (2000, April 13). *State and federal prisoners returning to the community: Findings from the Bureau of Justice Statistics.* Paper presented at the First Reentry Courts Initiative Cluster Meeting, Washington, DC.

Beck, A. J., Karberg, J. C., & Harrison, P. M. (2002). *Prison and jail inmates at midyear 2001* (Bulletin). Washington, DC: Bureau of Justice Statistics.

Beck, A. J., & Shipley, B. E. (1989). *Recidivism of prisoners released in 1983* (Bulletin). Washington, DC: Bureau of Justice Statistics.

Becker, H. (1963). *Outsiders: Studies in the sociology of deviance.* New York: Free Press.

Beckett, K., & Sasson, T. (2000). *The politics of injustice: Crime and punishment in America.* Thousand Oaks, CA: Pine Forge.

Behar, L. (1985). Changing patterns of state responsibility: A case study in North Carolina. *Journal of Clinical Child Psychology, 14,* 188-195.

Behar, L. (1986, May-June). A state model for child mental health services: The North Carolina experience. *Children Today,* pp. 16-21.

Belden, E. (1920). *Courts in the United States hearing children's cases.* Washington, DC: U.S. Children's Bureau.

Belenko, S. (2001). *Research on drug courts: A critical review, 2001 update.* New York: Columbia University, National Center on Addiction and Substance Abuse.

Belluck, P. (1998, February 11). Fighting youth crime, some states blend adult and juvenile justice. *New York Times,* pp. A1, A26.

Benda, B. B. (2002). Religion and violent offenders in boot camp: A structural equation model. *Journal of Research in Crime and Delinquency, 39,* 91-121.

Bennett, W. J., DiIulio, J. J., Jr., & Walters, J. P. (1996). *Body count: Moral poverty . . . and how to win America's war against crime and drugs.* New York: Simon & Schuster.

Bernard, T. (1992). *The cycle of juvenile justice.* New York: Oxford University Press.

Bernard, T. J., & Ritti, R. R. (1991). The Philadelphia Birth Cohort and selective incapacitation. *Journal of Research in Crime and Delinquency, 28,* 33-54.

Berrueta-Clement, J. R., Schweinhart, L. J., Barnett, W. S., Epstein, A. S., & Weikart, D. P. (1984). *Changed lives: The effects of the Perry Preschool Program on youths through age 19.* Ypsilanti, MI: High/Scope.

Best, J., & Hutchinson, M. M. (1996). The gang initiation rite as a motif in contemporary crime discourse. *Justice Quarterly, 13,* 383-404.

Beyer, M., Grisso, T., & Young, M. (1997). *More than meets the eye: Rethinking assessment, competency and sentencing for a harsher era of juvenile justice.* Washington, DC: American Bar Association, Juvenile Justice Center.

Beyers, J. M., Loeber, R., Wikstrom, P. H., & Stouthamer-Loeber, M. (2001). What predicts adolescent violence in better-off neighborhoods? *Journal of Abnormal Child Psychology, 29,* 369-381.

Bickman, L. (1996). A continuum of care: More is not always better. *American Psychologist, 51,* 689-701.

Bickman, L., Guthrie, P. R., & Foster, E. M. (1995). *A continuum of care: More is not always better—The Fort Bragg experiment.* New York: Plenum.

Bickman, L., Salzer, M. S., Lambert, E. W., Saunders, R., Summerfelt, W. T., Heflinger, et al. (1998). Rejoinder to Mordock's critique of the Fort Bragg evaluation project: The sample is generalizable and the outcomes are clear. *Child Psychiatry and Human Development, 29,* 77-91.

Bishop, D. M., & Frazier, C. E. (1991). Transfer of juveniles to criminal court: A case study and analysis of prosecutorial waiver. *Notre Dame Journal of Law, Ethics and Public Policy, 5,* 281-302.

Bishop, D. M., & Frazier, C. E. (1996). Race effects in juvenile justice decision-making: Findings of a statewide analysis. *Journal of Criminal Law and Criminology, 86,* 392-413.

Bishop, D. M., & Frazier, C. E. (2000). Consequences of transfer. In J. Fagan & F. E. Zimring (Eds.), *The changing borders of juvenile justice: Transfer of adolescents to the criminal court* (pp. 227-276). Chicago: University of Chicago Press.

Bishop, D. M., Frazier, C. E., Lanza-Kaduce, L., & White, H. G. (1999). *A study of juvenile transfers to criminal court in Florida* (Fact Sheet No. 1999-113). Washington, DC: Office of Juvenile Justice and Delinquency Prevention.

Bishop, D. M., Frazier, C. E., Lanza-Kaduce, L., & Winner, L. (1996). The transfer of juveniles to criminal court: Does it make a difference? *Crime & Delinquency, 42,* 171-191.

Biskupic, J. (1996, June 25). Civil forfeiture in drug case upheld, 8 to 1. *USA Today,* pp. 1A-3A.

Bittner, E. (1970). *The functions of the police in modern society.* Washington, DC: Government Printing Office.

Bjerregaard, B., & Lizotte, A. J. (1995). Gun ownership and gang membership. *Journal of Criminal Law and Criminology, 86,* 37-58.

Bjerregaard, B., & Smith, C. (1993). Gender differences in gang participation, delinquency, and substance use. *Journal of Quantitative Criminology, 9,* 329-355.

Blackwood, A. (2001, July 8). Boy's death puts spotlight on boot camps. *News and Observer* (Raleigh, NC), p. 15A.

Bleich, J. L. (1987). Toward an effective policy for handling dangerous juvenile offenders. In F. X. Hartmann (Ed.), *From children to citizens: Vol. 2. The role of the juvenile court* (pp. 143-175). New York: Springer-Verlag.

Block, C. R. (1993). Lethal violence in the Chicago Latino community. In A. V. Wilson (Ed.), *Homicide: The victim/offender connection* (pp. 267-342). Cincinnati, OH: Anderson.

Block, C. R., & Christakos, A. (1995). *Major trends in Chicago homicide: 1965-1994.* Chicago: Illinois Criminal Justice Information Authority.

Block, C. R., Christakos, A., Jacob, A., & Przybylski, R. (1996). *Street gangs and crime: Patterns and trends in Chicago.* Chicago: Illinois Criminal Justice Information Authority.

Block, R., & Block, C. R. (1993). *Street gang crime in Chicago* (Research in Brief). Washington, DC: National Institute of Justice.

Blum, A. (2001, July 13). Vance punishes 8 after probe of student tours of D.C. jail. *Washington Post,* p. B4.

Blumstein, A. (1995a, August). Violence by young people: Why the deadly nexus? *National Institute of Justice Journal, 229,* 1-9.

Blumstein, A. (1995b). Youth violence, guns, and the illicit-drug industry. *Journal of Criminal Law and Criminology, 86,* 10-36.

Blumstein, A. (1996). *Youth violence, guns, and the illicit drug markets* (Research Preview). Washington, DC: National Institute of Justice.

Blumstein, A., Cohen, J., & Nagin, D. (Eds.). (1978). *Deterrence and incapacitation: Estimating the effects of criminal sanctions on crime rates.* Washington, DC: National Academy of Sciences.

Blumstein, A., & Rosenfeld, R. (1999). Trends in rates of violence in the U.S.A. *Studies on Crime and Crime Prevention, 8,* 139-167.

Blumstein, A., & Wallman, J. (2000). *The crime drop in America.* Cambridge: Cambridge University Press.

Bonnie, R. J., & Grisso, T. (2000). Adjudicative competence and youthful offenders. In T. Grisso & R. G. Schwartz (Eds.), *Youth on trial: A developmental perspective on juvenile justice* (pp. 70-103). Chicago: University of Chicago Press.

Bonta, J. (1996). Risk-needs assessment and treatment. In A. T. Harland (Ed.), *Choosing correctional options that work* (pp. 18-32). Thousand Oaks, CA: Sage.

Bonta, J., & Gendreau, P. (1990). Re-examining the cruel and unusual punishment of prison life. *Law and Human Behavior, 14,* 347-372.

Borduin, C. M., Henggeler, S. W., Blaske, D. M., & Stein, R. (1990). Multisystemic treatment of adolescent sexual offenders. *International Journal of Offender Therapy and Comparative Criminology, 35,* 105-113.

Borduin, C. M., Mann, B. J., Cone, L. T., Henggeler, S. W., Fucci, B. R., Blaske, D. M., et al. (1995). Multisystemic treatment of serious juvenile offenders: Long-term prevention of criminality and violence. *Journal of Consulting and Clinical Psychology, 63,* 569-578.

Bortner, M. A., Zatz, M. S., & Hawkins, D. F. (2000). Race and transfer: Empirical research and social context. In J. Fagan & F. E. Zimring (Eds.), *The changing borders of juvenile justice: Transfer of adolescents to the criminal court* (pp. 277-320). Chicago: University of Chicago Press.

Bovard, J. (1999, May 27). Your car may be committing crimes. *USA Today,* p. 15A.

Boyle, P. (1999, September). Fatal hugs: Restraining enraged kids put youth workers in legal, moral morass. *Youth Today,* pp. 1, 42-47.

Boyle, P. (2001, April). A DAREing rescue. *Youth Today,* pp. 1, 16-19.

Braga, A. A., Kennedy, D. M., Waring, E. J., & Piehl, A. M. (2001). Problem-oriented policing, deterrence, and youth violence: An evaluation of Boston's Operation Ceasefire. *Journal of Research in Crime and Delinquency, 38,* 195-225.

Braga, A. A., Piehl, A. M., & Kennedy, D. M. (1999). Youth homicide in Boston: An assessment of supplementary homicide report data. *Homicide Studies, 3,* 277-299.

Braithwaite, J. (2001). *Restorative justice and responsive regulation.* New York: Oxford University Press.

Brantingham, P. J., & Faust, F. L. (1976). A conceptual model of crime prevention. *Crime & Delinquency, 22,* 284-296.

Bratton, W. (with Knobler, P.). (1998). *Turnaround: How America's top cop reversed the crime epidemic.* New York: Random House.

Brendtro, L. K., & Long, N. J. (1994). Violence begets violence: Breaking conflict cycles. *Reclaiming Children and Youth, 3,* 2-7.

Brendtro, L. K., & Ness, A. E. (1995). Fixing flaws or building strengths? *Reclaiming Children and Youth, 4,* 2-7.

Brennan, P., Mednick, S., & Kandel, E. (1991). Congenital determinants of violent and property offending. In D. J. Pepler & K. H. Rubin (Eds.), *The development and treatment of childhood aggression* (pp. 81-92). Hillsdale, NJ: Lawrence Erlbaum.

Brent, D. A., & Birmaher, B. (2002). Adolescent depression. *New England Journal of Medicine, 347,* 667-671.

Brewer, D. D., Hawkins, J. D., Catalano, R. F., & Neckerman, H. J. (1995). Preventing serious, violent, and chronic offending: A review of evaluations of selected strategies in childhood, adolescence, and the community. In J. C. Howell, B. Krisberg, J. D. Hawkins, & J. J. Wilson (Eds.), *A sourcebook: Serious, violent, and chronic juvenile offenders* (pp. 61-141). Thousand Oaks, CA: Sage.

Bridges, G. S. (1997). *A study on racial and ethnic disparities in superior court bail and pre-trial detention practices in Washington.* Olympia: Washington State Minority and Justice Commission.

Bridges, G. S., Crutchfield, R. D., & Simpson, E. E. (1987). Crime, social structure and criminal punishment: White and nonwhite rates of imprisonment. *Social Problems, 34,* 345-361.

Briscoe, J. (1997). Breaking the cycle of violence: A rational approach to at-risk youth. *Federal Probation, 61*(3), 3-13.

Bronfenbrenner, U. (1979). *The ecology of human development: Experiments by nature and design.* Cambridge, MA: Harvard University Press.

Brooks, K., Schiraldi, V., & Ziedenberg, J. (2001). *School house hype: Two years later.* Washington, DC: Justice Policy Institute, Center on Juvenile and Criminal Justice.

Brooks, T. R., & Petit, M. (1997). *Early intervention: Crafting a community response to child abuse and violence.* Washington, DC: Child Welfare League of America.

Brooks-Gunn, J., Graber, J. A., & Paikoff, R. L. (1994). Studying links between hormones and negative affect: Models and measures. *Journal of Research on Adolescence, 4,* 469-486.

Brown, J. M., & Langan, P. A. (1998). *State court sentencing of convicted felons* (Bulletin). Washington, DC: Bureau of Justice Statistics.

Brown, W. K., Miller, T. P., & Jenkins, R. L. (1991). The human costs of "giving the kid another chance." *International Journal of Offender Therapy and Comparative Criminology, 35,* 296-302.

Browning, K., & Huizinga, D. (1999). *Highlights of findings from the Denver Youth Survey* (Fact Sheet No. 1999-106). Washington, DC: Office of Juvenile Justice and Delinquency Prevention.

Brunk, M., Henggeler, S. W., & Whelan, J. P. (1987). A comparison of multisystematic therapy and parent training in the brief treatment of child abuse and neglect. *Journal of Consulting and Clinical Psychology, 55,* 311-318.

Bryant, D. (1989). *Communitywide responses crucial for dealing with youth gangs* (Program Bulletin). Washington, DC: Office of Juvenile Justice and Delinquency Prevention.

Buchanan, C. M., Eccles, J. S., & Becker, J. B. (1992). Are adolescents the victims of raging hormones? Evidence for activational effects of hormones on moods and behavior at adolescence. *Psychological Bulletin, 111,* 62-107.

Building Blocks for Youth. (2000). *Youth crime/adult time: Is justice served?* Washington, DC: Author.

Bullis, M., & Walker, H. M. (1996). Characteristics and causal factors of troubled youth. In C. M. Nelson, R. B. Rutherford, & B. I. Wolford (Eds.), *Comprehensive and collaborative systems that work for troubled youth: A national agenda* (pp. 15-28). Richmond, KY: National Juvenile Detention Association.

Bureau of Alcohol, Tobacco and Firearms. (1999). *The Youth Crime Gun Interdiction Initiative performance report.* Washington, DC: Author.

Bureau of Justice Assistance. (1997). *Urban street gang enforcement.* Washington, DC: Author.

Bureau of Justice Statistics. (2001). *Personal crimes of violence, 1999.* Washington, DC: Author. Retrieved from http://www.ojp.usdoj.gov/bjs/abstract/cvusst.htm

Bureau of Justice Statistics. (2002). *Prisoners in 2001* (Bulletin). Washington, DC: Author.

Burke, C., & Pennell, S. (2001). *Breaking Cycles evaluation: A comprehensive approach to youthful offenders.* San Diego, CA: San Diego Association of Governments.

Burns, B. J. (1991). Mental health services use by adolescents in the 1970s and 1980s. *Journal of the American Academy of Child and Adolescent Psychiatry, 30,* 144-150.

Burns, B. J., Costello, E. J., Angold, A., Tweed, D., Stangl, D., Farmer, E. M. Z., et al. (1995). Children's mental health service use across service sectors. *Health Affairs, 14,* 147-159.

Burns, B. J., & Goldman, S. K. (Eds.). (1999). *Promising practices in wraparound for children with serious emotional disturbances and their families: Systems of care.* Washington, DC: American Institutes for Research, Center for Effective Collaboration and Practice.

Burns, B. J., Goldman, S. K., Faw, L., & Burchard, J. (1999). The wraparound evidence base. In B. J. Burns & S. K. Goldman (Eds.), *Promising practices in wraparound for children with serious emotional disturbances and their families: Systems of care* (pp. 77-100). Washington, DC: American Institutes for Research, Center for Effective Collaboration and Practice.

Burns, B. J., Hoagwood, K., & Mrazek, P. J. (1999). Effective treatment for mental disorders in children and adolescents. *Clinical Child and Family Psychology Review, 2,* 199-254.

Burns, B. J., Landsverk, J., Kelleher, K., Faw, L., Hazen, A., & Keeler, G. (2001). Mental health, education, child welfare, and juvenile justice service use. In R. Loeber & D. P. Farrington (Eds.), *Child delinquents: Development, intervention, and service needs* (pp. 273-304). Thousand Oaks, CA: Sage.

Burns, B. J., Schoenwald, S. K., Burchard, J. D., Faw, L., & Santos, A. B. (2000). Comprehensive community-based interventions for youth with severe emotional disorders: Multisystemic therapy and the wraparound process. *Journal of Child and Family Studies, 9,* 283-314.

Burrell, S. (2000). *Pathways to juvenile detention reform: Vol. 6. Improving conditions of confinement in secure detention facilities.* Baltimore: Annie E. Casey Foundation.

Bursik, R. J., Jr., & Grasmick, H. G. (1993). *Neighborhoods and crime: The dimensions of effective community control.* New York: Lexington.

Burton, M. (2001). *Juvenile justice state legislation in 2000.* Denver, CO: National Conference of State Legislators.

Butterfield, F. (1997, July 21). With juvenile courts in chaos, some propose scrapping them. *New York Times,* pp. A1, A13.

Butterfield, F. (1998, July 15). Profits at juvenile prisons are earned at a chilling cost. *New York Times,* p. A1.

Butts, J. A. (1999, May). Feeding kids to the monster. *Youth Today,* p. 23.

Butts, J. A., & Adams, W. (2001). *Anticipating space needs in juvenile detention and correctional facilities* (Juvenile Justice Bulletin). Washington, DC: Office of Juvenile Justice and Delinquency Prevention.

Butts, J. A., Buck, J., & Coggeshall, M. (2002). *The impact of teen court on young offenders.* Washington, DC: The Urban Institute.

Butts, J. A., & DeMuro, P. (1989). *Risk assessment of adjudicated delinquents: Division for Children and Youth Services, Department of Health and Human Services, State of New Hampshire.* Ann Arbor: University of Michigan, Center for the Study of Youth Policy.

Butts, J. A., & Halemba, G. J. (1996). *Waiting for justice.* Pittsburgh, PA: National Center for Juvenile Justice.

Butts, J. A., & Snyder, H. N. (1997). *The youngest delinquents: Offenders under age 15* (Juvenile Justice Bulletin). Washington, DC: Office of Juvenile Justice and Delinquency Prevention.

Butts, J. A., & Travis, J. (2002). *The rise and fall of American youth violence: 1980 to 2000.* Washington, DC: Urban Institute.

Byrne, J. M., & Pattavina, A. (1992). The effectiveness issue: Assessing what works in the adult community corrections system. In J. M. Byrne, A. J. Lurigio, & J. Petersilia (Eds.), *Smart sentencing: The emergence of intermediate sanctions* (pp. 281-303). Newbury Park, CA: Sage.

Cairns, R. B., & Cairns, B. D. (1994). *Lifelines and risks: Pathways of youth in our time.* New York: Cambridge University Press.

Cairns, R. B., Cairns, B. D., Neckerman, H. J., Ferguson, L. L., & Gariepy, J. L. (1989). Growth and aggression: I. Childhood to early adolescence. *Developmental Psychology, 25,* 320-330.

California Board of Corrections. (2001). *Repeat Offender Prevention Program status report: July 2001.* Sacramento: Author.

California Council on Criminal Justice. (1989). *Task force report on gangs and drugs.* Sacramento: Author.

Capaldi, D. N., & Patterson, G. R. (1996). Can violent offenders be distinguished from frequent offenders? Prediction from childhood to adolescence. *Journal of Research in Crime and Delinquency, 33,* 206-231.

Capizzi, M., Cook, J. I., & Schumacher, M. (1995, March-April). The TARGET model: A new approach to the prosecution of gang cases. *Prosecutor*, pp. 18-21.

Caplan, G. (1976). Criminology, criminal justice, and the war on crime. *Criminology, 14*, 3-16.

Carroll, L., & Mondrick, M. E. (1976). Racial bias in the decision to grant parole. *Law and Society Review, 11*(1), 93-107.

Catalano, R. F., Arthur, M. W., Hawkins, J. D., Berglund, L., & Olson, J. J. (1998). Comprehensive community- and school-based interventions to prevent antisocial behavior. In R. Loeber & D. P. Farrington (Eds.), *Serious and violent juvenile offenders: Risk factors and successful interventions* (pp. 248-283). Thousand Oaks, CA: Sage.

Catalano, R. F., Berglund, M. L., Ryan, J. A., Lonczak, H. S., & Hawkins, J. D. (1999). *Positive youth development in the United States: Research findings on evaluations of positive youth development programs*. Seattle: University of Washington, Social Development Research Group.

Catalano, R. F., & Hawkins, J. D. (1996). The social development model: A theory of anti-social behavior. In J. D. Hawkins (Ed.), *Delinquency and crime: Current theories* (pp. 149-197). New York: Cambridge University Press.

Catalano, R. F., Kosterman, R., Hawkins, J. D., Newcomb, M. D., & Abbott, R. D. (1996). Modeling the etiology of adolescent substance abuse: A test of the social development model. *Journal of Drug Issues, 26*, 429-455.

Catalano, R. F., Loeber, R., & McKinney, K. (1999). *School and community interventions to prevent serious and violent offending* (Juvenile Justice Bulletin). Washington, DC: Office of Juvenile Justice and Delinquency Prevention.

Caulkins, J. P., Rydell, C. P., Everingham, S. S., Chiesa, J., & Bushway, S. (1999). *An ounce of prevention, a pound of uncertainty*. Santa Monica, CA: RAND.

Center for Evaluation Research and Methodology. (2002). *OJJDP project on effective delinquency programs*. Nashville, TN: Vanderbilt Institute of Public Policy Studies, Center for Evaluation Research and Methodology.

Center for Substance Abuse Treatment. (1999). *Strategies for integrating substance abuse treatment and the juvenile justice system: A practice guide*. Washington, DC: Author.

Center for the Study of Prevention and Violence. (1998). *CSPV blueprints fact sheet*. Boulder, CO: Author.

Center for the Study of Social Policy. (1995). *Building new futures for at-risk youth: Findings from a five-year, multi-site evaluation*. Washington, DC: Author.

Chaiken, M. R. (2000). *Violent neighborhoods, violent kids* (Juvenile Justice Bulletin). Washington, DC: Office of Juvenile Justice and Delinquency Prevention.

Chaiken, M. R., & Chaiken, J. M. (1991). *Priority prosecution of high-rate dangerous offenders* (Research in Action). Washington, DC: National Institute of Justice.

Chamberlain, P. (1994). *Family connections: Treatment foster care for adolescents with delinquency*. Eugene, OR: Castilia.

Chamberlain, P. (1998). *Treatment foster care* (Juvenile Justice Bulletin). Washington, DC: Office of Juvenile Justice and Delinquency Prevention.

Chamberlain, P., & Reid, J. B. (1998). Comparison of two community alternatives to incarceration for chronic juvenile offenders. *Journal of Consulting and Clinical Psychology, 66*, 624-633.

Chambliss, W. J. (1995). Crime control and ethnic minorities: Legitimizing racial oppression by creating moral panics. In D. F. Hawkins (Ed.), *Ethnicity, race, and crime: Perspectives across time and place* (pp. 235-258). Albany: State University of New York Press.

Chandler, K. A., Chapman, C. D., Rand, M. R., & Taylor, B. M. (1998). *Students' reports of school crime: 1989 and 1995*. Washington, DC: Bureau of Justice Statistics and National Center for Education Statistics.

Chard-Wierschem, D. (1998). *In pursuit of the "true" relationship: A longitudinal study of the effects of religiosity on delinquency and substance abuse*. Unpublished doctoral dissertation, University at Albany, State University of New York.

Cheatwood, D. (1993). Capital punishment and the deterrence of violent crime in comparable counties. *Criminal Justice Review, 18*, 165-181.

Chesney-Lind, M. (1997). *The female offender: Girls, women, and crime*. Thousand Oaks, CA: Sage.

Chesney-Lind, M., & Brown, M. (1999). Girls and violence. In D. J. Flannery & C. R. Huff (Eds.), *Youth violence: Prevention, intervention, and social policy* (pp. 171-199). Washington, DC: American Psychiatric Press.

Chesney-Lind, M., & Paramore, V. V. (2001). Are girls getting more violent? Exploring juvenile robbery trends. *Journal of Contemporary Criminal Justice, 17*, 142-166.

Chesney-Lind, M., & Sheldon, R. (1998). *Girls, delinquency, and juvenile justice*. Belmont, CA: West /Wadsworth.

Chicago Police Department, Gang Crime Section. (1992). *Street gangs*. Chicago: Author.

Children's Research Center. (1993). *A new approach to child protection: The CRC model*.

Madison, WI: National Council on Crime and Delinquency.

Chiricos, T. G., & Crawford, C. (1995). Race and imprisonment: A contextual assessment of the evidence. In D. F. Hawkins (Ed.), *Ethnicity, race, and crime: Perspectives across time and place* (pp. 281-309). Albany: State University of New York Press.

Clark, C. S. (1991). Youth gangs. *Congressional Quarterly Research, 22,* 755-771.

Clayton, R. R., Cattarello, A. M., & Johnstone, B. (1996). The effectiveness of Drug Abuse Resistance Education (Project DARE): 5-year follow-up results. *Preventive Medicine, 25,* 307-318.

Clear, T. R. (1988). Statistical prediction in corrections. *Research in Corrections, 1*(1), 1-39

Clear, T. R. (1994). *Harm in American penology: Offenders, victims, and their communities.* Albany: State University of New York Press.

Coalition for Juvenile Justice. (1997). *False images: The news media and juvenile crime* (1997 Annual Report). Washington, DC: Author.

Coalition for Juvenile Justice. (1994). *No easy answers: Juvenile justice in a climate of fear.* Washington, DC: Author.

Coalition for Juvenile Justice. (1998). *A celebration or a wake? The juvenile court after 100 years.* Washington, DC: Author.

Coalition for Juvenile Justice. (1999). *Ain't no place anybody would want to be: Conditions of confinement for youth.* Washington, DC: Author.

Cocozza, J. J., & Skowyra, K. (2000). Youth with mental health disorders: Issues and emerging responses. *Juvenile Justice, 7*(1), 3-13.

Cohen, L. E., & Vila, B. J. (1996). Self-control and social control: An exposition of the Gottfredson-Hirschi/Sampson-Laub debate. *Studies on Crime and Crime Prevention, 5,* 125-150.

Cohen, M. (1998). The monetary value of saving a high-risk youth. *Journal of Quantitative Criminology, 14,* 5-33.

Cohen, S. (1980). *Folk devils and moral panics: The creation of the mods and rockers.* New York: Basil Blackwell.

Coie, J. D., & Dodge, K. A. (1998). The development of aggression and antisocial behavior. In W. Damon (Series Ed.) & N. Eisenberg (Vol. Ed.), *Handbook of child psychology: Vol. 3. Social, emotional, and personality development* (5th ed., pp. 779-861). New York: John Wiley.

Coie, J. D., & Miller-Johnson, S. (2001). Peer factors and interventions. In R. Loeber & D. P. Farrington (Eds.), *Child delinquents: Development, intervention, and service needs* (pp. 191-209). Thousand Oaks, CA: Sage.

Coie, J. D., Watt, N. F., West, S. G., Hawkins, J. D., Asarnow, J. R., Markman, H. J., et al. (1993). The science of prevention: A conceptual framework and some directions for a national research program. *American Psychologist, 48,* 1013-1022.

Coleman, J. E., Jr. (Ed.). (1998). The ABA's proposed moratorium on the death penalty [Special issue]. *Law and Contemporary Problems, 61*(4).

Coleman, J. S. (1988). Social capital in the creation of human capital. *American Journal of Sociology, 94*(Suppl.), 95-120.

Commonwealth of Kentucky, Department of Juvenile Justice. (2002). *Residential facilities.* Frankfort: Author. (Retrieved from http://djj. state.ky.us/rsdntlfclts.htm)

Comprehensive Youth Strategies Project. (2000). *Comprehensive strategy for Texas youth: Manual and planning workbook.* San Marcos: Southwest Texas State University, Center for Initiatives in Education.

Conduct Problems Prevention Research Group. (1999a). Initial impact of the Fast Track prevention trial for conduct problems: I. The high-risk sample. *Journal of Consulting and Clinical Psychology, 67,* 631-647.

Conduct Problems Prevention Research Group. (1999b). Initial impact of the Fast Track prevention trial for conduct problems: II. Classroom effects. *Journal of Consulting and Clinical Psychology, 67,* 648-657.

Cook, P. J., & Laub, J. H. (1998). The unprecedented epidemic of youth violence. In M. Tonry & M. H. Moore (Eds.), *Youth violence* (pp. 27-64). Chicago: University of Chicago Press.

Cook, P. J., & Ludwig, J. (2001, June 10). Protecting the public in presidential style. *News and Observer* (Raleigh, NC), p. A31.

Coolbaugh, K., & Hansel, C. J. (2000). *The Comprehensive Strategy: Lessons learned from the pilot sites* (Juvenile Justice Bulletin). Washington, DC: Office of Juvenile Justice and Delinquency Prevention.

Cothern, L. (2000). *Juveniles and the death penalty: A report of the federal Coordinating Council on Juvenile Justice and Delinquency Prevention* (Juvenile Justice Bulletin). Washington, DC: Office of Juvenile Justice and Delinquency Prevention.

Cottle, C., Lee, R. J., & Heilbrun, K. (2001). The prediction of criminal recidivism in juveniles: A meta-analysis. *Criminal Justice and Behavior, 28,* 367-394.

Craig, W., & Pepler, D. J. (1997). Observations of bullying and victimization in the school yard. *Canadian Journal of School Psychology, 13*(2), 41-59.

Crick, N. R., & Grotpeter, J. K. (1995). Relational aggression, gender, and psychological adjustment. *Child Development, 66,* 710-722.

Cronin, R. (1996). *Fact-finding report on community assessment centers (CAC's): Final report.* Washington, DC: Office of Juvenile Justice and Delinquency Prevention.

Crowe, A. H. (1998). *Drug identification and testing in the juvenile justice system.* Washington, DC: Office of Juvenile Justice and Delinquency Prevention.

Crutchfield, R. D., Bridges, G. S., & Pitchford, S. R. (1994). Analytical and aggregation biases in analyses of imprisonment: Reconciling discrepancies in studies of racial disparity. *Journal of Research in Crime and Delinquency, 31,* 166-182.

Cullen, F. T., & Applegate, B. K. (1997). *Offender rehabilitation.* Aldershot, UK: Ashgate.

Cullen, F. T., & Gendreau, P. (1989). The effectiveness of correctional treatment: Reconsidering the "nothing works" debate. In L. Goodstein & D. L. MacKenzie (Eds.), *The American prison: Issues in research and policy* (pp. 23-44). New York: Plenum.

Cullen, F. T., & Gendreau, P. (2000). Assessing correctional rehabilitation: Policy, practice, and prospects. In J. Horney (Ed.), *Criminal justice 2000: Vol. 3. Policies, processes, and decisions of the criminal justice system* (pp. 109-175). Washington, DC: National Institute of Justice.

Cullen, F. T., Gendreau, P., Jarjoura, G. R., & Wright, J. P. (1997). Crime and the bell curve: Lessons from intelligent criminology. *Crime & Delinquency, 43,* 387-411.

Cullen, F. T., & Gilbert, K. E. (1982). *Reaffirming rehabilitation.* Cincinnati, OH: Anderson.

Cullen, F. T., Golden, K. M., & Cullen, J. B. (1983). Is child saving dead? Attitudes toward juvenile rehabilitation in Illinois. *Journal of Criminal Justice, 11,* 1-13.

Curry, G. D. (1998). Responding to female gang involvement. In J. Hagedorn & M. Chesney-Lind (Eds.), *Female gangs in America* (pp. 133-143). Chicago: Lakeview.

Curry, G. D., & Decker, S. H. (1998). *Confronting gangs: Crime and community.* Los Angeles: Roxbury.

Curry, G. D., & Decker, S. H. (2000). *Referrals and the referral process in the St. Louis family court.* St. Louis: Missouri Department of Criminology and Criminal Justice.

Curry, G. D., Decker, S. H., & Egley, A., Jr. (2002). Gang involvement and delinquency in a middle school population. *Justice Quarterly, 19,* 275-292.

Curry, G. D., Fox, R. J., Ball, R. A., & Stone, D. (1992). *National assessment of law enforcement anti-gang information resources: Final report.* Washington, DC: National Institute of Justice.

Curry, G. D., & Spergel, I. A. (1988). Gang homicide, delinquency and community. *Criminology, 26,* 381-405.

Curry, G. D., & Spergel, I. A. (1992). Gang involvement and delinquency among Hispanic and African-American adolescent males. *Journal of Research in Crime and Delinquency, 29,* 273-291.

Curtis, R. A. (1992). Highly structured crack markets in the southside of Williamsburg, Brooklyn. In J. Fagan (Ed.), *The ecology of crime and drug use in inner cities.* New York: Social Science Research Council.

Cuyahoga County Juvenile Court. (1996). *Assess, classify, and treat.* Cleveland, OH: Author.

Danegger, A. E., Cohen, C. E., Hayes, C. D., & Holden, G. A. (1999). *Juvenile Accountability Incentive Block Grants: Strategic planning guide.* Washington, DC: Office of Juvenile Justice and Delinquency Prevention.

Davidson, W. S., Redner, R., & Amdur, R. (1990). *Alternative treatments for troubled youth: The case of diversion from the justice system.* New York: Plenum.

Dawes, D. M., & Ross, P. (2000). *Fiscal year 1999 juvenile justice statistics for North Carolina: Juveniles adjudicated delinquent.* Raleigh: North Carolina Sentencing and Policy Advisory Commission.

Dawson, R. O. (1988). The third justice system: The new juvenile-criminal system of determinate sentencing for the youthful violent offender in Texas. *St. Mary's Law Journal, 19,* 943-1015.

Dawson, R. O. (1990). The violent juvenile offender: An empirical study of juvenile determinant sentencing proceedings as an alternative to criminal prosecution. *Texas Tech Law Review, 21,* 1897-1937.

Dawson, R. O. (1992). An empirical study of Kent style juvenile transfers to criminal court. *St. Mary's Law Journal, 23,* 975-1054.

Dawson, R. O. (2000). Judicial waiver in theory and practice. In J. Fagan & F. E. Zimring (Eds.), *The changing borders of juvenile justice: Transfer of adolescents to the criminal court* (pp. 45-81). Chicago: University of Chicago Press.

Dean, C. W., Brame, R., & Piquero, A. R. (1996). Criminal propensities, discrete groups of offenders, and persistence in crime. *Criminology, 34,* 547-574.

Dean, C. W., Hirschel, J. D., & Brame, R. (1996). Minorities and juvenile case dispositions. *Justice System Journal, 18,* 267-285.

Dean, C. W., & Reppucci, N. D. (1974). Juvenile correctional institutions. In D. Glaser (Ed.), *Handbook of criminology* (pp. 865-894). Chicago: Rand McNally.

Decker, S. H. (1996). Collective and normative features of gang violence. *Justice Quarterly, 13,* 243-264.

Decker, S. H., Bynum, T., & Weisel, D. (1998). A tale of two cities: Gangs as organized crime groups. *Justice Quarterly, 15,* 395-423.

Decker, S. H., & Curry, G. D. (2000). Addressing key features of gang membership: Measuring the involvement of young members. *Journal of Criminal Justice, 28,* 473-482.

Decker, S., & Curry, G. D. (2002). "I'm down for my organization": The rationality of responses to delinquency, youth crime and gangs. In A. R. Piquero & S. G. Tibbits (Eds.), *Rational choice and criminal behavior* (pp. 197-218). New York: Routledge.

Decker, S. H., & Kempf-Leonard, K. (1991). Constructing gangs: The social definition of youth activities. *Criminal Justice Policy Review, 5,* 271-291.

Decker, S. H., & Lauritsen, J. L. (2002). Leaving the gang. In C. R. Huff (Ed.), *Gangs in America* (3rd ed., pp. 51-67). Thousand Oaks, CA: Sage.

Decker, S. H., & Van Winkle, B. (1994). Slinging dope: The role of gangs and gang members in drug sales. *Justice Quarterly, 11,* 583-604.

Decker, S. H., & Van Winkle, B. (1996). *Life in the gang: Family, friends, and violence.* New York: Cambridge University Press.

DeComo, R. E. (1998). Estimating the prevalence of juvenile custody by race and gender. *Crime & Delinquency, 44,* 489-506.

Degnan, W. (1994). *Lifeskills post-parole treatment program.* Sanger, CA: Operation New Hope.

Degnan, W., & Degnan, A. (1993). *Lifestyle changes: One step at a time.* Sanger, CA: Operation New Hope.

Delaware Statistical Analysis Center. (1999). *Evaluation of the Delaware Juvenile Drug Court Diversion Program.* Dover: Author.

Dembo, R., & Rivers, J. E. (1996). Juvenile health service centers: An exciting opportunity to intervene with drug-involved and other high-risk youth. In C. B. McCoy, L. R. Metsch, & J. A. Inciardi (Eds.), *Intervening with drug-involved youth* (pp. 133-155). Thousand Oaks, CA: Sage.

DeMause, L. (Ed.). (1974). *The history of childhood.* New York: Psychohistory.

DeMuro, P. (2000). *Pathways to juvenile detention reform: Vol. 4. Consider the alternatives.* Baltimore: Annie E. Casey Foundation.

Derzon, J. H., & Lipsey, M. W. (1999, November). *The correspondence of family features with problem, aggressive, criminal, and violent behavior.* Paper presented at the annual meeting of the American Society of Criminology, Toronto.

Deschenes, E. P., & Esbensen, F. (1999). Violence and gangs: Gender differences in perceptions and experiences. *Journal of Quantitative Criminology, 15,* 53-96.

Deutsch, L. (2000, February 26). Los Angeles police officer gets five years. *USA Today,* p. 6A.

Developmental Research and Programs, Inc. (2000). *Communities That Care prevention strategies: A research guide to what works.* Seattle: Author.

Developmental Research and Programs, Inc., & National Council on Crime and Delinquency. (2000). *Comprehensive Strategy curriculum: The Comprehensive Strategy for Serious, Violent, and Chronic Juvenile Offenders.* Washington, DC: Office of Juvenile Justice and Delinquency Prevention.

DiIulio, J. J., Jr. (1995a). Arresting ideas. *Policy Review, 74,* 12-16.

DiIulio, J. J., Jr. (1995b, November 27). The coming of the super-predators. *Weekly Standard,* p. 23.

DiIulio, J. J., Jr. (1996a). *How to stop the coming crime wave.* New York: Manhattan Institute.

DiIulio, J. J., Jr. (1996b, Spring). They're coming: Florida's youth crime bomb. *Impact,* pp. 25-27.

Dishion, T. J., McCord, J., & Poulin, F. (1999). When interventions harm: Peer groups and problem behavior. *American Psychologist, 54,* 755-764.

Dodge, K. A., Bates, J. E., & Pettit, G. S. (1990). Mechanisms in the cycle of violence. *Science, 250,* 1678-1683.

Dolan, L. J., Kellam, S. G., Brown, C. H., Werthamer-Larsson, L. R. G. W., Mayer, L. S., Laudolff, J., et al. (1993). The short-term impact of two classroom-based preventive interventions on aggressive and shy behaviors and poor achievement. *Journal of Applied Developmental Psychology, 14,* 317-345.

Donohue, E., Schiraldi, V., & Ziedenberg, J. (1999). *School house hype: School shootings and the real risks students face in America.* Washington, DC: Justice Policy Institute, Center on Juvenile and Criminal Justice.

Drug Enforcement Administration. (1988). *Crack cocaine availability and trafficking in the United States.* Washington, DC: Author.

Duchnowski, A. J., & Kutash, K. (1996). A mental health perspective. In C. M. Nelson, R. B. Rutherford, & B. I. Wolford (Eds.), *Comprehensive and collaborative systems that work for troubled youth: A national agenda* (pp. 90-110). Richmond, KY: National Juvenile Detention Association.

Dunford, F. W., & Elliott, D. S. (1984). Identifying career offenders using self-reported data. *Journal of Research on Crime and Delinquency, 21,* 57-86.

Dunlap, E. L., & Roush, D. W. (1995). Juvenile detention as process and place. *Juvenile and Family Court Journal, 46*(2), 3-16.

Durlak, J. A. (1995). *School-based prevention programs for children and adolescents.* Thousand Oaks, CA: Sage.

Durlak, J. A. (1997). *Successful programs for children and adolescents.* New York: Plenum.

Durlak, J. A. (1998). Common risk and protective factors in successful prevention programs. *American Journal of Orthopsychiatry, 68,* 512-520.

Durlak, J. A., & Lipsey, M. W. (1991). A practitioner's guide to meta-analysis. *American Journal of Community Psychology, 19,* 291-332.

Durlak, J. A., & Wells, A. M. (1997). Primary prevention mental health programs for children and adolescents: A meta-analytic review. *American Journal of Community Psychology, 25,* 115-152.

Ebner, P. (2001). *Alameda County placement risk assessment validation, final report.* Oakland, CA: National Council on Crime and Delinquency.

Eddy, P., Sabogal, H., & Walden, S. (1988). *The cocaine wars.* New York: W. W. Norton.

Eggert, L. L., Thompson, E. A., Randall, B. P., & Pike, K. C. (2002). Preliminary effects of brief school-based prevention approaches for reducing youth suicide: Risk behaviors, depression, and drug involvement. *Journal of Child and Adolescent Psychiatric Nursing, 5*(2), 48-64.

Egley, A., Jr. (2000). *Highlights of the 1999 National Youth Gang Survey* (Fact Sheet No. 2000-20). Washington, DC: Office of Juvenile Justice and Delinquency Prevention.

Egley, A., Jr. (2003). *Levels of involvement: Differences between gang, gang-marginal, and nongang youth.* Unpublished doctoral dissertation, University of Missouri, St. Louis, Department of Criminology and Criminal Justice.

Egley, A., Jr. (2002a). *National Youth Gang Survey trends from 1996 to 2000* (Fact Sheet No. 2002-03). Washington, DC: Office of Juvenile Justice and Delinquency Prevention.

Egley, A., Jr. (2002b, November). *National Youth Gang Surveys: 1996-2001.* Paper presented at the annual meeting of the American Society of Criminology, Chicago.

Egley, A., Jr., & Arjunan, M. (2002). *Highlights of the 2000 National Youth Gang Survey* (Fact Sheet No. 2002-04). Washington, DC: Office of Juvenile Justice and Delinquency Prevention.

Egley, A., Jr., Major, A. K., & Howell, J. C. (2003). *National Youth Gang Survey: 1999-2001.* Tallahassee, FL: National Youth Gang Center.

Eisenberg, M., & Markley, G. (1987). Something works in community supervision. *Federal Probation, 51*(4), 28-32.

Elder, G. H., Jr. (Ed.). (1985a). *Life course dynamics: Trajectories and transitions, 1968-1980.* Ithaca, NY: Cornell University Press.

Elder, G. H., Jr. (1985b). Perspectives on the life course. In G. H. Elder, Jr. (Ed.), *Life course dynamics: Trajectories and transitions, 1968-1980* (pp. 23-49). Ithaca, NY: Cornell University Press.

Elder, G. H., Jr. (1986). Military times and turning points in men's lives. *Developmental Psychology, 3,* 215-231.

Elder, G. H., Jr. (1992). The life course. In E. F. Borgatta & M. L. Borgatta (Eds.), *The encyclopedia of sociology* (3rd ed., pp. 1120-1130). New York: Macmillan.

Elliott, D. S. (1994a). Serious violent offenders: Onset, developmental course, and termination. *Criminology, 32,* 1-21.

Elliott, D. S. (1994b). *Youth violence: An overview.* Boulder, CO: Center for the Study and Prevention of Violence.

Elliott, D. S. (1995, November). *Lies, damn lies and arrest statistics.* Paper presented at the annual meeting of the American Society of Criminology, Boston.

Elliott, D. S. (Ed.). (1998). *Blueprints for violence prevention.* Denver: C&M.

Elliott, D. S. (2000). Violent offending over the life course: A sociological perspective. In N. A. Krasnegor, N. B. Anderson, & D. R. Bynum (Eds.), *Health and behavior* (Vol. 1, pp. 189-204). Rockville, MD: National Institutes of Health.

Elliott, D. S., Huizinga, D., & Menard, S. (1989). *Multiple problem youth: Delinquency, substance abuse and mental health problems.* New York: Springer-Verlag.

Elliott, D. S., Huizinga, D., & Morse, B. (1986). Self-reported violent offending. *Journal of Interpersonal Violence, 1,* 472-514.

Elliott, D. S., & Menard, S. (1996). Delinquent friends and delinquent behavior: Temporal and developmental patterns. In J. D. Hawkins (Ed.), *Delinquency and crime: Current theories* (pp. 28-67). New York: Cambridge University Press.

Empey, L. T. (1974). Crime prevention: The fugitive utopia. In D. Glaser (Ed.), *Handbook of criminology* (pp. 1095-1123). Chicago: Rand McNally.

Empey, L. T. (1978). *American delinquency: Its meaning and construction.* Homewood, IL: Dorsey.

Empey, L. T., & Erickson, M. (1972). *The Provo experiment.* Lexington, MA: Lexington.

Empey, L. T., & Lubeck, S. (1971). *The Silverlake experiment.* Chicago: Aldine.

Empey, L. T., & Stafford, M. C. (1991). *American delinquency: Its meaning and construction* (3rd ed.). Belmont, CA: Wadsworth.

Eron, L. D., & Huesmann, L. R. (1987). Television as a source of maltreatment of children. *School Psychology Review, 16,* 195-202.

Eron, L. D., & Slaby, R. G. (1994). Introduction. In L. D. Eron, J. H. Gentry, & P. Schlegel (Eds.), *Reason to hope: A psychosocial perspective on violence and youth* (pp. 1-22). Washington, DC: American Psychological Association.

Esbensen, F. (2000). *Preventing adolescent gang involvement: Risk factors and prevention strategies* (Juvenile Justice Bulletin, Youth Gang Series). Washington, DC: Office of Juvenile Justice and Delinquency Prevention.

Esbensen, F. (2001). The national evaluation of the Gang Resistance Education and Training (G.R.E.A.T.) program. In J. Miller, C. L. Maxson, & M. W. Klein (Eds.), *The modern gang reader* (2nd ed., pp. 289-302). Los Angeles: Roxbury.

Esbensen, F., & Huizinga, D. (1993). Gangs, drugs, and delinquency in a survey of urban youth. *Criminology, 31,* 565-589.

Esbensen, F., Huizinga, D., & Menard, S. (1999). Family context and criminal victimization in adolescence. *Youth & Society, 31,* 168-198.

Esbensen, F., Huizinga, D., & Weiher, A. W. (1993). Gang and non-gang youth: Differences in explanatory variables. *Journal of Contemporary Criminal Justice, 9,* 94-116.

Esbensen, F., & Osgood, D. W. (1999). Gang Resistance Education and Training (GREAT): Results from the national evaluation. *Journal of Research in Crime and Delinquency, 36,* 194-225.

Esbensen, F., Osgood, D. W., Taylor, T. J., Peterson, D., & Freng, A. (2001). How great is G.R.E.A.T.? Results from a longitudinal quasi-experimental design. *Criminology and Public Policy, 1,* 87-117.

Esbensen, F., & Winfree, L. T. (1998). Race and gender differences between gang and nongang youths: Results from a multisite survey. *Justice Quarterly, 15,* 505-526.

Esbensen, F., Winfree, L. T., He, N., & Taylor, T. J. (2001). Youth gangs and definitional issues: When is a gang a gang, and why does it matter? *Crime & Delinquency, 47,* 105-130.

Eslea, M., & Smith, P. K. (1998). The long-term effectiveness of anti-bullying work in primary schools. *Educational Research, 40,* 203-218.

Espiritu, R. C., Huizinga, D., Crawford, A. M., & Loeber, R. (2001). Epidemiology of self-reported delinquency. In R. Loeber & D. P. Farrington (Eds.), *Child delinquents: Development, intervention, and service needs* (pp. 47-66). Thousand Oaks, CA: Sage.

Evans, M. E., & Boothroyd, R. A. (1997). Intensive in-home crisis services for children with serious emotional disturbances. In S. W. Henggeler & A. B. Santos (Eds.), *Innovative approaches for difficult to treat populations* (pp. 27-46). Washington, DC: American Psychiatric Press.

Executioners kick off 2000 with juvenile offenders. (2000, February). *Youth Today,* pp. 7-8.

Ezell, M. (1997). *TeamChild: Evaluation of the second year.* Seattle: University of Washington, School of Social Work.

Fagan, J. (1989). The social organization of drug use and drug dealing among urban gangs. *Criminology, 27,* 633-669.

Fagan, J. (1990). Social process of delinquency and drug use among urban gangs. In C. R. Huff (Ed.), *Gangs in America* (pp. 183-219). Newbury Park, CA: Sage.

Fagan, J. (1995). Separating the men from the boys: The comparative advantage of juvenile versus criminal court sanctions on recidivism among adolescent felony offenders. In J. C. Howell, B. Krisberg, J. D. Hawkins, & J. J. Wilson (Eds.), *A sourcebook: Serious, violent, and chronic juvenile offenders* (pp. 238-274). Thousand Oaks, CA: Sage.

Fagan, J. (1996). Gangs, drugs, and neighborhood change. In C. R. Huff (Ed.), *Gangs in America* (2nd ed., pp. 39-74). Thousand Oaks, CA: Sage.

Fagan, J., & Chin, K. (1990). Violence as regulation and social control in the distribution of crack. In M. E. De La Rosa, E. Y. Lambert, & B. Gropper (Eds.), *Drugs and violence: Causes, correlates, and consequences* (NIDA Research Monograph No. 103, pp. 8-43). Rockville, MD: National Institute on Drug Abuse.

Fagan, J., & Liberman, A. (2001, November). *Juvenile vs. criminal courts: Comparing the recidivism of adolescent felony offenders across court contexts.* Paper presented at the annual meeting of the American Society of Criminology, Atlanta.

Fagan, J., Rudman, C. J., & Hartstone, E. (1984). Intervening with violent juvenile offenders: A community reintegration model. In R. A. Mathias, P. DeMuro, & R. Allinson (Eds.), *Violent juvenile offenders: An anthology* (pp. 207-229). San Francisco: National Council on Crime and Delinquency.

Fagan, J., Slaughter, E., & Hartstone, E. (1987). Blind justice? The impact of race on the juvenile process. *Crime & Delinquency, 33,* 224-258.

Fagan, J., & Zimring, F. E. (Eds.). (2000). *The changing borders of juvenile justice: Transfer of adolescents to the criminal court.* Chicago: University of Chicago Press.

Farrell, A. D., & Meyer, A. L. (1997). The effectiveness of a school-based curriculum for reducing violence among urban sixth-grade students. *American Journal of Public Health, 87,* 979-984.

Farrell, A. D., & Meyer, A. L. (1998). *Social skills training to promote resilience in urban sixth-grade students: One product of an action strategy to prevent youth violence in high-risk environments.* Unpublished manuscript, Virginia Commonwealth University.

Farrington, D. P. (1983). Offending from 10 to 25 years of age. In K. T. Van Dusen & S. A. Mednick (Eds.), *Prospective studies of crime and delinquency* (pp. 17-37). Boston: Kluwer-Nijhoff.

Farrington, D. P. (1986a). Age and crime. In M. Tonry & N. Morris (Eds.), *Crime and justice: An annual review of research* (Vol. 7, pp. 189-250). Chicago: University of Chicago Press.

Farrington, D. P. (1986b). Stepping stones to adult criminal careers. In D. Olweus, J. Block, & M. R. Yarrow (Eds.), *Development of antisocial and prosocial behavior* (pp. 359-384). New York: Academic Press.

Farrington, D. P. (1989). Later adult life outcomes of offenders and non-offenders. In M. Brambring, F. Losel, & H. Skowronek (Eds.), *Children at risk: Assessment, longitudinal research, and intervention* (pp. 220-224). Berlin: De Gruyter.

Farrington, D. P. (1993a). Have any individual, family or neighborhood influences on offending been demonstrated conclusively? In D. P. Farrington, R. J. Sampson, & P. H. Wikstrom (Eds.), *Integrating individual and ecological aspects of crime* (pp. 7-37). Stockholm: National Council for Crime Prevention.

Farrington, D. P. (1993b). Understanding and preventing bullying. In M. Tonry (Ed.), *Crime and justice: An annual review of research* (Vol. 17, pp. 381-458). Chicago: University of Chicago Press.

Farrington, D. P. (1995). The development of offending and antisocial behavior from childhood: Key findings from the Cambridge Study in Delinquent Development. *Journal of Child Psychology and Psychiatry, 36,* 929-964.

Farrington, D. P. (1996). The explanation and prevention of youthful offending. In J. D. Hawkins (Ed.), *Delinquency and crime: Current theories* (pp. 68-148). New York: Cambridge University Press.

Farrington, D. P. (1998). Predictors, causes, and correlates of male youth violence. In M. Tonry & M. H. Moore (Eds.), *Youth violence* (pp. 421-475). Chicago: University of Chicago Press.

Farrington, D. P. (2000). Explaining and preventing crime: The globalization of knowledge. The American Society of Criminology 1999 Presidential Address. *Criminology, 38,* 1-24.

Farrington, D. P., Snyder, H. N., & Finnegan, T. A. (1988). Specialization in juvenile court careers. *Criminology, 26,* 461-487.

Farrington, D. P., & West, D. J. (1993). Criminal, penal and life histories of chronic offenders: Risk and protective factors and early identification. *Criminal Behavior and Mental Health, 3,* 492-523.

Faw, L. (1999). The state wraparound survey. In B. J. Burns & S. K. Goldman (Eds.), *Promising practices in wraparound for children with serious emotional disturbances and their families: Systems of care* (pp. 61-65). Washington, DC: American Institutes for Research, Center for Effective Collaboration and Practice.

Fearn, N. E., Decker, S. H., & Curry, G. D. (2001). Public policy responses to gangs: Evaluating the outcomes. In J. Miller, C. L. Maxson, & M. W. Klein (Eds.), *The modern gang reader* (2nd ed., pp. 330-344). Los Angeles: Roxbury.

Federal Bureau of Investigation. (1992). *Uniform crime reports 1991.* Washington, DC: Author.

Federal Bureau of Investigation. (2000). *Uniform crime reports, 1999.* Washington, DC: Author.

Feely, K. (2000). *Pathways to juvenile detention reform: Vol. 2. Collaboration and leadership in detention reform.* Baltimore: Annie E. Casey Foundation.

Feinberg, M. E., Greenberg, M. T., & Osgood, D. W. (2001). *Readiness, functioning, and effectiveness in community prevention coalitions: A study of Communities That Care.* University Park: Pennsylvania State University, Prevention Research Center.

Feindler, E. L., Marriott, S. A., & Iwata, M. (1984). Group anger control training for junior high school delinquents. *Cognitive Therapy and Research, 8,* 299-311.

Feld, B. C. (1977). *Neutralizing inmate violence: Juvenile offenders in institutions.* Cambridge, MA: Ballinger.

Feld, B. C. (1993). Criminalizing the American juvenile court. In M. Tonry (Ed.), *Crime and justice: An annual review of research* (Vol. 17, pp. 197-280). Chicago: University of Chicago Press.

Feld, B. C. (1998a). Abolish the juvenile court: Youthfulness, criminal responsibility, and sentencing policy. *Journal of Criminal Law and Criminology, 88,* 68-136.

Feld, B. C. (1998b). Juvenile and criminal justice systems' responses to youth. In M. Tonry & M. H. Moore (Eds.), *Youth violence* (pp. 189-262). Chicago: University of Chicago Press.

Feld, B. C. (1999). The honest politician's guide to juvenile justice policy in the twenty-first century. *Annals of the American Academy of Political and Social Science, 564,* 10-27.

Feldman, R. A. (1992). The St. Louis experiment: Effective treatment of antisocial youths in prosocial peer groups. In J. McCord & R. E. Tremblay (Eds.), *Preventing antisocial behavior: Interventions from birth through adolescence* (pp. 233-252). New York: Guilford.

Fernandez, M. E. (1998, November 15). An urban myth sees the light again. *Washington Post,* p. B2.

Fessenden, F. (2000, April 8). Rampage killers: A statistical portrait. *New York Times.* Retrieved from http://www.nytimes.com/library/national/040900rampage-killers.html

Fields, G. (1999, July 21). Senate hearing takes up debate over police seizures of property. *USA Today,* p. 6A.

Fields, G. (2000, April 18). Police group wants national study of justice system. *USA Today,* p. 7A.

Fight Crime: Invest in Kids. (2002). *A school and youth violence prevention plan.* Washington, DC: Author. Retrieved from http://www.fight-crime.org

Finckenauer, J. O., & Gavin, P. W. (1999). *Scared straight: The panacea phenomenon revisited.* Prospect Heights, IL: Waveland.

Finestone, H. (1976). *Victims of change.* Westport, CT: Greenwood.

Finkelhor, D., & Dziuba-Leatherman, J. (1994). Victimization of children. *American Psychologist, 49,* 173-183.

Finn, P., & Healey, K. M. (1996). *Preventing gang- and drug-related witness intimidation.* Washington, DC: Office of Justice Programs, National Institute of Justice.

Fisher, M. (2002). *Youth courts: Young people delivering justice.* Chicago: American Bar Association.

Fishman, J. (1923). *Crucibles of crime.* New York: Cosmopolis.

Flaherty, M. (1983). The national incidence of juvenile suicides in adult jails and juvenile detention centers. *Suicide and Life-Threatening Behavior, 13,* 85-94.

Fleisher, M. S. (1995). *Beggars and thieves: Lives of urban street criminals.* Madison: University of Wisconsin Press.

Fleisher, M. S. (1998). *Dead end kids: Gang girls and the boys they know.* Madison: University of Wisconsin Press.

Fleisher, M. S. (2000). (Counter-)transference and compassion fatigue in urban gang ethnography. *Focaal, 36,* 77-96.

Fleisher, M. S. (2002). Doing field research on diverse gangs: Interpreting youth gangs as social networks. In C. R. Huff (Ed.), *Gangs in America* (3rd ed., pp. 199-217). Thousand Oaks, CA: Sage.

Fleisher, M. S., Decker, S., & Curry, G. D. (2001). An overview of the challenge of prison gangs. *Corrections Management Quarterly, 5*(1), 1-9.

Forst, M., Fagan, J., & Vivona, T. S. (1989). Youth in prisons and training schools: Perceptions and consequences of the treatment-custody dichotomy. *Juvenile and Family Court Journal, 39*(1), 1-14.

Foshee, V. A., Bauman, K. E., Arriaga, X. B., Helms, R. W., Koch, G. G., & Linder, G. F. (1998). An evaluation of Safe Dates, an adolescent dating violence prevention program. *American Journal of Public Health, 88,* 45-50.

Fox, J. A. (1996a, October 10). The calm before the crime wave storm. *Los Angeles Times,* p. B9.

Fox, J. A. (1996b). *Trends in juvenile violence: A report to the United States attorney general on current and future rates of juvenile offending.* Washington, DC: Bureau of Justice Statistics.

Fox, J. A., & Levin, J. (1994). *Overkill: Mass murder and serial killing exposed.* New York: Plenum.

Fox, S. J. (1970). Juvenile justice reform: A historical perspective. *Stanford Law Review, 22,* 1187-1239.

Fraser, M. W., Day, S. H., & Schwalbe, C. (2002). *Risk assessment in juvenile justice: The reliability and validity of a risk assessment instrument protocol.* Chapel Hill: University of North Carolina, Jordan Institute for Families.

Fremon, C. (1995). *Father Greg and the homeboys.* New York: Hyperion.

Friedman, R. M., & Burns, B. J. (1996). The evaluation of the Fort Bragg Demonstration Project: An alternative interpretation of the findings. *Journal of Mental Health Administration, 23,* 128-136.

Friedman, R. M., Katz-Leavy, J. W., Manderscheid, R. W., & Sondheimer, D. L. (1996). Prevalence of serious emotional disturbances in children and adolescents. In R. W. Manderscheid & M. A. Sonnerschein (Eds.), *Mental health, United States* (pp. 71-88). Washington, DC: U.S. Department of Health and Human Services, Substance Abuse and Mental Health Services Administration, Center for Mental Health Services.

Fritsch, E. T., Caeti, T. J., & Hemmens, C. (1996). Spare the needle but not the punishment: The incarceration of waived youth in Texas prisons. *Crime & Delinquency, 42,* 593-609.

Fritsch, E. J., Caeti, T. J., & Taylor, R. W. (1999). Gang suppression through saturation patrol, aggressive curfew, and truancy enforcement: A quasi-experimental test of the Dallas anti-gang initiative. *Crime & Delinquency, 45,* 122-139.

Fulton, B. A., Stone, S. B., & Gendreau, P. (1994). *Restructuring intensive supervision programs: Applying "what works."* Lexington, KY: American Probation and Parole Association.

Funk, S. (1999). Risk assessment for juveniles on probation: A focus on gender. *Criminal Justice and Behavior, 26,* 44-68.

Furfey, P. H. (1928). *The gang age.* New York: Macmillan.

Gaes, G. G., Flanagan, T. J., & Motiuk, L. L. (1999). Adult correctional treatment. In M. Tonry &

J. Petersilia (Eds.), *Prisons* (pp. 361-426). Chicago: University of Chicago Press.

Gaouette, N. (1997, September 15). Hope rises at Homeboy Bakeries in L.A. *Christian Science Monitor*, pp. 1-3.

Gardiner, G. S., & McKinney, R. N. (1991). The great American war on drugs: Another failure of tough-guy management. *Journal of Drug Issues, 21,* 605-616.

Garmezy, N. (1985). Stress-resistant children: The search for protective factors. In J. E. Stevenson (Ed.), *Recent research in developmental psychopathology* (pp. 213-233). New York: Pergamon.

Garofalo, J., Siegel, L., & Laub, J. H. (1987). School-related victimizations among adolescents: An analysis of National Crime Survey narratives. *Journal of Quantitative Criminology, 3,* 321-338.

Garrett, C. J. (1985). Effects of residential treatment on adjudicated delinquents: A meta-analysis. *Journal of Research in Crime and Delinquency, 22,* 287-308.

Geerken, M. J., & Hayes, H. D. (1993). Probation and parole: Public risk and the future of incarceration alternatives. *Criminology, 31,* 549-564.

Gendreau, P. (1981). Treatment in corrections: Martinson was wrong. *Canadian Psychology, 22,* 332-338.

Gendreau, P. (1996a). Offender rehabilitation: What we know and what needs to be done. *Criminal Justice and Behavior, 23,* 144-161.

Gendreau, P. (1996b). The principles of effective interventions with offenders. In A. T. Harland (Ed.), *Choosing correctional options that work* (pp. 117-130). Thousand Oaks, CA: Sage.

Gendreau, P., & Andrews, D. A. (1990). Tertiary prevention: What the meta-analyses of the offender treatment literature tells us about what works. *Canadian Journal of Criminology, 32,* 173-184.

Gendreau, P., & Andrews, D. (1994). *The Correctional Program Assessment Inventory* (5th ed.). Saint John: University of New Brunswick.

Gendreau, P., Cullen, F. T., & Bonta, J. (1994). Intensive rehabilitation supervision: The next generation in community corrections. *Federal Probation, 58*(1), 72-78.

Gendreau, P., & Goggin, C. (1996). Principles of effective correctional programming. *Forum on Correctional Research, 8,* 38-41.

Gendreau, P., & Goggin, C. (1997). Correctional treatment: Accomplishments and realities. In P. Van Voorhis, M. Braswell, & D. Lester (Eds.), *Correctional counseling and rehabilitation* (3rd ed., pp. 271-279). Cincinnati, OH: Anderson.

Gendreau, P., Goggin, C., & Paparozzi, M. (1996). Principles of effective assessment for community corrections. *Federal Probation, 60*(3), 64-77.

Gendreau, P., Little, T., & Goggin, C. (1996). A meta-analysis of the predictors of adult offender recidivism. *Criminology, 34,* 575-607.

Gendreau, P., & Ross, R. R. (1979). Effectiveness of correctional treatment: Bibliotherapy for cynics. *Crime & Delinquency, 25,* 463-489.

Gendreau, P., & Ross, R. R. (1987). Revivification of rehabilitation: Evidence from the 1980s. *Justice Quarterly, 4,* 349-407.

General Services Administration. (2001). *Catalog of federal domestic assistance.* Washington, DC: Author. Retrieved from http://www.cfda.gov

Geraghty, T. F. (1997). Justice for children: How do we get there? *Journal of Criminal Law and Criminology, 88,* 190-241.

Gerber, J., & Fritsch, E. (1995). Adult academic and vocational correctional education programs: A review of recent research. *Journal of Offender Rehabilitation, 22*(1-2), 119-142.

Gibbons, D. C. (1999). Changing lawbreakers: What have we learned since the 1950s? *Crime & Delinquency, 45,* 272-293.

Gibbs, J. C., Potter, G. B., & Barriga, A. (1996). Developing the helping skills and prosocial motivation of aggressive adolescents in peer group programs. *Aggression and Violent Behavior, 1,* 283-305.

Gilliard, D. K. (1999). *Prison and jail inmates at midyear 1998* (Bulletin). Washington, DC: Bureau of Justice Statistics.

Gilliard, D. K., & Beck, A. J. (1996). *Prison and jail inmates, 1995* (Bulletin). Washington, DC: Bureau of Justice Statistics.

Gilliland, E. M., Hanke, P. J., & Liedka, R. V. (1996). *Risk assessment and placement classification for juveniles in custody in New Mexico.* Albuquerque: University of New Mexico, Institute for Social Research.

Ginsberg, C., & Loffredo, L. (1993). Violence-related attitudes and behaviors of high school students: New York City. *Journal of High School Health, 63,* 438-439.

Girls Incorporated. (1996). *Prevention and parity: Girls in juvenile justice.* Indianapolis: Author.

Glass, G. V, McGaw, B., & Smith, M. L. (1981). *Meta-analysis in social research.* Beverly Hills, CA: Sage.

Glueck, S., & Glueck, E. (1950). *Unraveling juvenile delinquency.* New York: Commonwealth Fund.

Goldman, S. K. (1992). Ventura County, California. In B. A. Stroul, S. K. Goldman, I. Lourie, J. W. Katz-Leavy, & C. Zeigler-Dendy (Eds.), *Profiles of local systems of care for children and adolescents with severe emotional disturbances* (pp. 287-338). Washington, DC: Georgetown University Child Development Center, CASSP Technical Assistance Center.

Goldman, S. K. (1999). The conceptual framework for wraparound: Definition, values, essential elements, and requirements for practice. In B. J. Burns & S. K. Goldman (Eds.), *Promising practices in wraparound for children with serious emotional disturbances and their families: Systems of care* (pp. 9-16). Washington, DC: American Institutes for Research, Center for Effective Collaboration and Practice.

Goldman, S. K., & Faw, L. (1999). Three wraparound models as promising approaches. In B. J. Burns & S. K. Goldman (Eds.), *Promising practices in wraparound for children with serious emotional disturbances and their families: Systems of care* (pp. 17-59). Washington, DC: American Institutes for Research, Center for Effective Collaboration and Practice.

Goldstein, A. P. (1993). Interpersonal skills training interventions. In A. P. Goldstein & C. R. Huff (Eds.), *The gang intervention handbook* (pp. 87-157). Champaign, IL: Research Press.

Goldstein, A. P., & Glick, B. (1994). *The prosocial gang: Implementing aggression replacement training.* Thousand Oaks, CA: Sage.

Goldstein, A. P., Glick, B., & Gibbs, J. C. (1998). *Aggression replacement training: A comprehensive intervention for aggressive youth* (Rev. ed.). Champaign, IL: Research Press.

Goldstein, H. (1979). Improving policing: A problem-oriented approach. *Crime & Delinquency, 25,* 236-258.

Goldstein, H. (1990). *Problem-oriented policing.* New York: McGraw-Hill.

Goodwin, T. M. (2000). *National Youth Court guidelines.* Lexington, KY: American Probation and Parole Association, National Youth Court Center.

Goodwin, T. M., Steinhart, D., & Fulton, B. (1996). *Peer justice and youth empowerment: An implementation guide for teen court programs.* Washington, DC: National Highway Traffic Safety Administration and Office of Juvenile Justice and Delinquency Prevention.

Gorman-Smith, D., & Tolan, P. (1998). The role of exposure to community violence and developmental problems among inner-city youth. *Developmental Psychopathology, 10,* 101-116.

Gottfredson, D. C. (1986). An empirical test of school-based environmental and individual interventions to reduce the risk of delinquent behavior. *Criminology, 24,* 705-731.

Gottfredson, D. C. (1990). Changing school structures to benefit high-risk youths. In P. E. Leone (Ed.), *Understanding troubled and troubling youth* (pp. 246-271). Newbury Park, CA: Sage.

Gottfredson, D. C. (1997). School-based crime prevention. In L. W. Sherman, D. C. Gottfredson, D. L. MacKenzie, J. Eck, P. Reuter, & S. Bushway (Eds.), *Preventing crime: What works, what*

doesn't, what's promising (pp. 5.1-5.71). Washington, DC: National Institute of Justice.

Gottfredson, D. C. (2001). *Schools and delinquency.* New York: Cambridge University Press.

Gottfredson, D. C., & Barton, W. (1997). *Closing institutions for juvenile offenders: The Maryland experience.* Lewiston, NY: Edwin Mellin.

Gottfredson, D. C., & Exum, M. L. (2002). The Baltimore city drug treatment court: One-year results from a randomized study. *Journal of Research in Crime and Delinquency, 39,* 337-356.

Gottfredson, D. C., & Gottfredson, G. D. (2002). Quality of school-based prevention programs. *Journal of Research in Crime and Delinquency, 39,* 3-35.

Gottfredson, D. C., Gottfredson, G. D., & Hybl, L. G. (1993). Managing adolescent behavior: A multiyear, multischool study. *American Educational Research Journal, 30,* 179-215.

Gottfredson, D. C., Wilson, D. B., & Najaka, S. S. (2002). School-based crime prevention. In L. W. Sherman, D. P. Farrington, B. C. Welsh, & D. L. MacKenzie (Eds.), *Evidence-based crime prevention* (pp. 56-164). London: Routledge.

Gottfredson, G. D. (1981). Schooling and delinquency. In S. E. Martin, L. B. Sechrest, & R. Redner (Eds.), *New directions in the rehabilitation of criminal offenders* (pp. 424-469). Washington, DC: National Academy Press.

Gottfredson, G. D. (1987). Peer group interventions to reduce the risk of delinquent behavior: A selective review and a new evaluation. *Criminology, 25,* 671-714.

Gottfredson, G. D., & Gottfredson, D. C. (2001). *Gang problems and gang programs in a national sample of schools.* Ellicott City, MD: Gottfredson Associates.

Gottfredson, G. D., Gottfredson, D. C., Czeh, E. R., Cantor, D., Crosse, S., & Hantman, I. (2000). *The National Study of Delinquency Prevention in Schools: Final report.* Ellicott City, MD: Gottfredson Associates

Gottfredson, M. R. (1979). Treatment destruction techniques. *Journal of Research in Crime and Delinquency, 16,* 39-54.

Gover, A. R., MacKenzie, D. L., & Armstrong, G. S. (2000). Importation and deprivation explanations of juveniles' adjustment to correctional facilities. *International Journal of Offender Therapy and Comparative Criminology, 44,* 450-467.

Gramckow, H. P., & Tompkins, E. (1999). *Enabling prosecutors to address drug, gang, and youth violence* (JAIBG Bulletin). Washington, DC: Office of Juvenile Justice and Delinquency Prevention.

Green, M. (1999). *The appropriate and effective use of security technologies in U.S. schools: A guide for schools and law enforcement agencies.* Washington, DC: National Institute of Justice.

Greenbaum, P. E., Dedrick, R. F., Friedman, R. M., Kutash, K., Brown, E. C., Larieri, S. P., et al. (1996). National Adolescent and Child Treatment Study (NACTS): Outcomes for children with serious emotional and behavioral disturbance. *Journal of Emotional and Behavioral Disorders, 4*(3), 130-146.

Greenberg, M. T., & Kusche, C. A. (1993). *Promoting social and emotional development in deaf children: The PATHS project.* Seattle: University of Washington Press.

Greene, J. A. (1999). Zero tolerance: A case study of police policies and practices in New York City. *Crime & Delinquency, 45,* 171-187.

Greenwood, P. W., Model, K. E., Rydell, C. P., & Chiesa, J. (1996). *Diverting children from a life of crime: Measuring costs and benefits.* Santa Monica, CA: RAND.

Griffin, P. (1999). Juvenile probation in the schools. *NCJJ in Focus, 1*(1), 1-10.

Griffin, P., Torbet, P. M., & Szymanski, L. (1998). *Trying juveniles as adults in criminal court: An analysis of state transfer provisions.* Washington, DC: Office of Juvenile Justice and Delinquency Prevention.

Grisso, T. (1996). Society's retributive response to juvenile violence: A developmental perspective. *Law and Human Behavior, 20,* 229-247.

Grisso, T., Barnum, R., Fletcher, K. E., Cauffman, E., & Peuschold, D. (2001). Massachusetts Youth Screening Instrument for mental health needs of juvenile justice youths. *Journal of the American Academy of Child and Adolescent Psychiatry, 40,* 541-548.

Grisso, T., & Schwartz, R. G. (Eds.). (2000). *Youth on trial: A developmental perspective on juvenile justice.* Chicago: University of Chicago Press.

Grossman, D. C., Neckerman, H. J., Koepsell, T. D., Asher, K., Liu, P. Y., Beland, K. N., et al. (1997). A randomized controlled trial of a violence prevention curriculum among elementary school children. *Journal of the American Medical Association, 277,* 1605-1611.

Grossman, J. B., & Garry, E. M. (1997). *Mentoring: A proven delinquency prevention strategy* (Juvenile Justice Bulletin). Washington, DC: Office of Juvenile Justice and Delinquency Prevention.

Grove, W. M., Eckert, E. D., Heston, L., Bouchard, T. J., Segal, N., & Lykken, D. T. (1990). *Clinical vs. mechanical prediction: A meta-analysis.* Unpublished manuscript, University of Minnesota, Department of Psychology.

Grove, W. M., & Meehl, P. E. (1996). Comparative efficiency of informal (subjective, impressionistic) and formal (mechanical, algorithmic) prediction procedures: The clinical-statistical controversy. *Psychology, Public Policy, and Law, 2,* 293-323.

Guarino-Ghezzi, S., & Loughran, E. J. (1996). *Balancing juvenile justice.* New Brunswick, NJ: Transaction.

Guest, T., & Pope, V. (1996, March 25). Crime time bomb. *U.S. News & World Report,* pp. 29-36.

Gugliotta, G., & Leen, J. (1989). *Kings of cocaine.* New York: Simon & Schuster.

Haapanen, R. A. (1990). *Selective incapacitation and the serious offender: A longitudinal study of criminal career patterns.* New York: Springer-Verlag.

Haapanen, R. A., & Britton, L. (2002). Drug testing for youthful offenders on parole: An experimental evaluation. *Criminology and Public Policy, 1,* 217-243.

Hagan, J., & Foster, H. (2000). Making corporate and criminal America less violent: Public norms and structural reforms. *Contemporary Sociology, 29*(1), 44-53.

Hagan, J., & McCarthy, B. (1997). *Mean streets: Youth crime and homelessness.* Cambridge: Cambridge University Press.

Hagedorn, J. M. (1988). *People and folks: Gangs, crime and the underclass in a rustbelt city.* Chicago: Lakeview.

Hagedorn, J. M. (1994). Homeboys, dope fiends, legits, and new jacks. *Criminology, 32,* 197-217.

Haggard, U., Gumpert, C. H., & Grann, M. (2001). Against all odds: A qualitative follow-up study of high-risk violent offenders who were not reconvicted. *Journal of Interpersonal Violence, 16,* 1048-1065.

Hahn, A., Leavitt, T., & Aaron, P. (1994). *Evaluation of the Quantum Opportunities Program (QOP): Did the program work?* Unpublished manuscript, Brandeis University, Heller Graduate School.

Hammer, H., Finkelhor, D., & Sedlak, A. (2002). *Runaway/thrownaway children: National estimates and characteristics.* Washington, DC: Office of Juvenile Justice and Delinquency Prevention.

Hamparian, D. M. (1987). Violent juvenile offenders. In F. X. Hartmann (Ed.), *From children to citizens: Vol. 2. The role of the juvenile court* (pp. 128-142). New York: Springer-Verlag.

Hamparian, D. M., Davis, J. M., Jacobson, J. M., & McGraw, R. F. (1985). *The young criminal years of the violent few.* Washington, DC: U.S. Department of Justice.

Hamparian, D. M., Schuster, R., Dinitz, S., & Conrad, J. P. (1978). *The violent few: A study of dangerous juvenile offenders.* Lexington, MA: Lexington.

Hannson, K. (1998, February). *Functional Family Therapy replication in Sweden: Treatment outcome with juvenile delinquents.* Paper presented at the Eighth International Conference on Treating Addictive Behaviors. Santa Fe, NM.

Harachi, T. W., Abbott, R. D., Catalano, R. F., & Haggerty, K. P. (1996). *The effects of risk and protective factors on antisocial behavior and academic success in the early primary grades.* Paper presented at the meeting of the Life History Research Society, London.

Harrell, A. (1996). *Intervening with high-risk youth: Preliminary findings from the Children-at-Risk program* (Research Preview). Washington, DC: National Institute of Justice.

Harrell, A., Cavanagh, S., & Sridharan, S. (1999). *Evaluation of the Children-at-Risk program: Results 1 year after the end of the program* (Research in Brief). Washington, DC: National Institute of Justice.

Harries, K., & Cheatwood, D. (1997). *The geography of execution: The capital punishment quagmire in America.* Lanham, MD: Rowman & Littlefield.

Harris, G. T., Rice, M. E., & Quinsey, V. L. (1998). Appraisal and management of risk in sexual aggressors: Implications for criminal justice policy. *Psychology, Public Policy, and Law, 4,* 73-115.

Harrison, P., Maupin, J. R., & Mays, G. L. (2000). Are teen courts an answer to our juvenile delinquency problems? *Juvenile and Family Court Journal, 51*(4), 27-33.

Hawkins, D. F. (Ed.). (1995). *Ethnicity, race, and crime: Perspectives across time and place.* Albany: State University of New York Press.

Hawkins, D. F., Laub, J. H., & Lauritsen, J. L. (1998). Race, ethnicity, and serious juvenile offending. In R. Loeber & D. P. Farrington (Eds.), *Serious and violent juvenile offenders: Risk factors and successful interventions* (pp. 30-46). Thousand Oaks, CA: Sage.

Hawkins, J. D. (1995, August). Controlling crime before it happens: Risk-focused prevention. *National Institute of Justice Journal, 229,* 10-12.

Hawkins, J. D. (Ed.). (1996). *Delinquency and crime: Current theories.* New York: Cambridge University Press.

Hawkins, J. D. (1999). Preventing crime and violence through Communities That Care. *European Journal on Crime Policy and Research, 7,* 443-458.

Hawkins, J. D., Arthur, M. W., & Catalano, R. F. (1995). Preventing substance abuse. In M. Tonry & D. P. Farrington (Eds.), *Building a safer society: Strategic approaches to crime prevention* (pp. 343-428). Chicago: University of Chicago Press.

Hawkins, J. D., & Catalano, R. F. (1993). *Risk-focused prevention using the social development strategy.* Seattle: Developmental Research and Programs, Inc.

Hawkins, J. D., Catalano, R. F., & Associates. (1992). *Communities That Care.* San Francisco: Jossey-Bass.

Hawkins, J. D., Catalano, R. F., & Brewer, D. D. (1995). Preventing serious, violent, and chronic juvenile offending: Effective strategies from conception to age 6. In J. C. Howell, B. Krisberg, J. D. Hawkins, & J. J. Wilson (Eds.), *A sourcebook: Serious, violent, and chronic juvenile offenders* (pp. 47-60). Thousand Oaks, CA: Sage.

Hawkins, J. D., Catalano, R. F., Kosterman, R., Abbott, R. D., & Hill, K. G. (1999). Preventing adolescent health-risk behavior by strengthening protection during childhood. *Archives of Pediatrics and Adolescent Medicine, 153,* 226-234.

Hawkins, J. D., Catalano, R. F., & Miller, J. Y. (1992). Risk and protective factors for alcohol and other drug problems in adolescence and early adulthood: Implications for substance abuse prevention. *Psychological Bulletin, 112,* 64-105.

Hawkins, J. D., Doueck, H. J., & Lishner, D. M. (1988). Changing teaching practices in mainstream classrooms to improve bonding and behavior in low achievers. *American Educational Research Journal, 25,* 31-50.

Hawkins, J. D., Farrington, D. P., & Catalano, R. F. (1999). Reducing violence through the schools. In D. S. Elliot, B. A. Hamberg, & K. R. Williams (Eds.). *Violence in American schools: A new perspective* (pp. 188-216). New York: Cambridge University Press.

Hawkins, J. D., Herrenkohl, T. I., Farrington, D. P., Brewer, D. D., Catalano, R. F., & Harachi, T. W. (1998). A review of predictors of youth violence. In R. Loeber & D. P. Farrington (Eds.), *Serious and violent juvenile offenders: Risk factors and successful interventions* (pp. 106-146). Thousand Oaks, CA: Sage.

Hawkins, J. D., Herrenkohl, T. I., Farrington, D. P., Brewer, D. D., Catalano, R. F., Harachi, T. W., et al. (2000). *Predictors of youth violence* (Juvenile Justice Bulletin). Washington, DC: Office of Juvenile Justice and Delinquency Prevention.

Hawkins, J. D., Hill, K. G., Battin-Pearson, S. R., & Abbott, R. D. (2000). *Long term effects of the Seattle Social Development Intervention on school bonding trajectories.* Seattle: University of Washington, Social Development Research Group.

Hawkins, J. D., & Lishner, D. M. (1987). Schooling and delinquency. In E. H. Johnson (Ed.), *Handbook on crime and delinquency prevention* (pp. 179-221). New York: Greenwood.

Hawkins, J. D., Von Cleve, E., & Catalano, R. F. (1991). Reducing early childhood aggression: Results of a primary prevention program.

Journal of the American Academy of Child and Adolescent Psychiatry, 30, 208-217.

Hawkins, J. D., & Weis, J. G. (1985). The social development model: An integrated approach to delinquency prevention. *Journal of Primary Prevention, 6,* 73-97.

Hayeslip, D. W., Jr. (1989). *Local-level drug enforcement: New strategies* (Research in Action No. 213). Washington, DC: National Institute of Justice.

Hemmens, C., Fritsch, E., & Caeti, T. (1997). Juvenile justice code purpose clauses: The power of words. *Criminal Justice Policy Review, 8,* 221-246.

Henggeler, S. W. (1997a). The development of effective drug abuse services for youth. In J. A. Egertson, D. M. Fox, & A. I. Leshner (Eds.), *Treating drug abusers effectively* (pp. 253-279). New York: Basil Blackwell.

Henggeler, S. W. (1997b). *Treating serious antisocial behavior in youth: The MST approach* (Juvenile Justice Bulletin). Washington, DC: Office of Juvenile Justice and Delinquency Prevention.

Henggeler, S. W. (1999). Multisystemic Therapy: An overview of clinical procedures, outcomes, and policy implications. *Child Psychology and Psychiatry Review, 4,* 2-10.

Henggeler, S. W., Cunningham, P. B., Pickrel, S. G., Schoenwald, S. K., & Brondino, M. J. (1996). Multisystemic Therapy: An effective violence prevention approach for serious juvenile offenders. *Journal of Adolescence, 19,* 47-61.

Henggeler, S. W., Melton, G. B., & Smith, L. A. (1992). Family preservation using multisystem therapy: An effective alternative to incarcerating serious juvenile offenders. *Journal of Consulting and Clinical Psychology, 60,* 953-961.

Henggeler, S. W., Melton, G. B., Smith, L. A., Schoenwald, S. K., & Hanley, J. H. (1993). Family preservation using multisystem treatment: Long-term follow-up to a clinical trial with serious juvenile offenders. *Journal of Child and Family Studies, 2,* 283-293.

Henggeler, S. W., Pickrel, S. G., & Brondino, M. J. (1999). Multisystemic treatment of substance abusing and dependent delinquents: Outcomes, treatment fidelity, and transportability. *Mental Health Services Research, 1,* 171-184.

Henggeler, S. W., Rowland, M. D., Randall, J., Ward, D. M., Pickrel, S. G., Cunningham, P. B., et al. (1999). Home based Multisystemic Therapy as an alternative to the hospitalization of youths in psychiatric crisis: Clinical outcomes. *Journal of the American Academy of Child and Adolescent Psychiatry, 38,* 1331-1339.

Henggeler, S. W., & Schoenwald, S. K. (1994). Boot camps for juvenile offenders: Just say "no." *Journal of Child and Family Studies, 3,* 243-248.

Henggeler, S. W., Schoenwald, S. K., Borduin, C. M., Rowland, M. D., & Cunningham, P. B. (1998). *Multisystemic treatment of antisocial behavior in children and adolescents.* New York: Guilford.

Hennepin County Attorney's Office. (1995). *Delinquents Under 10 in Hennepin County: A statistical analysis and practices and experiences of police jurisdiction.* Minneapolis: Author.

Hennepin County Attorney's Office. (1998). *Delinquents Under 10 in Hennepin County: A research update and program progress report.* Minneapolis: Author.

Herman, S. (1999). Challenges facing restorative justice. *Net Works, 14*(1), 1-3.

Herrenkohl, T. I., Hawkins, J. D., Chung, I., Hill, K. G., & Battin-Pearson, S. R. (2001). School and community risk factors and interventions. In R. Loeber & D. P. Farrington (Eds.), *Child delinquents: Development, intervention, and service needs* (pp. 211-246). Thousand Oaks, CA: Sage.

Herrenkohl, T. I., Huang, B., Kosterman, R., Hawkins, J. D., Catalano, R. F., & Smith, B. (2001). A comparison of social development processes leading to violent behavior in late adolescence for childhood initiators and adolescent initiators of violence. *Journal of Research on Crime and Delinquency, 38,* 45-63.

Heward, M. E. (2002). The organization and operation of teen courts in the United States: A comparative analysis of legislation. *Juvenile and Family Court Journal, 53*(1), 19-35.

Higgins, D., & Coldren, J. D. (2000). *Evaluating gang and drug house abatement in Chicago.* Chicago: Illinois Criminal Justice Information Authority.

Hill, K. G., Hawkins, J. D., Catalano, R. F., Kosterman, R., Abbott, R. D., & Edwards, T. (1996, November). *The longitudinal dynamics of gang membership and problem behavior: A replication and extension of the Denver and Rochester gang studies in Seattle.* Paper presented at the annual meeting of the American Criminological Society, Chicago.

Hill, K. G., Howell, J. C., Hawkins, J. D., & Battin-Pearson, S. R. (1999). Childhood risk factors for adolescent gang membership: Results from the Seattle Social Development Project. *Journal of Research in Crime and Delinquency, 36,* 300-322.

Hill, K. G., Howell, J. C., Hawkins, J. D., Catalano, R. F., Maguin, E., & Kosterman, R. (1995, November). *The role of gang membership in delinquency, substance abuse, and violent offending.* Paper presented at the annual meeting of the American Society of Criminology, Boston.

Hipwell, A. E., Loeber, R., Stouthamer-Loeber, M., Keenan, K., White, H. R., & Kroneman, L. (2002). Characteristics of girls with early onset of disruptive and antisocial behavior. *Criminal Behavior and Mental Health, 12,* 99-118.

Hirota, J. M. (1994a). *Children at risk: Profiles of a program at one year.* New York: Columbia University, National Center on Addiction and Substance Abuse.

Hirota, J. M. (1994b). *Children at risk: The second year.* New York: Columbia University, National Center on Addiction and Substance Abuse.

Hirschi, T. (1969). *Causes of delinquency.* Beverly Hills, CA: Sage.

Holsinger, A. M., & Latessa, E. J. (1999). An empirical evaluation of a sanction continuum: Pathways through the juvenile justice system. *Journal of Criminal Justice, 27,* 155-172.

Holt, N. (1997). *A new risk assessment model for parolees: Combining risk and stakes.* Sacramento: California Department of Corrections.

Horowitz, R. (1983). *Honor and the American dream: Culture and identity in a Chicano community.* New Brunswick, NJ: Rutgers University Press.

Horowitz, R. (1990). Sociological perspectives on gangs: Conflicting definitions and concepts. In C. R. Huff (Ed.), *Gangs in America* (pp. 37-54). Newbury Park, CA: Sage.

Howell, J. C. (Ed.). (1995). *Guide for implementing the Comprehensive Strategy for Serious, Violent, and Chronic Juvenile Offenders.* Washington, DC: Office of Juvenile Justice and Delinquency Prevention.

Howell, J. C. (1996). Juvenile transfers to the criminal justice system: State-of-the-art. *Law and Policy, 18,* 17-60.

Howell, J. C. (1997). *Juvenile justice and youth violence.* Thousand Oaks, CA: Sage.

Howell, J. C. (1998a, February-March). Abolish the juvenile court? Nonsense! *Juvenile Justice Update,* pp. 1-2, 10-13.

Howell, J. C. (1998b). Promising programs for youth gang violence prevention and intervention. In R. Loeber & D. P. Farrington (Eds.), *Serious and violent juvenile offenders: Risk factors and successful interventions* (pp. 284-312). Thousand Oaks, CA: Sage.

Howell, J. C. (1998c, March-April). Superpredators and the prophets of doom. *Youth Today,* p. 50.

Howell, J. C. (1998d). *Youth gangs: An overview* (Juvenile Justice Bulletin, Youth Gang Series). Washington, DC: Office of Juvenile Justice and Delinquency Prevention.

Howell, J. C. (1999). Youth gang homicides: A literature review. *Crime & Delinquency, 45,* 208-241.

Howell, J. C. (2000). *Youth gang programs and strategies.* Washington, DC: Office of Juvenile Justice and Delinquency Prevention.

Howell, J. C. (2001a). Juvenile justice programs and strategies. In R. Loeber & D. P. Farrington (Eds.), *Child delinquents: Development, intervention, and service needs* (pp. 305-322). Thousand Oaks, CA: Sage.

Howell, J. C. (2001b). Risk-needs assessments and screening devices. In R. Loeber & D. P. Farrington (Eds.), *Child delinquents: Development, intervention, and service needs* (pp. 395-404). Thousand Oaks, CA: Sage.

Howell, J. C. (2003). Youth gangs: Prevention and intervention. In P. Allen-Meares & M. W. Fraser (Eds.), *Intervention with children and adolescents: An interdisciplinary perspective* (pp. 493-514). Boston: Allyn & Bacon.

Howell, J. C., Curry, G. D., Pontius, M., & Roush, D. W. (2003). *National survey of youth gang problems in juvenile detention facilities.* East Lansing: Michigan State University, National Juvenile Detention Association, Center for Research and Professional Development.

Howell, J. C., & Decker, S. H. (1999). *The youth gangs, drugs, and violence connection* (Juvenile Justice Bulletin, Youth Gang Series). Washington, DC: Office of Juvenile Justice and Delinquency Prevention.

Howell, J. C., Egley, A., Jr., & Gleason, D. K. (2000, November). *Youth gangs: Definitions and the age-old issue.* Paper presented at the annual meeting of the American Society of Criminology, San Francisco.

Howell, J. C., Egley, A., Jr., & Gleason, D. K. (2002). *Modern day youth gangs* (Juvenile Justice Bulletin, Youth Gang Series). Washington, DC: Office of Juvenile Justice and Delinquency Prevention.

Howell, J. C., & Gleason, D. K. (1999). *Youth gang drug trafficking* (Juvenile Justice Bulletin, Youth Gang Series). Washington, DC: Office of Juvenile Justice and Delinquency Prevention.

Howell, J. C., & Hawkins, J. D. (1998). Prevention of youth violence. In M. Tonry & M. Moore (Eds.), *Youth violence* (pp. 263-315). Chicago: University of Chicago Press.

Howell, J. C., Hill, K. G., Battin, S. R., & Hawkins, J. D. (1996, November). *Youth gang involvement in drug trafficking and violent crime in Seattle.* Paper presented at the annual meeting of the American Society of Criminology, Chicago.

Howell, J. C., & Krisberg, B. (1998). Introduction. In J. C. Howell & B. Krisberg (Eds.), Juveniles in custody [Special issue]. *Crime & Delinquency, 44,* 483-488.

Howell, J. C., Krisberg, B., Hawkins, J. D., & Wilson, J. J. (Eds.). (1995). *A sourcebook: Serious, violent, and chronic juvenile offenders.* Thousand Oaks, CA: Sage.

Howell, J. C., & Lynch, J. (2000). *Youth gangs in schools* (Juvenile Justice Bulletin, Youth Gang Series). Washington, DC: Office of Juvenile Justice and Delinquency Prevention.

Howell, J. C., Moore, J. P., & Egley, A., Jr. (2002). The changing boundaries of youth gangs. In C. R. Huff (Ed.), *Gangs in America* (3rd ed., pp. 3-18). Thousand Oaks, CA: Sage.

Howell, M. Q. (2002). *Case study of a western North Carolina juvenile court.* Unpublished manuscript, University of North Carolina–Charlotte, Department of Criminal Justice.

Hoyt, D. R., Ryan, K. D., & Cauce, A. M. (1999). Personal victimization in a high-risk environment: Homeless and runaway adolescents. *Journal of Research in Crime and Delinquency, 36,* 371-392.

Hser, Y., Grella, C. E., Hubbard, R. L., Hseih, S., Fletcher, B. W., Brown, B. S., et al. (2001). An evaluation of drug treatments for adolescents in 4 US cities. *Archives of General Psychiatry, 58,* 689-695.

Hsia, H. M., & Beyer, M. (2000). *System change through state challenge activities: Approaches and products* (Juvenile Justice Bulletin). Washington, DC: Office of Juvenile Justice and Delinquency Prevention.

Huang, B., Kosterman, R., Catalano, R. F., Hawkins, J. D., & Abbott, R. D. (2001). Modeling mediation in the etiology of violent behavior in adolescence: A test of the Seattle social development model. *Criminology, 39,* 75-108.

Huesmann, L. R., & Miller, L. S. (1994). Long-term effects of repeated exposure to media violence in childhood. In L. R. Huesmann (Ed.), *Aggressive behavior: Current perspectives* (pp. 153-186). New York: Plenum.

Huff, C. R. (1996). The criminal behavior of gang members and non-gang at-risk youth. In C. R. Huff (Ed.), *Gangs in America* (2nd ed., pp. 75-102). Thousand Oaks, CA: Sage.

Huff, C. R. (1998). *Comparing the criminal behavior of youth gangs and at-risk youth* (Research in Brief). Washington, DC: National Institute of Justice.

Huff, C. R., & Shafer, K. H. (2002). Gangs and community-oriented policing: Transforming organizational culture. In C. R. Huff (Ed.), *Gangs in America* (3rd ed., pp. 131-146). Thousand Oaks, CA: Sage.

Hughes, R. H., & Dukes, R. L. (1997). The effects of gang membership on deviance in two populations: Secondary school students and adolescent serious habitual offenders. *Free Inquiry in Creative Sociology, 25*(1), 97-107.

Hughes, S. P., & Schneider, A. L. (1989). Victim-offender mediation: A survey of program characteristics and perceptions of effectiveness. *Crime & Delinquency, 35,* 217-233.

Hui, T. K. (2001, December 13). Suspended student on track for January graduation. *News and Observer* (Raleigh, NC), p. 3B.

Huizinga, D. (1995). Developmental sequences in delinquency. In L. Crockett & N. Crowder (Eds.), *Pathways through adolescence: Individual development in context* (pp. 15-34). Mahwah, NJ: Lawrence Erlbaum.

Huizinga, D. (1997). *Gangs and the volume of crime.* Paper presented at the annual meeting of the Western Society of Criminology.

Huizinga, D., & Elliott, D. S. (1987). Juvenile offenders: Prevalence, offender incidence, and arrest rates by race. *Crime & Delinquency, 33,* 206-223.

Huizinga, D., Esbensen, F., & Weiher, A. W. (1991). Are there multiple paths to delinquency? *Journal of Criminal Law and Criminology, 82,* 83-118.

Huizinga, D., Esbensen, F., & Weiher, A. W. (1996). The impact of arrest on subsequent delinquent behavior. In R. Loeber, D. Huizinga, & T. P. Thornberry (Eds.), *Program of Research on the Causes and Correlates of Delinquency: Annual report 1995-1996* (pp. 82-101). Washington, DC: Office of Juvenile Justice and Delinquency Prevention.

Huizinga, D., & Jakob-Chien, C. (1998). The contemporaneous co-occurrence of serious and violent offending and other problem behavior. In R. Loeber & D. P. Farrington (Eds.), *Serious and violent juvenile offenders: Risk factors and successful interventions* (pp. 46-67). Thousand Oaks, CA: Sage.

Huizinga, D., Loeber, R., & Thornberry, T. P. (1994). *Urban delinquency and substance abuse: Initial findings report.* Washington, DC: Office of Juvenile Justice and Delinquency Prevention.

Huizinga, D., Loeber, R., & Thornberry, T. P. (1995). *Recent findings from the Program of Research on Causes and Correlates of Delinquency.* Washington, DC: Office of Juvenile Justice and Delinquency Prevention.

Huizinga, D., Loeber, R., Thornberry, T. P., & Cothern, L. (2000). *Co-occurrence of delinquency and other problem behaviors* (Juvenile Justice Bulletin). Washington, DC: Office of Juvenile Justice and Delinquency Prevention.

Huizinga, D., & Schumann, K. F. (2001). Gang membership in Bremen and Denver: Comparative longitudinal data. In M. W. Klein, H.-J. Kerner, C. L. Maxson, & E. G. M. Weitekamp (Eds.), *The Eurogang paradox: Street gangs and youth groups in the U.S. and Europe* (pp. 231-246). Amsterdam: Kluwer.

Human Rights Watch. (1995). *Children in confinement in Louisiana.* New York: Author.

Human Rights Watch. (1996a). *All too familiar: Sexual abuse of women in U.S. state prisons.* New York: Author.

Human Rights Watch. (1996b). *Modern capital of human rights? Abuses in the state of Georgia.* New York: Author.

Human Rights Watch. (1997a). *Cold storage: Super-maximum security confinement in Indiana.* New York: Author.

Human Rights Watch. (1997b). *High country lockup: Children in confinement.* New York: Author.

Human Rights Watch. (1999). *No minor matter: Children in Maryland's jails.* New York: Author.

Human Rights Watch. (2000a). *Out of sight: Super-maximum security confinement in the United States.* New York: Author.

Human Rights Watch. (2000b). *United States—Punishment and prejudice: Racial disparities in the war on drugs.* New York: Author.

Human Rights Watch. (2001a, January 18). *Bush urged to promote human rights* (Press release). New York: Author. Retrieved from http://www. hrw.org/press/2001/01/bush0117.htm

Human Rights Watch. (2001b). *No escape: Male rape in U.S. prisons.* New York: Author.

Human Rights Watch. (2002a, May 24). *United States: Spare Texas juvenile offender* (Press release). New York: Author. Retrieved from http://www.hrw.org/press/2002/05/ death-pen.htm

Human Rights Watch. (2002b). *World report 2002.* New York: Author. Retrieved from http://www.hrw.org/wr2k2/children.html

Humes, E. (1996). *No matter how loud I shout: A year in the life of juvenile court.* New York: Touchstone.

Hunzeker, D. (1995, May). Juvenile crime, grown up time. *State Legislatures,* pp. 15-19.

Hutson, H. R., Anglin, D., Kyriacou, D. N., Hart, J., & Spears, K. (1995). The epidemic of gang-related homicides in Los Angeles County from 1979 through 1994. *Journal of the American Medical Association, 274,* 1031-1036.

Hutzler, J. (1982). Cannon to the left, cannon to the right: Can the juvenile court survive? *Today's Delinquent, 1,* 25-38.

Illick, J. E. (1974). *Child-rearing in seventeenth-century England and America.* New York: Psychohistory.

Illinois Criminal Justice Information Authority. (1999). Reducing youth gang violence in urban areas: One community's effort. *On Good Authority, 2*(5), 1-4.

Inciardi, J. A. (1986). *The war on drugs: Heroin, cocaine, crime, and public policy.* Palo Alto, CA: Mayfield.

Inciardi, J. A. (1990). The crack-violence connection within a population of hard-core adolescent offenders. In M. E. De La Rosa, E. Y. Lambert, & B. Gropper (Eds.), *Drugs and violence: Causes, correlates, and consequences* (NIDA Research Monograph No. 103, pp. 92-111). Rockville, MD: National Institute on Drug Abuse.

Inciardi, J. A., & Pottieger, A. E. (1991). Kids, crack, and crime. *Journal of Drug Issues, 21,* 257-270.

Institute of Medicine. (1990). *A study of the evolution, effectiveness, and financing of public and private drug treatment systems.* Washington, DC: National Academy Press.

Institute of Medicine. (1994). *Reducing risks for mental disorders: Frontier for preventive intervention research.* Washington, DC: National Academy Press.

International Association of Chiefs of Police. (2000). *A measured response to crime: IACP's call for a national commission.* Alexandria, VA: Author.

Ireland, T. O., Smith, C. A., & Thornberry, T. P. (2002). Developmental issues in the impact of child maltreatment on later delinquency and drug use. *Criminology, 40,* 359-400.

Jackson, P. G., & Rudman, C. (1993). Moral panic and the response to gangs in California. In S. Cummings & D. J. Monti (Eds.), *Gangs: The origins and impact of contemporary youth gangs in the United States* (pp. 257-275). Albany: State University of New York Press.

Jacobs, J. B. (1977). *Stateville: The penitentiary in mass society.* Chicago: University of Chicago Press.

Jacobs, R. (2001). *Race, media and the crisis of civil society: From Watts to Rodney King.* New York: Cambridge University Press.

Jang, S. J., & Johnson, B. R. (2001). Neighborhood disorder, individual religiosity, and adolescent use of illicit drugs: A test of multilevel hypotheses. *Criminology, 39,* 109-144.

Jang, S. J., & Smith, C. A. (1997). A test of reciprocal causal relationships among parental supervision, affective ties, and delinquency. *Journal of Research in Crime and Delinquency, 34,* 307-336.

Jensen, E. L., & Metsger, L. K. (1994). A test of the deterrent effect of legislative waiver on violent juvenile crime. *Crime & Delinquency, 40,* 96-104.

Jenson, J., Hartman, H., & Smith, J. (1997). *Evaluation of Iowa's juvenile crime prevention community grant fund program.* Iowa City: University of Iowa, School of Social Work.

Jessness, C. F., Allison, F. S., McCormic, P. M., Wedge, R. F., & Young, M. L. (1975). *Evaluation of the effectiveness of contingency contracting with delinquents.* Sacramento: California Youth Authority.

Jessor, R., & Jessor, S. L. (1977). *Problem behavior and psychological development: A longitudinal study of youth.* San Diego, CA: Academic Press.

Johnson, B. R., Li, S. D., Larson, D. B., & McCullough, M. (2000). A systematic review of the religiosity and delinquency literature. *Journal of Contemporary Criminal Justice, 16,* 32-52.

Johnson, C. A., Penz, M. A., Weber, M. D., Dwyer, J. H., Baer, N., MacKinnon, D. P., et al. (1990). Relative effectiveness of comprehensive community programming for drug abuse prevention with high-risk and low-risk adolescents. *Journal of Consulting and Clinical Psychology, 58,* 447-456.

Johnson, D. L., & Walker, T. (1987). Primary prevention of behavior problems in Mexican-American children. *American Journal of Community Psychology, 15,* 375-385.

Johnson, G., & Hunter, R. (1985). *Law-related education as a delinquency prevention strategy: A three-year evaluation of the impact of LRE on students.* Boulder, CO: Center for Action Research.

Johnson, K. (2000, February 10). Unready, unrehabilitated, and up for release. *USA Today,* p. 13A.

Johnson, K., & Wagner, D. (2001). *Missouri multi-county juvenile officer workload study report.* Madison, WI: National Council on Crime and Delinquency.

Johnson, K., Wagner, D., & Matthews, T. (2001). *Missouri juvenile risk assessment re-validation report.* Madison, WI: National Council on Crime and Delinquency.

Johnson, R. (1978). Youth in crisis: Dimensions of self-destructive conduct among adolescent prisoners. *Adolescence, 13,* 461-482.

Johnston, L. D., Bachman, J. G., & O'Malley, P. M. (1995). *Monitoring the Future.* Ann Arbor: University of Michigan, Institute for Social Research.

Johnston, L. D., O'Malley, P. M., & Bachman, J. G. (1999, December 17). *Drug trends in 1999 among American teens are mixed* (Press release). Ann Arbor: University of Michigan News and Information Services.

Joint Legislative Audit and Review Commission of the Virginia General Assembly. (1997). *The operation and impact of juvenile corrections services in Virginia.* Richmond, VA: Virginia General Assembly.

Jones, C. (2001, July 12). NYC, police union near deal with Louima. *USA Today,* p. 3A.

Jones, P. R. (1996). Risk prediction in criminal justice. In A. T. Harland (Ed.), *Choosing correctional options that work* (pp. 33-68). Thousand Oaks, CA: Sage.

Jones, R. S. (Ed.). (1997). Conditions of confinement [Special issue]. *Journal of Contemporary Criminal Justice, 13*(1).

Joshi, P. K., & Rosenberg, L. A. (1997). Children's behavioral response to residential treatment. *Journal of Clinical Psychology, 53,* 567-573.

Josi, D., & Sechrest, D. K. (1999). A pragmatic approach to parole aftercare: Evaluation of a community reintegration program for high-risk youthful offenders. *Justice Quarterly, 16,* 51-80.

Jung, S., & Rawana, E. P. (1999). Risk and need assessment of juvenile offenders. *Criminal Justice and Behavior, 26,* 69-89.

Kachur, S. P., Stennies, G. M., Powell, K. E., Modzeleski, W., Stephens, R., Murphy, R., et al. (1996). School-associated violent deaths in the United States, 1992-1994. *Journal of the American Medical Association, 275,* 1729-1733.

Kalb, L. M., Farrington, D. P., & Loeber, R. (2001). Leading longitudinal studies on delinquency, substance use, sexual behavior, and mental health problems with childhood samples. In R. Loeber & D. P. Farrington (Eds.), *Child delinquents: Development, intervention, and service needs* (pp. 415-423). Thousand Oaks, CA: Sage.

Kamradt, B. (2000). Wraparound Milwaukee: Aiding youth with mental health needs. *Juvenile Justice, 7*(1), 14-23.

Karoly, L. A., Greenwood, P. W., & Everingham, S. S. (1998). *Investing in our children.* Santa Monica, CA: RAND.

Katner, D. R. (2002). A defense perspective of treatment programs for juvenile sex offenders. *Juvenile Correctional Mental Health Report, 2*(2), 17-30.

Katz, L. R. (1970). Gideon's trumpet: Mournful and muffled. *Criminal Law Bulletin, 6,* 529-576.

Kaufman, J. G., & Widom, C. S. (1999). Childhood victimization, running away, and delinquency. *Journal of Research in Crime and Delinquency, 36,* 347-370.

Kazdin, A. E. (1994). Interventions for aggressive and adolescent children. In L. D. Eron, J. H. Gentry, & P. Schlegel (Eds.), *Reason to hope: A psychosocial perspective on violence and youth* (pp. 341-382). Washington, DC: American Psychological Association.

Keen, J. (2001, May 10). Bush, Ashcroft to announce zero-tolerance for gun crimes. *USA Today,* p. 5A.

Keenan, K. (2001). Uncovering preschool precursor problem behaviors. In R. Loeber & D. P. Farrington (Eds.), *Child delinquents: Development, intervention, and service needs* (pp. 117-134). Thousand Oaks, CA: Sage.

Kellam, S. G., Rebok, G. W., Ialongo, N., & Mayer, L. S. (1994). The course and malleability of aggressive behavior from early first grade into middle school: Results of a developmental epidemiologically-based preventive trial. *Journal of Child Psychology and Psychiatry, 35,* 259-281.

Kelley, B. T., Huizinga, D., Thornberry, T. P., & Loeber, R. (1997). *Epidemiology of serious violence* (Juvenile Justice Bulletin). Washington, DC: Office of Juvenile Justice and Delinquency Prevention.

Kelley, B. T., Loeber, R., Keenan, K., & DeLamatre, M. (1997). *Developmental pathways in boys' disruptive and delinquent behavior* (Juvenile Justice Bulletin). Washington, DC: Office of Juvenile Justice and Delinquency Prevention.

Kelley, B. T., Thornberry, T. P., & Smith, C. (1997). *In the wake of childhood maltreatment* (Juvenile Justice Bulletin). Washington, DC: Office of Juvenile Justice and Delinquency Prevention.

Kelling, G. L., & Coles, C. M. (1996). *Fixing broken windows: Restoring order and reducing crime in our communities.* New York: Free Press.

Kempf-Leonard, K. (1997). *Gender and juvenile justice in Missouri.* St. Louis: University of Missouri, Department of Criminology and Criminal Justice.

Kempf-Leonard, K. (1998). *Validation of pilot risk and needs assessment instruments* (prepared for the Office of State Courts Administrator). Jefferson City, MO: Office of State Courts Administrator.

Kempf-Leonard, K., & Tracy, P. E. (2000). The gender effect among serious, violent, and chronic offenders: A difference in degree rather than kind. In R. Muraskin (Ed.), *It's a crime: Women and justice* (pp. 453-478). Upper Saddle River, NJ: Prentice Hall.

Kempf-Leonard, K., Tracy, P. E., & Howell, J. C. (2001). Serious, violent, and chronic juvenile offenders: The relationship of delinquency career types to adult criminality. *Justice Quarterly, 18,* 449-478.

Kempf-Leonard, K., & White, N. (1999). *Assessing the impact of 1995 changes to the Missouri Juvenile Code: Waiver.* St. Louis: University of Missouri, Department of Criminology and Criminal Justice.

Kennedy, D. M. (1999, July). Pulling levers: Getting deterrence right. *National Institute of Justice Journal, 236,* 2-8.

Kennedy, D. M., & Braga, A. A. (1998). Homicide in Minneapolis. *Homicide Studies, 2,* 263-290.

Kennedy, D. M., Piehl, A. M., & Braga, A. A. (1996). Youth violence in Boston: Gun markets, serious youth offenders, and a use-reduction strategy. *Law and Contemporary Problems, 59,* 147-196.

Kent, D. R., Donaldson, S. I., Wyrick, P. A., & Smith, P. J. (2000). Evaluating criminal justice programs designed to reduce crime by targeting repeat gang offenders. *Evaluation and Program Planning, 23,* 115-124.

Kiessling, J. J., & Andrews, D. A. (1980). Behavior analysis systems in corrections: A new approach to the synthesis of correctional theory, practice, management and research. *Canadian Journal of Criminology, 22,* 412-427.

Kirby, L. D., & Fraser, M. W. (1997). Risk and resilience in childhood. In M. W. Fraser (Ed.), *Risk and resilience in childhood* (pp. 10-33). Washington, DC: National Association of Social Workers.

Kirigin, K. A., Braukmank, C. J., Atwater, J. D., & Worl, M. M. (1982). An evaluation of teaching-family (Achievement Place) group homes for juvenile offenders. *Journal of Applied Behavior Analysis, 15,* 1-16.

Klein, M. W. (1971). *Street gangs and street workers.* Englewood Cliffs, NJ: Prentice Hall.

Klein, M. W. (1995). *The American street gang.* New York: Oxford University Press.

Klein, M. W., Kerner, H.-J., Maxson, C. L., & Weitekamp, E. G. M. (Eds.). (2001). *The Eurogang paradox: Street gangs and youth groups in the U.S. and Europe.* Amsterdam: Kluwer.

Klein, M. W., & Maxson, C. L. (1989). Street gang violence. In M. E. Wolfgang & N. A. Weiner (Eds.), *Violent crime, violent criminals* (pp. 198-234). Newbury Park, CA: Sage.

Klein, M. W., & Maxson, C. L. (1994). Gangs and cocaine trafficking. In D. L. MacKenzie & C. Uchida (Eds.), *Drugs and crime: Evaluating public policy initiatives* (pp. 42-58). Thousand Oaks, CA: Sage.

Klein, M. W., Maxson, C. L., & Cunningham, L. C. (1991). Crack, street gangs, and violence. *Criminology, 29,* 623-650.

Knitzer, J. (1982). *Unclaimed children: The failure of public responsibility to children and adolescents in need of mental health services.* Washington, DC: Children's Defense Fund.

Kolvin, I., Miller, F. J. W., Scott, D. M., Gatzanis, S. R. M., & Fleeting, M. (1990). *Continuities of deprivation?* Aldershot, UK: Avebury.

Kosterman, R., Hawkins, J. D., Hill, K. G., Abbott, R. D., Catalano, R. F., & Guo, J. (1996, November). *The developmental dynamics of gang initiation: When and why young people join gangs.* Paper presented at the annual meeting of the American Society of Criminology, Chicago.

Kovacs, M. (1996). Presentation and course of major depressive disorder during childhood and later years of the life span. *Journal of the American Academy of Child and Adolescent Psychiatry, 35,* 705-715.

Kovandzic, T. V., Sloan, J. J., & Vieraitis, L. M. (2002). Unintended consequences of politically popular sentencing policy: The homicide-promoting effects of "three strikes" in

U.S. cities (1980-1999). *Criminology and Public Policy, 1,* 399-424.

Koyanagi, C., & Gaines, S. (1993). *All systems failure: An examination of the results of neglecting the needs of children with serious emotional disturbance.* Alexandria, VA: National Mental Health Association.

Kraemer, H. C., Kazdin, A. E., Offord, D. R., Kessler, R. C., Jensen, P. S., & Kupfer, D. J. (1997). Coming to terms with the terms of risk. *Archives of General Psychiatry, 54,* 337-343.

Krajicek, D. J. (2000, February). Boot camps get a kick in the head. *Youth Today,* p. A2.

Krisberg, B., & Austin, J. (1993). *Reinventing juvenile justice.* Newbury Park, CA: Sage.

Krisberg, B., Currie, E., Onek, D., & Wiebush, R. G. (1995). Graduated sanctions for serious, violent, and chronic juvenile offenders. In J. C. Howell, B. Krisberg, J. D. Hawkins, & J. J. Wilson (Eds.), *A sourcebook: Serious, violent, and chronic juvenile offenders* (pp. 142-170). Thousand Oaks, CA: Sage.

Krisberg, B., & Howell, J. C. (1998). The impact of the juvenile justice system and prospects for graduated sanctions in a comprehensive strategy. In R. Loeber & D. P. Farrington (Eds.), *Serious and violent juvenile offenders: Risk factors and successful interventions* (pp. 346-366). Thousand Oaks, CA: Sage.

Krisberg, B., Neuenfeldt, D., Wiebush, R. G., & Rodriguez, O. (1994). *Juvenile intensive supervision: Planning guide.* Washington, DC: Office of Juvenile Justice and Delinquency Prevention.

Krisberg, B., Onek, D., Jones, M., & Schwartz, I. (1993). *Juveniles in state custody: Prospects for community-based care of troubled adolescents.* San Francisco: National Council on Crime and Delinquency.

Krohn, M. D., Lizotte, A. J., Thornberry, T. P., Smith, C. A., & McDowall, D. (1996). Reciprocal causal relationships among drug use, peers, and beliefs: A five-wave panel model. *Journal of Drug Issues, 26,* 405-428.

Krohn, M. D., Thornberry, T. P., Rivera, C., & Le Blanc, M. (2001). Later careers of very young offenders. In R. Loeber & D. P. Farrington (Eds.), *Child delinquents: Development, intervention, and service needs* (pp. 67-94). Thousand Oaks, CA: Sage.

Krug, E. G., Brener, N. D., Dahlberg, L. L., Ryan, G. W., & Powell, K. E. (1997). The impact of an elementary school-based violence prevention program on visits to the school nurse. *American Journal of Preventive Medicine, 13,* 450-463.

Krysik, J., & LeCroy, C. W. (2002). The empirical validation of an instrument to predict risk of recidivism among juvenile offenders. *Research on Social Work Practice, 12,* 71-81.

Kumpfer, K. L., & Alvarado, R. (1998). *Effective family strengthening interventions* (Juvenile Justice Bulletin). Washington, DC: Office of Juvenile Justice and Delinquency Prevention.

Kupersmidt, J. B., DeRosier, M. E., & Patterson, C. J. (1995). Similarity as the basis for companionship among children: The roles of sociometric status, aggressive and withdrawn behavior, academic achievement, and demographic characteristics. *Journal of Social and Personal Relationships, 12,* 439-452.

Kupperstein, L. (1971). Treatment and rehabilitation of delinquent youth: Some sociocultural considerations. *Acta Criminologica, 4,* 11-111.

Kurz, G. A. (1999, July). *The Orange County 8% Early Intervention Program.* Paper presented at the National Youth Gang Symposium, Las Vegas.

Kurz, G. A., & Moore, L. E. (1994). *The "8 percent problem": Chronic juvenile offender recidivism.* Santa Ana, CA: Orange County Probation Department.

LaFree, G. D. (1980). The effect of sexual stratification by race on official reactions to rape. *American Sociological Review, 45,* 842-854.

Lahey, B. B., Gordon, R. A., Loeber, R., Stouthamer-Loeber, M., & Farrington, D. P. (1999). Boys who join gangs: A prospective study of predictors of first gang entry. *Journal of Abnormal Child Psychology, 27,* 261-276.

Lally, J. R., Mangione, P. L., & Honig, A. S. (1988). The Syracuse University Family Development Research Project: Long-range impact of an early intervention with low-income children and their families. In D. R. Powell (Ed.), *Parent education as early childhood intervention: Emerging directions in theory, research and practice* (pp. 79-104). Norwood, NJ: Ablex.

Land, K. C., McCall, P. L., & Williams, J. R. (1990). Something that works in juvenile justice: An evaluation of the North Carolina Court Counselors' Intensive Protective Supervision randomized experimental project, 1987-1989. *Evaluation Review, 14,* 574-606.

Land, K. C., McCall, P. L., Williams, J. R., & Ezell, M. (1998). *Alternatives to Detention Study: Final report.* Raleigh: North Carolina Administrative Office of the Courts.

Landreville, P. (1999). Electronic surveillance of delinquents: A growing trend. *Deviance Et Societe, 23*(1), 105-121.

Lane, J., & Meeker, J. W. (2000). Subcultural diversity and the fear of crime and gangs. *Crime & Delinquency, 46,* 497-521.

Langan, P. A., & Levin, D. J. (2002). *Recidivism of prisoners released in 1994* (Special Report). Washington, DC: Bureau of Justice Statistics.

Latessa, E. J., Cullen, F. T., & Gendreau, P. (2002). Beyond correctional quackery: Professionalism and the possibility of effective treatment. *Federal Probation, 66*(2), 43-49.

Latessa, E. J., & Holsinger, A. M. (1998). The importance of evaluating correctional programs: Assessing outcome and quality. *Corrections Management Quarterly, 2*(4), 22-29.

Latessa, E. J., & Holsinger, A. M. (1999). *Evaluation of the Ohio Department of Youth Services' community correctional facilities.* Cincinnati, OH: University of Cincinnati, Division of Criminal Justice.

Laub, J. H., & Lauritsen, J. L. (1993). Violent criminal behavior over the life course: A review of the longitudinal and comparative research. *Violence and Victims, 8*, 235-252.

Lauritsen, J. L., & Quinet, K. F. D. (1995). Repeat victimization among adolescents and young adults. *Journal of Quantitative Criminology, 11*, 143-166.

Lauritsen, J. L., & White, N. A. (2001). Putting violence in its place: The influence of ethnicity, gender, and place on the risk for violence. *Criminology and Public Policy, 1*, 37-60.

Le Blanc, M. (1998). Serious, violent, and chronic juvenile offenders: Identification, classification, and prediction. In R. Loeber & D. P. Farrington (Eds.), *Serious and violent juvenile offenders: Risk factors and successful interventions* (pp. 167-193). Thousand Oaks, CA: Sage.

Le Blanc, M., & Frechette, M. (1989). *Male criminal activity from childhood through youth: Multilevel and developmental perspectives.* New York: Springer-Verlag.

Le Blanc, M., & Lanctot, N. (1998). Social and psychological characteristics of gang members according to the gang structure and its subcultural and ethnic makeup. *Journal of Gang Research, 5*(3), 15-28.

Le Blanc, M., & Loeber, R. (1993). Precursors, causes and the development of criminal offending. In D. F. Hay & A. Angold (Eds.), *Precursors and causes in development and psychopathology* (pp. 233-263). New York: John Wiley.

Le Blanc, M., & Loeber, R. (1998). Developmental criminology updated. In M. Tonry (Ed.), *Crime and justice: An annual review of research* (Vol. 23, pp. 115-198). Chicago: University of Chicago Press.

LeClair, D. P. (1983). *Varying time criteria in recidivism followup studies: A test of the "crossover effects" phenomenon.* Boston: Massachusetts Department of Correction.

LeCroy, C. W., Krysik, J., & Palumbo, D. (1998). *Empirical validation of the Arizona Risk/Needs Instrument and assessment process.* Tucson: LeCroy & Milligan Associates.

Lederman, C. S. (1999). The juvenile court: Putting research to work for prevention. *Juvenile Justice, 6*(2), 22-31.

Leffert, N., Saito, R. N., Blyth, D. A., & Kroenke, C. H. (1996). *Making the case: Measuring the impact of youth development programs.* Minneapolis: Search Institute.

Leiber, M. J. (2002). Disproportionate minority confinement (DMC) of youth: An analysis of state and federal efforts to address the issue. *Crime & Delinquency, 48*, 3-45.

Leinwand, D. (2000, February 25). LAPD, neighborhood shaken. *USA Today*, p. 3A.

Leinwand, D. (2001, February 21). Some find "zero" tolerance intolerable. *USA Today*, p. 3A.

Lemert, E. M. (1951). *Social pathology: Human deviance, social problems, and social control.* New York: McGraw-Hill.

Lerman, P. (1991). Counting youth in trouble in institutions: Bringing the United States up to date. *Crime & Delinquency, 37*, 465-480.

Lerman, P. (2002). Twentieth-century developments in America's institutional systems for youth in trouble. In M. K. Rosenheim, F. E. Zimring, D. S. Tanenhaus, & B. Dohrn (Eds.), *A century of juvenile justice* (pp. 74-109). Chicago: University of Chicago Press.

Lerman, P., & Pottick, K. J. (1995). *The parents' perspective: Delinquency, aggression, and mental health.* Chur, Switzerland: Harwood.

Lerner, S. (1990). *The good news about juvenile justice.* Bolinas, CA: Common Knowledge.

Lester, D., & Van Voorhis, P. (1997). Cognitive therapies. In P. Van Voorhis, M. Braswell, & D. Lester (Eds.), *Correctional counseling and rehabilitation* (3rd ed., pp. 163-185). Cincinnati, OH: Anderson.

Levin, D. J., Langan, P. A., & Brown, J. M. (2000). *State court sentencing of convicted felons, 1996* (Bulletin). Washington, DC: Bureau of Justice Statistics.

Levitt, S. D. (1999). The limited role of changing age structure in explaining aggregate crime rates. *Criminology, 37*, 581-597.

Levrant, S., Cullen, F. T., Fulton, B., & Wozniak, J. (1999). Reconsidering restorative justice: The corruption of benevolence revisited? *Crime & Delinquency, 45*, 3-27.

Lewis, D. O., Pincus, J. H., Bard, B., Richardson, E., Prichep, L. S., Feldman, M., et al. (1988). Neuropsychiatric, psychoeducational, and family characteristics of 14 juveniles condemned to death in the United States. *American Journal of Psychiatry, 145*, 585-589.

Lewis, R. M. (1984). *Variables associated with the restrictiveness of placement of violent and assaultive youth prior to their certification as Willie M class members.* Unpublished doctoral dissertation, University of North Carolina.

Library Information Specialists. (1983). *Suicides in jails*. Boulder, CO: National Institute of Corrections.

Liebman, J. S., Fagan, J., & West, V. (2000). *A broken system: Error rates in capital cases, 1973-1995*. New York: Columbia University, School of Law.

Lipsey, M. W. (1992). Juvenile delinquency treatment: A meta-analytic inquiry into the variability of effects. In T. D. Cook, H. Cooper, D. S. Cordray, H. Hartman, L. V. Hedges, R. J. Light, et al. (Eds.), *Meta-analysis for explanation* (pp. 83-127). New York: Russell Sage Foundation.

Lipsey, M. W. (1995). What do we learn from 400 research studies on the effectiveness of treatment with juvenile delinquents? In J. McGuire (Ed.), *What works: Reducing reoffending* (pp. 63-78). New York: John Wiley.

Lipsey, M. W. (1999a). Can intervention rehabilitate serious delinquents? *Annals of the American Academy of Political and Social Science, 564*, 142-166.

Lipsey, M. W. (1999b). Can rehabilitative programs reduce the recidivism of juvenile offenders? An inquiry into the effectiveness of practical programs. *Virginia Journal of Social Policy and the Law, 6*, 611-641.

Lipsey, M. W. (2000a). Meta-analysis and the learning curve in evaluation practice. *American Journal of Evaluation, 21*, 207-212.

Lipsey, M. W. (2000b, July). *What 500 intervention studies show about the effects of intervention on the recidivism of juvenile offenders*. Washington, DC: Paper presented at the Annual Conference on Criminal Justice Research and Evaluation.

Lipsey, M. W., & Derzon, J. H. (1998). Predictors of violent or serious delinquency in adolescence and early adulthood: A synthesis of longitudinal research. In R. Loeber & D. P. Farrington (Eds.), *Serious and violent juvenile offenders: Risk factors and successful interventions* (pp. 86-105). Thousand Oaks, CA: Sage.

Lipsey, M. W., Howell, J. C., & Tidd, S. T. (2002). *A standardized program evaluation protocol for North Carolina's juvenile justice system programs*. Nashville, TN: Vanderbilt University, Center for Evaluation Research and Methodology.

Lipsey, M. W., & Wilson, D. B. (1993). The efficacy of psychological, educational, and behavioral treatment: Confirmation from meta-analysis. *American Psychologist, 48*, 1181-1209.

Lipsey, M. W., & Wilson, D. B. (1998). Effective interventions with serious juvenile offenders: A synthesis of research. In R. Loeber & D. P. Farrington (Eds.), *Serious and violent juvenile offenders: Risk factors and successful interventions* (pp. 313-345). Thousand Oaks, CA: Sage.

Lipsey, M. W., & Wilson, D. B. (2000). *Practical meta-analysis*. Thousand Oaks, CA: Sage.

Lipsey, M. W., & Wilson, D. B. (2001). The way in which intervention studies have "personality" and why it is important to meta-analysis. *Evaluation and the Health Professions, 24*, 236-254.

Lipsey, M. W., Wilson, D. B., & Cothern, L. (2000). *Effective interventions for serious and violent juvenile offenders* (Juvenile Justice Bulletin). Washington, DC: Office of Juvenile Justice and Delinquency Prevention.

Lipton, D., Martinson, R., & Wilks, J. (1975). *The effectiveness of correctional treatment: A survey of treatment evaluation studies*. New York: Praeger.

Lizotte, A. J., Howard, G. J., Krohn, M. D., & Thornberry, T. P. (1997). Patterns of illegal gun carrying among young urban males. *Valparaiso University Law Review, 31*, 375-393.

Lizotte, A. J., Krohn, M. D., Howell, J. C., Tobin, K., & Howard, G. J. (2000). Factors influencing gun carrying among young urban males over the adolescent-young adult life course. *Criminology, 38*, 811-834.

Lizotte, A. J., & Sheppard, D. (2001). *Gun use by male juveniles: Research and prevention*. Washington, DC: Office of Juvenile Justice and Delinquency Prevention.

Lizotte, A. J., Tesoriero, J. M., Thornberry, T. P., & Krohn, M. D. (1994). Patterns of adolescent firearms ownership and use. *Justice Quarterly, 11*, 51-73.

Lochman, J. E., Burch, P. R., Curry, J. F., & Lampron, L. B. (1984). Treatment and generalization effects of cognitive-behavioral and goal-setting interventions with aggressive boys. *Journal of Consulting and Clinical Psychology, 52*, 915-916.

Lochman, J. E., Coie, J. D., Underwood, M. K., & Terry, R. (1993). Effectiveness of a social relations intervention program for aggressive and nonaggressive, rejected children. *Journal of Consulting and Clinical Psychology, 61*, 1053-1058.

Locy, T. (2001, April 17). Problems with police not new. *USA Today*, p. 3A.

Loeber, R. (1988). Natural histories of juvenile conduct problems, delinquency, and associated substance abuse: Evidence for developmental progressions. In B. B. Lahey & A. E. Kazdin (Eds.), *Advances in clinical child psychology* (Vol. 11, pp. 73-124). New York: Plenum.

Loeber, R. (1990). Developmental and risk factors of juvenile and antisocial behavior and delinquency. *Clinical Psychology Review, 10*, 1-41.

Loeber, R. (1996). Developmental continuity, change, and pathways in male juvenile problem behaviors and delinquency. In J. D. Hawkins (Ed.), *Delinquency and crime: Current theories* (pp. 1-27). New York: Cambridge University Press.

Loeber, R., Burke, J. D., Lahey, B. B., Winters, A., & Zera, M. (2000). Oppositional defiant and conduct disorder: A review of the past 10 years, part I. *Journal of the American Academy of Child and Adolescent Psychiatry, 39,* 1-17.

Loeber, R., DeLamatre, M., Keenan, K., & Zhang, Q. (1998). A prospective replication of developmental pathways in disruptive and delinquent behavior. In R. Cairns, L. Bergman, & J. Kagan (Eds.), *The individual as a focus in developmental research* (pp. 185-215). Thousand Oaks, CA: Sage.

Loeber, R., DeLamatre, M., Tita, G., Stouthamer-Loeber, M., & Farrington, D. P. (1999). Gun injury and mortality: The delinquent backgrounds of juvenile victims. *Violence and Victims, 14,* 339-352.

Loeber, R., & Dishion, T. J. (1983). Early predictors of male delinquency: A review. *Psychological Bulletin, 94,* 68-99.

Loeber, R., Dishion, T. J., & Patterson, G. R. (1984). Multiple gating: A multistage assessment procedure for identifying youths at risk for delinquency. *Journal of Research in Crime and Delinquency, 21,* 7-32.

Loeber, R., & Farrington, D. P. (1998a). Conclusions and the way forward. In R. Loeber & D. P. Farrington (Eds.), *Serious and violent juvenile offenders: Risk factors and successful interventions* (pp. 405-427). Thousand Oaks, CA: Sage.

Loeber, R., & Farrington, D. P. (1998b). Never too early, never too late: Risk factors and successful interventions with serious and violent juvenile offenders. *Studies on Crime and Crime Prevention, 7,* 7-30.

Loeber, R., & Farrington, D. P. (Eds.). (1998c). *Serious and violent juvenile offenders: Risk factors and successful interventions.* Thousand Oaks, CA: Sage.

Loeber, R., & Farrington, D. P. (2000). Young children who commit crime: Epidemiology, developmental origins, risk factors, early interventions, and policy implications. *Development and Psychopathology, 12,* 737-762.

Loeber, R., & Farrington, D. P. (Eds.). (2001a). *Child delinquents: Development, intervention, and service needs.* Thousand Oaks, CA: Sage.

Loeber, R., & Farrington, D. P. (2001b). Executive summary. In R. Loeber & D. P. Farrington (Eds.), *Child delinquents: Development, intervention, and service needs* (pp. xix-xxxi). Thousand Oaks, CA: Sage.

Loeber, R., & Farrington, D. P. (2001c). The significance of child delinquency. In R. Loeber & D. P. Farrington (Eds.), *Child delinquents: Development, intervention, and service needs* (pp. 1-22). Thousand Oaks, CA: Sage.

Loeber, R., Farrington, D. P., Stouthamer-Loeber, M., Moffitt, T. E., & Caspi, A. (1998). The development of male offending: Key findings from the first decade of the Pittsburgh Youth Study. *Studies on Crime and Crime Prevention, 7,* 141-172.

Loeber, R., Farrington, D. P., Stouthamer-Loeber, M., & Van Kammen, W. B. (1998). *Antisocial behavior and mental health problems.* Mahwah, NJ: Lawrence Erlbaum.

Loeber, R., Farrington, D. P., & Waschbusch, D. A. (1998). Serious and violent juvenile offenders. In R. Loeber & D. P. Farrington (Eds.), *Serious and violent juvenile offenders: Risk factors and successful interventions* (pp. 13-29). Thousand Oaks, CA: Sage.

Loeber, R., & Hay, D. F. (1994). Developmental approaches to aggression and conduct problems. In M. Rutter & D. F. Hay (Eds.), *Development through life: A handbook for clinicians* (pp. 488-516). Oxford: Blackwell Scientific.

Loeber, R., Kalb, L., & Huizinga, D. (2001). *Juvenile delinquency and serious injury victimization* (Juvenile Justice Bulletin). Washington, DC: Office of Juvenile Justice and Delinquency Prevention.

Loeber, R., Keenan, K., & Zhang, Q. (1997). Boys' experimentation and persistence in developmental pathways toward serious delinquency. *Journal of Child and Family Studies, 6,* 321-357.

Loeber, R., & Le Blanc, M. (1990). Toward a developmental criminology. In M. Tonry & N. Morris (Eds.), *Crime and justice: An annual review of research* (Vol. 12, pp. 375-473). Chicago: University of Chicago Press.

Loeber, R., & Stouthamer-Loeber, M. (1996). The development of offending. *Criminal Justice and Behavior, 23,* 12-24.

Loeber, R., Wei, E., Stouthamer-Loeber, M., Huizinga, D., & Thornberry, T. P. (1999). Behavioral antecedents to serious and violent offending: Joint analyses from the Denver Youth Survey, Pittsburgh Youth Study and the Rochester Youth Development Study. *Studies on Crime and Crime Prevention, 8,* 245-263.

Loeber, R., & Wikstrom, P. H. (1993). Individual pathways to crime in different types of neighborhood. In D. P. Farrington, R. J. Sampson, & P. H. Wikstrom (Eds.), *Integrating individual and ecological aspects of crime* (pp. 169-204). Stockholm: National Council for Crime Prevention.

Loeber, R., Wung, P., Keenan, K., Giroux, B., Stouthamer-Loeber, M., Van Kammen, W. B., & Maughan, B. (1993). Developmental pathways in disruptive child behavior. *Development and Psychopathology, 5,* 103-133.

Logan, W. A. (1998). Proportionality and punishment: Imposing life without parole on juveniles. *Wake Forest Law Review, 33,* 681-725.

Loper, A. B. (2000). *Female juvenile delinquency: Risk factors and promising interventions* (Juvenile Justice Fact Sheet). Charlottesville: University of Virginia, Institute of Law, Psychiatry and Public Policy.

Losel, F. (1995). The efficacy of correctional treatment: A review and synthesis of meta-evaluations. In J. McGuire (Ed.), *What works: Reducing reoffending* (pp. 79-111). New York: John Wiley.

Louisiana Juvenile Justice Commission. (2001-2002a). *Goals.* Baton Rouge: Author. Retrieved from http://jjc.legis.state.la.us/ jjc-goals.htm

Louisiana Juvenile Justice Commission. (2001-2002b). *JJC history.* Baton Rouge: Author. Retrieved from http://jjc.legis.state.la.us/ jjc-history.htm

Louisiana Juvenile Justice Commission. (2001-2002c). *JJC process.* Baton Rouge: Author. Retrieved from http://jjc.legis.state.la.us/ jjc-process.htm

Lourie, I. S., & Katz-Leavy, J. W. (1987). Severely emotionally disturbed children and adolescents. In W. W. Menninger & G. T. Hanna (Eds.), *The chronic mental patient* (Vol. 2, pp. 159-187). Washington, DC: American Psychological Association.

Lovell, D., Cloyes, K., Allen, D., & Rhodes, L. (2000). Who lives in super-maximum custody? A Washington State study. *Federal Probation, 64*(2), 33-38.

Lubitz, R. (2001). *Strategies to reduce commitments to youth development centers.* Raleigh: North Carolina Department of Juvenile Justice and Delinquency Prevention.

Lurigio, A. J., & Rosenbaum, D. P. (1994). Community policing. *Crime & Delinquency, 40,* 299-468.

Lynch, J. P., & Sabol, W. J. (1997). *Did getting tough on crime pay?* Washington, DC: Urban Institute.

Lynskey, D. P., Winfree, L. T., Esbensen, F., & Clason, D. L. (2000). Linking gender, minority group status, and family matters to self-control theory: A multivariate analysis of key self-control concepts in a youth gang context. *Juvenile and Family Court Journal, 51*(3), 1-19.

Lyon, J. M., Henggeler, S. W., & Hall, J. A. (1992). The family relations, peer relations, and criminal activities of Caucasian and Hispanic-American gang members. *Journal of Abnormal Child Psychology, 20,* 439-449.

Lyons, D. (1997, May). Juvenile justice comes of age. *State Legislatures,* pp. 12-18.

MacBeth, G. (1993). Collaboration can be elusive: Virginia's experience in developing an inter-agency system of care. *Administration and Policy in Mental Health, 20,* 259-282.

MacKenzie, D. L. (2000). Evidence-based corrections: Identifying what works. *Crime & Delinquency, 46,* 457-471.

MacKenzie, D. L., & Souryal, C. (1994). *Multisite evaluation of shock incarceration.* Washington, DC: National Institute of Justice.

MacKenzie, D. L., Wilson, D. B., Armstrong, G. S., & Gover, A. R. (2001). The impact of boot camps and traditional institutions on juvenile residents: Perceptions, adjustment, and change. *Journal of Research in Crime and Delinquency, 38,* 279-313.

Macmillan, R. (2000). Adolescent victimization and income deficits in adulthood: Rethinking the costs of criminal violence from a life-course perspective. *Criminology, 38,* 553-587.

Maguin, E., & Loeber, R. (1996). Academic performance and delinquency. *Crime and Justice, 20,* 145-264.

Maguire, K., & Pastore, A. L. (Eds.). (1995). *Sourcebook of criminal justice statistics— 1994.* Washington, DC: Bureau of Justice Statistics.

Mahoney, A. R. (1987). *Juvenile justice in context.* Boston: Northeastern University Press.

Mahoning County Community Planning Team. (2000). *Mahoning County Strategic Plan for Youth and Families.* Youngstown, OH: Author.

Malcom, J. L. (2002). *Guns and violence: The English experience.* Cambridge, MA: Harvard University Press.

Males, M. A. (1996). *The scapegoat generation: America's war on adolescents.* Monroe, ME: Common Courage.

Males, M. A. (1997, Winter). Distorting "youth violence." *Juvenile and Family Justice,* pp. 21-22.

Males, M. A., & Macallair, D. (1998). *The impact of juvenile curfew laws in California.* San Francisco: Justice Policy Institute, Center on Juvenile and Criminal Justice.

Males, M. A., & Macallair, D. (2000). *The color of justice.* Washington, DC: Building Blocks for Youth.

Maloney, D., Romig, D., & Armstrong, T. (1988). Juvenile probation: The balanced approach. *Juvenile and Family Court Journal, 39*(3), 1-63.

Maltz, M. D. (1999). *Bridging gaps in police crime data* (Bulletin). Washington, DC: Bureau of Justice Statistics.

Manhattan Institute, Center for Civic Innovation. (1999). *"Broken windows" probation: The next step in fighting crime.* New York: Author.

Mann, C. R. (1993). *Unequal justice: A question of color.* Bloomington: Indiana University Press.

Marans, S., & Berkman, M. (1997). *Child development-community policing: Partnership in a climate of violence* (Juvenile Justice Bulletin). Washington, DC: Office of Juvenile Justice and Delinquency Prevention.

Martin, J., Nada-Raja, S., Langley, J., Freehan, M., McGee, R., Clarke, J., et al. (1998). Physical assault in New Zealand: The experience of 21 year old men and women in a community sample. *New Zealand Medical Journal, 111,* 158-160.

Martin, S. E., Sechrest, L. B., & Redner, R. (1981). *New directions in the rehabilitation of criminal offenders.* Washington, DC: National Academy Press.

Martinson, R. (1974). What works? Questions and answers about prison reform. *Public Interest, 35,* 22-54.

Martinson, R. (1979). New findings, new views: A note of caution regarding sentencing reform. *Hofstra Law Review, 7,* 242-258.

Matthews, B., Hubbard, D. J., & Latessa, E. (2001). Making the next step: Using evaluability assessment to improve correctional programming. *Prison Journal, 8,* 454-472.

Mauer, M. (1997). *Intended and unintended consequences: State racial disparities in imprisonment.* Washington, DC: Sentencing Project

Mauro, T. (2002, October 31). Should juvenile sniper be sentenced to death? *USA Today,* p. 15A.

Maxfield, M. G., & Maltz, M. D. (Eds.). (1999). The National Incident-Based Reporting System [Special issue]. *Journal of Quantitative Criminology, 15*(2).

Maxson, C. L. (1995). *Street gangs and drug sales in two suburban cities* (Research in Brief). Washington, DC: National Institute of Justice.

Maxson, C. L. (1998a). Gang homicide: A review and extension of the literature. In D. Smith & M. Zahn (Eds.), *Homicide: A sourcebook of social research* (pp. 197-219). Thousand Oaks, CA: Sage.

Maxson, C. L. (1998b). *Gang members on the move* (Juvenile Justice Bulletin, Youth Gang Series). Washington, DC: Office of Juvenile Justice and Delinquency Prevention.

Maxson, C. L., Curry, G. D., & Howell, J. C. (2002). Youth gang homicides in the United States in the 1990's. In S. Decker & W. Reed (Eds.), *Responses to gangs: Evaluation and research* (pp. 111-137). Washington, DC: National Institute of Justice.

Maxson, C. L., Whitlock, M. L., & Klein, M. W. (1998). Vulnerability to street gang membership: Implications for prevention. *Social Service Review, 72*(1), 70-91.

Mazerolle, P., Brame, R., Paternoster, R., Piquero, A. R., & Dean, C. W. (2000). Onset age, persistence, and offending versatility: Comparisons across gender. *Criminology, 38,* 1143-1172.

McArthur, A. V. (1974). *Coming out cold: Community reentry from a state reformatory.* Lexington, MA: Lexington.

McBride, A. G., Scott, R., Schlesinger, S. R., Dillingham, S. D., & Buckman, R. B. (1992). *Combating violent crime: 24 recommendations to strengthen criminal justice.* Washington, DC: U.S. Department of Justice, Office of the Attorney General.

McCarthy, T. (2001, September 3). L.A. gangs are back. *Time, 158.*

McConnaughey, J. (1996, November 8). La. law: 5-year-old is hauled off in cuffs. *USA Today,* p. 2A.

McCord, J. (1985). Deterrence and the light touch of the law. In D. P. Farrington & J. Gunn (Eds.), *Reactions to crime: The public, the police, courts, and prisons* (pp. 73-85). New York: John Wiley.

McCord, J., & Conway, K. (2000, November). *Unpacking age, co-offending, and crime relationships.* Paper presented at the annual meeting of the American Society of Criminology, San Francisco.

McCord, J., & Tremblay, R. E. (Eds.). (1992). *Preventing antisocial behavior: Interventions from birth through adolescence.* New York: Guilford.

McCord, J., Widom, C. S., & Crowell, N. A. (Eds.). (2001). *Juvenile crime, juvenile justice.* Washington, DC: National Academy Press.

McCorkle, R. C. (1992). Personal precautions to violence in prison. *Criminal Justice and Behavior, 19,* 160-173.

McDonald, D. C., & Carlson, K. E. (1992). *Federal sentencing in transition, 1986-90.* Washington, DC: Bureau of Justice Statistics.

McDowall, D. (2000). Juvenile curfew laws and their influence on crime. *Federal Probation, 64*(2), 58-63.

McDowall, D., Loftin, C., & Wiersema, B. (2000). The impact of youth curfew laws on juvenile crime rates. *Crime & Delinquency, 46,* 76-91.

McGarvey, E. L., & Waite, D. (2000). *Profiles of incarcerated adolescents in Virginia correctional facilities: Fiscal years 1993-1998.* Richmond: Virginia Department of Criminal Justice Services.

McKinney, K. C. (1988). *Juvenile gangs: Crime and drug trafficking* (Bulletin). Washington, DC: Office of Juvenile Justice and Delinquency Prevention.

McPartland, J. M., & Nettles, S. M. (1991). Using community adults as advocates or mentors for at-risk middle school students: A two-year evaluation of Project RAISE. *American Journal of Education, 99,* 568-586.

McShane, M. D., & Williams, F. P. (1989). The prison adjustment of juvenile offenders. *Crime & Delinquency, 35,* 254-269.

McWhorter, D. (1999, March 29). Killing by N.Y. police raises ghosts of past. *USA Today,* p. 17A.

Mears, D. P. (1998). Evaluation issues confronting juvenile justice sentencing reforms: A case study of Texas. *Crime & Delinquency, 44,* 443-463.

Mears, D. P. (2000). Assessing the effectiveness of juvenile justice reforms: A closer look at the criteria and the impacts on various stakeholders. *Law and Policy, 22,* 175-202.

Mears, D. P. (2001). Getting tough with juvenile offenders: Explaining support for sanctioning juveniles as adults. *Criminal Justice and Behavior, 28,* 206-226.

Mears, D. P., & Field, S. H. (2000). Theorizing sanctioning in a criminalized juvenile court. *Criminology, 38,* 983-1019.

Mears, D. P., & Kelly, W. R. (1999). Assessments and intake processes in juvenile justice processing: Emerging policy considerations. *Crime & Delinquency, 45,* 508-529.

Mears, D. P., & Kelly, W. R. (2002). Linking process and outcomes in evaluating a statewide drug treatment program for youthful offenders. *Crime & Delinquency, 48,* 99-115.

Mears, D. P., Ploeger, M., & Warr, M. (1998). Explaining the gender gap in delinquency: Peer influence and moral evaluations of behavior. *Journal of Research in Crime and Delinquency, 35,* 251-266.

Medaris, M. L., Campbell, E., & James, B. (1997). *Sharing information: A guide to the Family Educational Rights and Privacy Act and participation in juvenile justice programs.* Washington, DC: Office of Juvenile Justice and Delinquency Prevention.

Meehan, P. J., & O'Carroll, P. W. (1992). Gangs, drugs, and homicide in Los Angeles. *American Journal of the Disabled Child, 146,* 683-687.

Melton, G. B., Limber, S. P., Cunningham, P., Osgood, D. W., Chambers, J., Flerx, V., et al. (2000). *Violence among rural youth: Final report to the Office of Juvenile Justice and Delinquency Prevention.* Washington, DC: Office of Juvenile Justice and Delinquency Prevention.

Memory, J. M. (1989). Juvenile suicides in secure detention facilities: Correction of published rates. *Death Studies, 13,* 455-463.

Menard, S. (1987). Short-term trends in crime and delinquency: A comparison of UCR, NCS, and self-report data. *Justice Quarterly, 4,* 455-474.

Menard, S. (2000). The "normality" of repeat victimization from adolescence through early adulthood. *Justice Quarterly, 17,* 543-574.

Menard, S. (2002). *Short- and long-term consequences of adolescent victimization* (Fact Sheet). Washington, DC: Office of Juvenile Justice and Delinquency Prevention and Centers for Disease Control and Prevention.

Mendel, R. A. (2001). *Less cost, more safety: Guiding lights for reform in juvenile justice.* Washington, DC: American Youth Policy Forum.

Mennel, R. (1973). *Thorns and thistles: Juvenile delinquents in the United States, 1825-1940.* Hanover, NH: University Press of New England.

Mercy, J. A., & O'Carroll, P. W. (1988). New directions in violence prediction: The public health arena. *Violence and Victims, 3,* 285-301.

Merlo, A. V., Benekos, P. J., & Cook, W. J. (1997). Waiver and juvenile justice reform: Widening the punitive net. *Criminal Justice Policy Review, 8,* 145-168.

Meyer, A. L., & Farrell, A. D. (1998). Social skills training to promote resilience in urban sixth-grade students: One product of an action research strategy to prevent youth violence in high-risk environments. *Education and Treatment of Children, 21,* 461-488.

Miethe, T. D., & McCorkle, R. C. (1997a). *Evaluating Nevada's anti-gang legislation and gang prosecution units.* Washington, DC: National Institute of Justice.

Mihalic, S., Irwin, K., Elliott, D., Fagan, A., & Hansen, D. (2001). *Blueprints for violence prevention* (Juvenile Justice Bulletin). Washington, DC: Office of Juvenile Justice and Delinquency Prevention.

Mikkelsen, E. J., Bereika, G. M., & McKenzie, J. C. (1993). Short-term family-based residential treatment: An alternative to psychiatric hospitalization for children. *American Journal of Orthopsychiatry, 63,* 28-33.

Milakovich, M. E., & Weis, K. (1975). Politics and measures of success in the war on crime. *Crime & Delinquency, 21,* 10-20.

Miller, J. A. (2001). *One of the guys: Girls, gangs and gender.* New York: Oxford University Press.

Miller, J. G. (1973). The politics of change: Correctional reform. In Y. Bakal (Ed.), *Closing correctional institutions* (pp. 3-8). Lexington, MA: D. C. Heath.

Miller, J. G. (1991). *Last one over the wall: The Massachusetts experiment in closing reform schools.* Columbus: Ohio State University Press.

Miller, N. (1996). *Understanding juvenile waiver: The significance of system resources in case allocation between juvenile and criminal court.* Washington, DC: Institute for Law and Justice.

Miller, W. B. (1982, March-April). Youth gangs: A look at the numbers. *Children Today,* pp. 10-11.

Miller, W. B. (1992). *Crime by youth gangs and groups in the United States.* Washington, DC: Office of Juvenile Justice and Delinquency Prevention.

Miller, W. B. (2001). *The growth of youth gang problems in the United States: 1970-1998.* Washington, DC: Office of Juvenile Justice and Delinquency Prevention.

Minor, K. I., Hartmann, D. J., & Terry, S. (1997). Predictors of juvenile court actions and recidivism. *Crime & Delinquency, 43,* 328-344.

Minor, K. I., Wells, J. B., Soderstrom, I. R., Bingham, R., & Williamson, D. (1999). Sentence completion and recidivism among juveniles referred to teen courts. *Crime & Delinquency, 45,* 467-480.

Moffitt, T. E. (1993). Adolescence-limited and life-course-persistent antisocial behavior: A developmental taxonomy. *Psychological Review, 100,* 674-701.

Moffitt, T. E. (1997). Adolescence-limited and life-course-persistent offending: A complementary pair of developmental theories. In T. P. Thornberry (Ed.), *Developmental theories of crime and delinquency* (pp. 11-54). New Brunswick, NJ: Transaction.

Moffitt, T. E., Caspi, A., Rutter, M., & Silva, P. A. (2001). *Sex differences in antisocial behavior: Conduct disorder, delinquency, and violence in the Dunedin longitudinal study.* New York: Cambridge University Press.

Moffitt, T. E., & Silva, P. A. (1988). IQ and delinquency: A direct test of the differential detection hypothesis. *Journal of Abnormal Psychology, 97,* 330-333.

Montgomery, I. M., Torbet, P. M., Malloy, D. A., Adamick, L. P., Toner, M. J., & Andrews, J. (1994). *What works: Promising interventions in juvenile justice.* Washington, DC: Office of Juvenile Justice and Delinquency Prevention.

Moon, M. M., Applegate, B. K., & Latessa, E. J. (1997). RECLAIM Ohio: A politically viable alternative to treating youthful felony offenders. *Crime & Delinquency, 43,* 438-457.

Moon, M. M., Sundt, J. L., Cullen, F. T., & Wright, J. P. (2000). Is child saving dead? Public support for juvenile rehabilitation. *Crime & Delinquency, 46,* 38-60.

Moone, J. (1994). *Juvenile victimization: 1987-1992* (Fact Sheet No. 1994-17). Washington, DC: Office of Juvenile Justice and Delinquency Prevention.

Moore, E. A. (2000). Sentencing opinion: *People of the State of Michigan v. Nathaniel Abraham. Juvenile and Family Court Journal, 51*(2), 1-11.

Moore, J. W. (1978). *Homeboys: Gangs, drugs and prison in the barrios of Los Angeles.* Philadelphia: Temple University Press.

Moore, J. W. (1990). Gangs, drugs and violence. In M. E. De La Rosa, E. Y. Lambert, & B. Gropper (Eds.), *Drugs and violence: Causes, correlates, and consequences* (NIDA Research Monograph No. 103, pp. 160-176). Rockville, MD: National Institute for Drug Abuse.

Moore, J. W. (1991). *Going down to the barrio: Homeboys and homegirls in change.* Philadelphia, PA: Temple University Press.

Moore, J. W. (1993). Gangs, drugs, and violence. In S. Cummings & D. J. Monti (Eds.), *Gangs: The origins and impact of contemporary youth gangs in the United States* (pp. 27-46). Albany: State University of New York Press.

Moore, J. W. (1998). Understanding youth street gangs: Economic restructuring and the urban underclass. In M. W. Watts (Ed.), *Cross-cultural perspectives on youth and violence* (pp. 65-78). Stamford, CT: JAI.

Moore, J. W., & Hagedorn, J. M. (2001). *Female gangs* (Juvenile Justice Bulletin, Youth Gang Series). Washington, DC: Office of Juvenile Justice and Delinquency Prevention.

Moore, R. H. (1987). Effectiveness of citizen volunteers functioning as counselors for high-risk young male offenders. *Psychological Reports, 61,* 823-830.

Mordock, J. B. (1997). The Fort Bragg Continuum of Care Demonstration Project: The population served was unique and the outcomes are questionable. *Child Psychiatry and Human Development, 27,* 241-254.

Morgan, M., & Patton, P. (2002). Gender-responsive programming in the justice system: Oregon's guidelines for effective programming for girls. *Federal Probation, 66*(2), 57-65.

Morley, E., Rossman, S. B., Kopczynski, M., Buck, J., & Gouvis, C. (2000). *Comprehensive responses to youth at risk: Interim findings from the SafeFutures Initiative.* Washington, DC: Urban Institute.

Morrissey, J. P., Johnson, M. C., & Calloway, M. O. (1997). Evaluating performance and change in mental health systems serving children and youth: An interorganizational network approach. *Journal of Mental Health Administration, 24,* 4-22.

Motiuk, L., McGuire, J., & Gendreau, P. (2000). "What works" in corrections. *Forum on Corrections Research, 12*(2), 3-60.

Munger, R. L. (1998). *The ecology of troubled children: Changing children's behavior by changing the places, activities, and people in their lives.* Cambridge, MA: Brookline.

Murder case takes twist. (1998, August 25). *Las Vegas Review-Journal,* pp. 1, 3.

Murphy, H. A., Hutchinson, J. M., & Bailey, J. S. (1983). Behavioral school psychology goes outdoors: The effect of organized games on playground aggression. *Journal of Applied Behavior Analysis, 16,* 29-35.

Murray, C., & Cox, L. (1979). *Beyond probation.* Beverly Hills, CA: Sage.

Nagin, D. S., Farrington, D. P., & Moffitt, T. E. (1995). Life-course trajectories of different types of offenders. *Criminology, 33,* 111-139.

Nagin, D. S., & Land, K. C. (1993). Age, criminal careers, and population heterogeneity: Specification and estimation of nonparametric, mixed Poisson model. *Criminology, 31,* 327-362.

Nansel, T. R., Overpeck, M., Pilla, R. S., Ruan, W. J., & Simmons-Morton, B. S. P. (2001). Bullying behaviors among U.S. youth: Prevalence and association with psychological adjustment. *Journal of the American Medical Association, 285,* 2094-2100.

National Advisory Commission on Criminal Justice Standards and Goals. (1973). *A national strategy to reduce crime.* Washington, DC: Government Printing Office.

National Center for Education Statistics. (1997). *Principal/school disciplinarian survey on school violence, Fast Response Survey System* (FRSS No. 63). Washington, DC: Author.

National Center for Neighborhood Enterprise. (1999). *Violence-free zone initiatives.* Washington, DC: Author.

National Conference of State Legislatures. (1999a). *Comprehensive juvenile justice: A legislator's guide.* Denver, CO: Author.

National Conference of State Legislatures. (1999b). Serious juvenile offenders in the juvenile justice system. In National Conference of State Legislatures, *Comprehensive juvenile justice: A legislator's guide* (pp. 1-5). Denver, CO: Author.

National Council of Juvenile and Family Court Judges. (1990). *Minority youth in the juvenile justice system: A judicial response.* Reno, NV: Author.

National Council of Juvenile and Family Court Judges. (1998). *The Janiculum Project: Structural, procedural and programmatic recommendations for the future juvenile court.* Reno, NV: Author.

National Council on Crime and Delinquency. (1996a). *Nebraska juvenile risk assessment findings.* Madison, WI: Author.

National Council on Crime and Delinquency. (1996b). *Travis County juvenile risk assessment findings.* Madison, WI: Author.

National Criminal Justice Association. (1997). *Juvenile justice reform initiatives in the states, 1994-1996.* Washington, DC: Office of Juvenile Justice and Delinquency Prevention.

National Institute of Corrections. (1995). *Offenders under age 18 in state adult corrections systems: A national picture.* Washington, DC: Author.

National Institute of Justice. (2002, March). Preventing school shootings: A summary of a U.S. Secret Service Safe School Initiative report. *NIJ Journal, 248,* 10-15.

National Institute on Drug Abuse. (2000). *Monitoring the Future report, 1975-1999.* Rockville, MD: Author.

National Research Council. (1993). *Losing generations: Adolescents in high risk settings.* Washington, DC: National Academy Press.

National Research Council & Institute of Medicine. (2002). *Community programs to promote youth development.* Washington, DC: National Academy Press.

National Threat Assessment Center. (2000). *USSS Safe School Initiative: An interim report on the prevention of targeted violence in schools.* Washington, DC: U.S. Secret Service.

National Youth Court Center. (2002). *State youth court associations.* Lexington, KY: Author. Retrieved April 6, 2002, from http://www.youthcourt.net/statelist.htm

National Youth Gang Center. (1997). *1995 National Youth Gang Survey.* Washington, DC: Office of Juvenile Justice and Delinquency Prevention.

National Youth Gang Center. (1999a). *1996 National Youth Gang Survey.* Washington, DC: Office of Juvenile Justice and Delinquency Prevention.

National Youth Gang Center. (1999b). *1997 National Youth Gang Survey.* Washington, DC: Office of Juvenile Justice and Delinquency Prevention.

National Youth Gang Center. (2000). *1998 National Youth Gang Survey.* Washington, DC: Office of Juvenile Justice and Delinquency Prevention.

National Youth Gang Center. (2001a). *Assessing your community's youth gang problem.* Washington, DC: Office of Juvenile Justice and Delinquency Prevention.

National Youth Gang Center. (2001b). *Planning for implementation of the OJJDP comprehensive gang model.* Washington, DC: Office of Juvenile Justice and Delinquency Prevention.

Needle, J., & Stapleton, W. V. (1983). *Police handling of youth gangs.* Washington, DC: Office of Juvenile Justice and Delinquency Prevention.

Nelson, C. M., Rutherford, B. P., & Wolford, B. I. (Eds.). (1996). *Comprehensive and collaborative systems that work for troubled youth: A national agenda.* Richmond, KY: National Juvenile Detention Association.

New Jersey Juvenile Justice Commission. (1999). *National directory of juvenile detention alternative programs.* Trenton: Author.

New twist on juvenile boot camps: School-based programs. (2000, August/September). *Juvenile Justice Update,* pp. 4, 13.

Norfolk Community Services Board. (1999). *Norfolk Assessment Center.* Norfolk, VA: Author.

North Carolina Department of Health and Human Services. (2000). *Report to the governor and the General Assembly on the Special Populations Program (formerly known as Willie M.): 1999-2000.* Raleigh: Author.

North Carolina Department of Health and Human Services. (2002). *Final report to the General Assembly on the Comprehensive Treatment Services Program.* Raleigh: Author.

North Carolina Department of Juvenile Justice and Delinquency Prevention. (2001a). *Calendar year 2000 annual report.* Raleigh: Author.

North Carolina Department of Juvenile Justice and Delinquency Prevention. (2001b). *Court services policies and procedures.* Raleigh: Author.

North Carolina Department of Juvenile Justice and Delinquency Prevention. (2002). *Calendar year 2001 annual report.* Raleigh: Author.

North Carolina Division of Mental Health, Developmental Disabilities and Substance Abuse Services. (2000). *Child and family services.* Retrieved October 31 from www.dhhs.state.nc.us/mhddsas/childandfamily/index.htm

Novotney, L. C., Mertinko, E., Lange, J., & Baker, T. K. (2000). *Juvenile mentoring program: A progress review* (Juvenile Justice Bulletin). Washington, DC: Office of Juvenile Justice and Delinquency Prevention.

Obeidallah, D. A., & Earls, F. J. (1999). *Adolescent girls: The role of depression in the development of delinquency* (Research Preview). Washington, DC: National Institute of Justice.

Office of Juvenile Affairs. (2000). *1999 annual report.* Oklahoma City: Oklahoma Department of Health and Human Services, Office of Juvenile Affairs.

Office of Juvenile Justice and Delinquency Prevention. (1995). *Delinquency prevention works.* Washington, DC: Author.

Office of Juvenile Justice and Delinquency Prevention. (1997). *Title V incentive grants for local delinquency prevention programs: 1996 report to Congress.* Washington, DC: Author.

Office of Juvenile Justice and Delinquency Prevention. (2002). *2000 report to Congress: Title V Community Prevention Grants Program.* Washington, DC: Author.

Office of State Courts Administrator, Juvenile and Adult Court Programs Division. (2000). *Report on standards for the administration of juvenile justice.* Jefferson City, MO: Author.

Office of State Courts Administrator, Juvenile and Adult Court Programs Division. (2001). *Classification system risk and needs profile: 9th Circuit summary.* Jefferson City, MO: Author.

Office of State Courts Administrator, Juvenile and Adult Court Programs Division. (2002). *Missouri's juvenile offender risk and needs assessment and classification system: User manual.* Jefferson City, MO: Author.

Office of the Criminal Justice Coordinator. (1991). *Electronic monitoring at the Youth Study Center: An evaluation.* New Orleans: Author.

Oldenettel, D., & Wordes, M. (2000). *The community assessment center concept* (Juvenile Justice Bulletin). Washington, DC: Office of Juvenile Justice and Delinquency Prevention.

Olds, D. L., Henderson, C. R., Jr., Cole, R., Eckenrode, J., Kitzman, H., Luckey, D., et al. (1998). Long-term effects of nurse home visitation on children's criminal and antisocial behavior. *Journal of the American Medical Association, 280,* 1238-1244.

Olds, D. L., Henderson, C. R., Jr., Tatelbaum, R., & Chamberlin, R. (1986). Preventing child abuse and neglect: A randomized trial of nurse home visitation. *Pediatrics, 78,* 65-78.

Olds, D. L., & Kitzman, H. (1993). Review of research on home visiting for pregnant women and parents of young children. *Future of Children, 3*(3), 53-92.

Olweus, D. (1978). *Aggression in the Schools.* New York: John Wiley.

Olweus, D. (1979). Stability of aggressive reaction patterns in males: A review. *Psychological Bulletin, 85,* 852-875.

Olweus, D. (1991). Bully/victim problems among schoolchildren: Basic facts and effects of a school based intervention. In D. J. Pepler & K. H. Rubin (Eds.), *The development and treatment of childhood aggression* (pp. 441-448). Hillsdale, NJ: Lawrence Erlbaum.

Olweus, D. (1992). Bullying among school children: Intervention and prevention. In R. D. Peters, R. J. McMahon, & V. L. Quinsey (Eds.), *Aggression and violence throughout the life span* (pp. 100-125). Newbury Park, CA: Sage.

Olweus, D. (1994). Bullying at school: Basic facts and effects of a school based intervention programme. *Journal of Child Psychology and Psychiatry, 35,* 1171-1190.

Orange County Chiefs' and Sheriff's Association, County-Wide Gang Strategy Steering Committee. (1999). *The final report of the Orange County Consortium COPS Project.* Westminster, CA: Author.

Orange County Probation Department. (2000). *The 8% solution: A collaborative approach to prevent chronic juvenile crime.* Santa Ana, CA: Author.

Orlandi, M. A. (1996). Prevention technologies for drug-involved youth. In C. B. McCoy, L. R. Metsch, & J. A. Inciardi (Eds.), *Intervening with drug-involved youth* (pp. 81-100). Thousand Oaks, CA: Sage.

Osofsky, J. D., & Fenichel, E. (Eds.). (1994). *Caring for infants and toddlers in violent environments: Hurt, healing and hope.* Arlington, VA: Zero to Three/National Center for Clinical Infant Programs.

Padilla, F. M. (1992). *The gang as an American enterprise: Puerto Rican youth and the American dream.* New Brunswick, NJ: Rutgers University Press.

Palacios, W. R. (1996). Side by side: An ethnographic study of a Miami gang. *Journal of Gang Research, 4*(1), 27-38.

Palmer, T. (1975). Martinson revisited. *Journal of Research in Crime and Delinquency, 12,* 133-152.

Palmer, T. (1983). The effectiveness issue today: An overview. *Federal Probation, 47*(2), 3-10.

Papachristos, A. V. (2001). *A.D., after the Disciples: The neighborhood impact of federal gang prosecution.* Peotone, IL: New Chicago Schools Press.

Parent, D., Dunworth, T., McDonald, D., & Rhodes, W. (1997). *Transferring serious juvenile offenders to adult courts* (Research in Action). Washington, DC: National Institute of Justice.

Parent, D., Leiter, V., Livens, L., Wentworth, D., & Stephen, K. (1994). *Conditions of confinement: Juvenile detention and corrections facilities.* Washington, DC: Office of Juvenile Justice and Delinquency Prevention.

Parent, D., Wentworth, D., & Burke, P. (1994). *Responding to probation and parole violators* (Issues and Practices in Criminal Justice). Washington, DC: National Institute of Justice.

Parsons, K. J. B., & Meeker, J. W. (1999, November). *The connection between gangs and drugs: Drug-related analysis from the Gang Incident Tracking System.* Paper presented at the annual meeting of the American Society of Criminology, Toronto.

Paternoster, R., & Piquero, A. R. (1995). Reconceptualizing deterrence: An empirical test of personal and vicarious experiences. *Journal of Research in Crime and Delinquency, 32,* 251-286.

Patterson, G. R., Capaldi, D., & Bank, L. (1991). An early starter model for predicting delinquency. In D. J. Pepler & K. H. Rubin (Eds.), *The development and treatment of childhood aggression* (pp. 139-168). Hillsdale, NJ: Lawrence Erlbaum.

Patterson, G. R., DeBaryshe, B. D., & Ramsey, E. (1989). A developmental perspective on antisocial behavior. *American Psychologist, 44,* 329-335.

Patterson, G. R., Reid, J. B., & Dishion, T. J. (1992). *Antisocial boys: A social interactional approach.* Eugene, OR: Castalia.

Patterson, G. R., & Yoerger, K. (1993). Developmental models for delinquent behavior. In S. Hodgins (Ed.), *Mental disorder and crime* (pp. 140-172). Newbury Park, CA: Sage.

Pearson, F. S., Lipton, D. S., & Cleland, C. M. (1996, November). *Some preliminary findings from the CDATE project.* Paper presented at the annual meeting of the American Society of Criminology, Chicago.

Peeples, F., & Loeber, R. (1994). Do individual factors and neighborhood context explain ethnic differences in juvenile delinquency? *Journal of Quantitative Criminology, 10,* 141-157.

Pennell, S., Curtis, C., & Scheck, D. C. (1990). Controlling juvenile delinquency: An evaluation of an interagency strategy. *Crime & Delinquency, 36,* 257-275.

Peters, M., Thomas, D., & Zamberlan, C. (1997). *Boot camps for juvenile offenders.* Washington, DC: Office of Juvenile Justice and Delinquency Prevention.

Petersilia, J. (1983). *Racial disparities in the criminal justice system* (Paper prepared for the National Institute of Corrections). Santa Monica, CA: RAND.

Petersilia, J. (2001). When prisoners return to communities: Political, economic, and social consequences. *Federal Probation, 65*(1), 3-8.

Petersilia, J., & Turner, S. (1985). *Guidelines-based justice: The implications for racial minorities.* Santa Monica, CA: RAND.

Petersilia, J., & Turner, S. (1993). Intensive probation and parole. In M. Tonry (Ed.), *Crime and justice: An annual review of research* (Vol. 17, pp. 281-336). Chicago: University of Chicago Press.

Petersilia, J., Turner, S., & Peterson, J. (1986). *Prison versus probation in California: Implications for crime and offender recidivism.* Santa Monica, CA: RAND.

Pfeiffer, S. I., & Strzelecki, S. C. (1990). Inpatient psychiatric treatment of children and adolescents: A review of outcome studies. *Journal of the American Academy of Child and Adolescent Psychiatry, 29,* 847-853.

Pindur, W., & Elliker, J. (1999). *Norfolk Juvenile Justice Recidivism Evaluation Project.* Norfolk, VA: Old Dominion University.

Piquero, A. R., Paternoster, R., Brame, R., Mazerolle, P., & Dean, C. W. (1999). Onset age and specialization in offending behavior. *Journal of Research in Crime and Delinquency, 36,* 275-299.

Platt, A. M. (1977). *The child savers: The invention of delinquency* (Rev. ed.). Chicago: University of Chicago Press.

Podkopacz, M. R., & Feld, B. C. (1995). Judicial waiver policy and practice: Persistence, seriousness and race. *Law and Inequality, 14,* 101-207.

Podkopacz, M. R., & Feld, B. C. (1996). The end of the line: An empirical study of judicial waiver. *Journal of Criminal Law and Criminology, 86,* 449-492.

Podkopacz, M. R., & Feld, B. C. (2001). The back-door to prison: Waiver reform, "blended sentencing," and the law of unintended consequences. *Journal of Criminal Law and Criminology, 91,* 997-1071.

Poe-Yamagata, E., & Butts, J. A. (1996). *Female offenders in the juvenile justice system.* Washington, DC: Office of Juvenile Justice and Delinquency Prevention.

Poe-Yamagata, E., & Jones, M. (2000). *And justice for some.* Washington, DC: Justice Policy Institute.

Pollard, J. A., Hawkins, J. F., & Arthur, M. W. (2000). Risk and protection: Are both necessary to understand diverse behavioral outcomes in adolescence? *Social Work Research, 23*(3), 145-158.

Pope, C. E. (1995). Equity within the juvenile justice system: Directions for the future. In K. Kempf-Leonard, C. E. Pope, & W. H. Feyerherm (Eds.), *Minorities in juvenile justice* (pp. 201-216). Thousand Oaks, CA: Sage.

Pope, C. E., & Feyerherm, W. H. (1990). Minority status and juvenile justice processing (2 parts). *Criminal Justice Abstracts, 22,* 327-336, 527-542.

Pope, C. E., & Feyerherm, W. H. (1991). *Minorities in the juvenile justice system.* Washington, DC: Office of Juvenile Justice and Delinquency Prevention.

Porter, G. (2000). *Detention in delinquency cases, 1988-1997* (Fact Sheet No. 2000-17). Washington, DC: Office of Juvenile Justice and Delinquency Prevention.

Powell, K. E., & Hawkins, D. F. (Eds.). (1996). Youth violence prevention: Descriptions and baseline data from 13 evaluation projects. *American Journal of Preventive Medicine, 12*(Suppl.).

Pranis, K. (1998). *Guide for implementing balanced and restorative justice.* Washington, DC: Office of Juvenile Justice and Delinquency Prevention.

Pratt, G. (1994, December). *Community based comprehensive wrap-around treatment strategies.* Paper presented at the Juvenile Justice Research Symposium, Phoenix, AZ.

Pratt, T. C., & Maahs, J. (1999). Are private prisons more cost-effective than public prisons? A meta-analysis of evaluation research studies. *Crime & Delinquency, 45,* 358-371.

President's Commission on Law Enforcement and Administration of Justice. (1967). *The challenge of crime in a free society.* Washington, DC: Government Printing Office.

Presser, L., & Gunnison, E. (1999). Strange bedfellows: Is sex offender notification a form of community justice? *Crime & Delinquency, 45,* 299-315.

Previte, M. T. (1997, February). Preventing security crises at youth centers. *Corrections Today,* pp. 7-79.

Puritz, P., Burrell, S., Schwartz, R., Soler, M., & Warboys, L. (1995). *A call for justice: An assessment of access to counsel and quality of representation in delinquency proceedings.* Washington, DC: American Bar Association.

Puritz, P., & Shang, W. W. L. (1998). *Innovative approaches to juvenile indigent defense* (Juvenile Justice Bulletin). Washington, DC: Office of Juvenile Justice and Delinquency Prevention.

Puzzanchera, C. M. (2000). *Delinquency cases waived to criminal court, 1988-1997* (Fact Sheet No. 2000-02). Washington, DC: Office of Juvenile Justice and Delinquency Prevention.

Puzzanchera, C. M. (2001). *Delinquency cases waived to criminal court, 1989-1998* (Fact Sheet No. 2001-35). Washington, DC: Office of Juvenile Justice and Delinquency Prevention.

Quelling a crime wave. (2001, November 7). *Globe,* p. A22.

Rackauckas, T. (1999). *1998 annual report, Gang Unit and Tri-Agency Resource, Gang Enforcement Teams (TARGET).* Santa Ana, CA: Orange County District Attorney's Office.

Radelet, M. L. (1989). Executions of whites for crimes against blacks: Exceptions to the rule? *Sociological Quarterly, 30,* 529-544.

Radelet, M. L., Bedau, H. A., & Putnam, C. E. (1992). *In spite of innocence: The ordeal of 400 Americans wrongly convicted of crimes punishable by death.* Boston: Northeastern University Press.

Rand, M. R., & Strom, K. (1997). *Violence-related injuries treated in hospital emergency departments* (Special Report). Washington, DC: Bureau of Justice Statistics.

Redding, R. E., & Howell, J. C. (2000). Blended sentencing in American juvenile courts. In J. Fagan & F. E. Zimring (Eds.), *The changing borders of juvenile justice: Transfer of adolescents to the criminal court* (pp. 145-179). Chicago: University of Chicago Press.

Redondo, S., Sanchez-Meca, J., & Garrido, V. (1999). The influence of treatment programmes on the recidivism of juvenile and adult offenders: A European meta-analytic review. *Psychology, Crime, and Law, 5,* 251-278.

Regnery, A. S. (1986). A federal perspective on juvenile justice reform. *Crime & Delinquency, 32,* 39-51.

Reich, K., Culross, P. L., & Behrman, R. E. (2002). Children, youth and gun violence: Analysis and recommendations. *Future of Children, 12*(2), 5-19.

Reiner, I. (1992). *Gangs, crime, and violence in Los Angeles.* Los Angeles: Office of the District Attorney of the County of Los Angeles.

Reiss, A. J., Jr. (1988). Co-offending and criminal careers. In M. Tonry & N. Morris (Eds.), *Crime and justice: An annual review of research* (Vol. 10, pp. 117-170). Chicago: University of Chicago Press.

Rennison, C. M. (2001). *Criminal victimization 2000: Changes in 1999-2000 with trends for 1993-2000* (Bulletin). Washington, DC: Bureau of Justice Statistics.

Renouf, A. G., & Harter, S. (1990). Low self-worth and anger as components of the depressive experience in young adolescents. *Development and Psychopathology, 2,* 293-310.

Rich, T. (1999, October). Mapping the path to problem solving. *National Institute of Justice Journal, 236,* 2-9.

Richie, B. E., Tsenin, K., & Widom, C. S. (2000). *Research on women and girls in the justice system.* Washington, DC: National Institute of Justice.

Riddell, S. G. (1999, Winter). Juvenile drug courts showing great promise. *Juvenile and Family Justice Today,* pp. 12-13.

Righthand, S., & Welch, C. (2001). *Juveniles who have sexually offended: A review of the professional literature.* Washington, DC: Office of Juvenile Justice and Delinquency Prevention.

Risler, E. A., Sutphen, R., & Shields, J. (2000). Preliminary validation of the juvenile first offender risk assessment index. *Research on Social Work Practice, 10,* 111-126.

Risler, E. A., Sweatman, T., & Nackerud, L. (1998). Evaluating the Georgia legislative waiver's effectiveness in deterring juvenile crime. *Research on Social Work Practice, 8,* 657-667.

Rivara, F. P. (1995). Crime, violence and injuries in children and adolescents: Common risk factors. *Criminal Behavior and Mental Health, 5,* 367-385.

Rivard, J. C., Johnsen, M. C., Morrissey, J. P., & Starrett, B. E. (1999). The dynamics of interagency collaboration: How linkages develop for child welfare and juvenile justice sectors in a system of care demonstration. *Journal of Social Service Research, 25*(3).

Riveland, C. (1999). *Supermax prisons: An overview and general considerations.* Washington, DC: National Institute of Corrections.

Rivers, J. E., & Anwyl, R. S. (2000). Juvenile assessment centers: Strengths, weaknesses, and potential. *Prison Journal, 80,* 96-113.

Rivers, J. E., Dembo, R., & Anwyl, R. S. (1998). The Hillsborough County, Florida Juvenile Assessment Center: A prototype. *Prison Journal, 78,* 439-450.

Roberts, P. G., & Stratton, L. M. (2000). *The tyranny of good intentions: How prosecutors and bureaucrats are trampling the Constitution in the name of justice.* Roseville, CA: Forum.

Robertson, J. E. (1999). Cruel and unusual punishment in United States prisons: Sexual harassment among male inmates. *American Criminal Law Review, 36*(1), 1-51.

Robinson, D. A., & Stephens, O. H. (1992). Patterns of mitigating factors in juvenile death penalty cases. *Criminal Law Bulletin, 28,* 246-275.

Romano, E., Tremblay, R. E., Vitaro, F., Zoccolillo, M., & Pagani, L. (2001). Prevalence of psychiatric diagnoses and the role of perceived impairment: Findings from an adolescent community sample. *Journal of Child Psychology and Psychiatry, 42,* 451-461.

Romig, D. (1978). *Justice for our children.* Lexington, MA: Lexington.

Rosenbaum, D. P., Flewelling, R. L., Bailey, S. L., Ringwalt, C. L., & Wilkinson, D. L. (1994). Cops in the classroom: A longitudinal evaluation of Drug Abuse Resistance Education (DARE). *Journal of Research in Crime and Delinquency, 31,* 3-31.

Rosenbaum, D. P., & Hanson, G. S. (1998). Assessing the effects of school-based drug education: A six-year multilevel analysis of Project D.A.R.E. *Journal of Research in Crime and Delinquency, 35,* 381-412.

Rosenberg, I. M. (1993). Leaving bad enough alone: A response to the juvenile court abolitionists. *Wisconsin Law Review, 1993*(1), 163-185.

Rosenblatt, E. (Ed.). (1996). *Criminal injustice: Confronting the prison crisis.* Boston: South End.

Rosenfeld, R., Bray, T. M., & Egley, A., Jr. (1999). Facilitating violence: A comparison of gang-motivated, gang-affiliated, and nongang youth homicides. *Journal of Quantitative Criminology, 15,* 495-515.

Rosenheim, M. K., Zimring, F. E., Tanenhaus, D. S., & Dohrn, B. (Eds.). (2002). *A century of juvenile justice.* Chicago: University of Chicago Press.

Rossman, S. (2001, November). *Preliminary findings from the SafeFutures youth and caregivers surveys.* Paper presented at the annual meeting of the American Society of Criminology, Atlanta.

Roth, J. A., Ryan, J. F., Gaffigan, S. J., Koper, C. S., Moore, M. H., Roehl, J. A., et al. (2000). *National evaluation of the COPS Program—Title I of the 1994 Crime Act..* Washington, DC: National Institute of Justice.

Rothman, D. J. (1971). *The discovery of the asylum: Social order and disorder in the new republic.* Boston: Little, Brown.

Roush, D. W. (1996a). *Desktop guide to good juvenile detention practice.* Washington, DC: Office of Juvenile Justice and Delinquency Prevention.

Roush, D. W. (1996b). A juvenile justice perspective. In C. M. Nelson, R. B. Rutherford, & B. I. Wolford (Eds.), *Comprehensive and collaborative systems that work for troubled youth: A national agenda* (pp. 29-60). Richmond, KY: National Juvenile Detention Association.

Roush, D. W., & McMillen, M. (2000). *Construction, operations, and staff training for juvenile confinement facilities* (Juvenile Accountability Incentive Block Grants Program Bulletin). Washington, DC: Office of Juvenile Justice and Delinquency Prevention.

Roy, S. (1995a). Juvenile offenders in an electronic home detention program: A study on factors related to failure. *Journal of Offender Monitoring, 8*(2), 9-17.

Roy, S. (1995b). Juvenile restitution and recidivism in a midwestern county. *Federal Probation, 59*(1), 55-62.

Rubin, H. T. (2000). Teen Quest: Female-specific program services for Colorado's delinquent girls. *Juvenile Justice Update, 6*(3), 1-16.

Rubin, H. T. (2000-2001). Georgia Department of Juvenile Justice moves forward by moving back to the community. *Juvenile Justice Update, 7*(1), 1-2, 14-16.

Ruddell, R., & Mays, G. L. (in press). Examining the arsenal of juvenile gunslingers: Trends and policy implications. *Crime & Delinquency.*

Rumsey, E., Kerr, C. A., & Allen-Hagen, B. (1998). *Serious and violent juvenile offenders* (Juvenile Justice Bulletin). Washington, DC: Office of Juvenile Justice and Delinquency Prevention.

Rutter, M. (1986). The developmental psychopathology of depression: Issues and perspectives. In M. Rutter, C. Izard, & P. B. Read (Eds.), *Depression in young people: Developmental and clinical perspectives.* New York: Guilford.

Rutter, M. (1987). Psychosocial resilience and protective mechanisms. *American Journal of Orthopsychiatry, 57,* 316-331.

Rutter, M., Giller, H., & Hagell, A. (1998). *Antisocial behavior by young people.* New York: Cambridge University Press.

Ryan, G., Miyoshi, T. J., Metzner, J. L., Krugman, R. D., & Fryer, G. E. (1996). Trends in a national sample of sexually abusive youths. *Journal of the American Academy of Child and Adolescent Psychiatry, 35,* 17-25.

Sakamoto, W. (1996). *Gang and youth violence intervention: Creating a safe and secure school campus.* San Diego, CA: San Diego County Office of Education.

Samenow, S. E. (1984). *Inside the criminal mind.* New York: Times Books.

Samenow, S. E. (1998). *Straight talk about criminals: Understanding and treating antisocial individuals.* Northvale, NJ: Jason Aronson.

Sametz, L., & Hamparian, D. (1990). *Innovative programs in Cuyahoga County juvenile court: Intensive probation supervision and probation classification.* Cleveland, OH: Federation for Community Planning.

Sampson, E. H. (1985). *Dade youth gangs: Final report of the grand jury.* Miami, FL: Dade County District Attorney.

Sampson, E. H. (1988). *Dade County gangs: Final report of the grand jury.* Miami, FL: Dade County District Attorney.

Sampson, R. J., & Laub, J. H. (1993). *Crime in the making: Pathways and turning points through life.* Cambridge, MA: Harvard University Press.

Sampson, R. J., & Laub, J. H. (1994). Urban poverty and the family context of delinquency: A new look at structure and process in a classic study. *Child Development, 65,* 523-540.

Sampson, R. J., & Lauritsen, J. L. (1990). Deviant lifestyles, proximity to crime, and the offender-victim link in personal violence. *Journal of Research in Crime and Delinquency, 27,* 110-139.

Sampson, R. J., & Lauritsen, J. L. (1997). Racial and ethnic disparities in crime and criminal justice in the United States. In M. Tonry (Ed.), *Ethnicity, crime, and immigration: Comparative and cross-national perspectives* (pp. 311-374). Chicago: University of Chicago Press.

Sampson, R. J., & Raudenbush, S. W. (2001). *Disorder in urban neighborhoods: Does it lead to crime?* Washington, DC: National Institute of Justice.

Sanchez-Jankowski, M. S. (1991). *Islands in the street: Gangs and American urban society.* Berkeley: University of California Press.

Sanders, W. (1994). *Gangbangs and drive-bys: Grounded culture and juvenile gang violence.* New York: Aldine de Gruyter.

Sarnecki, J. (1986). *Delinquent networks.* Stockholm: National Swedish Council for Crime Prevention, Research Division.

Sarri, R. (1981). The effectiveness paradox: Institutional vs. community placement of offenders. *Journal of Social Issues, 37*(3), 34-50.

Sawicki, D. R., Schaeffer, B., & Thies, J. (1999). Predicting successful outcomes for serious and chronic juveniles in residential placement. *Juvenile and Family Court Journal, 50*(1), 21-31.

Scheb, J. M., & Scheb, J. M., Jr. (2002). *Criminal law and procedure* (2nd ed.). Belmont, CA: Wadsworth.

Schlosser, E. (1998, December). The prison-industrial complex. *Atlantic Monthly, 282,* 51-77.

Schmalleger, F. (1999). *Criminal justice today* (5th ed.). Upper Saddle River: NJ: Prentice Hall.

Schmidt, F. L. (1992). What do data really mean? Research findings, meta-analysis, and cumulative knowledge in psychology. *American Psychologist, 47,* 1173-1179.

Schneider, A. L. (1990). *Deterrence and juvenile crime: Results from a national policy experiment.* New York: Springer-Verlag.

Schneider, A. L., & Ervin, L. (1990). Specific deterrence, rational choice, and decision heuristics: Applications in juvenile justice. *Social Science Quarterly, 71,* 585-601.

Schneider, A. L., Ervin, L., & Snyder, J. Z. (1996). Further exploration of the flight from discretion: The role of risk/need instruments in probation supervision decisions. *Journal of Criminal Justice, 24,* 109-121.

Schumacher, M., & Kurz, G. (2000). *The 8% solution: Preventing serious, repeat juvenile crime.* Thousand Oaks, CA: Sage.

Schwartz, I. M. (1999). Will the juvenile court system survive? *Annals of the American Academy of Political and Social Science, 564,* 8-184.

Schweinhart, L. J., Barnes, H. V., & Weikart, D. P. (1993). *Significant benefits: The High/Scope Perry Preschool Study through age 27.* Ypsilanti, MI: High/Scope.

Scott, E. S. (2000). Criminal responsibility in adolescence: Lessons from developmental psychology. In T. Grisso & R. G. Schwartz (Eds.), *Youth on trial: A developmental perspective on juvenile justice* (pp. 291-324). Chicago: University of Chicago Press.

Sealock, M. D., Gottfredson, D. C., & Gallagher, C. (1997). Drug treatment for juvenile offenders: Some good and bad news. *Journal of Research in Crime and Delinquency, 34,* 210-236.

Sechrest, L., White, S. O., & Brown, E. D. (1979). *The rehabilitation of criminal offenders: Problems and prospects.* Washington, DC: National Academy of Sciences.

Seckel, J. P., & Turner, J. K. (1985). *Assessment of planned re-entry programs.* Sacramento: California Youth Authority.

Seitz, V., & Apfel, N. (1994). Parent-focused intervention: Diffusion effects on siblings. *Child Development, 65,* 667-683.

Sentencing Project. (2002). *Facts about prisons and prisoners.* Washington, DC: Author. Retrieved from http://www.sentencingproject.org/brief/pub1035.pdf

Sewer of the summit. (2002). *Youth Today, 11*(5), 2.

Shafer, K. (1999). *Mission aligned policing philosophy.* Columbus, OH: Columbus Division of Police.

Shannon, L. W. (1968). *Juvenile delinquency in Madison and Racine.* Iowa City: University of Iowa.

Shannon, L. W. (1988). *Criminal career continuity: Its social context.* New York: Human Sciences Press.

Shannon, L. W. (1991). *Changing patterns of delinquency and crime: A longitudinal study in Racine.* Boulder, CO: Westview.

Shannon, L. W. (1998). *Alcohol and drugs, delinquency and crime: Looking back to the future.* New York: St. Martin's.

Sharpe, D. (1997). Of apples and oranges, file drawers and garbage: Why validity issues in meta-analysis will not go away. *Clinical Psychology Review, 17,* 881-901.

Shaw, C. R., & McKay, H. D. (1931). *Social factors in juvenile delinquency: Report on the causes of crime* (Report No. 11). Washington, DC: Government Printing Office.

Shaw, C. R., & McKay, H. D. (1969). *Juvenile delinquency and urban areas.* Chicago: University of Chicago Press.

Shaw, M., & Robinson, K. (1998). Summary and analysis of the first juvenile drug court evaluations. *National Drug Court Institute Review, 1*(1), 73-85.

Shaw, M., & Robinson, K. (1999, Summer). Reports on recent drug court research. *National Drug Court Institute Review, 2*(1), 107-119.

Shelden, R. G. (1999). *Detention diversion advocacy: An evaluation* (Juvenile Justice Bulletin). Washington, DC: Office of Juvenile Justice and Delinquency Prevention.

Shepherd, R. E. (1999). The juvenile court at 100 years: A look back. *Juvenile Justice, 6*(2), 13-21.

Sheppard, D., Grant, H., Rowe, W., & Jacobs, N. (2000). *Fighting juvenile gun violence* (Juvenile Justice Bulletin). Washington, DC: Office of Juvenile Justice and Delinquency Prevention.

Sherman, L. W. (1990). Police crackdowns: Initial and residual deterrence. In M. Tonry & N. Morris (Eds.), *Crime and justice: An annual review of research* (Vol. 12, pp. 1-48). Chicago: University of Chicago Press.

Sherman, L. W., Gottfredson, D. C., MacKenzie, D. L., Eck, J., Reuter, P., & Bushway, S. (Eds.). (1997). *Preventing crime: What works, what doesn't, what's promising.* Washington, DC: National Institute of Justice.

Shichor, D., & Sechrest, D. K. (Eds.). (1996). *Three strikes and you're out: Vengeance as public policy.* Thousand Oaks, CA: Sage.

Short, J. F., Jr., & Strodtbeck, F. L. (1965). *Group process and gang delinquency.* Chicago: University of Chicago Press.

Shure, M. B., & Spivack, G. (1988). Interpersonal cognitive problem solving. In R. H. Price, E. L. Cowen, R. P. Lorion, & J. Ramos-McKay (Eds.), *Fourteen ounces of prevention: A casebook for practitioners* (pp. 69-82). Hawthorne, NY: Aldine.

Sickmund, M. (2000). *Offenders in juvenile court, 1997* (Juvenile Justice Bulletin). Washington, DC: Office of Juvenile Justice and Delinquency Prevention.

Sickmund, M. (2002). *Juvenile offenders in residential placement: 1997-1999* (Fact Sheet

No. 2002-07). Washington, DC: Office of Juvenile Justice and Delinquency Prevention.

Sickmund, M., Snyder, H. N., & Poe-Yamagata, E. (1997). *Juvenile offenders and victims: 1997 update on violence.* Washington, DC: Office of Juvenile Justice and Delinquency Prevention.

Sigda, K. B., Kupersmidt, J. B., & Martin, S. L. (1996, March). *Attitudes about prosocial and antisocial peers among incarcerated adolescents.* Paper presented at the annual meeting of the Society for Research on Adolescence, Boston.

Silberberg, N. E., & Silberberg, M. C. (1971). School achievement and delinquency. *Journal of Educational Research, 41,* 17-33.

Simons, R. L., Wu, C., Conger, R. D., & Lorenz, F. O. (1994). Two routes to delinquency: Differences between early and late starters in the impact of parenting and deviant peers. *Criminology, 32,* 247-275.

Singer, S. I. (1996). *Recriminalizing delinquency: Violent juvenile crime and juvenile justice reform.* New York: Cambridge University Press.

Skogan, W. G., Hartnett, S. M., DuBois, J., Comey, J. T., Kaiser, M., & Loving, J. H. (1999). *On the beat: Police and community problem solving.* Boulder, CO: Westview.

Skogan, W. G., Hartnett, S. M., DuBois, J., Comey, J. T., Kaiser, M., & Loving, J. H. (2000). *Problem solving in practice: Implementing community policing in Chicago.* Washington, DC: National Institute of Justice.

Skolnick, J. H. (1989). *Gang organization and migration.* Sacramento: Office of the Attorney General of the State of California.

Skolnick, J. H., Correl, T., Navarro, E., & Rabb, R. (1988). *The social structure of street drug dealing: Report to the Office of the Attorney General of the State of California.* Berkeley: University of California Press.

Slater, E. (2000, March 30). Scandal forces Chicago police to overhaul anti-gang unit. *Los Angeles Times,* p. A5.

Small, S. A., & Luster, T. (1994). Adolescent sexual activity: An ecological risk-factor approach. *Journal of Marriage and the Family, 56,* 181-192.

Smith, B. (1998). Children in custody: 20-year trends in juvenile detention, correctional, and shelter facilities. *Crime & Delinquency, 44,* 526-543.

Smith, C. A., Krohn, M. D., Lizotte, A. J., McCluskey, C. P., Stouthamer-Loeber, M., & Weiher, A. W. (2000). The effect of early delinquency and substance use on precocious transitions to adulthood among adolescent males. In G. L. Fox & M. L. Benson (Eds.), *Families, crime and criminal justice* (Vol. 2, pp. 233-253). Amsterdam: JAI.

Smith, C. A., Lizotte, A. J., Thornberry, T. P., & Krohn, M. D. (1995). Resilient youth: Identifying factors that prevent high-risk youth from engaging in delinquency and drug use. In J. Hagan (Ed.), *Delinquency in the life course* (pp. 217-247). Greenwich, CT: JAI.

Smith, C. A., & Thornberry, T. P. (1995). The relationship between childhood maltreatment and adolescent involvement in delinquency. *Criminology, 33,* 451-477.

Smith, D. A., Visher, C. A., & Davidson, L. A. (1984). Equity and discretionary justice: The influence of race on police arrest decisions. *Journal of Criminal Law and Criminology, 75,* 234-249.

Smith, K. (2000, August 18). Families of 6 teens killed while clearing roadside sue. *Las Vegas Sun,* p. 3.

Smith, S. L., Fairchild, M., & Groginsky, S. (1997). *Early childhood care and education: An investment that works.* Denver, CO: National Conference of State Legislatures.

Smith, W. R., & Aloisi, M. F. (1999). Prediction of recidivism among "second timers" in the juvenile justice system: Efficiency in screening chronic offenders. *American Journal of Criminal Justice, 23,* 201-222.

Smith, W. R., Aloisi, M. F., & Goldstein, H. (1996). *Early court intervention: A research and demonstration project.* West Trenton, NJ: Juvenile Justice Commission.

Snell, T. L. (1999). *Capital punishment 1998* (Bulletin). Washington, DC: Bureau of Justice Statistics.

Snyder, H. N. (1988). *Court careers of juvenile offenders.* Washington, DC: Office of Juvenile Justice and Delinquency Prevention.

Snyder, H. N. (1998). Serious, violent, and chronic juvenile offenders: An assessment of the extent of and trends in officially recognized serious criminal behavior in a delinquent population. In R. Loeber & D. P. Farrington (Eds.), *Serious and violent juvenile offenders: Risk factors and successful interventions* (pp. 428-444). Thousand Oaks, CA: Sage.

Snyder, H. N. (1999). *Juvenile arrests 1998* (Juvenile Justice Bulletin). Washington, DC: Office of Juvenile Justice and Delinquency Prevention.

Snyder, H. N. (2000). *Juvenile arrests 1999* (Juvenile Justice Bulletin). Washington, DC: Office of Juvenile Justice and Delinquency Prevention.

Snyder, H. N. (2001). Epidemiology of official offending. In R. Loeber & D. P. Farrington (Eds.), *Child delinquents: Development, intervention, and service needs* (pp. 25-46). Thousand Oaks, CA: Sage.

Snyder, H. N., & Sickmund, M. (1995). *Juvenile offenders and victims: A national report.* Washington, DC: Office of Juvenile Justice and Delinquency Prevention.

Snyder, H. N., & Sickmund, M. (1999). *Juvenile offenders and victims: 1999 national report.* Washington, DC: Office of Juvenile Justice and Delinquency Prevention.

Snyder, H. N., & Sickmund, M. (2000). *Challenging the myths* (Juvenile Justice Bulletin, 1999 National Report Series). Washington, DC: Office of Juvenile Justice and Delinquency Prevention.

Snyder, H. N., Sickmund, M., & Poe-Yamagata, E. (1996). *Juvenile offenders and victims: 1996 update on violence.* Washington, DC: Office of Juvenile Justice and Delinquency Prevention.

Snyder, H. N., Sickmund, M., & Poe-Yamagata, E. (2000). *Juvenile transfers to criminal court in the 1990's: Lessons learned from four studies.* Washington, DC: Office of Juvenile Justice and Delinquency Prevention.

Snyder, T., & Hoffman, C. (2001). *Digest of education statistics.* Washington, DC: National Center for Education Statistics.

Soler, M. (2001). *Public opinion on youth, crime, and race: A guide for advocates.* Washington, DC: Building Blocks for Youth. Retrieved from http://www.buildingblocksforyouth.org/advocacyguide.html

Soler, M., & Shauffer, C. (1990). Fighting fragmentation: Coordination of services for children and families. *Nebraska Law Review, 69,* 278-297.

Soler, M., & Warboys, L. (1990). Services for violent and severely disturbed children: The Willie M. litigation. In S. Dicker (Ed.), *Stepping stones: Successful advocacy for children* (pp. 61-112). New York: Foundation for Child Development.

Sondheimer, D. L., Schoenwald, S. K., & Rowland, M. D. (1994). Alternatives to the hospitalization of youth with a serious emotional disturbance. *Journal of Clinical Child Psychology, 23*(Suppl.), 7-12.

Sontheimer, H., & Goodstein, L. (1993). Evaluation of juvenile intensive aftercare probation: Aftercare versus system response effects. *Justice Quarterly, 10,* 197-227.

Spergel, I. A. (1995). *The youth gang problem.* New York: Oxford University Press.

Spergel, I. A., & Bobrowski, L. (1989). *Minutes from the "Law Enforcement Youth Gang Definitional Conference: September 25, 1989."* Rockville, MD: Juvenile Justice Clearinghouse.

Spergel, I. A., & Curry, G. D. (1990). Strategies and perceived agency effectiveness in dealing with the youth gang problem. In C. R. Huff (Ed.), *Gangs in America* (pp. 288-309). Newbury Park, CA: Sage.

Spergel, I. A., & Curry, G. D. (1993). The National Youth Gang Survey: A research and development process. In A. Goldstein & C. R. Huff (Eds.), *The gang intervention handbook* (pp. 359-400). Champaign, IL: Research Press.

Spergel, I. A., & Grossman, S. F. (1997a). *Evaluation of the Little Village Gang Violence Reduction Project.* Chicago: University of Chicago, School of Social Service Administration.

Spergel, I. A., & Grossman, S. F. (1997b). The Little Village project: A community approach to the gang problem. *Social Work, 42,* 456-470.

Spergel, I. A., Grossman, S. F., & Wa, K. M. (1998). *The Little Village Gang Violence Reduction Program: A three year evaluation.* Chicago: University of Chicago, School of Social Service Administration.

Spergel, I. A., Wa, K. M., Choi, S. E., Grossman, S., Jacob, A., Spergel, A., et al. (2002). *Evaluation of the Gang Violence Reduction Project in Little Village.* Chicago: University of Chicago, School of Social Service Administration.

Spohn, C., Gruhl, J., & Welch, S. (1987). The impact of the ethnicity and gender of defendants on the decision to reject or dismiss felony charges. *Criminology, 25,* 175-191.

Spohn, C., & Holleran, D. (2002). The effect of imprisonment on recidivism rates of felony offenders: A focus on drug offenders. *Criminology, 40,* 329-357.

Stack, B. W. (2002, June 18). Couch kids life: Teens walk away from home but don't go far. *News and Observer* (Raleigh, NC), pp. 1E, 3E.

Stahl, A. L. (2000). *Delinquency cases in juvenile court, 1997* (Fact Sheet No. 2000-04). Washington, DC: Office of Juvenile Justice and Delinquency Prevention.

Stanfield, R. (2000). *Pathways to juvenile detention reform: Overview. The JDAI story: Building a better detention system.* Baltimore: Annie E. Casey Foundation.

Starbuck, D., Howell, J. C., & Lindquist, D. J. (2001). *Hybrid and other modern gangs* (Juvenile Justice Bulletin, Youth Gang Series). Washington, DC: Office of Juvenile Justice and Delinquency Prevention.

Stattin, H., & Magnusson, D. (1991). Stability and change in criminal behaviour up to age 30. *British Journal of Criminology, 31,* 327-346.

Steffensmeier, D., & Harer, M. D. (1999). Making sense of recent U.S. crime trends, 1980-96/8: Age-composition effects and other explanations. *Journal of Research in Crime and Delinquency, 36,* 235-274.

Steinberg, L., & Schwartz, R. G. (2000). Developmental psychology goes to court. In J. Fagan & F. E. Zimring (Eds.), *The changing borders of juvenile justice: Transfer of adolescents to the criminal court* (pp. 9-31). Chicago: University of Chicago Press.

Steiner, H., Garcia, I. G., & Matthews, Z. (1997). Posttraumatic stress disorder in incarcerated juvenile delinquents. *Journal of the American Academy of Child and Adolescent Psychiatry, 36,* 357-365.

Steinhart, D. (2000a). *Pathways to juvenile detention reform: Vol. 1. Planning for juvenile detention reforms.* Baltimore: Annie E. Casey Foundation.

Steinhart, D. (2000b). *Pathways to juvenile detention reform: Vol. 9. Special detention cases: Strategies for handling difficult populations.* Baltimore: Annie E. Casey Foundation.

Stevens, A. B., Owen, G., & Lahti-Johnson, K. (1999). *Delinquents under 10: Target early intervention phase I evaluation report.* St. Paul, MN: Amherst H. Wilder Foundation, Wilder Research Center.

Stevens, D. J. (1997). Origins and effects of prison drug gangs in North Carolina. *Journal of Gang Research, 4*(4), 23-35.

Stewart, E. A., Simons, R. L., Conger, R. D., & Scaramella, L. V. (2002). Beyond the interactional relationship between delinquency and parenting practices. *Journal of Research in Crime and Delinquency, 39,* 36-59.

Stimmel, B. (1996). *Drug abuse and social policy in America.* New York: Haworth Medical Press.

Stoll, A., Dukes, R. L., & Smith, C. A. (1997). The impact of gangs and gang violence on contemporary youth: An assessment of the problem in Colorado Springs. *Free Inquiry in Creative Sociology, 25*(1), 75-86.

Stouthamer-Loeber, M., Loeber, R., Farrington, D. P., Zhang, Q., Van Kammen, W. B., & Maguin, E. (1993). The double edge of protective and risk factors for delinquency: Interactions and developmental patterns. *Development and Psychopathology, 5,* 683-701.

Stouthamer-Loeber, M., Loeber, R., Homish, D. L., & Wei, E. (2001). Maltreatment of boys and the development of disruptive and delinquent behavior. *Development and Psychopathology, 13,* 941-955.

Stouthamer-Loeber, M., Loeber, R., Van Kammen, W. B., & Zhang, Q. (1995). Uninterrupted delinquent careers: The timing of parental help-seeking and juvenile court contact. *Studies on Crime and Crime Prevention, 4,* 236-251.

Stouthamer-Loeber, M., Loeber, R., Wei, E., Farrington, D. P., & Wikstrom, P. H. (2002). Risk and promotive effects in the explanation of persistent serious delinquency in boys. *Journal of Consulting and Clinical Psychology, 70,* 111-123.

Strasburg, P. A. (1977). *Violent delinquents.* New York: Ford Foundation.

Streib, V. L. (1983). The American experience with capital punishment. *Oklahoma Law Review, 36,* 613-641.

Streib, V. L. (1998). Present death row inmates under juvenile sentences and executions for juvenile crimes, January 1, 1973 to October 31, 1998. In V. L. Streib, *Juvenile Death Penalty Today.* Cleveland, OH: Author.

Strom, K. J. (2000). *Profile of state prisoners under age 18, 1985-97* (Bulletin). Washington, DC: Bureau of Justice Statistics.

Stroul, B. A. (1996). *Children's mental health: Creating systems of care in a changing society.* Baltimore: Paul H. Brookes.

Stroul, B. A., & Friedman, R. (1986). *A system of care for severely emotionally disturbed youth.* Washington, DC: Georgetown University, Child and Adolescent Service System Program Technical Assistance Center.

Stroul, B. A., & Friedman, R. (1988). Caring for emotionally disturbed children and youth: Principles for a system of care. *Child Today, 17,* 11-15.

Styve, G. J., MacKenzie, D. L., & Gover, A. R. (2000). Perceived conditions of confinement: A national evaluation of juvenile boot camps and traditional facilities. *Law and Human Behavior, 24,* 297-308.

Surette, R. (2002). Self-reported copycat crime among a population of serious and violent juvenile offenders. *Crime & Delinquency, 48,* 46-69.

Sutherland, E. H. (1973). Development of the theory. In K. Schuster (Ed.), *Edwin Sutherland on analyzing crime* (pp. 13-29). Chicago: University of Chicago Press.

Sutphen, R. D., Thyer, B. A., & Kurtz, P. D. (1995). Multisystemic treatment of high-risk juvenile offenders. *International Journal of Offender Therapy and Comparative Criminology, 39,* 329-334.

Tapper, D. (1996). *Children at risk: Final report on the demonstration program.* New York: Columbia University, National Center on Addiction and Substance Abuse.

Taxman, F. S., Soule, D., & Gelb, A. (1999). Graduated sanctions: Stepping into accountable systems and offenders. *Prison Journal, 79,* 182-204.

Taylor, C. S. (1990). *Dangerous society.* East Lansing: Michigan State University Press.

Teplin, L. A. (2001). *Addressing alcohol, drug, and mental disorders in juvenile detainees* (Fact Sheet No. 2001-02). Washington, DC: Office of Juvenile Justice and Delinquency Prevention.

Thornberry, T. P. (1987). Toward an interactional theory of delinquency. *Criminology, 25,* 863-891.

Thornberry, T. P. (1994). *Violent families and youth violence* (Fact Sheet No. 1994-21).

Washington, DC: Office of Juvenile Justice and Delinquency Prevention.

Thornberry, T. P. (1996). Empirical support for interactional theory: A review of the literature. In J. D. Hawkins (Ed.), *Delinquency and crime: Current theories* (pp. 198-235). New York: Cambridge University Press.

Thornberry, T. P. (Ed.). (1997). *Developmental theories of crime and delinquency.* New Brunswick, NJ: Transaction.

Thornberry, T. P. (1998). Membership in youth gangs and involvement in serious and violent offending. In R. Loeber & D.P. Farrington (Eds.), *Serious and violent juvenile offenders: Risk factors and successful interventions* (pp. 147-166). Thousand Oaks, CA: Sage.

Thornberry, T. P., & Burch, J. H. (1997). *Gang members and delinquent behavior* (Juvenile Justice Bulletin, Youth Gang Series). Washington, DC: Office of Juvenile Justice and Delinquency Prevention.

Thornberry, T. P., Huizinga, D., & Loeber, R. (1995). The prevention of serious delinquency and violence: Implications from the Program of Research on the Causes and Correlates of Delinquency. In J. C. Howell, B. Krisberg, J. D. Hawkins, & J. J. Wilson (Eds.), *A sourcebook: Serious, violent, and chronic juvenile offenders* (pp. 213-237). Thousand Oaks, CA: Sage.

Thornberry, T. P., Krohn, M. D., Lizotte, A. J., & Chard-Wierschem, D. (1993). The role of juvenile gangs in facilitating delinquent behavior. *Journal of Research in Crime and Delinquency, 30,* 55-87.

Thornberry, T. P., Krohn, M. D., Lizotte, A. J., Smith, C. A., & Tobin, K. (2003). *Gangs and delinquency in developmental perspective.* New York: Cambridge University Press.

Thornberry, T. P., Krohn, M. D., McDowall, D., Bushway, S. D., & Lizotte, A. J. (2002, November). *General versus typological theories of antisocial behavior.* Paper presented at the annual meeting of the American Society of Criminology, Chicago.

Thornberry, T. P., Lizotte, A. J., Krohn, M. D., Farnworth, M., & Jang, S. J. (1994). Delinquent peers, beliefs, and delinquent behavior: A longitudinal test of interactional theory. *Criminology, 32,* 601-637.

Thornberry, T. P., & Porter, P. K. (2001). Advantages of longitudinal research designs in studying gang behavior. In M. W. Klein, H.-J. Kerner, C. L. Maxson, & E. G. M. Weitekamp (Eds.), *The Eurogang paradox: Street gangs and youth groups in the U.S. and Europe* (pp. 59-78). Amsterdam: Kluwer.

Thrasher, F. M. (1927). *The gang: A study of 1,313 gangs in Chicago.* Chicago: University of Chicago Press.

Tierney, J. P., & Grossman, J. (1995). *Making a difference: An impact study.* Philadelphia: Public/Private Ventures.

Tiet, Q. Q., Wasserman, G. A., Loeber, R., McReynolds, L. S., & Miller, L. S. (2001). Developmental and sex differences in types of conduct problems. *Journal of Child and Family Studies, 10,* 181-197.

Tobler, N. S. (1986). Meta-analysis of 143 adolescent drug prevention programs: Quantitative outcome results of program participants compared to a control or comparison group. *Journal of Drug Issues, 16,* 537-567.

Tolan, P. H., & Gorman-Smith, D. (1998). Development of serious and violent offending careers. In R. Loeber & D. P. Farrington (Eds.), *Serious and violent juvenile offenders: Risk factors and successful interventions* (pp. 68-85). Thousand Oaks, CA: Sage.

Tolan, P. H., & Guerra, N. G. (1994). *What works in reducing adolescent violence: An empirical review of the field.* Boulder, CO: Center for the Study and Prevention of Violence.

Tolan, P. H., Perry, M. S., & Jones, T. (1987). Delinquency prevention: An example of consultation in rural community mental health. *American Journal of Community Psychology, 15,* 43-50.

Tollett, C. L., & Benda, B. B. (1999). Predicting "survival" in the community among persistent and serious juvenile offenders: A 12-month follow-up study. *Journal of Offender Rehabilitation, 28*(3-4), 49-76.

Tollett, T. (1987). *A comparative study of Florida delinquency commitment programs.* Tallahassee: Florida Department of Health and Rehabilitative Services.

Tonry, M. (1994a). *Malign neglect: Race, crime, and punishment in America.* New York: Oxford University Press.

Tonry, M. (1994b). Racial politics, racial disparities, and the war on crime. *Crime & Delinquency, 40,* 475-494.

Tonry, M. (1999a). Community penalties in the United States. *European Journal on Criminal Policy and Research, 7*(1), 5-22.

Tonry, M. (1999b). *The fragmentation of sentencing and corrections in America: Sentencing and corrections issues for the 21st century* (Research in Brief, Papers from the Executive Sessions on Sentencing and Corrections). Washington, DC: National Institute of Justice.

Tonry, M. (1999c). Parochialism in U.S. sentencing policy. *Crime & Delinquency, 45,* 48-65.

Tonry, M., & Farrington, D. P. (Eds.). (1995a). *Building a safer society: Strategic approaches to crime prevention.* Chicago: University of Chicago Press.

Tonry, M., & Farrington, D. P. (1995b). Strategic approaches to crime prevention. In M. Tonry

& D. P. Farrington (Eds.), *Building a safer society: Strategic approaches to crime prevention* (pp. 1-20). Chicago: University of Chicago Press.

Torbet, P. M. (1999). *Holding juvenile offenders accountable: Programming needs of juvenile probation departments*. Pittsburgh, PA: National Center for Juvenile Justice.

Torbet, P. M., Gable, R., Hurst, H., Jr., Montgomery, I. M., Szymanski, L., & Thomas, D. (1996). *State responses to serious and violent juvenile crime*. Washington, DC: Office of Juvenile Justice and Delinquency Prevention.

Torbet, P. M., Griffin, P., Hurst, H., Jr., & MacKenzie, L. R. (2000). *Juveniles facing criminal sanctions: Three states that changed the rules*. Washington, DC: Office of Juvenile Justice and Delinquency Prevention.

Torbet, P. M., & Szymanski, L. (1998). *State legislative responses to violent juvenile crime: 1996-1997 update* (Juvenile Justice Bulletin). Washington, DC: Office of Juvenile Justice and Delinquency Prevention.

Tracy, P. E., & Kempf-Leonard, K. (1996). *Continuity and discontinuity in criminal careers*. New York: Plenum.

Tracy, P. E., & Kempf-Leonard, K. (1998). Sanctioning serious juvenile offenders: A review of alternative models. In W. Laufer & F. Adler (Eds.), *Advances in criminological theory* (pp. 135-171). New Brunswick, NJ: Transaction.

Tracy, P. E., Wolfgang, M. E., & Figlio, R. M. (1990). *Delinquency careers in two birth cohorts*. New York: Plenum.

Travis, J., & Petersilia, J. (2001). Reentry reconsidered: A new look at an old question. *Crime & Delinquency, 47*, 291-313.

Tremblay, R. E., & Craig, W. M. (1995). Developmental crime prevention. In M. Tonry & D. P. Farrington (Eds.), *Building a safer society: Strategic approaches to crime prevention* (pp. 151-236). Chicago: University of Chicago Press.

Tremblay, R. E., & LeMarquand, D. (2001). Individual risk and protective factors. In R. Loeber & D. P. Farrington (Eds.), *Child delinquents: Development, intervention, and service needs* (pp. 137-164). Thousand Oaks, CA: Sage.

Tremblay, R. E., Masse, L., Pagani, L., & Vitaro, F. (1996). From childhood physical aggression to adolescent maladjustment: The Montreal Prevention Experiment. In R. D. Peters & R. J. McMahon (Eds.), *Preventing childhood disorders, substance abuse, and delinquency* (pp. 268-298). Thousand Oaks, CA: Sage.

Tremblay, R. E., Pihl, R. O. P., Vitaro, F., & Dobkin, P. L. (1994). Predicting early onset of male antisocial behavior from preschool behavior. *Archives of General Psychiatry, 51*, 732-739.

Tremblay, R. E., Vitaro, F., Bertrand, L., Le Blanc, M., Beauchesne, H., Bioleau, H., et al. (2001). Parent and child training to prevent early onset of delinquency: The Montreal Experimental Study. In A. R. Piquero & P. Mazerolle (Eds.), *Life-course criminology*. Belmont, CA: Wadsworth.

Trulson, C., Triplett, R., & Snell, C. (2001). Social control in a school setting: Evaluating a school-based boot camp. *Crime & Delinquency, 47*, 573-609.

Trump, K. S. (1998). *Practical school security: Basic guidelines for safe and secure schools*. Thousand Oaks, CA: Corwin.

Tyler, K. A., Hoyt, D. R., & Whitbeck, L. B. (2000). The effects of early sexual abuse on later sexual victimization among female homeless and runaway adolescents. *Journal of Interpersonal Violence, 15*, 235-250.

Ullman, R. P. (2000). Federal juvenile waiver practices: A contextual approach to the consideration of prior delinquency records. *Fordham Law Review, 68*, 1329-1369.

U.S. Department of Health and Human Services. (1999). *Mental health: A report of the surgeon general*. Rockville, MD: Author.

U.S. Department of Health and Human Services. (2001). *Youth violence: A report of the surgeon general*. Rockville, MD: Author.

U.S. Department of Justice, Office for Victims of Crime. (1996). *Victims of violence: A new frontier in victim services*. Washington, DC: Author.

U.S. General Accounting Office. (1989). *Nontraditional organized crime*. Washington, DC: Author.

U.S. General Accounting Office. (1994). *Residential care*. Washington, DC: Author.

U.S. General Accounting Office. (1995). *Juvenile justice: Juveniles processed in criminal court and case dispositions*. Washington, DC: Author.

U.S. General Accounting Office. (1996). *Status of delinquency prevention programs and description of local projects*. Washington, DC: Author.

U.S. General Accounting Office. (1997). *Drug courts: Overview of growth, characteristics, and results*. Washington, DC: Author.

U.S. General Accounting Office. (1998). *Law enforcement: Information on drug-related police corruption*. Washington, DC: Author.

Uviller, H. R. (1999). *The tilted playing field: Is criminal justice unfair?* New Haven, CT: Yale University Press.

Valdez, A., Alvarado, J., & Arcos, R. (2000, November). *The effects and consequences of* selling and using heroin among Mexican American street gang members. Paper presented at the annual meeting of the American Society of Criminology, San Francisco.

Vance, E., & Sanchez, H. (1998). Creating a service system that builds resiliency. Raleigh: North Carolina Department of Health and Human Services and Department of Public Instruction.

VanDenBerg, J. (1999). History of the wraparound process. In B. J. Burns & S. K. Goldman (Eds.), Promising practices in wraparound for children with serious emotional disturbances and their families: Systems of care (pp. 1-16). Washington, DC: American Institutes for Research, Center for Effective Collaboration and Practice.

VanDenBerg, J., & Grealish, M. (1996). Individualized services and supports through the wraparound process: Philosophy and procedures. Journal of Child and Family Studies, 5, 7-21.

Van den Haag, E. (1975). Punishing criminals: Concerning a very old and painful question. New York: Basic Books.

Van Kammen, W. B., & Loeber, R. (1994). Are fluctuations in delinquent activities related to the onset and offset in juvenile illegal drug use and drug dealing? Journal of Drug Issues, 24, 9-24.

Van Kammen, W. B., Maguin, E., & Loeber, R. (1994). Initiation of drug selling and its relationship with illicit drug use and serious delinquency in adolescent boys. In E. G. M. Weitekamp & H.-J. Kerner (Eds.), Cross-national longitudinal research on human development and criminal behavior (pp. 230-241). Amsterdam: Kluwer.

Venkatesh, S. A. (1996). The gang and the community. In C. R. Huff (Ed.), Gangs in America (2nd ed., pp. 241-256). Thousand Oaks, CA: Sage.

Vigil, J. D. (1988). Barrio gangs: Street life and identity in Southern California. Austin: University of Texas Press.

Vigil, J. D., & Yun, S. C. (2002). A cross-cultural framework for understanding gangs: Multiple marginality and Los Angeles. In C. R. Huff (Ed.), Gangs in America (3rd ed., pp. 161-174). Thousand Oaks, CA: Sage.

Villalva, M. (2000, February 8). Parental survey reveals "clear" fear: Violence against, or by, their child. USA Today, pp. 8D, 10D.

Villarruel, F. A., & Walker, N. E. (2002). ¿Dónde está la justicia? A call to action on behalf of Latino and Latina youth in the U.S. justice system. Washington, DC: Building Blocks for Youth.

Vinter, R. (1976). Time out: A national study of juvenile corrections programs. Ann Arbor,

MI: National Assessment of Juvenile Corrections Project.

Violent and irrational—and that's just the policy. (1996, June 8). Economist, pp. 23-25.

Virginia Department of Criminal Justice Services, Criminal Justice Research Center. (2000). Evaluation of the Richmond City Continuum of Juvenile Justice Services Pilot Program. Richmond: Author.

Virginia Policy Design Team. (1994). Mental health needs of juveniles in Virginia's juvenile detention centers. Richmond: Virginia Department of Criminal Justice.

Visher, C. A., Lattimore, P. L., & Linster, R. L. (1991). Predicting the recidivism of serious youthful offenders using survival models. Criminology, 29, 329-366.

von Hirsch, A. (1976). Doing justice: The choice of punishments. New York: Hill & Wang.

Wagner, D. (2001, June 5). Risk and needs assessment for juvenile justice. Paper presented at the North Carolina Juvenile Justice Retreat, Burlington, NC.

Wagner, D., & Connell, S. (2002). North Carolina Department of Juvenile Justice Risk Assessment Profile. Madison, WI: National Council on Crime and Delinquency.

Wagner, D., & Wiebush, R. G. (1996). Validation of the Rhode Island Risk Assessment Instrument. Madison, WI: National Council on Crime and Delinquency.

Wagner, M., D'Amico, R., Marder, C., Newman, L., & Blackorby, J. (1992). What happens next? Trends in postschool outcomes of youth with disabilities. Menlo Park, CA: SRI International.

Wakeling, S., Jorgensen, M., Michaelson, S., Begay, M., Hartman, F. X., & Kalt, J. P. (2000). Policing on American Indian reservations: A report to the National Institute of Justice. Cambridge, MA: Harvard University, John F. Kennedy School of Government.

Waldorf, D. (1993). When the Crips invaded San Francisco: Gang migration. Journal of Gang Research, 1(4), 11-16.

Walker, K. E., Watson, B. H., & Jucovy, L. Z. (1999). Resident involvement in community change: The experiences of two initiatives. Philadelphia: Public/Private Ventures.

Walker, M. L., & Schmidt, L. M. (1996). Gang reduction efforts by the Task Force on Violent Crime in Cleveland, Ohio. In C. R. Huff (Ed.), Gangs in America (2nd ed., pp. 263-269). Thousand Oaks, CA: Sage.

Walker-Barnes, C. J., & Mason, C. A. (2001a). Ethnic differences in the effect of parenting on gang involvement and gang delinquency: A longitudinal, hierarchical linear modeling perspective. Child Development, 72, 1814-1831.

Walker-Barnes, C. J., & Mason, C. A. (2001b). Perceptions of risk factors for female gang involvement among African American and Hispanic women. *Youth & Society, 32,* 303-336.

Warr, M. (1996). Organization and instigation in delinquent groups. *Criminology, 34,* 11-37.

Warr, M. (2002). *Companions in crime: The social aspects of criminal conduct.* New York: Cambridge University Press.

Washington State Institute for Public Policy. (2002). *Washington State's implementation of aggression replacement training for juvenile offenders: Preliminary findings.* Olympia: Author.

Wasserman, G. A., Ko, S. J., & Jensen, P. (2002). *Guidelines for child and adolescent mental health referral.* New York: Columbia University, Center for the Promotion of Mental Health in Juvenile Justice. Retrieved May 6, 2002, from http://www.promotementalhealth.org

Wasserman, G. A., & Miller, L. S. (1998). The prevention of serious and violent juvenile offending. In R. Loeber & D. P. Farrington (Eds.), *Serious and violent juvenile offenders: Risk factors and successful interventions* (pp. 197-247). Thousand Oaks, CA: Sage.

Wasserman, G. A., Miller, L. S., & Cothern, L. (2000). *Prevention of serious and violent juvenile offending* (Juvenile Justice Bulletin). Washington, DC: Office of Juvenile Justice and Delinquency Prevention.

Wasserman, G. A., & Seracini, A. M. (2001). Risk factors and interventions. In R. Loeber & D. P. Farrington (Eds.), *Child delinquents: Development, intervention, and service needs* (pp. 165-190). Thousand Oaks, CA: Sage.

Webster-Stratton, C. (1984). Randomized trial of two parent training programs for families with conduct-disordered children. *Journal of Consulting and Clinical Psychology, 52,* 666-678.

Webster-Stratton, C. (1999). *How to promote social and emotional competence in young children.* London: Sage.

Webster-Stratton, C. (2000). *The Incredible Years training series* (Juvenile Justice Bulletin). Washington, DC: Office of Juvenile Justice and Delinquency Prevention.

Weisel, D. L., & Eck, J. E. (1994). Toward a practical approach to organizational change in community policing initiatives in six cities. In D. P. Rosenbaum (Ed.), *The challenge of community policing: Testing the promises* (pp. 53-74). Thousand Oaks, CA: Sage.

Weisel, D. L., & Painter, E. (1997). *The police response to gangs: Case studies of five cities.* Washington, DC: Police Executive Research Forum.

Weiss, F. L., Nicholson, H. J., & Cretalla, M. M. (1996). *Prevention and parity: Girls in juvenile justice.* Indianapolis IN: Girls Incorporated Research Center.

Weissberg, R. P., & Caplan, M. (1998). *Promoting social competence and preventing antisocial behavior in young urban adolescents.* Philadelphia: Temple University, Center for Research in Human Development and Education, Laboratory for Student Success.

Weissberg, R. P., & Greenberg, M. T. (1997). School and community competence-enhancement and prevention programs. In W. Damon (Series Ed.) & I. E. Sigel & K. A. Renninger (Vol. Eds.), *Handbook of child psychology: Vol. 5. Child psychology in practice* (5th ed., pp. 877-964). New York: John Wiley.

Weisz, J. R., Martin, S. L., Walter, B. R., & Fernandez, G. A. (1991). Differential prediction of young adult arrests for property and personal crimes: Findings of a cohort follow-up study of violent boys. *Journal of Child Psychology and Psychiatry, 32,* 783-792.

Weisz, J. R., Walter, B. R., Weiss, B., Fernandez, G. A., & Mikow, V. A. (1990). Arrests among emotionally disturbed violent and assaultive individuals following minimal versus lengthy intervention through North Carolina's Willie M. program. *Journal of Consulting and Clinical Psychology, 58,* 720-728.

Weisz, J. R., & Weiss, B. (1993). *Effects of psychotherapy with children and adolescents.* Newbury Park, CA: Sage.

Weitekamp, E. G. M. (2001). Gangs in Europe: Assessments at the millennium. In M. W. Klein, H.-J. Kerner, C. L. Maxson, & E. G. M. Weitekamp (Eds.), *The Eurogang paradox: Street gangs and youth groups in the U.S. and Europe* (pp. 309-324). Amsterdam: Kluwer.

Weitekamp, E. G. M., Kerner, H.-J., Schindler, V., & Schubert, A. (1995). On the "dangerousness" of chronic/habitual offenders: A re-analysis of the 1945 Philadelphia birth cohort data. *Studies on Crime and Crime Prevention, 4,* 159-175.

Weithorn, L. A. (1988). Mental hospitalization of troublesome youth: An analysis of skyrocketing admission rates. *Stanford Law Review, 40,* 773-838.

Werner, E. E., &. Smith, R. S. (1982). *Vulnerable but invincible: A longitudinal study of resilient children and youth.* New York: McGraw-Hill.

Werner, E. E., & Smith, R. S. (1992). *Overcoming the odds: High risk children from birth to adulthood.* Ithaca, NY: Cornell University Press.

Weston, D. A. (1969). Fines, imprisonment, and the poor: Thirty dollars or thirty days. *California Law Review, 57,* 778-821.

Whitbeck, L. B., Hoyt, D. R., & Yoder, K. A. (1999). A risk-amplification model of victimization and depressive symptoms among runaway and homeless adolescents. *American Journal of Community Psychology, 27,* 273-296.

White, J. (1985). *The Comparative Dispositions Study.* Washington, DC: Office of Juvenile Justice and Delinquency Prevention.

Whitlock, M. L. (2002). *Family-based risk and protective mechanisms for youth at-risk of gang joining.* Unpublished doctoral dissertation, University of California, Los Angeles.

Wickham, D. (1998, May 26). To save country, save kids from violence, AIDS. *USA Today,* p. 15A.

Widom, C. S. (1992). *The cycle of violence* (Research in Brief). Washington, DC: National Institute of Justice.

Widom, C. S., & Maxfield, M. G. (2001). *An update on the "cycle of violence"* (Research in Brief). Washington, DC: National Institute of Justice.

Wiebe, D. J. (1998, November). *Targeting and gang crime: Assessing the impacts of a multi-agency suppression strategy in Orange County, California.* Paper presented at the annual meeting of the American Society of Criminology, Washington, DC.

Wiebe, D. J., Meeker, J. W., & Vila, B. (1999). *Hourly trends of gang crime incidents, 1995-1998.* Irvine: University of California, Focused Research Group on Gangs.

Wiebush, R. G. (1993). Juvenile intensive supervision: The impact on felony offenders diverted from institutional placement. *Crime & Delinquency, 39,* 68-89.

Wiebush, R. G. (2000). *Risk assessment and classification for serious, violent, and chronic juvenile offenders.* Madison, WI: National Council on Crime and Delinquency.

Wiebush, R. G. (2001, November). *Recidivism in the IAP.* Paper presented at the annual meeting of the American Society of Criminology, Atlanta.

Wiebush, R. G. (Ed.). (2002). *Graduated sanctions for juvenile offenders: A program model and planning guide.* Oakland, CA: National Council on Crime and Delinquency and National Council of Juvenile and Family Court Judges.

Wiebush, R. G., Baird, C., Krisberg, B., & Onek, D. (1995). Risk assessment and classification for serious, violent, and chronic juvenile offenders. In J. C. Howell, B. Krisberg, J. D. Hawkins, & J. J. Wilson (Eds.), *A sourcebook: Serious, violent, and chronic juvenile offenders* (pp. 171-212). Thousand Oaks, CA: Sage.

Wiebush, R. G., & Hamparian, D. M. (1986). *Probation classification: Design and development of the Cuyahoga County Juvenile Court model.* Cleveland: Ohio Serious Juvenile Offender Project.

Wiebush, R. G., & Hamparian, D. M. (1991). Variations in "doing" intensive supervision: Programmatic issues in four Ohio jurisdictions. In T. L. Armstrong (Ed.), *Intensive interventions with high-risk youths: Promising approaches in juvenile probation and parole* (pp. 153-188). Monsey, NY: Criminal Justice Press.

Wiebush, R. G., Johnson, K., & Wagner, D. (1997). *Development of an empirically-based risk assessment instrument and placement recommendation matrix for the Maryland Department of Juvenile Justice.* Madison, WI: National Council on Crime and Delinquency.

Wiebush, R. G., & Wagner, D. (1995). *Rhode Island juvenile risk assessment findings.* Madison, WI: National Council on Crime and Delinquency.

Wiebush, R. G., Wagner, D., & Erlich, J. (1999). *Development of an empirically-based assessment instrument for the Virginia Department of Juvenile Justice.* Madison, WI: National Council on Crime and Delinquency.

Wiebush, R. G., Wagner, D., Healy, T., & Baird, C. (1996). *Development of a risk assessment instrument for adjudicated juvenile offenders in Virginia.* Madison, WI: National Council on Crime and Delinquency.

Wiebush, R. G., Wagner, D., Prestine, R., & Baird, C. (1992). *The impact of electronic monitoring on juvenile recidivism: Results of an experimental test in the Cuyahoga County Juvenile Court.* Madison, WI: National Council on Crime and Delinquency.

Wiebush, R. G., Wagner, D., Prestine, R., & Van Gheem, S. (1993). *Oklahoma Office of Juvenile Justice 1992 Workload Study: Final report.* Madison, WI: National Council on Crime and Delinquency.

Wikstrom, P. H., & Loeber, R. (2000). Do disadvantaged neighborhoods cause well-adjusted children to become adolescent delinquents? A study of male juvenile serious offending, individual risk and protective factors and neighborhood context. *Criminology, 38,* 1109-1142.

Williams, K., Cohen, M., & Curry, G. D. (1994, November). *Evaluation of female gang prevention programs.* Paper presented at the annual meeting of the American Society of Criminology, Miami, FL.

Williams, T. (1989). *The cocaine kids: The inside story of a teenage drug ring.* Reading, MA: Addison-Wesley.

Williamson, D., Chalk, M., & Knepper, P. (1993). Teen court: Juvenile justice for the 21st century? *Federal Probation, 57*(2), 54-58.

Willing, R., & Fields, G. (1999, December 20). Geography of the death penalty. *USA Today,* pp. 1A, 6A.

Wilson, D. B., & Lipsey, M. W. (2001). The role of method in treatment effectiveness research:

Evidence from meta-analysis. *Psychological Methods, 6,* 413-429.

Wilson, J. J. (2000, July 14). [Remarks made at BARJ Special Emphasis States Roundtable, San Diego, CA.]

Wilson, J. J., & Howell, J. C. (1993). *A Comprehensive Strategy for Serious, Violent and Chronic Juvenile Offenders.* Washington, DC: Office of Juvenile Justice and Delinquency Prevention.

Wilson, J. Q. (1995). Crime and public policy. In J. Q. Wilson & J. Petersilia (Eds.), *Crime* (pp. 489-507). San Francisco: Institute for Contemporary Studies.

Wilson, J. Q., & Kelling, G. L. (1982, March). Broken windows. *Atlantic Monthly, 249,* 29-38.

Wilson, S. J., & Lipsey, M. W. (2000). Wilderness challenge programs for delinquent youth: A meta-analysis of outcome evaluations. *Evaluation and Program Planning, 23,* 1-12.

Wilt, M. B. (1996). *Evaluation report to the Norfolk Interagency Consortium.* Richmond: Virginia Commonwealth University, Department of Psychology.

Winner, L., Lanza-Kaduce, L., Bishop, D. M., & Frazier, C. E. (1997). The transfer of juveniles to criminal court: Reexamining recidivism over the long term. *Crime & Delinquency, 43,* 548-563.

Wolf, M. M., Phillips, E. L., & Fixson, D. L. (1974). *Achievement Place: Phase II* (Report No. 1). Rockville, MD: National Institute of Mental Health, Center for Studies of Crime and Delinquency.

Wolfgang, M. E. (1982). Abolish the juvenile court system. *California Lawyer, 2,* 12-13.

Wolfgang, M. E., Figlio, R. M., & Sellin, T. (1972). *Delinquency in a birth cohort.* Chicago: University of Chicago Press.

Wolfgang, M. E., Thornberry, T. P., & Figlio, R. M. (1987). *From boy to man, from delinquency to crime.* Chicago: University of Chicago Press.

Wood, D. A., & Brown, J. W. (1989). *Juvenile electronic monitoring: Assessment report.* Champaign, IL: Community Research Associates.

Woodward, L. J., & Fergusson, D. M. (2000). Childhood and adolescent predictors of physical assault: A prospective longitudinal study. *Criminology, 38,* 233-262.

Wooldredge, J. D. (1988). Differentiating the effects of juvenile court sentences on eliminating recidivism. *Journal of Research in Crime and Delinquency, 25,* 264-300.

Wooldredge, J. D. (1998). Analytical rigor in studies of disparities in criminal case processing. *Journal of Quantitative Criminology, 14,* 155-179.

Wordes, M., & Jones, S. M. (1998). Trends in juvenile detention and steps toward reform. *Crime & Delinquency, 44,* 544-560.

Wu, B. (2000). Determinants of public opinion toward juvenile waiver decisions. *Juvenile and Family Court Journal, 51*(1), 9-20.

Wyrick, P. A. (2000). *Vietnamese youth gang involvement* (Fact Sheet No. 2000-01). Washington, DC: Office of Juvenile Justice and Delinquency Prevention.

Yablonsky, L. (1967). *The violent gang* (Rev. ed.). New York: Penguin.

Yoshikawa, H. (1994). Prevention as cumulative protection: Effects of early family support and education on chronic delinquency and its risks. *Psychological Bulletin, 115,* 1-27.

Yoshikawa, H. (1995). Long-term effects of early childhood programs on social outcomes and delinquency. *Future of Children, 5,* 51-75.

Young, M. C. (2000). *Providing effective representation for youth prosecuted as adults* (Bulletin). Washington, DC: Bureau of Justice Assistance.

Young, T. M., & Pappenfort, D. M. (1977). *Secure detention and alternatives to its use.* Washington, DC: Law Enforcement Administration.

Zaczor, B. (2002, September 8). Boys' case revives Fla. trial law debate. *News and Observer* (Raleigh, NC), p. 7A.

Zatz, M. S. (1987). Chicano youth gangs and crime: The creation of moral panic. *Contemporary Crises, 11,* 129-158.

Ziedenberg, J. (2001). *Drugs and disparity: The racial impact of Illinois' practice of transferring young drug offenders to adult court.* Washington, DC: Building Blocks for Youth.

Zimmerman, J., Rich, W., Keilitz, I., & Broder, P. (1981). Some observations on the link between learning disabilities and juvenile delinquency. *Journal of Criminal Justice, 9,* 1-17.

Zimring, F. E. (1981). Kids, groups and crime: Some implications of a well-known secret. *Journal of Criminal Law and Criminology, 72,* 867-885.

Zimring, F. E. (1996, August 19). Crying wolf over teen demons. *Los Angeles Times,* p. B5.

Zimring, F. E. (1998a). *American youth violence.* New York: Oxford University Press.

Zimring, F. E. (1998b). Toward a jurisprudence of youth violence. In M. Tonry & M. H. Moore (Eds.), *Youth violence* (pp. 477-501). Chicago: University of Chicago Press.

Zimring, F. E. (1999). The executioner's dissonant song: On capital punishment and American legal values. In A. Sarat (Ed.), *The killing state: Capital punishment in law, politics, and culture* (pp. 137-147). New York: Oxford University Press.

Zimring, F. E. (2000). The punitive necessity of waiver. In J. Fagan & F. E. Zimring (Eds.),

The changing borders of juvenile justice: Transfer of adolescents to the criminal court (pp. 207-226). Chicago: University of Chicago.

Zimring, F. E. (2002). The common thread: Diversion in the jurisprudence of juvenile courts. In M. K. Rosenheim, F. E. Zimring, D. S. Tanenhaus, & B. Dohrn (Eds.), *A century of juvenile justice* (pp. 142-157). Chicago: University of Chicago Press.

Zimring, F. E., & Fagan, J. (2000). The search for causes in an era of crime declines: Some lessons from the study of New York City homicide. *Crime & Delinquency, 46,* 446-456.

Zimring, F. E., Fagan, J. E., & Kupchik, A. (2001, November). *The effect of downward shifts in the maximum jurisdictional age of juvenile court on the age distribution of arrests: Reports on some national samples.* Paper presented at the annual meeting of the American Society of Criminology, Atlanta.

Zimring, F. E., & Hawkins, G. J. (1973). *Deterrence.* Chicago: University of Chicago Press.

INDEX

ABOUT THE AUTHOR

James C. (Buddy) Howell, Ph.D., worked at the federal Office of Juvenile Justice and Delinquency Prevention (OJJDP) in the U.S. Department of Justice for 21 years, mostly as Director of Research and Program Development. He also was Director, National Institute of Juvenile Justice and Delinquency Prevention, and Deputy Administrator of OJJDP. In addition, he was a member of the National Advisory Committee for Juvenile Justice and Delinquency Prevention and the Federal Coordinating Council for Juvenile Justice and Delinquency Prevention. He currently is Adjunct Researcher with the National Youth Gang Center in Tallahassee, Florida. He is an associate editor of the new interdisciplinary journal *Youth Violence and Juvenile Justice,* author of *Juvenile Justice and Youth Violence* (1997), and lead editor of *A Sourcebook: Serious, Violent, and Chronic Juvenile Offenders* (1995). Some of his recent research on juvenile delinquency has appeared in *Crime & Delinquency*, *Criminology, Journal of Research in Crime and Delinquency*, and *Justice Quarterly*.